THE FILMS OF LOUIS MALLE

THE FILMS OF LOUIS MALLE

A Critical Analysis

Nathan Southern *with* Jacques Weissgerber

RESEARCH ASSISTANCE BY HEATHER MCBRIER
FOREWORD BY JEAN-CLAUDE CARRIÈRE

McFarland & Company, Inc., Publishers
Jefferson, North Carolina, and London

All photographs courtesy of Nouvelles Éditions de Films

LIBRARY OF CONGRESS CATALOGUING-IN-PUBLICATION DATA

Southern, Nathan C., 1978–
The films of Louis Malle : a critical analysis /
Nathan Southern with Jacques Weissgerber ;
research assistance by Heather McBrier ;
foreword by Jean-Claude Carrière.
p.   cm.
Includes bibliographical references and index.

ISBN 0-7864-2300-5 (illustrated case binding : 50# alkaline paper)

1. Malle, Louis, 1932–   — Criticism and interpretation.
I. Weissgerber, Jacques, 1949–   II. Title.
PN1998.3.M34S68   2006   791.4302'33'092 — dc22   2005022635

British Library cataloguing data are available

Cover photograph: Louis Malle frames a shot on the set of *Alamo Bay* (1985)

Manufactured in the United States of America

McFarland & Company, Inc., Publishers
Box 611, Jefferson, North Carolina 28640
www.mcfarlandpub.com

For Lisa Anne
With my deepest admiration and gratitude.
— N.S.

Acknowledgments

Without the time, assistance and generosity of an enormous number of individuals, this project never would have happened: foremost, Marie-Christine Breton, Manuel Malle, Vincent Malle and the staff of Nouvelles Éditions de Films, for advice, copies of unreleased films, interviews, interview contact information and written permission to access Louis Malle's private papers and make research dubs.

I never could have completed the text without the diligence, encouragement and inexhaustible energy of Jacques Weissgerber, one of the best coresearchers and translators I could ever have hoped for — he has been a godsend. Heather McBrier, our executive assistant, was consistently a great help and continued to work for us through a difficult pregnancy and after the arrival of her first child.

Thanks to: Stéphanie Grégoire, who did her thesis and a documentary on Louis — she was also a great help, sending unproduced Malle scripts, articles, etc., and sharing insights on the director; Heather McBrier's sister, Alicia Abernethy, for putting us in touch with Heather initially; everyone outside of NEF who took time from busy schedules to participate in interviews, offering insights and reflections on Louis Malle: Brigitte Bardot, Candice Bergen, Fred Berner, Alain Bernheim, Renato Berta, James Bruce, Keith Carradine, Leslie Caron, Jeff Fiskin, George Gaynes, André Gregory, John Guare, David Hare, Ed Harris, Justine Malle, Ross Milloy, Donald Moffat, Philippe Noiret, Michel Piccoli, Polly Platt, Susan Sarandon, Diana Scarwid, Brooke Smith and Alexandra Stewart.

An extra-special thanks to Jean-Claude Carrière, for our interview and his exceptional foreword.

Additional thanks to Fabienne Vonier, of Mk2–Paris, for logistical detail on how Malle financed *Au revoir les enfants*; Karen Pedersen (librarian at the Writer's Guild of America library, Los Angeles) for help contacting interviewees; Elinor Hernon (librarian in Newton, Mass.) who pulled in hundreds of articles on Malle for my research; Ruta Abolins and Margie Compton of the University of Georgia Library Media Center and Peabody Awards Collection for selling us a dub of *And the Pursuit of Happiness*; Leanne Hall from the Australian Center for the Moving Image for running a telecine of *Les Dernières Vacances* (and Chantal Girondin for clearing the rights); Drs. Claretta Tonetti and T. Jefferson Kline of Boston University and Dr.

Tom Conley of Harvard University for advice and encouragement on critical material; Molly Haskell, formerly of Columbia University and *The Village Voice*, currently of Sarah Lawrence College, who offered suggestions for contextual resources in my background research on *Damage*; Régis Robert and Nadie Tenèze of the BiFi in Paris for research assistance on Appendix A, highlighting much of Louis's unproduced work; Bob Rothstein and the staff of the Geddes Language Center at Boston University and Janet Kent of Atwood's Camera in Newton, Mass., for transfers; Jerry Ohlinger for stills; Kenneth Carroll for use of his recording equipment in taping interviews; Mary Drouillard for help translating and transcribing *Place de la République*; Will Burton for contextual references; Tom Southern for publishing advice; and Martha Luttrell at ICM, Louis's agent for years, who initially put me in touch with the Malles in February 2001.

Thanks to my friends Jonathan Richards, Bill Darmon, Bill Phillips, the late Agnes Richard, David Selkovits and Laura McKellar for encouragement and suggestions, and Michelle (née) Lieder for giving me the hefty dose of encouragement that I needed to get this project under way, in the late summer of 2001, as well as my mother, Tangie, and brother, Alex, for their unflagging encouragement.

But I would most like to thank Christopher Jenkins, Elan Bair, Donna Caney and the clientele of Home Instead of Newton, Mass., who supported me with a salaried position for two of the three-and-a-half years when this book was being researched and written, and my father, Gary, who helped support me during the final nine months of writing and revision. To a significant degree, they — above all others — were the ones who made this volume possible.

— N.S.

Contents

Foreword

Louis Malle, the Elusive One

by Jean-Claude Carrière

(translated by Jacques Weissgerber)

Louis Malle has not made two films that are alike. Each one could have been imagined, written and produced by a different author interested, on this planet, in a thousand things.

Thus, through his films, his whole life was an endless search for subjects he wanted to treat, as well as ways of bringing them to the screen.

He was, indisputably, the first director of the *Nouvelle Vague*, with *Elevator to the Gallows*, yet he always refused to let himself be labeled, pegged in a class, a generation, a school. By instinct, he stayed clear of any categorization, constantly going from fiction to documentary, from original work to adaptation, from laughter to tragedy, from today to yesterday, from here to elsewhere. He used to say that the two countries that interested him most were the United States and India. And so he filmed both. He lived driven by curiosity, he embodied independence, diversity, the unforeseen — while keeping what he miraculously possessed from the start, a technical mastery so refined that it had become invisible.

The man was not exactly the mirror image of his work. His charm, his thoughtful intelligence remained the same from year to year, from one encounter to the other, as did his loyalty in friendship. But he always kept a keen eye on the lookout for the world, for things, for men, for women. One always felt he was on the go.

Elegant in his clothing as in his thought, often surprising in his choices— with a marked preference for those years in life when an adolescent suddenly turns into a man, encompassing a mixture of discoveries, surrender, fears, as well as dangers (one thinks of *Murmur of the Heart*, or *Lacombe, Lucien*).

I always thought that the Buddhist concept of *Beginner's Mind* perfectly applied to him: Each of his films was a beginning. A statement by Master Suzuki had struck me concerning Louis: "In the beginner's mind there are many possibilities, but in the expert's there are few." "One can say that Louis Malle dedicated all his energy to never becoming an expert.

And so novelty, exploration and risk-taking are his work's, as well as his life's, lesson.

Preface

During his 40-year career and posthumously, the brilliant director of *Les Amants*, *Le Feu follet*, *Le Souffle au cœur*, *Atlantic City* and *Au revoir les enfants* has received an insubstantial amount of formal, book-length critical attention in France and the United States.[1] From the early sixties through 2004, only six texts on Louis Malle appeared in the United States, France and Great Britain, four of which never received an English translation: the 1964 Henry Chapier–edited volume on Malle of the infamous series *Cinéma d'aujourd'hui* (which follows the director's career through *Le Feu follet*); the 1979 compilation *Louis Malle par Louis Malle* (which ends with *Pretty Baby*); René Prédal's 1989 critical monograph *Louis Malle* (published immediately following *Au revoir*); and Pierre Billard's 2003 *Louis Malle: Le Rebelle solitaire*, a biography that eschews critical discussions of Malle's work.[2] Of the two remaining English-language texts, Hugo Frey's 2004 *Louis Malle* analyzes the director's major endeavors (*Murmur of the Heart, Lacombe, Lucien, Pretty Baby*) but gives short shrift to his lesser-seen films, while Faber and Faber's *Malle on Malle* (1993, rev. 1996) contains a series of transcribed interviews that Philip French and Oren Moverman conducted with the director. As such, it incorporates fascinating thoughts, anecdotes, and reflections from Malle about his life and the production of his films, and can only be called a masterful, essential work, but it omits film criticism *per se*.

No formal, detailed critical analysis of Louis Malle's entire *œuvre*, covering *The Silent World* through *Vanya on 42nd Street*, has yet been written and published, for two major reasons. The first is logistical: although most of Malle's 30 films reached American art theaters or public television affiliates upon release, many have never received home video distribution and are seldom screened in repertory. The films thus evade critical discussion by virtue of going unseen. *Le Monde du silence* (1956), *Vive le tour* (1962), *Bons Baisers de Bangkok* (1964), *Le Voleur* (1967), *Phantom India* (1969), *Humain, trop humain* and *Place de la République* (1972), *Black Moon* (1975), *Close Up* (1976), *God's Country* (1985), and *And the Pursuit of Happiness* (1986) fall into this category.

The second reason for the critical neglect of Malle's work is that although his career flourished concurrently with the Nouvelle Vague, his cinematic *démarche* cuts against the grain of Sarrisian auteurism, which has led many journalists to brush him aside as a dilettante. This is a gross misperception; though seldom recognized as such, Malle was actually far more successful than his auteurist contemporaries in carrying the modernist conception of "art as expression of a singular identity" into cinema. He found a more authentic way to accomplish that goal, and thus passively and unintentionally cast a discerning light on the likes of Truffaut, Rohmer, Chabrol and Godard, raising the question of their authenticity as individually expressive "authors." Had this been recognized during his lifetime, Malle would certainly have become more scandalous and controversial than even Makavejev or Pasolini.

The marginalization of Louis Malle's work is unfortunate and should be rectified, for few familiar with Malle's films will dispute his status as one of the most gifted and consistently inspired directors of the late twentieth century. Exceedingly rare are those cineastes who not only remain prolific but who continue to work at a brilliant level from project to project; Malle represents an exception and thus can only be called a visionary. Some have dismissed his work as too commercial; those detractors overlook the pleasures inherent in mainstream filmmaking, *sans* running threads, particularly given a director intimately familiar with the medium.

This book, then, attempts to compensate for Malle's lack of critical attention with an analysis of his entire *œuvre*, from *Le Monde du silence*—the director's 1956 Palme d'Or–winning documentary collaboration with Jacques-Yves Cousteau—through his swan song, *Vanya on 42nd Street* (1994). For Malle's features, I devote one chapter to each work, and each chapter uses a four-phase approach: a brief exploration of the events that inspired Malle to create the motion picture; a synopsis; a detailed analysis of the film; and a summary of critical reactions upon release.

For Malle's documentaries (aside from *Le Monde du silence*), I analyze two films per chapter: *l'Inde fantôme* and *Calcutta* as one discussion (Chapter 9), *Humain, trop humain* and *Place de la République* as a second (Chapter 11), and *God's Country* and *And the Pursuit of Happiness* as a third (Chapter 19). In Chapter 24 ("Brief Encounters"), I have grouped together analyses of three Malle-directed shorts: his "William Wilson" episode of the 1969 film-as-sketch *Spirits of the Dead* and his little-seen documentaries *Vive le tour* and *Bons Baisers de Bangkok*. This volume omits *Close Up* (1976), a 26 minute documentary on the fashion model and actress Dominique Sanda (*Une Femme douce*), set to the music of Erik Satie. According to Louis's son Manuel, Sanda asked Malle to shoot that film as a personal favor, but decided "not to let anyone see it,"[3] rendering it unavailable for viewing or study.

By necessity, I examine Malle's features on a self-referential basis, with the guideline of how Malle and his collaborators use the techniques appropriate for the film at hand to best evoke the "themes, tropes, and preoccupations" of the material. This is how Malle approached fictional narratives: nontheoretically and guided by instinct. Conversely, I analyze the documentary material as a series of variations on the theory of cinema direct, for Malle shot nonfiction films according to its principles.

The introduction to this book and several of the background sections of the chapters incorporate extracts from a series of interviews that I conducted from February 2003 through December 2004 with a number of Malle's family members and collaborators who agreed to discuss their interaction with the director. Because many of the artists who worked with Malle early in his career are no longer living, or—in a few rare cases—could not participate due to physical infirmity, most of the individuals whom I interviewed knew or worked with Malle during his last three decades. Aside from a few exceptions—Brigitte Bardot, for instance, and the distinguished Philippe Noiret—interview material is thus weighted more toward the end of the book. I regret my inability to interview those individuals whom we failed to reach despite many attempts to work through representation, and those who died before we contacted them, such as Christine Gouze-Renal, the producer of *Vie privée*, who passed away in October 2002, and the extraordinary Phoebe Brand (Nanny in *Vanya on 42nd Street*) who died in July 2004.

The interview process did present one frustrating conundrum. Biographer Pierre Billard and Louis Malle's daughter, Justine, have each noted the director's habit of gently reinventing episodes from his life. Because Malle had this tendency, the details he recounts in published interviews occasionally diverge from the details recalled by our interviewees for this book, and my attempts to establish a linear history of certain episodes from Malle's life (such as the origin of *Crackers*) were problematic. To further complicate matters, interviewees occasionally disagreed with one another. Some of this may be a casualty of the rashomon effect, or an illustration of how memory shifts over time. Regardless of the reason for it, I present multiple versions of the same events wherever I have observed discrepancies, without attempting to offer a definitive history.

Appendix A contains a record of Malle's unproduced films from 1956 through 1995. As is the case with many filmmakers, Malle began a number of compelling projects throughout his career that never saw the light of day. *Louis Malle par Louis Malle* lists a number of these endeavors through 1979, and *Malle on Malle* also references several of the unfinished films, which the writer-director was forced to abandon in mid-development for various reasons. Among the more significant: *Moon over Miami*, a John Guare–written political satire on Abscam, to star Dan Aykroyd and John Belushi (as offshore tax evasion swindler Shelley Slutski) circa 1981–82, but terminated after Belushi's death at the Château Marmont[4]; *Jelly Roll*, a cinematization of Jelly Roll Morton's memoirs, co-written with Jack Gelber and abandoned in 1967 when Malle felt dissatisfied with the script (elements would eventually find their way into *Pretty Baby*)[5]; a late 1970s documentary on the phenomenon of the American shopping mall, scrapped when the production became too boring[6]; and various onscreen incarnations of Henry James's *What Maisie Knew*, all crafted by Guare,[7] the last of which was the infamous Marlene Dietrich biopic *Dietrich and Marlene* (with Uma Thurman as Dietrich and Stephen Rea as Josef von Sternberg), slated to go into production in mid–1995 but postponed and eventually terminated by Malle's death from lymphoma.[8] It is apparent, from even this cursory list, that many of the abandoned projects are more fascinating than the fully realized works. In including and editing Appendix A, I am indebted to Stéphanie Grégoire, who spent weeks of research at the BiFi in Paris digging up material on these curios; the only drawback is that it was often impossible for her to tell, from Malle's private papers, *why* he abandoned many of the projects. And such an appendix could never be comprehensive: according to Guare, Malle was the kind of person who had a thousand ideas a day and wanted to make every single one; the two men would often meet in the evening and brainstorm new projects into the small hours, so that one could write a whole book on this subject.

Countless reviews of Malle's films, articles covering the production detail of his films, interviews with Malle and his collaborators, and screenplay extracts of his films appeared, globally, between 1956 and 1995. I have thus narrowed the scope of the Select Bibliography to articles on Malle, falling within this 40-year time span, from the following sources: all major American popular periodicals; *Daily Variety*; the British publications *Sight and Sound* and *The Monthly Film Bulletin*; and all major French newspapers and film periodicals. This bibliography absorbs the ones in Faber's *Malle on Malle* and René Prédal's 1989 *Louis Malle* and expounds upon those citations by including full references whenever possible; yet complete citations were not always feasible in the case of the French sources, because of the expense and time associated with retrieving citation information from the Bibliothèque Française. I have tried to avoid overlapping with the bibliographic data in Nicholas Thomas's *International Dictionary of Films and Filmmakers*, Vol. I., so that my bibliography can be thought of as a companion piece to Thomas's work. Thomas places heavy emphasis on a number of British film journals largely inaccessible in the States.

At the moment, the *œuvre* of Louis Malle is poised to receive a great deal of renewed attention, including a retrospective touring that began at Lincoln Center Plaza in June 2005, and DVD reissues of 15 of Malle's major works, through the Criterion Collection series scheduled to continue through mid–2006. Those endeavors and this book (I am happy to announce) are benefiting from the full cooperation and endorsement of Malle's family and production company, Nouvelles Éditions. I hope that this resurgence of awareness yields serious critical reestimation of Louis Malle as an artist and that the tide of rekindled interest in his films encourages new generations to discover the exciting body of work he left in his wake — rich in thematic and stylistic diversity, rife with the energy of a man who lived for exploration — as the tenth anniversary of his death approaches.

Nathan Southern
Beverly Hills, Michigan
October 2005

Introduction

Louis Malle —
Mainstream Iconoclast

"Without tradition, art is a flock of sheep without a shepherd. Without innovation, it is a corpse."
— Winston Churchill

"The more minimal the art, the more maximum the explanation."
— Hilton Kramer

"Louis lived his life in service to the material — he always worked through the lens, a process by which he was uniquely gifted and special. Every Malle film presents a solid story, that has been realized in a uniquely creative, affectionate, and humanistic way."
— Fred Berner, Producer of *Vanya on 42nd St.*,
Assistant director on *Alamo Bay*

At the outset of Louis Malle's cult comedy *My Dinner with André* (1981), acclaimed playwright Wallace Shawn (*Our Late Night, Uncle Dan and Aunt Lemon*) invites us to join him for dinner with an old friend: the distinguished and erudite, legendary stage director André Gregory. Through the sheer power of words and imagery, Gregory — portraying a character based on himself — describes his globe-trotting adventures to Shawn and the audience, guiding us through a two-hour series of fantastic, surrealistic voyages, across landscapes illuminated only to the mind's eye. We follow André to the mystical Scottish colony of Findhorn, through a death and rebirth ceremony on craggy Montauk, and out into the middle of the vast, empty Sahara by night, beneath an endless canopy of stars.

The consistent passion in André's voice and mannerisms overpowers us. He radiates contagious enthusiasm, the thrill of ceaseless discovery sets his words afire, and he becomes — through his self-characterization — a nearly perfect representation of Louis Malle. Just as Gregory projects a need to continually explore, discover and expand his horizons, accounts of Malle's highly transitional life paint a portrait of a restless, footloose artist whose need to engage in wayfaring, boundary-pushing, and

7

sailing repeatedly into uncharted waters became an integral component of his life at an early age, and thus laid the groundwork for his outlook and his trajectory as a filmmaker during adulthood.

Malle's deep-seated need to explore first blossomed during early adolescence, when he experienced a series of mildly upsetting physiological restraints. He suffered from a heart murmur that prevented him from engaging in strenuous activity[1] (an obvious inspiration for *Le Souffle au cœur*) and temporarily kept him from attending school. While cloistered in his home, he responded to his physical limitations by charting the world vicariously through literature, which temporarily suppressed his sense of confinement and suspended the illusions of physical movement and global exploration within his mind. Once he overcame his debilitating condition and gained an increased capacity for physical exertion, he did everything in his power to escape from the limitations of the past. Yet, according to his son Manuel, he periodically experienced health problems over the next few decades and even spent one summer holiday wearing a heart device.[2] Although Malle ultimately died from lymphoma and not a coronary ailment, he had open-heart surgery in late 1990 and doctors cautioned him not to strain himself.[3] It seems, from all these accounts, that the possibility of death from a coronary condition lingered with Louis Malle for many years. At the very least, the memories of physical restraint during boyhood hung over Malle's head like a dark shroud. And given these recollections, Malle's overwhelming need to explore the world as a form of liberation only grew in intensity. Filmmaking ultimately became his tool for canvassing the world around him, and he spent most of his adult life probing countless, unfamiliar vistas of experience with his movie camera: Bangkok (*Bons Baisers de Bangkok*); India (*L'Inde fantôme, Calcutta*); Algeria (unreleased documentary); and the American Midwest (*God's Country*),[4] to name but a few. Malle's wanderlust also expanded the scope of his subject matter, by catalyzing his need to constantly push into new cinematic territory from project to project—a kind of restless, intra-medium exploration — which is why, as writer-director, he never leads his audience into the same onscreen world twice. In commentaries, Malle constantly alludes to "reinventing" and expanding his cinematic sphere of reference with changes of focus; new subjects; untapped themes, genres and emotional subtexts; and, significantly, geographical transitions. His oeuvre can thus be seen as an ongoing series of excursions into uncharted cinematic waters—from undersea documentary work (*Le Monde du silence* [1956]); to provocative, explicit dramas that peel back the layers of the bourgeois (*Les Amants* [1958], *Damage* [1992]); to quietly funny, understated character comedies (*Atlantic City* [1980], *Le Souffle au cœur* [1971]); to—in one case—surrealistic, enigmatic Freudian fantasy (*Black Moon* [1975]). This diversity existed from the very beginning, and even became evident in the multifarious works that inspired Malle to pick up a camera: motion pictures such as Jean Renoir's *Rules of the Game* (1939), Roger Leenhardt's *Les Dernières Vacances* (1948), and Josef von Baky's Nazi-funded *Münchhausen* (1943) could hardly be more disparate.[5]

As a by-product of Malle's own taste for exploration, he used his filmmaking to carry viewers' minds into new realms, and the limitless horizon concept of the Shunryu Suzuki text *Zen Mind, Beginner's Mind* (a work that influenced Malle tremendously), became an integral spatio-temporal component of his cinematic praxis, evident as early as 1956, via his contributions to *The Silent World*. Ergo, throughout his *œuvre*, Malle makes frequent use of abrechtian kinesthesia and spatial relationships, doing his utmost to suspend the sensations of physical limitation and stasis in the viewer's mind. To varying degrees in all of his films aside from *Zazie dans le Métro* (the one "odd duck" in his catalogue — the film that plays by unique ontological rules), Malle presents the viewer with a hyperreal onscreen environment by tearing down the "fourth wall" between the audience and the characters. He is thus able to suspend the illusion of a fully dimensional world beyond the confines of the screen and immerses the audience in a sphere of hyperrealism, to the same degree that Brecht constantly reminded the audience of the artificiality of the theatrical experience. Stylistically speaking, this explains Malle's careful avoidance of all Brechtian alienation devices— his disinclination for jump-cuts; one-shot or stagy scenes; theatrical, expressionistic *mise en scène*; and cinematographic stasis. Instead, he often gravitates to a highly mobile camera, deep-focus, and extraneous sounds that suggest a continually unfolding world in the distance — devices most apparent in his films *Ascenseur pour l'échafaud*; *Le Feu follet*; *Lacombe, Lucien*; and *Black Moon*. The abrechtianism also explains his cross-genre pollination, his multilayered (astereotypical, unreadable) characters and his structural experimentation that enables his characters to arc so dramatically that they gravitate not simply to new stages of development, but to multiple onscreen *worlds* within the same film, that have distinct aesthetic qualities and spatial relationships (most evident in *Les Amants* and *Viva Maria*)—a technique that Kubrick would later use in *Full Metal Jacket* (1987) and Neil Jordan in *The Crying Game* (1992).

Despite the obvious appeal of Malle's adventurous diversity from film to film and his capacity for immersing his audiences in the cinematic experience, his eclecticism has given him a sizeable number of detractors—critics and viewers who, instead of perceiving topical, thematic, and stylistic disparity as great strengths, view those qualities as insurmountable handicaps. Bound to the New Wave idea of "personal style," these commentators brush Malle aside. Their consequent ambivalence has ultimately become a wall, separating the writer-director from the serious attention his work so consistently and passionately demands, and a reminder that by clinging to nonconformity, Malle took a broad, risky leap without a safety net.

As Pauline Kael keenly observes:

> The only quality common to the films of Louis Malle is the restless intelligence one senses in them. A new Chabrol or a Losey is as easily recognizable as a Magritte, but even film enthusiasts have only a vague idea of Malle's work. Had Malle gone on making variations of almost any one of his films, it is practically certain he would have been acclaimed long ago, but a director who is impatient and dissatisfied and never tackles the same problem twice gives reviewers trouble and is likely to be dismissed as a dilettante.[6]

In striking fulfillment of the Kaelian prophecy, the *Village Voice's* Andrew Sarris observes in a *Lacombe, Lucien* review, "There seemed to be something irremediably *dilettantish* in Malle's artistic temperament. He seemed to be following the public pulse more closely than his own inner voice."[7] Likewise, in his massive reference volume *French New Wave*, Jean Douchet limits the discussion of Malle to a cursory paragraph and concludes with, "His work includes a few successful films that are primarily the result ... of good scripts and an interesting story."[8] The author also incorporates a shockingly hollow observation from *Cahiers du cinéma*: "[Malle] is still in search of a 'subject.' Disturbing, honest, hard working, he's looking for 'his' vision of the world, but ... so far it's managed to evade him."[9]

In her essay "Approaching Artaud," Susan Sontag writes that "Modern literature projects ... the romantic conception of writing as a medium in which a singular personality heroically exposes itself."[10] If one extends this logic to the *auteurists* of the Nouvelle Vague, it suggests that Truffaut, Chabrol, Rohmer and Godard staked a claim to the title of "cinematic modernists," each a purveyor of a singular identity via a unique set of aesthetic and stylistic trademarks. But Malle believed their claim aberrant, and on some level found Bazinian auteurism distasteful. The director's brother, Vincent Malle, reflects, "One of the things that [Louis] was the most proud [of] is that ... he never ... did the same film [twice].... And that's why he was completely [irritated] ... when people compared him with Truffaut ... because [Louis] kept saying that Truffaut does the same film over and over and over again."[11] Malle held a conviction that the auteurist concept as "one set of preoccupations representative of a singular id" is inherently false, because it fails to take into account the constantly evolving worldview and ever-shifting perception of the artist. It was this fallacy that Malle's stylistic and thematic fluidity critiqued so stringently and indirectly rectified, via its own eclecticism. The director thus rewrote the rules that Bazin, Truffaut, and Sarris established, and, in turn, raised the question of whether filmmakers who share his eclecticism in their *œuvres* (e.g., Ruiz, Aléa, Bertolucci, Mizoguchi) should not be considered more authentic harbingers of personal expression than Truffaut, Rohmer, Chabrol and Godard.

Malle's *modus operandi* for choosing subject matter bears close comparison to Sontag's assessments about Artaud: his tastes, interests and thematic preoccupations were guided by some level of instinct that he could not control on a conscious and rational level. The rapidity with which his instincts shifted, in turn, accelerated his personal growth to a greater degree than most directors, multiplying and broadening the number of stages through which he evolved psychologically, spiritually, intellectually, emotionally, creatively, within any set period — and thus made it that much clearer to him that he needed to retain thematic and topical fluidity from film to film if his motion pictures were, in any way, to continue to function as personal statements.

For these reasons, it is not exactly accurate to classify Malle as an "anti-auteur." Moreover, despite surface-level inconsistencies, Malle's work does encompass a few running threads from film to film:

(1) *"The World Through a Child's Eyes"*: Throughout his career, Malle placed adolescents or pre-adolescents at the center of a countless number of features. As Susan Sarandon observes, "[Louis] was definitely somebody who was locked into an adolescent's point of view. I mean, if you look at all of Louis's really good films, they're all about a boy or a girl of that age, or slightly older. And there's clearly something to that."[12] A great many of these films, in turn, investigate the "loss of innocence"

in children, as Malle felt transfixed by that moment when the corruption and defilement of the adult world brings an adolescent in touch with reality.[13] Examples include *Zazie dans le métro*; *Le Souffle au cœur*; *Lacombe, Lucien*; *Black Moon*; *Pretty Baby*; *Alamo Bay*; and *Au revoir les enfants*; Malle's unproduced, Guare-written script for *Dietrich and Marlene* is structured around the same conceit.

(2) *Subtlety:* A surprisingly large number of mainstream critics and lay viewers respond identically to each new Malle film after an initial screening: most feel dramatically underwhelmed. Leonard Maltin tags a mediocre rating onto *May Fools* (1990) with the observation, "It's all rather slight."[14] The editors of *The Motion Picture Guide* lace their review of *May Fools* with the criticism: "[*Milou en mai*] seems more akin to the fluffy inconsequentiality of *Cousin, Cousine*," and attack the picture's aesthetic as "visually undistinguished in a generically handsome way." [15] Although Roger Ebert hails *Lacombe, Lucien* as a masterwork, he "wasn't sure of [it's] point"—as if he expected some grandiose "message" that Malle failed to deliver. [16] And Maltin dismisses *Pretty Baby* as "distressingly low-key."[17]

From observer to observer, one notices the astonishing similarity of these comments; countless like examples littered the press following the release of each new Malle film. Few of Malle's detractors stopped to consider another possibility: subtlety, understatement, and dramatically "low-key" material are as integral to the cinema of Louis Malle as—say—time-fractured narratives are to the films of Alain Resnais. Ergo, one's complaints about "underwhelming" material point not to the director's errors, but to the viewer's myopic inability to lock into Malle's minimalist vision by adopting a new perspective. This shift of focus and abandonment of expectation is essential if one wishes to understand and appreciate Louis Malle's work. Malle thus worked extremely well with subtle, ahistrionic actors, capable of delivering understated performances, and it is hardly surprising that Jean Douchet describes Maurice Ronet (to whom Malle gave two of the finest roles of his career) as "a subtle actor whose sense of the contingency of things prevented him from becoming the star he could have been."[18] Ronet required a director keenly enough attuned to his quiet dramatic technique, with a similar gift for understatement; Malle fit the bill perfectly.

(3) *Socially exiled main characters:* Philip French highlights another exception to the heterogeneity of Malle's films: many of Malle's main characters are "outsiders, people who feel alienated from the society they live in."[19] Consider *Les Amants'* Jeanne Tournier, *Le Voleur's* Georges Randal, *Pretty Baby's* E.J. Bellocq, *My Dinner with André's* André Gregory, *Atlantic City's* Lou Pascal, *Feu follet's* Alain Leroy, and *Damage's* Stephen Fleming, among others.

(4) *Heightened ethos via negation and irony:* Countless Malle features employ moral negation, by refusing to levy ethical judgment against the main character(s) (as in the case of *Lacombe, Lucien*) or moral irony, by deliberately playing the devil's advocate and adopting a perverse or objectionable moral stance. The major examples of the latter include: *Pretty Baby*, given its "polite view of (child) prostitution"[20]; *Murmur of the Heart*, with its acceptance of mother-son incest; and even *Atlantic City*, where cocaine dealing becomes the *deus ex machina* that enables "nickel and dime" numbers man Lou Pascal (Burt Lancaster) to live out his gangster fantasies. Malle's

"immoral" stances sprung from his own mischievousness — the charge he pulled from scandalizing audiences with seemingly "objectionable" content and messages. Manuel Malle recalls attending a repertory screening of *Le Souffle au cœur* with his father in late 1993, on the upper West Side of Manhattan. The Malles sat behind two elderly women who were unfamiliar with the picture's subject matter and unaware of its "shocking" finale. With one eye on the ladies, Malle waited anxiously for the "consummation" of the mother-son relationship in the film, where 12-year-old son Laurent (Benoît Ferreux) begins to undress his intoxicated mother Clara (Léa Massari) and "accidentally" makes love to her in a moment of drunken euphoria. As the elderly women squealed and gasped, Louis burst into peals of laughter.[21] He knew what he was doing, all right: for he only adopted his controversial moral perspectives ironically, to impel his viewers to reexamine their own hypocrisies and social mores. "I've always liked to ... [force] people to reconsider preconceived ideas," Malle stated in an interview.[22] In this light, the films emerge as more morally triumphant than other mainstream films, Malle as more morally conscientious than his contemporaries.

André Bazin's introduction to his essay "The Myth of Total Cinema" offers a nearly perfect metaphorical insight into the genesis of Malle's nontheoretical method for making stylistic choices on feature films:

> Paradoxically enough, the impression left on the reader by Georges Sadoul's admirable book on the origins of the cinema is of a reversal, in spite of the author's Marxist views, of the relations between an economic and technical evolution and the imagination of those carrying on the search. The way things happened seems to call for a reversal of the historical order of causality, which goes from the economic infrastructure to the ideological superstructure, and for us to consider the basic technical discoveries as fortunate accidents but essentially second in importance to the preconceived ideas of the inventors. The cinema is an idealistic phenomenon. The concept men had of it existed so to speak fully armed in their minds, as if in some platonic heaven, and what strikes us most of all is the obstinate resistance of matter to ideas rather than of any help offered by techniques to the imagination of the researchers.[23]

One may reduce Bazin's "conceptual → mechanical" transition to the microcosmic level of personal discovery as it newly recurs for each future filmmaker during his or her childhood years (temporarily ignoring the macrocosmic level of social trends and phenomena). Given storytelling as a "conceptual" phenomenon (particularly as it arises in literature, the clearest distillation of storytelling into a medium), and cinema as a "mechanical" phenomenon (a vehicle for storytelling), many young cineastes follow the reverse transition (i.e., mechanical → conceptual) during the early stages of intellectual and artistic development. These directors' recollections of their early childhood are thus rife with accounts of cinephilia — stories of attending film screenings two, three, four, five times a week, and feeling drawn to the medium *per se* (desiring, on some instinctive level, involvement in the process of creating motion pictures without a full understanding), but only later turning to stories, as subject matter or fuel for the cinematic process. In other words, the conceptual need to tell stories follows, and thus becomes subservient to, the overpowering discovery of the mechanical medium of cinema. Truffaut offers a classic example in the volume of collected interviews *Le Cinéma selon François Truffaut*. He recalls first turning to film as an escape from family travails and the family's loathsome camping trips, long before any recollections of literary discovery.[24,25]

Such is not the case with Malle. Anecdotes from his boyhood reveal explicitly that because of his heart murmur, his discovery of storytelling (through literature) took a front seat to his discovery of cinema. Malle dove into a succession of literary works before he encountered motion pictures. He observes of his adolescence, "I was very much immersed in literature. I read almost anything — I even read Nietzsche when I was fourteen!... My passion for the cinema came ... after that."[26]

The fact that literature predates motion pictures as a formative influence in Malle's life is a critical point. It suggests that upon discovery of cinema, he brought to it a preexistent, unusually strong appreciation for storytelling, instead of beginning the road to his career by studying ideas about what film can and cannot do, and turning to literature later, as fuel for his cinematic craft. In other words, during Malle's boyhood, cinema became subservient to the need to tell a story — or a vehicle for storytelling — instead of vice versa, as was the case with his contemporaries.[27,28]

Appropriately, Louis Malle's son, Manuel, recalls that his father regarded himself primarily as a storyteller.[29] And later on, in the 1950s, the very fact that Malle chose to drop out of the IDHEC film school to work with Jacques Cousteau on the *Calypso* illustrates the same idea. By joining Cousteau, Malle eschewed days he would have otherwise spent in a classroom, debating heady, dry cinematic theories with fellow students, and instead spent countless hours learning the hands-on of how to tell a story visually, filming fish and sealife underwater. As a result, he became better prepared, technically, than the *Cahiers* founders, and high polish and technical proficiency graced his features.[30]

Because the need to tell a strong story with fleshed-out, multidimensional characters remained Malle's chief artistic purpose, he sought to use techniques appropriate for the subject, characters, themes, and dramatic situations at hand; the diversity of subject, in turn, explains the lack of stylistic consistency throughout his career. For example: because *Zazie dans le métro* paints the adult world through a child's eyes, Malle employs playful techniques: The camera whips in and out, the actors accelerate and decelerate, the *mise en scène* shifts. And because *My Dinner with André* turns the viewer into an unseen member of a three-person dinner conversation, Malle uses a simple series of two shots and close-ups, cutting back and forth between Wally Shawn and André Gregory until the edits become subliminal. Thus, Malle uses a kind of cinematic self-referentiality, where each of his motion pictures carries an appropriate style relative to content, and where each picture must thus be studied independently of the others that precede and follow it.[31]

Such an interpretive mode — the idea of returning to story as the most rudimentary, nontheoretical functional element of the cinematic narrative — may appear too simple, which could explain why so many critics and film historians have overlooked it. Yet, to the contrary, this mode remains far more complex and demanding than the auteurist approach. It required Malle to continually attempt to define a much broader and more ambitious trope than his contemporaries— not simply, "How can I develop a set of recurrent visual and aural cinematic metaphors to carry and represent my own obsessions, idiosyncrasies, and general worldview," but epistemologically, "How can I single out and objectively summarize the platonic nature of the link between 'content' and 'form appropriate to content' that will retain validity in all cases?"

On a broader level, Malle sought an answer to this question within the boundaries of *mainstream* narrative cinema for his feature films. If John Cassavetes exemplified the value of working spontaneously, against the grain of convention, to expand the possibilities of the filmic form, Malle reminds us of the value of holding to preestablished methods, and using the constancy (and reliability) of approach to master the cinematic craft over several decades and sculpt "amazingly good films in several styles."[32] In the autobiographical section of *Louis Malle par Louis Malle,* the director reflects:

> I am convinced, there are two categories of creators: those who quickly and spontaneously throw out the best they can offer, and those who, throughout their entire lives, never stop perfecting their work, in a slow, often necessary evolution. A filmmaker like Jean-Luc Godard belongs to the first category. From his very first film he found his entire sensibility and, over 60 years, his outlook has been completely unique, and superior to everyone else's. This isn't a matter of talent, but of genius, of extraordinary intuition. He will throw out images onto the celluloid, in a carefully controlled improvisation, with a very sure instinct. And he doesn't preoccupy himself with deepening these sensibilities. Since 1968, he has searched for something different, something unique, and now he proceeds by trial and error. God knows how different we are, but I admire him; he fascinates me. I would like to see all of his films, right away. At the other end of the spectrum from this spontaneous creator, in the fashion of Gericault, there is the long progression appropriate to Delacroix or Matisse. Within my means, this is the type of destiny that tempts and inspires me.[33]

And yet, given this nontheoretical *démarche* for feature films, Malle crafted his documentaries, in some respects, on a theoretical basis. The grand paradox is that although he worked within the theoretical boundaries of *cinema direct* for the nonfiction films, playing by the rules of temporal and spatial continuity, synchronous sound, and the construction of a cinematic first-person perspective, he operated instinctively from moment to moment while shooting the documentaries.

———————————

According to *Alamo Bay* producer Ross Milloy (*Lord of the Flies*), Louis Malle patterned the trajectory of his personal and professional life after an unusual biological principle. Milloy reflects:

> [Louis] was always ... trying to go someplace new. And I remember he once told me that he liked to ... totally change himself and his environment every seven years.... [following the teachings of] some yoga swami.... He mentioned

it to me in the context of ... your skin changing every seven years ... [human] skin refreshes itself, regenerates itself, every seven years ... and ... [Louis] ... said [because of that] he always liked to try and kind of recreate himself and his environment every seven years, which ... prompted [his] move to America.[34]

In other words, Malle periodically reinvented himself throughout his life. At several watershed points, he wiped the slate clean, "rewriting" his thought process and sensibilities by starting afresh with not simply a new film or genre, but a new environment altogether.[35] It began by accident in 1956, when an ear infection sent him to a New York hospital and physiologically prevented him from continuing his documentary work with Cousteau, at which point he turned to the narrative fiction of *Ascenseur* and *Les Amants*. It happened in 1967 when feelings of personal stasis and *Le Voleur*'s disappointing critical reception turned him off to conventional drama and the disillusioned filmmaker dropped out of society, shooting *L'Inde fantôme* in exile, in India. It happened in 1976, when Malle moved from the Causse de Limogne to Los Angeles and began making Hollywood studio pictures. And it happened in 1993, when, following the insults that the press unjustly heaped onto *Damage*, Malle headed to New York and made the low-budget, "hands-on" indie film *Vanya on 42nd Street*, a decision Candice Bergen calls "one of the best moves Louis ever made."[36] But of these instances, the director's Indian exile impacted his subsequent work more dramatically than any other transition. The director's brother, Vincent Malle, observes:

> The trip to India changed [Louis] considerably.... [India] ... is [a country] that he was completely fascinated by ... because he could not apply any of his ... very classical analysis to what was around him.... He was in a completely different world. And although he had done documentaries before and went traveling a lot, this was the first time he was completely in a country that was mesmerizing and flabbergasting and everything, and so he decided to just drift along ... like Stendhal, becoming a mirror on the road, basically.... And so that was ... very scary, and at the same time very liberating. He certainly was *more* [of a *raissoneur* before India] ... extraordinarily well-read, and knew a lot of philosophy, and stuff like that, and logic, and ... he always tried to put to analysis what was happening to him, and then compared it to things that he had read about or knew about ... [put everything into] into some kind of a classification. Whereas with India, he couldn't do that because it doesn't work ... everything is so much ... bang ... in your face ... you cannot try to think about Pascal, and Descartes, and all of that ... it doesn't work at all! India [challenged the preconceptions Louis had] ... [for in India], once ... you think you have understood something, something else comes upon that is ... the complete opposite of what you thought you had understood.[37]

Indeed, despite all of the thematic and topical reinvention from project to project in the director's filmography, one can safely divide Malle's work into "pre–India" and "post–India" without incurring complications, and "the Indian documentaries"— *Phantom India* and *Calcutta*—mark the great divide in Louis Malle's filmography: the watershed point of complete (or near complete), multileveled artistic regenesis for the filmmaker. This regenesis found its source in an internal transmutation: to

an inestimable degree, Malle almost completely abandoned classical Western reasoning following India. Vincent Malle observes:

> One of the things that India did ... and ... May '68, too ... is that [Louis] ...
> learned to let go much more than he used to. He was ... less guarded and less
> distant with his emotions ... or at least [would] let his emotions speak and react.
> He was more instinctive ... after India, than he was before. So ... that did change
> the way he wanted to tell stories, and the way he related to people.[38]

On set, Malle began operating according to pure reflex and instinct; for example, according to Candice Bergen, he learned to rely on sound as his key reference
point in determining which take to use. He would stand on the edge of the set, chew-
ing gum with his eyes closed, while he listened to takes through a set of headphones.[39]
And Vincent Malle observes, "One of [Louis's] favorite phrases after [India] was to
approach everything with *approximation successif* ... successive approximations.
Which is ... you try something, it doesn't work; you try something else ... you make
your circles smaller and smaller until you think you have some kind of a field where
you feel comfortable."[40]

But heightened instinct only represents part of the equation; the additional internal changes that Malle experienced are almost too numerous to mention. Only by
dropping out and heading for the East did he find the means to hone and develop his
behavioral perception as a visual anthropologist, an ability he would transpose to his
direction on the set of *Le Souffle au cœur*; *Lacombe, Lucien*; *Pretty Baby*, and many
other works, ascending to a level of awareness that transcended reason and almost
became a sixth sense. Only via the Indian experience did Malle attain the self-
knowledge to grasp the significance in his own life of relinquishing his ongoing search
for a personal style and embrace the prospect of challenging his own sensibilities
from film to film: It imparted greater and greater acuity of self-perception, so that
he could retain a constantly-sharpening awareness of his feelings and intuitions about
the events that unfolded around him. And only at this point did the director — near-
suicidal in 1967[41] — discover a way to save himself in a period of extreme emotional
and personal crisis (c. 1967), with a simple method of creative recharge: India made
hands-on, 16mm documentary filmmaking *per se* a cathartic vehicle for Malle until
his death.

India also drew out a level of humanism in Malle's work that meant accepting
a whole person — embracing their weaknesses along with their strengths, and loving
the individual, despite shortcomings and not without traces of humor. The firsthand
knowledge that Malle gained, in India, of non–Judaeo-Christian value systems abetted this acceptance. The experience of being plunged into an alien culture out of
sync with Western ethos enabled Malle, upon returning to France, to accept the
immorality and hypocrisy of the French bourgeois *classe* to which he belonged as a
child, and helped him observe the seeds of a "sexually liberated" society in 1950s bourgeois France[42] — perceptions most apparent in *Murmur*. More broadly, Malle became
a moral relativist, adopting a brand of situational ethics that helped him take an
accepting, nonjudgmental view of such issues as mother-son incest, wartime collab-

oration, and child prostitution, by empathetically assuming the perspectives of those at the center of the controversies.

Narratively, Malle's internal transformation emerged alongside a gradual, step-by-step liberation from any conventional Western dramatic structure, as the director progressed from *Murmur* to *Lacombe* to *Black Moon* to *Pretty Baby*. The Eastern-influenced structural liberation is most overwhelming in the first half of *Pretty Baby*, where Malle, cinematographer Sven Nykvist, and scenarist Polly Platt merely set up their actors in scenes and let those scenes unfold, relying exclusively on the behavior of the actors to provide dramatic momentum, tension, and conflict.[43] Taken together, the reliance on quasi-improvisatory, documentary-like behavioral observation and the gradual loss of Western dramatic architecture — abilities that Malle acquired and honed as the '70s progressed — embodied major strides toward realism.[44]

Malle's heightened instinctiveness sharpened and strengthened a philosophy that he had acquired before his Eastern exile. Throughout his career, Malle — as a documentarian — was most interested in photographing a preorchestrated, predetermined performance, in lieu of creating one. David Hare observes:

> Louis was a director who expected people to come and offer something to him. If you look at his greatest work ... *My Dinner with André* ... *Lacombe, Lucien* ... *Atlantic City* ... the greatest stuff often involves something that's already there. And then this man comes and photographs it ... Louis liked to be offered something. He didn't like to have to *create* something from the ground up ... basically, what he wanted to do is photograph something that's happening. And then mold it and shape it. He [wasn't] good at making it happen in the first place.[45]

Sarandon echoes this insight about Malle by affirming the idea that he "was not an actor's director in that he gave you notes."[46] In fact, she describes a level of extreme discomfort that Malle expressed when directing anyone. For example, when problems arose on the set of *Atlantic City*, Malle sent Sarandon to talk to Lancaster, and gave Lancaster suggestions through her. She characterizes Malle as particularly uncomfortable directing children, as he demonstrated on the set of *Pretty Baby*:

> Brooke [Shields] had difficulty. And I would be off-camera, doing the lines in a little tiny voice that always made her laugh. So I just came to the set when I wasn't working to try to help work with her. Because [Louis] wasn't comfortable working with her. I was there to try to act as ... [an] interpreter for Louis. The "go-between" if he wanted something."[47]

To partially steer around directing actors, Malle used razor-sharp strategic casting; he would seek out performers who had some intimate connection with or understanding of their characters. In the case of *Lacombe, Lucien*, for example, Malle hired unknown Pierre Blaise because "I could see right away that he could completely identify with the character."[48]

Malle's hesitancy to offer overt direction to actors points to both his conviction that actors need to do very little onscreen (given the camera's ability to catch every nuance that unfolds before it) and to his love of minimalism. In those cases where Malle gave explicit direction, he almost always asked for less intensity. Ergo, John Guare remembers Malle's direction to Burt Lancaster in *Atlantic City*: "Louis kept saying, 'Burt: *down*. Less, less, less, less, less.'"[49] And when Malle videotaped André Gregory rehearsing for *Dinner*, he beseeched Gregory to subdue his performance with, "It would win a Tony, but it would never win you an Oscar."[50] Other instances of Malle's hesitancy to give performance-related direction demonstrate his heightened sensitivity to actors' feelings, as when he took Brooke Smith aside on *Vanya* and whispered suggestions into her ear, in lieu of calling out instructions, simply to avoid embarrassing her in the presence of other actors. Smith recalls, "Sometimes when I'm working with a director and they direct me in some kind of intimate adjustment and they do it out loud in front of everybody, that ... is very jarring.... [Louis] wouldn't do that at all.... He would come over and talk quietly with you."[51] Malle evinced the same level of consideration with innumerable performers.

According to David Hare, Malle's economic model for filmmaking by the end of his life became Rainer Werner Fassbinder; he admired Fassbinder's method of assembling a small crew and budget and using limited resources to produce a beautiful onscreen aesthetic. Hare comments:

> Being a prodigiously intelligent man, [Louis] had concluded that American filmmaking was becoming hopelessly elephantine, that it takes all day to get a shot, you know, that films all have to be ... [he takes on an affected accent] huge, and important, and major motion pictures ... and that there is a pomposity among the artists in American film now, that is matched by the elephantiasis of the budget, and you might say the ridiculous emphasis on the aesthetic ... that the lighting cameraman now rules the roost.... [And Louis] ... used to say, "Look at Fassbinder. He doesn't light the shot, he just uses what lighting is there, and yet he creates, accidentally, effects that are far more beautiful than the effects that are created by Vittorio Storaro spending five hours lighting. And, come on, we've gotta be quicker about [it] ..." so that, you know, he was in Heaven, making both the things he made with Wally, you know, when he was making *My Dinner with André*, or when he made *Vanya*. That was [Louis's] idea of filmmaking. He loved it! He loved carrying the camera himself, ... he'd hold the sound boom. He'd be perfectly happy working sound![52]

This provides another explanation for why Malle gravitated to hands-on, 16mm filmmaking—working with light, extremely mobile crews, after debacles like *Vie privée* (when he shot *Vive le tour*) and the twin calamities of *Crackers* and *Alamo Bay* (when he shot *God's Country* and *Pursuit*). Hands-on filmmaking became a mode of escape from studio gigantism. It renewed his interest in directing.

But in the end, the equation was perhaps a bit more complex. According to Candice Bergen, Malle spent his life chasing a paradox, identified, on the most local and immediate level, by René Prédal in his 1989 book *Louis Malle*. Prédal suggests that Malle's American experience revolved around his ongoing quixotic mission to accomplish the impossible. He writes, "After *Atlantic City* ... Louis wanted to enter into the System and direct an American film in a way that would give him enough elbow room to make it exactly as he wanted it."[53] The "way" Predal references is, of course, the European way; Malle wanted to make a Hollywood studio film that became a commercial and critical triumph, yet retain the flexibility everpresent for European directors on their home turf. Candice Bergen echoes Prédal's insight about her late husband, on a broader level, when reflecting on the miserable *Crackers* experience:

> I think he was taking [*Crackers*] in part to have a film that might be a commercial film, because he was always frustrated by ... trying to make a film that was faithful to his talent and his gifts and his taste as a filmmaker, but that would also be a commercial success.... He was always sort of chasing this kind of elusive critical and commercial success, while at the same time being fairly contemptuous of commercial success and commercial films. He ... would have liked to have had the commercial success, but not to have compromised himself, and I think he felt that with *Crackers*, which was very good, easy money ... that he compromised himself.[54]

But generally speaking, these compromises were rare in Malle's life and experience. He remains, above all else, a director who never (*Crackers* aside) compromised on the intelligence of his work. His failure to meld the combination of artistic integrity and depth with the status of a Hollywood blockbuster is merely a reflection on the impossibility of that goal.

1
Le Monde du silence (The Silent World)—1956
Plunging Through the Fourth Wall

"Free water. Free to pour seaward through the Gate. Beholden to no man. Free to link up with the California Current beyond the Farallones and head for the Bering Sea. To curve west and roam for months toward Asiatic shores. To slip southward into the blue arms of tropic seas roiled by the northeast trade, then to range on and on, not far above the line...."

"Wandering is an art in itself."
— Sterling Hayden, *Wanderer*

"Confined indoors by ill health and winter weather, [Teddy] wheezed restlessly from room to room in search of further entertainment. For a while he amused himself with *objets d'art* in the parlor: a Russian moujik pulling a tin sledge across a snowfield of malachite; a carved Swiss hunter chasing chamois goats around an improbably small mountain."
— Edmund Morris,
The Rise of Theodore Roosevelt

BACKGROUND

In 1951, after finishing one year at the Institut d'Études Politiques in Paris, 19-year-old Louis Malle applied and gained acceptance to the prestigious, ultra-competitive Institut des Hautes Études Cinématographiques (IDHEC) film school, a division of the Université de Paris. Malle managed to convince his wealthy parents—dubious about his future in cinema—to fund enrollment in degree programs at both universities, while he studied politics and film concurrently. Yet after a year, Malle grew dissatisfied with IDHEC's strong theoretical approach to cinema.[1] After directing and editing only one highly formalist five-minute short, the January 1953 film "Crazéologie,"[2] a Brechtian work that reflected "the early works of Beckett and Ionesco"[3] starring his brother Bernard and Louis Bataille,[4] Malle began to suffer from a pronounced sense of ennui, and longed to cultivate his filmmaking abilities with additional hands-on experience, using cameras and editing equipment. The poorly-funded university, however, offered little assistance. Malle's solution arrived in the spring of 1953, when a seasoned oceanographer and French *cause célebré* walked into the IDHEC director's office.[5]

Jacques-Yves Cousteau had broken new scientific ground several years earlier by inventing the aqualung, and garnered worldwide acclaim in 1950 following the publication of *The Silent World*, a 250-page record of his oceanographic accomplishments.[6] His reputation also spread with the release of several underwater shorts distributed by Universal, one of which, *Par dix-huit mètres de fond* (Sixty feet down), won an award for Best Short Film at Cannes in 1942.[7] Armed with a love of cinema, a passion for oceanic exploration, and an overhauled exploratory vessel christened *Calypso*, Cousteau convinced British Petroleum's chief geologist that aqualung divers could be useful in underwater oil prospecting. The oceanographer thus managed to secure his first major contract with British Petroleum. Though the contract did not fund undersea exploration *per se*, it enabled Cousteau to hire and train a young, enthusiastic, restless film student as a cameraman. The captain foresaw filming the crew's adventures on a long voyage with his new apprentice, and editing the footage into a feature-length documentary.

Cousteau visited IDHEC and requested a student interested in working aboard *Calypso* during the summer. Malle, then class president, volunteered for the task.[8,9] After three months of learning to direct, shoot, edit and dive on the British Petroleum voyage, Malle dropped out of IDHEC to work with Cousteau full time. He spent 1953 cutting his teeth on the crew's equipment, and on January 7, 1954, the crew sailed out of Marseilles,[10] traversing the Red Sea, the Mediterranean, the Persian Gulf, and the Indian Ocean, where filming for *The Silent World* (*Le Monde du silence*) began. In a 1956 *New York Times* article, Cousteau notes, "our fourteen divers logged 5,000 individual descents in the 11 months we were at sea filming *The Silent World*."[11] Given Malle's equal participation in the cinematography, direction, and editing of the film, Cousteau willingly offered the young, aspiring filmmaker co-directorial credit on the picture.

The filmmakers employed revolutionary cinematographic techniques for the shoot, including "The SM-2 Submarine Cinecamera, a "custom-built 35-mm motion picture camera that takes a 200-foot load of color or black and white film,"[12] equipped to change speeds and lenses underwater.[13] For lighting, the team used "pyrotechnic torches housing a battery at the base and wires leading to a detonator at the top. [The] battery [would ignite the] air bag at top starting [an] underwater flame which lasts for sixty seconds."[14] Malle and Cousteau supplemented this light with several dozen 6,000 watt flood lamps, powered by underwater cable that ran from the ship.[15]

SYNOPSIS

As an 86 minute[16] filmed document of the Cousteau team's exploratory voyage across the Red Sea and into the Seychelles, *Monde du silence* incorporates the following sequences, respectively: (1) In an underwater epilogue, divers ignite torches and descend to the ocean floor, where they film sealife. (2) On the Calypso's deck, an unseen narrator introduces the audience to Cousteau and his crewmen for the first time. (3) The Cousteau team "unexpectedly" encounters a team of Greek sponge divers underwater, who violently chop off and collect coral samples. (4) In-house film technician André Laban accidentally stays underwater for an excessive amount of time, and suffers from drunkenness induced by nitrogen narcosis; Cousteau forces Laban to stay trapped in a decompression chamber while his shipmates enjoy a feast of succulent lobster. (5) Numerous dolphins surround the Calypso and leap out of the water (a sequence Cousteau edits into a Disneyesque "dance of the porpoises"). (6) In a nighttime sequence, divers Frédéric Dumas and Albert Falco carry underwater torches to a record depth of 247 feet below sea level, and reveal colors never before observed by men. (7) Members of the Cousteau team plant dynamite on the ocean floor, to kill sealife *en masse* and stuff the specimens into formaldehyde-filled research jars. (8) Cousteau informs his crew, "a munitions ship went down in 1941, somewhere in the channel, at about one hundred feet,"[17] and implores the divers to search for the ship, which leads to an extended discovery and exploration of a shipwrecked vessel, *The Thistlegorm*. (9) *The Calypso* runs into a monsoon storm. (10) In an infamous, harrowing series of events, *The Calypso* accidentally crashes into a mother whale, and her calf ensues, lacerating itself on the ship's propeller. To end the whale's torment mercifully, Dumas draws a rifle and puts a bullet through the calf's head. Thirty bloodthirsty sharks approach the whale corpse, and feast orgiastically. Angered by the sight, Cousteau's crewmen avenge the baby's demise by hauling the brute sharks onto the deck and beating them to death with large mallets. And, in a comical footnote, (11) The crewmembers go ashore where Bonnard, the ship's pet daschund, plays with tortoises.

ANALYSIS

The Silent World's lasting value as a motion picture lies almost exclusively in two broad contributions from Louis Malle: his ontological experiments and his early evocation of cinema direct. In each arena, however, Cousteau's shallow contrivances offset and threaten to drown out Malle's innovations.

Ontologically, André Bazin — in his essay on *Monde du silence*— alludes to the idea that the production of the film enabled Malle, Cousteau, and the crewmen to "revisit secrets within themselves."[18] He argues that one of the fundamental mythical elements (or secrets) entails a man's need to surpass the ontological limitations imposed on him — specifically, his desire to be "[liberated] from the chains [of gravity] that tie him to the earth" by entering and conquering the new, untamed oceanic realm.[19]

Cousteau, like Malle, suffered from physical maladies as a young man that restrained his activity. Chronic enteritis, a "painful inflamation of the intestines," forced young Jacques to stay indoors, preventing him from participating in sports and undertaking extensive physical exploration of the outdoor world. And Cousteau, like Malle, felt an overwhelming need for the liberation Bazin describes, and responded to his physiological constraints by diving into books and exploring the world vicariously through literature, which suspended the concept of restraint and perpetuated the illusions of physical movement and global exploration within his mind. Once Cousteau overcame his disability and gained the capacity for physical movement, he responded as Malle reacted to his own heart murmur, taking full advantage of every opportunity to escape from past constraints by physically exploring countless, unfamiliar realms: the world's oceans, Antarctica, the Amazon.

In sum, the filmmakers shared a highly unusual, highly individualistic metaphysical quality: the link between exploration as an escape from physical restraint in their personal lives and their pursuit of filmmaking as an exploratory tool. This quality led both men into the cinematic arena, pulled them together for the production of *Monde du silence*, and contributed to an unspoken level of understanding between the two artists. The most significant difference between the two men involves their varying abilities to carry this principle into the cinematic realm. Cousteau's contributions to *The Silent World* remain unsophisticated and simplistic, his spatial and ontological concerns confined to the subject matter of the film — the shallowest level — without penetrating technique. His technique thus works against and detracts from the ontological subtext of *Monde*'s subject, whereas Malle's approach continues to evoke, underscore, and flesh out the material's metaphysical components (via ontological and spatial principles) 50 years after the film's release.

In his unauthorized biography of Cousteau, Axel Madsen alludes to the captain's beliefs about time as a component of art:

> Cousteau believed cinema was the supreme art form because movies encompassed many other art forms and because they had an almost organic duration. Painting, sculpture, and architecture, he believed, tried to defy time, to be frozen in eternity, whereas theater, ballet, music, poetry, and film used time as raw material. "I prefer to admit that we are here like a flower, to bloom and die," he said. "The supreme art has to deal with this, to cope with it and to use time as a building block in a piece of art you are making."[20]

Madsen makes it clear, in the above passage, that Cousteau (like Malle) was wholly conscious of time as a cinematic device. Yet Cousteau's approach to editing eliminates all spatio-temporal continuity. In an unplanned sequence that contains the film's most powerful moments, the Calypso literally runs into a herd of sperm whales. A mother whale crashes into the ship's bow; her young calf follows, but accidentally penetrates the whirring blades of the front propeller, lacerating its small body and filling the ocean with warm clouds of blood. On board, panic ensues. Cousteau attempts to convey the horror and confusion that erupt among members of the crew with a manipulative, carefully edited sequence that combines real-time footage of the wounded calf, floating in the ocean, with inserted "reaction shots" from himself, the various crew members, and even the ship's pet dachshund, Bonnard, who runs onto the deck to investigate the confusion.

To some viewers in the 1950s, with a poorer understanding of editing techniques than contemporary audience members, the contrivances in this sequence may not have been as apparent as they are today, and perhaps, in their minds, the picture gained authenticity with supplemental reaction shots. Bosley Crowther, of *The New York Times*, even celebrates the film for "avoiding [the] trickery" that became a hallmark of Disney *True-Life Adventure* films.[21] Yet the Cousteau approach to editing, which chops up sequences into brief, telling fragments, is problematic, for it eliminates all sense of real time in the viewer's mind and subtly reminds the contemporary viewer of the filmmaker's presence in the editing room, thus heightening the subjectivity of shot selection and detracting from the horror and the onscreen reality of the experience that the viewers are asked to share. Kinesthetically, Cousteau's editing undercuts the fluidity of the film, and this sequence cuts against the grain of cinematic time by virtually obliterating all sense of continuity.

Rife with abrechtianism, Malle's ontological contributions to *The Silent World* lie at the opposite end of the spectrum: the filmmaker extends and protracts the spatio-temporal components of the motion picture, and avoids fragmentation whenever possible. He plunges the audience into real time and makes us believe, through the use of prolonged time and visceral movement, that our bodies are physically traveling through the aquatic depths with the divers. One of Malle's most breathtaking sequences in *Le Monde du silence* illuminates this point perfectly. Following the *Calypso*'s arrival in the tropics, the emergence of dolphins, and one diver's descent to the observational window at the bottom of the ship, we experience a succession of shots where Louis has attached the camera to the front of a scooter. Several meters undersea, with the sunlight gleaming and bouncing off the surface of the ocean, the filmmaker runs the scooter at high speeds and shoots while he rides behind the dolphins, allowing "reality to unfold" before the lens—unbroken, unedited. We watch the dolphins swim in front of us, and experience the sun filtering through the surface of the ocean, as the water whips past us. Of all the cinematic elements we encounter in this shot (light, texture, etc.), movement—the illusion of our bodies' kinesthetic movement through the water—drowns out the rest. We actually believe on a visceral level that we have somehow become a porpoise, speeding along with the other porpoises, and the kinesthesia is so overpowering that we almost completely forget our static viewing experience, in the dark of the movie theater or living room. This, at its very core, constitutes a nearly flawless example of Malleian abrechtian kinesthesia.

According to Louis Malle, the structure and basic concepts of *The Silent World* belong entirely to Cousteau. But this is only partially accurate; Malle's contributions emerge vividly within the film, and (as in the ontological realm) cut so directly across the grain of Cousteau's techniques that the motion picture becomes a schizophrenic work torn between conflicting documentary methods: the manipulatively structured *cinéma mensonge* of the captain and the ambiguous, open-ended, multiplicative cinema direct of Malle. The primary distinction, in turn, between the two *démarches* involves a differing estimation of the audience's intellectual capacities.

Solely responsible for the architecture of the film, Cousteau utilized a structural approach of contrivance and gross oversimplification in the editing room. Having instructed underwater cinematographers Malle, Dumas, and Falco to emphasize the mysterious, the wondrous, and the spectacular during the shoot, the captain arranged *Monde du silence* sequentially (some events planned, a few recorded spontaneously), and laced each sequence with various onscreen "wonders" that turned the picture into a carnivalesque series of novelties. He intercut raw footage, inserted reaction shots, and short reenactments to give the events greater fluency, and divided the picture into 11 conceptualized, themed sequences, carrying the project away from free-form documentary and toward a more carefully structured nonfiction narrative.

Although Cousteau places his strongest emphasis on spectacle and novelty, most of the images that were unique and unfamiliar to viewers in 1956 (for instance, dolphins frolicking in the warm seawater, and the multicolored coral of the ocean depths) have since grown so tired and overly familiar that all novelty has dissipated. If one restricts one's critical focus to content (temporarily ignoring form), we may feel tempted to argue that *Monde*'s scientific insights have lost all novelty, as well, now that 50 years of oceanographic exploration and discovery have dated the film. After all, a contemporary viewer with even a rudimentary grasp of basic oceanographic principles will feel his or her attention beginning to lag during the film, for the underwater explorer Cousteau insists on revealing only the simplest, most transparent scientific insights to viewers through his narration. "Porpoises," the captain informs us, "are not fish, but warm-blooded mammals, a lot like dogs."[22] One might argue that ocean science was simply primitive in 1956 — infinitely more primitive than today — and time itself inflicted inevitable casualties on the motion picture. Yet an examination of two oceanographic texts from the same period, using the level of scientific insight as a constant variable, imparts a much different impression of Cousteau's narration in the film. An excerpt from the seminal work *The Sea Around Us* by Rachel Carson (published in 1961):

> Caisson disease, which is caused by the rapid accumulation of nitrogen bubbles in the blood with sudden release of pressure, kills human divers if they are brought up rapidly from depths of two hundred feet or so. Yet, according to the testimony of whalers, a baleen whale, when harpooned, can dive straight down to a depth of half a mile, as measured by the amount of line carried out. From these depths, where it has sustained a pressure of half a ton on every inch of body, it returns almost immediately to the surface. The most plausible explanation is that, unlike the diver, who has air pumped to him while he is under water, the whale has in its body only the limited supply it carries down, and does not have enough nitrogen in its blood to do serious harm. The plain truth is, however, that we really do not know, since it is obviously impossible to confine a living whale and experiment on it, and almost as difficult to dissect a dead one satisfactorily.[23]

And an excerpt from the book *The Silent World*, by Captain Cousteau (published in 1953, three years prior to the film's release):

> Some fish have internal ears with *otoliths*, or ear stones, which make attractive necklaces called "lucky stones." But fish show little or no reaction to noises. The evidence is that they are much more responsive to nonaudible vibrations. They have a sensitive lateral line along their flanks which is, in effect, the organ of a sixth sense. As a fish undulates, the lateral receiver probably establishes its main sense of being.[24]

Three observations are significant here. First, the most obvious: the scientific verbiage and insights in the above texts—written within a few years of *The Silent*

World's production—are sophisticated enough to prove that, even in a 1950s context, the narrative observations in the Cousteau-Malle film ("I can hardly believe my ears! The giant whale squeaks like a mouse!") have been grossly watered down to a patronizing level, suitable for young children. Therefore, one can infer that Cousteau deliberately oversimplified the narration, widening the intellectual chasm between the explorers and the audience. As Bosley Crowther affirms in a 1956 *New York Times* article, viewers never learn what knowledge Cousteau, Malle, and the other crewmembers gained on the voyage.[25] And one cannot assume that the onscreen revelations and the crew's newfound knowledge are identical, despite Cousteau's declaration, in the *Times*, that he wanted viewers to "share [the crew's] experiences."[26]

Second, Cousteau-as-author addresses readers on a far deeper and more scientifically precise level than Cousteau-as-filmmaker, which leads one to question his faith in the depth and illuminating potential of the cinematic medium as opposed to literature (as we shall see, his technical approach to the film underscores this idea as well).

Third, Rachel Carson is more willing than Cousteau to acknowledge her own lapses in scientific information: "The plain truth is, *we really do not know...*"[27] In her work, Ms. Carson provides that which the Malle-Cousteau documentary so unwisely omits: a snapshot of exactly where ocean science and the oceanographers stood in the late fifties—which discoveries had already been made, and which had yet to be made. This is why, even if one looks beyond the dilution of scientific insights in the film, and makes the valid argument that any documentary on undersea exploration will become dated with time (particularly given the lightning-paced advances in oceanographic research and development as the years and decades pass), the argument loses validity: because "dated" content would not become an issue, if the form were more carefully premeditated.

Examining the film strictly on an architectural level: Cousteau could have improved the work 1000 percent by utilizing a looser structure, simply recording the events and the discoveries as they occurred—unabetted by rehearsed dialogue, "trick" editing, mood music, reaction shots, reenactment,[28] interpretation, or flowery "literary" narration.[29] In this way, he could have enabled the audience to learn scientific truths along with the crewmembers, an accomplishment similar to that of Carson's book. And *The Silent World* might have become a valuable historical record of the contributions to science made by the oceanographic team. Unfortunately, Cousteau did not follow this path. And the novelty-based, contrived structure of the picture (though it did not affect the audience response in 1956) has since eliminated historical significance as a possibility.[30]

The dachshund shot in the baby whale sequence reveals another problem: Cousteau's method enables him to act not just as filmmaker, but as god—nailing down black-and-white interpretations of the onscreen events, in the viewer's mind, through Eisensteinian montage and image association. Suddenly, in the viewer's mind, Bonnard leaps frantically from one of the ship's interior rooms onto the deck to investigate the injury of the whale, when (in reality) the dog's reaction was probably entirely unconnected to the accident. Thus, the Cousteau approach eliminates all multiplicativeness in the viewer's mind. Given the subject matter of the film, this device (in principle) is extremely problematic — Cousteau and Malle, not unlike the viewers, were still somewhat unfamiliar with oceanic exploration in 1956. This level of unfamiliarity should undergird the entire film, evoking a sense of wonder, of mystery, of the unknown, colossal, perhaps even threatening forces within our world's oceans. When Cousteau hands his viewers an explanation of every onscreen event, he bludgeons and ultimately destroys the mystery so desperately needed for the film to maintain power and integrity.

Conversely, the opening sequence belongs almost entirely to Louis Malle, and harnesses a dramatically different set of techniques that form the foundation of cinema direct documentary filmmaking, heightening the viewer's sense of the ambiguous and unknowable. The film opens with a loud burst from underwater torches, seizing the viewer's attention and announcing the arrival of a film that will fully envelop the senses and make us forget our extra-cinematic reality. In a series of six takes, prior to the title sequence, Malle places us in a realm of hyper-subjectivism. We observe the descent of the scuba divers from numerous angles, yet the camera's location within the ocean shifts only slightly. Here, an event that could arrive and pass quickly has been protracted onscreen, minute details (such as the rapid rise of oxygen bubbles) heightened and accentuated. The extension of time, almost to an approximation of real time, creates the (hyper-real) illusion that we are actually in the ocean, alongside the divers, perhaps floating above them, yet we begin to enter a cinematic fourth dimension that allows us to move into a succession of various angles and perspectives.

The role of Malle as cameraman and editor is critically important here. Cinematic subjectivity is inevitable in documentary work, but whereas in Cousteau's approach to editing and shot selection, subjectivity detracts from the viewing experience (by viscerally reminding each audience member of their spatial limitations and subservience to the whims of the filmmaker-cinematographer), the Malle approach to editing and shot selection hands the viewer a level of heightened subjectivism. This approach affirms the transferred subjectivity that occurs when the sequence begins, and allows each viewer to step into the role of the cameraman's first-person perspective. Yet the multiple shot and multiple angle selection of the divers' descent, for example (or, in the use of a mobile camera, the horizons that continually unfold before the audience, as in the breathtaking Malleian scooter shots) enable the filmmaker to give the audience an almost godlike omnipresence through the protraction of the cinematic time-space continuum.[31] In other words, in the Cousteauian technique, reality is fragmented, via editing, in a way that reduces the viewer's options. Yet through Malleian technique, onscreen reality is extended and fleshed out. And the viewer, in turn, gains a sense of empowerment *from* the filmmaker, instead of forced submission *to* the filmmaker.

Subsequently, (following the credits) Malle carries the subjectivization even further, when the viewer himself subtly becomes an "extra diver" with the soft addition of breathing sounds over the soundtrack and an extended shot, wherein the camera descends to the sea floor and approaches the divers. Significantly, we never discover exactly what the divers are filming (the focus of their work remains shrouded in mystery) or the specific identity of the strange black shapes created when the sun hits the equipment that ascends with the divers (in the final, dreamlike shot of the opening sequence).

One of the picture's most famous sequences — the exploration of the Thistle-gorm shipwreck — employs the very same set of techniques. Malle (the mind behind this sequence) eliminates all narration, and throws a series of cryptic images onto the screen: countless shapes and forms that defy identification. In other words, Malle is placing in the viewer's hands the difficult tasks of image analysis and identification that accompany heightened subjectivity. And even if our ability to identify a few of the images (an ancient bicycle, a coral-covered diving bell, a rotted boot) might initially seem to detract from the sequence's powerful ambiguity, we must also navigate our way through the multi-layered significance of the objects' platonic identities. In sum, Malle, unlike Cousteau, is doing everything in his power to construct and preserve the multiplicity, the ambiguity, and the mystery of human experience by building a cinematic first-person perspective. Such a perspective — when coupled with Abrechtian kinesthesia and time protraction — is the essence of cinema direct.[32]

Thus, to recap: the fundamental ideological elements of cinema direct filmmaking as used by Malle in *The Silent World* are self-led viewer observation, multiplicative ambiguity, and transferred subjectivity during the viewing experience, from "viewer-as-self" to "viewer-as-cameraman," fostered by the construction of a first person perspective, time protraction, and abrechtian kinesthesia that spring from the limitless mobility of the camera person.

Yet one senses, at certain moments in the film, that Cousteau works on a conscious and deliberate level to deflate the myths that Malle carefully establishes through the ambiguity of cinema direct. For instance, the scenes with the divers, as we have seen, are wondrous, majestic, and delightfully mysterious: the men become mythical heroes, in the tradition of the great explorers. Yet in the following scene (which, according to Malle, was entirely Cousteau's idea), the divers climb up onto the deck of *The Calypso* and instantly regress into absurd, freakish figures — men bearing tremendously heavy equipment, flapping along in their scuba gear awkwardly. Conceptually speaking, the scene is amusing, yet one would be hard pressed to imagine a clearer or more effective way to defeat the effect of the onscreen mythology established so carefully by Malle.

Little wonder, then, that for ontological and structural reasons, Malle long refrained from accepting co-authorship of *The Silent World,* insisting that it is — at heart — a Cousteau film, and not one of his own (despite the picture's shared directorial credit). He had his reasons: had Malle helmed the picture alone, one can envision an unrecognizably different documentary that would simply record the unbroken, uninterpreted reality of the Red Sea voyage as a lasting record of the crew's discovery process (particularly given the content and form of Malle's later documentaries). The later nonfiction works, as we shall see, can even be interpreted as Malle's stylistic rebellion against the contrivances and "docudrama" imposed on him by Captain Cousteau during the production of *Monde du silence* — a series of full, unadulterated plunges into the murky waters of cinema direct.

A close examination of film history in reference to *Monde du silence* yields an astonishing revelation about Louis Malle, generally unacknowledged by film historians. In his *Documentary* reference text, Erik Barnouw traces the evolution of direct cinéma from 1948 (i.e., just under a decade prior to *Monde du silence*) to 1973. Barnouw lists Richard Leacock as the pioneer of the cinema direct movement,[33] and states that until 1960, the primary ideological elements of the movement that documentarians had woven into their work were those of *observation* and *multiplicative ambiguity* (principles Barnouw credits largely to Leacock, Robert Flaherty, and the three most influential harbingers of the British "Angry Young Man" School: Lindsay Anderson, Karel Reisz, and Tony Richardson, all of whom crafted short documentaries before turning to features).[34] Barnouw reminds us that such directors (as illustrated by their technical experimentation) could foresee the next ideological advancement in the evolution of cinema direct — heightened subjective reality, via the future arrival of cinematographic mobility and synchronous sound — even if they did not yet have the mechanical capability for realizing their vision(s).[35,36]

But Barnouw's history is somewhat erroneous. He implies — incorrectly — that the full construction of an onscreen first-person perspective through direct cinema could not (and therefore, generally did not) occur prior to 1960–1961, because of the technical roadblocks that needed to be overcome by Leacock and his business partner, Robert Drew.[37] Actually, the 1956 Malle-Cousteau documentary reveals an ironic loophole: by simply shifting to a more mobile filmmaking environment (that not only freed the cameramen from the constraints of gravity but from the constraints of synchronous sound — hence, *The **Silent** World*), Louis Malle and Jacques Yves-Cousteau were able to leap ahead of these technical stumbling blocks several years earlier than Leacock or Drew. Malle recalls:

> We had to invent the rules — there were no references; it was too new. The camera by definition — because were underwater — had a mobility and fluidity; we could do incredibly complicated equivalents of what, on land, would be a combination of crane movements plus enormous tracking shots, and we would do it just like breathing because it was part of the movement of the diver.[38]

Taking it a step further: thanks to his realization and easy grasp of how to take full ideological advantage of the environmental loophole, Malle alone (*sans* Cousteau) built a cinematic first-person perspective as the cornerstone of cinema direct, about four years ahead of Leacock and other contemporaries. [Hence his statement that the "(camera movement) was part of the movement of the diver."] Malle thus became one of the first filmmakers to realize the full extent of the new cinema direct ideology through successful hands-on experimentation.

CRITICAL RESPONSE

One must put *The Silent World* in a historical context to grasp how revolutionary it appeared to 1956 audiences. Though three additional oceanographic films emerged earlier that year, none found a niche with audiences, so that most viewers who attended a screening of *Monde du Silence* were unacquainted with underwater documentaries.[39] Images as simple as a turtle laying and burying its eggs in the sand

and the ability of the sea anemones to stun and devour little fish mesmerized viewers foreign to the sights. The film enabled audiences—for the very first time — to
shift away from preconceived notions of an anthropocentric universe and abandon
the fallacy that other species lack biological functions as complex as those in *Homo
sapiens.* Through the film, viewers gained their first impressions of symbiosis (note
the images of the cuttlefish traveling close to the sharks' bodies) and their first sense
that many other species can adapt more easily to the natural environment than
humans. Ontologically, *The Silent World* opened up "new vistas of experience" for
mankind, enabling viewers to travel into spheres that, for centuries, had gone unseen
and were only accessible to the mind's eye. André Bazin writes, "we can permit ourselves to indicate that [*The Silent World*'s] beauties are indescribable, and that they
constitute the greatest revelation that our small planet has given mankind since the
early days of heroic terrestrial exploration."[40]

Additional critics and the public sided with Bazin: in a short time, *The Silent
World* garnered phenomenal success outside of Paris: it won the coveted Palme d'Or
at Cannes '56 and the Academy Award for Best Documentary, and ran for several
months after opening at the Paris Theater in Manhattan on Monday, Sept. 24, 1956.
The film received unanimously positive reviews; just as Bazin (the most prominent
critic in France at the time) celebrated *Monde*'s ontological achievements, Crowther
refers to the film as "an hour and twenty-six minutes of pictorial (and piscatorial) marvels and thrills," and celebrates its "wonderful intimacy."[41] *The Monthly Film Bulletin*
proclaims, "The sea is Cousteau's kingdom, and its kaleidoscope of movement and
colour comes vividly alive in the hands of the cinema's first underwater poet."[42] Likewise, *Variety* praises the film by commenting, "There have been many underwater
exploration pix of late, but this emerges by far the most original," and "new hues down
below and much editing and commentary weld this into a taking documentary of high
calibre."[43] Yet ironically, as Malle observes, the Parisian public greeted *The Silent World*
more apathetically than audiences in other countries. "The film," he notes, "which had
already been released in Paris, prior to Cannes, was shown with a polite indifference."[44]

Similarly, contemporary critics often levy complaints against *The Silent World*,
observing that it has dated terribly, given the "spectacle-laced" structure Cousteau
demanded and his awkward style of filmmaking — perhaps one of the reasons, almost
50 years later, the film is screened so rarely and generally unavailable for rental or
purchase outside of France. In *Malle on Malle*, Philip French criticizes the techniques
that have weakened *Monde* over the years, including prewritten dialogue and the
editing of footage into contrived sequences.[45]

Prince Rainier and the newly-coronated Princess Grace of Monaco attended a
screening of *Monde du silence*; it inspired Rainier to beef up the protectorate's tourism
by pumping hundreds of thousands of dollars into the National Oceanographic Institute and adding a museum. Influenced heavily by Grace and Rainier, the institute's
board of directors named Cousteau as president — a position Jacques held for most
of his adult life.[46] Malle, only 23 years old and already a recipient of the Golden Palm,
found his future as a filmmaker secured. Consequently, *Monde*'s success enabled the
young director to travel back to Paris and (ultimately) to commence work on his first
feature, *Elevator to the Gallows.*

2

Ascenseur pour l'échafaud (Elevator to the Gallows)—1957

The Illusions of a Romantic

"It had occurred to her early that in her position — that of a young person spending, in framed and wired confinement, the life of a guinea pig or a magpie — she should know a great many persons without recognizing the acquaintance."

— Henry James, "In the Cage"

"Since for the time being there is no possibility whatever of a causal explanation, we must assume provisionally that improbable accidents of an acausal nature — that is, meaningful coincidences — have entered the picture."

— Carl Jung, "On Synchronicity"

BACKGROUND

The conception, production and release of *Ascenseur pour l'échafaud* signify the outset of a key seven-year period (1957–1963), when the neophyte director Louis Malle completed a loosely connected (though not unbroken)[1] string of four successful adaptations, each source novel written by a highly respected European belletrist. The films include: *Ascenseur pour l'échafaud* (*Elevator to the Gallows*, a.k.a. *Frantic*, a.k.a. *Lift to the Scaffold*), from a *policier* by Noël Calef, screenplay by Malle and Roger Nimier; *Les Amants* (The Lovers), from a nineteenth century novel *Point de Lendemain* by Baron Dominique Vivant Denon, co-adapted by Malle and Louise de Vilmorin; *Zazie dans le métro* (Zazie in the Subway), from an experimental novel by Raymond Queneau; and *Le Feu follet* (The Fire Within), from an existential Fitzgeraldesque novel by suicide victim Pierre Drieu La Rochelle.

In his landmark essay "*Le Journal d'un curé de campagne* and the Stylistics of Robert Bresson," André Bazin[2] introduces the first of two principles that — when juxtaposed — can be read as a two-axiom philosophy on screen adaptations of literary works. Citing Bresson's *Diary of a Country Priest* (1950) as a quintessential example,

Munitions manufacturer and war veteran Julien Tavernier (Maurice Ronet) carries out plans to murder the boss he is cuckolding, Simon Carala (Jean Wall), and frame it as a suicide, in Louis Malle's debut noir, *Ascenseur pour l'échafaud* (Elevator to the Gallows).

Bazin condemns austere, ascetic faithfulness to source material during the adaptation process. He demonstrates that because the governing rules of literary and cinematic mediums sit in strict opposition, true faithfulness to a text requires cinematic equivalence: identification of the literary craftsman's voice, technique, and basic themes, and the reconstruction of those elements in a filmic context —

> If we praise Bresson for his fidelity, it is for the most insidious kind of fidelity, a most pervasive form of creative license. Of course, one clearly cannot adapt without transposing. In that respect, (Georges) Bernanos was on the side of aesthetic common sense. Literal translations are *not* the faithful ones... A character on the screen and the same character as evoked by the novelist are not identical... If he had really been faithful to the book, Bresson would have made quite a different film. Determined though he was to add nothing to the original — already a subtle form of betrayal by omission.[3]

The second idea, discussed less frequently and traditionally credited to François Truffaut, suggests that, to craft an interesting adaptation, the scenarist (or writer-director) can often locate and acquire the rights to B and C grade source novels (even run-of-the-mill drugstore paperbacks) with interesting central concepts yet poor characterization and underdeveloped themes. During the adaptation process, the scenarist(s) flesh out and improve the material substantially in screenplay form, signifying a grand departure from the original text.[4]

It is startling and disconcerting that although these ideas can be traced to Bazin and Truffaut, respectively, Malle was one of the first (if not *the* first) to put both principles to the test by stepping behind the camera. In the case of the first rule, *Zazie dans le métro* enabled Malle to demonstrate (thanks to the extreme stylistic playfulness within Queneau's book) how separate and distinct voices, dialects, literary devices, and writing styles can be translated into their respective onscreen visual equivalents. Thus, it can be argued that *Zazie* was one of the very first films to fully realize the extent and implications of the Bazinian cinematic equivalence rule, and of the cinematic adaptation process.[5] Chapter 4 (on *Zazie*) addresses this idea more fully.

Malle's revolutionary evocation of the second axiom pertains specifically to *Ascenseur*. Its status as a debut feature aside, *Elevator to the Gallows* occupies a unique position in the pantheon of Malle adaptations, thanks to the unusual creative process that belies the genesis of the picture. Noel Calef's source novel of *Elevator* is significantly weaker and thinner than Malle's film version. According to Malle, Roger Nimier, an accomplished French literary craftsman,[6] found Calef's text foolish, but agreed to retain only the fascinating ironic twist that lies at the heart of the story, and to build an original narrative around it.[7] Thus, the produced film became infinitely more complex (and fascinating) than the book, and has since demonstrated longevity. As the film represents a deliberate, immeasurable improvement on a B-grade *roman policier*, one should interpret the entire picture in the light of cinematic expansionism: the ability of the filmmakers and scenarists (i.e., Malle and Nimier) to transition the source novel from uninteresting and limpid throwaway genre pulp to a complex piece of finely-crafted revisionist noir, by imbuing the screenplay with genre deconstructionism, multiplicative themes, literary archetypes, multi-dimensional character and an oblique tone. Nearly every significant aspect of the picture is grounded in this idea, however indirectly.

But this approach to a debut feature did not arrive in Malle's frame of reference overnight; it took shape over the course of several months. Indeed, *Elevator to the Gallows* might not exist in its current form, had Malle not pursued a number of false leads to a new project, in the months following *The Silent World*'s debut at Cannes.

The surreal experience of moving from the underwater realm of the Mediterranean and Captain Cousteau's Paris-based editing room into an unfamiliar world of "producers [and] actors" overwhelmed the 23-year-old Malle and left him incredulous. He traveled to Cannes '57, and found the glitziness of the European cinematic world ugly and distasteful, notably the experience of landing on the cover of *Paris-Match*, surrounded by starlets.[8] Yet the young filmmaker also thrilled at the professional contacts afforded by the experience. He returned to Paris immediately after the festival ended, just prior to the issuance of the awards. Ironically, the judges, in disagreement over whether to award the Golden Palm to Bergman's *Smiles of a Sum-*

mer Night (1955), opted as a compromise to select the Cousteau-Malle documentary as the recipient.[9]

During the ensuing months, a number of opportunities arose for Louis Malle that never came to full fruition. Jacques Tati offered Malle the position of camera-man on his 1958 *Mon Oncle*. Yet—at about the same time—Robert Bresson pro-posed that Malle work as assistant director and research assistant on his 1958 film *Un Condamné à mort s'est échappé* (*A Man Escaped*). As a greater admirer of Bresson, Louis rejected Tati's offer and accepted the second position. Authenticity weighed heavily in Bresson's mind, and the director—insistent on precise realism in every min-iscule detail of the film's *mise en scène*—foresaw Malle's unusual background in docu-mentary filmmaking as a significant asset.[10] Bresson thus assigned Malle to detail supervision, and even asked the young filmmaker to scout nonprofessional cast mem-bers for the picture. But once the shoot began, Bresson already had a full crew and didn't particularly need an assistant director; moreover, Malle found the role boring and unproductive, and in the mean time, another opportunity arose to work with Cou-steau, filming the wreck of the *Andrea Doria* off the coast of Nantucket. Empathetic to Malle's frustration, Bresson encouraged him to leave the production and join Cousteau. Yet only a few weeks later, a severe ear infection sent Malle to a New York hospital.[11]

Throughout his recovery, Malle's documentary instincts remained intact. After leaving the hospital, he carried a 16mm camera to Budapest to film the 1956 anti–Rus-sian Hungarian Revolution, but missed the climactic action by several days, and the project collapsed.[12] Returning to Paris in the autumn and winter of 1956, Malle penned a biographical script about a young man's heartbreak from a broken love affair at the Sorbonne. Numerous distributors rejected the project. Finally, Alain Cavalier, a friend of Malle's, found a B-grade *roman policier*, admired the interesting prem-ise, and suggested that Malle adapt it as a debut feature. He pitched the idea to a producer, who agreed to back the picture if Malle agreed to cast B-movie star Jeanne Moreau as the female lead. Malle consented, and eventually enlisted famed literary stylist Roger Nimier as co-scenarist.[13] The picture debuted in France on January 29, 1958, but did not open in New York City until June 10, 1961.

Synopsis

Algerian war veteran and ex-paratrooper Julien Tavernier (Maurice Ronet), a top-level executive employed by munitions manufacturer Simon Carala (Jean Wall), becomes entangled in a steamy adulterous affair with Florence (Jeanne Moreau), Mr. Carala's wife. Near the end of a Saturday, while Julien works at the office, the lovers exchange romantic platitudes over the telephone. Julien plans to do away with Simon, so that he and Florence can be together permanently. The lovers make an impassioned promise to meet that evening, following the murder. Acting with extreme forethought and precision, Tavernier asks his secretary not to be disturbed, and slips through the outer window of his office. He scales the outside of the building with a grappling hook and steps into Carala's office, confronting Simon with a gun. Using the com-pany's war profiteering as an excuse, Julien puts a gun to his boss's head and pulls the trigger. Tavernier takes every precaution to frame the murder as a suicide: he commits the act with Carala's own gun, latches all of the doors on the way out of the office, and locks the remaining door from the inside, by sliding a knife in-between the door frame and the deadbolt as he leaves.

Tavernier slips away from the building nonchalantly. Meanwhile, across the street, teenage florist Veronique (Yori Bertin) and her boyfriend Louis (Georges Poujouly) quarrel. To make Louis envious, Veronique begins to fawn over Julien as he climbs into his car. Tavernier prepares to drive off when, at the last second, he instinctively glances up and spots a lingering piece of incriminating evidence: the grappling hook, dangling from Carala's office window. Frustrated, he abandons the running automobile, runs back into the office building, and catches the elevator to the top floor. Yet in mid-flight, the security guard pulls the power on the lift and Julien finds himself stuck, in-between floors.

Outside, Louis — determined to impress Veronique — decides, impulsively, to steal Julien's car and drive through Paris. While the teenage couple cruise out of the city and toward the freeway, Mme. Carala spots Veronique in the passenger's side of Julien's car, but cannot see the driver with his convertible top raised. Assuming that Julien is driving, she tries to push the worst conclusion out of her mind: betrayed by her lover, who backed out of the murder like a coward and took off with the teenage florist.

Night falls. Julien remains trapped in the elevator, and searches desperately for a method of escape. Meanwhile, Florence combs the city for her lover, questioning everyone she encounters. And after circling the same stretch of the freeway several times, the young lovers are cut off by a middle-aged German couple in a Mercedes, the Benckers. Irritated, Louis tails the sportscar to a roadside motel.

Meanwhile, Julien uncovers a trapdoor on the bottom of the lift; he lowers himself down into the shaft, but at that exact minute, a guard restores power, which sends Julien hurtling to the bottom as he clings to the rope. At the last moment, the guard cuts the power again; a terrified Julien climbs back up into the elevator and collapses from exhaustion.

Florence continues to wander through the city. Instinctively, she visits the locked office building, yet a small schoolgirl interrupts her. A minute or two after Florence accompanies the girl away from the building, the girl suddenly runs back to the steps and notices the grappling hook, which blew off of Simon's window in a rainstorm and fell onto the wet sidewalk. She seizes it, removing the last piece of evidence that ties Julien to the Carala murder, which suggests that Julien may still emerge unscathed.

At the motel, Horst Bencker (Ivan Petrovich) and his wife (Elga Andersen) entertain Louis and Veronique (who pose as M. and Mme. Julien Tavernier) with champagne in a private room. Mme. Bencker borrows Julien's camera from Vero and silently snaps three photos of Louis and Horst, infuriating Louis. Vero slips when she refers to her boyfriend as "Louis" instead of Julien, so that Horst accuses an embarrassed Louis of posing as Tavernier.

Veronique drops off the roll of film at the motel film developer. Later, in the middle of the night, thunder jostles Louis awake. Still irate at the Germans, and hell bent on revenge against Horst for discovering his identity, he attempts to abscond with Vero, in Horst's car, without paying for the room. But the Benckers foil Louis's plot when Horst emerges from the hotel room with a gun and confronts the young thief. Shaken and terrified, Louis instinctively whips Julien's gun from his trench-coat and commits a double homicide. Vero and Louis return to Veronique's apart-ment and—faced with the certainty of arrest—attempt to kill themselves by swallowing Gardenal.

Dead from exhaustion, Florence drags herself into the police station to inquire about Julien. All evidence has led the police to connect Julien to the murder of two Germans at the roadside motel, not the Carala murder. Thus, early on Sunday morn-ing, the papers issue photograph-accompanied "Most Wanted" announcements regarding Tavernier, and when Julien finally manages to leave the elevator, he stands little chance of escape. The police confront Tavernier and drag him to an interroga-tion room, pinning him with the double murder. The truth forces Julien to remain silent, as he understands that the facts would only implicate him in Carala's death and make the situation stickier.

Florence slowly puts the pieces together. After she confronts Veronique and Louis at the apartment (who only took enough pills to knock themselves out), Louis suddenly recognizes the value of the undeveloped photos at the motel. Minutes later, he winds up on a moped, racing to the scene of the crime (Florence in pursuit), to retrieve the undeveloped film. Louis bolts into the motel darkroom, with Florence behind him, in an attempt to collect and destroy the incriminating evidence. But a police officer is already present. Wise to the truth, he waits eagerly as his two per-petrators enter the lab. Inspector Cherier (Lino Ventura) accuses Florence and Julien of Carala's death, and tags Veronique and Louis with the Bencker murder. Pho-tographs of Julien and Florence, locked in each other's arms, float in the tray, finally uniting the estranged lovers.

ANALYSIS

Ascenseur pour l'échafaud constitutes an exercise in revisionist noir. Given Malle's two admitted cinematic influences for *Elevator* (in *Malle on Malle*) one may be tempted to interpret the film theoretically, as a Bressonian deconstruction of Hitch-cock. After all, *Elevator* does—on the most obvious level—address Hitchcockian style themes, yet ignores the tendency so common to suspense-filled thrillers of mov-ing quickly and economically to a resolution and denouement, and instead utilizes a *lenteur* common to the cinema of Bresson.

This approach is problematic; it leads one to tag the languor as a flaw, when— if one eschews a stylistic interpretation or approach—it becomes clear that the pace deepens and fleshes out the themes of the narrative. Because *Cahiers* writers used filmic style as their main criterion for analysis, the journal naturally attacked the "crawl" of the narrative as a stylistic lapse. "The film's flaws," the magazine observed, "are those which, by necessity, accompany youth ... first of all, a slowness, or, more specifically, a certain *inertia* that the rapidity of movements and the frequency of short cuts cannot shake."[14]

Nontheoretically, one French journal's observation — that the themes of romantic angst, loneliness, and separation lie at the core of *Elevator*[15] — is accurate. These ideas constitute the foundational theme of the work, and Malle places the heaviest thematic emphasis on romantic separation between Julien and Florence, which accounts for the film's pace. (By extending the temporal element and using extremely long takes during Mme. Carala's walk through Paris, Malle enables viewers to feel Florence's angst, frustration, and hopelessness, viscerally.) Consequently, the sequences with Florence Carala wandering through the city (combing the streets for her lover) deliver the most powerful emotional impact and give the picture longevity, enabling it to withstand repeated viewings. Ergo, when contemporary viewers reflect on *Ascenseur*, they often recall Mme. Carala's stroll through nighttime Paris, and forget the thriller subtext.[16]

But the themes of romantic separation run far deeper (and the film is more pessimistic) than one might anticipate. Malle repeatedly underscores the inability of two individuals to *ever* fully know each other. In Malle's eyes, the trans-emotional, intellectual, psychological and spiritual union of lovemaking is full and complete, but fleeting and impermanent. Given a modernist society, the prison of subjective consciousness, and the vast differences between genders, the Jungian concept of "paradoxical unity" can never be realized. Thus, Florence's thoughts reveal her incomplete knowledge of Julien, which plagues her with doubt about the possibility of her lover eloping with the florist. Out-of-touch with the complications that have arisen, she questions Julien's faithfulness and emotional attachment to her, accusing him of cowardice and disloyalty.

The opening shot of *Ascenseur* thus includes a visual trick that reveals the incongruities and the incomplete unity that are unavoidable in a male-female relationship. Malle opens on a close-up of Florence's softly-lit face, as she utters passionate words of love to Julien; the viewer assumes — erroneously — that the lovers have managed to achieve some level of romantic union (even — on the simplest level — their presence in the same room, perhaps in bed together). By concealing the telephone and suddenly disclosing its presence with a zoom-out, Malle carries his viewers from a point where they share the lovers' self-deception and illusion of possible romantic unity, to a broader perspective (accompanied by a dramatic shift in tone) that symbolically unveils the inevitability of their separation between Julien and Florence.

Granted, one may be tempted to believe — particularly if one ignores the stylistic clues and listens to the characters — that a permanent emotional, spiritual, and sexual union is possible. "I'll wait at the cafe, as usual. When you're done, you'll take your big car. You'll stop opposite, and I'll climb in beside you," Florence whispers to her paramour. "And we'll be free, Julien."[17] Yet from the very first shots in the prologue, the director-scenarist is revealing visually (and aurally) to the audience a truth that the illicit lovers have not yet realized: that self-mythologized romantic union is quite literally impossible. From this point, the same visual trope recurs throughout the narrative. During the credits, the Miles Davis music becomes a cool, anesthetizing aura that encases the two lovers and the audience in a "romantic prism." But because Malle has already carried the audience outside of this prism (and will do so again after the opening credits), the viewer understands just how illusory it is. The ultramodern, dehumanizing architecture (which divides the human characters into tiny, squared-off offices); the separation of the two main characters until the closing scene; and, more significantly, Malle's objective, deliberately cold, voyeuristic approach to the subject matter add to the nihilistic futility of the lovers' unfulfillable romantic promises to each other.

Ideologically speaking, voyeurism lies at the heart of *Elevator to the Gallows*. Malle and Nimier take advantage of the Conradian "fascination with the abomination"—the viewer's (generally unadmitted) delight in watching the convoluted mechanics of a heinous crime unfold. Countless American film noirs of the 1940s share the basic premise — two illicit lovers (a married femme fatale and her illicit bedmate) conspire to murder the woman's husband and elope together, but the plan goes awry. [The two most obvious influences are Wilder's *Double Indemnity* (1944) and Tay Garnett's *The Postman Always Rings Twice* (1946)]. Nevertheless, to understand how voyeurism emerges in *Ascenseur* stylistically, a more general categorization is necessary.

All suspense-based noir films take advantage of the viewer's inability to know the full details of the events in the forthcoming acts (as suspense, by its very definition, necessitates information about future events that the director and scenarist[s] hide or obscure from the audience). But such films fall into one of two tonal categories, depending on the emotional texture that accompanies the narrative (see table).

These principles (and a discussion of the other films) help contextualize *Elevator*. Malle and Nimier approach Julien's preparation for the homicide by turning it into a coldly objective example of an observational crime noir, and Malle's technique thus holds to all of the rules listed in the first category. The filmmaker employs a voyeuristic shot-by-shot method in the film: following the credit sequence, we objectively watch every single detail of Julien Tavernier's homicide preparation, from the most significant to the most inconsequential aspect, frame by frame. Shot: Julien opens his desk drawer and carefully removes a pair of gloves, a gun, and a grappling hook. Shot: Julien dons the gloves, puts the gun in his pocket and the grappling hook over his shoulder. Shot: Julien opens the window and steps out onto the ledge. And so forth. Aside from one image of Simon Carala (from Julien's perspective), Malle carefully avoids "look shots" and first person camerawork. Each viewer remains detached — an objective observer, hooked to the onscreen events by his or her fascination with Tavernier's morbid and immoral actions. Malle openly shares and encourages the audience's obsession with the crime, allowing the camera to linger over every single detail of Julien's preparation.

Oddly, the murder itself occurs offscreen; the sound of the gunshot is inaudible, muffled by the secretary's electric pencil sharpener. A more graphic depiction of the murder could destroy the delicate tonal balance of the film by tipping audience empathy away from Julien. Malle's goal (again) is to help the audience remain objective and unbiased — neither completely opposed to Tavernier's actions nor completely supportive of Tavernier's homicide. If Malle and Nimier employed a highly subjective approach, we might feel a surging level of suspense, fearing for Tavernier's safety and asking the question, "Will he emerge unscathed?" But Malle has already rendered complete empathy impossible by deliberately avoiding moments that enable

Two Variants of Cinematic Emotional Texture
in the Film Noir and Postnoir Periods[18,19,20]

Observational (Detached)	*vs.*	*Empathetic (Involved)*
Tends to retain a godlike perspective over the events of the narrative		Tends to retain a first-person (protag. based) perspective over the events of narrative
The viewer retains a level of emotional distance from the protagonist		The viewer remains, almost constantly, in shoes of protagonist
Fear for the protagonist (and hence for ourselves) generally nonexistent		Film takes advantage of fear attributable to unpredictability of protagonist's fate.
Saturated with voyeurism, which the director/scenarists often heighten by using an oblique tone (with aid of negative/multidimensional char. traits, or vagueness in character[s]). This erects an emotional wall between chars. and viewers, and makes full empathy difficult, if not impossible.		Tone is clear-cut and positive, because the scenarists construct the characterizations in such a way that leads us to empathize/side with the protagonist.
Dynamic (i.e., narrative may suddenly and unexpectedly evolve into an empathetic suspenser).		Static (tends to remain empathetic, if tone is stable).
Suspense revolves around question of what will happen in narrative as a whole.		Audience worries constantly about the protagonist. Suspense thus revolves around question of the protagonist's fate.
Examples: ***Elevator to the Gallows***, *The Stranger*, *Blood Simple* (transitory), *Double Indemnity*, *The Postman Always Rings Twice*, *In Cold Blood* (transitory)		Examples: *Experiment in Terror, Mirage, The Woman in the Window, Body Heat, D.O.A., Psycho* (1960; transitory)

the audience to side with Julien completely. Granted, the tone of the film tips audience empathy more toward Julien than Carala: Malle includes a deliberately uncomfortable shot of Julien, immediately after he enters Simon's office, when he resembles a deer, caught in headlights, and Carala makes his first off-camera appearance — noisy, obnoxious, irksome. ("Asseyez-vous, Monsieur Tavernier," he whines gratingly.) Julien's victimization becomes palpable at this moment. But Tavernier's fate never completely concerns the audience.

Before the murder, Malle so distances the audience from Julien and Florence that he renders it impossible for the viewer to fully empathize with the conspirators. The telephone conversation that opens the film is oblique enough and stylized enough to hold the audience at an emotional distance. And indeed, the fact that one never observes the lovers together and witnesses their interaction — their geographical division throughout the story — makes it extremely difficult for the audience to feel their mutual passion.

The film's complex three-subplot structure enables Malle to intercut the stories of Louis and Veronique, Julien, and Florence. It imparts a sense of godlike omniscience to the viewer and, functionally, recalls the kinesthetic audience empowerment that Malle employed in *Le Monde du silence*. Like the stylistic devices in the opening scenes, the structure enables the audience to rise above the level of subjective empathy with (or fear for) one protagonist that is a standard for the suspense-thriller genre, to a more coolly detached observational plateau. And this ultimately enables Malle to establish one of the picture's most important elements: the deconstruction and redefinition of fate.

Fate—as critic Philip French notes in his introduction to *Malle on Malle*[21]—plays a central role in *Elevator to the Gallows* (as in other Malle films). Yet the director-scenarist uses *Ascenseur* to dissemble and reconstruct the viewer's notions of fate's basic constitutional elements. The events that lead up to Tavernier's indictment demonstrate that one's traditional definition of *fate*—"the supposed miraculous force or power that determines events"—is illusory, created by the power of individuals evoking consequences collectively and actively (i.e., through causal relationships) and perpetuated by the distortion of one's own egocentrism.

Malle heightens the film's Jamesian multiplicativeness in the first act (prior to Florence's voice-over monologues) by remaining on an observational plateau, without penetrating the inner workings of the characters' minds.[22,23] This reintroduces the concept of audience empowerment, for the omniscient viewpoint necessitates that each viewer draw his or her own conclusions regarding each character's subjective interpretation of the unfolding events (i.e., a subjective take on the subjective). Florence's voice-over monologues represent the first, deliberate lapses in this ambiguity—the first clarifications of her subjective thoughts.

Later in the film, although Malle dramatizes Julien's interrogation at the hands of the police and his frustration at his inability to offer an alibi that would implicate him in another crime, Malle avoids depicting Julien's response in reference to the source of the accusations. Granted, the character will find it impossible to escape from an ironic reaction—the unforeseen and inexplicable experience of wandering out of the elevator and being arrested not for Carala's framed suicide, but for the murder of two Germans, which occurred 50 miles away from the elevator where he spent the night. Yet because Malle cuts away from Julien at the cafe (when the police roll up) and wisely avoids the use of a voice-over in this sequence, the viewer must guess as to Julien's conclusions regarding the source of the mix-up, given that the elevator literally and metaphorically imprisoned him and sealed him off from knowledge of the night's unfolding events.

One may, for instance, deduce that the conclusions within Julien's mind bear closest similarities to the synchronicity introduced by Carl Jung, who defined and described "meaningful coincidences": the simultaneous occurrence of two strikingly similar yet causally unrelated events.[24] If such is the case, Julien would subsequently be tempted to guess the presence of a Jungian "cosmic organizing principle" behind his arrest for the wrong murder—God, destiny, or (most likely) the force of fate—which will inevitably implicate him in a homicide—any homicide, by any means possible, simply because he is guilty of *a* murder. In a Calvinistic sense, Julien's guilt-driven belief in automatic divine punishment for committing a moral infraction would help drive this notion home.[25]

Regardless of how Julien explains the coincidence, Malle's narrative structure defeats the possibility of any all-controlling fatalistic force in the viewer's mind, for it allows the audience to follow three interlocking stories and four interlocking major characters simultaneously. Malle thus helps the audience understand that the consequences for Julien Tavernier are not by any means inexplicable or mysterious. Each small, seemingly inconsequential action taken by each character is, on the most fundamental level, attributable to the power of his or her own free will. These choices, in turn, trigger additional consequences and other characters' choices. The power one character might perceive as "fate" is, in fact, comprised of the collective power of his own and the other characters' decisions, woven together, which will ultimately lead to Julien's indictment in the Bencker murder.

At least one godlike element in the film functions beyond the realm of the characters' free wills, and nudges the narrative forward. In a moment so subtle that it risks being overlooked, Louis and Veronique lie in bed together, asleep in their motel room, when a roll of thunder jostles Louis awake. Still outraged at Horst Bencker, Louis attempts to steal the Benckers' car, which immediately leads to the murder. Without the thunder, the murder might never have occurred.

Given the basic existence of thunder as an effectual element in the film, one could infer that in Malle's eyes, the unstoppable, deific power of "fate" does exist, in addition to "the sum total of human choices" so often mislabeled as "destiny"; that the two work together in the same direction to produce ultimate consequences; and that neither element could function independently of the other. This interpretation is fallacious: in the world of *Ascenseur*, the uncontrollable elements may indirectly influence the characters' fates within the boundaries of causal relationships, but natural forces in the film do not all move in the same direction and point to the same end. The same rainstorm that jostles Louis awake (indirectly eliciting murder for which Julien will be held responsible) also blows the last lingering piece of the Carala murder off of the building and onto the sidewalk (helping to free Julien from conviction of Carala's murder). Malle is thus simultaneously toying with the audience's fatalistic notions (by including the thunder) and ultimately discrediting them by highlighting the Janussian randomness of supra-human events.

On another level, Malle slightly exaggerates the schematics of the film and the interconnectedness of the characters' decisions. The consequences of the characters' decisions work together so ingeniously to produce the desired result (Julien wandering out of the elevator and being arrested for another murder) that they call attention to Malle's own role, as the god of the film — the orchestrator of the characters' fates — and blur the line between onscreen and offscreen reality. (This also recalls Malle's description of *Elevator* as an "exercise.")

Given Malle's fervent opposition throughout his career to Godardian jump-cuts, and his constant use of abrechtian onscreen depth (particularly in *Ascenseur*) it may appear surprising or slightly paradoxical that *Elevator* aligns itself ideologically (though not structurally or presentationally), with Brecht's early interpretations of Marlowe's Elizabethan drama. In Brecht's eyes, "[Marlowe's] noblemen ... who betray their country for their private interests are judged very harshly, and *by the events themselves.*" This corresponds, in *Ascenseur*, to Julien's decision to pursue the private interest of an affair with Florence, at the expense of his obligations to M. Carala, which would (of course) constitute betrayal. Malle's deconstruction of fate (and his corresponding argument that individuals are somewhat in control of their destinies) might seem to constitute a fundamental difference — that is, until we recall Brecht's similar belief that "each human relationship is founded on an exact economy, and because of this, miracles are excluded,"[26] and his corresponding affirmation that characters "do not submit absolutely to their destiny."[27]

Some critics have misread *Elevator to the Gallows* as an inherently satirical film,[28] which (though understandable) is untenable. Satire typically entails overt or implied, humor-laced criticism of a social, cultural, or artistic convention, and (though often overlooked) the suggestion of efficacy through a preferable alternative (without which, it would simply become invective). *Elevator*'s genre revisionism and deconstruction work against the conventions of the "Hitchcockian thriller" (just as satire cuts against the grain of convention in the ideological sense) yet true satire inevitably incorporates humor and criticism. In *Ascenseur*, Malle does not attempt to openly criticize and tear down the original genre conventions with humor, but rather (in the opposite sense) augments genre conventions with a multilayered narrative, themes, and characters, accompanied by a challenging structure. Furthermore, as we have already seen, the director not only examines *Ascenseur*'s theme of unavoidable and irreconcilable emotional separation between a man and a woman, but gives it a straight interpretation. The theme itself is neutral, but the (subjective) approach Malle uses to evoke the theme could not be wrought more soberly or pessimistically. (Malle's follow-up, *Les Amants,* addresses the same themes and preoccupations as *Elevator,* but does so in a humorous, anti-bourgeois vein, and revels in satire).

Malle and Nimier eliminate humor from much of *Ascenseur*, with one exception. Malle depicts Louis and Veronique in an extremely lighthearted, mildly comic manner. Louis's acts of rebellion (he spends the drive through Paris playing with Tavernier's windshield wipers and repeatedly circles the same stretch of freeway) and his short, clipped dialogue ("Tu me nerves") suggest Malle's desire to "kiss off" the image of the American rebel as introduced and promulgated far more soberly by American youth cinema. And on another note, Malle uses Louis and Veronique instruments to carry and deliver the central irony of the piece. But these humorous elements are so fleeting that they can hardly be used to defend the entire film as a "satire."

To a large degree, *Ascenseur* itself functions as a running commentary on the American and French *film noir* and *postnoir* periods. Most of the noirish elements (the nighttime sequences; Florence Carala's romantic voice-over monologues; the Freudian, rain-slicked streets; the central fatalistic elements of the motel shooting and the rainstorm) occur during the second act. Bookending this lengthy sequence, Malle interpolates a pre-nighttime series of events and (toward the end of the film) an "Early Sunday morning" series of events, grounded in intense, unstylized, a-expressionistic realism. Again, Malle, Decae, and Nimier underscore the tension between the self-projected romantic illusions of the amorous pair (second act) and the dehumanizing, hard-edged realism of the modernist world that ultimately makes their union impossible.

Ergo, the shots in the first and third acts take advantage of Wellesian deep focus, three-dimensional onscreen space, and (significantly) a real-time narrative pace, to persuade each viewer that he or she is actually glimpsing an authentic world, *sans* any spatial boundaries. Malle and Decaë utilize a very matter-of-fact, time-protracted, shot-by-shot storytelling method to convey Julien's homicide, his entrapment in the elevator at the Carala building, and his arrest for the wrong murder, and the audience witnesses every significant event, moment by moment.

In light of this aesthetic, spatial and temporal realism, one of the film's most important shots follows Simon Carala's murder. Julien Tavernier glances up and notices a black cat, walking coolly past the office window, on the top of the terrace railing, several hundred feet above the ground. It stops to watch him. Ignoring the obvious (and contrived) superstitious implications of this image (and the fact that it may be interpreted as the embodiment of Julien's guilt-ridden conscience, or of his neurosis), the cat is such an unusual, random, and unanticipated subject that it calls attention to itself. On a deeper level, it is an abrechtian object, implying that a real world exists beyond the edge of the frame — that the cat ultimately came from a specific location, just happened to pass behind the office window, and will reach an offscreen destination. The shot thus carries what Pauline Kael referred to as a "dailiness"[29]; intertextually, the feline in *Ascenseur* recalls the black and white cat that walks up one side of the glass roof and down the other above the housemaid's bed in De Sica's *Umberto D.* (1955), as both share this onscreen matter-of-factness: the writer-director reveling in the ordinary, the mundane, the unspectacular. The active world beyond the confines of the screen. The ominous connotations of the cat in *Elevator* thus obscure the animal's realist (and dimensional) significance.

The first and third acts of *Elevator* thus align themselves aesthetically with Italian neorealism, one of the most influential cinematic movements prior to 1957, for both movements attempt to heighten onscreen reality. Like the neorealists, Malle views onscreen deception as inevitable and embraces it; as in *Le Monde du silence*, his abrechtianism in *Elevator* works to fully envelop the viewer in an ultra-reality, and lies at the opposite end of the spectrum from expressionism (high stylization characterized by constant, Brechtian reminders of the director's stylistic presence).

Yet even if Malle and the neorealists pursued the same goal, *Elevator*'s visual approach cuts against the grain of neorealist technique in its first and third acts. If one examines *The Bicycle Thief* and *Umberto D.*, for example, one will notice that the films use a gritty, unpolished, often hand-held filmmaking (and a rough aesthetic) to heighten the "reality" of the onscreen images. Malle's technique subtly calls this approach into question, by suggesting that a rough aesthetic acts as a Brechtian distancing device by distracting each viewer continuously (i.e., the crudeness of the film's look becomes a constant reminder of the cinematic experience). In the first and third acts of *Elevator to the Gallows*, Malle thus presents the audience with the opposite approach: a cinematic world so carefully lit and designed that it becomes hyper-real — one that takes advantage of the viewer's familiarity with the aesthetic conventions of cinema by holding to and heightening those conventions. A wholeness of time and a wholeness of space — without interruption — and a smooth photographic quality, that work together to engulf the viewer.

Despite some on-location scenes, Malle and Decaë light the objects and settings in the with controlled, high-contrast lighting. Appropriately, Malle recalls that he filmed a great deal of *Ascenseur* and *Le Feu follet* in the studio. He also notes that Decae shot with black-and-white Tri-X film, to increase the realism of the aesthetic.[30] A pallor hangs over the entire pre-elevator sequence — a bleakness, a profound sense of inhumanity, and an aura of environmental repression. And the overall sensory effect — thanks to the realism — is one of complete authenticity and believability. This forces us to see through the paper-thin falsehood of the noirish stylization and romantic conventions that Malle sets up in the second act — conventions that, in an unrevisionist, textbook noir picture, one would accept, unblinkingly, as "reality."

CRITICAL RESPONSE

French critics and the public greeted *Elevator to the Gallows* with general warmth and acceptance, if not unqualified praise. Jean Herman, writing for the French journal *Cinéma*, described his enthusiasm after becoming acquainted with Malle as a director through *Ascenseur*, categorized the picture with such groundbreaking classics as Chabrol's *Le Beau Serge* and Truffaut's *Les Mistons*, and remarked, "It enables us to affirm the fact that this young director is capable of making excellent films and facing the task of pulling together a commercial motion picture."[31] Pauline Kael observed, "Jeanne Moreau's ... sullen, sensual mask is just right for this limited but absorbing policier..." and "the film has an unusual sense of control and style, considering that the plot itself is third-rate."[32] As we have already seen, *Cahiers du cinéma* generally admired the film's performances and its *mise en scène*, yet perceived the slow pace and the use of soliloquy as lapses in style.

In a November 1958 *Cahiers du cinéma* article (concurrent with the release of *Les Amants*), Jacques Doniol-Valcroize reflects on Malle's own initial displeasure with *Elevator*, and his insistence that *Les Amants* is a far more personal, fully-realized work:

> Several months ago, Louis Malle admitted to himself that he didn't deserve the Prix Louis-Delluc for *Elevator to the Gallows* and said that, were it up to him, he would have awarded it to Vadim's *Sait-on Jamais*. He said it was unfortunate that the juries did not wait one year to give him the award, because *Les Amants* represents an ideal film for the Louis-Delluc. All of the promises that Malle delivered in his first film — a film far removed from his temperament; [the film] constituted nothing for him but a departure and a stylistic exercise.[33]

With time, Malle's own reactions to *Ascenseur* drifted from lukewarm acceptance to enthusiasm. Thirty years later, he confided to Philip French that *Ascenseur* is, "weirdly enough ... closer to me than *Les Amants*." As French observes:

> *Ascenseur* contains most of the characteristic themes, tropes, and preoccupations, if only in embryonic form, that were to get more considered treatment later: a fascinated contempt for the hypocrisies of the middle class; jazz music; suicide; the adult world observed by the dangerously innocent young; a polit-

ical background that frames and is reflected in the protagonists' conduct; characters trapped in some web of fate; the destructive power of sexual passion; a gift for seizing a society at a precise moment of social change; the urge to disrupt and disconcert; a refusal to make direct moral judgements. Anticlericalism is one of the few missing elements.[34]

    Elevator also won the 1957 Prix Louis-Delluc. Despite small critical reservations, *Ascenseur*'s success contributed to Malle's unmitigated directorial autonomy on the set of his next project, *Les Amants*. Yet, more impressively, the film imparted widespread autonomy to young French filmmakers *per se*. Like Vadim's *...And God Created Woman* one year before it, and Chabrol's *Le Beau Serge* three years later, *Elevator*'s success helped open the floodgates for new directors in the watershed years to follow, by proving that the "jeunesse" could craft commercially and critically viable films. Without *Ascenseur*, seminal works such as Truffaut's *Les Quatre cents coups* and Godard's *Breathless (À bout de souffle)* could never have been realized as easily.

3
Les Amants (The Lovers)—1958
Restoration of the Sacred

"From these ... principles were produced male and female ... together they bring forth the 'Incorruptible One,' the *quinta essentia...*"
— Carl Jung, "The Conjunction"

"Your daughter and the moor are now making the beast with two backs."
— Iago, Shakespeare's *Othello*, Act I, sc. 1

BACKGROUND

Given the positive public and critical reception of *Elevator to the Gallows*, Malle gained the freedom to craft a far "more personal"[1] follow-up. Through Jeanne Moreau, he became acquainted with writer Louise de Vilmorin, a French *cause-célèbré* and author of the novel *Madame De* (adapted by Max Ophuls eight years prior), remembered as much for well-publicized affairs with literary giants including de Saint-Exupery and Malraux, as for her *romans* on the French *noblesse*, rife with *savoir-fair* and meticulous dramatic construction.[2]

Malle wasted no time approaching de Vilmorin. On January 29, 1958 — the night of *Ascenseur*'s premiere — he presented Louise with a copy of an eighteenth century *conte libertin* written by Baron Dominique Vivant Denon, regarding a countess, trapped in an unhappy marital relationship, who finds an escape from the mundanity of monogamous life when she falls instantly in love. Malle proposed a contemporization of Denon's story: a film about the wife of a provincial French newspaper publisher in the late 1950s who, for the first time in her life, discovers the physical pleasure of lovemaking outside of marriage and is so redeemed and permanently altered emotionally and sexually that she abandons her family for her new lover.[3]

Malle and de Vilmorin started their collaboration in late January or early February 1958, and production commenced in May of that year. Although Malle never perceived the film as autobiographical material *per se*, one of his close female friends had left her husband for an extra-marital lover, an affair that led to tragedy. Malle

An icy emotional barricade has arisen between bourgeois housewife Jeanne Tournier (Jeanne Moreau) and her husband, Henri (Alain Cuny), that will lead Jeanne into an impassioned extra-marital affair in Louis Malle's *Les Amants* (The Lovers).

felt intrigued by this series of events and wanted to explore it onscreen, and he was eager to establish his own reputation as a blossoming provocateur.[4]

Amid a professional and personal (amorous)[5] relationship with Jeanne Moreau (who would appear in two of his later directorial efforts), Malle envisioned the Denon adaptation as a Moreau vehicle, and thus planned to cast her in the central role of Mme. Tournier, the listless provincial housewife.[6] Malle considered Jean-Louis Trintignant—fresh from the international acclaim of Vadim's *...And God Created Woman* (1956)—for the role of Bernard Dubois-Lambert (Tournier's lover), but ultimately enlisted Jean-Marc Bory to play the part.[7] Malle and de Vilmorin changed the title from Denon's *Point de lendemain* (Point of No Tomorrow) to *Les Amants* (The Lovers). Malle began production of the film in May 1958, and cut the picture with editor Leonide Azar late that summer. *Les Amants* premiered at the Venice Film Festival in September, and reached French screens on November 5, 1958.

SYNOPSIS

Spring, 1958. Jeanne Tournier, the provincial wife of Henri Tournier (Alain Cuny), owner-publisher of the *Moniteur de Borgogne* newspaper, feels increasingly dissatisfied with her home life. Suffering from ennui compounded by her solipsistic husband's neglect, apathy, and inability to give or receive healthy affection, she begins to take increasingly long sojourns away from her Dijon house, to the Paris home of wealthy childhood friend Maggy Thiébaut-Leroy (Judith Magre). On long afternoons, Jeanne and Maggy covet handsome athlete Raoul Florès as he gallops across the polo field. Though Raoul demonstrates romantic interest in Jeanne (and Maggy encourages their extramarital relationship), Jeanne feels dissatisfied inside, and uncertain as to whether she returns Raoul's feelings.

After she returns home, Jeanne drops hints to her husband that she needs affection. She kisses Henri on the forehead, but he only questions her motives for displaying physicality, criticizes her choice of words, and insists that she check on dinner. Over their meal together, the cold, patronizing Henri—suspicious of his wife's fidelity—begins to toy with Jeanne antagonistically, dropping hints to "challenge" her capacity for unfaithfulness.

During a second trip to Paris, Jeanne expresses her doubts about Raoul to Maggy; Maggy reminds her best friend that Raoul is a miracle in the flesh, there to be taken, that over 30 women would give anything to be his lover. Jeanne's equivocation only builds.

One night, Jeanne follows Henri on a late-night trip to the *Moniteur,* and happens to meet her husband's young, voluptuous secretary. Henri—selfishly displeased and insensitive to his wife's need for attention—forces Jeanne to leave. A few nights later, he staggers into the house drunk and partially undressed, which suggests to an indignant Jeanne that he hasn't actually been working late and pushes their relationship even closer to the brink. To make matters worse, Henri insists that Jeanne invite Maggy and Raoul as overnight guests, the following weekend.

During her next visit to Paris, Jeanne invites Maggy and Raoul to stay at her house for the weekend; they accept. On Jeanne's drive out of the city and back to Dijon, however (with Maggy and Raoul a great distance behind her), her engine fails. She pulls off to the side of the road and hitches a ride with a young man, Bernard Dubois-Lambert (Jean-Marc Bory). During their time together in the car, Bernard first exasperates Jeanne by stopping to drop off some books at an old professor's house, but then manages to get on Jeanne's good side by ridiculing her husband. He openly envisions Henri as an "old bear" who "wears a cap" and "hugs anyone who offends him," and, when he spots Maggy and Raoul on Jeanne's lawn, describes them as "two corpses on chairs." Jeanne bursts into a fit of uncontrollable laughter.

That evening, Henri invites Bernard to stay for dinner and spend the night at the house. For Jeanne, dinner is a "disaster." In an attempt to sway Raoul away from his wife, Henri plays the part of an amorous husband. Raoul falls into the trap, convinced so defiantly of Henri's sincerity that Jeanne brushes him aside and begins to regard him as an idiot.

That night, Jeanne spurns Raoul's advances and, enrobed in a white nightgown, strolls downstairs and out the back door, where she unexpectedly encounters Bernard. The two walk together through a field and the woods surrounding the house, and begin to make passionate love. The lovemaking continues in Jeanne's bedroom and in her bathtub. In the morning, Jeanne and Bernard awaken in each other's arms and plan to run off together. Jeanne saunters past her astonished friends and shocked husband, climbs into Bernard's car, and speeds off with her new paramour. The two stop to have breakfast at a roadside diner, and continue down the road together. Though Jeanne looks doubtfully toward an uncertain future, she regrets nothing.

ANALYSIS

The Lovers recounts one woman's emotional and sexual emancipation through the mechanism of an adulterous affair. It begins with Jeanne Tournier, a housewife and mother who feels miserably unhappy and unfulfilled at her core, yet remains so bound by an ungiving, frigid husband, the shackles of bourgeois social convention, and her own inexperience that she lacks a firm conception of her needs. Jeanne has never known sexual or romantic pleasure, either extramaritally or with her husband; the affair with Bernard thus comes as a revelation so unexpected and emotionally affirming that it turns Jeanne's world upside down and transforms her into a completely different person.

A comparison of *Ascenseur pour l'échafaud* and *Les Amants* reveals the cinematic maturation Malle experienced between the production of the two films. Though immensely enjoyable and successful on its own terms, *Elevator* (as Jacques Doniol-Valcroze observes in *Cahiers du cinéma*)[8] is essentially an *exercise*—an attempt to carve a story out of a gimmick (man commits murder, gets trapped in elevator, is released but immediately arrested for another murder, for which all evidence points directly to him) to heighten the audience's sense of irony, and the supplementation of that plot device with deeper and more multi-layered themes. Thus, with regard to approach, the film stands as a typical debut work for a burgeoning *cineaste*.

Les Amants, however, captures the essence of classic character-driven narrative structures in literature and film (no doubt explained hugely by novelist de Vilmorin's status as a co-scenarist). Eric Rohmer praised the film in an *Arts* essay because, "Unlike Aurenche and Bost, who chop their screenplays into playlets, the director of this film has provided this precious jewel with a setting of extreme refinement, while providing the flow of his story with the freedom of written narrative."[9] This freedom is completely tied into the fact that the film recounts one character's arc in a clear, well-written, and emotionally resonant fashion—the romantic and emotional evolution and burgeoning self-discovery of Jeanne Tournier—and allows that arc to drive the story. As Rohmer observes, "suspense comes not from fate, as in *Ascenseur*, but from the characters' emotions."[10] Despite increased familiarity with Jeanne throughout the picture, one may still find it difficult to predict her actions or the consequences of her actions; Malle and de Vilmorin craft the character so well that one literally believes she could carry the story in any direction she so chooses. Hence, the film captures the mystery, ambiguity and contradictions of one character's free will.

Granted, it would be inaccurate to suggest that Malle completely omits destiny from the film; a few elements in the picture that drive the narrative on a minor level (notably Jeanne's auto breakdown, which leads to her fateful meeting with Bernard) lie beyond Jeanne Tournier's control and can in fact be attributed to fate.[11] But these elements remain tertiary.

While *Elevator to the Gallows* is a cineaste's film — a film made by and for film lovers, with largely cinematic influences (Robert Bresson, Alfred Hitchcock) most of Malle's influences for *Les Amants* are extra-cinematic: the literature of Gustave Flaubert (one thinks immediately of Emma in *Madame Bovary*, particularly given the book's theme of sexual liberation and pessimistic conclusion); the symphonies by Brahms that unfold on the soundtrack; the pre–Napoleonic European goddess literature of the *salonnieres*; and the tableaux of Caspar David Friedrich.[12] (The love-making scenes may remind one of Friedrich's "Moon Rising Over the Sea," "City at Moonrise," "Landscape with Oak Trees and Hunter," and "Cross in the Mountains," in particular.) In the way of cinematic influences, many critics have traced *Les Amants* (thanks in part to the scandals that both films elicited) to Gustav Machaty's notorious *Ecstasy* (1933), starring Hedy Lamarr as Eva, a woman who, like Jeanne Tournier, is defined and driven by her need for sexual fulfillment.

The first post-credit shot sequence of *Les Amants* conveys a significant piece of information about the film. It is a longshot, set on the edge of a polo field, from such a far distance that it is impossible to identify any of the spectators, who are reduced to tiny black shapes as they walk across the screen. A team of polo players gallops across the field just past the fans. Given the group imagery, and Decaë's subsequent transition to an even smaller group and finally to an individual (accompanied by the Moreau voice-over), Malle is revealing that the film will unfold on a dualistic level. It is simultaneously an allegory about French society during the late 1950s, and the story of one character's progression: Jeanne Tournier.

Similarly, the film offers an astonishing ontological transition from the first to the second image. An action-filled medium shot of the polo players follows the long shot. Almost no discernible time lapses in between the two shots, and the second shot is an enlarged *segment* of the first — as if Decaë, gifted with an omnipresent ability to move to different depths, is (through the use of individual shots) actually conveying the meaning of all images to follow: singular shots as three-dimensional fractions of a four-dimensional world, with limitless time, space, and depth. It would be difficult to find a clearer visual representation of the trope of the cinematographic process *per se*; Malle and Decaë employ this groundbreaking use of onscreen space throughout the film.

As Malle mentioned to Philip French, the first half of *Les Amants* draws a satirical portrait of the late 1950s French bourgeois. Given Malle's own background — he grew up independently wealthy, heir to the Beghin sugar fortune in Thumeries, a northern French industrial town —coupled with his description of *Les Amants* (following the film's release) as far "more personal" than *Ascenseur* ("something closer to me"[13]) and his outspoken contempt for his family's abundant wealth, it becomes apparent that Malle crafted an anti-bourgeois satire as an expression of contempt for his origins. (In his autobiography, he recalls hiding his place of birth and the wealth of the Malle family, and attempting to secure as much financial independence as possible.)[14] *Les Amants* offers insight into the nature of the French aristocracy in the late fifties, by coloring the bourgeois as an elitist group so small and so tight that all the French families in the same social strata are acquainted, each family tied to one particular industry (for instance, the sugar manufacturing of the Beghins). The characters echo the astonishingly small size of the French power structure when Jeanne Tournier just "happens" to be picked up by a random stranger, discovers that his surname is "Dubois-Lambert," and not only realizes that she knows his cousin, Jacques, but that he is familiar with Maggy Thiébaut-Leroy by industry and reputation:

BERNARD   (introducing self; tips hat) Bernard Dubois-Lambert.

JEANNE   Dubois-Lambert?! I know a Dubois-Lambert, who golfs at St. Cloud. Eh … Jacques Dubois-Lambert.

BERNARD   My cousin. I can't stand him.

JEANNE   But he's charming.
           (pause)
           Is your family related to the Klebers, the sugar people? And do you know the Thiébaut-Leroys? They're in wool. Maggy's my best friend!

BERNARD   Poor you.

JEANNE   Do you know her?

BERNARD   Only by reputation, thank God. I avoid all those people.[15]

Beyond the film's effort to convey the story of a woman's sexual and emotional emancipation from her entrapment in a confining social sphere, Malle and de Vilmorin begin with a character in desperate need of a singular identity *per se*. Jeanne's bourgeois social identification in this film cloaks her protectively; as long as she can wrap herself in the cover of middle and upper-class society (with her role as a social-climbing housewife), she need not worry about discovering herself as a socially liberated (and individualized) woman; she can simply become a "Maggy clone." And yet, though Malle and de Vilmorin situate Jeanne in an elitist environment *physically*, amid members of the same social strata (particularly Maggy Thiébaut-Leroy), the dissatisfaction and hesitancy on Jeanne's face (in the opening scene) and her reflexive third-person voice-over (on the soundtrack) lend the impression of one who feels unsettled and displaced. One never believes that Jeanne belongs to this group of phonies. With a level of insight keen enough to zero in on Jeanne's Achilles' heel, Henri attacks her clonish behavioral emulation of Maggy. ("I'll be back in two ticks," she assures her husband. "That's Maggy talk," he responds, to which she turns away indignantly.) Jeanne's dialogue at dinner is overwhelmingly shallow; she rambles on about the latest hairstyles in Paris—further echoes of Maggy, and Jeanne's own lack of individuality.

Though unapparent until the group dinner (a key scene, just prior to the third act), Malle and de Vilmorin place Maggy Thiébaut-Leroy and Henri in the same tonal category: as inhibitors of Jeanne's liberation. Ergo, the average viewer will experience a similar distaste for both characters. As one French critic observes, Maggy Thiébaut-Leroy embodies every negative quality Malle and de Vilmorin associate with the prototypical late 1950s social-climbing elitist: materialistic, phony, shallow, hypocritical. He writes, "Malle and de Vilmorin amused themselves by instilling in

Maggy all those exasperating faults of the species they knew all too well: the mundane, stupid snob."[16]

Similarly, the average viewer will never fall short of feeling sheer disgust for Henri. Malle uses dark techniques reminiscent of horror films to make the viewer fully aware (on a gut level) of Jeanne's subjugation; Alain Cuny plays Henri as a tall, domineering, ursine figure who (literally and figuratively) glares down at his wife, lumbers through the house drunkenly, and suffocates Jeanne with an evil grin. His footsteps up the stairs through the dark house ring the toll of death knells. The disaffection Henri projects toward Jeanne shapes the tone of his character, via a direct emotional connection with the audience; because an individual's need to receive affection from a spouse is so rudimentary and so primal, the average viewer will recognize Henri's contempt and respond positively (with justification) to Jeanne's familial abandonment.

Maggy and Henri find each other deplorable; if one weighs either individual's comments about the other too heavily, one may find oneself siding with him or her and overlooking the similar natures of the two characters. Naturally, if an individual belongs to a social group (e.g., the French bourgeois) with ugly characteristics, one will regard everyone else as diseased and oneself as upright.

The tonality of the relationship between Jeanne and the audience lies at the opposite end of the spectrum. The viewer sympathizes with Jeanne from first frame to last, and understands that, on the most primal level, she must undergo a slow transition. At the outset of the film, Jeanne remains emotionally and intellectually incomplete, and her liberation could not occur without a gradual build in self-knowledge. During the opening scenes, Jeanne willingly accepts the marital subjugation forced upon her by Henri. (Note how she kneels before her husband, takes his hand, and almost *begs him* to admire and accept Raoul Florès— as if playing the role of the mid-adolescent daughter, beseeching her father for permission to go on a date.) Jeanne senses the need to break out of her bourgeois shackles sexually from the beginning of the story, but her sensory perception first emerges on a level so subterranean and so buried in her psyche that she follows her instincts blindly without a conscious acknowledgement of her destination, groping for an answer.

The option of an affair with Raoul Florès leads Jeanne and the audience to a dead end. Jeanne's rebellious instincts must be accompanied by her intellectual realization that Henri and Raoul share the same bourgeois social status and many similar attitudes. Jeanne's doubts about Raoul build during the first and second acts, and will only reach a conscious, decisive level upon her pivotal discovery—following the group dinner conversation, when Raoul buys into Henri's pretense of an emotionally tight relationship with Jeanne— that Raoul belongs in the same boat as her husband. Florès lies completely out of touch with Jeanne's marital dissatisfaction and her emotionally fueled sexual desires, and thus initially refuses to consummate their affair because he wants to avoid disrupting the "marital harmony" of the Tournier household.

What Jeanne has, then (when faced with Raoul as a prospective lover) is the option of bourgeois intra-rebellion. Though she could (ostensibly) opt to follow this path by consummating her affair with Raoul, it would leave her in the same social sphere in which she began, with the same clonish absence-of-identity and the same void at her core. In other words, the sexual rebellion with a bourgeois partner, who rears the same ugly, insensitive, thick head as Henri, would be akin to the bourgeois rebelling within itself. The affair would become self-gratifying and ultimately futile, or masturbatory, instead of producing the newfound inner reality and self-emancipation that the affair with Bernard Dubois-Lambert yields, because Bernard cuts against the grain of the bourgeois; he is a social outcast, an outsider, a rebel who detests Maggy Thiébaut-Leroy and who gains Jeanne's support by mocking her society friends openly. Lovemaking with Bernard will thus enlighten and illuminate Jeanne, and enable her social and spiritual self-reinvention.

An unusual painting, entitled "La Carte du tendre," appears behind the opening credits of *Les Amants* and ties closely into the film on two levels. Art historian Vincent Lavoie reflects on the origin and significance of the painting in *Parachute* magazine. He describes "Carte du tendre" as

> An ancient literary source, [authored by] Madeleine de Scudery, and one of the most celebrated pages in her suite of historical novels *Clélie* (1654–60). The map in question, a symbol of amorous casuistry, proceeds from an allegorical topography of sentiments, a type of map in vogue in the Seventeenth century. The initiative journey proposed by this precious map leads to the principle of friendship, or even to the love, platonic or otherwise, of a woman.[17]

Malle recalls that de Scudery ran a salon — a critical observation. In 1929, Valerian Tornius authored and published a brilliant work entitled *Salons: Pictures of Society through Five Centuries*. One of the theses of Tornius's book (as well as the thesis of Robert Graves's *White Goddess* and one of the central points of Bogdanovich's *Killing of the Unicorn*) is that matriarchal pagan society, guided by matriarchal religion, preceded patriarchal society, and thus can be seen as foundational to human behavior and all social interaction. Salons, from the era of Boccaccio until Napoleon turned the tables, were a key European social fixture and a sphere of social and relational control for women. Moreover, Tornius implies that one of the hallmarks of a female-driven (and matriarchal) European society involved a decisive lack of monogamy. Guided by their emotions, each salonnière had affairs with countless men, but would seldom consider the patriarchal Christian option of marrying into a fixed relationship with a husband and thus becoming subservient to one man. They perceived the two paths as contradictory.[18]

On one level, *Les Amants* can be interpreted as an affirmation of the pagan ideal. Through the film, Malle suggests that true emancipation for Jeanne Tournier will involve shedding the monogamous idea *per se*; this is why her comment at the end suggests a complete liberation. She does not know how long the relationship will last ("Already, at the hour of dawn, she had doubts"), but neither does she regret her escape from a suffocating marital relationship. Moreover, by drifting into a fleeting romantic relationship, guided by her heart, Jeanne heads toward an embrace and affirmation of an anti-monogamous lifestyle.

Granted, Malle admits to Philip French that he left the conclusion of *Les Amants* open-ended. But prior to the intentionally ambiguous epilogue, the film's stylistic approach underscores the theme of a classicist return to the fundamental quality of female-driven relationships, guided by emotion and opposed to anti-feminine monogamous subjugation. The picture thus employs a "classicist aesthetic" that evokes the feeling of a return to Renaissance Europe. Ironically, though Malle set *Les Amants* in 1958, it has the look and feel of a period piece: long-held takes (and occasionally, an entire scene comprised of only one take), rich "classical" lighting, a widescreen DyaliScope format, Wellesian deep focus (as in *Ascenseur*), a *mise en scène* so rich with detail that it can almost be called baroque, a formalist structure with planned sequences of exactly three minutes in length. With the addition of Brahms' "Opus 18 (String Sextet No. 1 in B Flat Major)" on the soundtrack, particularly during the outdoor nighttime scenes, the film (as Malle notes) takes on a lyrical tone, and what could simply be a depiction of graphic coitus evolves into emotionally charged lovemaking and an uninhibited celebration of passionate eroticism.

On another level, the core of *Les Amants* involves Jeanne Tournier's *progression* to higher self-knowledge through romance, it is thus ideal to depict a "romantic progression" on a map, and would be difficult to imagine a more appropriate or meaningful painting than the portion of *La Carte du tendre* that appears behind the credits of *Les Amants*. This opening image of the film sets up a basic metaphor that will recur throughout the picture; the *lack* of geographic progression during the first and second acts, in turn, underscores the redundancy and the stasis in Jeanne Tournier's current life. Malle interpolates several driving sequences, yet unlike the abrechtian qualities of *Monde du silence* (for example) one senses a lack of geographic progress—a redundancy. Concurrent with Jeanne's contemplation and rejection of an affair with Raoul Florès, Malle intercuts several scenes of Jeanne traveling back and forth, repeatedly, on a singular stretch of road between her home in Dijon and society milieux in Paris. Similarly, many of the scenes in the first half of the film are stagy for a Malle feature (most of the action in the first and second acts unfolds in the Tournier home and beside the polo field). In particular, these sequences anticipate the "road" metaphor of Buñuel's thematically similar anti-bourgeois piece *The Discreet Charm of the Bourgeoisie* (1972), where the director cuts periodically to existential scenes of the main characters walking repeatedly on the same endless stretch of road, "symbol of their stasis."[19] Appropriately, in *Les Amants*, the most dramatic environmental shifts in the narrative accompany the most notable emotional transitions in Jeanne's evolution: as Jeanne and Bernard drive down the road, the morning after lovemaking, headed toward an uncertain future, and, prior to this, when Jeanne enters the celestial realm.

The cinematic architecture of *Les Amants* renders it incredibly unique. The only viable intertextual comparison one can make (involving an aforementioned principle, from the introduction to this text) is to Neil Jordan's groundbreaking drama *The Crying Game*. Just as Jordan's film offers a groundbreaking structural experiment by following the progression of its central character, Fergus (Stephen Rea), from a sphere appropriate to one film (a Northern Ireland terrorist camp) into another environment (the London underground) that seems to exist and function in a completely different motion picture, as a mirror of Fergus's dramatic internal and external transmutation,[20] *Les Amants* incorporates two worlds, as an indicator of Jeanne Tournier's dramatic internal progression. In Malle's conversations with Philip French about the picture, the director recalls: "There were two sides to [*Les Amants*], and I suppose if I were to make it today I would be more capable of integrating the two sides. The first half is a comedy of manners, a satire on the mores of the upper class in the late 1950s; the second part is almost an homage to the German romantic painter Caspar David Friedrich."[21] Granted, a closer integration of the two sides might align the film more closely with conventional Hollywood cinematic architecture, but it would also threaten to damage the thematic relevance of the film's fascinating structure.

The second environment in *Les Amants* is a nighttime world of romantic initiation that Jeanne Tournier must enter to undergo an emotional, sexual, and psychological transmutation. Full of coital imagery (e.g., water; twisting trees; lush, fertile vegetation), the French countryside in which Jeanne and Bernard wander and make love under the moonlight (in a field, in a boat on a lake, on a bridge beside a water mill, etc.) is appropriately ethereal, quasi-celestial. Malle and Decaë film Moreau and Bory with a narrow depth of field, to leave the backgrounds slightly out of focus and cast a "dreamlike" appearance onto the surroundings.

Jeanne's internal evolution entails throwing off the shackles of restraint and inhibition. Visually speaking, she literally appears to evolve into a goddess. One French critic refers to her as an "apparition," drifting toward Bernard in her white nightgown; American critic Danny Peary writes, "Moreau is something special: when she lets down and brushes her hair and walks outside in her white nightgown, she makes the quickest transition from dowdy to ethereal in cinema history."[22] The transformation has occurred internally, as well: as if she were a Boccaccian goddess, she takes the upper hand in her relationship with Bernard; *leading* him along, and resisting his advances initially and only reciprocating *when she is ready*.

Jeanne's physical transmutation (as a product of her inner evolution), is why Maggy's comment to her, "You're unrecognizable" (in reference to a change in her external state as a result of "falling in love" with Raoul Florès) is one of the funniest lines in the film. Jeanne may go through the formality of telling Raoul that she loves him, but her countenance (and her unwillingness to have coitus with Raoul in the third act) suggest otherwise. We notice no change in Jeanne's appearance relative to her encounters with the milquetoast Raoul Florès. In light of Jeanne's physical transmutation just prior to lovemaking with Bernard, Maggy's comment is hysterical.

Speaking literally (given the transience of the nighttime) and allegorically, it would be impossible for the second "world" of *Les Amants* to represent a permanent state for the characters. Thanks to the temporality of the internal and external shifts, the lovers perceive the dawn ("l'aube") as cruel for their countenances. Driven by the throes of sexual passion, their exchanged promises — impassioned words of forever, of permanence — are thus as fleeting as the proverbial orgasm itself. As the sun rises, passion wanes and Jeanne herself regresses into a state of deep physical imperfection; Malle films her with a kerchief around her head, a swollen, unmade face, and puffy eyelids. Self-conscious and embarrassed by her own appearance, she warns Bernard not to look at her.

The same basic idea drives *Les Amants* and *Ascenseur* (and traces of it will highlight *Le Feu follet*): in all three films, Malle ultimately affirms the impermanence of romantic love, the tentativeness of sexual pleasure, and the impossibility of complete emotional, intellectual, and spiritual union between a male and a female. Jeanne thus begins to doubt the security of her new relationship with Bernard immediately after the dawn breaks; Malle wanted to imply that the romance may not endure, but admired Jeanne's insistence on forging down the path of liberation despite lingering uncertainties.[23]

But even considering the pessimistic subthemes shared by *The Lovers* and *Elevator*, *Les Amants* remains a far more optimistic work. Despite the likelihood that Jeanne's relationship with Bernard will end soon, her positive evolution to complete liberation through her exposure to impassioned lovemaking is now embedded in her psyche, an inextricable component of her self-knowledge (a theme *Ascenseur* completely fails to explore). This, in turn, is why Jeanne regards the experience as a positive step in her own emotional development and (in voice-over) embraces the events of the prior evening.

The voice-overs are an integral element of *Les Amants*. During Jeanne Moreau's third-person narration (one should consider the differences between the implications of this voice and the implications of *Ascenseur*'s first-person stream-of-consciousness narration), we must ask ourselves if Moreau reads narration about her character as a separate individual, or if Tournier narrates her own story. The third person voice may tempt one to argue that Moreau narrates her character's story, as it might seem absurd for Tournier to speak of herself with distant objectivity. Nevertheless, the latter interpretation carries decisively more interesting implications.

If true, the voice-over would almost certainly be a reflection on the *past*, for the narration reveals a heightened self-knowledge of Jeanne Tournier's internal state, of which Tournier at the story's outset is only aware on the most instinctive, subconscious level. The third-person voice-over with buried self-reflexivity suggests a heightened, melodramatic self-mythologization — as if, following her self-evolution, Jeanne is looking back and interpreting her own story in a grandiose literary mold, as a kind of neo-Victorian classicist arc that carried her into romanticism; here, the line between film and literature begins to blur. Appropriately, the mood and the vocal quality of the narration are romantically effusive. But the voice-over also implies Tournier's desire to self-consciously bury the pride in a third-person shell, presumably unaware of the fact that the third person voice actually heightens the audience's sense of her own self-importance.

Moreover, Decae's first close-up of Moreau lingers on her face for a noticeably *extended* period of time — so long that Tournier actually begins to fidget, becoming increasingly ill at ease (and making the audience uncomfortable as well). This reflects the dissatisfaction and the bourgeois displacement of the character per se, but on another level, if one accepts the hindsight theory (that Tournier recounts the beginning of her story in a biased, albeit *a*-rose-colored autobiographical flashback), one can almost read Jeanne's present awareness of her past self-importance, visualized through the facial expressions on her character (i.e., making her past self uncomfortable with the self-obsessive narcissism inevitable in centering an entire story around herself). Again, this suggests a desire, in the present, to shirk herself of obsessive pride by criticizing her past narcissism visually (her onscreen expression seems to say: "I'm uncomfortable when the camera focuses on me ... I'm not that important") which ironically has the opposite effect in the eyes of the audience because Tournier is the one who is doing the reflecting and putting herself at the center of the story.

CRITICAL RESPONSE

In her outstanding monograph on Bernardo Bertolucci, Claretta Micheletti Tonetti recalls that when the director's critically hailed masterpiece, *Last Tango in Paris* (1972)—once hotly contested as "Art or Pornography?"—returned to European theaters in the early '90s (after Italian censors banned the picture 20 years prior), university students—desensitized by the looser mores of the post-sexual revolution years—found *Ultimo Tango*'s sexual content rather tame and struggled to understand the furor Bertolucci elicited in 1972.[24] One can imagine similar contemporary reactions to *Les Amants*. It may be difficult for a viewer under the age of 40 to understand just how scandalous Malle's film first appeared to audiences. But during the late fifties, with the Hays Code still in effect, *The Lovers* reached American cinemas and broke countless pre-established censorship rules, which induced the ratings board to tag it with an "X" certification and drew ire from the Catholic Legion of Decency. Consequently, numerous states red-flagged the picture. In a September 1958 caption, *Variety* predicted, "Since it is adultery and fairly lucid, a la *Ecstasy*, by which it was obviously influenced, Legion of Decency trouble is in store. If these scenes have to be cut there isn't much left in the pic."[25] Film historian Martin Quigley, Jr., recalls, "Prosecution of a theater manager in Cleveland Heights, Ohio, on the grounds of showing an obscene film, engendered a lawsuit that finally made its way to the U.S. Supreme court, which ruled that the picture did not come under the legal definition of obscenity. The case against the manager was dismissed."[26]

In *The Lovers*, Malle pushed the content line farther than had ever been pushed in a non-underground, commercial film. Nude shots of Moreau during coitus with most of her left breast exposed, and the long-held shot on her face during cunnilingus (when she orgasms), followed by her hand dropping limply onto a pillow, infuriated the film's more conservative viewers and critics. But beyond the basic (and shallow) question of *which* physical details are exposed, the film's "message"—perceived by many as a propagation of adultery—fueled the virulent hostility of right wing critics.

Les Amants became one of the key films of the late fifties that not only wore down and eventually abolished cinematic censorship, but paved the way for the sexual revolution itself 10 years later, with its unabashed celebration of extramarital carnality as a form of anti-bourgeois rebellion. In this sense, *The Lovers* falls into the same category as Vilgot Sjoman's groundbreaking (and far more explicit) arthouse classic *I Am Curious ... Yellow* (1967).[27] Thus, the impact of Malle's film on cultural standards and on sexual mores *per se* in the United States and Europe cannot be overestimated. It marked the first instance in Louis Malle's career when the filmmaker attempted to openly shock viewers into rethinking conservative Western attitudes toward sex, but would by no means be the last.

In the United States, *Les Amants* received a less-than-enthusiastic critical reception. When some narrow-minded American critics condemned the film, their remarks resembled nervous, thinly-veiled attempts to attack the picture's erotic content and sexual liberalism. The same *Variety* article that predicts trouble for the film attacks what it perceives as "fairly banal dialogue ... diminish(ed) vitality ... and direction that dwells on too many unessential points and lacks the true feel for this woman's plight to make her emotional release effective drama."[28] And writing for *The Monthly Film Bulletin*, film journalist Eric Rhode complains, "For the most part the film is too uncertain ... its resolution is intentionally ridiculous."[29]

Yet according to Malle, the film became "a phenomenon" in Europe.[30] Rohmer, as we have seen, praises the film, proclaiming, "Finally, we are presented with a film that can sustain a comparison with the best that literature has produced throughout the ages ... the excellence of the screenplay never detracts from the film's naturalness."[31] Writing for the British journal *Sight and Sound*, journalist Richard Roud refers to *The Lovers* as "a film as promising as Chabrol's *Le Beau Serge*," and observes, "Never before has one seen CinemaScope breadth so successfully combined with the suggestion of depth ... the dryness [of de Vilmorin's dialogue], its concision and exactness beautifully counterpoint the ease and fluidity of Decae's camerawork and of the musical score."[32] Significantly, *Les Amants* won the Special Jury Prize at the Venice Film Festival in 1958, and made the 26 year old Malle an internationally acclaimed cinematic giant.

Malle, always his own harshest critic, recalls his initial, latent displeasure with *Les Amants* after the film left the editing table, insisting in hindsight that while the first two features remained well crafted and delivered a strong emotional and intellectual impact on many viewers, neither of the contrasting styles of *Ascenseur* and *Les Amants* were close enough to him.[33] He felt that *Les Amants* projected a "naive, shallow, and maladroit"[34] image of himself as an artist, and the film's strict formalism (with long takes of predetermined, equal length) ran contrary to his instincts. So Malle continued to search, gradually yet tenaciously, for the quintessential cinematic metaphor of his own emotional and intellectual vision.

4

Zazie dans le métro (Zazie)—1960

The World as Carnival

"Just above him, twelve feet overhead, Teddy Bloat is about to fall out of the minstrels' gallery, having chosen to collapse just at the spot where somebody in a grandiose fit, weeks before, had kicked out two of the ebony balusters. Now, in his stupor, Bloat has been inching through the opening, head, arms, and torso, until all that's keeping him up there is an empty champagne split in his hip pocket, that's got hooked some-how—/ By now, Pirate has managed to sit up on his narrow bachelor bed, and blink about. How awful ... how bloody awful ... above him, he hears clothes rip. The Special Operations Executive has trained him to fast responses. He leaps off of the cot and kicks it rolling on its casters in Bloat's direction. Bloat, plummeting, hits square amidships with a great strum of bedsprings. One of the legs collapses. 'Good morning,' notes Pirate."

— Thomas Pynchon, *Gravity's Rainbow*

BACKGROUND

Around the early winter of 1959, while Louis Malle struggled, futilely, to launch planned adaptations of Joseph Conrad's *Victory* and Phyllis Hastings's *Rapture in My Rags* through Nouvelles Éditions, *Zazie dans le métro*, French belletrist Raymond Queneau's 13th novel, made its initial appearance in European bookstores and became a cult sensation.[1] The story of the work—a foul-mouthed gamin of unspecified age[2] (roughly between 13 and 15 years old) travels from her rural French village to Paris to stay with her female impersonator uncle and discovers the duplicitousness and deception of the adult world—enchanted Malle. But he felt even more captivated by *Zazie*'s anarchic, mischievous style: the phonetic orthography, literary parodies, sophisticated word play and double-entendres that fill Queneau's pages. Malle felt so taken with the literary playfulness of the novel, in fact, that he immediately attempted to option *Zazie* through NEF. But the French powerhouse producer Raoul

Aunt Albertine (Carla Marlier) clowns with her impudent, mischievous niece, 10-year-old Zazie (Catherine Demongeot) during the girl's surrealistic trip to Paris in *Zazie dans le métro.*

J. Lévy, of Iéna Productions (*Et Dieu créa la femme, Les Orgueilleux*) had already acquired the rights to the material, with René Clément (*Forbidden Games, Purple Noon*) slated to direct.[3] Here, events took an interesting and unexpected turn. For some indeterminate reason, Lévy and Clément withdrew from the project; Malle speculated, years later, that the men simply found the material intractable.[4] Still, it took Lévy and Clément months to give up on *Zazie*, and NEF's ongoing attempts to option the *roman à clef* thus stretched into the autumn of 1959.[5]

Malle's initial plan for the adaptation entailed a quick, simple transposition of events from page to screen, shot in black-and-white, on a minuscule budget — without complex adaptive work and minus any cutting.[6] But in time, he rejected this strategy in favor of doing a lengthy, big-budget Technicolor version with his close friend, screenwriter Jean-Paul Rappeneau (*A Very Private Affair, That Man from Rio*); the two men began an eight-month adaptation process that involved finding cinematic equivalents for Queneau's attacks on conventional literature.[7] In adapting the work, Malle planned to draw, onscreen, from such cinematic influences as the Marx Brothers, Tex Avery, Looney Tunes, Mack Sennett, Jacques Tati and the entire surrealist movement.

Preproduction on *Zazie* saw a number of bureaucratic and logistical shifts among the crew. Billard documents Malle's decision to change assistant directors repeatedly; he began with Alain Cavalier, whom he replaced with Rappeneau (doubling as A.D.), whom he replaced with Volker Schlöndorff, whom he replaced with Philippe Collin, one of Louis's schoolmates at IDHEC.[8]

Malle asked Collin to find an actress to portray Zazie, on whom the entire film would hinge. Though Collin's specific démarche has gone undocumented, he ultimately landed on Catherine Démongeot — at the time a 10 year old with no film experience, but one unanimously chosen as the lead. Philippe Noiret (*The Clockmaker, Life and Nothing But*), who portrays Zazie's uncle Gabriel in the film, recalls:

> [Malle and Collin] had to conduct lots of screen tests, and the casting was an extremely delicate matter, not to mention terribly long, certainly, but one rewarded with great success when they found this little girl who was absolutely *ideal* for the role of Zazie, who had a spirit, vivacity, and intelligence exceptional for a girl of that age, and a gift for comedy that was real. These were qualities almost impossible to find in a ten year old.[9,10]

As for Noiret himself and the supporting cast, Malle sought out those actors balanced between experience on the stage and experience in vaudevillian farce, who could travel to both extremes in performance. Noiret reflects on how he and the other players became involved:

> What most drew Louis to the idea of casting me — what most seduced him — was that he had seen me in two completely different exercises. One was playing in theatrical pieces, mostly the classic plays, major works of the stage... But at the same time, I did a number with my partners in this theatrical troupe, in the halls of the Left Bank, that was carbaret, or music hall, if you like ... [Louis wanted] to have someone who on the one hand, had just come from playing Macduff in *Macbeth* ... and at the same time who spent his nights playing in the cabarets of the Left Bank of the era, and could also do comedy ... it interested [Louis] to have two sides in the same actor... This was [also] the case with ... several other actors who were in *Zazie* ... Jacques Dufilho and Hubert Deschamps in particular.[11]

Malle's insistence on actors with theatrical experience was hardly indiscriminate; according to Noiret (who, at the time, had only appeared in one additional film, by Agnes Varda), the performances in *Zazie* required greater projection than a typical feature — were more grossly exaggerated, more deliberately caricatured, poetic in lieu of realistic. Malle engaged the actors in a broad array of improvisation; for instance, the entire Eiffel Tower sequence, Noiret recalls, including his "dream ballet," is ad libbed.[12] The Eiffel sequence reveals another interesting point: Malle had many of the actors do their own stunts. For instance, none of Gabriel's astonishing, dizzying onscreen balletics at La Tour Eiffel are matted or shot in a studio. In fact, when Noiret asked the director, sardonically, if he would be expected to climb to the top of the Eiffel Tower antenna while Malle filmed, Malle responded with an emphatic yes and insisted on shooting Noiret doing exactly that.[13,14] Malle also asked the leads, on occasion, to act more slowly, while he reduced the camera speed and instructed his extras to perform at normal speed; as a result, his actors appear to be playing at normal speed while everyone around them is accelerated.

Another of Malle's unusual strategies on *Zazie* involved casting the same group of 13 professional actors as a recurrent group of extras throughout the movie — each one playing a slightly different extra in each new appearance. In doing so, Malle established a level of rapport between the actors that would have been absent, were *Zazie* cast with new extras in every scene; the use of preestablished, experienced actors enabled him to use performers comfortable and familiar with improvising, to the extent that they could be relied on to ad lib actions in their particular corner of the frame. The result is an Altmanesque tapestry, with a dozen actions unfolding at once in every crowd scene.[15]

Malle and cinematographer Henri Raichi (*Les Amants*, *Le Voleur*) shot *Zazie* in Paris in mid–1960; it debuted in France on October 28 of that year and in the States on November 20, 1961.[16] By Malle's own account, the film drew a decidedly odd reaction during its initial theatrical run in France. The first week, *Zazie* sold out and broke box office records; a few days later, the theaters emptied and merely drew handfuls of viewers, rendering *Zazie* a financial failure. Yet, despite its initial box-office disappointment, the film became a cult sensation in time and has since been playing in Parisian theaters, regularly, for over 40 years.[17]

SYNOPSIS

Ten-year-old Zazie Lalochère (Catherine Démongeot) travels to Paris on the train with her mother, Jeanne (Odette Piquet). They plan to meet her Uncle Gabriel (Philippe Noiret), a female impersonator and cabaret dancer, at the Gare de l'Est for a 36-hour Parisian visit. Upon arrival, Jeanne abandons Zazie and Gabriel for a lover, and promises to reconnect with her daughter in two-and-a-half days. Loud, impudent, and vulgar for her age, Zazie greets Gabriel by pinching him on the leg, and demands to see the Paris Métro, but is outraged to discover that the iron gates to the subway have been locked in observance of a strike. Zazie and Gabriel pile into the taxi chauffered by Gabriel's friend, Charles (Antoine Roblot), the vehicle crammed to the brim with passengers.

Gabriel, Zazie and Charles visit the café below Gabriel's flat, an establishment run by Turandot (Hubert Deschamps), a scrawny little man with a hearing aid in one ear (which Zazie naughtily tugs) and a green parrot, Laverdure, who repeatedly squawks, "Yakety yak, that's all you guys can do." Gabriel and his wife, Albertine (Carla Marlier) treat Zazie to a dinner of consommé at their home that evening, while the neon lights of the boulevard flash through the windows. The following morning, Zazie awakens with Gabriel still asleep; she slips outside and sprints toward the Métro, but Turandot catches sight of her, chases her down the street and seizes her. Zazie screams out to passers-by and deceitfully informs them that Turandot is a child molester who whispered obscenities into her ear; Zazie, in turn, whispers the obscenities the ear of a woman; the horrified pedestrians begin a game of operator, whispering the obscenities into each other's ears, one after another, until the man at the end of the line expresses confusion, and the woman beside him withdraws a small notebook and illustrates the obscenity for him.

Zazie finally manages to slip away from the ruckus, and next runs into Pedro

Trouscaillon (Vittorio Caprioli), a slightly fat and homely, yet affable, mustachioed prankster whose occupation and appearance shift continuously, and whom Zazie initially mistakes for a cop; Trouscaillon accompanies Zazie to a flea market and buys her some blue jeans, then treats her to a feast of mussels and French fries at a café. When Zazie digs into the mollusks, however, she sprays Trouscaillon with saltwater, drawing crowd of spectators, who hover around the glass window behind Trouscaillon and inspect the diners nosily.

Zazie's subsequent attempt to escape from Trouscaillon falls flat; she tries to pull another con by accusing Trouscaillon of predatory sexual behavior within earshot of tourists, as she did to Turandot, but Trouscaillon manages to gain the crowd's sympathy against Zazie by insisting that she is a little thief who stole a pair of blue jeans from him. Arguments erupt among the members of the mob, and the disagreements lapse into a noisy brouhaha from which Zazie and Trouscaillon barely manage to escape. Trouscaillon chases Zazie from one side of Paris to another, the pursuit sparked by scattershot gags. At the wildest moment, Zazie throws the blue jeans to Trouscaillon, but a stick of lit TNT falls into his hands and explodes in cartoonlike fashion; at another, Zazie and Trouscaillon stop in a mirrored hall to take photographs of one another with a camera on a tripod.

Rearriving at Gabriel's flat, Zazie awakens her still-sleeping uncle and introduces Trouscaillon as a cop; Trouscaillon falls for Aunt Albertine and infuriates Gabriel by accusing him of being gay; this plants the idea in Zazie's mind that her uncle might be a "hormosessual" (though she has no idea what that means); she spends the remainder of her time in Paris pumping Gabriel with questions about his sexual orientation and can never get a straight answer from him. Zazie eventually concludes that being a "hormosessual" might have something to do with Gabriel's wearing the perfume Barbouze by Fior. Later in the day, Gabriel and Charles takes Zazie up to the top of the Eiffel tower, in an elevated car full of noisy, hyperactive tourists; when they arrive at an observation platform, however, Zazie makes her uncle terribly nervous by leaning over the side of the railing. As he cranes forward and attempts to hang onto her, his eyeglasses drop from his face and fall several stories, landing squarely on the nose of a woman who is sitting at the base of the tower and reading a newspaper. Without his glasses, Gabriel stumbles along the observation platforms at the highest levels of the tower, and veers dangerously close to the edge; he lapses into a kind of dream state, chanting a poetic soliloquy in voice-over. Gabriel eventually latches onto a helium balloon and floats to the base of the tower, retrieving his glasses, while Zazie and Charles descend on the Eiffel staircase. During their long descent, Zazie demands that Charles take romantic interest in her and marry her; he stubbornly refuses.

The group meets the silver-haired widow Mouaque (Yvonne Clech), who drives a purple luxury car and wears a dress of the same color; she develops an infatuation with Gabriel, but he is waylaid and essentially kidnapped by a group of crazed tourist girls, who spirit him off on a bus. Gabriel manages to escape in time for his nightclub act and performs backstage, in top hat, with a bunch of dancing girls, but realizes that he has forgotten his dress, and races over to the pay phone, making several unsuccessful attempts to reach Albertine through Turandot and his lover, the red-headed Mado (Annie Fratellini). Mado eventually agrees to rush up to the flat and retrieve the dress from Albertine in time for the act. Shortly after she does so, however, Trouscaillon appears at the window — without being seen by the two women — and, dressed as Mado, manages to push Mado out of the room and get close to Albertine by taking Mado's place; Albertine fails to notice the deception.

Following Gabriel's act, the entire group hustles off to a café and sits down to dinner, but arguments erupt that descend into a cataclysmic riot that destroys the restaurant; Zazie, who has fallen fast asleep, remains oblivious and imperturbable. Seconds after Trouscaillon barges in, leading an army of Mussolini-esque Black Shirts, Albertine reappears, made up as a man dressed in a police outfit and rechristened Albert, and leads the entire group out of the violent mob, via an elevator that carries them to the Paris Métro. Zazie does finally ride on the subway, but continues to sleep as she is taken to meet her mother once again at the Gare. On the way home, Jeanne asks Zazie what she did in Paris, and she admits, "I've aged."

ANALYSIS

As an adaptation of Raymond Queneau's 1959 novel, *Zazie dans le métro*— Louis Malle's third feature — represents Malle's attempt to master "cinematic language"[18] with some of the most intractable source material for an adaptation imaginable, shy of Joyce or Nabokov: an experimental *roman* that functions as a kind of digest of literary techniques— a book rife with sophisticated puns and word play. But the tricky adaptive process behind the film only represents the first of its many significant components. Like Malle's later feature *Viva Maria* (1965),[19] *Zazie* pursues so many goals that (although many of its individual aims succeed) the picture as a whole becomes hopelessly weighty by virtue of its own excess. Thus, while *Zazie* cinematizes Queneau's experimental techniques on a foundational level, Malle adds many additional dimensions, and the film becomes (alternately) an investigation of modernist reality, a work that uses experimental cinematographic techniques to make pop psychological observations about children, a celebration of the pagan tradition of comedy, and, to a lesser degree, a work that invented film orchestration years ahead of its time.

Referencing André S. Labarthe and Malle, Stéphanie Grégoire argues, in the sections of her thesis covering *Zazie*, that Malle's film assaults the conventional "cinematographic eye" just as Queneau upends the conventional "literary voice."[20] This process of deconstruction and dissimulation (a fulfillment of the Geller-honed "rule of equivalences" for adapting modernist literature)[21] emerges, on the most immediate level, via Malle's attempts to find filmic correlatives for several of Queneau's individual literary techniques. First, Queneau utilizes a kind of "semantic acceleration" by uniting monosyllabic words into polysyllabs. Consider the opening sentence of the novel: "Howcanaystinksotho?"[22] This is Queneau's most common trope — he scatters slight variations on it, innumerable times, throughout the novel: "the chapshutistrap,"[23] "Tsnot healthy,"[24] "Zthat you,"[25] "Charlesbuggadorff?"[26] Just as Queneau has compressed the smaller semantic units by piling a few words or an entire sentence query into one word, and thus leaves the reader with a sense of hyperactive verve, Malle periodically films at a slower speed than 24 frames-per-second (his most common trope in the picture). By his own admission, he often shot at twelve or eight,[27] which makes the actors appear pumped up on amphetamines; they become hyperactive cartoons.

A more sophisticated yet slightly less pervasive technique in the novel involves a kind of word play, wherein Queneau reinvents a polysyllabic word by breaking it apart, and rewrites the syllables so that he not only makes the larger word correspond to a juvenile phonetic orthography, but turns each syllable into a thematic variant on the meaning of the larger compound polysyllab. (This semantic invention constitutes an unmistakable nod to James Joyce.) For instance: in Queneau's hands, "Homosexual" becomes "Hormosessual." Beyond the orthographic respelling, the two halves of the word embody variations (loosely, anagrams) on "hormone" and "sensual," each with an unmistakable thematic connection to "Homosexual." Malle, in turn, finds an onscreen parallel for this technique. The film frame itself — the onscreen ontological sphere of action — becomes analogous to the framework of the word unit. Though *Zazie* is a highly Brechtian, alienating film, Malle paradoxically takes full habitual and temperamental advantage of his own abrechtian qualities by opening up spaces within the main space, and new dimensions can emerge anywhere in the frame, at any time. In other words, Malle has buried multiple dimensions in the ontological sphere, just as, in Queneau, words are buried within words. The two best examples arrive near the end of the picture: first, when the zombie-like waiters emerge from the floor-level cupboards beneath the spigots in the bar, and later, when Trouscaillon leads the black-shirted fascists and they literally appear to emerge from the movie screen that lies behind him. And, as yet another parallel in Queneau, each of these events bears strong thematic connection to the ideas generated by the larger scene.

Two of the equivalences in Malle's film spring from the presence of an absence in Queneau, and thus might easily risk being overlooked. Gilbert Adair reflects:

> There is, in the first instance, *Zazie*'s narrative rhythm, the mercurial plotting and pacing, near-Voltairean in their unfussy speed and lightness, that whisk the characters from one end of Paris to another with little of the prosy, pragmatic connective tissue, the statutory passages of expositional description — what, in the cinema's terminology, are called establishing shots — that novelistic scene-shifting appears even now to require.[28]

Adair intertwines two distinct observations in the above passage. The first involves Queneau's almost complete[29] omission of paragraphs that detail connecting actions, carrying the characters ontologically and kinesthetically, from one scene to another. Malle preserves this via a device that Adair later references: the jump-cut. But whereas the jump-cuts of a director like Godard (consider the close-ups of Belmondo's face in the car at the outset of *Breathless*) are so quick and fleeting that they merely involve excising a second or two from a continuous action, Malle's often involve splicing out the entire middle passage of an action to zip characters from origin to destination 10 times as quickly. Consider the scene in which Zazie, Charles, and Gabriel exit from the car outside of Turandot's café. In lieu of walking from the car to the café steps in a continuous action, they vanish from the car and appear instantaneously on the steps. Similarly, in the dining room of Gabriel's house: when Zazie leans up to kiss her uncle goodnight, she appears at his cheek and disappears, like a flash of lightning.

The second of Adair's points, though subtle, involves Queneau's complete or near-complete omission of scenic description from his narrative. Though the idea of finding an exact filmic equivalent for this technique is virtually impossible and might risk alienating everyone (how could Malle completely blot out *mise en scène* when working in a visual medium?) the director finds an effective and unusual equivalent: by utilizing hyper-artificial, Brechtian sets of hideously bright, often uniform color, he almost completely alienates the viewer from the backdrops and draws full attention to the foregrounded actions. The spatial brechtianism of a work like Zazie—much of which feels (regardless of the on-location work) filmed on a studio backlot—thus stands at the opposite end of the spectrum from the abrechtian neorealist ontology of, for example, De Sica's *Umberto D.* (1952), Malle's own *Feu follet* (1963), and the first half of Payne's *About Schmidt* (2002), which explains why those films involve the viewer not only in the characters' actions, but in the onscreen space. *Zazie* avoids this route—the environment *per se* holds the viewer at a coldly unfamiliar distance via emotional alienation. Ergo, when the director strained himself technically to retain the same background for both sides of a two-ended dinner conversation between Zazie and Pedro Trouscaillon (because he thought it would amuse viewers), no one noticed—they were focusing too intently on the foregrounded action.[30]

On the broadest adaptive level, Grégoire's interpretations of *Zazie* as an attack on the conventional cinematographic eye—in the sense that Queneau attacks the concept of a more pedestrian literary voice[31]—withstand even the toughest scrutiny. The film's opening train shot provides the best example. It is a quintessentially abrechtian, Malleian shot, but its continuity is shredded apart with jump cuts, and it thus assaults Malleian spatial fluidity. Malle similarly avoids sustaining ontological or temporal flow for any length of time, throughout the picture. An inestimable number of scenes in the picture feel as if they have been shot with at least 10 to 15 setups *each*. This dissimulation functions not reflexively, but as a kind of egressive microscopic illumination, concurrently shining a light on—and dissecting—films of greater spatio-temporal wholeness, including (on a note of amusing irony) the rest of Malle's entire filmography. In other words, the dissimulation deeply calls into question, in the viewer's mind, the illusions of continuity that feature films at the alternate end of the ontological spectrum work to sustain, and *Zazie* thus dissects western cinematic convention *per se*. The dissimulation also points to a much larger philosophical context in which the motion picture operates: that of modernity, of which spatio-temporal dissolution is one of the most critical aspects. *Zazie* qualifies as "classically modernist" in the same sense as the jazz idiom and the impressionist idiom: it celebrates the broken whole. Consider Dr. Norman Cantor's observation in light of Malle's film:

> A fourth quality of modernism was a penchant for the fragmented, the fractured, and the discordant. In opposition to the Victorians, who showed a predilection for the finished and the harmonious, modernism foregrounded

the disharmonious and the unfinished, the splintered world, the piece that had
broken off—the serendipitous—and pursued this preference to the point of
making it an aesthetic principle.[32]

Cantor later affirms, "Modernism [is] antihistoricist. It [does] not believe that
truth lay in telling an evolutionary story.'"[33] *Zazie* is, on some levels, highly nonlin-
ear and thus quintessentially modern. Grégoire implies that Malle's cinematization
of *Zazie* preserves not only the basic order of events in Queneau's narrative but prop-
agates narrative linearity *per se*[34]; this assessment is valid, but only on the most literal level—the level on which the motion picture officially begins at the outset of
Zazie's 36-hour Parisian visit and progresses forward in time to her departure.
Though accurate in this sense—which could lead one to distinguish *Zazie* from, say,
the surface-level alinearity of a work such as, say, Resnais's *L'Année dernière à Marien-
bad* (1961), true narrative linearity—in the core sense—must be evaluated by looking beneath the film's surface-level aspects, and analyzing it on a deeper level, for it
remains contingent on character arcs that drive the narrative forward. Thus, even if
a film operates chronologically within its own time sequence, it is still possible for
it to lack any internal progression.[35] As Adair observes, the characters in *Zazie* have
"been granted no interiority."[36] Such an interiority is a prerequisite for the existence
of arcs; because these arcs, in turn, are absent from the book and the film, one feels
unceasingly, throughout the novel, that the events could ostensibly roll on forever,
so random and helter skelter is the progression of the *récit*. A clue to this lack of progression is the parrot Laverdure's rhythmic maxim, "Talk, talk, that's all you can do"[37]
(or "Yakety-yak, that's all you guys can do"[38] in the film), which (though more deceptively comical and lightweight) cannot help but recall Vonnegut's death refrain "So
it goes" from *Slaughterhouse-Five*, and that novel's achronological structure; Laverdure's observation carries a similar overtone of existential limitlessness—of a non-
linear, random progression of events into eternity.
    Zazie also constitutes a modernist work in that the events of the *récit*—as Malle
interprets Queneau's novel—are highly subjective filtrations through the eyes of an 11
year old; thus, Malle twists the onscreen world, aesthetically, spatially, logically, into
childlike contortions. The film's post-credit establishing shot provides one of the
sharpest indicators of this filtration *per se*: Gabriel, in medium shot, stands behind a
row of passengers. As he complains loudly and mischievously about the stench ema-
nating from those before him (as an obnoxious child might), Malle films from a low
angle, as if a child is watching the events unfold before herself. It is as if Zazie has projected her impudence onto everyone and everything around her, even prior to her
arrival, so that—interpretively—external factors become pop psychological indicators of her reasoning. These indicators fall into several behavioral patterns in the film.
First: Zazie engages in a childlike compartmentalization and expects others to do the
same. The best example is her attempt to con passersby into believing that Turandot
and (later) Trouscaillon are each child molesters, simply by virtue of their being middle-
aged men who associate with a little girl *per se*. Second: as illustrated by Malle's use of
slower or occasionally faster camera speeds, to accelerate and decelerate his actors,
respectively, Zazie, like many children, has a highly variable, highly fluid temporal

span; she can protract time if an event she experiences is desirable (note the inter-
minable length of her chase sequence with Trouscaillon) or compress time if she grows
impatient, such as the aforementioned instances when Malle omits connective action,
and Zazie zips, instantly, from one side of the frame to another. Zazie also demonstrates
the extent of childlike egocentrism ("The entire world is meant to revolve around me.")
For instance, when she first runs up to the metro and shakes the iron gates vigorously,
she mutters, "I can't believe the bastards did this to me." Again: in her eyes, it is as if
they made a deliberate, conscious attempt to frustrate Zazie and Zazie *alone* (never mind
the rest of the inconvenienced world), pouring all of their energies into ensuring that
she will never ride the Métro during her Paris visit.

And finally, Zazie perceives (and Malle, in turn, gives us) a world devoid of consequence, that points to the extent to which children lack a firm conception of the
results of their actions. For example, Mouaque casually abandons her car amid a
bumper-to-bumper traffic jam — she simply lets it glide along, pushed by the cars
behind it and pushing the cars ahead of it — climbs out, wanders around Paris with
Zazie and a few of the others, and happens back upon the car at another location10
minutes later. She mentions nothing of the vehicle's abandonment or of her inability to find the car upon wanting to retrieve it; it merely appears before her. Again:
irresponsible actions, such as the abandonment of a luxury car in the middle of a
crowded Parisian boulevard, have no consequence, an idea that an inherently anarchic child of Zazie's age might certainly take for granted.

Etiologically, *Zazie* celebrates the pagan comic tradition in lieu of (and as
opposed to) the Judaeo-Christian comic tradition. If — as referenced elsewhere in
this text — the latter depends on an unshakeable belief in mankind's "fall from grace,"
and the chasm that has opened up between a viewer's expectations of behavioral perfection and the sobering reality of evil (i.e., the failure to meet those expectations
that produces laughter),[39] the pagan comic tradition sits at odds to this. It springs
from such ancient sources as Euripedes' *Bacchaë*, a beautiful illustration of anarchic
revel without form or order, the drunken chaotic merriment that elicits intense,
crazed laughter. Much classic screen comedy falls neatly into one category or the
other; Chaplin and Keaton exemplify the first, the off-the-wall absurdity of the Marx
Brothers the second. Again, *Zazie* falls squarely into the pagan sphere: Malle presents the audience with an insane, anarchic world, robbed of any logic or predictabil-
ity, and if the insanity occasionally fails to elicit laughter, this happens because Malle
intentionally pushes to such an extreme that the sources of the comedy become over-
apparent. The film's conclusion, a virtual descent into Armageddon, led by Trouscaillon's black-shirted fascists, can hardly be termed "accidental": it represents the
logical fulfillment of the deceptively cheerful and happy off-the-wall insanity of the
prior 70 minutes. Malle is essentially extrapolating the basis of the comedy from the
previous hour by removing the comic outer layers for a sobering, horrifying glimpse
of the chaotic, lawless, insane and cruel world that lies beneath.

One final thought about the stylistic element of *Zazie*. A number of sequences
from the motion picture utilize clear-cut film orchestration and thus predate similar cinematic work of artists like Bob Fosse by several years. Pauline Kael writes of
Zazie, "Many of the modern styles in film editing ... generally thought to derive from

Alain Resnais or Richard Lester, have an earlier source in *Zazie*."[40] One of Malle's most profound innovations in editing is rooted in cinematic orchestration. The most vivid example emerges shortly after Zazie's initial trip (with Charles and Gabriel) to Turandot's café. Malle alternates, musically, between quick shots of blinking neon signs outside of Gabriel's flat (later visible in an interior shot, through the semi-transparent curtains on the windows) and a long-held reverse tracking medium shot of Carla Marlier (i.e., Aunt Albertine) as she walks toward the camera carrying a bowl of consommé. His editing and the high pitched violin notes have been timed to the blinking of the neon lights (a leg kicking a soccer ball; a bow crossing a fiddle), and Malle establishes a rhythmic alternation between this quick repetition and the long held reverse track down the hallway, wherein the long-held, low pitched violin draw on the soundtrack corresponds to the continuous movement of Marlier toward the camera.

CRITICAL RESPONSE

As noted earlier in this chapter, *Zazie* qualified as a colossal financial and critical disaster in France. Worldwide, most critics assessed *Zazie* as an uneven and predominantly unsuccessful work. Indicative of the American reaction is Gene Moskowitz, writing for *Variety*, who affirms, "Instead of springing full blown from the inventiveness of the makers this has been reworked for the screen. Result is an uneven texture that runs from inspired scenes to repetitive bits and overstraining in the symbolism of the story."[41] In the British *Sight and Sound*, Geoffrey Nowell-Smith writes, "The film is, in the last analysis, a failure. The mayonnaise of slapstick, parody and social satire is not homogeneous: the elements remain obstinately separate."[42]

French reactions were only slightly more positive; writing for *Cinéma*, Marcel Martin admires Malle's cleverness in finding cinematic equivalents for Queneau's literary games, and perceives *Zazie* as a "lucid diagnostic of the turmoil and disarray of the contemporary world."[43] Yet Martin also criticizes the film's excessively abrupt transition from humor to grave reflection (in the final apocalyptic sequence) as a structural flaw.[44] Reviewing for *Cahiers*, André Labarthe types *Zazie* as an inevitable failure, a film that successfully disintegrates the sense of onscreen reality but is unable, by its very nature, to transgress the reality principle that governs cinema; he also perceives Malle's attack on conventional genres as unwise and inefficient, arguing that *Zazie* belongs to a genre and thus undoes itself.[45]

5

Vie privée (A Very Private Affair)—1961

The Myth of Emptiness

"Woody Allen is poignant here in the same way that Chaplin was poignant, and it's creepy, because you feel that these rich, gifted, accomplished writer-director-comedians who have won their artistic freedom, who have many friends and are attractive to lovers, who are admired the world over, are showing you the truth of how at some level they still feel utterly alone and lost, like sad, wormy nothings."
— Pauline Kael, review of *Zelig* (1983)

"...it is the signal to go straight
Down like a glorious diver   then feet first   her skirt stripped
    beautifully
Up   her face in fear-scented cloths   her legs deliriously bare   then
Arms out   she slow-rolls over   steadies out   waits for something
    great
To take control of her."
— James Dickey, "Falling"

BACKGROUND

Two flagrant blunders or "accidents" marred Louis Malle's otherwise successful career. The first, 1961's *Vie privée* (*A Very Private Affair*),[1] could hardly have arrived at a more disadvantageous moment for the 27 year old wunderkind.[2]

Two years earlier, Malle's desire to adapt a cult novel by Raymond Queneau (*Zazie*) represented not so much a career gamble, as a deliberate, conscious relinquishment of box office demands. Three prior successes imparted the confidence necessary for Malle to "take a dive," getting away with one large scale, purely arcane experimental project—*Zazie dans le Metro*—used almost exclusively (and self-indulgently) to hone his adaptation skills, at the expense of commercial success. The problem with such a leap: following *Zazie*'s box office failure in late 1960,[3] it put twice the pressure on Malle's shoulders to produce a new triumph and free himself from

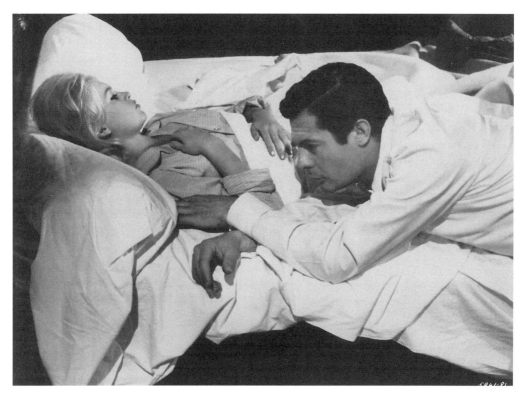

The sex kittenish movie star and model Jill (Brigitte Bardot) and her lover, newspaper publisher
Fabio Rinaldi (Marcello Mastroianni), grow restless and bored while hiding from the paparazzi
in a Spoleto hotel room in Louis Malle's ode to the shallowness of celebrity life, *Vie privée* (A
Very Private Affair).

industry perception as a financial liability. Such did not happen: *Vie privée* not only
failed to collect substantial box office receipts, but became the first Malle film to
bomb critically, as well.[4] And with two back-to-back flops, the director would soon
fight a Herculean battle to secure funding for a new project.

Vie privée originated as the brainchild of slick French commercial producer
Christine Gouze-Rénal (*L'Affair d'une nuit*, *La Femme et le pantin*, *Escapade*), who
sought to pair Malle and screenwriter Henri Jeanson (*Montparnasse 19*) in the creation of a Brigitte Bardot vehicle, a remake of the Noel Coward-Sidney Franklin *Private Lives*. Malle objected to the Coward adaptation and the Jeanson partnership
(with whom he did not feel a strong connection)[5] but agreed to cast Bardot in a cinematic investigation of her own image with biographical elements. He co-wrote a
treatment with Jean Ferry and Jean-Paul Rappeneau, and wove in specific episodes
from Bardot's life. Bardot observes, "[*Vie privée*] re-creates, with reserve (restraint?),
important moments of my life. I had a hard time with some episodes that were still
too painful for me at the time... There is a lot of truth, somewhat fictionalized, but
the basis of the events [in the film] remains true."[6]

Malle grudgingly agreed to cast Marcello Mastroianni as the male lead, despite
the mutual animosity between Mastroianni and Bardot. Given Bardot's tight sched-

ule and a miniscule window of time to complete the film, Malle and his co-writers were unable to finish the script before production began, and resigned themselves to write the final act at night, while shooting during the day. It was a small sign of impending disaster: during the immensely troubled production, Mastroianni and (later) Malle himself tried to pull out on various occasions, in vain; the director threw in the towel during the third act, resigned to accept the film's failure; and numerous fights erupted between the two leads.[7] Production commenced in the spring of 1961 and wrapped during the Spoleto festival, in early July 1961. The film reached European screens in early 1962.

SYNOPSIS

Jill (Brigitte Bardot) is a "young French girl" who hails from a wealthy, bourgeois family. Though in her twenties, she still lives with her single mother in Switzerland. She spends the summer days indulging in ballet lessons with her best friend, Carla (Ursula Kubler), swimming in Lake Geneva, and romancing her choreographer boyfriend Dick (Dirk Sanders). One evening, Carla's husband, Fabio Rinaldi (Marcello Mastroianni) ("one of Geneva's most successful publishers of art books and theater magazines") returns on a plane trip from London, and Jill accompanies Carla to the airport to pick him up. Jill falls instantly, hopelessly, yet Fabio's commitment to Carla prevents Jill from making an advance. She sees no option but to accompany Dick on a move to Paris, against the objections of her mother.

Jill begins by supporting herself as a dancer, but this ends alongside her romance with Dick, and—faced with no other option—she "scrapes by" as a photographer's model and actress in Paris. Her career triumphs raise her into the limelight over the next three years. Yet fame reveals its dark underbelly, as tabloid reporters and paparazzi constantly surround Jill, hound her to death, and stir up nasty rumors from her string of casual lovers and her loose, promiscuous lifestyle.

Following an implied nervous breakdown from the chastisement of a maid, Jill longs for the solemnity and the anonymity of the private life. Half-frazzled, she escapes from Paris and travels back to Geneva, incognito, to discover that her mother's house has been locked and barred. At the last minute, she visits Fabio at his office, and learns, to her delight, that Fabio and Carla have divorced. Fabio takes Jill in his arms and leads her back to his flat, where the two begin a passionate, heated romance. Yet Rinaldi soon has a theatrical commitment at the annual Spoleto festival, where he will direct his own translation of a play. Fabio persuades Jill to stay indoors in Geneva (safe from the paparazzi), yet Jill defies his orders and sneaks off to the Spoleto festival to find her lover. Her only means of escape from the reporters and photographers involves hiding incognito in Fabio's hotel room, yet this proves ineffective when the press learns of her whereabouts and paparazzi begin to track her all over the hotel. She even befriends one photographer, Alain, but Fabio smells a rat and throws Alain out of the room. Storming off furiously, Alain vows revenge.

Jill's vehement insistence on finding a way to watch Fabio's production leads her to a high ledge above the amphitheater. Spotting his object of prey, Alain slips up on

Jill from below and flashes several pictures of her. As the flashes blind her, she slips from the railing and falls to her death.

ANALYSIS

With *A Very Private Affair*, Louis Malle, Jean-Paul Rappeneau, and Jean Ferry attempt to investigate what lies behind the shallowness of a celebrity image by establishing the "star mythos" onscreen and penetrating it. Using Brigitte Bardot as the sexual and spiritual embodiment of the "celebrity" phenomenon, *Affair* purports to move beyond the surface glitter and gloss of Bardot's image and to expose the deeper underlayers.

On critical and commercial levels, *Affair* became one of Malle's two unequivocal failures (alongside *Crackers*). On the broadest level, Malle and his co-writers erred gravely when defining the architecture of the motion picture. Malle's self-admitted intent for the film — to reexamine Bardot as a mythical phenomenon — could occur most pointedly if the co-scenarists liberated the film from the trappings of a fictional narrative, perhaps (for instance) directing a documentary on the real-life Bardot making a film that reinforces her image, thus setting up and establishing a distinction between the two entities. "Jill" may epitomize (point-for-point) one of Bardot's characterizations, but as Malle and his co-scenarists set up the character, Jill is *all myth*. The film only presents one side of Bardot: the onscreen "image" with which viewers are already familiar.

This is not necessarily an unrectifiable problem. Pauline Kael's central criticism of *Vie privée*—"[Malle] seems to be trying to show what's under a star's myth, but we don't experience the myth, only the shallowness underneath,"[8] identifies the critical focal point of the motion picture as shallowness. Yet Kael's myopic comment only begins to hint at the overwhelming problem posed by the film. The motion picture's central flaw remains far broader than simply the shallowness of Bardot's character. If Kael's inferences and observations about the film were accurate, one could argue, justifiably, that Jill's shallowness is one of the film's subtextual issues, and thus confined to a critical locus— the film's message that beneath the "media star" facade lies only more shallowness (a valid theme). Instead, the medium becomes a poor substitute for the message: we never once sense the shallowness in Jill *per se*, only the shallowness of the screenplay itself (context), which robs the motion picture of credibility. In other words, *Vie privée* suffers from the externalization of the critical focal point (shallowness), which envelops the context of the material and overtakes the film. If *Feu follet* (see Chapter 6) uses negative spaces to its advantage, subtextually, to build the viewer's awareness of absences in a character's life (by filtering the world expressionistically through Alain Leroy's pathological observation),[9] *A Very Private Affair* draws attention to negative spaces that represent the scenarists' and directors' unfulfilled responsibilities for filling in gaps in characterization and the narrative. One can thus primarily criticize the film for what it does not do, and any attacks on the motion picture's content risk becoming a laundry list of complaints, all related to absences. Most significantly, Malle, Rappeneau, and Ferry fail to imbue Jill with any depth in the first act of the motion picture[10]—they take no time and no care to set up a credible character with understandable, empathetic motivations (instead relying on voice-over narration to reveal key information about Jill and seal up gaps in the narrative — so often a sign of a troubled production). For the duration of the first few scenes, cinematographer Henri Decaë bathes Bardot's head in a halo of suffused light, sculpting her image as a piece of religious iconography. The halo catches the viewer's eye as a visually persistent metaphor and — through its very existence — must be affirmed on some level. It also comments self-effacingly on our needs to deify Bardot as an audience, and (as Donald Gutierrez observes in his essay on fame) to "mak[e] gods and goddesses of mass-media celebrities,"[11] becoming (via stasis and one-dimensionality) a symbol of its own shallowness.

Malle's central message is clear: "celebrity" represents an inborn gift; destiny will propel Jill to the top. And one might guess, from the pseudo-religious aesthetic motif coupled with the dramatic set-up (where Jill enjoys an ephemeral boy-girl relationship with Dick yet yearns, on a deeper level, for the warmth and sincerity of a relationship with Fabio) that Malle plans to layer two levels of Jill's character, consistent with Kael's assessment about the unfulfilled intent of the motion picture: a static, shallow, mythical "celebrity" layer, atop a dynamic, breathing, pulsating underlayer. We assume that a complex, more authentic person will emerge when circumstances strip away the celebrity layer. This assumption is incorrect: Jill never reveals more than one dimension.

One prospective theme for the motion picture might be the idea that shallowness gradually builds as an accompaniment to (or a casualty of) fame, wealth, and glamour. Malle, Ferry, and Rappeneau could thus situate Jill's burgeoning shallowness in a larger context, and give us (for example) a scenario where fame robs her of palpable depth that exists during the first act of the story. In this instance, the insight inherent in the arc representing "Jill's loss of depth" (context) would counterbalance the growing shallowness in Jill (subtext), imparting to the audience a basic critical framework from which to judge the regression of Bardot's character.[12] Such does not happen.

A broader problem associated with the film involves its desperate need for a deeper and more thorough investigation of the phenomenon of celebrity. Malle's instinct during his initial project meeting with Gouze-Renal was correct: "the aura of fame" and a filmic dissection of Bardot's myth could offer potentially fascinating film material. Various texts have been written on "celebrity" over the past few decades, addressing such questions as: "Are celebrities born, or made?" "What is the relationship between fame and immortality?" "What are the behavioral liabilities—and benefits—of fame?" and "Is celebrity typically predestined by a specific physiological trait?"[13] The fact that even these long-researched, carefully written books fail to provide a single set of answers suggests the limitless depth inherent in the subject. But *Vie privée* never plumbs this depth.

Anticipating Woody Allen's *Stardust Memories* (*Affair*'s closest cinematic descendant and an infinitely more grotesque film), *A Very Private Affair* essentially begins with one basic idea — the problem of celebrities being swamped, eaten alive, and drained of privacy by reporters and paparazzi — and reiterates it 40, 50, 60 times over, until the motion picture itself becomes an unforgivable series of one-notes. Malle glosses over the questions of: Jill's rise to fame (courtesy of a three-year flash-forward); the behavioral liabilities of fame, and, significantly, the explanations for Jill's magnetism. We never once watch Jill model for a photographer or (aside from a few seconds), act in front of a movie camera — Malle seems to believe Bardot's appeal will emerge, *de nature*, when he places her in front of his cameras. Regarding fame-driven behavioral vices: Malle not only holds Jill's sexual indiscretions off camera, raising doubts as to their very existence, but presents Jill as the ultimate, Burgessian victim, fallen prey to the unstoppable tide of success and her own inborn, sumptuous irresistibility.

Malle omits explicit depictions of Jill's vices as a clever ploy, to gently sculpt the tone of the film as it applies to audience perception of Jill's (Bardot's) mythos. In this light, *Privée* does begin to work somewhat on an obscure level, as a cinematic transliteration of the mythical "feminist hero" crafted by Simone De Beauvoir in her 1960 book, *Brigitte Bardot and the Lolita Syndrome*.[14] Recalling Malle's tonal omissions in *Affair*, one of De Beauvoir's central theses explores Bardot's need to stay eternally youthful, a nymphette who, because she lacks a past, cannot be held accountable for her actions[15]:

> BB has not been marked by experience. Even if she has lived — as in *Love Is My Profession* — the lessons that life has given her are too confused for her to have learned anything from them. She is without memory, *without a past*, and, thanks to this ignorance, she retains the perfect innocence that is attributed to a mythical childhood.[16]

Affair cinematizes additional points from Beauvoir, as well. In the film, Jill becomes Beauvoir's "erotic hoyden," led exclusively by instinct (which leads the emotionally ransacked, mentally dulled Jill back to Fabio's offices); this same instinct drives her to witness Fabio's play, risking public recognition (and, unknowingly, death) in the process. Yet on the broadest level, the De Beauvoir cinematization weakens the motion picture, as *Affair* remains trapped within the mythical framework of an essay that has long since faded into obscurity. ("If we want to understand what BB represents," Beauvoir writes, "it is not important to know what the young woman named Brigitte Bardot is really like."[17])

Recalling the extreme Hollywood narrative structure of Von Sternberg's *Blonde Venus* and anticipating (over the next few decades) the lurid cinematizations of Sidney Sheldon novels, the blinking intertitle "THREE YEARS LATER..." that appears just after Jill begins her rise to fame functions as nothing more than an overtly Brechtian interruption. Not only does the use of such a device run explicitly contrary to Malle's cinematic tradition (given his passionate avoidance of brechtian devices and his frequent abrechtian set-ups, both kinesthetically and ideologically) but in the basic framework of the sequence, the device is wildly inappropriate, for it contradicts the ideological intentions of Brecht himself! In Walter Weideli's monograph on the theatrical director, he writes, "Evidently Brecht ... refus[es], as he was to say in his poem on Empedocles, 'to obscure any further what is already obscure in itself.' To his way of thinking, each human relationship is founded on an exact economy, and ... miracles are excluded."[18] Brecht used intertitles to clarify and break through artificial conventions. Yet in *Affair,* Malle's intertitles further obscure the "mystery" behind Jill's (or Bardot's) rise to fame. The narrator underscores this intention with, "Between this face and this machine something clicked, something mysterious, a magical meeting that was to make of Jill, whether she wanted it or not, a great star, a queen, a freak, a goddess." Why would Malle use these devices to only further obscure a myth whose constitutional elements lie out of the viewer's basic intellectual grasp prior to the outset of the film? The improper use of the intertitles will only compound audience infuriation.

In *Malle on Malle,* the writer-director claims that he perceives the final act of *Affair* (when Jill and Fabio visit the Spoleto festival) as the most successful sequence, without question[19]—a dubious claim. Esthetically, the shots in the closing act may carry the "organic, sensual" quality Malle describes, but the Spoleto sequence (unlike the rest of the film) lacks narrative drive—it feels insecure, as if nothing significant is driving the story forward. (Likely a product of Malle's inability to finish the ending during pre-production, and his decision to co-write the conclusion with Ferry and Rappeneau at night, while the cameras rolled during the day.) In Spoleto, Jill simply sits in her room and complains of her inability to leave (her frustration building), scene after scene, until, exasperated, she slips out of the room and literally meets death at the hands of the paparazzi. One can understand why MGM chopped 20 minutes out of the final sequence: even in its edited state, it drones endlessly.

The closing shot provides not only the most fascinating moment in the film, but one of the most enigmatic images in film history: as Jill slips from a stone ledge and plummets to her death, Malle closes in on Bardot's body, falling perpetually against a shifting backdrop, her face lit by unaffected, sunny happiness, hair streaming upward.

As Bardot affirms, the shot succeeds visually and aesthetically: "The final scene," she declares, "is a masterpiece of beauty, emotion, esthetics and pain."[20] Yet ideologically, the shot fails. Jill's serenity during the extenuation of her fall almost necessitates a mention of Dickey's poem "Falling" (1967) wherein a stewardess accidentally falls from the emergency exit of an aircraft, in mid-flight. The subtext of Dickey's poem never ceases to fascinate—in Dickey's hands the stewardess's fall represents the universal "womb to grave" journey, and paints the atheistic belief that mankind's only purpose involves learning to live every day to its fullest as the span of life passes in the blink of an eye.[21] But despite almost identical imagery and ironies in *Affair* (i.e., the happiness on the casualty's face prior to death, and the extenuation of the fall) such themes could not possibly apply here, given the context of the film, which leaves the viewer with an unanswered question: ideologically and thematically, what could this bizarre shot possibly add to *Vie privée*? Because Bardot recalls that "there was no discussion [about the meaning of the image] ... we shot it live in complete silence,"[22] its significance remains an inscrutable mystery.

CRITICAL RESPONSE

A Very Private Affair bombed terribly and MGM subsequently withdrew the film from distribution for 30 years. The picture received short shrift from dozens of critics on opposite sides of the Atlantic. In the States, Pauline Kael writes, "Malle provides prankish, lively moments, though the story, with its many parallels to Bardot's own life, produces a sense of discomfort. It's one of the least interesting of Malle's films."[23] British critics also panned the film. Tom Milne dismisses *Privée* in *The Monthly Film Bulletin* with, "The hypothetical film-star, played in one long, scarcely-broken pout, is such a conventional piece of cardboard that whether or not she commits suicide is never of much moment; and Mastroianni has a hard time of it to make anything ... out of the magazine-fiction lover... Still, it *looks* good."[24] But in France, one finds an exception to the rule. Writing for *Cinéma,* Marcel Martin raves about the picture's aesthetic, which he perceives as revolutionary, "a dazzling poem of sumptuous and glistening images" and the first film shot in the mode of the impressionist painters; Martin defends the film against those who attack its absence of sociology, arguing that it is, at heart, a drama (not a sociological document), and praises it as a compelling, fascinating investigation of celebrity life.[25]

6

Le Feu follet
(The Fire Within)—1963
Falling into the Gray Void

"Gatsby believed in the green light, the orgastic future that year by year recedes before us. It eluded us then, but that's no matter — tomorrow we will run faster, stretch out our arms farther... And one fine morning..."
— F. Scott Fitzgerald, *The Great Gatsby*

"I thought in my heart, 'Come now, I will test you with pleasure to find out what is good.' But that also proved to be meaningless. 'Laughter,' I said, 'is foolish. And what does pleasure accomplish? I tried cheering myself with wine, and embracing folly...'"
— Ecclesiastes 2:2–3a

BACKGROUND

In a brief state of self-imposed exile from feature films, Malle shot two 16mm documentaries in 1962: an untitled film on French involvement in Algeria (never edited or released)[1] and "Vive le tour," on the annual Tour de France bicycle race (see Chapter 24).[2] Financially comfortable in-between projects from the success of his first three pictures[3] and his familial wealth,[4] Malle slipped into the role of the quintessential Parisian night owl: writing until two or three in the morning; hitting clubs until dawn; living on the high of spirits and jazz.[5]

Buoyed by an infectious sense of freedom, and similarly at ease after dark, Maurice Ronet had befriended Malle on the set of *Elevator to the Gallows*. Both men understood the late-night high life intimately and had grown tighter than brothers by the early sixties. So it seemed fitting that their second film collaboration, *Le Feu follet* (*The Fire Within*; a.k.a. *The Maddening Flame, Will o' the Wisp*) not only reflected, to a degree, on their shared lifestyle,[6] but that it — by virtue of its familiarity with its subject matter and the trust established between the two men — became one of the most powerful and accomplished French films of the early '60s.

After spending months in detox at a Versailles sanitarium, the emotionally fragile ex-playboy Alain Leroy (Maurice Ronet) reaches out to society friend Solange (Alexandra Stewart) as he searches for a reason to continue living in Louis Malle's existential psychodrama *Le Feu follet* (The Fire Within).

The central concept of the picture evolved gradually. It began as a meditation on the life and suicide of one of Malle's acquaintances, a writer who told his frends he was planning to leave town, bade them farewell, retreated alone to his bedroom and shot himself.[7] Malle devised an original scenario based loosely on this event, where a young Parisian alcoholic spends one endless *soir* in the City of Lights, and — depressed and debauched after the sun rises— puts a bullet through his chest.[8] Dissatisfied with the treatment, (which he perceived as too close to himself and self-indulgent) Malle turned instead to a book from his parents' library, *Le Feu follet*, controversial fascist writer Drieu La Rochelle's fictionalization of surrealist poet Jacques Rigaut's life and suicide.[9] Malle crafted the adaptation single-handedly, and (with time) transitioned the time and setting from one long night in Paris to the last 48 hours in the life of a Gatsbyesque playboy, Alain Leroy, after his release from a Versailles sanitarium where he spent six weeks receiving treatment for alcoholism.

Oddly (given Malle's closeness to Ronet and Ronet's resemblance to Leroy), Malle did not initially plan to cast Ronet as Alain. He instead drew inspiration from the playboys who surrounded him in Paris nightclubs, and — in a move doubtless inspired by his creative admiration for Bresson, who worked only with non-thespians— sought to find and cast a real-life playboy as the lead. Countless nighthawks around Malle captured the essence of his vision for the main character: perpetually adolescent on the surface, but beneath it all, sodden, satiated from wild living yet empty inside, and disillusioned with the transience, dissatisfaction, and emptiness of hedonistic pursuits. "Old young men" who used alcohol as a cushion against the disappointment of relationships. "Feu follets," or "maddening flames."[10]

Unfortunately, as Malle reveals in his autobiographical account, he could not find a real-life playboy who managed to be convincing or persuasive enough in the role, and thus approached Ronet.[11] The terribly excited actor embraced the role of Alain Leroy while working on the set of Autant-Lara's *Le Meurtrier*, and lost almost 45 pounds to force his chubby frame into underweight, gaunt, "post-detox" shape.[12] Malle enlisted Lena Skerla to play the secondary role of Lydia, Alain's lover.

Synopsis

Thirty-year-old Alain Leroy (Maurice Ronet) is a former alcoholic, in the final days of detox treatment under the aegis of Dr. La Barbinais (Jean-Paul Moulinot), at a Versailles sanitarium. Once a reckless, freewheeling adolescent, Leroy has come face-to-face with the unresolvable contradiction of turning 30 and yet feeling the need to protract his youth. Life has become an empty, meaningless series of exercises, and Leroy faces deep, inescapable depression.

As the story opens, Alain stares sadly into the eyes of his lover, Lydia (Lena Skerla) as they lie in bed together in a Versailles hotel room. Later, he rolls over and lights a cigarette. As Lydia dresses and prepares to leave, kneeling on the bed and leaning over to the nightstand, Alain throws his arms around her, in a final, desperate attempt to prevent her from leaving. One step at a time, Leroy begins to relinquish all of his material possessions: he tips a charwoman at the hotel with an expensive watch and drops a huge bill into a cabbie's hand, telling him to "keep the change." Alain and Lydia catch a cab back to the sanitarium.

Dorothy — Alain's wife and Lydia's close friend — resides in Manhattan, estranged from her husband. She sent Lydia to check up on Alain, but responds to his telegrams with immutable silence. These indications of her apathy so remind Alain of his inability to handle marriage that he shies away from Lydia's marriage proposals, believing at his core that he will ruin her life, just as he ruined Dorothy's. Yet the thought of losing Lydia as she prepares for a return to Manhattan so torments Alain that in the cab the closes his hand around hers, squeezes tightly, and implores her not to leave Versailles. Only at the very last moment — when Alain leaves the cab, and enters the clinic, slamming the door behind him — does Lydia catch a brief, uncertain glimpse of her lover's impending suicide. She screams out to stop him, but her shout goes unheard.

Alan believes that a release from the sanitarium will destroy him — that he cannot cope if the doctor turns him out on the street. Yet La Barbinais refuses to acknowledge Alain's illness, and fails to recognize his desperation. And to Alain, disillusioned by his wife's cold apathy, La Barbinais's reminders to telegram Dorothy, to wait patiently for her response — his insistence that Dorothy cares — are jokes. "That's what you think," Alain tells the physician, "Because it suits you." Alain ekes out the tedium of life in his clinic bedroom, filled with knickknacks, meaningless souvenirs of a life lived and worn thin: still photographs of Dorothy, miniature hats, tiny American flags. He toys with a luger, scratches entries in a journal and tears them up, cuts out random news clippings on the deaths of young girls and pins them to his wall. Anything to bide the time.

The following day, Alain begins to search — weakly and halfheartedly — for a reason to live. He hitchhikes to Paris with two lorry drivers, revisit his old friends, all fresh from smooth transitions into adulthood. But their new goals and motivations fail to convince: ex-playboy friend Dubourg (Bernard Noël) married a smug, smirking woman, started a family, and throws himself, each night, into writing a text about Egypt; lesbian painter Jeanne (Jeanne Moreau) lost her partner in an automobile accident, and escapes from pain by anesthetizing herself with drugs and surrounding herself with snobbish poets; brothers Jerome and François Minville (Romain Bouteille and François Gragnon) became OAS domestic terrorists who plant bombs throughout Paris and wound harmless citizens to protest French involvement in Algeria. Ex-girlfriend and lover Solange (Alexandra Stewart) married an aristocrat, Cyrille (Jacques Sereys) and entertains rich, indifferent, right-wing intellectuals. Unspeakably depressed, disappointed, and emotionally scarred, Alain takes his first drink of wine in months.

The next morning, Leroy awakens in his clinic bedroom with a hangover. Solange phones to remind him of a lunch invitation; he cuts her off and asks the maid not to be disturbed until noon. Alain finishes reading Fitzgerald's *The Great Gatsby*, pulls out his luger, puts the barrel up to his heart, and pulls the trigger. His final telegram to Dorothy (heard in voice-over), states, "I'll kill myself because I did not love you, because you did not love me. The bonds between us were loose; I'll kill myself to tighten them. I leave a stain on you, an indelible stain."[13]

ANALYSIS

The Fire Within enters the arena of intense psychodrama by plunging headlong into the mind of an emotionally and psychologically disturbed character. Alain Leroy is a perpetual adolescent, a man who "spent his youth carousing" (as one homosexual character in the film puts it) and who once used the tools of anesthetization to delude himself: an escape through the intoxication of alcohol, the fleeting pleasure of sex, and living for the next high. His paper-thin, illusory goals not only masked deep-seated self-doubt and the unwillingness to shirk adolescence and face adult responsibility, but set the stage for profound disappointments later on. Tragedy erupts, then, when Alain's cushions are ripped away violently — by an excruciating alcoholism treatment at the La Barbinais sanitarium ("If I had known what it was, I couldn't have done it"); by his age (pushing 30); by the horrifying discovery that days steeped in alcohol have brought entrapment, instead of the liberation he anticipated ("When [Dorothy and I] got married," Alain tells Lydia sadly, "I swore I'd stop drinking"); by the deflation of his own self-mythology (note his self-doubt about his ability to give Lydia orgasms, in the opening scene ["I'm sorry"], and the deep-seated belief in his inability to handle a marital relationship that prevents him from accepting Lydia's proposal and moving to Manhattan); by sterilization at the clinic; and, above all else, by the horrifying, paralyzing discovery that the adolescent pursuits of his past were temporal. Alain thus continually bemoans impermanence, particularly his inability to retain a hold on women. Most disturbingly, he feels suffocated and trapped in an emotional bell jar. "The cure" for alcoholism obliterated his ability to feel. Now, he is simply numb.

Leroy falls into a no-win situation: he consistently refuses to grow up, but finds a return to the adolescent pursuits of his past impossible, and thus realizes slowly that his only remaining option is to die a young man by committing suicide. The central narrative follows Alain as he combs his old haunts and reconnects with old friends, searching weakly, dispassionately, for a reason to keep going.

Le Feu follet covers a period of approximately 48 hours—the last two days in Alain Leroy's life. The Leroy of years past (prior to detox) bears little, if any, relation to his character in the film; he once lived the life of Jay Gatsby, and strongly resembled the Gatsbyesque mythical archetype constructed by Scott Fitzgerald through Nick Carraway's narration. Jay and the old Alain share the same unrestrained high spirits. The love of money, alcohol, women, sex. The protracted adolescence. An African character in *Le Feu follet* recalls how Alain Leroy brought celebratory acts of drunken merriment to Paris, such as Go-Karting in the Parisian streets and hijacking a tourist bus to give the passengers a lecture *on Scott Fitzgerald*. Eerily, Leroy finishes reading *The Great Gatsby* seconds before his suicide. Malle is thus wholly conscious of the tie-ins between Gatsby and Leroy. But Alain has ultimately traveled down a much different road than Jay.

As a character, Leroy embodies a tragic counterpoint between the Gatsbyesque playboy life of early sixties, late night Paris, and the deaths of those who allowed the lifestyle to destroy them and committed suicide (illustrated by the bitter ends of Jacques Rigaut, Malle's unnamed friend, and Drieu La Rochelle). *Feu follet* meditates on the motivations for deep-seated depression and suicide; simply put, it crafts an explanation for why one with Leroy's history would opt to kill himself. The picture became a cathartic tool not only for Malle (who devised and crafted the La Rochelle adaptation to deal with a close friend's suicide),[14] but will prove useful to all viewers anguished by the suicide of a friend, relative, or loved one, who continually ask that one question to which the victim(s) are unable to respond. As Malle had to face "the irreversibility of suicide" through his friend's death, it lies at the foundation of the film, simply through the basic irreversibility of a preestablished cinematic narrative with a pessimistic conclusion, and through Alain's friends' long-winded struggles to turn him around, particularly Dubourg, who begins to resemble Don Quixote fighting windmills.

One of the most fascinating aspects of Louis Malle's transition from *Elevator* to *Les Amants* to *Feu follet* (excluding *Zazie dans le métro*) involves the gradually decreasing significance of "plot devices" and tangible events as a driving factor for the narrative(s). It would be difficult to imagine a more event-driven film than *Elevator* (the film suffers from a complete absence of character arcs); in *Les Amants*, Jeanne Tournier's evolution drives the story, but also influences larger, plot-related events (bourgeois dinner, nighttime stroll, lovemaking, abandonment of family, early morning breakfast at a roadside diner, etc.). *The Fire Within* represents the next step in this evolution: it is, at its core, a character study (or, more specifically, a study of a character's perspective and world), so unadulterated by "events" in the narrative progression that the challenge and aim of the film simply involve watching Alain Leroy spiral downward as he searches, without success, for a reason to live. Ergo, *The Fire Within* is rooted almost entirely in behavioral observation. *Feu follet* explains suicide on a dualistic level, bringing us simultaneously to apexes of emotional and intellectual empathy with Alain Leroy.

On one level, Malle uses external cinematic devices to offer deep, profound insights into Leroy's internal state (recalling the cinema of Jean Renoir, and anticipating the stage work of playwright John Guare).[15] The best example of this occurs in the film's most euphoric scene: following the dinner scene at the institution, Alain walks out onto the balcony, and leans against the railing, staring into the distance. Malle and editor Suzanne Baron gently overlay Satie's "Gnossienne #2" atop the lyrical, elegiac images, as Alain coolly glimpses the outside world. Children playing ball on the lawn. A woman shaking out her laundry. The rhythm of life. But Alain cannot enter the flow. He stands nearby and watches silently, passively, a prisoner locked within himself as the world unfolds before his eyes.

It might be easy to overlook the implications of this sequence. An almost identical moment ensues, later in the film. In both instances, a resident of the institution arrives—first, Mademoiselle Farnoux (Yvonne Clech), and later, Dr. La Barbinais—and they unintentionally drown out the rapture of Alain's solitude with the crudeness of their interruptions. Though non-diegetic, the music functions as a projection of Alain's internal state, a strong indication of Alain's feelings, and a lens through which Alain perceives the world (just as the cool, anesthetizing Miles Davis jazz emanates from the lovers' self-mythologized romantic union in *Ascenseur*). Malle is implying that Alain, like many alcoholics, is more suited to his role as a passive observer than as one forced to interact, awkwardly, with people, which is why, for him and for the viewer (guided by the music), the moments of passive observation, without additional characters, are infinitely more soothing and relaxing than the moments when Alain finds himself in a group. In *Feu follet*, the external can thus be interpreted as a projection of the internal — the flight of Alain's inner perspective out of him, until it fills the screen and overtakes the viewer's senses. Indeed — in a 1971 interview with Guy Braucourt, Malle reflects on *Feu follet*'s emotional union —*un accord*—"between the hero and the music of Erik Satie,"[16] Ergo, *The Fire Within* encompasses proto-modernist cinematic expressionism. Yet the film also incorporates a significant deviation from expressionist aesthetic philosophy. Whereas in classical expressionism, the artist uses his or her own subjective perception as an aesthetic base, Malle relies on aesthetic transference in *Feu follet*, allowing the overall esthetic and style to emanate from a character and not himself.

Malle thus filters the Sisyphian futility of life through Alain's eyes, and weaves an aesthetic representation of his perspective into the cinematography and shot selection, and the film offers a relentlessly bleak picture of the chronic depressive's nihilist mindset: cinematographer Ghislain Cloquet employs eternally long takes and sequences which literally exhaust the viewer (anticipating Malle's anti-capitalist documentary *Humain, trop humain*); constant, pervasive, suffocating close-ups; the high-contrast lighting of *Elevator to the Gallows*, here used to "blot out" emotion and warmth from the screen, like a cloud blocking the sun.

Yet, alongside the internal perspective of Leroy imparted to the audience, the writer-director concurrently treats Leroy as a case study, and full appreciation of the film requires acute clinical examination of Alain's actions. Viewers who have known suicide victims, and particularly those familiar with depression who once contemplated suicide themselves, will recognize the haunting tell-tale signs of Alain's impending death: he tells friends, "I'm going on a trip," and asks (when they fail to catch his hint), "Don't you understand?"; Alain informs the doctor, "Don't worry, I'll be gone by this weekend"; Alain relinquishes his possessions—his watch, his money—to complete strangers; he is convinced, unshakably, that because Dorothy hasn't yet written him, she never will; he feels inextricably tied to failure and locked into the certainty that if he makes another emotional commitment (with Lydia) he will drive her away. Alain shaves, packs his belongings, and puts his things in order minutes before his death—echoes of countless suicides.

Bits of dialogue in *Le Feu follet* highlight another cause of depression and suicide: introversion. Shortly before his lorry ride to Paris, Alain Leroy steps into a cigar shop. His exchange with the merchant:

ALAIN	Give me Sweet Aftons, please.
MERCHANT	What's that?
ALAIN	Irish cigarettes.
MERCHANT	(shakes head) We don't stock them.
ALAIN	You should.
MERCHANT	Not enough demand.
ALAIN	I'm demanding.
MERCHANT	One's not enough. The entire stock would perish.

"*I'm* demanding." Though subtle, the exchange reveals Leroy's belief that everything revolves around himself. The same egocentrism here and lack-of-regard for the existence of everything and everyone else (and others' feelings) lie at the heart of suicide: the ultimate act of self-absorption.

Brilliantly and ingeniously, although the audience remains locked into external behavioral observation of Alain, we simultaneously begin to share Leroy's thought patterns, guided by the aesthetic. Instead of simply observing just how pervasive Alain's negative thoughts have become—where every solution introduced by an old friend becomes an "alibi," beaten down by Alain with contradictory arguments—others' comments are stripped bare through Alain's perspective, as ridiculous, naive pieces of optimism. For instance, the physician's insistence that Dorothy will eventually write back: merely a transparent, desperate, laughable attempt to teach Alain "positive thinking." Dubourg's melodramatic plea that Fanny and the children are "part of his passion": a shallow, unconvincing attempt to justify his own miserable existence.

It would be farsighted to describe Alain Leroy as a "static" character simply because his evolution is not dramatic enough to warrant a permanent shift away from suicide. Though he fails to change in the most fundamental way (i.e., remains locked into self-inflicted death), his desperation builds over the course of the story, and he becomes—relatively speaking—more resigned to suicide as the narrative rolls on. Concurrent with this regressive emotional spiral, Malle offers a structural recurrence. In the second act, the same basic event occurs four times: Alain visits friend, after friend, after friend, after friend, and in each of the four major sequences (Dubourg; Jeanne; Minvilles; Solange and Cyrille), Alain learns just how useless that person's newfound reason for living appears to him (static, recurrent) and becomes slightly more resigned to suicide (dynamic). Aside from the downward shifts in Alain's arc, the only major variants are the friends' identities and their reasons for living per se (i.e., alibis), which, by themselves, help maintain viewer interest.

On a broader level, the erroneous argument that Alain Leroy is a "static" character may be delivered by viewers unattuned to Leroy's gradual, subtly building intensity and desperation. This points to the film's greatest hazard: *Fire* may run the risk of becoming too minimalist, and far too understated for unprepared viewers. Malle constructed the film by directly omitting the elements one typically anticipates in a narrative feature. In other words, he works against viewer expectations in order to make the audience more conscious of negative spaces. The film becomes so minimalist that it is akin to an exercise in sensory deprivation. A first and second screening simply involve audience conditioning, and a release of each viewer's basic expectations. Thus, the viewer must begin to lock into the relentlessly slow pace, gradually, and accept the picture's abundance of non-events. The absence of narrative *is* the point: anticipating Chantal Akerman in her groundbreaking *Jeanne Dielman, 23 Quai du Commerce, 1080 Bruxelles* (1975), we feel the tedium, monotony, and depression in Alain's life through the events that do not happen (e.g., he does not receive a telegram from Dorothy, or opt to move to New York City with Lydia, or run out into the world and embrace life). The meaningless, fruitless non-events in Alain's room asphyxiate the viewer, as the camera focuses on hundreds of details without purpose: an existential commentary on the futility of life that recalls the absurd, eternal "hat swapping" games of Vladimir and Estragon in Beckett's *Waiting for Godot*. Alain doodles with a marker beside his journal. Alain pops the head off of a tiny doll. Alain fidgets with a miniature flag. Alain adjusts a proof sheet of Dorothy, attached to his bedroom wall. Alain toys with a tiny hat (a nod to Beckett, perhaps?),[17] and so on, and so forth. Ostensibly speaking, the actions could unfold endlessly.

Likewise, Malle constructs the picture's emotional framework around a great void. The filmmaker presents an emotionally sterile character who searches, desperately and without success, for a source of joy, a passion. The prospect of retaining an emotional hold on the film during the opening scenes is thus impossible. The director omits almost all humor and warmth from the film in subsequent scenes, making the viewer conscious of the emptiness. One of the only occasions when Alain smiles or laughs is when he discusses young pop stars with Dubourg's children and (in the process) temporarily, instinctually reverts to adolescence himself. (Alain [smiling]: "You like Françoise Hardy?" "No? Who then?" Little girl: "Sylvie Vartan!"

Dubourg: "Who's that?" Alain [to Dubourg, smiling]: "A pop star. You're getting very old!"). The sudden appearance of happiness in Alain's eyes is (deliberately) jarring. Again, Malle seeks to help the audience identify so fully and completely with the depressed and emotionally displaced Leroy that each viewer carries a deadening weight, on the gut level, as the film progresses—conscious of his or her own sudden inability to experience joy and warmth.

Though it marks only one instance in the film, Malle uses one of the key scenes to conduct an interesting experiment: he attempts to wean the audience off of artificial stylistic elements that abet each viewer's emotions. Malle exposes the audience to two almost identical sequences: one of Leroy standing on a balcony and watching life in the distance (cited earlier) where Malle and editor Suzanne Baron overlay a Satie piece on the soundtrack and (subsequently) a remarkably similar sequence of Leroy gazing through a window, accompanied by an empty soundtrack, where (in "look shot") a pedestrian walks beside the road, carrying a musical instrument case, and another gentleman lifts the trunk of his broken-down auto in mid-lane. As noted previously, characters from the institution "interrupt" Alain's solitude in each instance. Yet in the second scene, Malle carefully avoids music. The Satie piece isn't necessary here, because—given the similarity of the two scenes—we automatically "read the music" into the film. The first instance, on the terrace, was so powerful that the Satie piano notes continue to resonate in our heads,[18] and once again, we find ourselves thinking lyrically, like Alain Leroy, but now without the artificial element of added music to guide us.

Aesthetically and stylistically, *The Fire Within* employs the same basic set of techniques as the first and third acts of *Ascenseur*: high-contrast black-and-white cinematography, with a meticulous, shot-by-shot, documentary-like attention to even the most mundane details; a real-time pace; and Wellesian depth. The mood thus remains inevitably dark and somber. But why do the stylistic devices in question seem so much more focused and deliver a far more powerful impact in *Le Feu follet* than in *Ascenseur*? The answer recalls Malle's observation (from the introduction) about the slow, tentative development of his stylistic and thematic instincts over many years. In *Elevator*, the realist techniques at the outset and conclusion of the film fully elicit the sober (and realist) thematic underpinnings described earlier: romantic separation, the inevitability of fate (collective and supra-human), and the dehumanization of the urban setting. The film carries two grave limitations, however. First, Malle primarily uses the motion picture's realist style (in the first and third act) to critique stylization within film noir *per se*. Ergo, the realist aesthetic carries less weight with this added contextual commentary than it would if it simply undergirded the thematic core material of the film. Second, the basic dramatic architecture and the Woolrichesque "ironic twist" of *Ascenseur* turn it into highly contrived exercise that works against the aforementioned universal themes.

Feu follet travels beyond this by eliminating contrivances and approaching an even deeper level of realism than *Elevator*'s subthemes of romantic separation: psycho-realism. Malle elicits this, in turn, via stark, overwhelming aesthetic and spatio-temporal realism woven throughout the motion picture. In other words, *Le Feu follet* penetrates the inner workings of a suicide's mind — a dramatic level so dark, and so intimate, that the material can only be called the "ultimate justification" for the harsh realist lighting, suffocating close-ups, exhausting use of real-time, and succession of existential images and events. In fact, the subject matter of *Le Feu follet* blends so smoothly with the film's dark aesthetic and stylistic elements that the combination immolates with passion and depth.

Malle's stylistic approach to *Feu follet* draws heavy influence from neorealism, yet the revolutionary quality of the film involves Malle's specific decision to take this neo-realist aesthetic and couple it with psychodrama. That approach — a kind of "psycho-realist aesthetic" — was so unique that it almost went unprecedented in 1963, but it became *en vogue* right around the time of *Feu follet*'s release, and appears, along with Roman Polanski's *Knife in the Water* from the year prior, to have ignited a trend of slightly less accomplished films with a hauntingly similar, almost uniform approach to the aesthetic evocation of onscreen psychodrama. Roughly, this lasted from 1962 to 1963 (when *Knife* and *Fire* were released), to about 1967. Cross-cultural examples abound, particularly in the States and in England. In Britain, films such as Bryan Forbes's *Séance on a Wet Afternoon* (1964) and *The Pumpkin Eater* (1964) demon-strate aesthetic influence by the Polanski and Malle films. From the U.S., *David and Lisa* (1962); *Lady in a Cage* (1964); *Bunny Lake Is Missing* (1965); *Mickey One* (1965); *Who's Afraid of Virginia Woolf?* (1966); and *In Cold Blood* (1967) appear to have been influenced by *Knife* and *Fire*. Though diverse and disparate on the surface, all of the aforementioned motion pictures belong to the same subgenre (psychodrama) in the sense that all of the characters engage in some level of psychological struggle or battle a mental illness. Examples abound: after grappling with alcoholism for several months, Ronet's character in *The Fire Within* prepares to commit suicide at a sanitar-ium; driven by the obsession of proving her own telepathic abilities to the outside world, Kim Stanley's emotionally crazed phony psychic in *Séance* forces her husband (Richard Attenborough) to kidnap a child; the two serial killers in the Capote-Brooks collaboration *In Cold Blood* flee authorities after butchering a helpless family. More-over, all are shot in an identical photographic style: high-contrast black and white cinematography, carefully controlled lighting, and Wellesian depth, filmed in real time, with an emphasis on existentially mundane subjects. Moreover, the films typically unfold in urban milieux, with a majority of scenes set in the late afternoon, under gloomy, cloudy, pre-storm skies; the central idea is that, metaphorically speaking, clouds lie on the horizon. In any given scene, a storm is constantly brewing, ready to pour down on the heads of the disturbed characters. The impending tragedy reflects the charac-ters' inner turmoil, and the state of constantly teetering on the edge of a breakdown.[19]

CRITICAL RESPONSE

Given *Le Feu follet*'s influence on subsequent films, Malle's powerful stylistic approach to *The Fire Within* did not go unheralded or unnoticed among his contem-poraries. Yet, it would be easy to oversimplify the critical response that *The Fire Within* received, both during and after its initial release. Not unlike the directors who adopted Malle's psycho-realism in subsequent years, film journalists currently regard *The Fire Within* as Malle's masterpiece, his most perfect blend of form and content. (Indeed, in discussions with Malle, Philip French refers to the motion picture as "one of your finest films—one with few, if any, flaws."[20]) Yet a closer examination of the critical response suggests that many observers carry sharply divided feelings about the picture.

In a 1971 *New Yorker* review of *Le Souffle au cœur,* Pauline Kael heralds *Follet* as a triumph, referring to it as, "the film that first convinced me that Malle was a superb director ... it shows the influence of Bresson but is without the human pride ... that poisons some of Bresson's later work ... directed in a clean, deliberate style."[21] Kael later offers some insights into the film's almost indescribable box-office failure in the United States, observing that (through 1971, anyway) most Americans never saw *The Fire Within*—either because it "got tangled in distribution problems," or because it "was not commercial in American terms."[22] Indeed, despite a small, devoted following, and "some generous reviews," the picture never caught on in the States. A 1963 article from *Variety*, that arbiter of cinematic bankability in the U.S., seems to offer an answer to Kael's conundrum, for the publication (such a critical force in determining a motion picture's box office) almost single-handedly drowns out the possibility of an American following with the statement, "It is still fairly offbeat fare ... and looms mainly as an art bet abroad, where it will call for a personal and inventive sell due to its fragile if tragic structure."[23] The same publication criticizes the film's emotional void: "Pic can't generate much emotional drive since it is about a man who has already made up his mind to die and will not to take a stand and change his life."[24] Yet *Variety* also praises the film by observing, "The basis of the film lies in its excellent notations, dialog, commentary, and acting," and, "It does deal with a palpable human theme and keeps interest in the character throughout, in spite of its one-track outlook."[25]

These comments mirror the basic, dichotomous critical response to the film in Europe, where—though the positive reception was far from unanimous—*Le Feu follet* at least received complete distribution and more widespread consideration from film journalists. The British press praised *Le Feu follet*'s technical accomplishments. Writing for *The Monthly Film Bulletin*, British journalist Peter John Dyer writes, "For the most part the film is outstandingly self-assured, nowhere more so than in the minute exploration of Alain's room, shot (by Ghislain Cloquet) and edited (by Suzanne Baron) with fine, jagged intensity ... the visual compositions throughout are flawlessly pieced together, their classical building of mood soberly backed by Satie's music and Bernard Evein's assiduously detailed art direction."[26] Yet many French critics judged *Le Feu follet* rather harshly upon release, attacking the picture's icy emotional core. Nowhere is this more obvious than in a *Télé-Ciné* review by Pierre Loubière, who opens the critique by observing:

> Why does *Feu follet* strike me as far too cold, and thus inhuman? Is this simply the film's argument? Or is it Malle's temperament? In this film, which often revolves around a question of love, all the characters are icy and the hero writes that he'll kill himself because no one loved him and he loves no one. The *mise en scène* evokes far more clinical insight than the passionate attention of an amorous director from his characters. How unfortunate.[27]

7

Viva Maria—1965

Only a Paper Moon

"To make an omelette you need not only those broken eggs but someone 'oppressed' to break them: every revolutionist is presumed to understand that, and also every woman, which either does or does not make
fifty-one percent of the population of the United States a potentially revolutionary class..."
— Joan Didion, "The Women's Movement"

"In Breughel's *Icarus*, for instance: how everything turns away
Quite leisurely from the disaster; the ploughman may
Have heard the splash, the forsaken cry,
But for him it was not an important failure; the sun shone
As it had to on the white legs disappearing into the green
Water; and the expensive delicate ship that must have seen
Something amazing, a boy falling out of the sky,
Had somewhere to get to and sailed calmly on."
— W.H. Auden, "Musée des Beaux Arts"

BACKGROUND

The small scale of *Le Feu follet* afforded Malle the flexibility necessary to go over
schedule and slightly over budget when necessary.[1] Yet the director's immersion into
the film's suicidal mindset and his emotional attachment to the existential piece only
increased his depression. Malle returned to his Paris flat one day in mid-shoot, and–as
so often occurred[2]– decided to cut against the grain of *Fire* thematically, stylistically
and tonally for his next film. He envisioned a picaresque Technicolor-Panavision
romp, cast against a Third World backdrop, packed with wall-to-wall cabaret music
and rollicking, bawdy humor. From the beginning, the director wrote the treatment
as a conceptual gimmick: a star vehicle carried by Brigitte Bardot and Jeanne Moreau,
two of France's most illustrious sex symbols, as striptease artists–cum–Latin American revolutionaries.[3]

The approach backfired when the press launched pre-production tabloid rumors
of a bitter rivalry between the two bombshells and delivered the film's premise to the

Flanked by Maria I (Jeanne Moreau) and the cockney gunman Rudolfo (Claudio Brook), strip-tease artist-cum-revolutionary Maria II (Brigitte Bardot) draws her rifle, seeking vengeance on a military dictatorship that has enslaved hundreds of defenseless Latin American peasants in **Viva Maria.**

public as a "battle between the stars." Later, the French, American, and Italian paparazzi—repeating the pattern of *Vie privée*—swooped down onto Bardot and Moreau during the first day of the shoot, robbing the project of any seclusion or nonchalance. During the production of *Viva Maria*, Malle married Anne-Marie Deschodt. Their marriage would last two years.[4]

Viva Maria marks the first of three credited[5] collaborations between Malle and Jean-Claude Carrière (*Le Voleur, Milou en mai*), one of Europe's most prolific screenwriters and one of Malle's best friends. Malle cites his experiences writing the screenplay with Carrière as "great fun."[6] The scenarists used, as a reference point, the book-bound republications of late nineteenth and early twentieth century French magazines that became a major formative influence in their childhood (notably *Le Monde illustré* and *Journal des voyages*). Carrière remembers, "[Louis and I agreed] that the film should [evoke] 'the dreams of eroticism and adventure of a young European teenager from the beginning of the century.'"[7]

Cinematically, Malle and Carrière wanted to pay homage to the American male buddy adventure films of the 1940s and the 1950s, particularly *Vera Cruz* (*Maria*'s biggest filmic influence),[8] starring Burt Lancaster and Gary Cooper, and directed by

Robert Aldrich. Malle hoped to turn *Viva Maria* into a pastiche of Aldrich's Mexican odyssey, but the fantasy book influence, an unanticipated political subtext and a distinct genre blend imparted to *Maria* a body and edge that set it apart from competitors.

Maria premiered in France on November 22, 1965, and opened one week before Christmas in the States, on December 18, 1965. It extended to Germany, Italy, Belgium, and Denmark from January through June of 1966.

Synopsis

Six-year-old Maria O'Malley (a.k.a. Maria II) helps her Republican terrorist father (Fernando Wagner) dynamite a British fortress by rolling a fuse through an open field. A legend unfolds as the two spend the next 15 years spreading terror across the countryside, planting bomb after bomb to protest British colonialism. In 1907, Maria's father suffers mortal wounds at the hands of colonial troops while attempting to dynamite a central American bridge. To save herself, the now-voluptuous, 21-year-old Maria (Brigitte Bardot) blows the soldiers and her father sky high by obliterating the bridge with TNT.

Maria emerges unscathed and slips into the guise of a grubby urchin boy, tucking her pretty blonde Melisandish tresses beneath a cockney cap. Drifting through the jungle, she stumbles onto a vaudevillian circus train, en route through Central America, where Janine (Adriana Roel) and Maria I (Jeanne Moreau) perform as chanteuses. As fate would have it, Maria II happens upon the circus at exactly that moment when Janine, suffering from unrequited love, slips into her empty caravan and kills herself, leaving Maria I devoid of a partner. Subsequently, Maria II hides unseen, as a stowaway atop one of the freight cars, and swings down into the startled Maria I's trailer, playfully hijacking the woman with a knife and stealing milk from a saucepan. Little by little, pretense disappears, and the two girls form a bond. As the caravan rolls into the Republic of San Miguel, Maria I invites Maria II to join the song and dance act — despite Maria II's lack of stage experience and ignorance of libretto.

What begins as an unpolished, even clumsy act before scores of drunken, rowdy Latin American men soon evolves into a triumph of mythical proportions. When Maria II accidentally rips off part of her dress onstage and decides to continue removing the fabric, layer by layer, she unintentionally invents the world's first striptease. Still wet behind the ears, Maria II also finds her first sexual initiation from a group of male performers in the circus. Meanwhile, Maria I tells her new partner of a mysterious, dark-eyed gentleman, who once threw roses at her feet after a performance. Forced to abandon her lover as the caravan rolled onto a new town, she left the sleeping stranger in the darkness. He soon reappears and identifies himself as Florés (George Hamilton), a chained and yoked ex-revolutionary leader for the peasants of San Miguel. When the two women witness the brutal enslavement and torture suffered by the Miguelian citizens, Maria II grabs a gun and fires at one of the captors. Within minutes, armed guardsmen of the military dictatorship take the entire caravan hostage, and the women wind up — with their performing troupe —chained in a dank prison cell.

The scar-faced local leader, Rodriguez (Carlos Lopez Moctezuma), has the two Marias led to his room and attempts to seduce the women with a piece of classical music, but the Marias hypnotize him. Meanwhile, Rodolfo (Claudio Brook), the troupe's cockney gunslinger, leads a break from the prison, but Florés takes a mortal wound from a bullet during the escape. Deeply smitten, Maria II vows to carry the revolution in Florés's name and rouses the peasants with Mark Antony's "friends, Romans, countrymen" speech from *Julius Caesar*. She joins forces with bomb and gun expert Maria I, and the two lead the peasants in revolt against the military dictator, El Presidente (Jose Angel Ferresquilla), polishing off battle after battle and even managing to defeat the dictator's artillery-laden "train of death" by placing a live beehive in the middle of the track that sends the passengers scurrying. The head priest attempts to incarcerate and torture the Marias, who have by now attained deific status among the children, but this fails when the instruments of torture he uses (from the inquisition) fall apart after centuries without use. Ultimately, the Marias— rescued from the prison by Rudolfo and his compatriots seconds before assassination — depose El Presidente and the priest, who continues to live despite his decapitation from a bomb. The Marias continue to perform throughout Europe, and become legends in their own time.

ANALYSIS

In *Viva Maria*, Louis Malle crafts a bawdy postmodern legend, embodied by two female revolutionaries who demonstrate feminine voluptuousness and intuition yet exude masculine brawn, centuries ahead of their time. At its core, *Maria* represents an attempt to deftly blend contemporary myth and tall tale. The haunting, lingering tone of the *chanteur*-narrator in the prologue, and the final image of the epilogue, where the two women stand side-by-side in a second-person shot and hypnotically chant their names back and forth, letting the name "Maria" roll off their tongues in a kind of mythically persistent echo, establish and bookend the film's evocation of myth. Yet, lest viewers read the mythmaking too soberly, Malle weaves elements of tall tale into the story as well, those details that might with successive generations become barroom legends, notably the crooked gun with a mirror attached that shoots around corners and Bardot's "accidental" invention of the striptease. (The striptease invention in *Maria* suggests a blue revisionist parody of the legends of Paul Bunyan and Pecos Bill, with their use of outrageous stories to explain natural phenomena).[9]

Viva Maria earns its place as a watershed motion picture in light of its groundbreaking onscreen depiction of femininity, yet not as the first "female buddy film" per se. Rather, it became the harbinger of a key subgenre. In *Films by Genre*, cinéma historian Daniel Lopez asserts that "female bonding films are practically nonexistent."[10] Not only does *Maria*'s existence cast the light of incredulity on Lopez's maxim, but a cursory examination of film history reveals two or three dozen earlier

and subsequent motion pictures in which leading female characters form a tight
emotional bond (see table on page 95).

As the table illustrates, *Viva Maria* became one of the first female "buddy films"
of feminist substitution. Within this small, often ignored subgenre, scenarists imbue
their female characters with classically masculine traits, and drop the characters into
a standard "male buddy framework." Of this framework, Lopez writes, "Whenever
men have found themselves in isolated environments or in situations of danger, a
bond has sprung up among them ... this bond is usually between two men."[11] Thus,
in *Viva Maria*, Malle and Carrière hold fast to the "male bonding" formula: two
female characters, surrounded by danger (the bellicosity of a Latin American military dictatorship, Inquisition-era instruments of torture, bombs, violence, bloodshed, death), from which an emotional bond emerges. To put it another way: by
placing the women in what are essentially action-oriented male roles, with male characteristics (or substituting female characters for male characters in male roles), *Maria*
attempts to prove the constitutional equality and synonymy of the two genders.[12]
When coupled with the film's *fin de siècle* setting, the message of gender synonymy
gains a level of universality and timelessness, and thus becomes more powerful than
it would if Malle simply set *Viva Maria* in Central America circa 1965.[13]

On a sociopolitical level, *Maria* liberates its two female main characters from
the trappings of the traditional constraints that surrounded the average Western
female in the post–World War II years. The film thus espouses the same brand of
"classical feminism" that became the ideological cornerstone of the sexual revolution in the late sixties and early seventies. Yet the average viewer may experience some
confusion, for the striptease sequences seem to contradict this proto-feminist reading by apparently celebrating the objectification of women. Indeed, viewers often mis-
construe *Viva Maria* as an exploitation film, and dismiss the picture as commercial
fluff, thanks to Malle's heavy emphasis on sensationalism (two French sex symbols
in a contrived story that places great weight on violence and innuendo). Such a reading errs gravely by focusing too heavily on the first half of the motion picture, and
consequently misses the film's all-encompassing dramatic structure, which follows
the pattern of classic satire.

A single architectural split cuts through the middle of *Maria*'s dramatic structure, dividing the story in half between the cabaret sequences and the "revolution-
oriented" subplot that rounds out and polishes off the motion picture.[14] Though
prior to the revolutionary sequences, *Maria* spends 45 minutes depicting lusty male-
fueled conceptions of feminine physicality (in the striptease scenes), the film's more
straight-faced approach to its action sequences (with the "liberation" of the Marias)
can be read as a critical reaction to the innuendo-filled first half of the film. The first
half, in turn, gains a more tongue-in-cheek, satirical tone in hindsight, and the film
begins to qualify as a social satire on the objectification of women. The character arcs
follow this pattern as well, as the women cast off the chains of enfranchisement. And
again, we have the classic satirical structure: a mocked behavior, followed by a proposed superior alternative. Yet Malle buries his satire deeply enough to avoid the pit-
fall of didacticism.

Maria II, for instance (i.e., Bardot) initially demonstrates her own acceptance

Female Bonding Films

Buddy Films of Feminine Evocation

To varying degrees, films rooted in an ancient reverence for the feminine that goes back thousands of years. Valerian Tornius traces it back to the Renaissance, but it also lies at the foundation of ancient goddess cults, where matriarchal civilizations first took root.

Films establish their own dramatic framework, which begins with the complete or partial emotional isolation of female characters, presented as a casualty of superiority to men. (Cukor's *The Women,* for example, uses the literal elimination of men from the screen as an emotional metaphor.)

The literal or metaphoric isolation of women often leads to intense scenes of emotional bonding, confession, sharing, etc. Behavior may be grounded in a friendship, occasionally accompanied by fierce competition, rivalry, backbiting, or a combination of the above.

Can be summarized as motion pictures that, to varying degrees, celebrate "classical femininity" unabashedly.

Culturally, the most recent films in this category represent a definitive counter-reaction to the perceived hypocrisy (and buried misogynistic objectification) of the sexual revolution.

Major Examples (Chronological)

The Women (George Cukor, USA, 1939; a harbinger of its subgenre)
Old Acquaintance (Vincent Sherman, USA, 1943)
Our Hearts Were Young and Gay (Lewis Allen, USA, 1944)
How to Be Very, Very Popular (Nunnally Johnson, USA, 1955)
The Turning Point (Herbert Ross, USA, 1977)
Foxes (Adrian Lyne, USA, 1980)
Heartaches (Donald Shebib, Canada, 1981)
Rich and Famous (George Cukor, USA, 1981)
Entre Nous (Diane Kurys, France, 1983)
Bagdad Cafe (Percy Adlon, West Germany, 1988)
Beaches (Garry Marshall, USA, 1988)
Shag (Zelda Barron, USA, 1989)
Steel Magnolias (Herbert Ross, USA, 1989)
Eating (Henry Jaglom, USA, 1990)
Antonia & Jane (Beeban Kidron, UK, 1991)
Fried Green Tomatoes (Jon Avnet, USA, 1991)
Strangers in Good Company (Cynthia Scott, Canada, 1991)
Heavenly Creatures (Peter Jackson, New Zealand, 1994)
Boys on the Side (Herbert Ross, USA, 1995)
How to Make an American Quilt (Jocelyn Moorhouse, USA, 1995)
Girls' Night (Nick Hurran, UK, 1998)

Buddy Films of Feminist Substitution

Originated with angry or irritated reactions to the rise of films emphasizing male camaraderie and friendship (see quote in text from Lopez), and, as such, did not really begin to emerge until the late sixties and early seventies, as a cultural byproduct of the sexual revolution.

Films preserve the same dramatic architecture and framework as the male buddy film, wherein two or three characters experience an emotional bond as a response to real or perceived physical (perhaps violent) danger. Films simply substitute female characters for male characters within this framework.

The drama itself may often involve intense displays of action or violence in response to external danger(s), such as scenarios where one of two female characters "rescues" the other from rape or attack (see *Thelma & Louise* and *Messidor*).

As a result of the above, films attempt to downplay or erase entirely all elements of "classical femininity" painted (often beautifully) by films of evocation.

On a social level, demonstrates a desire for equality through a feminist belief in the synonymy of gender constitution.

Major Examples (Chronological)

Viva Maria (Louis Malle, Italy/France, 1965; again, a harbinger of its subgenre)
And Soon the Darkness... (Robert Fuest, UK, 1970)
Julia (Fred Zinnemann, USA, 1977)
Messidor (Alain Tanner, France/Switzerland, 1979)
Outrageous Fortune (Arthur Hiller, USA, 1987)
Leaving Normal (Edward Zwick, USA, 1991)
Thelma & Louise (Ridley Scott, USA/Australia, 1991)

of self-objectification by allowing herself to be treated as a whore by men on the afternoon of her sexual initiation (joining a number of cabaret workers for implied group sex in a caravan). Yet she subsequently declares her independence by helping her partner confront (and reject the sexual advances of) local leader Rodriguez, demonstrating emotional maturation and an adverse reaction to the initial sexual chains she bore.

Maria also benefits from an anti-capitalist satirical reading. Malle remembers how, at Berlin University in the mid-late sixties, Rainer Werner Fassbinder and his contemporaries interpreted the film as a political allegory on two conflicting means of protest: the bloodshed and force of Maria II (Bardot), versus the passive resistance and legal reformations of Maria I (Moreau); Malle admits that his intentions for the film (and Carrière's) were never this deep or complex.[15] To expound on Fassbinder's Marxist assessment: the story begins with two characters, both women, neither one of whom evinces political consciousness. Maria II (Bardot) may traipse around the British empire, letting bombs slide from her fingertips in defiance of colonialism, but she only does so in the tracks of (and out of admiration for) her father. (If her only "political consciousness" involves following another's lead, blindly, it cannot be called an individual politicization at all). Maria I, on the other hand, demonstrates *no* political insight whatsoever. In this light, the women begin the story as fundamentally reactionary, a quality demonstrated by their gleeful participation in the cabaret show — not only a symbol of capitalist subjugation through gender, but quite literally an enterprise where the women celebrate capitalism unwittingly by becoming commodities themselves in celebrating the exchange of money for the exhibition of their bodies. The politically naive Maria I and Maria II follow along blindly within the troupe, *until* they witness the gut-wrenching enslavement of the San Miguelians. Appropriately, this is one of the only sequences in the entire film completely devoid of puns or sight gags: the peasants are lassoed, whipped, treated like caged animals, brutally and grotesquely.

By default, Malle must omit humor from this sequence, for a sober politicization of the two Marias renders their burgeoning consciousness credible. Moreover, a graphic and explicit depiction of San Miguelian slavery preserves the tone of the film by enabling viewers to share and empathize with the women's transformation. The film's depiction of Hispanics takes a brilliant 180-degree turn at this point: by initially presenting the men as lecherous, filthy, stupid, drunken Central Americans in the cabaret audience, and suddenly pulling back to reveal the doglike treatment of the San Miguelian citizens, Malle not only turns the tables and points an accusatory finger at viewers (forcing the audience members to reexamine their own delight in the racial stereotypes of the barroom scenes) but critiques the racism inherent in a prejudicial dictatorship that would relegate men to such a pathetic social strata. Appropriately, the two Marias soon become revolutionaries who embody opposite approaches to revolt (as Fassbinder described). But purely on the level of character, the two women will eventually begin to share and exchange revolutionary methods, complementing each other, as a product of a tighter emotional bond.

With a closer reading, one realizes that the central split is not the sole architectural division in the film. It is only the most obvious division, and several smaller splits emerge, that turn *Maria* into a chain of mini "loosely-knit" spectacles: a storybook myth, a striptease act, sight gags, and a revolutionary story-within-a-story. By weaving several forms of entertainment into the fabric of a cinematic narrative, the director and co-scenarist are attempting to erect a "vaudevillian" dramatic structure, *en homage* to the "cabaret-style" variety shows of the late 19th and early 20th centuries, the mini-"acts" linked only by the scenarists' desire to liberate the film itself from the trappings of story and deliberately present unadulterated entertainment at the expense of depth, which, of course, is closely aligned with the purpose of cabaret itself (and, more broadly, exploitation cinema). Thus, one could ostensibly argue that the entire film is a deliberately vapid exercise in sensationalism, and part of *Maria*'s brilliance involves its ability to function as either an anti-capitalist, proto-feminist satire with great depth or as a piece of exploitationist fluff, depending on the depth of one's gaze.

Within the vaudevillian structure, we encounter a significant degree of redefinition as Malle attempts to rewrite the viewer's notion of the "cinematic experience." Using onscreen geographic hyper-realism as a visual foundation (note the almost Herzogian detail of the landscape shots, such as the tiny, jerry-built shack that appears in the background of one train shot and serves no purpose other than establishing an ultra-real abrechtian backdrop), Malle and Carrière immerse the audience into an abrechtian world, obscuring the boundaries at the beginning and end of the motion picture. (Notably, the mythically-oriented prologue and epilogue carry a visual and aural persistence that seem to bleed off into the reality of the theater and linger with viewers.) Atop this careful attempt to plunge unsuspecting viewers fully and completely into an ultracinematic, hyperaesthetic realm with blurred boundaries, Malle constructs and presents the revolutionary story as a "sub-film," as if it were the "feature presentation" in a variety hour. Here, the cinematic illusion of *Viva Maria* as a motion picture is obscured, and the subfilm-within-the-film becomes its own self-referential text, or the central motion picture.

Prior to this, Malle uses the cabaret and striptease sequences to redefine the role of the spectators inside the cabaret and the role of us, as viewers. When Malle introduces us to the milieu of the cabaret audience, a subtle transition occurs. He begins his cabaret sequences with a shot of a mirror—a platonic symbol tied connotively to an *antithesis* of reality. Our first glimpse of the barroom audience (before the shot changes) appears solely as a reflection in the mirror, lending to all subsequent cabaret-related images a pronounced degree of falseness and illusion. The members of the cabaret audience, become, in essence, participants in the stage show, as the surrealistic gags and visual illusions flow equally from the onstage magician-performers and the Latin American audience members. The best example is the gun-wielding Mexican, in the audience, who shoots the magician's dove, and the magician who completes the act by resurrecting the bird—*both* work to bring the gag full circle, and we are the only ones who do not actively contribute to the gag. Later, when we encounter one of the film's first and wildest sight gags (a Mexican on a horse rides out of the men's room), the original mirror reappears in the background, and it becomes a Pavlovian associative symbol, reminding us of the intra-textual illusions of what we are witnessing on screen—in other words, underscoring the "magical" or fake surrealist quality of the entire cabaret realm, and our role, as viewers: we become passive recipients of the entertainment: as if we are actually sitting in the cabaret (an extension of the abrechtian landscape) and watching a series of visual magic tricks on stage. Later, the transition comes full circle. While Bardot and Moreau perform (over the course of several scenes) they shift their gazes, gradually, from an oblique angle (as if addressing the crude, filthy, sex-thirsty audience members in the cabaret) to a vertical angle, and the culmination of this transition leads to a second person-perspective, wherein the intra-frame cabaret audience disappears (visually *and* aurally), and the two striptease-dancers are simply addressing the in-theater audience (or, more literally, Malle's camera). In other words, Malle temporarily redefines the entire cabaret reality as the "stage" and redefines the audience members as the members of the cabaret audience.

Maria also revisits the basic constitutional elements of surrealism. In conversations with Philip French, Malle laments *Maria*'s evolution into a "real" adventure film. Yet in context, the film's authenticity becomes absolutely essential, as Malle, Carrière, and cinematographer Henri Decaë use geographic realism as a visual foundation that works symbiotically with the film's *sur*realist elements. We repeatedly experience the same basic phenomenon in the film: on the broadest level, a painstakingly rendered Central American detail-filled landscape painted with dark browns and greens, and, atop this, a series of bright, flashy, outrageously out-of-place objects (the loudly-painted caravan wagons, the women in their frilly period dresses, the vaudeville troupe) that seem to burst forth from the landscape. Here, the surreal becomes a visually concrete extension of the real.[16]

Ideologically, Malle and Carrière most often use the bizarre, absurdly exaggerated surrealistic events to create humor, and surrealism falls into two categories: first, it becomes an extension of the basic foundations of traditional humor and second, it elicits a bizarre series of surprises that bound over the chasm of human limitation unexpectedly. The first category recalls theologian K.L. Billingsley's observation that "True comedy is very serious business indeed and a consequence of the fall, which left human beings in a no-man's land between the perfection they can conceive and the utter imperfection of what they are and do."[17] In the opening sequence, six-year-old Maria gambols through an open meadow, "rapturously," and sings merrily to herself. The unfamiliar viewer will undoubtedly read this image as a gentle and sacred, reverent embodiment of *innocence unbound*, until the darker, more delightfully wicked, surrealistic truth becomes apparent: she is a preschool-aged terrorist, who delights in planting bombs, and laughs emerge from the chasm between expectation and reality. Yet *Maria* doesn't only incorporate characters who fall through the chasm when we expect them to "bound over gracefully": it also involves characters who triumph when we expect them to stumble. We encounter characters rife with grungy humanness (the cockney gunsmith, the strongman) who surprise us by transcending perfection and accomplishing tasks on the surrealistic level: the marksman polishes off assassinations by firing a gun bent to shoot around corners, the muscleman's strength enables him to lift an entire train car, and so forth.

Additionally, Malle often uses the set-ups of *Viva Maria*'s gags to hone and perfect the classic "double punchline." An example: during one of the cabaret sequences, the magician begins a trick that involves seemingly pulling coins from his assistant's ear. The money-hungry cabaret audience members rush up onto the stage and grab the woman, turning her upside-down and attempting to shake excess money out of her. But this constitutes only the first half of the gag: Malle cuts to a close-up of the woman, minutes later, standing in the wings and asking herself, stupidly, "Why do they always do that?"

If *Viva Maria*'s humor qualifies it as parody, it remains an intertextual parody, devoid — like *Ascenseur* and *Zazie* — of stable reference points outside the cinematic realm. (Indeed, the republic of San Miguel is itself a fictional country). The title *Viva Maria* suggests a tongue-in-cheek parody of both Jack Conway's *Viva Villa!* (1934), where Wallace Beery fights for Pancho Villa in the Mexican republic, and of Elia Kazan's *Viva Zapata!* (1952) starring Marlon Brando in a similarly straight-faced role as the mythical revolutionary Emiliano Zapata. As Malle observes, *Maria* borrows heavily from more sober "male buddy" variants (such as *Vera Cruz*), and from films such as George Cukor's vaudeville-in-the-old-west romp *Heller in Pink Tights* (1960). The core idea of turning Maria and Maria into military leaders, in itself, a parodic idea: an attempt to fill the dignified roles of revolutionaries with two woefully undignified figures: striptease artists, the most base profession imaginable, short of whores, thieves or con men.

The intra-cinematic nature of the parody explains why one cannot classify *Maria* as a Doctorowian legend (ala *Ragtime*). In discussions with Philip French, Malle summarized *Maria* as a film about two striptease artists who "end up fighting for Pancho Villa," yet Pancho Villa's name never emerges from the women's mouths, and we never see the characters interacting with Villa or Villa's henchmen, for a valid reason: *Maria* represents not an exercise in historical anachronism — placing two proto-feminist revolutionaries on a historically accurate Latin American landscape — but a critique of cinematic illusionism: an attempt to set up a genre-familiar environment (the western environment of the male buddy pictures) and to constantly, ruthlessly cut through the surface of the landscape, exposing the absurdity beneath those ridiculous facades that the audience accepts, blindingly, as "truth" in a stereotypical genre western. Ergo, the revolutionary peasants pull up stalks of green onions from the ground — and remove ammunition from the bulbs. A male revolutionary reaches into his baby's swaddling clothes — and withdraws a gun. Another figure cuts through his soft mattress — and exposes an arsenal of weapons. Though such a comparison risks insulting Malle's film, these elements of *Viva Maria* anticipate (ideologically) the desperate conclusion of Mel Brooks's *Blazing Saddles* (1974), where Brooks's characters run through the desert and suddenly crash into the wall of a movie set, which comes crashing down, exposing a Hollywood studio. Though much more subtle and artful in its approach, *Maria* similarly parodies the conventions of the western genre by exposing phoniness and absurdity that lie just out of the camera's reach, just beyond the field of vision.

Examining *Viva Maria*'s strengths and weaknesses more broadly, the film carries two major flaws. First, it suffers from excessive length. Malle could have accomplished the same tasks, and told the same story, in an 80-minute film. Instead, he crafted a motion picture that runs almost two hours, and the revolution sequences (in particular) seem to unfold endlessly. *Maria* also relies overwhelmingly on paper-thin sight gags that lose their punch with repeat viewings[18]: to gain longevity, the gags need to be attached to some deeper meaning that will impart ideological resonance to the humor. Paradoxically, the film's greatest strength is also its greatest weakness: it attempts to accomplish far too much.

CRITICAL RESPONSE

The reaction to *Viva Maria* mirrors the critical pattern that emerged for *Atlantic City*[19] and *Alamo Bay*. Just as those culturally sensitive films fell prey to a schizoid response in the press, torn between conflicting reactions in Europe and America, *Maria* bombed in the States (its chances ruined by terrible English dubbing)[20] but triumphed in Europe. Typical of the American journalists is Ralph Blum, who complains in *Vogue* that the picture is overbaked, a disparate conglomeration of two unrelated films strung together that do not hold together: "*Viva Maria* is a lesson in when to say 'When.'"[21] Critics in the UK, however, found *Maria* delightful: *Sight and Sound*'s Tom Milne lauds, "*Maria* is just as richly inventive [as *Zazie*], but the gags are never forced ... Decaë's Eastman Colour camerawork is a constant source of delight ... the whole film is ... littered with pleasing fancies."[22] In France, the picture received qualified praise. "*Viva Maria*," Marcel Martin writes in *Cinéma*, "isn't the best Louis Malle film so far, but it's a beautiful and great spectacle.... Malle and his co-screenwriter Jean-Claude Carrière ... take pleasure in concocting onscreen adventures that explode with infectious force."[23] Yet he also admits, "*Maria* is a solemn film, and that is, perhaps, the source of the dissatisfaction it provokes ... one gets the impression that Louis Malle didn't know how — or didn't want — to choose between the comic and the serious."[24] Similarly, in *Image et Son*, François Chevassu applauds Malle for acknowledging cinema's capacity for spectacle, yet acknowledges that it falls below par given the director's ability and past accomplishments, and that Malle falls into the trap of becoming picturesque in the revolution sequences.[25]

8

Le Voleur
(The Thief of Paris)—1967

Deflected Emotion and
the Art of Memory

"As to just what this ineffable quality was ... it was not bravery in the simple sense of being willing to risk your life ... No, the idea here ... seemed to be that a man should have the ability to go up in a hurtling piece of machinery and put his hide on the line and then have the moxie, the reflexes, the experience, the coolness, to pull it back in the last yawning moment."

— Tom Wolfe, *The Right Stuff*

"The most unambiguous statements by the patients give proof of the effort of will, the attempt at defence, upon which the theory lays emphasis; and at least in a number of cases the patients themselves inform us that their phobia or obsession made its first appearance after the effort of will had apparently succeeded in its aim."

— Sigmund Freud, "The Neuro-Psychoses of Defence"

BACKGROUND

The first act of Louis Malle's career — encapsulating everything prior to his self-imposed 1967–68 Indian exile (his first two decades in narrative fiction film) — illustrates beautifully the self-aggrandizement that cultivated ability and the hand of fate can deal. By 1965, though Malle had only 30 years on the plate, success had already propelled him to the forefront of the European cinematic *literati*. Yet a wave of nausea and panic swept over the young writer-director in the winter of 1965–1966. Perhaps borne of the ease with which he reeled in a two-picture deal at United Artists, perhaps borne of the global media frenzy that the press strung to *Maria* and *Les Amants*, and certainly borne of the comfort and pleasure that accompanied wealth, a new level of self-realization disarmed Malle. Suddenly aware of his own bourgeois

Gentleman thief Georges Randal (Jean-Paul Belmondo) must be physically restrained from lash-
ing out in fury when one of his close friends and accomplices, the thief Cannonier (Charles
Denner), is shot dead at his feet in the period drama *Le Voleur* (The Thief of Paris).

mindset, he worried he had somehow come full circle, drawn back to the suffocating, stilted upper-class attitude he initially abandoned by turning down his wealthy
future in the sugar beet industry in favor of a self-made career.[1] Herein lies the central explanation behind Malle's transition from *Maria* to *Le Voleur*.

Logistically speaking, *Maria* and *Voleur* are "sister films"—not only back-to-
back Malle-Carrière collaborations, but twin products of Malle's 1964 United Artists
two-picture contract[2] (and indeed, both films are cut from the same "studio cloth").
Aesthetically and stylistically, these films mirror the expensive, internationally-
produced widescreen period pieces UA turned out in the sixties and early seventies
(such as *Tom Jones, Once upon a Time in the West, Burn!,* and *The Private Life of Sher-
lock Holmes*). But, at heart, *Le Voleur* lies closest to *Feu follet*. As with *The Fire Within*,
Malle crafted *The Thief of Paris* (a.k.a., *The Thief*) as a meditation on his own life:
in this instance, the bourgeois status that had re-entrapped him as an accoutrement
of money, power, fame, and success. Malle writes:

> *Le Voleur* is a film about a disillusioned character, written and directed by a
> disillusioned filmmaker. With one key difference between us: I sensed that I

was becoming bourgeois—not socially, for I always held this status—but intellectually. While directing the film, at the Saint-Maurice studio, I remarked to Henri Decaë, the most gifted cameraman of my early films, that we were in the process of installing, in the same place, on the same platform, the same shot we used in *Les Amants* six years prior. That made Henri laugh, but it scared me. I sensed I was retracing my footsteps and I didn't like that.[3]

Georges Darien—a surrealist, suspected terrorist, and by all accounts an unsavory character (with a shadowy life and origins), penned and published the source novel of *Le Voleur* in 1897. Malle and Carrière struggled to work the 500-page epic into a two-hour script, but generally held fast to their source material by wrapping the backbone of the story arc around Darien's central irony: a thief who enters a life of crime to rebel against the bourgeois becomes magnetized and addicted to theft, gradually, helplessly, until his acquired wealth re-entraps him in the bourgeois mindset.

SYNOPSIS

One late summer evening in *fin-de-siècle* France, Georges Randal (Jean-Paul Belmondo), a young man clad in bourgeois attire, strolls down the street, travel bag in-hand, and stops beside the stone wall encircling an ancient Parisian manor. After scanning the area for signs of movement, Randal removes a grappling hook from his case, heaves his bag over the stone wall, and scales his way to the top. Upon hitting the ground, Randal slips up to the house gingerly, gracefully. He withdraws a crowbar from his case, and forces his way into the building; therein begins a night of wild and unrestrained, orgiastic thievery. In voice-over, Randal explains not only that burglary is his passion, but that he goes to great lengths to "do it dirty," never once worrying about leaving the furniture intact or the rooms in order.

Flashback to Randal's childhood. Orphaned at an early age, and raised by his piggish, reactionary and self-centered Uncle Urbain (Christian Lude), Georges fell helplessly in love with his beautiful cousin Charlotte. Upon Georges's return to Urbain's estate after a 14-year collegiate and military exile, the roof fell in—Charlotte (Genevieve Bujold) announced her engagement to a wormy manchild, Armand (Christian de Tillière) and Urbain revealed his slimy delight in piddling away Randal's money through various unscrupulous modes of embezzlement, and hid behind the cloak of good intent.

Infuriated, Randal upturned the evening's bill-of-fare by bedding Marguerite, the maid at Armand's estate (Bernadette Lafont) and using her to steal the jewels that tie Charlotte to Armand's family. Without the jewels, the distraught and livid Urbain felt obligated to sever the engagement of his daughter to Armand. Though Charlotte soon discovered the truth behind the disappearance of her dowry and threatened to rat out her cousin, she ultimately hid the jewels from Urbain, protecting Georges. Nonetheless, Charlotte also refused to elope with Georges. Soon after, Randal left home.

At the engagement party, Georges happened upon L'Abbe la Margelle (Julien

Guiomar), a priest who moonlights as a thief. Gifted at weaseling money out of the bourgeois and funneling it into the construction of missions and churches in China, Margelle mentored Randal, guiding him into a world of organized thievery. The two caught a train to Europe, and Randal soon accepted an apprenticeship under Roger la Honte (Paul le Person) a more-experienced thief. Years passed; Randal entered and abandoned an endless string of meaningless affairs with countless women — unhappy wives, mistresses, and girlfriends— meanwhile breaking into house after house and amassing an astonishing array of wealth and opulent accessories.

Randal encountered Cannonier, a shadowy figure of almost mythical proportions in the French underground, at a right-wing banquet. Working hand-in-hand, the two managed to slip all of the valuables out of a rich woman's room, but Cannonier— recognized by a gun-wielding policeman in the crowd below—fell dead from a bullet wound.

Charlotte returned to London and took up with Georges; the cousins finally consummated their love affair and moved in together. Randal suddenly discovered (thanks to Charlotte) that Urbain was on his deathbed; working in tandem with L'Abbe la Margelle, Randal forged a will; Urbain awoke, discovered the ploy, and — reaching for a handgun — attempted to stop his nephew, but fell dead at the last moment.

Given the new will, Georges and Charlotte inherited Urbain's fortune (at which, the executor reasoned that Urbain must have experienced a last-minute change of heart). The Abbe revealed his decision to leave for China, and soon departed. Charlotte urged Georges to stop his thievery, but George had become addicted — emotionally obligated, at all costs, ransack the mansion of a local industrialist who was on vacation.

The story returns to the present, at dawn. Georges finishes collecting valuables from the estate he is robbing and, suitcase-in-hand — boards a Paris-bound train at a local station.

ANALYSIS

Louis Malle co-adapted and directed *The Thief of Paris* as an introspective tool. He perceived the same Catch-22 of bourgeois-reentrapment in the life of Georges Randal that he had experienced, and thus not only felt an understandable kinship with Randal, but believed an adaptation of Darien's book would allow him to study this ironic "circular path" onscreen. *Le Voleur* thus represents an externalization of Malle's own fears, the director perhaps guided by the logic that in actualizing those fears cinematically, he could somehow free himself from the fate of remaining in the same social, emotional, and psychological trap as Randal.[4] Unfortunately, *The Thief of Paris* falls flat on all counts. While it encompasses a series of fascinating narrative, temporal and tonal experiments that one can expect from a Malle feature, such devices deprive the film of excitement and warmth, rendering *Le Voleur* less emotionally resonant than even *Vie privée* or *Crackers*.

Malle and Carrière wrote *Le Voleur* as a quasi-autobiographical, sociopolitical allegory. An unusual allegorical narrative structure thus supports the film, where the co-screenwriters abandon the classic "allegorical dramatic architecture" of literature and film (with the literal placed atop the ideological, and both presented simultaneously). Instead, the screenwriters build the entire film as an extended two-hour flashback and gently peel apart the story's literalism and allegorization, isolating the two levels from each other by using the literalism as the subtext for the flashback sequences, and using anti-capitalist allegory as the subtext for the present sequences, and never bringing the two together into a single, dual-layered series of actions.

Thief thus opens with a sequence, set in the present, where Georges Randal spends one long Parisian night ransacking a mansion, and as he does, the film cuts away to the chronological story of his life, explaining exactly how and why Randal entered a life of burglary. The flashback device in *Le Voleur* functions as more of a colored lens than a transparent window. Intertextually and functionally, this device withstands close comparison to, for example, the narrative structure of Blake Edwards's underrated Truffaut remake, *The Man Who Loved Women* (1983). But while Edwards's bittersweet comedy uses the flashback structure as an emotional lens (opening with a funeral and tingeing the farcical sexuality of the past with the melancholia of death-from-obsession), *Le Voleur* remains emotionally neutral and uses its flashback structure as a purely metaphoric lens, bombarding the audience with — in the sequence set in the present — a flood of angry allegorical images suggesting anti-capitalist violence and hatred and Randal's quasi-sexual addiction to thievery. The film impels the viewer to read these themes into the past events, through the heavily symbolic lens of the present. Ergo, the film opens with a barrage of metaphors: a massive, decaying estate — representative of the crumbling bourgeois capitalist order — and Randal's incriminating acts (e.g., busting open and splintering the rosewood chest) imply not simply the level of anti-bourgeois rebellion inherent in his vandalism, but establish a protracted metaphor of sexual violence that Malle sustains throughout the story. In this sense, the distinctly vaginal shape of the multi-layered entrance (doors-within-doors, leading to an inner door) underscores the simile that the film establishes between robbing a safe (stealing the wealth of the bourgeois) and deflowering a young woman through rape (robbing her of irreplaceable virginity without permission); both are inherently tied to the theft of a victim's identity.

The flashbacks also establish the film's theme of memory — anticipating Malle's *Au revoir les enfants* 20 years later, *Le Voleur* meditates on how one can project oneself into a mental restructuring of one's past through the art of memory — as one might impart form to a dream, or, on the level that Malle is reflecting on his own life in Randal's stead, as one shapes and structures a screenplay. Malle is not only subtly placing himself in the framework of the film — where the tool of "hindsight" becomes useful for the director, as a mode of self-investigation — but (on a concrete level) placing Georges Randal in the same position and inviting the more bourgeois members of his audience to turn their critical gazes inward via empathy with him.

Yet, as integral components of the film's dramatic structure, the flashback device and the literal-allegorical separation also yield several of the film's most staggering weaknesses. The events set in the past are so concrete and Randal's Uncle Urbain is such a palpable, detestable villain that the audience experiences no tonal ambivalence about him. Most striking is the brilliantly framed close-up of Urbain's leering, half-grinning fat face in the background with the foregrounded image of Georges reading stock sheets and discovering Urbain's theft of his assets. Indeed, the average viewer not only will loathe and detest Urbain for cutting straight to the heart of Randal's desires (Charlotte, inheritance) and ripping them away like some smarmy, prankish bully, but will crave some satisfactorily violent, cathartic revenge against Urbain on Randal's behalf. Malle's transition from Urbain's den back to the mansion setting that opens the film indicates revenge against Urbain, but only in the metaphoric sense — the extent to which Urbain symbolizes a piggy fat cat and a capitalist scoundrel (again, the events of the past filtered through the *purely allegorical* lens of the present). This symbolism is potent, but not potent enough to quench the audience's lust for revenge against Urbain: we want to see Georges immediately enact some sort of concrete vengeance — for example, ransacking Urbain's estate, burning the mansion to the ground, or maiming his uncle — without leaving behind a trail of his own guilt.[5] Again: if Malle and Carrière did not insist on separating the literal and allegorical into distinct time frames, it would leave open the option of combining anti-capitalist revenge (metaphoric) and anti–Urbain vengeance (concrete, tangible) into a single, multi-layered action.[6]

Most problematically, *Le Voleur*'s fractured time sequence robs the film of suspense. Malle pitched *The Thief of Paris* to United Artists as an thrilling Belmondo vehicle.[7] One can imagine UA executives in the screening room, hearts sinking as they realized the grim truth: that the film never touches the raw, nervous energy or suspends the uncertainty-of-outcome needed to maintain suspense and excitement. The audience never — even temporarily — forgets that the onscreen events are unfolding in Randal's *past* (reminded constantly of this by the periodic returns to the present, Randal's voice-over narration, and the simple fact that Malle and Carrière have not yet allowed the audience to move forward-in-time *from* the "night of robbery" that opens the motion picture). With the outcome of the story (i.e., Randal's physical and mental well-being) clear from the opening scenes, the co-screenwriters can never once fully suspend the illusion in the flashback scenes that Georges Randal might be caught red-handed in the middle of a break-in, shot by policemen, or guillotined for larceny. Malle and Carrière thus inadvertently kill off any suspense in viewers' hearts, and *Le Voleur* loses its ability to convey excitement altogether.[8]

The loss of suspense yields another fatal flaw, as well: it drives a tonal wedge of perception in between "past Georges" and the viewer.[9] Ideally speaking, the audience needs to be plunged fully into the character of "past Georges" where the thief's opaque, limited foresight merges with the opaque, murky foresight of the viewer. With the story's outcome unclear, the co-screenwriters must, in turn, help the audience grasp the extent to which Georges is committed to and obsessed with thievery: he will potentially sacrifice his own life and safety (those most sacred risks) to feel the orgasmic thrill of breaking into a house and ripping off others' possessions. The audience must also sense the palpable risk on Georges's shoulders, the risks that induce him to push the envelope as close to the brink of orgasm (climax, or capture) as possible. Concurrent with this rise in suspense, the audience's gradually increasing sense of danger and thrill-seeking along with Randal would most certainly accompany the rise of slow, sickened horror in viewers' minds, as they realize, *along with* Randal, that he has become hopelessly, helplessly addicted to theft — sinking into a massive, seductive whirlpool of crime and ultimately being rendered immobile. Such does not happen in *Le Voleur*; the co-screenwriters instead err gravely by unifying the audience, tonally, with "present Georges." One can observe that Randal is "hooked" as a thief at the beginning of the film and thus feel immediately distanced from him, instead of sharing his obsessions.

Yet these tonal omissions do not (by any means) negate an analysis of the film that posits Georges Randal as an obsessive-compulsive character. The most pointed and incisive reading of *Le Voleur* comes from the mind of *New Yorker* critic Pauline Kael, who observes, "Malle shows none of the seaminess of thievery; this is a study of compulsion."[10] Indeed, an analysis of *Le Voleur* as a study of obsessive-compulsive behavior concurs with Malle's view of Georges Randal: "[Randal] has to keep doing it, knowing at some point he'll be caught ... he is hooked, addicted, he has to do it."[11]

Hence, the key to unlocking Randal's psyche lies in the basic definition of "compulsive acts": an inability to give up a pattern of addictive behavior (e.g., gambling, overeating, alcoholism, drug abuse, erotomania, larceny), despite risking the loss of more sacred assets (family, home, love, health, life itself). This definition concurs with Randal's self-admitted addiction to thievery, but Randal's verbal admission of compulsive behavior fails to dramatize his addiction convincingly. In a motion picture, the risk of losing more sacred assets must be visible and palpable onscreen.[12] As a fleeting shot of another thief at the guillotine suggests, Georges may risk losing his head in *fin de siècle* France, but the audience's sense of risk should not be implied ever so slightly — it must be developed continuously, sustained, and gradually heightened throughout the entire narrative structure, via the tonal unification described earlier. Such does not happen here: given our knowledge of Georges's sound mind and health at the end of the story, we never once believe that Georges runs a personal risk.

It might be possible for Malle and Carriere to preserve the flashbacks and yet put external factors from Randal's life at risk — for instance, perhaps Charlotte could refuse to stay with her cousin if he continues burglary — but Malle and Carrière never once show Georges taking such a risk onscreen, and the only evidence we have of Georges's compulsion is his verbal declaration to Charlotte that theft has become an addiction, that he is physically and emotionally unable to stop. The result is a dull and limpid series of unconvincing staged robberies.

If (the operative word) one accepts that Georges Randal carries the obsessiveness and compulsion that are never played out onscreen, he emerges as one of Malle's more complex lead characters, with an intriguing aetiology. As a deeply pathological individual, prone to obsessive-compulsive behaviour, a violent and anarchic spirit lurks in Georges beneath a placid exterior, evidenced by the destruction and vandalism he enjoys enacting against the houses of the wealthy. In Freud's groundbreaking paper "The Neuro-Psychoses of Defence," the Viennese psychoanalyst traces the origin of obsessive thoughts and acts, phobias, and hysteria to a common source:

For these patients whom I analyzed had enjoyed good mental health up to the moment at which an occurrence of incompatibility took place in their ideational life — that is to say, until their ego was faced with an experience, an idea, or a feeling which aroused such a distressing affect that the subject decided to forget about it because he had no confidence in his power to resolve the contradiction between that incompatible idea and the ego by means of thought-activity.[13]

Georges Randal's burglary and penchant for anti-capitalist violence fall under the rubric of compulsions, or — in Freudspeak —"obsessive acts." To evidence the aetiology and origin of these pathologies, Malle hands the audience two basic "occurrences of incompatibility" in Randal's past. Most prominently, Malle and Carrière dramatize the incompatibility between Randal's expectations of inheritance and his disappointments after returning from college (his uncle's theft of the fortune, Charlotte's engagement to Armand). Randal must somehow deal with the traumatic conflict of interest (incompatibility), and initially does so by seizing his terrified uncle and throwing the old man, violently, onto the couch. But suddenly, Randal projects repression through a highly visible shift in his words and actions: "I am sorry. I will try to control myself, uncle," he whispers, lifting the worthless stock sheets from his uncle's desk. Malle and editor Suzanne Baron interpolate a haunting kinesthetic transition here: a split second later, the film returns to the mansion from the beginning of the story and a shock cut of Georges hurling the plate glass from a jewel case onto the floor, where it shatters into a thousand shards. The kinesthetic relationship demonstrates beautifully that the leftover energy from the ego's experience of incompatibility has been redirected to violence against Randal's victims' houses. Because Randal could still — ostensibly — acknowledge his hatred of Urbain at the end of the story, and may even be able to grasp the relationship between his anti–Urbain revenge and his compulsion to commit thievery, Georges's repression occurs purely on an emotional level, not on a mnemonic level — recalling Freud's description of those case studies where distressing ideas and experiences are present in an individual's memory, simultaneously, with compulsions.

On a more buried level, Georges witnessed his mother's horrific demise, as he reveals to Ida (Françoise Fabian) in the train car: "She fell, right under the wheels. The train passed over her. Sad end for the mother of a family." Though the passivity and apathy with which Randal describes the incident to Ida might seemingly negate its traumatic impact on him, the opposite is true — Randal's failure to demonstrate the inevitable sadness, remorse, or guilt suggests that his ego simply displaced those emotions. Freud indicates that repression in a patient's mind leads to denial when that person is confronted in the conscious state about the traumatic effects of the event — the residual energy, or the sum of excitation from the displaced traumatic effect, must be put to another use. In Randal's case: thievery and anti-bourgeois destruction.

Of these obsessive acts, the anti-bourgeois destruction and the violence are infinitely more significant than the theft. *Je fais une sale métier, mais j'ai une excuse, je le fais salement...* "I work in a dirty job, but I have an excuse: I do it dirty." Georges goes to great lengths to increase the devastation of his victims beyond the emotional impact of lost property — exhibiting intense, ugly violence against their houses and valuables — not protesting a sense of social unfairness *per se* (which is the L'Abbé la Margelle's Robin Hood–like motivation) or projecting envy (after all, Georges has forcibly reclaimed his inheritance by the end of the story, so the items themselves mean little to him) so much as an intense loathing of the bourgeois. Yet a tragic irony lies buried here. Because Randal, of course, belongs to the bourgeois himself by the end of the story (note the subtle shifts in Randal's attire between the outset, in his ratty brown coat, and the final flashback scenes, when he appears slicked up and enrobed in a tuxedo), his anti-bourgeois violent acts qualify as a mode of self-destruction. His repressed guilt for his mother's death has resurfaced in violent acts of self-loathing.[14]

Malle builds *Le Voleur* around the (easily confused) visual strategies of *emotional deflection* and *cinema interruptus*. To distinguish between the two: the deflective strategy typically surfaces as a directorial or editing technique, where shots are directed and orchestrated to avoid emphasizing the main character's emotional reactions. Yet the interruptus strategy emerges and gestates on the narrative level, with dramatic situations that fail to deliver an emotional payoff, or emotionally crippled or repressed characters who seldom allow themselves to experience emotional release. *Le Voleur* places an inestimably stronger emphasis on deflection, as a means of fueling subject-viewer role reversal. The events of *Le Voleur* clearly generate emotion in viewers' hearts, but Malle directs and re-orchestrates the shots (brilliantly) to avoid explicit onscreen revelation of Belmondo's emotional reactions. Though Belmondo gives an extremely subdued, almost errantly mute performance, he at least delivers facial and bodily gestures — as only the most astute and perceptive viewers will note, for the gestures surface when Belmondo has his back half-turned to the audience, his face barely visible. Note, for example, the scene when Charlotte reveals her engagement to Armand. Malle carefully avoids a clear glimpse of Georges's face, shoots the scene from over Belmondo's shoulder, and never cuts to a reaction shot. This recurs throughout the motion picture, and in each instance, we find the emotional component of our viewing experience deflected — redirected from sharing Belmondo's reactions to drawing our own reactions from the external events that swirl around Belmondo. Malle is attempting to liberate the audience from the trappings of being told how to feel by avoiding explicit depiction of his central character's emotions, and by using the Randal character himself as a variable — an emotionally ambiguous cipher. Randal, in turn, assumes the role of the passive cinematic viewer: simply standing back and allowing the world to swirl around him. This not only grounds the film in a firmly fatalistic worldview (implicitly rejecting deterministic ideas), but continues the viewer-subject role reversal experiments that Malle began in *The Silent World* and *Viva Maria*: the director attempts to swap the roles of the character and viewer by deflecting the viewer's emotions from empathy (with Georges Randal) to a kind of tabula rasa, response dependent on each particular viewer's emotional reaction.

Malle uses *cinema interruptus* strategy less frequently in *Le Voleur*, and it may be tied to one of the material's most intrinsic dramatic flaws. The prospect of building a narrative around a lead character who does not even begin to approach detec-

tion, arrest, or capture, and a structure which basically (by its very nature) eliminates all suspense guarantees that the film's emotional payoffs will be minimal; but
Malle and Carrière never even come close to having Randal detected, captured, or
(aside from one scene) chased. Consider for instance, the scene in which Randal lifts
a woman's pearl necklace from her home in broad daylight, slips out the door, and
is accidentally waylaid by an old friend on the stairway. Though the police ultimately
stop the gentlemen, they never even begin to suspect Randal or to frisk Randal, and
Malle cuts to a scene of L'Abbé la Margelle and Randal laughing, without following
through on the frisk.[15]

The other significant reason for the emotionally repressive visual strategies (the
deflection *and* the interruptus) as used in *Le Voleur* simply involves Malle's desire to
weave a level of acid social commentary into the film, on late Victorian Era Europe —
a period when society attempted to repress the modes and degree of emotional
response in the middle class and the same drives emerged from the repressed in baser,
more prurient, and more anarchic ways; hence the rise and tremendous success of
Freud and Freudian theory.

CRITICAL RESPONSE

Le Voleur failed to draw widespread attention in the States and Britain, where
the reaction was lukewarm, at best. It appeared and disappeared quickly, passing
almost unnoticed. Pauline Kael's comments typify the attitude of the American press:
"Malle shows none of the seaminess of thievery ... though it's well shot by Henri Decaë,
it lacks substance and is tedious."[16] Less typical is the reaction of seminal *Variety* critic
Gene Moskowitz, who expresses some concern over the film's "cold detachment" and
warns, "there is still a [coldness] in Malle's work," yet praises the film's "excellent
color, fine costuming, and expert thesping down the line," and concludes, "Based on
an anarchistic novel of the early 1900s, it is transcribed to film with a visual grace
and finesse. It is a solid, intriguing pic full of top-notch production values."[17]

Yet nothing could brace Malle for the poisonous reaction to *Le Voleur* in Europe,
where few — if any — of the major critics responded favorably to the film. The ugly
reactions struck the director with a grave amount of self-doubt and shock, for Malle
had become so personally attached to the material that he emerged from the production slightly blinded to the film's flaws (in 25 year anticipation of his reaction to
Damage— see Chapter 22, "Double Standards.") Most French critics shared a simple complaint about the film: they attacked Malle for taming the actions of a bourgeois thief: eliminating the action, the violence, the suspense, and (in Kaelspeak) the
"seaminess." Writing for *Humanite*, Samuel Lachize concludes, "I am content to
admire the beautiful work of Louis Malle: it's amusing, sympathetic, intelligent —
but it doesn't explode! What a shame!"[18] Long-time Malle admirer Jean-Louis Bory
concurs in *La Nouvel Observateur*: "Louis Malle has put a bowler hat on his camera.
He has confused the manner and behavior of the thief with the popular, elegant conception of the bourgeois— one of propriety and prettiness, and one that is
respectable."[19]

Yet a few critics wrote even nastier attacks on the film. In *France-Nouvelle*, Albert Cervoni writes, "With *Le Voleur*, Malle has created a film that one mustn't take seriously, with the presence of humor sometimes forceful, often as grating as a knife blade."[20] More poisonous and cynical are the words of Janick Arbois, writing for *Telerama*: "After having spit into the soup one mustn't eat it. It isn't appetizing."[21]

Little wonder that, shortly after the release of *Le Voleur* and the production of "William Wilson," Malle temporarily decided to abandon feature filmmaking altogether, dropped out of society, and headed for India.

9

Calcutta and *Phantom India* (L'Inde fantôme) — 1968–1969

The Universe Through a Looking Glass

"He stands in the middle of the road, his shoulders drooping, a copy of *Playboy* in his hand, and gazes along the road, as far as he can see. Somewhere up towards the western horizon he can make out an animal of some type crossing the road. It is not a kangaroo. It is something else but he doesn't know exactly what."
— Peter Carey, "A Windmill in the West"

"But closed in one room, in a world apart, I am glad to travel in my memory to that other world, hedged in by custom and sorrow, cut off from History and the State, eternally patient, to that land without comfort or solace, where the peasant lives out his motionless civilization on barren ground in remote poverty, and in the presence of death."
— Carlo Levi, *Christ Stopped at Eboli*

BACKGROUND

In the autumn of 1967, a grave fear of stagnation began to accrue in Louis Malle. Beset by self-doubt while shooting *Le Voleur*[1,2] and mild suicidal tendencies during the *tournage* of "William Wilson,"[3,4] with his two-year marriage to Anne-Marie Deschodt on the brink of collapse, the director fell into a great personal crisis during his 34th year. He wanted to break his pattern of helming a major French feature every couple of years, and needed to turn everything upside down, let go of his preconceptions about life and the world around him, and start from scratch.[5] Meanwhile, he accepted the invitation of the French Ministry of Foreign Affairs to host a film series of eight recent French titles including *Le Feu follet*— pictures generally representative of the *Nouvelle Vague*—in four Indian metropolises: Calcutta, Delhi, Madras and Bombay.[6] In Calcutta, he also visited the legendary Satyajit Ray (*The*

112

A maharaja rides his heavily adorned elephant through a packed, sweltering crowd in a sequence from Louis Malle's legendary epic documentary series **Phantom India** (L'Inde fantôme).

World of Apu, *Pather Panchali*, *Devi*) who, by bringing Malle to his Calcutta screening room and showing him Indian films unseen in Europe, and by virtue of being in the same profession, provided some familiar ground for the French director.[7]

When asked to describe the subject matter that typically drew her late husband to projects, Candice Bergen reflects, "Louis was ... fascinated by *phenomena*."[8] One can imagine the director's mesmerization upon being plunged into India for the first time. After the initial shock of the noise, odor, filth and clamoring mobs began to fade,[9] he discovered — beneath the chaos — not a series of isolated social phenomena, but a whole society rotating on different wheels — morally, ethically, spiritually, culturally — than anything known to him from the west. Infatuated with the country, Malle began to conceive a new idea for a documentary project — traveling throughout India for many months and capturing the journey on film. He later reflected:

> It is certain that India is the one nation that lends itself most poorly to being filmed. Just the same, it's the nation ... that has best resisted the steamroller of western civilization, and that will continue to resist it for a long time, because it has, in contrast to the west, a perfectly structured, coherent civilization that has existed for a long time.[10]

To jump-start the venture, the director returned briefly to Paris and assembled a lightweight crew of two close friends, sound engineer Jean-Claude Laureux and director-of-photography Étienne Becker, who would assist Malle in shooting the Indian voyage, each cinematographer using an Éclair and Beaulieu 16mm camera. Malle contacted American producer Elliott Kastner (*Harper*, *Sol Madrid*), a longtime friend who handed him 50,000 francs[11] to back the minimum expense needed for supplies, including film stock and power for the equipment. Francis Doré, the cultural councillor at the French Embassy in India, solicited permission for the director to shoot whatever he wished, as he wished; it was the first time in the history of cinema that the embassy granted this privilege to a filmmaker.[12] Malle's plan: "total improvisation."[13] The crew would tour India and shoot for an indefinite period of time, riding solely on instinct, filming whatever piqued their curiosity and inspired them. In an interview, the director recalls:

> It was a film of chance encounters. The process consisted of going somewhere and filming ... without any preconceived ideas, without attempting at all to tell a story or to have a game plan in advance. Similarly, there were certain things I filmed without knowing at all what they would be about ... it would have to be a completely unpolished film. I eliminated altogether the idea of a *mise en scène*. It was very simple yet at the same time required us to develop a rapport with the subjects we were shooting.[14]

The trip spanned January 5, 1968, through May 1, 1968.[15] As one leg of the journey, the team visited and filmed Calcutta between mid–January and February, and their footage on that kaleidoscopic city would later become a separate documentary (synopsized and discussed below). Yet when Malle returned to Paris in mid–May and sat down with Suzanne Baron to screen 30 hours of rushes at the editing table, the two hit a wall. The co-editors worried openly about the danger of organizing the "accidental material," afraid a significant amount of cutting would mean imposing a "supplementary" structure on the picture and sacrificing the freshness, the vitality of the footage that so many cinema direct documentaries lose at this stage. Malle foresaw such an occurrence as "disastrous,"[16] but the thought of projecting 30 hours of rushes, back-to-back, seemed not only unlikely but impossible, for a mainstream *or* an art-house audience.[17] Baron recalls:

> It was an editing process quite different than the one typically used: when I first saw the rushes from the film, I had the impression, from this collection of images, of actually going to India. It's that purity, that rawness, that we had to preserve in the editing and that would be lost if we organized the images effectively.[18]

They began cautiously, by removing all of the Calcutta footage and editing it together as the 105-minute documentary feature *Calcutta*.[19] With the remaider of the raw India stock, Malle and Baron spent over a year —from late May of 1968 through the summer of 1969 — meticulously cutting the rushes into the 378-minute cinema direct epic *Phantom India*, or *L'Inde fantôme*, and subdividing that footage into seven segments of approximately 54 minutes per episode, the sequences in each episode bound together under a loose thematic heading.[20]

It is a grand testament to their shared adroitness at the editing table that Malle and Baron managed to weave the material together in a way that preserves the "freshness of eye and mind" with which Malle and Becker initially shot the footage yet never once feels doctored, contrived, or manipulative. In fact, of all the praises heaped onto the film, critics speak most highly of Malle's postproduction work with Baron. Writing for *Cahiers du cinéma*, Jean-Pierre Oudart observes, "In the editing, one doesn't find a trace of that careless sentimentality ... the limitless 'respect' for the reels of film ... aesthetic 'finishing touches' in the editing ... [or] the indicators of an irritating narcissistic amateurism."[21]

Calcutta reached European audiences ahead of its follow-up documentary *Fantôme*, debuting at the Cannes Festival in May of '69.[22] Episode One of *L'Inde* ("La Caméra Impossible") premiered on the French television network Antenne-2 later that same year, on Friday, July 25,[23] and a successive episode aired every Friday evening for seven weeks, culminating with the final episode on September 5, 1969.[24,25] U.S. handling of the films differed slightly: *Calcutta* premiered on WNET Channel 13, New York City's PBS affiliate, on Tuesday evening, December 7, 1971[26]; *Phantom India* opened at the New Yorker Theater (*sans Calcutta*) on Saturday, May 20, 1972,[27] where the segments were shown individually, each successive episode running for about two weeks straight, appearing nightly as the second feature on the cinema's double bill. The arthouse worked its way to Episode Seven by late September 1972.[28,29]

Synopses

I. Calcutta

As an impressionistic cinema direct documentary composed of slightly reorganized footage taken between January 25 and February 17, 1968,[30] and covering Louis Malle, Étienne Becker, and Jean-Claude Laureux's exploration of Calcutta, capital city of West Bengal, *Calcutta* incorporates the following sequences, respectively.

The picture opens with a lengthy montage of Indian men dunking ritualistically and bathing in the polluted Ganges, and occasionally staring into the camera, bewildered, while the clamor of the urban center makes a slow build to chaotic madness around them — Indians chanting, yelling, screaming, wailing; ships droning. Men drive piled-high carts of dung and hay surrealistically through a hectic mob, and a beggar sits oblivious in the middle of a crowded road as cars hurtle around him. A man herds a flock of sheep, goats, and cattle through the street. Another beggar sits on the pavement and screams out in Hindi, presumably for alms. The camera shuffles through an array of faces, including that of a disfigured leper, before lingering on a hermit who says he comes from "far away" and has relinquished wealth to spend his time on Earth as an endless wanderer, begging for food and visiting the holy places. Life, he says, is a great illusion. A visit ensues to the temple of Kali, where the Nuns of the Order of Mother Teresa tend to the sick and the dying. There follows a visit to the governor's palace at the time when Calcutta is under strict martial law and the recently overthrown government strictly forbids assemblies of more than five individuals from gathering. Despite the ordinance and the high risk of arrest, the members of a women's organization flout rebellion, parading before the palace and toting orange flags with religious symbols. Later, an (unrelated) religious ceremony unfolds, commencing with a street music festival and concluding with an immersion ceremony, where students from the University of Calcutta spin effigies of Sarasvati, wife of Brahma, and toss her statues into the Ganges.

At Tallygunge, in the center of the city, with the Queen Victoria Monument visible in the distance, a contingent of Anglicized Indians gathers around a racetrack and a number of Indians tee off at the Royal Calcutta Golf Club; Malle reveals, in voice-over, that an insurmountable wall divides the upper-crust English area of Calcutta from the squalor and filth of the Indian ghettoes. The film visits the jute and rice fields and factories, introduces the Saddhus (world-renouncing and emotionally troubled hermits who have secluded themselves from civilization and live from the charity of others), and journeys to funerary and cremation ceremonies, where a deceased Indian woman with a mongoloid point is bound tightly while priests deliver recitations in Sanskrit and evoke the four elements over her. They smother her body with sticks, anoint the corpse, and set it ablaze.

During an exploration of an impoverished shantytown, Malle reveals that "the living conditions of inhabitants grow continually worse"[31] and the population continues to surge. In another corner of the city, the Biharis build a contemporary skyscraper without the advantage of modern equipment; Indian women carry stacks of heavy bricks on the tops of their heads, and 12 burly laborers unite to raise steel rods from the street by pulling a rope. Malle discloses the shocking fact that each laborer earns an average of only 75 rupees, or 10 dollars, per month. Moving on, the film visits the railway running between Calcutta and its rural outlands, and a religious ceremony that follows. In one of Calcutta's night markets, a man splits packages of cigarettes, selling individually portioned fags for a few coins per. At a bourgeois Indian wedding, the bride is carried aloft into the room.[32] Malle and co. draw attention to her dowry of money and jewels, and subsequently visit a grand banquet funded by the bride's father, who paid 50,000 rupees to cover the three-day meal, where the guests will eat in shifts.

Students from the United Front demonstrate tumultuously before the governor's palace, proclaiming political allegiace to the Vietcong, but are soon inundated by 10,000 policeman and soldiers who burst in with guns and wire hand shields; in mid-conflict, everyone ceases fighting to allow a religious procession to roll through. Seconds later, the clamor and the violence recommence.

In a street circus, pole sitters and acrobats do turns and flips from atop a tall pole and swing a small girl around by a rope that is attached to her waist. In the film's final sequence, Malle incorporates a lengthy montage of the Calcutta slums, visually detailing the slime, muck, filth, and skeletal bodies and haunting faces of emaciated children as they stare into the camera.

II. *Phantom India* (*L'Inde fantôme*)

<hr>

A. Episode One—"La Caméra impossible," or "Descente vers le sud" ("The Impossible Camera")

<hr>

The epic opens with a montage of interviews with highly Occidental, English-speaking Indians, who espouse their views on Communism and their heavy influence by western concepts and ideals; in voice-over, Malle indicates his fear that he is missing the real India, the unanglicized nation. He feels it important and necessary to dig deeper, go beneath the surface. In the following sequence, two women kneel in the dirt and pluck grass; when Malle and his crew approach, one runs away cursing and screaming that she doesn't want to be photographed. Later, the filmmakers visit shepherds by night on the road to Alvar who, with their expressions and gesticulations, alternately mock the filmmakers and evince mild concern. The filmmakers subsequently visit pyramid builders cutting stone on the outskirts of a village, and soot-covered, father and son dancers celebrating the Muharam to percussive music that becomes hypnotic in its persistence and intensity.

Over the course of the episode, subjects begin to stare pointedly, curiously, awkwardly into the camera, for extended periods of time. Malle, Laureux, and Becker visit a traditional Hindu wedding, a group of brickmakers, and a tribe of "untouchable" women, also known as the "backward classes." As the director and his crew subsequently "follow the trees" with their camera, tooling down a country road, Malle observes that he and his teammates are letting the camera guide them.

A visit to the celebration of Shiva reveals to Malle his (and the others') propensity for interpretive error. The director studies men and women in rags; we assume, as he did initally, that they are beggars, until he discovers—and informs us narratively—of our overriding misjudgement: the beggars are deliberately poor brahmins, the highest members of the caste, yet—paradoxically—far from the most respected individuals in Indian society. Further deepening and fleshing out the complexity here, Malle mentions that Indians divide the Brahmin caste into 1800 subdivisions; intracaste relations and marriage are strictly verboten.

We accompany Malle and his team to a strange, unplaceable, Felliniesque circus atmosphere held by "Catholic Christians ... on the edge of Kerala,"[33] where a heavily made-up transvestite pantomimes and makes histrionic facial gestures while waving his hands frantically, and another gleeful participant rides his cycle in circles. According to Malle, "[It] is equivocal, indecent, completely unbelievable in a country whose puritanism never ceases to amaze us."[34] A few minutes later, Malle, Becker, and Laureux stop beside a rural road to film a flock of vultures gorging themselves on a buffalo carcass; the birds will eventually strip the corpse bare. Malle concludes, "To us, it was a tragedy, a drama in several acts ... to the Indian accompanying us, it was ... the picture of life and death, their quiet alternation."[35]

A jeweler hosts a feast for his friends and relatives, women draw religious symbols on the sidewalk, and the filmmakers attend a ceremony for an arranged marriage, declaring that in India, everything is planned in advance. Yet an exception to the rule lies just around the corner: the filmmakers stumble upon a young girl and boy cuddling, and "[film] these lovers religiously."[36] Malle indicates that Indian newspapers are almost completely devoid of accounts of sexual violence (rapes, sodomy, exhibitionism, sadistic acts, etc). The director describes (in voice-over) traditional Indian wedding advertisements. The filmmakers visit the temple of Konarak, with its explicit bas-reliefs depicting sexuality and eroticism. Malle highlights implicitly the contradiction between this and the Victorian-influenced puritanism of Indian cinema — where no kissing is seen.

The team encounters two Frenchmen in their twenties, "hippies" or "beatniks" who have dropped out of western society and moved to India as inveterate wanderers. Though they initally project exuberance and enthusiasm and describe their ideas of giving up currency altogether, of becoming as contented as the Indians in the face of poverty, a follow-up reencounter with them reveals a change of heart. One has grown sick; distrustful of Indian medicine, his parents have sent him money to fly home. The other, a bit more tenacious, will now head for Goa and Pakistan. In a later scene, another wanderer, an Italian naturalist, declares that he moved to India in pursuit of Gandhi's ideals but could not find evidence of them. In the final sequence, the crew members find themselves on the beach, and Malle nostalgizes about his experience 15 years prior, filming on the shores of the Seychelles with Jacques Cousteau. He describes how challenging it is for him to avoid imposing a structure on his material. In the last few minutes, an economic dispute arises between a caste of shore fishermen and an outside trader.

B. EPISODE TWO — "CHOSES VUES À MADRAS"
("THINGS SEEN IN MADRAS")

Film two documents Malle, Becker, and Laureux's sojourn to Madras, opening with a lengthy temple celebration at Kapaleshvara in the outlying areas of the great city, where hundreds of surbanites heave a towering, elephantine float and guide it on a one kilometer journey that will take five hours, the structure resting every 20 meters. The cinematographers film from below (with the monolith hovering threateningly above them) and from a great height above the city.

The film segues into an exploration of the political canvas of Madras, beginning with a visit to a stage theater, where regional actors perform a scathing political satire in the language of Tamil. In the comedy, penned by a playwright named Chau, the Moghul despot Muhammad bin Tughlaq returns to contemporary India and claims a seat as prime minister before unveiling himself as a charlatan who set out to prove the absurdity of the Indian political system to the natives. In his narrative reflection, Malle comments on the status quo of Indian politic, describing the structure and aim of the D.M.K., and the Tamil-led bloody strife that unfolds in the south, led by T.R. Janarthanan.

Malle, Becker, and Laureux tour the Family Planning Ward at the Madras Fair, where a government official makes a feeble attempt to restrain the population surge by giving a birth control demonstration that will show his audience I.U.D. and condom procedures. Malle discloses the fact that in recent years, such demonstrations and the issuance of birth control devices have almost completely proven ineffective, that the government has grown so desperate as to even "[offer] condoms to men who agree to undergo sterilization."[37] He observes bemusedly that "the spectators will be fighting over these, beginning with a 10-year-old boy who gets a whole stock of them."[38] According to the director, the Indians point fingers at the British for contributing to the population surge by cutting down on epidemics and infant mortality without assisting economic development.

Malle and his assistants visit the Madras film industry and glimpse snippets from the behind-the-scenes production of *Thillana Mohanambal* (1968)[39] a kitschy melodrama of love-at-first-sight starring the 'Jean-Paul Belmondo of India,' Sivaji Ganeshan, as a clarinet player who wins the love of a young woman. Malle marvels at the "complete absence of psychology and constant intervention of magical forces"[40] in the film product of Bombay and Madras, cinema commonly despised by Indian intellectuals. A lengthy tour of the Kalak-Shetra Dance School, "conservatory of the choreographic tradition in the South,"[41] and a theosophical, pluralistic institution, constitutes the episode's final sequence. Therein, young girls perform Kathakali and Bharata Natyam dances before the cameras until the school forces the filmmakers to leave.

C. EPISODE THREE — "LA RELIGION" ("THE INDIANS AND THE SACRED")

Film three opens with an image of bizarre grotesquerie: in a cathartic attempt to repudiate the physical, corporal world and "break out of the cycle of reincarnation,"[42] a yogi winces as he bears the weight of a colossal steel cage, from which protrude hundreds of needles and rods piercing his tongue, back, stomach, groin. Barely able to move his legs, he makes feeble attempts to walk as the sun blazes down on him. Malle characterizes the image as a "tapa, an ascetic exercise, one of countless ... cruel methods to mortify [and] constrain ... [the] body."[43] In the following sequence, the crew members visit a statue of Nandi the Bull next to the city of Mysore in south Karnataka, and witness pujas that are "at once prayer, offering, and ritual ceremony,"[44] conducted by peasants, families, and young children whose shaved heads point to their prior religious initiation, while priests distribute sacred water.

Malle, Laureux, and Becker drift into the deep south where traditional Indian religions are more alive and prominent; in voice-over, Malle references Indian essayist Nusrat Chowdhury, who traced the Indian renunciation of the world to the always-extreme meteorological conditions of the country. The team meets a temple employee who works as a water-fetcher; later, they visit the Tirukkalikundram Temple, built atop a rocky summit, where, on a daily basis, devotees ascend the hillside and feed a pair of eagles at 11:30 A.M. In voice-over, Malle reflects on the misuse of traditional Indian religions in which "robber-priests" con offering funds out of magnanimous belivers, and he details the status and function of the arrogant Brahmins within the caste system. A trip to the ashram of Tiruvvamalai incorporates a glimpse of the lingam, a great phallic stone, purified alternately with water and milk, and lavished with floral offerings and incantations. Malle discusses the role and the multifacetedness of Shiva, the god of sexuality.

The crew visits Madurai, the most venerated temple in the southern part of the country, and films 12 gopurams, pillars covered with mythological scenes that are painted brightly, often to the chagrin of western tourists. Malle reminds us how the visitors—in their anger—tend to forget that Greek and medieval cathedrals were painted in a like manner. Upon attempting to shoot inside of the temple, the filmmakers run into some resistance from the temple administrators, but are ultimately able to buy their way in (unshown). As they film, a great pantheon of believers approaches—a comingling of local residents and the nomads, ascetics, and mendicants who make pilgrimages from across the nation. Men and women bathe inside of the temple, soaking and scrubbing obsessively; Malle notes the irony that despite this fixation on cleanliness, the locals drink the water, "[which] swarms with larvae and fish."[45] As he mentions this detail, larvae squirm just below the surface of the water as the Indians lap it up.

The filmmakers linger in a *garbhagriha*, or a room housing an image of a tutelary god. Malle reflects on the paradox—so strange and disconcerting to one from the west—that Hinduism boasts a cohesion to rival even Christianity, and yet lacks one central deity binding it all together. In front of the altars, dozens of believers do their pujas. A visit to the port of Rameshvaram with its massive temple is followed by an examination of world-renouncing hermits, including a subgroup, the *saddhus* (also referenced in *Calcutta*), mystical, shaman-like figures who are, according to Malle, "bizarre, sometimes scary. Among them there are many asocial, unstable, abnormal individuals."[46]

The film segues into the image of an elderly saddhu who walks alone down a country road, eyes fixed into the distance, mind on another plane, never once affirming the existence of Malle and the others. The episode concludes with an 87-year-old woman climbing the stairs at the Ramajirukha sanctuary, an offshoot of a larger temple, where—in Indian myth—Rama returned to India after slaying Ravana.

D. Episode Four—"La Tentation du rêve"
("Dreams and Reality")

As the segment opens, a cattle-laden coterie of migrants lumbers down a dusty road in a great caravan, and a flock of peasant women with goods stacked on their heads approaches in the distance. Time protracts and appears to stop altogether, and Malle mentions in his narration that for the Indians, minutes and seconds do not exist. The filmmakers feel the loss of time as well; they are becoming unified in spirit with their subjects.

In a follow-up sequence a group of priests gather on a beach and conduct religious gestures and rites with their hands—simple, yet mysterious and highly poetic, the meanings obstuse and unknown. Malle concludes, "Their gestures elude us... But it's no longer important. Without understanding them, we are in an intuitive relationship with these men and women; we share their sense of harmony with nature."[47] Similar events transpire by the head of the Kaveri river: at dawn, a priest sits in solitude and lets his hands flow in a pattern discernible in its motions, but disconnected from its origins and significance.

Concurrent with Malle's declaration that he has learned to expect and accept anything in India, the filmmakers happen upon the surrealistic—a man pushes a sewing machine down a vacant road in the hot sun; and the ominous—a covey of bats, suspended from tree branches, bursts into a torrent of black wings. A nearby village reevokes reminders of British influence as colonialism rears its ugly head again: half-demolished train cars lie dormant in the grass, piled atop one another in a heap of scrap. Nearby lie traces of the British rail system, notably a slow, anachronistic railway twice as long as China's. Meanwhile—in the mountains of Kerala—pickers in a tea plantation earn scant daily wages under the thumbs of capitalist supervisors while straining to maintain a hectic pace. The tea, Malle informs us, will be "sent to the nearby harbor of Quilon [and] ... shipped to England."[48]

A meditation on the gradual extinction of wild animals in India follows, including a tour of a contrived and artificial animal sanctuary, and horrifying glimpses of "slave" elephants who, with ropes tied to their tusks, throw all of their weight into heaving wood for a sawmill. One of the film's only glimpses of a tiger—characterized by Malle as "ultimate mockery"[49]—comes not in the wild, but from a domesticated tiger, with the quirks and mannerisms of a house pet, treated by his master like an oversized pussycat in a cage at the local zoo. Malle details the heartbreaking facts of the *shikar*, in which wealthy Indians organize game hunts with the aid of hundreds of friends, and tigers may even be deliberately drugged to become easier prey.

Malle, Becker, and Laureux visit Cochin, along the coast, where fishermen make their living by trawling with "Chinese nets" onshore and offshore, for fish and shrimp; they later return to the inland lagoons. The film segues into a tour of the political landscape of Kerala, one of the hotbeds of Indian communism, and features extended interviews with Keralan prime minister Elankulam Manakkal Sankaran Namboodiripad, general secretary of Bengali communists Jyoti Basu, Keralan minister of Alimentation Ghori Thomas (and her husband Teve Thomas), Muslim League member Mohamed Koyas, and Bombay city councilwoman Ms. Rangnekar. The episode ends with an elephant that Malle and the others follow as it travels from house to house as part of the Sarasvati festival, being worshipped and fed with buckets of grain.

E. Episode Five—"Regards sur les castes" ("A Look at the Castes")

Episode Five opens on an interview with an idealistic, 20-something American, Thomas Howard, from the state of Madras—one of 700 men and women (among 560,000 Indian towns) each of whom settles briefly in an Indian village and teaches the locals how to live more effectively. Howard spends his days emphasizing advancements in farming techniques to his villagers. A visual examination of rural peasant life ensues, initially without mention or external sign of castes, focusing simply on rich and colorful detail including the preparation of *chapatis* (or pancakes), a woman spinning on a spinning wheel, a man and a young girl cutting mustard weed, an extended music festival conducted solely for the filmmakers' benefit.

Malle and Laureux (with Becker filming) appear onscreen for the first time in the motion picture, making their way through a heavy crowd, followed by a pack of curious children. The filmmakers emphasize additional details of peasant life, notably the frequent use of dung for fuel. A blatant indication of caste surfaces abruptly: women fetch water outside of wells, each woman assigned to a different well site based on her caste. In his narration, Malle outlines the four basic caste divisions in Indian society (Brahmin, Kshatria, Vaishya, Sudra) yet reminds the audience that these divisions are meaningless and that subdivisions number into the thousands.

Haunting close-ups of wide-eyed children fill the screen. A visit to one village — where women carry water jugs on their heads— reveals that most of the feminine faces have been concealed with saris. An sequence with the Harijans, or "untouchables" — referred to by Gandhi as "God's children" — is followed by a meeting with several Indian men who sit on the ground and smoke a hookah, hands cupped over the pipe to avoid contaminating others of varying castes. A trip to the public baths prompts caste-related questioning from Malle, but the bathers are unable to respond directly to his queries.

The filmmakers journey to an outdoor school on the roof of the public baths, and — a few scenes later — discover a blind camel dragging a millstone around and around in endless circles, day and night, an image perceived by Malle (mentioned explicitly in his narration) as a metaphor for Indian society. A return to the well system, where a man periodically draws water, suggests the idea — and prompts Malle to affirm the fact — that within the caste structure, each man is given his own role and singular task, and he must never take on additional responsibilities outside of his assigned work. Society is entirely compartmentalized.

A local village houses the most extreme societal outcasts in the area, more ostracized than even the *harijans*: hut-dwellers who "[descended] from the mountain tribe [and] ... came down to the plains to 'proletarize' themselves."[50] At a local river, a surrealistic scene unfolds, with the village washermen, or *dhobis*— a bottom-of-the-barrel caste — laundering *en masse* on the banks of the water.

Malle recounts the history of the caste system and later tours the Red Fort in Delhi, dyers standing in front who color long swathes of fabric to be woven into turbans. At a Bombay shantytown, the caste structure has yielded an even tighter cohesion in the community, binding individuals of like strata together. At a funeral, the participants project joy, laughter, and exuberance, tooting "For He's a Jolly Good Fellow" on instruments. Their joy can only be explained by their faith that the deceased will ultimately break out of the reincarnation cycle. In voice-over, Malle offers detailed explanation of this belief. In a related propitiation ceremony, priests invoke the gods with cantations, anoint the corpse with floral and scatological offerings, and place balls of rice on the dead man's tongue.

Episode Five ends with a brief depiction of the village sport — a combination of *jeu de barre* and Greco-Roman wrestling — and a trip to the Panchayat, a city assembly with a *Sarpanj* as chief, where Malle expresses delight and surprise (in voice-over) after inferring that he is seeing democracy at work, but is disappointed to learn that he is actually witnessing an investigation into accusations of usury against the chief.

F. Episode Six — "Les Étrangers en Inde" ("On the Fringes of Indian Society")

Episode Six highlights and explores the subcultural nuances of several isolated minority groups within Indian society. It initially unfolds with images shot after Malle, Becker, and Laureux had to "drive for a whole day on impossible trails, then climb a mountain for six hours."[51] Following this journey, the filmmakers encounter the Bandos, an antediluvian, somewhat brutish tribe — its vulgate completely disconnected and dissociated from any of the major Indian tongues — and a race that (according to Malle's opening narration) exists in only about a hundred villages in the heart of Orissa. The sequence opens in the Bando village of Mudlipoda. Malle cites the Bandos' aboriginal origin; they indeed appear similar, ethnologically, to Australian aborigines or to an African tribe — black skin; ear and nose rings; loincloths. Many of the women appear onscreen (and apparently function from day-to-day) without clothes, but wear a series of heavy, stacked brass rings encircling their necks. Mudlipoda functions as the Bandos' administrative center, comprised largely of a number of grass huts, and a series of comparatively modern, white administrative buildings. Malle remarks in his narration that the tribe is anomalous in India, where bovine are sacred — as they make a practice of slaughtering and feasting on cattle.

A visit follows to the nearby village of Chrisampada, its Bando residents so skittish, they vanish instantly when Malle and his assistants arrive, only appearing — fleetingly, transiently, a bit comically — in the corner of the frame. Yet a couple of tribesmen evince more resilience and — less camera-shy — opt to stick around, building a cob house before Malle's cameras. As one local constructs a roof, Malle reflects in voice-over on the "sexual dormitories" established by the local tribes where young men and women are encouraged to indulge in sexual promiscuity prior to marriage. Prior to the filmmakers' departure, the village chief addresses the challenge of living conditions in an area where the Department of Land and Water Conservation has claimed much of the territory.

With his narration, Malle underscores the profound and overwhelming sadness that is already apparent visually, sketched out on the villagers' faces, and ponders the Bandos' pagan mythos of sun-worship and fertility ceremony. During a trip the Bando market, the women carry stacks of the only village commodity — whisk brooms — and exchange the items for a pithy sum, spent entirely on more necklaces. A few of the women trade rice for peppers. Malle informs his audience that in Bando society, patronymic names are nonexistent; parents name their children after days of the week. Malle discloses the idea that the tribe is becoming integrated into mainstream Indian society and thus literally vanishing — their culture evanescent. The filmmakers also happen upon a Communist proselytizer, around whom the villagers rally.

The film next explores the subcultures of Indian Christianity and Judaism, primarily with visits to several local churches; as a congregation streams out of one church door and down the steps, Malle reasons that Christians appear out of place, ill-at-ease when confronted with Hinduism, that Christianity has largely failed in India. Several Jews appear onscreen, assembling around a synagogue. Malle draws attention to the fact that they appear sickly and degenerate, a quirk perhaps traceable to the absence of miscegenation. A follow-up sequence explores an ashram, founded by Sri Aurobindo and run by a vague figure called "The Mother." "The Mother" refuses to appear onscreen, depicted only in a series of still photographs, over which she expostulates on the ashram's philosophy. A trip to Aurobindo's tomb (a holy site) yields many interviews with residents who proclaim their own peace and happiness, but (to Malle's eventual irritation) "see themselves as the saviors of mankind."[52] The filmmakers also tour and film the ground on which "Auroville," the collective's "ideal city for the future of man," will soon be built.

As a final note in Episode Six: an encounter with the Todas tribe, a wildly primitive yet idealistic community of Sumerian ancestry that lacks "war, hunger, prudishness, injustice"— reason enough for Malle to ponder their societal fabric. We learn that in this community, all 13-year-old girls experience coital initiation at the hands of the same older and sexually experienced man (a "teacher"), and that — as in the rest of India — the Todas worship their bovines and live from the milk. A group of Todas children sing, dance, and improvise poetry in which they mock the filmmakers' arrival and intrusion; Malle reveals the Todas' unusual beliefs (that humanity came into existence after being pulled from a river by a bull's tail, that the deceased go to live in a valley close to the tribe). The Todas dance to celebrate the arrival of an infirmary truck that will inoculate them and — making no distinction between "good" and "bad" news— dance upon learning that the Forest Department will infringe on their pasture and that the community may be wiped out.

G. EPISODE SEVEN—"BOMBAY" ("BOMBAY—THE FUTURE INDIA")

Per its title, Episode Seven of *Phantom India*— the final segment in the series— examines the many facets of Bombay. It opens by positing the great Muslim city geographically, with a lengthy coastal shot of the Arabian Sea (where sailboats and other ships glide past languidly) but segues into a glimpse of Bombay's horrid slums, the poverty-stricken masses crowded into an endless series of dilapidated, shanty-like buildings. The commuter train, packed to capacity, glides through; a few residents push heavily laden carts and pull rickshaws up steeply-sloped roads.

In a specialized neighborhood, Muslim artisans— stencillers, goldworkers, potters, others— practice their craft on a small scale. Malle reflects (in voice-over) on the dating of local Islamic influence back to Moghul rule, and on the formation of Pakistan by Muslims around 1947. The muezzin —completely blind, eyes white and malformed — rolls his head around and chants indecipherably; upon hearing his voice (broadcast over speakers) the devout make a daily pilgrimage across the ocean shallows, when the water recedes, to the Haji Ali Mosque — "situated on a rock five hundred meters from the shore [and] cut off from land at high tide."[53]

Several dozen young Indian men stand on a road at night and watch one of Bombay's petrochemical plants, the red light playing on their faces, as gases burst into the air from atop its high columns. Later, Malle and his crew visit the "red-light district" of Bombay, a series of cell-like, brightly-colored rooms, visible from the street through bar-covered windows, where young prostitutes watch passersby and await clients. The filmmakers draw a spectrum of reactions from the hookers — intrigue, attraction, embarrassment, fear, mockery. Malle ponders the irony that although prostitution is open and even encouraged in Bombay, the consumption of alcohol — a violation of Islamic law — is strictly forbidden.

Upon a visit to the Bombay stock exchange — where Indian businessmen gather *en masse* and shout and scream and wave their fists at the figures before them — Malle reflects on the similarities between this scene, the floor of the NYSE, and the exchange in Milan. A lengthy interview follows with Pachavai Patel, a wealthy Indian industrialist who has built a personal fortune from selling agricultural equipment. Therein, he discusses the policies and beliefs of the right-wing political party Svantantra — the party of capitalists.

A wedding of two "Parsis" — "the pioneers of Indian capitalism"[54] — takes place in another part of the city, "following the ritual of the Mazdean religion whose founder was Zarathustra."[55] At a yoga class, Yehudi Menuhin's teacher instructs his students on how to assume various meditative positions. Malle and his co-filmmakers then visit the home of a fabulously wealthy, "unnamed" socialist intellectual, who, at first glance, sits in his living room surrounded by a square of iridescent pillows and *objets d'art*. In an interview, "V.P." describes the political unity he so desires, through socialism, for India, and it becomes clear that numerous outside powers — Pakistan, China, Britain, the United States — hope for India's demise.

The film visits a textile mill that has become almost completely automatized, an auto factory manufacturing new jeeps,[56] a noisy communist demonstration that somehow turns into a musical celebration with dances and parades, and (at the other end of the political spectrum) a frightening political rally of Shiv Sena, the ultra-racist, reactionary group led by Bal Thackeray, whose followers propagate systematic violence against South Indian immigrants. A visit to the South Indians — predominantly Catholic — precedes an extended interview with Rajani Desai, a hauntingly beautiful and Oxford-educated young Indian woman, who speaks of India with cool detachment and — hugely optimistic — predicts that much of her country will industrialize and westernize, and achieve eventual economic self-actualization.

Episode seven concludes with the temple celebration in the village of Rajevzari, on the outskirts of Bombay, in which numerous Indians — a return to the "leitmotif" of the journey — stare, wide-eyed, into Malle's cameras, and where others make their way up the temple steps in a grand procession. A brief trip to the salt marshes follows. The film's final image is that of several Indian men straining to push a heavy, bag-laden cart up a hill and through traffic. After hopping onto the cart themselves, the men ride it down the slope of the next hill.

A group of middle-aged Indian men cluster on the steps of a temple in *Calcutta* (1969), a feature-length documentary shot by Louis Malle during his six-month exile in India. The Indians'
confused and bewildered stares into the camera become one of the leitmotifs of the film.

ANALYSIS

As two "sister documentaries," cut from the same basic experiential cloth in
Malle's life — his four-month decision to drop out of western society and enter self-
imposed exile in India — *Phantom* and *Calcutta* claim a unique status in the pantheon
of Malle films: the two cinematic accomplishments by which the director felt most

gratified at the end of his life[57] and his two most critically acclaimed documentaries.[58] The films represent attempts to push the boundaries of cinema direct documentary filmmaking as far as it can possibly go—to the very edge of the medium. The documentaries thus function reflexively: stretching the principles to this extent means that the focus and critical investigation of the motion pictures must, by necessity, double back on themselves, directing the audience's focus toward itself and the filmmakers instead of outward toward the subjects. This represents a blatant, deliberate, and hugely defiant reaction against the egressive form of the travelogue. Through voice-over narration, Malle repeatedly reminds his viewers of his own ignorance, his inability to resolve the contradictions that lay before him on the tapestry of India, his fear of being unable to shake his western judgements and preconceptions. Malle's self-doubt and indecisiveness have the immediate psychological effect of director-audience unification, in intellect and spirit.[59] Through this brand of introspection, in turn, one gains insight into others on the screen.

Yet to treat the India footage as a pure investigation of (and experimentation with) cinema direct — and thus, a pair of projects in which subject has no relevance — would be erroneous. While Malle does use the reflexive nature of the material in *Calcutta* and *L'Inde* to explore the documentary-making process, and thus places an overwhelming emphasis on the limitations of the form in the hands of an alien traveler (a western traveler), subject and form compliment each other in *Phantom* and *Calcutta*, evidenced by a couple of brilliant and wonderfully ironic analogues from which the films draw much of their power.

The first analogue recalls Malle and Baron's fear of structural imposition at the editing table. Faced with a seemingly insurmountable problem, the editors reached two solutions: (1) Divide the material into subgroups based on general thematic consistency (e.g., Episode Two—"Things Seen in Madras"; Episode Three—"Religion"; Episode Four—"The Caste System," etc.), not merely as a direct parallel to the same "transition to opacity" that Oudart traces it (see below), but—far more significantly—to establish a structural metaphor for the overwhelming, caste-produced compartmentalization of Indian society. (2) Toy deliberately with the chronology, to remove the individual sequences from consecutive order and—via aurally dated "journal entries" at the outset of sequences in Episodes One through Four[60]—remind the audience, constantly, of this almost Vonnegutian time scheme. For example, within Film One, Malle jumps from January 18th to January 25th to April 9th, back to February 19, ahead to March 2nd, and Back to February 18th, and then ahead to April 5th, so the audience is experiencing the depressing absence of linear progression (progression in the western sense) that one finds in Indian society. As V.S. Naipaul writes, "This is precisely the saddening element in Indian history: this absence of growth and development ... There is only a series of beginnings, no final creation ... 'the depressing chronicle of a succession of castles built on the waste sand of the sea shore.'"[61] In both instances (the categorization of the narrative and the achronology of the time sequence), Malle and Baron realized that the use of these narrative devices could only heighten the material by "drawing out" and complimenting structures already present in Indian society, instead of deflating the material by imposing a foreign and ill-fitting narrative structure onto it.

The montage of the Indian documentaries also reveals a gentle counterbalance between the creation of an onscreen subjective (isolated in a powerful sequence such as the "unfolding tree-lined road" of Episode One), and Malle's attempts to place the subjective in a larger framework by cutting together the footage that he shot and the footage that Becker shot, and thus transcending the subjective (i.e., the first real extension and maturation of Malle's hyper-subjectivity in *Monde du silence*). It means building limited visual omnipresence via cross-cutting[62] to give each viewer a broadened spectrum of visual options and — far more importantly — imparting the audience with a sense in which the same objective reality ("The There" in Yeatsspeak) can be filtered through multiple perspectives simultaneously — recalling Andrew Sarris's conclusion about the apotheosis of *Lacombe, Lucien*: that the same event can be detailed from innumerable vantage points.[63]

Jean-Pierre Oudart works toward an understanding of the second analogue in his analysis of *Calcutta*, "Les trajets et les lieux," published in *Cahiers du cinéma*. Oudart's reading is grounded in a concept he terms "syntagmatic paralysis"[64]: the loss of interpretive meaning and the resultant emphasis on surface image. Though the deliberation of this move on Malle's part is uncertain, the director has chosen as his focus a culture where both the political and the polytheistic religious structures (Hindu and Islamic) that lie at the foundation of all aspects of everyday life have become syntagmatic, "abstracted from"[65] the "significances" and "meanings" of their rituals for the common man (though not for the priests).[66] In other words, for all intents and purposes, such meanings are nonexistent in the scheme of everyday India.[67] In his 1964 social commentary on India entitled *An Area of Darkness*, V.S. Naipaul writes:

> Religious enthusiasm derived, in performance and admiration, from simplicity, from a knowledge of religion only as ritual and form ... Religion was spectacle, and festivals, women veiled ... the ceremonial washing of the genitals in public before prayers; it was ten thousand simultaneous prostrations. It was this complete day-filling, season-filling mixture of the gay, the penetential, the hysterical and, importantly, the absurd ..."I am a bad Muslim,"[68] the medical student had said ..."I believe in evolution ..." But he rejected none of the forms, no particle of the law ... [And] it was in politics as it was in religion.[69]

Taking this idea one step further: when Malle posits Indian culture, with all of its syntagma, as the subject of a highly reflexive, inegressive cinema direct documentary, he indirectly establishes this very absence, this loss of cultural meaning, as a deconstructionist metaphoric substitution for his and the audience's shared ignorance of deeper meaning, a casualty that the limitation of the documentary form — within the context of cinema direct — imposes, *de facto*, on the audience. And when Malle continually proclaims his own limitations, his own inability to penetrate the surface, such proclamations are also a direct commentary on India itself. Ergo, Oudart writes of a "series of [onscreen] images that, by virtue of the syntagmatic paralysis that they carry, lay down ... the problems that, appear to be ... the most crucial in India: that of the series [of rituals, of traditions] in all of its ambiguity."[70]

The syntagmatic paralysis and the abstraction of image from meaning carry an important aftereffect that lies at the foundation of the motion picture: the ideolog-ical omissions automatically force the audience's perspective to a purely instinctive level for the duration of the film — to the level of image, shape, sound, color, move-ment, emotion — not as a product of any directorial attempts to "educate" viewers, but as yet another facet of the psychological, emotional, and spiritual unification between the filmmaker and the viewer, who will exist on the same exegetical plane as a result of this process. Though one could draw instances from literally any sequence in *Calcutta* or *Phantom*, two quintessential examples emerge in Episode One. Most overpowering is an encounter with a pair of Muslims. An adult man (pre-sumably a father) and tiny boy (presumably a son, an adorable miniature replica of his father) dance frenetically, covered with black soot from head to toe, a white skele-ton painted on each of their bodies. Rhythmic and mesmerizing, it pulls the audi-ence immediately in, with no interpretation outside of the knowledge that these men are dancing the "Tiger's Dance" and celebrating the Muharam. Similarly, on an emo-tionally interpretive level: an encounter with shepherds on the road to Alvar, at night, as they gather around a fire. As Malle announces, in voice-over, "The shepherds watch us filming them ... somewhat mocking," one notices something one might not notice without this aural clue-in: a couple of the shepherds do indeed make mock-ing gestures, lightly poking fun of the filmmakers and mimicking their movements. The observation is terribly funny, and it establishes a direct line of emotional uni-versality between the subjects, the filmmaker and the audience. Yet Malle never hands one a detailed analysis or explanation of the shepherds' sociological role or their rea-son for meeting before the fire; such is not his role.

Early in the *Phantom* epic and in the same montage that recurs at the outset of each episode, Malle intercuts a series of second-person shots— Indians staring directly into the camera lens, behind the rolling credits. At one point, he declares, "These stares will become the leitmotif of our journey."[71] Indeed, a similar series of images reemerges periodically throughout *Calcutta* and *Phantom*. The stares serve two key functions—first, as in "Bons Baisers de Bangkok" and other films, the glances call into serious question the ethic of Malle and his filmmakers carrying cameras into a foreign country, and our ethic, as viewers, participating in such a venture. Yet even more significantly, as a central, triumphant metaphysical accomplishment, Malle uses the two films to establish a connection between the onscreen subjects and the viewers.

Given the subjects' penetrative stares, the line-of-sight between the subject and audience so overpowers the viewer that one feels the camera and screen have tem-porarily vanished. At no point in the film is this more evident than in Episode Three of *Phantom* ("La Réligion"), featuring one of the most terrifying moments in the his-tory of world cinema. Malle introduces us to the sadhus, world-renouncing hermits who cast themselves to the very edge of the social fabric, gather in sects, and prac-tice a bizarre variant of occultism. Visually similar to mystics or shamans, a few *sad-hus* appear onscreen, one at a time. Malle observes in voice-over, "They are bizarre, sometimes scary. Among them, there are many asocial, unstable, abnormal individ-uals." As Malle utters these words, the film cuts to a close-up of one *sadhu*, a par-ticularly deranged and psychotic-looking individual, probably possessed by an evil spirit (or a group of spirits), who appears to be staring beyond his environs, through the screen, and into the viewer's heart, a malevolent, knowing grin half-cocked on his face. Experiencing this, we reason that his perception of us must, of course, be a visual illusion, but his gaze is so direct and penetrating, and so strips the viewer emotionally, that we immediately feel our blood run cold and our skin harden. It is too overwhelming. We are compelled to look away.

At the opposite end of the spectrum — and illustrative of the same technique — lies an incomparably *erotic* moment in the final sequence of Episode Two ("Choses vues à Madras,") set in a dance school for young women. By this point in the film, many viewers will have already resigned themselves to the lack of ideological interpretation, so that, when one hears Malle characterize the dancing as a "body language" known only to the indigenous Indian girls, one infers that the dancing process for these girls involves a complete immersion into a spiritual world unknown to westerners, and accepts his or her inability to interpret the individual bodily movements ideologically. Thus, one cannot possibly prepare oneself for the delightful surprise that follows. While Malle films one of the beautiful young women in close-up, she temporarily diverts her eyes from the dance instructor, and, bending over in a series of extended bows, casts a subtle and erotic sidelong glance into Malle's camera — as if conveying the message that, at this very moment, she cares nothing for spiritual matters — she is moving her body for us, dancing only for our pleasure and gratification and letting us know with her eyes.

In this instance and at other moments throughout the films, Malle radiates humanism. It soon becomes apparent that he has transcended western concepts of beauty, perceiving the glorious in every Indian he encounters—consider, for instance, how he lingers over even the leper's deformed face in *Calcutta*, how — in Episode Three of *Phantom*— he captures the exuberance in the facial detail and the vocal tones of the temple priest. This is particularly a key sequence because it showcases Malle's humanism despite the disappointing, the imperfect — Malle clearly sees both. He first draws attention to the priest's humor, his ebullience, before subsequently unveiling the man's greed and hunger for offerings. One does not negate the other. Taken together, they demonstrate Malle's sheer optimism, and his ability to see the core of goodness— of hope — in the face of the fallen.

A few key distinctions exist between *Calcutta* and *Phantom India. Calcutta* functions as an orchestral overture to *Phantom*— a motion picture not necessarily intended to be viewed and studied prior to Malle's epic, but more effective if examined in this light. Topically, it summarizes rather neatly and succinctly (per the city itself) most of the major themes and concerns of *L'Inde*. Stylistically, *Calcutta* adjusts the viewer to the approach of *Phantom* by "easing the audience into" the material with a highly impressionistic opening montage. The director withholds narration from the audience for almost 15 minutes, offering instead a visual panorama of the city — a magnetic panorama, that quite literally pulls or forces the audience into an instinctive pattern of interpretation.[72] Because this is the same highly instinctive, sub-ideological mindset into which India seduced Malle, the hyper-imagistic style of the film runs parallel to the offscreen effect of the culture. Malle only presents narration when it becomes absolutely necessary — when a mendicant begins babbling unintelligibly in Hindi, it is the first moment when we enter a complete void of understanding, when the need becomes so great that the dialogue itself demands interpretation.

A phenomenon similar to the narrative postponement transpires on a temporal level. The immediate and psychologically overwhelming protraction of time withholds the fulfillment of audience expectation, via the postponement of voice-over narrative — a delay that both slows the viewer's thought processes and encourages the reflection and anthropological observation that are central to *L'Inde*. This viewer approach is intrinsically linked to an ability to connect with the entire series and appreciate the onscreen subtleties and nuances that unfold spontaneously before Malle's cameras. The postponement also communicates sharply the need to avoid reliance on Malle for interpretation.

In certain respects, *Calcutta* is also more telling and renders Malle more vulnerable than *L'Inde*, because its images and commentary reveal the director falling, helplessly, into the trap of a western viewer — becoming a bit too emotionally affected and too grief-stricken (evidenced by the degree of visual emphasis) on the poverty and destitution of India and a little too swayed by ideological ideals, intent on viewing the Tallygunge-slum division as a lingering evil of capitalist Britain and thus on politicizing it (while *L'Inde* itself is defiantly unpolitical). Such are the casualties of footage shot early, prior to Malle's plunge into the heart of India, prior to his near-complete relinquishment of western thought processes and his onscreen and offscreen quest for metaphysical truth. Conversely, Malle remains defiantly apolitical and accepting of poverty, *sans* judgment, in *Phantom*.

The intention to create and sustain a unified perspective between Malle and the viewer is evident from the first frame of *Calcutta* (a shot taken from behind three black shadows— representative of the film crew—framed against a door leading out into Calcutta), yet this film — to an even greater degree than *Phantom*— leans more heavily on the isolated subjective camera than on the Malle-Becker multiperspective editing, and thus, the camera here becomes an inveterate representation of the overwhelming loneliness and psychological isolation of the self that is evident throughout the documentary.

CRITICAL RESPONSE

From their initial French releases in 1969 through mid–2005, *Calcutta* and *Phantom India*— two pieces of groundbreaking cinema — have somehow disappeared in repertory revival and in the video revolution of the eighties and nineties. Thus, the films have largely gone unseen ever since the early seventies; for some reason, they received very scant critical attention even at that time. Yet the critics who had the foresight to view and critique the Indian documentaries praised the films unanimously, on both sides of the Atlantic. Most of the published reviews refer only to *Calcutta*, perhaps because of *Phantom*'s origins on television.

In the U.S.: Pauline Kael proclaims the feature and the epic "masterful personal documentaries..." and refers specifically to *Calcutta* as "an incomparable vision of

the poetic insanity of India."[73] Reviewing *Calcutta* for *Variety*, Gene Moskowitz characterizes the film as "a discerning documentation of this overpopulated Indian city.
It eschews picturesqueness and ... is not preachy ... Commentary is terse, sets scenes
well, and rarely tries to ... give glib solutions ... [The film] may be a bit diffuse but
does give an absorbing aspect of a general problem..."[74] (referring to the city's poverty
and class divisions). In Britain, Jan Dawson praises *Phantom India* in *The Monthly
Film Bulletin* as follows:

> The most singly disconcerting and admirable aspect of Louis Malle's approach
> to an alien land and civilisation in *Phantom India* is the self-scrutinizing hon-
> esty with which he refuses to follow familiar lines. Articulately aware of the
> temptation to explain his material in accordance with western sensibilities, he
> steadfastly resists it ... Malle dares to interweave pessimism with admiration
> and bafflement, to admit the limits of his own comprehension. By so doing ...
> he achieves a new kind of travelogue: one which creates international under-
> standing by acknowledging the limits of the concept.

In France, critics and the public responded glowingly to both works. Writing
one of the only published commentaries on *Phantom India* (in *Écran*) for the 1975
French rerelease of the series, Max Tessier praises the work as a "surprising, kaleidoscopic film on the discovery of a completely different world and civilization than
the west," and summarizes the series's strengths with, "If the film maintains our
interest today, and for a long time, that isn't only thanks to the impact of the filmed
scenes, but also because Malle has refused to be didactic, and — to the contrary, he
confesses almost constantly his failure to comprehend India in its complexity."[75] A
bit less enthusiastic about *Calcutta* — though still favorable — is Gauston Haustrate,
writing for *Cinéma*, who cites his own hesitancy to regard *Calcutta* as a masterpiece,
but concludes, "Outside of Malle's politic, and beyond what is shown on the screen,
it is important to recognize that the film shows us a way of seeing that isn't negligi-
ble ... The editing together of *Calcutta* reflects well the disorientation of the director
when confronted with the incomprehensible."[76]

10

Le Souffle au cœur
(Murmur of the Heart) — 1971
East Meets West

"I can tell you, and I will.
Apollo said through his prophet that I was the man
Who should marry his own mother, shed his father's blood
With his own hands. And so, for all these years
I have kept clear of Corinth, and no harm has come —
Though it would have been sweet to see my parents again."
— Oedipus in Sophocles' *Oedipus Rex*, Scene III

"In today's fast-moving, transient, rootless society, where people meet
and make love and part without even really touching, the relationship
every guy has with his own mother is too valuable to ignore. Here is a
grown, experienced, loving woman, one you do not have to go to a party
or a singles bar to meet ... There are hundreds of times when you and
your mother are thrown together naturally. All you need is a little presence of mind to take advantage of the situation."
— Ian Frazier, "Dating Your Mom" (1978)

BACKGROUND

April 1968: central India. On the cusp of a blazing summer, under the pressure
of physical exhaustion, Étienne Becker, Jean-Claude Laureux, and Louis Malle threw
in the towel on *L'Inde fantôme* and Malle flew back to Paris with over 30 hours of
undeveloped, unedited documentary stock under his arm.

Returning to France was like awakening from a dream. Reinvigorated on
emotional, spiritual, and creative levels, Malle now carried a broader perspective
(a *global* perspective) of Western logic and ethos. He now saw the entire philosophical approach of Western civilization begin to appear in context, as only a miniscule
part of a much larger and more relativistic global framework. The state of Paris in
May of '68 — besieged by 24 hour protests and demonstrations, and on the threshold of a possible Communist revolution (with DeGaulle *in absentia*) — only added to

133

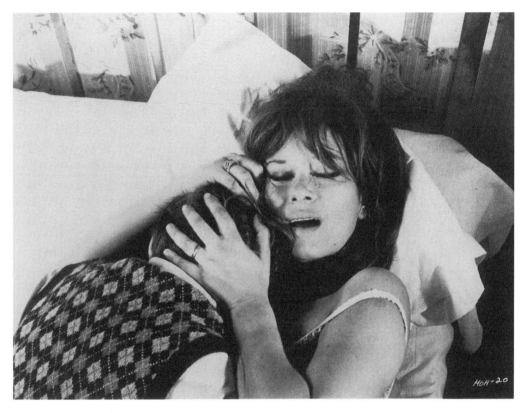

Following a Bastille Day (July 14) party at the mountain spa where they are sharing a room, Dijon housewife Clara (Léa Massari) and her 15-year-old son Laurent (Benoît Ferreux) become swept up in a moment of drunken euphoria and rewrite the rules of maternal love in *Le Souffle au cœur* (Murmur of the Heart).

Malle's sense of disorientation and his ongoing need to question everything around him.[1]

Meanwhile, a threatening dilemma lurked ominously in the back of the film-maker's mind: with the artist's canvas turned upside down and inside out, what would come next? How could this European anti-auteur — once such a mainstream, western filmmaker, with a *haute bourgeois* background and a framework of meaning often grounded in satirical rebellion from Judaeo-Christian ethos— even begin to consider a return to narrative feature filmmaking? Disoriented, Malle fumbled about, blindly, for a solution.[2] Between 1969 and 1970, he spent time with Pierre Kast and Jean-Claude Carrière preparing the treatment for *Mort de l'utopie*, a European alle-gorical fantasy on the final days of a sequestered village in the Andes, a modern day Eden.[3] The writer-director researched the concept of an "ideal society" by attending philosophical and anthropological conferences and lectures hosted by such notables as Margaret Mead, Robert Ardrey, and Marshall McLuhan,[4] but realized, somewhere along the line, that the creation of a "perfect society" would never work cinemati-cally — lacking the conflict necessary to sustain dramatic tension onscreen.[5]

With an astonishing degree of unpredictability and remarkable force, the director's childhood memories came flooding back,[6] and — having moved beyond the anti-bourgeois rebellion of youth and adolescence — Malle discovered a level of peace with his *classe* and upbringing for the first time in 38 years. He also began to acknowledge the passionate feelings for his mother, Françoise Beghin Malle, that he carried during childhood. This yielded what Pauline Kael terms the "obligatory first film"[7]: Malle's attempt to follow in the footsteps of the "prototypical debut feature on adolescence" that became common for *Nouvelle Vague* directors, by coming to terms with the events of his own pubescent sexual discovery onscreen. Though the filmmaker first decided to adapt *Ma Mère*, Georges Bataille's deeply tragic and melancholic (yet unfinished) story of incest, Malle recognized the need to filter the subject through his own voice.[8] Quickly and immediately, without premeditation (in the "automatic writing" mode) the basic story of *Le Souffle au cœur (Murmur of the Heart)* flowed out of the writer-director's mind and onto the page, and assumed a rather unusual form: Malle began with a series of events from his early teenage years, and imbued the story with imagined events and reconstructed characters, emerging with "partly-invented autobiography."[9] In truth, the adolescent Malle spent time at an Alsatian spa and wound up sharing a room with his ultra-devout, conservative mother, circa 1946.[10] In fiction, Malle omitted Françoise from the story, substituting an Italian immigrant mother radiant with passionate exoticism, whose relationship with her son begins tenderly, with mutual compassion and shared understanding, and ultimately transcends all familial, moral, ethical, and physical boundaries in its intimacy.

SYNOPSIS

In springtime France, circa 1954, shortly prior to the French surrender at Dien Bien Phu, the *haute bourgeois* Chevalier family lives together under one roof in Dijon, where the father, Charles, (Daniel Gélin) runs a gynecological practice out of the home. The freewheeling, anarchic 15-year-old Laurent Chevalier (Benoît Ferreux) enjoys stealing phonograph records of the jazz greats he worships (notably Charlie "Bird" Parker) and lifting erotic novels (Reage's *The Story of O*) from his parents. Deep in the throes of sexual exploration, Laurent masturbates alone, with his brothers, and with the help of the family cat, Joseph.

He spends his days attending a strict Catholic school under the tutelage of Father Henri (Michel Lonsdale), a man who has made a vow to chastity and scolds Laurent for "abusing himself," yet enjoys putting his hands seductively around Laurent's thigh.

Laurent's gorgeous, earthy, free-spirited, vampish mother Clara (Léa Massari), who grew up "like a savage" as the Italian daughter of an anti–Fascist refugee and Mussolini oppositionist, dotes on her youngest and refers to him with great affection and warmth as "Renzino," yet worries constantly about the future of her older sons, the hyperkinetic Thomas (Fabien Ferreux) and Marc (Marc Winocourt). Laurent's brothers steal wads of cash from their mother's purse, play "spinach tennis" by flinging forkfuls of the green mash through the air and catching them on plates, harass the family's obnoxious maidservant, Augusta (Ave Ninchi), and spend their nights having sex with older prostitutes. The boys all adore their vivacious mother, yet loathe and detest their indifferent gynecologist father, and regard him as an unsympathetic idiot.

Laurent grows enraged, indignant and jealous upon learning, with horror, that his mother is having an extramarital affair. He bursts into his father's office spitefully to inform Charles of Clara's infidelity (interrupting a gynecological session), but the doctor angrily forces his son out before learning the news. Meanwhile, the boy finds initiation into the realm of adulthood when his brothers steal their father's car and pilot it to a bar and brothel, L'Orée du Bois. Laurent follows an engaged prostitute, Freda (Gila von Weitershausen) into one of the back rooms, undresses, and gently mounts her, but his soused brothers burst into the room and drag his kicking and screaming naked body off of the bed. An infuriated Laurent tells Marc to "go to hell" and refuses to accept an apology.

Upon contracting a heart murmur at summer camp, Laurent gets shuffled off to an Alsatian spa for an electrocardiogram, mother-in-tow. Thanks to a logistical error made by her husband's secretary, Clara winds up sharing a suite with her 15-year-old son (though the two bed in separate, adjoining rooms). Once there, Laurent flirts with two girls his own age, Daphné (Corinne Kersten) and Hélène (Jacqueline Chauvaud), but reveals envy and possessiveness when his mother draws the attentions of a teenage boy, Hubert (François Werner), and when Clara's lover whisks her away from the resort for two days.

Yet Clara and Laurent grow ever closer during their stay. Clara returns in tears because her lover jilted her, allowing Laurent to demonstrate amazing resourcefulness and empathy. Tears come to his mother's eyes as he reassures her, sticks up for her, and tells her he's on her side and will always be her "friend." That night, at the spa's Bastille Day celebration, Clara becomes inebriated, and—upon assisting her back to the room—Laurent sits next to his mother on the bed and helps her undress. Under the aura of intoxication, the two caress and instinctively begin to make love.

When Clara awakens in the middle of the night (the alcohol having worn off) she tells her son softly that she hopes he doesn't regret the intercourse; it will be a special moment they will always remember together, and will never "be repeated." Laurent admits he isn't sorry. Sometime later that same night, he dresses, leaves his sleeping mother in the bedroom, and slips down to Hélène's room. He makes a play for her sexually, but—disgusted—she yells at him and pushes him away. Not to be deterred, Laurent heads for Daphné's room, and the two go to bed together.

The next morning, Laurent shuffles back to his room, shoes-in-hand, and comes face-to-face with his entire family, who have arrived at the spa to pick him up. Glimpsing the shoes (and no doubt believing they have a full understanding of the situation), Charles, Marc, and Thomas chuckle to themselves. After Clara and Laurent exchange a nervous (telling) glance, they too begin to giggle, and everyone bursts into peals of unbridled laughter.

ANALYSIS

The genesis of *Murmur of the Heart* can be traced back to 1968. As Malle confides in a 1971 interview with Guy Braucourt, *Souffle* could never exist in its current form (and mightn't exist *per se*) had the director not plunged headfirst into central India as preparation for *l'Inde fantôme*.[11] Malle observes:

> The [Indian] voyage(s) liberated, within me, a certain number of inhibitions (which one might call prudishness, restraint, self-censorship) that held me back from expressing myself fully, and caused me to take departures in my career, such as adaptations of others' works and allegorical subjects, whereby I wouldn't express myself directly, only indirectly, through writers that came between me and the subjects.[12]

The filmmaker who spent years fleeing his background, locked into constant shame over and denial of his own bourgeois tendencies, discovered inner peace in 1968 India,[13] and—given his newfound knowledge of the vast differences in ethical perception between the east and the west—became a relativist, which liberated many of his subsequent features from the ethical judgment many directors levy against their characters.[14] Malle's acceptance of his own bourgeois social status made his confidence surge, freed him from the cage of disgust for his origins, and turned him into an anomaly among European filmmakers with bourgeois backgrounds: with *Murmur*, he instinctively discovered the newfound ability to accept the morally hypocritical bourgeois on its own terms, to view the ethical duality of the higher European social strata (the prim and proper surface and the bubbling and crackling hedonistic passions beneath) with a marked, unusual degree of fondness and affection.

This explains why readings of the film as an anti-bourgeois social satire (a common critical misconception) fail. Though it became fashionable in the sixties and seventies for leftwing, pro-socialist European directors to launch savage attacks against the bourgeois with the cultivation of a satirical voice, Malle never attacks or condemns his characters in *Murmur*.[15] Instead, he shares and celebrates the ethical recklessness and anarchy of the Chevalier family. As Alexandre Astruc writes of the film, "Everything [presented] is all too pure, healthy, funny, and natural."[16] The Chevaliers are thus gleefully, carelessly happy and content, and Kael observes, "It is perhaps the first time on film that anyone has shown us the bourgeoisie enjoying its privileges."[17]

The classification of a film as "satire" presupposes some level of attack or criticism within the narrative.[18] In *Films by Genre*, Daniel Lopez writes, "Satire seeks to make us aware of human faults and follies by ridiculing them."[19] Consider also Danny Peary's observations about Buñuel's *The Discreet Charm of the Bourgeoisie*, one of the most acclaimed anti-bourgeois satires of the past 50 years, which he terms a "surprisingly subtle *attack* on the rich, the church, the military [and] police."[20] This reveals the distance between *Murmur* and traditional satire. In *Souffle*, Malle has no target of attack *per se*. Instead, he grafts a relativistic, eastern-influenced moral framework onto a traditional western dramatic structure.

Uncoincidentally, *Souffle* follows May of 1968 (regarded by many leftwing intellectuals as the closest twentieth century Europe ever came to a completely success-ful, peaceful Communist revolution), and Malle's attempt to construct a cinematic utopia with *Mort de l'utopie*. Following India, the director attempted to envision a completely sexually and emotionally liberated society, and saw the seeds of this lib-eration in the underlayers of the morally dualistic (hypocritical) European bourgeois of the 1950s. In this sense, *Murmur of the Heart* qualifies as a modernist classic, yet its modernism remains confined to content: the characters are modern in the sense that their value structures have begun to collapse; the director loosens them from the confines of western morality, a projection of his own moral and sexual liberation (see the above quote from Malle, on India). Herein lies the significance of the film's frenetic jazz score, its glowing numbers performed by Charlie "Bird" Parker and New Orleans clarinetist Sidney Bechet: returning to the very foundations of jazz as a mod-ernist art form (the collapse of cohesive systems of meaning, expressed by a coher-ent melody broken into improvisatory, often unrecognizable riffs), Malle uses the film's score to paint a portrait of the characters' "moral liberation" and ethical loos-ening, an accompaniment to the loosened, broken up, dizzied, and amelodic notes. Malle tells Guy Braucourt, "There is ... an accord of sensibility between the boy [Lau-rent] and the music of Charlie Parker ... a little similar to the accord in *Feu follet*, between the hero and the music of Erik Satie."[21] *Murmur* is only "a little similar," in the sense that although Malle uses the Satie music in *Feu follet* as an expressionistic device, to merge the mind and emotions of the audience with the sensibility of Alain Leroy (i.e., music as tonal evocation) the filmmaker uses the Parker and Bechet jazz in *Murmur of the Heart* to define the film's context aurally (i.e., music as contextual evocation). The ethical liberation of *Murmur* is not confined to Laurent: it extends to Thomas, Marc and Clara, and Malle subtly implies that Charles Chevalier faces the prospect of sexual and moral lib, when the doctor (in one of the film's funniest moments) turns away from a gorgeous blonde patient in his gynecological office and confesses, "In this profession, one has to be a saint."

The confinement of *Souffle*'s modernist elements to content and character behav-ior cannot be overstressed: on the surface, Malle never attempts to create a "mod-ernist" dramatic architecture, by dissembling the narrative structure of the film and eliminating temporal and spatial continuity, as in Buñuel's *L'Age d'or* and *Un Chien Andalou*, or Resnais's *Hiroshima, Mon Amour*. Instead, the film's modernist, relativis-tic ethos rests atop a traditional western narrative structure. Malle's authorship and direction of *Souffle au Coeur* represents, to some degree, an attempt at east-west philosophical reconciliation through this coupling, as much within the director's own mind as within the film. Yet, paradoxically, a deeper level of "architectural mod-ernism" lies buried in *Souffle*: by eliminating western ethos as an effectual force in the film, Malle scratches out those elements that guide an audience's sense of "right" and "wrong" within the developmental framework of a story, and an audience's expec-tations of how the story should or should not unfold. This liberates the governing rules for the narrative, and opens up options for the trajectories of the story and char-acter arcs.

The Judaeo-Christian code of ethic still exists in ghostly form in *Souffle*, but Malle treats it almost as a joke, a purposeless, antiquated series of rituals and empty, meaningless phrases, holding together the weak, rickety, rusty social structures around the characters. Ergo, seconds after Father Henri reprimands Laurent for "abusing" himself, and warns his young pupil of the dangers of the flesh, he puts his hand around Laurent's bare thigh.[22]

In her review of *Murmur*, Pauline Kael presents an unsolved conundrum. "I'm not sure," she writes, "how the picture was sustained and brought off so that we see the stuffiness and snobbery of the privileged class on the outside and the energetic amorality underneath."[23] In fact, Malle invents and employs a "tonal split" in *Souffle*, to impart his central character of Laurent with dual layers. The director begins by using three of the characters from the Chevalier family as social archetypes: Charles Chevalier (Gélin) embodies bourgeois "stuffiness and snobbery," Clara Chevalier (Massari) bourgeois "energetic amorality," and Laurent emerges with a combination of the two. Each parent offers a window (a "projection") into a distinct level of their youngest son's psyche: Charles mirrors the outer; Clara the inner, or the core (one of the reasons mother and son are able to bond so deeply). In other words, Laurent Chevalier (Ferreux) has inherited multidimensionality; the resultant relationship that Malle constructs between Laurent and the audience is the product of a "tonal split" between the attitude toward each parent (or each level of the son's psyche). And consequently, the tonal relationship between Laurent and the audience could not be more oblique. As Kael notes, "You're never quite sure how you feel about Laurent...."[24] Laurent, in turn, becomes an archetypal bourgeois adolescent, indicative of others his age, and with the film — with an archetypal figure at its core — gains a macrocosmic, social dimension.

Murmur of the Heart thus unfolds on two tiers simultaneously — the individual and the societal — united by the theme of liberation. Hence the observation of *Monthly Film Bulletin* critic Philip Strick, "it is a film about the difficulty of liberation, both within the family unit and outside it...."[25] But while Strick perceives Dien Bien Phu correctly as an important extension of the "pro-lib" theme (liberation from colonialism), the failed colonial expedition is little more than a footnote within the story, an attempt to give the narrative contextual grit, and subservient to the more-important running correlation between Laurent's sexual liberation (given his function as a prototypical "bourgeois youth") and the societal liberation that lurks unexpressed in the background,[26] as an allegorical extension of Laurent and Clara's archetypal natures. In *Souffle*, Malle demonstrates an uncanny ability to lead the audience gently into rethinking the sinfulness of mother-son incest. The relationship that the screenwriter-director builds between Clara and Laurent (one of the most authentic and moving in the film) long prior to any implication of lovemaking, suggests that the two can give and share emotionally on an almost unprecedented level, and demonstrates the irony that Laurent's understanding of Clara far supersedes that of her husband or her adulterous lover. Thus, many viewers will find it quite easy to accept the incest on Malle's terms; he uses it — ironically — as a physical outpouring of the Christian concept of *agape*. Yet (returning to the macrocosmic, social level of meaning) Malle ultimately acknowledges the impossibility of a "liberated" society, particularly in 1954 Dijon. The director knows better than to present an ending in which the incestuous relationship would continue beyond one evening (for instance, a conclusion where Clara and Laurent run off together, as lovers). Such would be a completely ridiculous and implausible development, because these characters (despite whatever liberating impulses they may carry, and whatever degree of behavioral license they may have reached) still live in western Europe circa 1954, and must still acknowledge their subservience to western ethos and to the family unit. Despite Kael's assertion to the contrary, incest is still something of a taboo to these characters, evidenced by the fact that only through the *deus ex machina* of inebriation can the inhibitions fall away and the darker, buried Freudian impulses emerge. Once the drunkenness fades, Clara reassures Laurent that "the moment will never be repeated." In other words, for all of their looseness and recklessness, the mother and son are still too grounded in the mores of the bourgeois to have incest by any means other than as an accident, and Malle reveals that the heretofore apparently "surface" bourgeois morality runs a bit deeper than we may think. The characters' reversion to western mores recalls not only the failure of May 1968, but the failure of *Mort de l'utopie,* the director's subsequent realization that "the reconstitution of a perfect society" (a utopia) "would probably be very naive, and quite dull," and the director's acknowledgement of the characters' extreme distances from full, unbridled sexual lib circa 1954. The writer-director's observations about his trips into the Eastern Hemisphere in *Malle on Malle* can be applied, equally, to the morality and ethos of the characters in *Souffle.* The filmmaker muses, "of course, I knew there was no way one could become Indian or Hindu — that's ridiculous. A lot of Westerners were trying to do that in those years."[27] One might rehash the quote rather easily, as follows: "I knew there was no way for an individual who grew up in Europe could break completely free of Western ethos and adopt a sense of eastern morality — that's ridiculous."

By presenting a French social class with a significantly looser moral and behavioral code, Malle also suggests that sexual behavior *per se* finds its degree of pathological severity (and, more broadly, its designation as "healthy" or "pathological") within a social framework. How telling that, in regard to Laurent's relationship with Clara, he possesses several behavioral characteristics listed in Freud's lecture "A Special Type of Object-Choice" under the heading of "psychoneurotics," yet cannot be correctly termed a "disturbed" adolescent in any significant way, having been raised by a mother (and within an environment) where his incestuous impulses are never treated as pathological. Thus, the boy chooses a woman as his love-object who is attached to another man (Dr. Chevalier) *and* to an adulterous lover; Freud asserts: "The [psychoneurotic] in question shall never choose as his love-object one who is disengaged."[28] Laurent chooses a woman whose reputation is particularly unchaste and earthy; Freud observes: "[The psychoneurotic's] loved one ... should be like a prostitute,"[29] and "[this] is connected with the experiencing of jealousy, which appears to be a necessity for lovers of this type."[30] (Note Laurent's indignant rage when he discovers Clara's infidelity to Charles, rage that outlines the boy's jealousy and possessiveness, where his simultaneous ability to demand that she not take a lover and his need to see her as earthy and sexy become "symptomatic of his confusion."[31]) And Laurent evinces a tendency and need to come to Clara's aid emotionally after her lover deserts her, while Freud notes: "Most startling ... is the urge they show to 'rescue' the woman they love."[32]

Yet most striking is Freud's final deduction: he discusses all of these symptoms in the context of taking a lover *per se*, without reference to familial relationships—until he concludes:

> The object-choice, which is so strangely conditioned, and this very singular way of behaving in love, have the same psychical origin as we find in the loves of normal people. They are derived from the infantile fixation of tender feelings on the mother, and represent one of the consequences of that fixation. In normal love only a few characteristics survive which reveal unmistakably the maternal prototype of the object-choice, as, for instance, the preference shown by young men for maturer women; the detachment of libido from the mother has been effected relatively swiftly. In our type, on the other hand, the libido has remained attached to the mother for so long, even after the onset of puberty, that *the maternal characteristics remain stamped on the love-objects that are chosen later, and all these turn into easily-recognizable mother surrogates.*[33]

As noted earlier, Malle's "loosened moral framework" opens up trajectories for the narrative. It enables the screenwriter-director to rewrite Freudian psychoanalytic theory, implementing not only the aforementioned morally revisionist versions of Freudian pathological traits, but rewriting Freud's conclusion: instead of a pathology where Laurent remains psychologically attached to his mother, and future lovers are all attempts to preserve and perpetuate the incestuous experience, the mother-son incest becomes, within the context of the 1954 Dijon bourgeois, a liberating experience — instead of disabling and crippling, it frees Laurent from the imprisonment of his inner-self by enabling him to move onto other lovers and perpetuating his sexual development. It frees him from psychoneurosis. Thus, liberation succeeds on the personal level and fails on the social.

CRITICAL RESPONSE

Like *Les Amants* 12 years prior (and *Pretty Baby* seven years hence), *Murmur of the Heart* drew a firestorm of global controversy. Even prior to release, Malle attempted to gain a grant from the French Movie Commission, which at the time demanded preapproval on screenplays, and threatened to ban the film. American critics were most vitriolic in their castigation, and — sadly — many comments reveal astonishing ignorance, a lack of keen perception, and a towheaded inability to grasp Malle's purpose or intent. Such is the case with Robert Hatch, writing for *The Nation*: "What [Malle] appears to be saying is that life is a great joke because nobody ever gets hurt. That point of view is bad enough in Tom and Jerry cartoons; when applied to alleged human beings it becomes moronic."[34] Malle collaborator Jeff Fiskin interprets the denouement similarly when he reflects, "The one time that [Louis] falsified everything was in *Souffle au cœur*... It was this marvelously romanticized version of a world that is in fact ... doesn't work the way he presented it."[35] And Stanley Kauffmann, writing for *The New Republic*, chides, "The script, which [Malle] wrote, is the epitome of a mediocre writer's idea of sensitivity and daring."[36]

Malle fared better from the pen of American critic Richard Schickel (of *Life*), who writes, "It is a tribute to a previously undemonstrated skill that Malle makes not a single misstep as he treads a line as delicate as any director has recently drawn ... and created from [the details] an evanescent mood that makes us not only receptive to his difficult work but grateful for it as well."[37] And Pauline Kael, as we have seen, hails *Murmur* as one of the cinematic masterpieces of the early seventies—an "exhilarating ... irresistible film."[38]

Though Alfred Fabre-Luce pans the film with a reactionary letter in *Le Monde* attacking Malle as immoral, French critics were generally rapturous in their praise. Alexandre Astruc writes, "It is not enough to say *Murmur of the Heart* is Malle's best film — it's his first true film... What's unique in the case of Malle is his ability to give the film its proper dimension, that's to say, in addition to its tenderness and gentleness ... the joyous humor he evinces."[39] And, noting the influence of directorial maturity on Malle's film, Guy Braucourt observes, "It's wonderful that Malle has waited close to 15 years to treat such an essential theme: he has returned to a freshness, a spontaneity, a tension as much in the scenario and the dialogue as in the *mise en scène*, that astonishes, much like a young director who is suddenly revealing his talent for the first time."[40]

Souffle faded from view for about 15 years, yet in spring 1989, Malle and Orion Pictures Classics (doubtless encouraged by the success of *Au revoir les enfants*) opted to rerelease the film and gave it its first video issue. In an '89 *New York Times* interview, Malle reflects, "I saw the film last year. I was surprised at how direct it was, how funny it was."[41] Indeed, *Murmur*'s critical reputation has aged and mellowed as beautifully as the film itself—despite the initial disgust of critics in the Hatch and Kauffmann vein, millions now regard the film as a classic — one of Malle's undisputed masterpieces.

11

Humain, trop humain and *Place de la République* — 1972 (released 1974)

On the Road Again

"A preference for the off-camera is a preference for ordinary life — 'the drama of the doorstep,' the legendary Scottish producer John Grierson called it. Ordinary people don't lose their dignity when they're caught off camera, because they're always off camera. It's on camera, in fact, where most people appear awkward and undignified...."
— Louis Menand, "Nanook and Me"

"Chance acquaintances are sometimes the most memorable, for brief friendships have such definite starting and stopping points that they take on a quality of art, of a *whole* thing, which cannot be broken or spoiled."
— William Saroyan, *Chance Meetings*

BACKGROUND

As two little-seen feature-length documentaries that Louis Malle produced in 1972 and shelved for two years, *Humain, trop humain* and *Place de la République* did not emerge from a period of creative ferment, but around the end of one of Malle's rare dry spells. Sandwiched in-between *Souffle au cœur* and *Lacombe, Lucien* lay a frustrating span (a creative dead zone) when several of Malle's proposed endeavors, including *Amazonie*, *Electric Sun*, and the long-termer *Robinson Crusoé*, died in the water.[1] Malle became something of a gun for hire during this period, spending much of the early summer of 1972 supervising the French-language dubs of Coppola's *Godfather* (under the French title of *Parrain*), at the request of Paramount.[2] Ergo, in slight contrast to his decision to make American docus during 1985 — a point when he longed to return specifically to a hands-on form of 16mm filmmaking *versus* the studio environment of *Alamo Bay* and *Crackers* — Malle's two documentary undertakings in 1972 revealed his need to return to filmmaking *per se*.

The idea behind *Humain, trop humain*— a protracted cinematographic study of assembly line work at a European automobile manufacturer — had lingered with Malle for years, but given his inability to overcome legal blockages from the major French auto plants, Simca and Citroën (who assumed that the left-leaning filmmaker would want craft a revolutionary political tract on the exploitation of workers) Nouvelles Éditions could never launch the project. Nonetheless, for some unknown reason, Citroën changed its mind in 1972 and opened its doors to Malle. He shot the documentary in three "movements," the first and the third at Citroën in Rennes, Brittany and the second at the Paris auto exposition in October of 1972.

One month prior, in September 1972, Malle began work on a documentary entitled *Paris '72*; according to Billard, the original game plan involved earmarking about 40 locations around Paris in more than 12 *arrondisements*, and both throwing out questions to pedestrians and using professional actors to "provoke" situations in public, while filming in full view. Over the weeks, Malle and his "two-man" team of Becker and Laureux narrowed the scope to a single Parisian locale — the Place de la République, where they drew more intriguing reactions and enthusiasm from passersby — and eliminated the concept of actor provocation, limiting their strategy to open-ended questions. *Humain, trop humain* and *Place de la République* debuted simultaneously in Paris, about three months after the January 30, 1974, premiere of *Lacombe, Lucien*.

SYNOPSES

Humain, trop humain

As a study of the French automobile culture, *Humain* incorporates three distinct movements. In the first, Louis Malle, Jean-Claude Laureux, and Étienne Becker visit the Citroën auto plant in Brittany, France circa July, 1972, and follow the production of a motor vehicle from its original form — as an undistinguished sheet of metal — to its final stages at the tail of the assembly line. In the second, Malle, Laureux and Becker tour the Paris auto exposition in October 1972 and nonchalantly film attendees discussing the performance qualities of the vehicles on display with representatives from various auto manufacturers. In the third, also filmed at Citroën during the July '72 visit, Malle, Laureux, and Becker zero in on individual workers and linger on their repetitive, mechanistic movements until the images become obsessive and exhausting.

Place de la République

In autumn 1972, Louis Malle, Jean-Claude Laureux, Étienne Becker and Fernand Mozskowicz tour the Place de la République in Paris, carrying their 16mm cameras and microphones on the small strip in between the rue du Temple and the boulevard Beaumarchais.[3] Therein, Malle and Mozskowicz stop a number of pedestrians and inquire about their lives, feelings, and interests. At one point late in the film, an attractive young woman initially subjected to an interview takes Malle's camera and conducts interviews herself.

ANALYSIS

Taken together, *Humain, trop humain* and *Place de la République* illustrate a decisive ideological split within the rubric of documentary theory that — historically — yielded two opposite approaches to cinema direct filmmaking. Although Malle directed both films, the works paradoxically take opposing stances within the cinema direct debate.

Celebrated documentarian Richard "Ricky" Leacock (*Happy Mother's Day*; *Lambert, Hendricks & Co.*; *A Stravinsky Portrait*) reflects on one approach to cinema direct when he observes:

> What is it we filmmakers are doing, then? The closest I can come to an accurate definition is that the finished film — photographed and edited by the same filmmaker — is an aspect of the filmmaker's perception of what happened. This is assuming that he does no directing ... It's no less objective to be selective. Objectivity has to do with, "Am I causing this to happen or is it happening irrespective of my being there?" That's one thing. Now selection is something else. The physicist is a very objective fellow, but *he is very selective*. He's much more selective than we [documentarians] are. He tells you *precisely* and *only* what he wants you to know. All the rest is irrelevant....[4]

Humain embraces the Leacock approach wholeheartedly. Appearances to the contrary, *Humain* does not constitute a nonfiction film with preconceived ideas behind it; Malle's claim about not intending to make a political statement[5] is valid, for he did shoot according to instinct, with no preconceptions. Vincent Malle observes, "[*Humain*] wasn't [preplanned at all]! That's what's amazing. [Louis] just came ... and we took two days, and we just went in and filmed! ... But ... he'd never been in ... a car factory before, and he absolutely didn't know what to expect."[6]

The picture does use structural impositions to draw out and give voice to ideas that emerged, naturally, from the spontaneous filmmaking, but according to Vincent, Louis introduced this structural element in the editing room,[7] a decision that underscores the selection process described by Leacock. Malle divides the motion picture into three distinct "movements" (as in an opera) that, when unified, function as a kind of reverse-satirical deconstruction. The first movement parodies linear social progression; Malle implies, facetiously, that the ordered *démarche* from a piece of metal into an automobile, with a beginning, a middle, and an end is indicative of a macrocosmic linearity. Yet the pseudo-religious choral music on the track (accompanied by organ swells) provides clear indications of how the images should be read — as sharply-honed irony — and when the automobiles arrive in the customer-laden showroom, all sense of progression ends; Malle dissects the "thematic whole" of industrial production from the first "movement" into pieces for clearer inspection, to unsheathe the chaos and anarchic lack of progression that lie beneath. And just as, in the second movement, the showroom dialogue deliberately takes the audience nowhere — it feels circular, pointless, superficial and shallow, and laced with gentle irreverence — the third "movement" shares this purpose but carries it one step beyond: Malle lingers on the repetitive motions of the workers 10, 12, 20, 30 times in a row, until he produces physical exhaustion and mind-numbing boredom in the viewer.

Humain thus cannot help but recall a feature of like purpose, Chantal Akerman's *Jeanne Dielman, 23 Quai du Commerce, 1080 Bruxelles* (1976). Dielman is arguably *Humain*'s closest cinematic counterpart, for the films encompass like trajectories, each opting to wear down the spectator and to create not simply viewer-subject tonal identification, but tonal *unification* on such a level that the oppression of the onscreen subjects becomes palpable for the audience. The potential problem that arises from *Humain*, of course, is the same that impacts *Dielman*: the knowledge that one's feelings of oppression as a viewer may transcend the subjects' feelings of oppression simply because the viewer lacks the opportunity to participate, physically, in the onscreen activity; passive observation, in other words, becomes a form of oppression in and of itself (that the onscreen subjects lack), doubling one's feelings of emotional and psychological torture as a viewer.

Humain has fallen prey to harsh criticism in some quarters because of its ideological preconceptions and its sequence preorchestration; writing for *Cahiers du cinéma*, Thérèse Giraud issues the most strident complaints. "*Humain, trop humain* ... is neither a documentary on the O.S. or on the auto exposition ... it isn't anything other than a fiction constructed from pieces of the cinematic eye, a juxtaposition that produces the 'truth.'"[8] The extent to which one ascribes to this criticism and regards it as valid depends entirely on one's acceptance of the Leacock school of cinema direct, for in complaining of an inherent ideology in the Malle film (read: a directorial perspective), Giraud is essentially objecting to the process of directorial and editorial selection that Leacock perceives as inevitable. One must, of course, consider the fact that on a purely technological level, *Humain* most certainly qualifies as direct cinema: it utilizes an observationist approach *via* the cinematographic mobility and sync sound that became inextricable benchmarks of the *direct* school.

Poised at the other end of the ideological spectrum from Leacock is Albert Maysles (*Salesman, Gimme Shelter*) who observes of his method of cinema direct:

> Actually, where I have been interested in writing has always been in diary form, which is similar to a factual style of making movies. You experience something, and without pressing much of a form on it, you immediately set it down — in this case, in print. In other words, a form of expression that comes as directly from your feelings as possible. At least in the filmmaking part, our style of making movies is totally spontaneous in the photography and in the event we're filming. People are doing something and there is no time lag in-between the event and the filming of it.[9]

As an ideological model, this summary aligns perfectly with *Place de la République. Place* is exactly what Maysles references: both a filmed record of direct subjective experience (Malle, Mozskowicz, and their unnamed female participant interviewing random subjects one-on-one, on the Place, in Paris) and, more deeply and significantly, a work pulled as directly from Malle's heart and feelings as any in his *œuvre*. Certainly, there are few films that lie closer to the core of Malle's humanist worldview.

The specific behavioral and facial details and preoccupations of the interviewees retain far less significance, here, than the underlying principle, which is that the camera eye — Malle's eye —falls in love with the diversity of the individuals who take turns standing before it, and the director attempts to carry viewers along with him; this encompasses a bold and unspeakably brave attempt on Malle's part to dramatically narrow the range and increase the depth of the audience's vision, drawing the viewer's attention not simply to the subjects' words, but to the beauty of their gestures and mannerisms, the variance of their interests. And on still another level, a key component of this diversity involves the pedestrians' reactions to the presence of a broadly disclosed movie camera. Malle has taken two constant variables—the 16mm camera and microphone — and, exposing the same setup to numerous individuals, draws a unique reaction in each instance and thus manages to achieve the seemingly impossible, externalizing the psychological uniqueness of each subject. In theory, given its concept, *Place* could also constitute a meditation on the ethics of approaching strangers with a camera. But because the documentary utilizes the opposite approach of, say, *Candid Camera*, and is shot in public, with the cinematographic apparatus in full view, Malle and his crew escape from this sphere and operate on ethically neutral ground throughout the motion picture.

CRITICAL RESPONSE

Humain, trop humain and *Place de la République* went virtually unseen in the United States and were only screened a handful of times in Europe. The only extant critical review in English of either film is Pauline Kael's capsule review of *Humain* in her *5,001 Nights at the Movies* that brushes the work aside as a bore. She writes, "Malle's film is so open and neutral a look at the work process that although one may feel that it gets beyond the usual bromides, it still doesn't seem to go very deep. The surfaces of the auto industry are very photogenic, but there are no revelations in this film."[10] The pictures received more substantial attention across the Atlantic — given their short runs in French cinemas— but the French writings steer around value judgments, instead dissecting form and intent. In *Cinéma*, Tristan Renaud assesses the works as deliberate exultations of banality (*les neutres*) and argues that Malle uses *Place* to facilitate communication — to establish running bonds between the onscreen participants and the audience and the filmmakers, epitomized by the young woman's decision to hold Malle's camera. For Renaud, the camera functions strictly as a purveyor of evidence; he also comments, bemusedly, on the irony that Malle avoids accosting passersby yet the reverse often happens.[11] He surmises *Humain* as a kind of critique of "conspicuous consumption," and affirms, "The overture, a long traveling shot on the rolling bridge that transports the enormous rolls of sheet metal, sacred music supporting the imagery, is completely unambiguous."[12] In *Jeune Cinéma*,

Jean Delmas describes *Humain* as a kind of vicious attempt to slice through and destroy whatever preconceptions the audience might have about assembly line work, for the sake of "transmitting the real."[13] He also describes the environment into which the audience is plunged as a "hell of noise,"[14] and states that "*Humain* makes an excellent contrast with more verbal political films ... for once image and sound, without the least bit of commentary — seem capable of carrying a concept."[15]

12
Lacombe, Lucien — 1974
The Politics of Detachment

"'God,' people say. 'But there were old men, women, and children.' I tell you: I had this mission, and I was intent upon it: I only saw, *They're enemy.* Of course, I still was in South Vietnam. I knew, *There are old men, women, and children in South Vietnam.* It was common sense: sure, but in combat there is damn little common sense."
— Lieutenant William J. Calley, Jr., as told to John Sack

"It is exciting and emancipating to believe we are one of nature's latest experiments, but what if the experiment is unsuccessful?"
— V.S. Pritchett, "The Scientific Romances"

BACKGROUND

Several of Louis Malle's most accomplished and acclaimed projects blossomed through long, creative preproduction periods, the filmmaker taking months or even years to weave into a cohesive whole the influences he wished to explore — in his mind and on paper — before crafting the screenplays. Over the period of maturation for each new motion picture, Malle's basic themes remained static, while his settings, major characters, and aesthetic and musical choices evolved around them. Not only does the genesis of *Lacombe, Lucien* epitomize this idea, but it springs from one of the longest periods of development in Malle's life, the ideas taking root nearly a decade before the filmmaker sat down with Patrick Modiano to co-write the first draft of the motion picture.[1,2] Though *Lacombe*'s central concept — the banality of evil as it bleeds into wartime collaboration — never wavered, the period and setting shifted rapidly with the passage of time, vital components of a long, oft tedious gestation.

Malle first conceived the project in mid–1954, when he became acquainted with two notorious intellectual fascists: journalist-author Lucien Rebatet (*Les Deux Etendards*) and Pierre Cousteau (Jacques's brother), editor-in-chief of *Je suis partout*. Though the French government initially sentenced both men to death as reparation

149

A machine gun slung over his shoulder, the brutish, instinctive farm boy turned Gestapo member Lucien Lacombe (Pierre Blaise) leans coolly against the back of a Nazi jeep, shouldered by one of his SS superiors in *Lacombe, Lucien.*

for wartime collaboration with the Nazis, Rebatet and Cousteau later received amnesty. As a young man, Malle spent several evenings at the home of Daniel Cousteau (Jacques and Pierre's father), keeping company with Pierre and Lucien. He found himself rapt, sucked into a whirlpool of political debate with the two right-wing intellectuals. In his autobiography, Malle characterizes their statements and observations as bitter, sententious, monstrous. The men were "released from prison more convinced [of the fascist stance] than ever," and Malle wondered, openly, how two intelligent adults could conceivably arrive at such abominable, ahumanistic conclusions regarding the fate of mankind and the surrounding world. For the young socialist filmmaker, it was a long, slow and dark prelude to the discovery of evil.[3]

Eight years later, with the French-Algerian war grinding a halt —(just prior to the Evian accords and the flight of French colons from the country),[4] Malle finished shooting raw documentary stock on Algeria that would eventually go unedited and unreleased.[5] Accompanied by assistant director Volker Schlondorff and a journalist friend from *Paris-Match*, the 30-year-old filmmaker spent several days at the Aletti Hotel in Algiers, but left for Kabylie after a short time. The three bunked down in a mountain-based army fortress with a group of die-hard paramilitary fascists— colons, protesting De Gaulle's decision to grant independence to the Algerian nationalists of the Front de Libération Nationale (FLN). In the mess hall, one of the aspiring officers — (later characterized by Malle as an idiot) — violently raided a local village at around 11 P.M. The bloodthirsty officers burst into a tiny hamlet, kicked in the doors of the mechtas, slapped a feeble old man on the mouth "who didn't respond quickly enough,"[6] and violently seized two innocent Algerians, to wheedle Malle, Schlondorff, and the journalist away from quasi-socialist political stances. Had Malle's protests not silenced the raid, it would certainly have continued, unabated, until morning. Later that same night, Malle roomed with an aspiring, gentle young accountant from Lille in his early twenties. A man who faithfully wrote daily letters to his fiancée, couldn't wait to return to his hometown, and happened to be in charge of torturing civilians.

Two related themes fascinated the writer-director — the inner corruption of the everyman and the moral ambiguity of simply "following one's orders" in wartime (even if it meant massacring thousands of innocents).[7] The task of weaving these themes into a narrative fell upon Malle's shoulders, and though his basic story never changed — (a young, naive man enlists, and joins the wrong side for the right reasons, and is eventually executed), the period and setting evolved through two additional stages before Malle zeroed in on World War II.

Europe, 1970: after reading a 1969 *Esquire* article on Lt. William J. Calley, Jr. — a soldier court-martialed for the My Lai massacre in Vietnam, who insisted he was "only doing his job" — Malle perceived yet another correlation to his collaboration project, and briefly considered filtering his themes through the lens of American involvement in southeast Asia. Yet as soon as the idea hit, he realized he needed to place the subject in another time and period: the ongoing Vietnam War would be far better suited for an American filmmaker.

Mexico, 1971: shortly after the release of *Souffle au coeur*, actress Gila von Weitershausen gave birth to Louis Malle's only son, Manuel Cuotemoc, just outside of Mexico City. Meanwhile, the director and his paramour watched in horror as chaos engulfed the country around them. Though the 1968 revolutions had long since ended, student protests continued, and the Mexican government responded by pulling juvenile delinquents ("Halcones") from the slums and — in lieu of throwing them into jail — trained the youth as para-military police, programmed to infiltrate student protests and deliberately create havoc with guns, clubs, and knives, slaying dozens. Malle considered the "banality of evil" angle from the haunting perspective of one of the infiltrators (or "halcones"), and spent weeks working on a Mexican phase of his collaboration project, tentatively called *Los Halcones*.[8] Though the police had hidden the Halcones deliberately, Malle managed to track down one or two of them and wrote a 20-page treatment.[9] Yet he concludes:

> Of course, I could not do this film. Rodolfo Etcheveria, the [Mexican] president's brother, an actor on his way to becoming a director of Mexican cinema, told me sadly, "You shouldn't touch the "Halcones," that's a subject much too delicate, too scandalous! My brother is on his way to trying to eliminate police corruption, but he has to take into account the strong opposition within his party. You are welcome to do it, but for pity's sake, choose another subject![10]

Etcheveria's discouragement carried Malle back to the idea of keeping his "collaboration project" within the boundaries of World War II (i.e., Nazi collaboration within France). Released only two years prior, Marcel Ophüls's legendary documentary *La Chagrin et la pitié*—the first mainstream nonfiction treatment of French collaboration—opened at a small cinema on the Parisian left bank (on April 5, 1971) and became an international *succès d'estime*. Despite waves of controversy that it generated among right-wing factions, Ophüls's film opened the door for Malle to explore collaboration within the boundaries of fiction.

Around 1972, with *Humain, trop humain* and *Place de la République* in the can, Malle settled into Coual (his house on the Causse du Lot) and began preproduction research. By this point, *Lacombe* had gone through its full evolution. Malle located a Toulouse historian with a filing cabinet full records and names of citizens, tracked down some of the individuals, and convinced them to talk, in confidence. He subsequently enlisted the help of 27-year-old novelist Patrick Modiano as co-screenwriter, a man whose three prior novels (*La Place de l'Étoile, La Ronde de nuit, Les Boulevards de ceinture*) dealt explicitly with the themes of "humiliation, cowardice, treason, and—across all of its manifestations—the quest for an identity" in World War II.[11] Though Malle and Modiano originally began with the concept of two main characters—a young country boy who journeys to Toulouse, where he becomes a bodyguard to a trafficker on the black market—the co-writers ultimately dismissed the idea as a cliché, and stuck to the concept of one figure, a boy in his late teens who simply joins the Gestapo out of misconstrued loyalty to his country, and is executed for his actions. Little did they foresee the controversy that would accompany this angle, or the wounds it would reopen in the collective unconscious of their countrymen.

Synopsis

Southwest France, June 1944. Following the Allied invasion of Normandy, a 17-year-old farm boy named Lucien Lacombe (Pierre Blaise) works at a local geriatric hospital under the aegis of several nuns, where he spends his days mopping floors and emptying chamber pots. After killing a thrush with a slingshot, he finishes his shift, climbs onto his bicycle, and heads back to his village. But upon arriving home, he is enraged to discover his father's incarceration as a P.O.W. in a German camp and his mother's ongoing affair with the landlord. Mme. Lacombe's decision to rent the house to strangers only compounds Lucien's aggravation. Lucien's brother, Joseph, is now an integral part of the Resistance.

Eager to do his part for France as well, Lucien shoots several hares with a rifle and carries the carcasses to Peyssac (Jean Bousquet), the village schoolteacher, who doubles as the local head of the underground. Lucien tries to use the rabbits as a leverage point for enlistment in the *maquis*, but Peyssac dismisses Lucien as "too young." Later, while cycling down a country road, Lucien accidentally punctures the tire of his bicycle and pushes it back to the village, arriving in town past curfew. Gestapo agents arrest Lucien and drag him into a hotel that doubles as their headquarters.

Accepted warmly and plied with cocktail, Lucien soon discovers that his favorite cycling champion, Aubert (Pierre Decazes) is now a Gestapo agent (who resides at the hotel), which impresses him immensely and begins to sway his loyalties. Questioned about the leader of the local resistance, Lucien — still reeling from rejection — squeals on the infuriated Peyssac. The Gestapo agents drag the resistance leader off to be tortured; Lucien joins their ranks the next morning.

Now inducted into the den of evil, Lucien accepts a gun from his superiors and accompanies Nazi aristocrat Jean-Bernard de Voisin to be fitted for a suit by the infamous Jewish tailor Albert Horn (Holger Löwenadler). Albert has been unofficially granted asylum in the town with his beautiful daughter France (Aurore Clément) and his elderly mother (Thérèse Giehse) in exchange for assisting the Nazis with his tailoring skills. Over time, Lucien falls in love with the urbane and sophisticated France Horn, to the chagrin and disgust of her father, whom Lacombe bullies and intimidates constantly. Though France initially refuses to return Lucien's affections, she eventually agrees to accompany him to a Gestapo dance and, reeling from the anti–Semitic insults that one of Lucien's jilted ex-lovers hurls at her, runs to Lucien's arms. The two make love in one of the back rooms of the hotel turned Gestapo outpost, and Lucien moves into the Horn household.

Repulsed and revolted, Albert dons his finest suit and heads down to the Gestapo hotel one afternoon to talk "man-to-man" with Lucien; the boy attempts to guide Horn out unnoticed, but a Gestapo agent, Faure (René Bouloc), catches the two and arrests Horn, dragging him off to a concentration camp. Lucien and a soldier head back to the Horn household to arrest France and her grandmother, but the soldier steals Albert's watch, leaving Lucien indignant. While Lucien follows the Horns out of the apartment (with the soldier leading the way), he whips out a gun and shoots down the Gestapo officer. Stealing the soldier's vehicle, Lucien, France, and Mme. Horn flee into the countryside and move into an abandoned farmhouse after the auto breaks down. For the next several months, Lucien provides for the women by hunting and trapping game. A final intertitle informs us that Lucien was tried, sentenced to death, and executed by a Resistance military tribunal in October 1944.

ANALYSIS

None of Louis Malle's films—not even *Souffle au cœur* or *Pretty Baby*—have been as misunderstood or as steeped in ill-advised controversy as *Lacombe, Lucien*. Often misread as an impassioned apologetic for French Nazi collaboration during World War II, the deliberate moral and philosophical ambiguity of the piece lifts it above such accusations.

Two traditional interpretations flank the motion picture: Pauline Kael's reading — about "a boy who doesn't achieve a fully human identity ... who has an empty space where feelings beyond the purely instinctual are supposed to be"[12]— paints Lucien Lacombe as a sociopathic figure, a psychological cripple. Yet Manuel Malle traces the horror generated by his father's film to "the sobering realization that anyone is capable of the atrocities 17-year-old Lucien Lacombe indirectly perpetuates."[13]

This suggestion points to a Nietzschean inversion — the Marxist flipside of *der Über-mensch,* where the everyman fills the role of the overman, fueled by the power surging through the proletariat. The schism of interpretation between (Manuel) Malle and Kael can be primarily attributed to cultural lensing.

Throughout the motion picture, co-screenwriters Malle and Modiano draw striking parallels between the instinctive predation and conscienceless bloodshed necessary for survival as a member of French bucolia, and the torture and violence necessary to succeed as Gestapo terrorist. Ergo, the scenarists flood the audience with a barrage of hunting metaphors — Lucien shoots rabbits, beats a chicken unconscious and knocks its head off with his fist, slingshots a thrush. As Manuel Malle observes, the common American interpretation of such acts as uniquely "barbaric" or "sociopathic" is a cultural distortion. Not only are hunting rabbits and beheading chickens second nature to a southern French farm boy, but (as the striking close-ups of Pierre Blaise reveal while he guns down hares) trigger-pulling yields an almost visceral physical pleasure for him. Malle and Modiano showcase, ever so disturbingly, how such behavior shares a common psychological origin with grisly bloodshed or torture of war prisoners: it requires one to operate purely on the level of animal instinct — not necessarily abandoning conscience altogether,[14] but doing so to the extent that one can see one's task through to its conclusion ("as workaday as running an office") without allowing the question of another creature's feelings to paralyze the central course of action. This also explains the shocking moment of transition in scene 24 when Malle depicts a group of Gestapo militiamen (including Lucien) advancing with rifles on members of the *maquis,* yet has Lucien wheel around and blow away a rabbit.

Yet in the end, the two aforementioned readings of the film hold equal weight and complement each other. In the Kaelian sense, the inability of rural citizens to think hyper-instinctively qualifies as an intrinsically pathological trait, illustrated by Lucien's failure to display a healthy conscience or to intervene in the face of Nazi torture. Yet in the (Manuel) Malleian sense, the screenwriters suggest repeatedly that this psychological handicap represents a universal quality among agrarian citizens in Europe. Farm workers and shepherds have subconsciously confined themselves to a para-instinctive spectrum of *vita activa* as a prerequisite for day-to-day survival, so that anyone — on a lower, bucolic social tier — could theoretically fall into Lucien's behavioral pattern. Consider Blaise's haunting insight: "I can understand Lucien. He was a country boy ... like me, and in the country you're too busy, if you're poor, to worry about principles. It's the next meal that counts."[15] A combination of the two ideas remains far more daring and scathing than a piece of Nazi apologetic because it suggests a horrific truth: like the Black Plague, the virulent disease of "animalistic, ultra-instinctive behavior" permeates the pastoral classes of French society.[16]

John Simon observes, "*Lacombe, Lucien* is remarkable, first, because it brings to film perhaps better than ever before ... the sense of the banality of evil."[17] Indeed, Malle and Modiano characterize "evil" and "dark" impulses as so widespread that they transcend political persuasion, demagogy evolving on both ends of the ideological spectrum. In one of the film's most haunting scenes (epitomizing this idea), schoolteacher-cum-*maquis* leader Peyssac turns a backward student into the butt of a class joke, with himself as comedian:

PEYSSAC (*excessively*): Maurice, I'm afraid there's not much hope for you.... Your case is hopeless. Do you see what you did? ... No, I don't mean the smudges on the paper from your dirty hands. I mean your spelling: you think "stormy" is written "S-T-A-U-R-M-Y"? Well (*shrugging his shoulders*) what can I say? I also have to admit one doesn't have to know how to spell to be a shepherd. (*He tosses Maurice's text back onto his desk, in a gesture of weariness.*)

Peyssac's little joke draws a predictably easy response from the other pupils, who burst out laughing.[18]

Dr. Claretta M. Tonetti (*Bernardo Bertolucci: The Cinema of Ambiguity*) comments, "Though it may sound paradoxical, *Lacombe, Lucien* manages to be self-deterministic and fatalistic concurrently."[19] In this regard, Malle captures perfectly the eternal Christian paradox—the interwoven tapestry of alternately Calvinistic and Arminian threads—that form Lucien's destiny. As a grand tragedy in the Shakespearean mold, seemingly uncontrollable forces work hand-in-hand with Lucien's choices to propel him toward Resistance-fueled death.

Fatalistically, Lucien's socially cultivated instinctiveness may correspond perfectly to the suitability of his Gestapo role, yet this fatality is idiosyncratic. It would be shortsighted to interpret Manuel Malle's observation as an indication that the ill-destined boy is a cipher, into which any individual could be plugged. Even Sarris counterbalances his comment—"Malle's eponymous non-hero ... represents every neatly-dressed wretch who ever hit the streets in search of a job"—with, "Then one day, the Gestapo offers a position of power and authority," suggesting that the world around Lucien—or, more specifically, that his unique familial dynamic—imparted a nihilistic sense of futility and impotence that the boy must overcome psychologically, via his Nazi enlistment. Paternally shorn, saddled with feelings of maternal neglect and betrayal—because Mme. Lacombe has "adopted" members of another family as boarders in the absence of her husband and sons—insignificance and helplessness at the sight of another family in his home (and using his father's items) overwhelm Lucien and push him not in the direction of fascism *per se*, but simply in the direction of a surrogate family.[20] The flat tire (like the thunder that awakens Georges Poujouly's character, Louis, in *Ascenseur*) contributes to Lucien's Nazi recruitment yet lies completely beyond his control.

Critic Jan Dawson's characterization of Lucien's choice as "A heads or tails affair"[21] is accurate and perceptive, yet reveals a hidden truth about the film: *Lacombe* gives equal weight to fatalism and self-determinism, but evokes self-determinism modernistically, in a void of action. The film's Calvinism runs hand-in-hand not with Lucien's pronounced series of decisions, but with a vacuum encapsulating Lucien's failure to take an active role—a use of purely reactionary behavior as political dissection. The most common misperception of the film involves the assumption that because Lucien consistently fails to look beyond the moment in his response patterns, Malle and Modiano render him completely helpless and impotent: "a passive, spineless marshmallow,"[22] and a marionette (along the lines of Billy Pilgrim, in the Vonnegut novel and Stephen Geller adaptation of *Slaughterhouse-Five*).[23] Such is not the case — Lucien may function as a purely, even pathetically reactionary character (possessor of a will and instinct that change by the moment depending upon the situation at hand), but he is still capable of shaping his destiny — the platonic nature and force of self-determinism unaltered. The film's conclusion underscores this fact: though the audience feels certain that Lacombe will allow France and her grandmother to be captured and deported by the Gestapo, the one small gesture of the guard pocketing Lucien's watch (and one must realize, given Lucien Lacombe's nature, that *only* this theft, nothing beyond the moment, not even the larger force of romantic love, influences Lucien) demonstrates the power — heretofore unused — of Lucien to shape his own destiny, when he whips out a gun and murders the guard in front of France Horn and her grandmother. It is a power that — prior to this scene — could have been interpreted as completely absent. Such is not the case.

Lacombe thus fulfills philosophical precepts introduced by Malle two decades prior, in *Ascenseur pour l'échafaud*. Yet here, instead of simply dissecting fate and revealing it as a collective phenomenon (*Elevator*), Malle demonstrates — inversely — how, in the hands of a reactionary character, the force of collective fatality can shape the mold almost completely for individual decisions. The moral ambiguity of Lucien's path springs from the co-scenarist and director's deliberate refusal to trace responsibility for actions to the fatalistic or deterministic levels. This explains why interpretations of the film as a piece of apologetics fail under the weight of critical myopia: the truth hangs, suspended, between the Calvinist and Arminian poles.[24]

Lacombe operates in Malle's favorite realm — the gray area between the black and white extremes of Western ethos. As French critics noted, *Lucien* is the quintessential amanichean Malle picture.[25] Malle depicts Lucien's bullying behavior, his condemnable need to belittle others (as when he threatens Albert Horn by using his finger as a gun and poking the old man in the chest), and his passivity in the face of darkness — both of which render him guilty — yet Malle also illustrates "just how far the [Nazi ideology] is from anything Lucien has ever thought about,"[26] partially absolving his iniquity. With *Lacombe*, Malle delves into some of the same philosophical territory as Hannah Arendt's memoir *Eichmann in Jerusalem* — just as Arendt claims that Eichmann was only doing his job, Lucien's crime is that he has followed orders. Yet the implications of Malle's case study are more horrifying and upsetting than Arendt's: unlike Eichmann, Lucien remains ignorant of anything outside of himself (ignorant of the Holocaust, and probably incapable of even comprehending the broad philosophical framework that belies fascism). Arendt's account thus lacks the tragic overtones of *Lacombe* — the simple gesture of Lucien working through the Pétain broadcast, unaffected, undeterred, and his pure, astonishing ignorance of current events (Malle's decision to situate the film in 1944, following the Allied deployment at Normandy, was highly deliberate) are interwoven into a grand, sweeping tragic tapestry. One could, at the worst, accuse Malle of deliberately seeking out and shaping for his cameras that one particular situation with a murky ethos, as a manipulative ploy to support his relativist allegory, were it not for the film's overwhelming credulity. During background research for *Lacombe*, Malle even located a boy named Hercule, in a village similar to that of the narrative, whose life and trajectory bear a note-for-note resemblance to Lucien's.[27]

The film demands that each viewer independently define the extent to which Lucien — a character who operates in a sphere slightly severed from reality — should claim responsibility for his or her actions. In one sense, Lucien Lacombe anticipates the observation made by André Gregory in Malle's *My Dinner with André*— walking around in "an insane dream world," Lucien Lacombe — like a primitive animal — never seems to carry full self-awareness. Following lovemaking, as he lies beside France Horn's nude body, he must actually put his hand out and stroke her bare back, as if attempting to reestablish tactile contact with the external world.

Visually, Malle and cinematographer Tonino Delli Colli's approach for *Lacombe* challenges the director's aesthetic evocation of *The Fire Within* (see Chapter 6). Whereas in *Le Feu follet* director Malle and cinematographer Ghislain Cloquet create a distinctive aesthetic (a high-contrast, black-and-white, psycho-realist aesthetic) that permeates and defines the onscreen characters and events— an active aesthetic — *Lacombe* utilizes a passive aesthetic: a deliberately distant, flat perspective, with an undefined visual quality, to eliminate distractions and draw emphasis solely to the field of action, to the characters' mannerisms and faces. This heightened reliance on observation enables the audience to self-reflexively contemplate the nature of voyeurism itself.

While *Lacombe* never completely sacrifices Malleian depth (note the deep focus of the opening shot, where Malle calls attention to Lucien's diligence in the foreground by first directing audience attention to Lucien less energetic co-worker, in the background and accentuating the contrast between the two); this is the exception and not the rule — the picture is, spatially, one of the most two-dimensional of Malle's endeavors. In this way, the director accentuates a level of contrast, where the characters stand out, in all of their wonderful psychological and ethical multi-dimensionality, against the flatness of the *mise en scène*.

Moreover, *Lucien* attempts the kinesthetic opposite of *Monde du silence*. *Lacombe*'s aesthetic has added political implications; the audience is never granted kinesthetic empowerment, but held at a distance, viewers more potently aware of their own helplessness and sheer inability to act or intervene in the face of a slowly-unfolding European tragedy, particularly in the countless instances when Lucien Lacombe fails to take a stand and carve his own path. This imposition of passivity correlates markedly to the nature of a "forced reactionary" political attitude in the audience, and — of course — ironically makes each viewer more acutely aware of the need for political progressivism. Moreover, Malle and Modiano cull terror from the chasm between the audience's recognition and Lucien's utter ignorance, in several distinct areas: idelogically (his blindness to the dangers of the politic to which he contributes), psycho-sexually (given the gentle and subtle implications of sado-masochism in the Nazi camp, between M. Tonin and Lucienne) and historically (Lucien remains profoundly ignorant of the news broadcasts which reveal the Allied foothold).

Critics such as Andrew Sarris who attack the deliberately slow, stated pace of *Lacombe* are missing the point. The film is a wholly observational work — one watches it as one watches a documentary — a technique promulgated and enabled by Malle's abandonment of classic narrative structure. Events in *Lacombe* appear to unfold (*déroule*) independently of a larger architectural schema; hence the picture's overwhelmingly slow, deliberate, stated pace, and its non-ending, its absence of resolution.

Yet the temptation to interpret *Lacombe* as a piece of Nietzschean nihilism must be avoided. Even though Malle deliberately, consciously and wisely refuses to provide a moral or allegorical resolution — a tidy, upbeat ending to Lucien's life — it would be fallacious to interpret this (see Ebert's comment, referenced in the Introduction) as the "absence of a message" in the film. One must remind oneself that the story unfolds almost entirely within the Gestapo camp. The *film-as-a-whole* carries perhaps more concrete meaning than any other Malle feature, but if one interprets the events in the light of Nietzschean futility, they must be interpreted as such within the framework of Lucien's life and his decision-making process (harkening back to Malle's layer of self-determinism), and one can argue that Lucien's path has yielded the consequence of nihilism because he belongs to a Gestapo camp whose belief in the tenets of Nietzsche is a "self-fulfilling prophecy." The philosopher may have grounded *The Will to Power* in philosophies which — to Hitler and his cronies — suggested that the Nazis would triumph above all and assume the status of a "super race," but he also wrote in the same volume that within the context of nihilism, "becoming has no goal."[28] It would seem (not only given Lucien's fate but given the fate of the entire Gestapo camp) that the Nazis focused too heavily on one aspect of Nietzsche's philosophical structure yet ignored a second — the futility that yields destruction. The meaningless non-ending of the film echoes this — but how better to demonstrate the deception, the illusoriness — of Lucien's "progression" within the Gestapo camp than to reveal that his constant belief in becoming something important *via* the assumption of power, status, etc. is nothing more than an unadulterated lie? By blindly following his Gestapo contemporaries, Lucien — a figure completely ignorant of philosophy and, daresay, incapable of even comprehending philosophy — has unknowingly trapped himself in their self-perpetuating psychological and philosophical, Nietzschean prison that sends the Nazis careening helplessly toward death, shaping *Lucien* as Malle's great modern tragedy.

CRITICAL RESPONSE

American critics responded favorably to *Lucien*; the most positive acclaim comes from Pauline Kael, who hails it as one of the most accomplished films of the early seventies and "one of the least banal films ever made."[29] She declares, "Malle is looking for something that he doesn't have the tools or the temperament to grab hold of, and he's catching it anyway.... Somehow ... he gets sounds that nobody's ever heard before."[30] Andrew Sarris summarizes his response by concluding, "[Malle's] enactment of the banality and bureaucracy of evil plays somewhat slowly because of the inexperience of the lead players, but many images stay in the mind with a fateful force."[31] Bruce Williamson, of *Playboy*, looks somewhat unfavorably upon the film, writing, "[*Lucien*] hardly deserves to be called a masterpiece," yet affirms, "Malle's direction is flawless—restrained and compassionate but never sentimentalized."[32]

Most of the significant objections to the film came from Europe—as previously noted, *Lacombe* divided French critics in half. An April 1974 published debate between Rene Andrieu and Malle in *Humanité dimanche*, reveals the misinterpretation of *Lucien* as a piece of Nazi apologetic. Though Andrieu opens by writing, "*Lacombe, Lucien* isn't a film that leaves us unscathed, whether or not we have experienced the Occupation. The situations and characters established by Malle strike us personally and directly,"[33] he systematically attacks the film as sympathetic to the Nazi cause by citing Malraux's quote that "anyone risks becoming fascistic if he doesn't have fidelity behind him."[34] A more positive response came from the pen of Marcel Martin, who, writing for *L'Écran*, declares, "Here we have a grand and beautiful film, the best film, no doubt, of Louis Malle, a work that is both intelligent and accomplished, that captivates and yet disturbs."[35]

In a tragic turn of events, 23-year-old actor Pierre Blaise—a close friend of the Malles—died in an automobile crash one year after *Lacombe*'s release, on August 31, 1975, on the outskirts of Montauban, France.[36] He appeared in only three additional films before his untimely passing: Roger Coggio's *Noces de porcelain* (1974), Mauro Bolognini's *Per le antiche scale* (1975), and Dennis Berry's *Le Grand Délire* (1975).

13

Black Moon — 1975

Timeless, Placeless, Senseless

> "Accompanying will be a phantasmagoria, a real one, rushing toward the screen, in over the heads of the audiences ... the images often changing scale so quickly, so unpredictably, that you're apt now and then to get a bit of lime-green in with your rose, as they say. The scenes are highlights from Pirate's career as a fantasist-surrogate, and go back to when he was carrying ... the mark of Youthful Folly growing in an unmistakable Mongoloid point, right out of the middle of his head."
> — Thomas Pynchon, *Gravity's Rainbow*

> "Reason flies / When following the senses, on clipped wings."
> — Dante Aligheri, "Paradiso," 2, *The Divine Comedy*

BACKGROUND

Louis Malle's psychological and spiritual rebirth in India yielded a gradual transformation of his work between 1968 and 1975.[1] If *Le Souffle au cœur* (see Chapter 10) manifests the director's near-abandonment of Western ethos as a guiding force for the narrative yet preserves traditional dramatic architecture, *Lacombe, Lucien* carries Malle to the next outpost in his East-West passage, combining his fresh humanism with the partial abandonment of Western narrative structure, for a work that approaches the level of docudrama and lifts its scenes above scripted conflict, encouraging the audience to rely largely on behavioral observation. Pauline Kael thus caps her review of *Lacombe* with a hauntingly incisive perception:

> Malle's early films were very precise, the work of an orderly, classical mind; they were films by a Frenchman who believed in reason, and although the Indian series brought out the humanist in him, he remained the *raissoneur*. This time, he's working on a subject that can't be thought out, and he's going on instinct ... He's looking for something he doesn't have the tools or the temperament to grab hold of, and he's catching it anyway. He's in the process of turning himself inside out.[2]

Fifteen-year-old Lily (Cathryn Harrison) receives "messages" from the male warrior Lily (Joe Dallesandro) when he seductively moves his fingers up and down her back in the Freudian fantasy *Black Moon.*

Between 1974 and 1975, Malle traveled one step beyond *Lacombe*, emerging with *Black Moon*, an experimental dystopian fantasy that carried him ever closer to Warhol-Mekas-Anger territory. Though the film never completely abandons narrative architecture, Malle drops all ideological threads that link *Moon*'s scenes and acts coherently (and couples this with a humanistic moral suspension), emerging with an arcane fantasist parable that defies categorization and interpretation.

Perhaps because *Black Moon*'s origins are so sketchy and mysterious—indeed, purportedly unclear to Malle himself—in no published source does the director tell a full and smooth story about the parturition of the film. Surrealist expert and frequent Malle collaborator Jean-Claude Carrière—when asked if Louis ever approached him to co-write the piece—reflects, "*Black Moon* ... Louis wanted to make as a very personal experience, no doubt about it. He didn't even talk to me about it."[3] A conversation did transpire between stage legend Thérèse Giehse (France's grandmother in *Lacombe, Lucien*) and Malle on the set of *Lacombe*, that indirectly precipitated *Black Moon*. The filmmaker confessed his professional adoration of Giehse to her and mentioned how much he would love to re-collaborate with her on a second film project, giving her a more centralized role. Having observed Malle's skill at eliciting subtle, telling behavior from his actors, Giehse recommended that he script and direct a film entirely devoid of dialogue.[4]

Malle issued contradictory stories about the timing of the ideas that inspired the plot points of *Black Moon*—ideas that came to him while staying in his family's country home in the south of France. According to the director's reminiscences in *Louis Malle par Louis Malle*, inspiration hit while he edited *Lacombe*[5]—probably in the late winter of 1973, for *Lucien* debuted in French movie houses on January 30, 1974.[6] Yet in *Malle on Malle*, the director places the same inspiration slightly later—in the middle of the debates *Lucien* elicited, weeks or months after the film's release. This would posit the genesis of *Moon* in the late winter or early spring of 1974.[7,8]

Regardless, Malle's recollections paint a picture of him returning to the Beghin house on the Causse du Lot in complete or near-complete isolation (as he did so often in the early seventies in-between projects, to "recharge" creatively), and having a series of vivid and surrealistic dreams that inspired him to write the motion picture. Malle felt that, "*Lacombe* and *Souffle* having earned substantial box office, the time was ripe for experimentation."[9] Capitalizing on his great respect for (and envy of) the surrealists, he attempted to recapture in film form the Bretonian technique of automatic writing, by weaving a melange of his dreams into a screenplay. The director wanted to begin with an unusually short script, and improvise dramatic events and character development on-set, on a scene-by-scene basis. In the only dream from this period that Malle recounts in detail (which crept into the film), Thérèse Giehse (France Horn's grandmother in *Lacombe, Lucien*) lay confined to Malle's bed and would not budge.[10] The director later listed a number of disparate dream-spun details that also found their way into the picture: "a badger run over by a car in the middle of the road ... a young girl who discovers a civil war and loses herself in the savage environs of my house; the house itself becoming a labyrinth, a maze, Noah's Ark; a quick-tempered rat, a sententious unicorn ... a universe that came from far off ... from my childhood."[11]

The director assembled a motley cast including Giehse; 15-year-old Cathryn Harrison (Rex's granddaughter, fresh from her first appearance, at 12, in Altman's *Images*); Alexandra Stewart (of *Feu follet*); and American underground star Joe Dallesandro (made famous by Warhol and Morrissey in their "Factory" productions *Flesh*, *Trash*, *Heat*, *Lonesome Cowboys*, and *Andy Warhol's Dracula*), who took the role when Malle's first choice—Terence Stamp (*The Mind of Mr. Soames*) declined.[12] The director wove together a short, fantasy-laced screenplay with much room for experimentation and improvisation, hiring Joyce Buñuel, Luis's daughter-in-law (*Tattoo*) to write minimal patches of dialogue for the film. *Black Moon* began shooting during the winter[13] of 1974-5, and arrived at French cinemas on September 24, 1975.[14]

Synopsis

At some point in the not-so-distant future, the world has descended into a dystopian state. As a badger noses its way across a country road just after dusk, a compact car speeds by and flattens the creature. The driver, a fair-haired girl of about 15 years named Lily (Cathryn Harrison), stops, climbs out of the car and inspects the roadkill. When the distant sputtering of gunfire fills the air, she climbs back into the vehicle and continues driving. On the car radio, she hears a broadcaster (Louis Malle, uncredited) bemoan "the crime and vice that are being committed in the large cities of the world."

Early the following morning, while still driving down the same highway, Lily discovers evidence of a massive, grotesque civil war that has erupted between genders: a battered, bloodied female corpse lies beside the road, and a platoon of all-male soldiers control a roadblock that prevents Lily from continuing her journey unscathed. Stopping the car abruptly, Lily witnesses one of the soldiers kissing a terrified woman — presumably his significant other — before joining his compatriots to extinguish all of the females (in a line-up) with subatomic machine guns. One of the generals approaches the car and discovers Lily's gender when he remove her hat and her blonde hair cascades down. Shaking with fear, she slams on the accelerator and speeds around the blockage, the men firing volleys at her car in an unfruitful attempt to end her flight.

Lily subsequently arrives at a pasture, inhabited by a flock of sheep, whose shepherd hangs, his body limp, from a tree branch. The animals bleat, whine, and stomp their feet, stampeding toward Lily furiously; the terrified girl races back to her car and continues driving. After making a brief stop at a clearing where a platoon of female soldiers laughingly torture one of their own, Lily flees her car on foot and winds up at a huge, rambling country house. Later, she rests languidly in the pasture outside of the estate, lazily watching a black caterpillar descend a leaf. She encounters a shaggy black unicorn (voiced by Thérèse Giehse — uncredited in this role) galloping through the pasture, flowers that squeal when they are stepped on, a female warrior (Alexandra Stewart) who trots past, wordlessly, on horseback, and a group of ever-screaming naked children who chase a giant sow.

Upon entering the house, Lily approaches a huge kitchen table with a tall glass of milk atop it; as she lifts the glass to drink, a smaller pig on a chair grunts angrily at her. Venturing upstairs, she discovers a cat who plays the piano by strolling up and down the keyboard, and a vicious, cantankerous old woman (also Giehse) who lies confined to her bed, stricken by illness, yet corresponds with a giant black rat atop her nightstand (in an unintelligible, unidentifiable dialect) and periodically is summoned by an unseen figure on a ham radio, to whom she voices complaints and insulting observations about Lily.

The woman stops moving abruptly and evinces no sign of breath. Assuming she is dead, Lily — who suddenly hears a gentleman singing an aria outside — races over to the window and espies a male warrior (Joe Dallesandro), a fraternal twin of the female warrior she encountered previously, tending a huge bonfire. Lily races down, grabs him, and attempts to notify him of the woman's death, but he appears oblivious and begins to stroke her face and upper body seductively, while — in the distance — the female warrior rides past, herding the naked boys and girls and the pig around the side of the house.

The male warrior runs his fingers along the upper part of Lily's back and shoulders, and she speaks his thoughts aloud: he insists his name is Lily, as well. The sister reappears; she and her brother venture into the house. Lily races after them, shouting that the old woman, who she believes is their mother, has died. Upon entering the house, Lily finds the brother and sister feasting, a dead lamb on the table before them; they offer her a piece of meat, but she declines to partake. The twins continue upstairs, and as the sister hums a tune, and the brother places an antique hand mirror in front of the elderly woman's face, she is magically, inexplicably revived back to life. When she smacks her lips hungrily, the female warrior sterilizes her own breast and offers the teat to the woman, who nurses on it.

Lily falls asleep beside the fire; while she dozes, the male warrior kneels before her and begins to run his hands up her thigh, massaging it sensually. A smile spreads to Lily's lips, yet when the old woman observes the brother's behavior, she screams at him and forces him to leave the room, infuriating Lily, who shouts "Again, again!" at the window, browbeating the old woman and tearing her room apart in a fury.

Later, echoes of the war recur outside; Lily questions the woman about it, who bursts into hysterical laughter when Lily's underwear falls off (twice) and photographs Lily pulling up her panties. Vexed, Lily seizes the camera, rips the film out, and hides the apparatus. She eats a piece of cheese covered with ants and is nearly bitten by a garden snake who crawls out of one of the woman's drawers, then spends a period of time leafing through the old woman's photo album. After respotting the shaggy black unicorn, rambling through the garden, from the upstairs window, Lily leaves the bedroom by climbing through the window and scaling down the side of the house. She helps the brother bury an enemy (whose corpse she discovers being pecked over by chickens) and—after a chase—finally happens on the unicorn who speaks with the old woman's voice and accuses her of being an "emmerdeuse" (obnoxious or irritating person).

At dusk, Lily ventures back to the house, where the sister feeds the naked children around a giant table. After supper, she joins everyone upstairs; the children gather, surrounding a baby in a box of jewels (Louis Malle's newborn daughter Justine, uncredited) and two of the children sing *Tristan and Isolde* while Lily accompanies them on the piano. The next morning, as night fades into dawn, a massive eagle flies through the window, and the sword-wielding brother decapitates it. The brother and sister engage each other in a duel outside as the war encroaches upon the house and explosions blow the garden to pieces. Lily returns to the bedroom, climbs into the old woman's now-empty bed, and toys with the ham radio; a black snake appears and crawls up her bare leg and under her skirt. As flocks of sheep gather around the house, the unicorn reappears in front of Lily. She sterilizes her own breast, preparing to offer it to the creature.

ANALYSIS

As a post-apocalyptic fantasy overlaid with fairy tale elements, *Black Moon* explores the neuroses associated with a post-pubescent girl's burgeoning corporeal awareness and sexual consciousness. Because it qualifies as Louis Malle's most cryptic and eccentric endeavor, *Moon* never ceases to confound viewers or to split critical opinion. In fact, the motion picture so divided French critics upon release that their published essays interpret the same imagery in completely incongruous ways, with little overlap.

Moon also represents Malle's one and only plunge into the murky waters of the hardcore fantasy-laced art cinema that became *en vogue* among European directors of the mid-seventies, joining the ranks of Polanski's *What?* (1973), Zeno's *Vase de noces* (a.k.a. *Wedding Trough*, 1973), Berlanga's *Tamaño Natural* (1974), Arrabal's *¡Viva la muerte!* (1970) and Blier's *Calmos* (1976).[15] Like the aforementioned directors, Malle bathes his film in psychedelic residue from the late sixties and imbues the narrative with sexual themes, yet in Malle's hands, these themes remain buried, ever so delicately, on the level of subterranean Freudian symbolism.

Jean de Baroncelli writes of *Black Moon*, "When confronted with such a film, two attitudes are possible. We can try to decrypt the film by applying each image to a psychoanalytical grill ... or we can take in the film as an explosion of fantastic images, like a voyage that is a mixture of the marvelous and nightmarish."[16] The problem with the latter approach is that it means directly or indirectly interpreting the motion picture as a "dream film" (as many have)—a major redundancy. As Susan Sontag observes in an interview with Malle, "The 'dream idea' doesn't merit any attention. The cinema always consists of dreams, by definition."[17] And David Mamet echoes this idea in *On Directing Film*, when he writes, "The dream and the film are the juxtaposition of images ... to answer a question ... all film is, finally, a 'dream sequence.'"[18] More problematically, the "dream film" categorization fails to make the critical distinction between Malle's use of dreams as source material and his onscreen intentions, when the two are mutually exclusive.

Though documented many times that Malle pulled a series of "sensual images" from his own dreams to write the screenplay (Prédal: "*Black Moon* nourishes itself on dream images that the cineaste has dreamed for a long time, noting them meticulously, one at a time"),[19] *Black Moon* carefully avoids that quality of dreams to which Mamet most often alludes: their marvellous variation. Instead, the filmmaker travels to the opposite extreme, reveling in constant imagistic repetition. To build a narrative structure (and provide underpinnings to his gossameric story) Malle isolates eight to ten archetypes from a cross-cultural mélange of mythologies—a badger, a horse, twin warriors, a unicorn, a rat, a group of savage naked children chasing a pig, a war between genders, an eagle (ultimately decapitated), a cat, the lily flower, the black moon itself—and reiterates them eight, ten, twelve or more times in various couplings and behavioral patterns. Malle characterizes his own narrative architecture for *Black Moon* as highly musical in nature, with recurrences of the archetypes substituted for classical riffs, and Lily's risk-filled, near-catastrophic journey to the house as "l'ouverture"—the orchestral overture of the piece.[20]

Similarly, *Black Moon*'s cinematographic approach carries it away from the visual quality of dreams. The picture never once employs dreamlike aesthetic or spatial distortion. At no time does *Moon* capture or even attempt to catch the off-kilter visual quality of the nightscape, rendering it incomparable to—for example — Maya Deren and Alexander Hammid's *Meshes of the Afternoon* (1943, rev. 1958) or Chris Marker's *La Jetée*. Malle and famed Bergman cinematographer Sven Nykvist shoot the motion picture realistically, with an afantasist aesthetic,[21] not only emphasizing excessively gloomy, overcast skies and naturalist barren landscapes, but preserving the abrecht-ian depth of Malle's previous works. As in *Ascenseur* and *Feu follet*, life constantly seems to be unfolding in the distance, just beyond the confines of the frame, lend-ing proof of its existence to the audience with faint aural clues. The latter is most obvious when Lily periodically hears volleys of gunfire from miles away (the sugges-tion that the war is encroaching) and when — in a moment of sheer terror — the pack of furious, revenge-thirsty, shepherd-shorn rams and ewes make a shocking reap-pearance in front of the house at the film's conclusion. This beat implies that the ani-mals have been stalking Lily — and making their way toward the house — for the duration of the picture. The realist aesthetic and hyper-dimensionality of the film decrease the distance between the audience and the events by lending the onscreen environment credibility. *Moon* is surrealistic in the sense that Breton defined "objec-tive chance": "situations ... that ... appear to belong *at the same time* to the real series and to the ideal series of events."[22] By juxtaposing fantastic archetypes with a real-ist aesthetic and the realist mundanity of narrative repetition, Malle and Nykvist have cut straight to the heart of "the form of manifestation of necessity" that defines Surrealism.[23]

Some critical opinions to the contrary, *Black Moon* does not lack a narrative; rather, Malle buries its dramatic structure. Hence Susan Sontag's comment to Malle, "*Moon* functions ... as a succession of sensual moments that hide the narrative."[24] The disembodied voice on the radio (Malle's own) at the outset of the film provides the first significant clue, forewarning, "Shall I describe to you the crime and vice that is being committed in the large cities of the world?"[25] The inexplicitness of the sug-gestion renders the audience's glimpse that much more powerful: a fleeting vision of a point when the world has become so corrupt, so morally deviant and perverted and blood-soaked with stomach-turning cruelty that Armageddon has erupted, tor-turing the innocent and virginal. The central story of *Black Moon* in many ways resembles that of Malle's *Milou en mai:* in a time of sweeping upheaval, a small band of outsiders have fled into the country to avoid involvement. Some critics have inferred that prior to the film's outset, Lily is fleeing from an urban center (Paris? London? Vienna?) into the countryside,[26] only to run headfirst into more violence. It would be irresponsible to posit this conclusion as definitive, but the idea itself is semi-plausible. If we accept everything onscreen as literal and asymbolic, Lily must surely have fled from a self-destructing metropolis — it is one of the only sound pos-sibilities. Yet if we read everything onscreen as allegorical, it means placing Lily's ori-gins into the same category as — say — Ned Merrill's (Burt Lancaster) origins prior to the outset of Frank Perry's *The Swimmer* (1968). In other words, if *Black Moon* operates in a purely allegorical, heavily symbolic realm, Lily's origins are nonexist-ent, for her journey simply represents an excursion into her own mind. Instead, the answer to the question of Lily's origins prior to the outset of the film — like the pic-ture itself — lies somewhere between the extremes of pure allegory and concealed narrative.

Malle's "buried narrative" carries a number of additional implications. Notably, the concepts of "life" and "death" have acquired unusual connotations for the bedrid-den old woman and the other residents of her country home. Within the realm of the story, death is no longer an absolute: one who appears dead in the permanent sense can suddenly be revived, but, in experiencing a resurrection, regresses psychically (hence the old woman's reversion to infantile behavior, smacking her lips and sucking on the female warrior's breast). Malle also implies that communication, in this microcosmic realm, can be accomplished nonverbally, by sending "messages" through the person's skin via touch. This is how Dallesandro's male warrior is able to send the young girl Lily messages without actually opening his mouth.

It is hardly accidental that the archetypes themselves should have multiple — even countless—connotations, or that Louis Malle should become so enmeshed in the idea of pulling off a Henry James adaptation later in life (*What Maisie Knew*). Like James, he wants to heighten imagistic multiplicativeness, enraptured by the process of audience interpretation. Thus, to fully appreciate the picture, one must not only acknowledge the deliberate, unavoidable plurality of interpretation, but agree to play Malle's game by devising a subjective interpretation of one's own. The table following this section provides a full assessment of the film's symbols for the adventurous; what follows is a very loose interpretation of the film's archetypal meaning — one of many possible readings.

Lily's name can be traced to the lily flower — a symbol of purity.[27] As Malle himself noted, *Black Moon* is a film that explores a young girl's neuroses and conflicting feelings when confronted with the onset of sexual maturation.[28] One can read the "black moon" symbol itself as the ghostly manifestation of Lily's neurosis. For her, passing from a chaste childhood into adulthood means facing the "presence of the absence" of childhood, and entering the "void of loneliness" typically symbolized by the "black moon."[29] The symbol, in turn, acquires a ghostly nature because it remains a neurosis, the product of Lily's mind, and never actually materializes. As "Lily," (the white flower) she is pure and virginal at the outset of the film, but the guns carried by the soldiers on the roadblock are most certainly phallic symbols to be used for symbolic rape. This is, in addition to the literal reality that the soldiers will kill Lily, exactly why she flees from them: the certainty that she is in danger specifically because of her gender — she feels threatened sexually. Taking this one step further, the caterpillar that Lily watches enables her to witness her own sexual maturation, externalized in front of her. The house itself that Lily visits could be emblematic of her own inner consciousness, or the visualization of that consciousness, where such a transformation will take place.

Later, though the male warrior begins to guide Lily through a sexual initiation by sliding his hands up her thigh and preparing to give her an orgasm, the old woman screams out to stop him. Not until the final scenes does Malle facilitate Lily's transformation from girl to woman, by hitting the audience with a shocking metaphor: a phallic snake slides up under Lily's dress, and the camera holds on her face for an uncomfortably long time. Once she has undergone this transition to womanhood — the metaphoric vaginal penetration[30] — she enters the maternal phase, and prepares her own breast for the unicorn as a kind of maternal rite-of-passage.

Meanwhile, a broader external reality unfolds around Lily. In the larger social realm, the degradation of mankind to the savage state is represented not only literally (via the soldiers) but allegorically, by the pig chased and surrounded by naked children.[31] The sow itself, the emblem of slime and filth, becomes a kind of maternal creature guiding the children in the ways of the old pre–Olympian world, the chthonic.

Malle counterbalances the film's human regression with a kind of super-evolution of the rest of the animal kingdom (outside of the sow), to the point where nature, after years of abuse at the hands of its caretakers, is rising up and reclaiming a position superior to mankind, usurping man's place in the absence of more sensible and moral behavior from the human populace. Hence the complaints of the squealing flowers, the rams' and ewes' thirst for revenge and their need to turn Lily into a scapegoat (Did they themselves somehow hang their shepherd as a kind of betrayal, or did the shepherd kill himself, betraying the animals?). This also explains the cat's attempts to play the piano, and the smaller pig's protests when Lily attempts to drink its milk, with quasi-human grunt-grunts.

The unicorn is an extremely ambiguous, multiplicative archetype. Malle tells Sontag, "She is very old, doubtless immortal. She was there before the humans, she stays after they are gone...." And yet, the director also affirms the more interesting possibility that "[The unicorn] may be the reincarnation of the old woman"[32]—an idea underscored by the fact that the creature speaks with the old woman's voice. Given the prior implications of mankind's descent into corruption ("the crime and the vice that are being committed in the large cities of the world") and the unicorn-as-godhead symbolism, one cannot help but draw parallels between the Giehse-reincarnation theory and the work of William Butler Yeats, who, in his poem "The Second Coming," advanced a theory of mankind's periodic descent into corruption, depravity, and violence, after which a rebirth would occur and homo sapiens would advance to a new evolutionary state.[33] Though the Giehse character lacks the moral corruption associated with a Yeatsian death prior to evolution, she does in fact suffer physiologically, and her maladies can be read as emblematic of mankind's spiritual and moral illness. It would thus make perfect sense that—ignoring the unicorn's earlier appearances in the garden and in Giehse's photo album—once the old woman dies, the unicorn would reappear in her stead, as her next "evolutionary form."

Although *Black Moon* functions well on some surrealistic levels, it is not a fully successful work. It needs to be more visually fantastic, and to have a clearer allegorical and metaphoric sublayer. An old-school surrealist would claim that to whatever degree the film fails, this is attributable to Malle's inability to fully adapt to the surrealist writing process, because—as the director later admitted—the *démarche* of on-set improvisatory filmmaking did not mesh with his sensibilities.[34] "Open realism," as Breton defined it, demands the systematic erosion or abandonment of all rational thought during the creative process. Automatic writing entails refusing to interpret one's work until that work has been finished, which is why Malle partially failed—he reveals that he couldn't help but (instinctively) reinterpret some of the images that came to him automatically. A film can be written and planned ahead of time, so if Malle sought to make a surrealist film, why did he not limit the automatism to the script-writing phase (for which it would be much more conducive) in lieu of attempting the impossible and employing automatism on a chaotic movie set? In addition to the logistical improbabilities of this route, Malle's recollections of the

Black Moon shoot suggest that he kept instinctively working toward the rational, trying to find a way to "work out" each scene,[35] instead of beginning with a surrealistic screenplay and filming it note-for-note, *sans* interpretation.

How ironic that although Malle seems to have concluded surrealist *automatism* impossible within the medium of cinema, Dalí and Buñuel most certainly accomplished it with their shorts *Un Chien Andalou* and *L'Age d'or*. An even greater irony lies in the fact that Breton himself, the veritable founder of automatism, responded to the idea of "surrealist cinema" with, "Three cheers for darkened rooms!"[36]

Major Symbols in *Black Moon*—
Mythological and Astrological Connotations

Black Moon—Personified by Lilith, Adam's first wife, this emblematizes the great void of nothingness and isolation—and, ofttimes, an inestimably destructive force that obliterates everything it touches. Yet it may either become a destructive or regenerative force depending on the chastity of the individual who comes into contact with it, and can represent the concentration of forbidden inner passions that must ultimately be conquered. May symbolize—paradoxically—either the concentration of chthonic elements, or the presence of the immaterial. Represented, geometrically, as two crescent moons set point to point with a straight line cutting through the nexus.[37]

Lily (the flower)—Represents, by turns, a symbol of purity, one of sexual potency (a tool of impregnation), and, like another symbolic flower—the violet—the concentration of unbridled lust and passion. Like the unicorn and the black moon, the lily can either exalt or obliterate.[41]

Rat—One of the twelve incarnations of the Chinese New Year. In both eastern and western cultures, it may hoard (hence the expression "pack rat"); the Chinese see it as "an emblem of timidity and meanness."[43] In western cultures (and Greek and Roman myth), indicative of chthonic earth-bound elements—dirt, soil and excrement. Is an avatar of tremendous prosperity and yet—because of its dishonest qualities, its propensity for theft—is typically distrusted.[44]

Caterpillar—In the *Upanishad*, symbolizes the process of becoming, transitioning from one stage of life into another, progressing

Unicorn—Often the embodiment of chastity. Symbolizes godhead, with the single horn (which, in Chinese mythology, only appears on the forehead of the male) representing the mongoloid point, a concentration of divine power. Its horn may represent a midpoint—a cosmic nexus—between sexual fertility and the psychic oneness that is a product of coital union.[38] In ancient medieval tapestries, the unicorn represents the Mother Goddess, and an embodiment of the pre-patriarchal feminine state.[39] Asian mythologies see it as the concentration of all positive behavioral qualities, and as a detector of purity and a predictor of wise regality. In such eastern cultures, often tied to the lunar, and, as such, reputed to have waged great battles against the sun.[40]

Badger—May represent one of two behavioral extremes—either a combination of sloth and culpability, or—from an eastern perspective—well-honed, yet clever and even deceitful, advanced intelligence and discernment.[42]

Eagle—In Asian cultures, represents temerity, fearlessness, acuity of vision and insight, power and leadership.[45] It can also appear as a destructive talisman or—conversely—in Greek mythologies, because of its capacity for flight (for ascending above the earth) as the purest essence of the Olympian, associated with the sun and commonly perched on the shoulder or scepter of Zeus. Across multiple cultures and belief systems, including Christianity (where it appears throughout Revelation), seen as the embodiment of the deific.[46]

Pig—A coprophagous creature that revels in dung, filth, muck, symbolizing egocentrism, gulosity. Almost universally (aside from Viet-

through various physical, spiritual, sexual, and biological evolutionary stages. In Roman cultures, it symbolizes the avaricious and the hideous.[47]

Horseman—Generally imbued with two polar opposite meanings—one involves triumph and a mastery of self-control (and the inner contentment that it produces), the other a completely opposite loss of inner control and control over external elements, and the terror and restlessness this may produce.[49]

Twins—As a somewhat unusual occurrence, a twin birth can suggest intervention from the gods; psychoanalytically, twins can symbolize the conflicting desires or warring impulses within the divided self. In the case of Castor and Pollux, for example, or Romulus and Remus, twins are often perceived, in innumerable cultures, as the offspring of deity and moral. Indian cultures—particularly the Pueblos—see twins as those who pave the way for a new world and do away with the old.[51]

namese cultures) seen as a filthy, gluttonous, stupid animal that savors and revels in mud and excrement. Egyptian cultures represented their goddess Nut as a sow in charge of a litter of piglets, and thus gave the essence of the porcine highly maternal connotations.[48]

Snake—Biblically, represented as the incarnation of evil—of extreme cunning and deception. In Freudian symbolism, the snake is a highly sexual, phallic animal. Asian cultures perceive it as a source of co-mingled fear and awe; in the first sense, can drain the life force of anyone with whom it comes into contact.[50]

House—Macrocosmic symbol that encapsulates the universe. If Buddhist symbolism ties the house to the human body,[52] Freudian and Jungian symbolism—particularly as it relates to dream imagery—perceive the house as the representation of the human consciousness. The Celtic saw the house as an indicator of the relationship between mankind and the gods; it may also emblematize the womb or—more broadly—the maternal.[53]

CRITICAL RESPONSE

Black Moon fared poorly in Europe and the United States, alienating viewers with its arcanum. Most critics panned the film. Particularly vicious and cutting is Pauline Kael, who writes in *The New Yorker*, "The surreal effects Malle uses don't connect with anything in his imagination, so there's no instinctive wit in them, no ambivalence, no friction. It's deadly … [Malle's] carried eclecticism too far with this apocalyptic *Francis, the Talking Unicorn*. Not everyone has it in him to be a fantasist."[54] And writing for *Cinéma*, Jean Roy comments, "What is really inadmissible here is that Malle has everything: 20 years of experience behind the camera; Thérèse Giehse, the creation of Brecht; Joe Dallesandro of *Andy Warhol's Dracula*, in which he showed us the acting potential he had hidden; Sven Nykvist, Bergman's cinematographer for 30 years. And with all this, the film accomplishes nothing."[55]

Yet one discovers a few happy exceptions: Susan Sontag finds the film mesmerizing and underrated and offers up fascinating, bristling insights in her interview with Malle, interpreting it on a level unknown to even the writer-director. According to Malle, the film fascinated child psychologists upon release, who analyzed it *ad nauseam*.[56] Gilles Colpart, writing for *La Révue du cinéma*, exalts the film wholeheartedly, commenting:

> This most recent film of Malle's functions as the outcome of an evolution in expression, of naturalism (fiction filmed like a documentary), of a formal and visual liberation. All the themes crystallize, in an explosion of representation of objects and forms, clearly marked by surrealism, that—at first glance—can't help but surprise the viewer.[57]

Moreover, Gene Moskowitz champions the film in *Variety* and calls *Moon* "strikingly photographed by Sven Nykvist" and "both intriguing and ambitious," and even "riveting." Even as he acknowledges that it "goes astray" in its second half, he remarks, "[*Moon*] still leaves an effect long after the pic ends ... could find its away on its extraordinary workmanship."[58] Alas, despite Moskowitz's positive response, his predictions for its box office — he felt it would do best with "savvy placement" among "selective audiences"[59] — may have led to poor handling by the film's distributor, Twentieth-Century Fox. The studio opted to release it in America, yet relied most heavily on small runs in Midwestern college towns such as Bloomington, Indiana,[60] where it hoped to find Malle or Dallesandro devotees. And Fox refused to release *Black Moon* in many countries, including Great Britain, simply because it anticipated a poor response.[61]

14

Pretty Baby (La Petite) — 1978

A Tainted World
Through Innocent Eyes

"There is nothing either fundamentally good, nor anything fundamentally evil; everything is relative, relative to our point of view ... It is extremely possible that something, perfectly indifferent in itself, may be indeed distasteful in your eyes, but may be most delicious in mine; and immediately I find it pleasing ... should I not be a fool to deprive myself of it merely because you condemn it?"
— The Marquis de Sade, *The 120 Days of Sodom*

"Long legged, thin armed, with high small buttocks — a small childish figure no longer quite a child, not yet quite a woman — [Temple] moved swiftly, smoothing her stockings and writhing into her scant, narrow dress. Now I can stand anything, she thought quietly, with a kind of dull, spent astonishment; I can stand just anything."
— William Faulkner, *Sanctuary*

BACKGROUND

The period of 1975 to 1977 incorporated a bold and dramatic transition in Louis Malle's life. Despite a "*carte blanche*" status that enabled him "to make any film he want[ed] in his native country,"[1] the filmmaker grew tired and listless and ready for a new challenge. Accepting the invitation of former UA studio head David Picker (a close friend and colleague since the mid-sixties, when he shepherded *Viva Maria* and *Le Voleur* through the Hollywood distribution channels),[2] Malle packed his bags and moved to Los Angeles in 1976.

Appointed president of Paramount's motion picture division that year,[3] Picker became a professional guardian to Malle in the States and mentored him on the logistics of the Hollywood system,[4] helping him secure a two-picture deal.[5] Acknowledging Malle's brilliance, Picker obliged the director's two stipulations: Malle wanted to self-produce his first American film, a request somewhat unusual for a new arrival in late seventies Hollywood (even given the director's European track record), and

Following his marriage to child whore Violet (Brooke Shields), the emotional photographer E.J. Bellocq (Keith Carradine) prepares to shoot pictures of a farewell party held for the ex-prostitutes of Madame Nell's brothel, on the banks of the Mississippi River, in the controversial period drama *Pretty Baby*.

because of Malle's uneasiness writing an English-language screenplay, he insisted on partnering up with an American scenarist.[6,7]

Picker put Malle in touch with Polly Platt,[8] an esteemed production designer on *The Last Picture Show* (1971), *Paper Moon* (1973) and *A Star Is Born* (1976),[9] who, in the late seventies, hoped to segue into screenwriting. Because her plans to co-script Altman's *Nashville* fell through in 1974,[10] Platt's only prior experience in scriptwriting circa 1978 was a co-story credit on ex-husband Peter Bogdanovich's *Targets* (1968).[11] Picker read Platt's unproduced adaptation of Malamud's novel *The Assistant* and gave the screenplay to Louis based on the "quality of the writing,"[12] and Malle and Platt met for the first time. Though Malle originally expressed interest in making a movie about the Californian mistreatment of illegal Mexican immigrants, Platt dissuaded him from this path, feeling it disastrous for a foreign director to arrive in a country and author a picture critical of that nation's policies.[13,14] When Platt asked Malle what interested him about the United States, he responded, "The music that came from New Orleans, in the early 1900s."[15,16]

Days later, while immersed in background research for *The Praying Mantis*, a forthcoming Henry Hathaway project about "killer prostitutes" in Amsterdam, Platt picked up a copy of Lee Friedlander's *E.J. Bellocq: Storyville Portraits* at the Museum of Modern Art. As the monograph contained haunting images of Storyville whores, she felt it would be superb contextual material for the Hathaway project. Yet more interesting discoveries were afoot: Platt learned from the text that the photographs were taken by "rediscovered" New Orleans photographer E.J. Bellocq, an ugly, hydro-cephalic dwarf who shot portraits of Storyville prostitutes and opium dens, and somehow managed, despite his extraordinary eye for beauty, to sink into obscurity. When the Hathaway project collapsed during the following weeks, Platt brought the Friedlander book to Malle and suggested that they make a film about Bellocq; the director shared her enthusiasm. Malle and Platt found themselves drawn to the same elements of the character: though curious about Bellocq's bizarre physiology and genetics, they were far more captivated and intrigued by the asexuality and naiveté of the photographs, "[the subjects'] innocence in spite of the fact that they were all prostitutes working at that time," and the detail that Bellocq's brother, a Catholic priest, destroyed as many of the negatives as he could find. Platt capitalized on Malle's love of period music by weaving it into the *récit*, promising the director that they could put the music in the whorehouse (as much of it, historically, was written and performed in bordellos).[17] She recalls:

> I went down to New Orleans, to Tulane University, and there's an oral history there, on the music ... and Jelly Roll Morton's down there, talking about his music on tape. That's where I got the title [of the film], because Jelly Roll Morton was singing on the tape the way *he* conceived the song "Pretty Baby." It had been a hit on Broadway and it was very fast-paced and innocent, completely non-sexual, and when Morton sang it, he slowed the pace ... way down ... and he sang a very sexually explicit version ... and I said, "Oh, my God! What a perfect title for the movie!"[18]

Platt traces the remaining elements of the *Pretty Baby* screenplay to a discovery from years prior. In preproduction on *The Last Picture Show* (circa 1970) she scouted locations for an unfilmed Mexican road trip sequence, and happened upon Mexican houses of prostitution, or "cribs." At that moment, she was struck by a haunting observation that she carried into the heart of her Malle script:

> I realized that prostitutes have children and families and they are normal and they're just like us, there's nothing different about these women. They just happen to work as prostitutes.... A friend had some still pictures from the forties of these houses of prostitution in Mexico and I noticed that ... the women looked happier to me than the men! ... I was very influenced by the sort of desperate search for love through sex, or ... life through sex, that obviously was not working according to these photographs ... So I had this idea that I would start the movie with the birth of a child ... the idea was that the child would be a boy, and that, for the first time in the history of any motion picture [laughs] you would have people being disappointed ... because what's the use of a boy in the house of prostitution? ... That gave me a way "into" the movie and Louis loved it, and I said ... we can shoot it ... [and] write it in such a way that you won't know whether [the mother giving birth] is in the throes of sex or ... the throes of labor.[19]

As for the character of a young girl that Malle and Platt placed at the center of their film, its origins were extremely personal for Platt. "I wanted," she recalls, "to investigate in the screenplay *amorality*. Because I felt that a child who was raised where prostitution was a way of making a living, that she would be completely without sexual hang-ups of any kind, and that character fascinated me."[20] Platt's daughter Antonia, nine years old at the time,[21] was "a very troubled child" who provided some inspiration. "She was completely naive," Platt observes, "and she couldn't have cared less what I did for a living."[22] Platt concluded that even if she herself were a prostitute, Antonia would probably not respond any differently to her.[23] Meanwhile, Malle happened to find a story of just such a young girl, a trick baby to whom Al Rose gave the pseudonym "Violet" in his nonfiction volume *Storyville, New Orleans.*[24] Platt and Malle ultimately decided it would be interesting to couple Violet and the photographer E.J. Bellocq in a love affair, which would form the dramatic framework of the film.

Malle and Platt enlisted Brooke Shields to portray Violet before casting anyone else in the picture. Malle knew her mother and father through his older brother, Jean-François, before beginning the project.[25] It is common knowledge that Brooke was "toughened" emotionally as a model at an early age; the producers thus happened upon a nearly perfect choice for a profoundly difficult role. Susan Sarandon observes, "Brooke lived a life that was very similar [to that of her character] ... you know ... the closest thing to a child prostitute, would be a child actor-model, in this day and age. [Brooke] was already an incredibly mature kid and I don't think it's any secret that she was ... asked to grow up very quickly."[26,27]

Then the conflicts erupted. Platt left for Arizona to write the screenplay, *sans* Malle, and though Malle paints a picture of this departure as a professional move—Platt's need to free herself from his input and assert her own creative independence[28]—Platt suggests otherwise, stating that "I went off to Arizona and wrote the script, and [Louis] wanted to come out and stay with me, and ... my ... boyfriend would not have it! It was very funny."[29] Regardless of whether her decision to exclude Malle from the scriptwriting process was professionally or personally oriented, it signaled rising tensions between them that intensified through the casting stage.

A great chasm exists between the slick, handsome, romanticized Bellocq portrayed by Keith Carradine in *Pretty Baby* and accounts of the real-life E.J. Bellocq (a five-foot, hydrocephalic duck-waddler with "a very, very high forehead that came to a point"[30]). Therein lies a tale. Upon finishing the screenplay, Platt—a longtime friend of Jack Nicholson's—could only foresee Nicholson playing Bellocq, because of "his chameleon-like ability, and [because] Jack has never really been successful as a sexual leading man." She recalls, "I just thought Jack would get it ... he would learn about what Bellocq was really like, and he would gain weight, and I just knew Jack would be perfect."[31]

Nicholson read the script and seized the opportunity. Yet Malle, upon hearing that Platt had approached a prospective lead without his input, grew livid and refused to even consider Nicholson, stating indignantly that he would never even think of working with a Hollywood star on his first American picture. Platt remembers, "I was just *furious*. I said ... 'He's not difficult at all!' I knew Jack very well, and Jack is *not* difficult, and I just couldn't convince Louis ... it was a mistake in my opinion, and ... I was not happy about the choice [Louis made]."[32]

To cast Bellocq, Louis consulted David Picker, who helped him scope out Paramount's A-list of actors. Malle met with Carradine, who, after doing some background research on Bellocq, expressed sheer bewilderment at the director's interest in casting him for this role:

> I went in to meet Louis, and sat down with him, and said, "Louis, you know, I'm honored to be here, and I think it's an extraordinary piece, but frankly, I can't imagine why you'd think *I* was right for this. I mean, E.J. Bellocq was virtually a dwarf. Very strange in appearance, and very odd, and physically, I certainly bear no resemblance to the guy." I think I might have even recommended another actor when I was in the room! [laughs] ... I suspect that what Louis saw in me at that point in my life — who I was then, and as an actor — I think he was looking for someone whose personal nature would mitigate the more prurient aspects of the [Violet/Bellocq] relationship.[33]

Complications beleaguered the production itself. According to Carradine:

> I think the tensions I witnessed were ... almost a cultural rift that stood between Louis and the crew. He was trying to do something that was obviously from a very continental, cosmopolitan viewpoint. And he was surrounded by this sort of thuggish group of teamsters, and your typical New Orleans crew who were sort of bored by the whole process, and these were guys who would be more interested in filming violence and car chases. Something as sweet as what Louis was trying to do was just ... alien to them.[34]

Platt notes that Malle liked continual rehearsal — a source of great frustration to the American crews, who simply wanted the director to do one rehearsal and allow them to set up lights.[35] She also remembers the outrageous complications brought on board by Brooke's mother, Teri Shields: "We had terrible troubles. [Teri] was a drunk, and she was obstreperous ... she got arrested for drunk driving with Brooke in the car, she punched the policeman in the face...."[36] More problematically, Platt believes Mrs. Shields's behavior adversely affected her daughter's ability to perform effectively, and diminished Brooke's emotional range:

> Brooke could not act when [her mother] was on the set.... If anything, I think [her mother's behavior] hindered her performance, because she had to be responsible for her mother. There was always that on her mind, and it made her more of what we would call a "control freak." So it was difficult for Brooke to cry ... to kiss Bellocq's character, you know? It was difficult for her to do a lot of things. Because she had to be the adult, and an actress, generally speaking, should be free of such constraints, in order to do her job.[37]

Despite all complications, Malle, Platt, Carradine, Shields and the rest of the crew eventually finished the film and — accompanied by a spate of controversy over the subject matter — it reached American cinemas on April 5, 1978.

Synopsis

Storyville, New Orleans, 1917. Twelve-year-old Violet (Brooke Shields), a "trick baby" conceived during one of her prostitute mother Hattie's (Susan Sarandon) sessions, now comes of age in a brothel, raised by Hattie and the house madam, Nell Livingston (Frances Faye). As Violet watches in tense, rapt fascination one night, the bed-bound Hattie screams, moans, curses and jostles her head back and forth on her pillow while dripping with sweat and pounding the mattress with her fist. One assumes she is caught in the throes of sex, but it soon becomes apparent that Hattie is in the throes of labor, as a midwife enters the room to assist. Hattie gives birth to Violet's new little brother, Will; Violet races through the bordello, first stumbling into one of the bedrooms and nearly interrupting a trick to pass the news on to one of her prostitute "sisters." Seconds later, she slides down the banisters and runs up to the house's black piano player, Claude, a.k.a. "The Professor" (Antonio Fargas) to share the announcement. The Professor celebrates by pouring out a rag onto the piano while Violet moves in time to the music joyously.

New Orleans photographer E.J. Bellocq (Keith Carradine) arrives at the bordello and pays Madame Nell for permission to shoot portraits of the prostitutes over the following weeks. A conflict erupts when Hattie's client Highpockets (Gerrit Graham), an ungainly, thick-headed lout, awakens to discover that Hattie has abandoned him after he paid for the entire night. Still inebriated, he stumbles in front of Bellocq's camera and attacks Hattie, ripping the emerald earrings from her ears that he gave her as a present, and toppling her; the two fall into each others' arms and roll around in the dirt, laughing.

The whores concur that Bellocq is "odd" because he never beds them, yet they feel so enchanted by Bellocq's portrait of Hattie that they ask him to photograph them, as well. Violet grows extremely attracted to Bellocq, spurred on by his elusive answers to her barrage of questions. Her possessiveness and emotional attachment build when Bellocq photographs Hattie several times, nude and clothed, and Violet, desperate for attention, damages one of Bellocq's glass plates. When he grabs and slaps her furiously, she runs into the adjoining room and throws herself onto the bed, crying and pounding her fists on the mattress. When she accuses Bellocq of "loving" Hattie, he retorts exasperatedly, "Don't tell me how I feel."

Though Violet is still a virgin, Nell and Hattie encourage her to participate in a "mother-daughter act," wherein she delivers (offscreen) oral sex to clients (dubbed the "French act") prior to Hattie's straight sex with them. Nell and the whores approach Violet's defloration as a grand ceremony: the madam invites a cadre of senators and other politicians to dine at the house, and, as an after-dinner "delicacy," has Violet hoisted aloft and carried on a platform, while dressed as the Grand Maja and toting a sparkler. Nell auctions off Violet's virginity for $400 to the highest bidder (Don K. Lutenbacher), to whom Violet declares coyly, "I'm glad it's you ... I can feel the steam rising right through my dress." When the whores notice the client hurrying out the door without a word, they race up to the bedroom and find Violet prostrate and unconscious on the bed, though she eventually lifts her head and opens her eyes, laughing and chiding, "What took you so long?"

Violet's mother informs everyone at the bordello of her engagement to Alfred Fuller (Don Hood), a longtime "client" who plans to marry Hattie, take her to St. Louis, and make her a respectable housewife. Hattie has lied to Fuller about Violet, claiming the young girl is actually her sister. Violet, by now entrenched and learned in the ways of the whorehouse, refuses to accompany her mother. An indignant Bellocq confronts Nell about Violet's fate without Hattie ("She's only twelve!") to which the madam responds, "She can do as she please" and informs Bellocq that his having fallen in love with Violet is overwhelmingly obvious. Embarrassed, Bellocq denies this, but displays great pleasure when Violet confronts him in the attic and, planting a kiss on his face, chides, "I love you once, I love you twice, I love you more than beans and rice!"

Hattie moves to St. Louis and Bellocq disappears from the whorehouse; when Violet encourages one of the African American boys to fornicate with her, she has her rear whipped with a belt. Mortified, Violet packs her suitcase and moves out of the brothel, visiting Bellocq at his house; the photographer is delighted to see her and, upon encouraging her to move in, becomes her lover. She sits for a number of portraits and accepts the gift of a doll from her new protector, but all is not well: the childish, high-strung Bellocq cannot tolerate or handle Violet's disobedience and throws temper tantrums when she disobeys, at one point threatening to kill her.

The authorities enter Storyville and begin to close down the whorehouses, cleaning the furniture out of Nell's house; Nell, believing that her money will now be worthless, burns large bills to ashes with a candle and the girls whisper that she has lost her mind. Meanwhile, despite their conflicts, Bellocq and Violet eventually marry, the ceremony preceded by a picnic on the river with the girls who used to work as Madame Nell's whores. Violet continues to live in Bellocq's house, where he allows her complete autonomy though she takes advantage of this freedom by sleeping until noon, living off of dessert, and — presumably — never enrolling in school or learning to read.

On their last day together, Bellocq and Violet enjoy lunch when Hattie and Alfred Fuller reappear at the house and forcibly reclaim Violet, using the law of "parental consent" as a weapon. Ripped apart emotionally, Bellocq screams that he cannot live without Violet, and accuses Hattie of abandoning the child. The ex-prostitute, now "Mrs. Fuller," casts aside Bellocq's words. As Violet — now dressed primly and properly in schoolgirl attire — prepares to board the train to St. Louis, Alfred Fuller turns to snap a picture of his new daughter with a brownie box camera. Frozen in the frame, bewildered, Violet has nowhere to run.

ANALYSIS

Al Rose's nonfiction book *Storyville, New Orleans* weaves together several pseudonymous testimonials of red-light district prostitution. These accounts unfold against the backdrop of a social phenomenon so rare and unique that it must surely qualify as a sociologist's dream: a city (Storyville) that functions as a modern day societal petri dish — an area separated legally from the rest of the country, and thus isolated, morally and spiritually, from the surrounding world. Within this sociological framework, Rose's volume poses a question long thought unanswerable: if children are subjected to behavior that qualifies as child abuse by Judaeo-Christian standards, yet raised in an isolated subculture where such behaviors are treated as normal or run-of-the-mill, would those children be adversely affected as adults? This question drew Louis Malle and Polly Platt to Rose's book and inspired them to create *Pretty Baby*. In the haunting testimony of a young girl referred to as "Violet," a "trick baby" born and raised in a brothel, Malle and Platt saw the definitive answer.

By middle–American standards, the details of Violet's account qualify the girl's short memoir as one of the most jarring, disturbing and graphic journalistic accounts of "legally accepted" child abuse in modern history. She recalls:

> One night when I was ten years old I walked into the bedroom where my mother turned her tricks. The john was in there with her and he had his pants off. She was, you know, washing off his prick with a wash cloth. She said this is my kid. He said don't I think a good little girl ought to help her mother. They both laughed. My mother asked me if I wanted to help and she held up the wash cloth. I didn't think nothin' of it. You know, like I said, I seen so much of this from the time I was born ... Pretty soon all the other girls were laughing about it, and then my mother used to get me to do the wash-up act every time she turned a trick.[38]

And later:

> [The johns] liked to have me around in the room while they fucked. One time Cora, one of the girls, had a john and she was sucking him off. It was nothing new to me. I seen it plenty of times before but only lately I'd be in the room while they were doing it. I said, "I can do that." So we took turns ... then he fucked her while I felt his balls ... I made five dollars for my end of that one, and then I started turning tricks myself just by blowing. I was still only ten years old so I didn't fuck. It was two more years before I did that.[39]

Violet's account grows even more heartbreaking and satanically perverse as she continues; she relays a situation where a "john" asked her if she wanted cunnilingus (still about 10 years old, she obliged him) and recalls that she and a friend of like age ("Liz") became acts in the notorious Emma Johnson's[40] sex circus, where Liz had to fornicate with a pony on stage, before an audience.[41]

But the "catch" in all of this—the central piece of information that, for Platt and Malle, made the girl's testimony remarkable and fascinating cinematic material—is the irony that Violet never felt sexually abused. According to her memoir, she grew up to become a perfectly normal housewife with three teenage daughters, and one devoid of sexual hang-ups. Violet concludes her testimony by reflecting, "'I know it'd be good if I could say how awful it was and like crime don't pay, but to me it seems just like anything else—like a kid whose father owns a grocery store. He helps him in the store. Well, my mother didn't sell groceries.'"[42] For the filmmakers, Violet's surroundings became a definitive litmus test of subjective versus objective ethos, and her adult reaction to her sexual activities during childhood provided the ultimate politically progressive answer to this test: proof positive that social conditions and structures, not an innate or inborn moral code, are the primary forces to determine the nature and boundaries of evil within civilization.

Many of the film's critics observe this irony while reviewing Rose's source work, and several chide or attack the motion picture for "sanitizing" prostitution, because they perceive the film's romanticized view of whorehouse life as innately false.[43] Such criticisms are ill-advised. Looking beyond the obvious — that it would be legally impossible and morally reprehensible for the filmmakers to cinematize the sexual acts Violet describes in Rose's book (because the scenes involve minors) — Malle and Platt take this impossibility and turn it around, deliberately "aestheticizing and muting"[44] all sex in the film and using this technique to their advantage. Their goal involves deliberately "setting up" the audience's expectations of onscreen kinkiness and deviancy, but instantly undercutting viewers' anticipations and thus unifying the audience's moral perspective with Violet's innocence and naivete. By filtering the story through Violet's eyes, yet holding explicit sex offscreen for the duration of the film (thus altering or "cleansing" the reality that unfolds around Violet), the filmmakers are enabling middle American or bourgeois European viewers to accept the whorehouse on their own moral terms, as a substitution for Violet's moral terms. Criticisms of historical inaccuracy here are moot, for Malle and Platt have extracted from Al Rose's book — and are working on — a level of truth far deeper than which sexual acts are depicted or implied: the truth that "everything Violet perceives in the brothel she regards as morally acceptable." In other words, the alteration of the events themselves, both actively (Danny Peary writes, "Nell's whores are well paid, well fed, healthy, and cheerful"[45]) and passively (no onscreen depictions of straight sex, oral sex, bestiality, etc., involving Violet or otherwise) merely exists to give the audience, like Violet, the experience *per se* of concurring ethically with the *idea* of "events transpiring within a whorehouse." *Pretty Baby* thus becomes a carefully constructed apologetic for moral relativism.

The onscreen fulfillment of this idea is encapsulated in an astonishing moral reversal that transpires in the picture's opening sequence. In a sustained shot that provides the most telling moment in the motion picture, Violet's face fills the screen, and she stares, mesmerized, while orgasmic cries pierce the air. The filmmakers are peaking and capping the prurient-minded audience's need for hot, kinky, and explicit sexual content, and thus working hand-in-hand with viewer expectations. Yet seconds later, Malle defeats these expectations instantly; the following image to which he and editor Suzanne Baron cut is a "look shot," taken from Violet's perspective, and the image at hand (Hattie giving birth) could not be any purer or more innocent. Again: Malle and Platt give the audience an inveterate understanding of Violet's open-mindedness by unifying viewers' perspectives with hers.

This strategy of "cleansing" the film of sex also belied Malle's marketing strategy for the picture. As a provocateur, he made a concerted effort to build prerelease expectations of explicit and raunchy content, by orchestrating a crafty and devious PR campaign. As early as fall 1977, *Pretty Baby* gained notoriety thanks to a strategic Joan Goodman article in *New York* magazine tagging the film as "*Lolita*, only in period costume and much more explicit." Months later, in January 1978, the film drew a great deal of pre-release publicity from a couple of photographs of 12-year-old Brooke Shields — made up as Violet — in the January edition of *Playboy* magazine (under the banner, "Film Directors' Erotic Fantasies")[46] and from a massive March 1978 article in *Playboy* that praises Malle for pushing cinema into previously unacceptable territory.[47] This was entirely hype: the "eroticism" of the Shields *Playboy* photographs is dubious at best — she appears fully clothed in both images and is not posed seductively, nor does she wear a seductive expression.[48] But the *New West* and *Playboy* tie-ins were deliberate moves on Louis's part; Vincent Malle observes:

> [Louis's marketing strategy] was absolutely deliberate! ... It was not something ... imposed on him by Paramount ... If anything Louis wanted [the prerelease publicity] to be more provocative and ... controversial than Paramount was comfortable [with] ... so, yes, the use of Brooke Shields and the use of nude photographs ... absolutely was not ... done behind Louis's back. Absolutely *not!* ... He was absolutely, completely in control of every part of the campaign.[49]

In sum, Malle realized that by leading viewers to expect "sophisticated kiddie porn," but carrying the film's content to the opposite extreme (inexplicitness), the contrast between audience expectations and onscreen reality — the power derived from the modernistic interplay of opposites within the framework of anticipation — would make the film's message of relativistic ethos that much clearer in the audience's mind.

Malle and Platt understood that the absence of scenes depicting 12-year-old Violet's sexual activity, when coupled with Violet's rather unfazed (neutral) response to her sex life, would yield two immediate consequences. First: the offscreen acts lose a component of reality (an element of visual legitimacy) by virtue of unfolding outside of the viewers' frame of reference. Ergo, although Malle and Platt subtly imply Violet and Hattie's joint participation in a mother-daughter sex act with Violet performing fellatio, and suggest that Violet's first client deflowers her roughly, with no tenderness, these occurrences are hugely drained of emotional impact because they are not seen. The unfulfilled expectations, in turn, draw even greater attention and emotional impact to the film's visual plane, on which the life of the motion picture unfolds most broadly.

The filmmakers understand this process; Malle and cinematographer Sven Nykvist emphasize the onscreen visual elements of the film more intensely than in any of the director's works other than *Le Feu follet*. Aesthetically, Malle singles out two key aspects of E.J. Bellocq's photographs, later underscored by Loïc Malle (no relation) in her introduction to a book of Friedlander's Bellocq recommissions. She begins by writing that for Bellocq, "being a prostitute is a state, like being John Doe or a celebrity."[50] Recognizing this aspect of Bellocq's photography, Malle and Platt attempt to capture this aspect of Bellocq's work cinematically. By largely depriving their prostitutes of individual personalities (Diana Scarwid's sexy and hilarious "Frieda" aside) they restrict and direct focus solely to the role of the women — to their career status — and thus make the lack of depicted individuality that much more explicit. One senses symbolically that the profession itself has severed a part of these women, has drained their inner vitality by placing unusual emphasis on the exterior, the superficial; Malle and Platt are thus making a sociological comment. The glimpse of the prostitutes on a functional basis entails a radical redefinition of the cinematic process, particularly as it demands that Malle and Platt rewrite the role of the audience, and that Malle align himself, virtually point-by-point, with Bellocq's sensibilities of the women — that the director attempts to return to the state of grace and naivete that Bellocq carried.

Loïc Malle continues by observing, "What captured Friedlander's interest was not just the emptiness that surrounds the women but also that with which Bellocq treated them — in other words, the liberty he granted them ... 'He just lets them act out whatever they had in mind for themselves.'" Following suit, (Louis) Malle and Platt build and approach the film as quasi-documentary material, turning it into an exercise in impressionistic narrative deconstructionism. Though the director cited the paintings of Vuillard as his primary visual inspiration, the motion picture carries cinema into the impressionist realm,[51] providing brief, brushstroke-like glimpses of whorehouse life; via Malle and Platt's decision to lace the narrative structure through a few major story developments and omit well-defined character arcs, they comment sociologically on the stasis, the lack of progression, imposed on prostitutes by whorehouse life. This explains why Violet's illiteracy and lack of emotional maturation (by the end of the story) build in impact, and it accounts for the drama of the visual leap from the confinement of the whorehouse to the freedom of the outdoor picnic. Moreover, resuming the progression of *Murmur of the Heart*, *Lacombe, Lucien*, and *Black Moon*, the director continues his attempts to free drama from a rigid Hollywood narrative structure[52] by physically building a depthless environment, orchestrating two dozen or so actors in mid-performance, and having them *live out their environment*, relatively free of his control.[53] He simply places his camera in the middle of the actors, relying on his ability catch nuances and gradations of human behavior and allowing this to "hook" the audience; Platt reminds us that the nature of the material — the subject matter — served her and Malle by demanding this approach.[54] This spatial depth carries another important side effect, as well: in line with Malle's abrechtian tendencies, the filmmakers actively sustain the illusion of an ere-unfolding four-dimensional historical environment throughout the motion picture. From Nykvist's opening shot — a miniature Storyville photographed at night, from above, while broken jazz strains play on the soundtrack — Malle is obsessed with reconstructing the past, and creates not simply a nostalgic film but an *investigation of* nostalgia.

Visually, Malle and Nykvist also draw power from the sharp, surrealistic contrast between this use of a continually unfolding world in the distance[55] and the film's Vuillardian flatness, in which characters seem to become part of the wallpaper or furniture and everything exists on a like plane (accomplished by the elimination of backlighting).[56] The effect of the chasm between the flatness and depth is that of a constantly active transition in the viewer's mind — flat paintings springing to life.

Malle, Nykvist and Platt construct the film's milieu in spheres, the innermost of which is the whorehouse; Violet stands at the center as the world whirls around her. The director gives us two lead characters whose gazes are constantly directed outward. Danny Peary notes, "Malle makes Violet curious about *everything* but her own body."[57] This is hardly accidental — given her absence of sexual hang-ups, she would naturally lack self-awareness. Moreover, it establishes the film's central perspective, and it directs the audience's focus to a broader, largely unseen sphere from which elements drift into the whorehouse: the world of the bourgeois. Malle scatters small, telling, subtle details throughout the film that point to the moral hypocrisy of American society, particularly Don Lutenbacher's wedding ring, the senators' attendance of the defloration ceremony, and the African American maid of the house, " a good churchgoing woman" by her own standards who supports whoring by her presence yet is morally repulsed when Violet attempts to have sex with an African American boy because "whites and coloreds can't be together."[58] Yet most scathing, certainly, is the conclusion, in which Malle and Platt suggest, via Hattie's transformation into bourgeois homemaker, that underneath it all, American bourgeois housewives are essentially whores, as hypocritical and as deviant as anyone by their own standards.

The attempt to rewrite the historical photographer E.J. Bellocq as a man in a child's body smacks of writer's convenience; perhaps it would have been far more interesting and more ambiguous to incorporate a male character that is completely asexual and unreadable. In all fairness to Platt, Malle insisted — to her chagrin — on writing and directing Bellocq as a kind of delayed adolescent, instead of the creepy asexual Bellocq whom Nicholson surely would have evoked. The director thus gave Carradine a list of physical characteristics to pay attention to in the part — behavioral characteristics of a typical adolescent — and instructed Carradine to try to remember the experiences of his youth; in the scene in which Violet is auctioned off, Carradine reflects, "What I can remember is from the character's point of view, feeling as though the adults were stealing her away in a funny way, that she was being sold off into the adult world, and that I was going to lose my childhood sweetheart."[59]

CRITICAL RESPONSE

Pretty Baby divided Malle's critics sharply. On the negative end, Molly Haskell, writing for *New York*, observes, "In leaving out the shame and degradation of prostitution, Malle gives us a view that is close to the traditional fantasy of the colorful, uninhibited natives who exist as a reproach to the uptight, churchgoing community. But freed from shame, they are also denied its corollary — spiritual aspiration."[60] Writing for *Progressive*, Kenneth Turan reveals decidedly mixed feelings about the film: though he found elements of the Shields performance "chilling," and feels that in the auction scene, "the strange horror of the situation comes through with a kind of uneasy intensity," he ultimately concludes, "For much of *Pretty Baby* this kind of force is absent. Part of the problem is that Malle, for reasons of his own, probably involving fear of local censorship, has adopted a flat, uninvolving directorial style ... Like its protagonist, *Pretty Baby* is something of a carnival attraction, nothing more."[61] Responding more favorably and eloquently with his review is Richard Corliss, writing for *New Times*, who summarizes the film with, "The only voluptuousness is in ... Malle's imagery, and this is appropriate." Though Corliss complains that "The trouble is the dialogue provided by screenwriter Polly Platt ... it means to be as ornate and stylized as the ad copy the whores provided by *The Blue Book*," he concludes, "These are minor flaws ... what stays in the mind is the irresistible force that draws two people together over all kinds of immovable emotional objects; and the realization that, whatever natural or perverse bonds tie us to the people we love, we're still, irrevocably, as alone as an oddball picture-taker and his child bride."[62] Reactions were equally mixed across the Atlantic: reviewing for *Écran*, Gilles Cebe attacked *Baby* as a "vain aesthetic exercise," and writes, "The story written by Polly Platt and Louis Malle must have had a strength on paper ... unfortunately, the finished product only captures a vague reflection of this."[63] Yet Henri Behar (writing for *Révue du cinéma*) responds more favorably to the film, complaining only of the "certain ... coldness we find again on all levels of the film" and — having dismissed this as a minor flaw — praising the "fragile and delicate" film for its "sumptuous elegance."[64]

Certainly, the question of *Pretty Baby*'s timing is far more important than its critical response, and — understandably — continues, all these years later, to raise eyebrows at Malle's judgment. The production and release of the film probably became the most important instance of moral controversy for Malle during his entire stateside career. Danny Peary writes:

> The picture was released during a peak period for public outrage over child abuse, child pornography, and child prostitution, and its critics were right to be disappointed that Malle refused to portray Violet's life in a brothel in a negative light.... The sledgehammer "selling of Brooke Shields as a pubescent sex symbol," which gained momentum because of this film, was truly tasteless. At least Malle didn't exploit his hot property as much as others did.[65]

And Sarandon affirms this:

> [*Pretty Baby*] came out at a weird time ... right when there was some heavy press emphasis on the discovery all of a sudden of child prostitution. And so it just happened to coincide with that, so it was banned in Canada ... and that's ridiculous ... ! They were looking for something. The film was disturbing ... [yet] clearly when you look at it, it doesn't have anything graphic. Even at that time it was pretty tame. And so they just had to find something ... they were just grasping at straws, and definitely threatening to give it an X rating, which is insane! ... And so ... everybody got in an uproar. But ... it was definitely just odd timing.[66]

15

Atlantic City— 1980
Dreams and Visions of Self

"[Jack Kerouac's] essence lay in a romantic vision of himself. It lay in his fantasies ... through everything returning again and again to the only fantasy that always held him, the vision of being a child permanently cut adrift in a darkening universe. This stream of fantasies, visions, myths, dreams, vanities— Kerouac used all these words for them — made up his life. They were the legend that he felt his life became. And they became more than this. In the intensity of the vision he had of his confused life he caught the dreams of a generation."
— Ann Charters, *Kerouac: A Biography*

"Our ideas of castles, formed in childhood, are inflexible, and why try to reform them? Why point out that in a real castle thistles grow in the courtyeard, and the threshold of the ruined throne room is guarded by a nest of green adders?"
— John Cheever, "The Golden Age"

BACKGROUND

The 18-month span following the production of *Pretty Baby*—from January 1978 through early July of 1979—constitutes a murky and poorly documented period of Malle's career, marred with numerous dead ends, project after project cropping up quickly and dying in the water. These failed endeavors include (but are not limited to): a documentary done with and about Stevie Wonder; an off-the-wall plan to rewrite Dreiser's *American Tragedy* as a farce entitled *An American Comedy*; a 16mm documentary chastising Disneyland as an evil, Pleasure Island-esque monstrosity, out to seduce small children with excessive commercialization; a brief reassessment of *The Boy* (Malle's defunct 1976 Jean-Pierre Gorin collaboration about wetbacks) without the participation of Gorin or Polly Platt; and most significantly, Malle's fruitless attempt, ongoing for many, many months, to realize one of his "lifelong dream projects": bringing Joseph Conrad's *Victory* to the screen as a Paramount-funded American epic.[1] A 1978 edition of *New West* also references a post–*Pretty Baby* Malle script about a suburban couple in the United States that, from the description in the arti-

185

Lou Pascal (Burt Lancaster), an aging numbers runner with fantasies of gangsterhood, is reduced to spending humiliating days catering to the whims of the testy ex–beauty queen Grace Pinza (Kate Reid) in Louis Malle's second English-language film, *Atlantic City.*

cle, sounds similar to a late-seventies *American Beauty*.[2] (These unrealized efforts receive additional attention in Appendix A.)

It is apparent, from even this cursory glimpse, that in Los Angeles circa 1978, Malle felt unsettled, ill-at-ease, highly distractible, and unwilling to commit to anything—flitting restlessly from idea to idea without focus. Yet two of his project ideas did make it to the production stage during this era: the first half of a documentary on Glencoe, Minnesota, titled *God's Country*, filmed during June 1979 (appended, edited and produced for PBS in 1985 — see Chapter 19 for a more detailed discussion), and *Atlantic City*, a feature regarded as one of the director's finest cinematic accomplishments.

Atlantic first took shape in mid–1979. A meeting occurred in late June or early July of that year between Malle and French mega-producer Alexandre Mnouchekine (*L'Emmerdeur*, *Préparez vos mouchoirs*).[3] Mnouchekine hoped to take advantage of the Capital Cost Allowance (CCA) 100 percent tax write-off for Canadian films by overseeing a motion picture co-produced by three Canadians under his aegis: Joseph Beaubien (*L'Homme en colère*), John Kemeny (*The Apprenticeship of Duddy Kravitz, Ice Castles*) and Denis Heroux (*The Little Girl Who Lives Down the Lane, Tomorrow Never Comes*). Speaking on behalf of his three business partners, Mnouchekine offered Malle a budget of just under five million to direct an adaptation of Laird Koenig's crime thriller *The Neighbor*. Only one catch: to take advantage of the CCA, the film had to wrap by December 31, 1979.

Malle read Koenig's book, hated it, and tossed it.[4] Yet, perhaps banking on his reputation, he somehow convinced the producers to let him take the five million and make an unrelated project.[5] In return, he agreed to stay within the boundaries of the romantic thriller genre and to honor Kemeny, Beaubien and Heroux's insistence on top male and female box office draws for the two central roles. The director had only two requests: in the female slot, he insisted on casting Susan Sarandon, his then live-in-lover of three years,[6] and after considering options for screenwriters, he refused to commit unless the producers allowed him to work with John Guare,[7] the New York–based playwright who became an off-Broadway cult sensation during the 1970s with the staging of his plays *The House of Blue Leaves*, *Marco Polo Sings a Solo*, *Landscape of the Body,* and *Bosoms and Neglect*.

When asked to describe his early association with Louis Malle, Guare recalls that the director attended a performance of *Landscape* at the Public Theatre back in 1977 and, deeply impressed, phoned him two years later:

> [Louis] said he had money for a thriller, to star Susan Sarandon and a bankable male star. [Louis's attempt to adapt *The Neighbor*] had fallen apart. He just couldn't find anything in it ... it had just collapsed. So, to make one last stab at it ... because he had all this money, because there was a 100% tax write-off for every dollar put into film production that year—1979—and, did I have any ideas for a movie? ... I was very fascinated with Atlantic City because a friend of my parents who was our neighbor when I was a kid was the man who had brought gambling to Atlantic City. He was the manager of the Chalfonte-Haddon Hall, which he turned into Resorts International Hotel & Casino.[8]

Malle's decision to seek out Guare of all possible candidates to work on the Canadian project can hardly be termed an accident. Just over a year prior, the screenwriter took a loose gamble by sidling up to Malle after an early screening of *Pretty Baby* and criticizing the film. Nonplussed, he informed the director rather coolly, "It's a shame you didn't work with a writer on this movie, it could have been good."[9] With this gentle negation, Guare was lamenting what he perceived (quite rightly) as a complete lack of structure in *Pretty Baby*—a European "languor"—and Malle knew it. More than a not-so-subtle attempt to bring the American critics' widespread complaint about *Pretty Baby* home to Malle in a decisive yet unhurtful blow, Guare's critique carried an implicit promise that if he worked on a Malle picture, he would, of course, impart a far more definite narrative structure to the script than *Pretty Baby* had incorporated. And it wasn't as if this promise existed without foundation: dramatic structure has long been one of the playwright's fortes. As Guare devotee Pauline Kael observes, "When I see a Guare play, I almost always feel astonished; I never know where he's going until he gets there. Then everything ties together. He seems to have an intuitive game plan."[10] In other words, Guare offered Malle (per his reputation as a writer) the option to retain a dramatic framework and yet (per his offbeat voice) the ability to remain fresh and unexpected. By virtue of Guare's carefully arranged narrative architecture, *Atlantic City* would thus mark the sudden and decisive end of Malle's progressive attempts (which began with *Souffle au cœur* and continued through *La Petite*) to free fictional cinematic narrative from the constraints of western dramatic structure altogether — an end that, owing to American audience demands, arguably should have been ushered in with *Pretty Baby*.

Guare continues his story:

> That day ... I told [Louis] about Atlantic City and I said, "It's a place that you should see!" He said, "This is my problem: today is the 29th of July," he said. "This movie, in order to qualify for the tax day ... there is a rabbi from Winnipeg[11] who has raised money. It has to complete shooting by December 31, 1979." So we went down the next day ... I called up Tony Raye, who said he would show us around ... a day after that, within the next two days, Louis came here early in the morning and we drove down and spent about ... eight to ten hours in Atlantic City[12] with Tony Raye showing us around.

As Malle and Guare were influenced heavily by Altman's 1975 opus *Nashville*,[13] both men felt drawn to the notion of crafting a Byzantine narrative with multiple storylines that converge by the end of the picture, and loved the idea of stripping the exterior of a geographic milieu to reveal the inner layers, the various social strata.[14] Guare observes, "What was interesting and what we liked about [Atlantic City] was there were so many rules ... This area of Atlantic City was being torn down to build [casinos] ... there just seemed to be all these different social stratas ... that Tony Raye took us through that day."[15] Guare's detailed account of the trip reveals the extent to which it became a blueprint for the finished film:

> We walked into Resorts International ... there was a clam bar. There were all these pretty girls working there, and we said, "Who are those girls?" And they said, "Well, they want to be dealers, but in order to qualify for being a blackjack dealer, you have to work for three to four months in a job to show that you'll stick around!" [We said], "Oh, well, that's Susan, right there!" And in a bookstore, there was an Atlantic City scrapbook that had a picture of a Gangster's Convention in 1929 — and at the top of the picture, in the far left corner, there was ... a big smiling boy ... and it seemed to be that that gangster — that that gangster's assistant up in the top corner — would grow up to be our man today, fifty years later ... And meeting ... [Skinny] d'Amato ... we just said, "Oh!" He lived in a humiliating situation.[16] And because of Miss America ... that there was an old beauty contest winner that he would be involved with. So those were the things— we wanted to get Miss America ... we wanted to get all those layers of Atlantic City ... into our story.[17]

Malle returned to France the following day. Upon request, Guare wrote *Atlantic City* in two weeks, and flew to La Coual with the script under his arm; the two men revised for another two weeks and eventually performed the piece for Heroux, Beaubien, and Kemeny. In Guare's hands, the tale about Atlantic City became "a lyric farce" in which several characters "realize their dreams through a series of accidents and several varieties of chicanery."[18] As Guare recalls his trip to New Jersey with Malle 25 years later, the primary characters in the comedy went straight from the

Malle-Guare Atlantic City experience to page to screen. These colorful characters include: Lou Pascal, a 70-something nickel-and-dimer who ran numbers in his youth for Capone and Meyer Lansky, loves to wax nostalgic about the golden age of Atlantic City, and fantasizes constantly about gangsterhood but never had the grit to enter the Mafia; Sally Matthews, a young immigrant from Moose Jaw, Saskatchewan who dreams of becoming a professional dealer and juggles a day job in an Atlantic City oyster bar with croupier classes; and the bedridden and elderly Grace Pinza, widow of small-time gangster "Cookie Pinza" who participated (as a young girl) in the Betty Grable Lookalike Contest on the boardwalk 40 years ago but has employed Lou as a caregiver and part-time stud since mobsters rubbed out her late husband.

Susan Sarandon reflects on the elements of *Atlantic City* that drew Malle to the project, and how Guare transitioned the story from Koenig's original novel:

> The whole voyeuristic [aspect] is what made [*Atlantic*] really interesting for Louis.... Originally ... it was just this movie about a kind of minor drug figure getting killed and putting other people in jeopardy, and then he has the money, and he holds onto the money.... When [Guare] changed it, I think [what] really made it interesting for Louis was the voyeurism and then the possibility that if you cast it correctly, that [Lou Pascal] wasn't some horrible old man but an elegant guy, so maybe there's actually the possibility that something might happen ... That's where the French point-of-view, or Louis's point-of-view, or the European sensibility came to play, whereas if an American had done it, it probably would have been just a heist film.... [Louis] did film it in a way that emphasized [the voyeurism].[19]

The need to find an "elegant" male star that Sarandon references presented a great dilemma in casting. According to Guare, he and Malle immediately thought of Henry Fonda as Pascal.[20] Yet Fonda—physically weak and debilitated in 1979 from a heart condition that would end his life three years down the road—posed such a grave insurance risk that Heroux and Co. forbade the filmmakers from hiring him, as Fonda's agent restricted the actor to a minimal number of minutes per day, and no fast walking or running. Likewise with James Mason, Jimmy Stewart, Laurence Olivier. Subsequently, Robert Mitchum's name popped up. "Louis went to see ... Mitchum," Guare recalls."[Mitchum] opened the door, and said, 'I just had my face lifted, and I only play under 45 now.'"[21] But after all these dead ends, "the inevitable man"[22] still waited in the wings. A well-known, barrel-chested actor of gangster iconography. A man who gained infamy over 30 years prior in Siodmak's quintessential film noir *The Killers* (1946), the first screen adaptation of Hemingway's short story. According to the insurance company, Burt Lancaster was "in perfect health, willing to play his age, and in great shape."[23] Lancaster read the screenplay and thrilled at the opportunity to take on such a dynamic, compelling role.

With Lancaster and Sarandon as the two leads, Guare and Malle set about finding a suitable candidate for Grace. Ginger Rogers (of Rogers and Astaire fame) was the only alternate choice prior to Kate Reid. Rogers read the script and shot off an immediate response, burning grievously: "'How *dare* you! At this stage in my career, that I'm going to end up in this filth!'...."[24] Guare recalls, "[Ginger was] insulted by the role. Insulted by the film — insulted by how lewd it was and how filthy it was. And so, we didn't know [who else to ask].... Betty Grable was dead ... we just didn't know...."[25] The brilliant Canadian actress Kate Reid — rescued by Malle and Guare from Z-grade Canadian horror fare like *Plague* (1978) and *Death Ship* (1980), and fresh from stage work with Guare only two months prior as the blind and bedbound, acid-mouthed Henny in *Bosoms and Neglect* — agreed to take the role without even reading the script first. The rest of the cast consisted entirely of Canadians[26] — Robert Joy, Hollis McLaren, Al Waxman, Bob Goulet.

Even if Malle and Guare concur that Lancaster's massive ego presented a challenge, their recollections of the shoot differ significantly. Malle presents a fairly mild version, where he and Burt got along swimmingly after discovering a mutual admiration for Visconti,[27] while Guare relays a prolonged, tumultuous conflict between Lancaster's vision of the role and Louis's attempts to elicit a more subdued performance from Burt, who insisted on being alternately difficult and offensive:

> There's a scene where Burt Lancaster is running up the stairs and he says, "I'm a lover!" Very hammy. That's what Burt had been playing the part like, all through it, and Burt embarrassed Louis — on the set — because Louis kept saying, "Burt: *down*. Less, less, less, less, less." And so Burt turned to the crew at one point and he said, "Okay." He said, "We're gonna do this next shot two ways. We're gonna do it the way the little frog wants it, and then we'll do it the way it's supposed to be done." And ... for a number of weeks on the picture, there were two versions shot of each scene. And Louis said, he said, "Ohhhh ... that bastard!" Burt was ... *awful* to Susan ... and insulting to Louis. And Louis said ... "If I didn't care so much, I would put the performance Mr. Lancaster wants — onscreen, to ruin his career!" But ... [Burt] came to see rushes at one point and ... looked up and ... saw what it was that Louis was doing and what he wanted. And it took a few weeks for Louis to gain Burt's respect.[28]

Susan Sarandon similarly recalls an on-set anecdote that illustrates Malle's attempt to transition Lancaster's approach from a performance of intensity to one of subtlety:

> It was very specifically written, the scene where I kind of offer myself to [Lancaster]. [As it is] described by John Guare, "the sun [is] coming through the blinds, and [Lou is] sitting there, unwrapping something, and speaking, and [Sally is] like a deer in the headlights, and his voice is mesmerizing." Well, when we got to that scene, Burt really felt compromised because he felt that it was expected of him to grab me, rip off my clothes and throw me to the ground ... and kind of ravage me, and that was what he wanted to do, and what he felt his audience expected of him.... Much to Burt's credit, he eventually tried it, and beautifully did it in the way that it was intended according to the script.[29]

Nor was *Atlantic City* particularly easy to distribute. Between 1979–81, Paramount invested hugely in Warren Beatty's *Reds* and Milos Forman's *Ragtime*, dropping about $25 million into each picture — a significant overinvestment, as the films only recouped about $20 million each. Though Malle claimed, years later, that he had a two-picture deal with Paramount in the late seventies[30]— presumably the same contract that gave him backing for *Pretty Baby* and *Atlantic City*— neither Polly Platt nor John Guare have any knowledge of such an arrangement, and the claim appears dubious given Paramount's careless rejection of *Atlantic City* on the first go-around. In fact, *numerous* studios rejected the picture. Sarandon observes, "[*Atlantic*] has such eccentric dialogue and everything, that when it was finished, nobody knew what to do with it. So that also sat around and couldn't get distribution for the longest time."[31] The turning point came only when the board at the Venice Film Festival co-awarded *Atlantic City* and Cassavetes's *Gloria* with the Golden Lion; Frank Mancuso and the Paramount brass, indignant that a picture with a budget of under five million could trump their multi-million dollar epics for overseas profitability and festival awards, picked up the film to avoid embarrassment.[32]

Atlantic City went into production in mid–October of 1979 with the exteriors filmed on location and the interiors shot in Montreal. It wrapped two-and-a-half months later, on December 31, 1979, just barely making the deadline for the tax write-off. Its entanglement in distribution problems delayed the picture's release in the states for over a year (until April 3, 1981)[33] lining it up for the 1981 Academy Awards (in March of '82). Despite minor bureaucratic problems, however, it went on to become one of Malle's critical and commercial triumphs and one of the sleeper hits of 1981.

Synopsis

In the popular resort town of Atlantic City, New Jersey, shortly following the legalization of casino gambling in the late seventies, Lou Pascal (Burt Lancaster), an elderly ex-numbers runner for La Cosa Nostra, now lives in a shabby tenement building off the boardwalk and acts as caretaker and part-time gigolo to the aging beauty queen Grace Pinza (Kate Reid). Grace spends her days in bed, sitting in her gaudy, knickknack-filled room with her pet poodle Peppy, watching television, and making demands on Lou's time and whereabouts. Sally Matthews (Susan Sarandon) lives opposite Lou's apartment—a 20-something, aspiring blackjack dealer who takes courses in dealing under the tutelage of the lecherous Frenchman Joseph (Michel Piccoli), supports herself by working in the casino oyster bar, and is in the process of fixing up a beachfront house with several other would-be dealers.

On a nightly basis, Lou spies on Sally through the window in his apartment facing her kitchen as she conducts her mysterious evening ritual of dropping her blouse, slicing and squeezing lemons, and rubbing the juice across her bare breasts and arms while she plays an aria from *Norma* on her stereo. Meanwhile, in Philadelphia, as a drug runner hides a cocaine stash in a glass phone booth, Sally's grody and skanky hippie ex-husband Dave (Robert Joy) watches from a distance. When the coast is clear, Dave slips into the phone booth and pockets the dope. Together, he and Sally's younger sister, the flower child Chrissie (Hollis McLaren)—who is pregnant with his baby—venture to Atlantic City and into a casino, and confront Sally at the oyster bar, demanding a place to crash.

Indignant at their arrival, Sally insists that they leave; Dave and Chrissie refuse and reveal their plans to spend the night at Sally's apartment. The couple follows her back to the building, where Lou watches them enter from above the stairs. Lou visits Grace; while she talks about her dreams, Lou hears the aria cascading down from Sally's apartment. Upstairs, Dave taunts Sally with talk of her humble origins and sexually offensive comments; Sally confronts him and punches him in the stomach.

Dave finally agrees to leave, but slips Sally's pocketbook out of her purse on his way out of the apartment, shortly after Lou leaves Grace's to take Peppy to the groomer and runs numbers for the boardwalk residents. The two men ultimately wind up in the same bar at the same time — Lou turning his number collections in to Fred O'Reilly, Dave approaching Fred as the drug connection through which he can make good on the cocaine. When Dave makes the fatal error of mentioning to Fred where he found the drugs, Fred refuses to help and, writing the name and phone number of the buyer on a piece of paper, flushes the paper down the toilet. Dave manages to pull the paper out in time and calls the drug buyer, Alfie (Al Waxman), snubbing Lou as Lou attempts to make conversation with him. Irritated, Lou leaves the bar. Yet upon discovering, from Fred, that Lou is a former gangster's assistant, Dave chases Lou down and claims (via pure, hot-aired invention) to have heard about Lou through Lou's reputation as a mobster — in Las Vegas. Flattered, Lou walks Dave back to their building and entertains him with stories of old Atlantic City. Dave offers to pay $100 to use Lou's apartment and asks to borrow a scale; Lou consents and pilfers one from the furious Grace.

Once inside of Lou's apartment with the shades drawn, Dave whips out the cocaine, mixes it with baby laxative, weighs the mixture on Grace's Weight Watchers' scale and impresses Lou by informing him of the steep payoff he will garner from selling the dope. He and Lou venture down to the hotel together for the drug drop-off; Dave asks a hesitant Lou to make the sale for him, and offers to meet him again outside of the hotel. Lou tentatively agrees, but when Dave ventures back outside (alone) O'Reilly pulls up in a Cadillac with two thugs, Felix (Moses Znaimer), and Vinnie (Angus MacInnes) who jump out and chase Dave down side streets; Dave leaps onto an animate hydraulic parking structure and rides it to the top; Vinnie dogs him down with a switchblade and stabs him to death, high above Atlantic City.

Inside the hotel, Lou makes the sale to Alfie, and encounters an old friend, Buddy O'Brien (Sean Sullivan) in the men's washroom; the two wax nostalgic about the good old days of Atlantic City. The authorities return Sally's wallet and inform her of Dave's death at the oyster bar; she later visits the new Frank Sinatra Wing of the Atlantic City Medical Center to identify Dave's body. While she does, Robert Goulet celebrates the opening of the hospital wing in the lobby by doing a song-and-patter number with a score of chorus girls and television cameras.

Lou meets up with Sally in the hospital and — identifying himself — takes the responsibilities for Dave's funeral and burial on his shoulders, having six dozen roses sent to the family, phoning Dave's parents for Sally, and paying for the body to be flown back to Canada. He begins to court an initially dubious Sally; the two gradually form a bond. The following morning, Lou buys a white leisure suit and white derby hat, sells more of the cocaine to Alfie, and donates his old suit to Buddy. Pretending to be a wealthy gangster with years of "pull" in Atlantic City, Lou treats Sally to an expensive lunch and eventually follows her back to the house she's renovating. Alone in the upper floors of the house, Lou reveals to Sally his habit of spying on her, and begins to seduce her with his words. She comes to him, with tears in her eyes and her blouse unbuttoned, and he rubs his hands over her breasts. The two make love offscreen.

On the way back to their building, after lovemaking, Lou and Sally are attacked by Angus and Vinnie; they tear Sally's dress and break her cassette recorder in half in an attempt to search for the drugs; Lou stands back, cowardly and helplessly, and fails to protect Sally while she is violated and he is threatened verbally. The two return to their building, mussed up and tattered, to discover with horror that the thugs have trashed Sally's apartment; Grace discloses Lou's old nickname ("Numbnuts") and tells Sally he has long been a coward, never showing the gumption to stand up for himself or to protect others. Lou tears off into his room, humiliated, and packs his suitcase, pocketing the rest of the cocaine and a handgun; he visits Alfie and, pawning off all but a small amount of the remaining cocaine, makes off with $4,000; he asks Alfie to tell Fred to "Tell those hoods to leave the women alone; what they're looking for, I got."

Meanwhile, Chrissie breaks down and informs Sally of the dope sale, and Sally deduces that Lou's money actually belongs to her. At Sally's croupier class that afternoon, Mr. Shapiro (Louis del Grande)—the representative for the gaming commission—fires her because of her connection with Dave; Sally confronts Lou furiously while he sits at one of the casino tables, and demands her money back; Lou refuses to talk to her. Joseph appears, and attempts to pawn Sally off to a lonely, middle aged man at one of the tables; she attacks him and screams at him and calls him a pimp. She is thrown forcibly out of the casino while Lou slips out and jumps into a cab, headed for the bus station; Sally follows.

By pretending that Lou is her senile father who forgot his medication, Sally manages to trick one of the bus drivers into throwing Lou off the bus; the two storm off together into the night, bickering over the money, and are once again confronted by Felix and Vinnie (who pulls a knife on Sally), but this time, Lou whips out a gun and mows both men down. He and Sally jump into the car triumphantly and soar out of Atlantic City, stopping for the night at a motel where they learn on the news that the cops have tied the double murder to a mob killing. Lou is overjoyed at the news and at the sketch of the gunman, which vaguely resembles him.

Lou and Sally discuss plans for the future and realize that their paths will diverge; Sally hopes to start a new life in France or Monte Carlo, while Lou plans to move to Florida. Nevertheless, Lou makes an informal proposal to take Sally down to Florida with him and protect her. The next morning, Lou awakens first and calls an incredulous Grace from the bathroom, taking responsibility for the two murders. He looks out into the main bedroom and spots Sally stealing his money; after Lou hangs up, the two have a brief exchange about going out for pizza, communicating, without direct acknowledgement, that Lou will let Sally abscond with the car and the money to start a new life for herself in France.

Pascal returns to Atlantic City; Grace sells the last $1000 of the cocaine to Alfie while Lou stands in the middle of the hotel hallway (behind her) and applauds. The two walk arm-in-arm down the boardwalk together while — looming above them — a building that is set to be demolished refuses to collapse under the weight of a wrecking ball.

Analysis

On its surface level, *Atlantic City* constitutes a "wish fulfillment fantasy." John Guare summarizes the picture as "[A film] about a man [Lou Pascal] who always wanted to be a gangster and never had a chance to be one, and finally gets a chance to live that out."[34] This is flush with the themes and tropes of Guare's major works. In *Atlantic*, as in Guare's two most critically and commercially successful stage plays, *The House of Blue Leaves* and *Six Degrees of Separation*, the playwright explores two of his chief dramatic preoccupations: characters' humiliations at the hands of their dreams (as he notes in his introduction to *Blue Leaves*)[35] and the constant chasm between the glow of those dreams and the depressing weight of reality — the chasm from which Guare pulls humor. Critic Gene Plunka writes, "The existential dilemma that Guare poses is how individuals can possess a sense of dignity and humanism in a world that is essentially fradulent."[36]

Yet to regard *Atlantic* only as a one-joke farce bathed in an aura of Calvinist irony, without ever moving beyond this surface level, means oversimplifying the picture and failing to acknowledge its depth and dimension. Guare builds the script on a rich foundation of heterogeneous intertextuality culled from three predominant sources: the mythology, history and sociology of Atlantic City, New Jersey; the psychology of self-myth and mythmaking[37]; and, to a much lesser degree, American cinematic *film noir* and its iconography. The distinctly American grain of two of these sources explains the picture's failure in France (as Malle mentions, North Americans seem to appreciate it more than Europeans)[38]: viewers who live or have come of age abroad may be more apt to miss the picture's cultural references.

Through the use of careful juxtapositions, *Atlantic City* draws an implicit, running correlation between its central characters and the New Jersey resort town; this occurs preponderantly on a mythical level, and it applies most to Lou Pascal. One should note that Pascal is — in every sense — a man divided at the outset of the story, the victim of a psychic split between reality (the depression of his day-to-day life with Grace Pinza) and fantasy — his idealistic self-vision of being a powerful mobster with connections, a contemporary version of the "dinosaurs" such as Capone and Lansky from the Halcyon Days of Prohibition-Era Atlantic City. ("I was Bugsy Siegel's cellmate!" Lou screams at a bus driver. "People come to see me from Las Vegas!") At the outset of the film, Malle and Guare present Pascal's "gangster myth" as purely false. It appears to be a complete or near-complete fabrication, to have sprung from a void — from nothingness, evidenced by the fact that he has adopted a mobster persona ("Mr. Ten Most Wanted") but is reduced to a degrading and humiliating life, cutting out money saver coupons for a cranky, bedridden old woman and to walking a poodle down the boardwalk. Still, his vision of himself persists and will eventually triumph, finding some foundation in reality.

Atlantic City itself carries almost identical mythological resonances. Around the turn of the century, the resort town became known as something of a fantasist's city, because it seemed, as an urban center, to have sprung literally from nothing, constantly imparting the illusion of a lush tropical resort, when in fact it is built on a mud marsh, half-frozen for much of the year. Jonathan Van Meter writes:

> Atlantic City was built on an unremarkable ten-mile-long strip of sand. There is a beach, but the character of the island before it was transformed in the late 19th century was one of windswept isolation, with a landscape of fine, white sand dunes that reached as high as 50 feet, cedar oak and holly trees, duck ponds, swamps, and briar thickets. In the summer, the place swarmed with mosquitoes and greenhead flies. Black snakes, foxes, rabbits, muskrats, and mink infested the island. Not exactly a paradise in waiting. But that is precisely what made Atlantic City's first heyday in the Victorian era so incredible — it had created so much from so little so quickly.[39]

And subsequently, Van Meter quotes Charles Funnell, revealing an even more astonishing correlation between the characters in *Atlantic City* and the resort itself:

> "Unlike the conventional city, Atlantic City had a single purpose. The Boardwalk was a stage, upon which there was a temporary suspension of disbelief, behavior that was exaggerated, even ridiculous, in everyday life was expected at the resort. The rigidities of Victorian life relaxed, permitting contact between strangers and the pursuit of fantasies.... The town was a gargantuan masquerade, as visitor deceived visitor.... And people wanted to be deceived, to see life other than it was, to pretend to be more than they were."[40]

Lou is thus a mythical symbol who has imbibed and embodies the very spirit — the very mythology — of Atlantic City, in much the same way that Paul "Skinny" d'Amato (who began his life in the thick of impoverishment) and Enoch L. "Nucky" Johnson personified the spirit of the city. He thus constantly dreams of being more than he is, lives out fantasies that seem to have come from nowhere.[41]

As the film progresses, however, a change occurs. Lou continues to deny the reality before him intensely and overwhelmingly, and while one might expect this to make Lou run the risk appearing delusional in the eyes of the audience, the opposite is true. His sense of a "possible self" (in the terminology of Dr. Dan McAdams and psychologist Hazel Markus)[42] — is so strong that it takes over and begins to gain tonal authentication as a result of its force, pulling viewers inside of Lou's fantasy and turning him into a walking anachronism. In other words: Lou's age aside, it eventually appears that Malle and Guare have literally pulled Pascal out of Prohibition-era Atlantic City and dropped him onto the boardwalk in the middle of 1979. His spirit of nostalgia is this strong and this persuasive to audiences. This persuasion is evoked largely through Guare's ear for detail, which is why the playwright, for much of *Atlantic City*, draws from ultra-specific references to the history of the area. Without these indicators, the audience would never believe Lou's recollections as readily. Most significantly: in a dialogue between Lou Pascal and Buddy O'Brien in the men's washroom of the hotel where Alfie resides, Guare invokes the spirit of a former kingpin and Atlantic City mayor — perhaps the most famous mayor in the history of twentieth century New Jersey — whose name is, in itself, a piece of local mythology and a household word in Atlantic City:

BUDDY   (laughing) Remember the time Nucky Johnson sent us out to buy a hundred
           boxes of rubbers? The *look* the guy gave us? A hundred boxes of rubbers — for
           two guys?!

LOU   (smiling). Buddy, you live too much in the past...

BUDDY   Yep. But them were the days![43]

The use of Enoch L. "Nucky" Johnson's name in the context of the story even transcends the framework of history; the fact that Lou and Buddy worship halcyon days centered around Johnson is key, absolutely central, to their characterizations and to the meaning of the film. Johnson himself — according to Van Meter and other Atlantic City historians — could certainly never have existed or thrived in his position without a "system" against which he could rebel, and this came in the form of Prohibition. It thus makes perfect sense that Lou would desire, and eventually obtain, a "Prohibition equivalent" — cocaine dealing becomes the contemporary substitute for illegal alcohol distillation and distribution.

At other points throughout the film, Guare has the characters mention Harry Cohn, Meyer Lansky, Bugsy Siegel — using their names to resurrect a forgotten era. Lou cites details whose very esotericism renders them vivid and credible: an old Fats Waller tune, "Flat Foot Floogie" ("Oh, the flat foot floogie with a floy, floy") and presumably a Cab Calloway tune ("Hep Cat's Love Song," which Lou shortens to "Hep Cat"). The past thus begins to gain legitimacy in the audience's eyes, through Lou's historical reevocation, and Lou gains audience sympathy — the audience learns that he is more than simply a fabricator, that the era really did, in fact, exist and thrive, decades prior, and that Lou was involved with the mafia, however small the capacity. And the audience begins to learn along with Pascal — over the course of the picture — that he truly does have a gangster's panache inside of him.

Yet even if Lou's vision of himself gains legitimacy, it does so while revealing just how selective and revisionist Pascal's memory is, and thus bears some thematic resemblance to Malle's far less successful *Le Voleur* of 12 years prior. Guare provides a window into the mnemonic process Lou undergoes and thus enables viewers to study it. For instance, Dave's (ludicrous) claim that he heard about Lou in Vegas — "It was in a crowd of people — your name popped up ..." — its fraudulence revealed by Dave's inability to even utter "Harry Grapke's" name and by the visual clarity of his "on-the-spot invention" — is, only a few scenes later, altered by Lou into, "This is Dave ... came to see me from Las Vegas. *Good friend* of Harry Grapke's." Even if evidence suggests that Lou was, on some level, legitimately a part of the mob in the "old days," one begins to get the impression that he was only on the fringe and longed, desperately, to be at the center. Taking the "art of selective memory" concept one step further, one should note the extent to which Lou's memories attain a Doctorowian quality — Guare's telling story about how the character of Pascal came to him and to Malle inevitably recalls Pauline Kael's summary of the Woody Allen film

Zelig as a *Ragtime*-like film in which Woody Allen "inserts this little lost sheep into the corner of the frame."[44] The physical position of "the big smiling boy" in the gangster's convention photograph—he was located in one of the top corners of the frame—makes Lou-as-a-boy *and* his real-life equivalent the proverbial "lost sheep." And Lou's constant nostalgizing in the contemporary setting provides a bittersweet commentary on how one who merely stood at the fringe of a broad and sweeping historical movement, at the edge of a larger-than-life, overpowering period and milieu, could somehow imbibe the sociological spirit of the era and allow that spirit, that energy, to become the vehicle for self-reinvention, whereby he reposits himself at the center of the mnemonic frame. This selective memory can, in turn, easily be defined as the core of the process of "waxing nostalgic"—a dissection of the platonic concept of nostalgia by Malle and Guare. It explains—for example—how one who was merely Bugsy Siegel's cellmate on a drunk and disorderly charge for 10 or 15 minutes can suddenly, in his mind, use this one small and telling detail to reinvent himself as Siegel's cellmate for many months or years, positing himself on the same level with Siegel, perhaps in for crimes of the same magnitude—murder, arson, bootlegging, racketeering, blackmail. This is all inveterately tied to the spirit of deception, of masquerade, of self-reinvention, that—as Van Meter notes above—Atlantic City is known for propagating because of the city's very constitutional (geographic) nature.

Any investigation into the sociological background of Atlantic City (pre– *or* post–1978) reveals a kind of psychic split that acts as an economic and social status barrier. As Van Meter suggests, the resort originally had two sides to it—the cheap, garish, family-oriented side, which, thanks to its impoverishment, tackiness and lack of class, resembled Coney Island; and the slick, chic, dark underworld, of impossibly hip, high class and (most important) economically well-to-do gangsters. Malle and Guare employ structural parallelism in the sense that Lou and Sally are each torn between the same two worlds—the world of the classy and polished (represented by: Sally's full-time croupier work and French lessons, fine wine, the aria on Sally's stereo, Lou's cigarette case and white suit) and the world of the everyday, the grotesque and gaudy (represented by Dave and Chrissie's hippie garb, Grace's knicknacks, her professional portrait of Peppy on the wall, Peppy himself, Grace's fantasy about platform shoes with goldfish in the heels, Dave's rock music). Moreover, Grace functions as the embodiment of tackiness and tastelessness against which Lou must rebel, and Dave bears the same relationship to Sally. (Note the physical blocking of the scene in Sally's apartment that opens with Dave half-kneeling, in a dark and distant corner of the room, like some slimy demonic creature; as he stands up, creeps over to Sally's stereo, and changes the music from the poetic aria to skanky and grungy rock 'n' roll.)

The psychic split that Lou and Sally each struggle to overcome points to an even deeper reality in the film. On a mythical level—in Ruckian terms—Lou and Sally share the same spiritual goal: to ascend from the chthonic to the Olympian. This is equally valid for Lou and for Sally, though practically speaking, it means something different for each of them: in Sally's case, it means the ability to start a new life in Europe, facilitated by Lou and his money; in Lou's case, it is a bit more complicated. Pascal—at the beginning of the story—has an image but no "self-myth" to attach to it, in the sense that psychoanalyst Dan McAdams defines the term — "a special kind of story that each of us naturally constructs to bring together the different parts of ourselves and our lives into a purposeful and convincing whole."[45] If the "imago" that Lou seeks to legitimize within his own self-myth is that of a gangster (or, according to McAdams's list of types, a combination of lover and warrior),[46] he must first live out life, legitimately (for however short of a period of time) in this gangster role. *Atlantic City* thus incorporates a double narrative: in addition to the external story — which includes everything in the dramatic structure of the motion picture (Dave's death, Lou's drug sales, Sally getting fired from the casino, etc.) — Lou's opportunity to "live out" gangsterhood and to make his spiritual ascendancy means essentially writing his own mythical story, an inner story, within the context of the drama — creating his self-myth as it applies to that role, and fostering a story he can pass along to others, for the purpose of *generativity* — producing his own legend that will outlive him: "The Man who Brought the Mob back to Atlantic City." Simply put, the process itself means ascending from run-down nickel-and-dimer (flawed human) to legendary mobster (godlike status) — when Lou turns this process into a narrative (as he certainly will in successive weeks) he creates his own self-myth.

Within this process of spiritual elevation, Lou and Sally help each other ascend, and the wonderful irony of the story, of course, is that Lou's exalted vision of Sally is partially an illusion — just as her vision of him ("Teach me stuff ...") is based on fantasy. Lou essentially perceives Sally as something of an Olympian goddess, his ticket to spiritual redemption. In a moment that is nothing short of inspired, just after Grace sits on her bed and rhapsodizes about pumps with goldfish swimming in the heels, Malle overlays the beginning of the aria on the soundtrack, and what begins, for the first few seconds, as non-diegetic — a parody of Grace's sense of class and sophistication — soon reveals itself to be diegetic. It is, in fact, Sally's recording of *Norma*, descending from upstairs; Lou begins to drink from his bottle of wine but slowly raises his head and closes his eyes and absorbs the music as if the goddess herself is casting down her blessings. He gazes upward, to the ceiling, as if toward Heaven. Similarly, one should note that in the second scene that details Sally's "nightly ablutions" with the lemons, the blue soap, and the aria, she is filmed very realistically upon first glance. Only after Malle details Lou watching her does he cut to what is carefully shown as a *look shot* of Sally bathed (as Dick Ciupka shoots her) in a rosy glow — shot bare-breasted, as if she were the Madonna — and the audience understands that she has become the embodiment of holiness for Lou. In other words: using objective reality to define the role of Lou's subjective perception and of subjective perception *per se* (as a platonic concept) within "the there." The two major shifts in Lou's perception of Sally arrive when he learns of Dave's real nature ("He was a shit!" Sally screams. "You'd marry him too, to get out of Saskatchewan!") and when Pascal discovers Sally's theft in the conclusion. Sally's disillusionment as far as her perception of Lou comes, of course, from Lou's failure to protect her (note the extent to which she cozies up to him, physically, just prior to the first attack from Vinnie and Felix) and from her conversation with Grace in the apartment building — when she learns, to her chagrin, that Lou is actually an imposter — poor, with no legitimate history in the mafia.

As for the temptation to read Atlantic City as a Calvinist work (ala Schrader or Scorsese), this interpretation fails to withstand closer analysis. More accurately, the picture falls into the same camp as *Ascenseur pour l'échafaud* (see Chapter 2), and in this sense, it is inherently, inveterately Malleian — a playful, mildly mischievous blend of the Calvinist and the Arminian, as in the extra-cinematic realm, where fatalistic and self-deterministic forces work hand-in-hand to produce destiny.

Atlantic City can also be read as a subtle *homage* to American film noir. When one of Malle and Guare's friends suggested Lancaster for Pascal, the filmmakers immediately harkened back to Lancaster's debut performance in *The Killers* (1946), one of the first examples of American *noir* and considered by many — 60 years later — to be the quintessence of this cinematic period. *The Killers*— like its follow-up, Siodmak's 1948 *noir* picture *Criss Cross* (Lancaster's two best known efforts from the era) is significant in that it established a persona for Lancaster that cut against the grain of Jimmy Cagney, Edward G. Robinson, Fred MacMurray. Unlike the aforementioned, Lancaster plays, in the Siodmak pictures, a generally nice guy who is led down the wayward path by virtue of circumstance and falls into the life of the seedy, the underhanded, the dark and twisted and morally corrupt underworld — decisions that his lead characters Ole Anderson (a.k.a. "The Swede") and Steve Thompson will eventually come to regret. It is thus on an affectionate, lightly comic note that Malle and Guare have Lancaster toying with the screen image he established in the late forties by making his character aspire to the opposite, Pascal dreaming constantly of entering gangster life but finding, in the end, that he's simply too kind and decent to be a cold-blooded murderer. ("I never killed anyone before in my life," Lou tells Sally in the motel; "I never thought you did," she admits.) *Atlantic City* also contains— by virtue of its geographic location — a sweet, low-key nod to *The Killers*: one of the key plot points in the backstory of Siodmak's film involves the Swede and his lover, Kitty Collins (Ava Gardner) absconding with over $200,000 and fleeing to a hotel in Atlantic City.

A final note. While *Casablanca* (1941) could never be termed a noir in the conventional sense, the conclusion of *Atlantic* bears striking similarities to the wrap-up of Curtiz's film, in which Rick lets Ilsa go. Guare, however, failed to cite Curtiz as an influence, perhaps because Lancaster devised the ending of the film.[47]

CRITICAL RESPONSE

Atlantic City received multiple Oscar nominations including Best Picture, Best Director, Best Original Screenplay, and Best Actor for Lancaster, yet — to everyone's surprise and chagrin —failed to win any. Critically, *Atlantic* (as foreshadowed earlier) scored hugely in North America and in many European countries including Britain, aside from France, where it was received with some indifference. In the States, Pauline Kael lavished praise onto the film, writing:

> *Atlantic City* has a lovely fizziness. Everything goes wrong and comes out right.... Louis Malle is in full control and at ease, and his collaboration with John Guare produces a rich, original comic tone. Sometimes the most pleas-

urable movies seem very slight, because they don't wham you on the noggin.
Malle's skill shows in the way he keeps this picture in its frame of reference,
and gives it its own look. Visually, it's extraordinary.[48]

More dissatisfied (and, for that matter, almost a lone dissenter in American critical
circles) is David Denby, who writes, "*Atlantic City* ... is sweet, funny, and affectionate, but there's not much narrative or poetic drive in it.... Guare has a tendency to
repeat his conceits as if they were profound or brilliantly funny, and the movie's
humanism grows faintly watery and tedious after a while."[49] But *Playboy* praises the
film; Bruce Williamson writes, "Opposite Sarandon, Burt Lancaster gives his best performance in years ... Guare's trenchant dialogue and screenplay are a good part of
the reason for *Atlantic City*'s success as an odd, amoral comedy ... rather weird but
at long last irresistible."[50] In Britain, Philip French gave the film the highest praise
it received anywhere, proclaiming it a masterpiece in his *Observer* review. He writes:

> A screenplay by the American playwright John Guare ... is as elegant in con-
> struction as it is quietly elegant in its dialogue.... This is a very funny, precise,
> ironic, deeply sad movie that escapes being aridly cynical or sentimentally
> patronising because of the wry affection with which Malle and Guare observe
> the central characters. The film scarcely puts a foot wrong, and Lancaster gives
> one of the major performances of his career.[51]

Far less enthusiastic are the French reviews, many of which brush the film aside
curtly. Typical of these pans is Claude-Michel Cluny's review for *Cinéma*. He writes,
"We need to report that there isn't anything wonderful to write about *Atlantic City*,
a film that slips away, transparently, with its simplistic dramatic set-ups."[52] But France
was a lone — and rather odd — exception in its response *Atlantic*, and even a few
French reviewers dissented, praising the film. Writing for *La Révue du Cinéma*, for
instance, Max Tessier comments, "*Atlantic City* ... is a nice surprise ... a script that's
quite solid, interesting and more or less detailed characters, and brilliant technique...."[53]

Thus, by and in large, *Atlantic City* triumphed critically and commercially, gar-
nering a reputation in the States and Britain as one of Malle's undisputed masterpieces. And on a personal note, it marked the beginning of an ongoing friendship,
one of the deepest friendships and creative partnerships Malle would ever
encounter — "a wonderful working relationship"[54] — between Louis and John Guare,
though the writer-director team would never again see any films through to completion.

16
My Dinner with André — 1981
Notes on Generativity

"I don't know why it is that you can know someone so well and not really know them at all. I guess it goes back to that old saying: 'A child is one person, a man is many.'"
— Barnaby Saltzer, Earl Mac Rauch's *Dirty Pictures from the Prom*

"In the room, the women come and go, talking of Michelangelo..."
— T.S. Eliot, "The Love Song of J. Alfred Prufrock"

BACKGROUND

The interim between the wrap of *Atlantic City* and the production of Malle's follow-up, *My Dinner with André*, spanned about 11 months—from December 31, 1979, to the end of November 1980.[1] In retrospect, Malle hit the zenith of his stateside career during the 1979–82 period: *Atlantic* and *André* would go on to become five-star critical and commercial triumphs, widely considered the director's two most accomplished English-language pictures. But this double success was still indeterminate in spring 1980, with *Atlantic* more than a year from distribution in the United States and *Dinner* months from pre-production.[2] In fact, the director worried that *Atlantic* mightn't even be issued, and spent months trying to prevent his masterpiece from falling between the cracks by persuading Barry Diller and Frank Mancuso to pick it up for distribution (see Chapter 15).[3] And though the Wally Shawn-André Gregory script for *Dinner* looked promising, its unusual subject matter (a two hour filmed conversation, *sans* cutaways) complicated the solicitation of funding several times and delayed production through the summer and autumn of 1980.[4]

As the eighties dawned, Malle's personal affairs proved equally capricious. His private life hit rock bottom given the emotionally shattering break-up of his three-year, love affair with Susan Sarandon.[5] But within a month of this split, his romantic life crescendoed once again. He met American actress Candice Bergen (*Carnal Knowledge, Getting Straight, Starting Over*) for the third or fourth time and the two fell deeply in love. The Malle-Bergen courtship debuted with a fateful romantic lunch

In a posh Manhattan restaurant, the age-old friends and colleagues Wally Shawn, a beleaguered Everyman struggling to get through his days, and André Gregory, a shamanlike theatrical guru fresh from globetrotting, share a moment of laughter and warmth before their long dinner conversation in *My Dinner with André.*

at the Russian Tea Room one wintry Sunday afternoon in late February 1980. They would be married only eight months later, on the Causse de Limogne in *sud-ouest* France.[6]

In his massive 2003 biography *Louis Malle: Le Rebelle solitaire*, Pierre Billard suggests a connection between the life-changing Bergen lunch, which somehow ballooned into a *four-hour* conversation on art, politics, cinema and philosophy,[7] and the two-hour dinner conversation of *André*.[8] The experience at the tea room may have heightened Malle's interest in the script; moreover, an amusing correlation exists between the Russian lunch and Malle's direction *André*'s final scenes. Bergen and Malle apparently stayed in the Tea Room long past lunch time, until their presence interfered with the staff's attempts to set up for dinner[9]; this possibly explains Malle's amusing interpolations of glances from the exasperated waiter (Jean Lenauer) into the final scenes of *André*. (Lenauer's reactions do not appear in the Shawn-Gregory script.)

Yet Malle had no influence over the subject matter *per se*; the drama's conception long predates his involvement, and it marks one of only two instances in his 40-year career where he signed on to helm a prewritten screenplay.[10] The story behind the script actually commenced a decade earlier, with two individuals: Wallace Shawn (b. 1943), son of the famous *New Yorker* editor William Shawn, and André Gregory

(b. 1934), the son of a Russian Jewish financier and something of a child prodigy. Both men grew up in Manhattan amid considerable wealth; both graduated from Harvard, about ten years apart.[11] Gregory became a hugely successful and iconoclastic New York City theatrical director, founder of a controversial touring stage ensemble known as "The Manhattan Project" (1968–1975)[12]; Shawn eked out a meagre living for several years writing stage plays in the early 1970s, and turned to acting in 1978, instantly becoming one of the most recognizable American character players with bit roles in such features as *All That Jazz* (1979), *Lovesick* (1983), *Micki and Maude* (1984), *Radio Days* and *The Princess Bride* (both 1987).

While riding his wave of directorial success in the early seventies, Gregory discovered Shawn's play *Our Late Night* and staged it in 1972 under the aegis of Joseph Papp, thereby giving Shawn his first official credit as playwright. Thus began the men's loose professional association and friendship. But Gregory hit a midlife crisis around 1975 that led to the dissolution of The Manhattan Project. He began mysteriously dropping out of society for short periods and disappearing altogether, his whereabouts unknown even to his family. Marie Brenner's words:

> By the early 1970s, André ... was feeling isolated by his theater ... he felt overcome by *skuchna* again. Slowly, he was beginning to realize that the times had moved past him and his dreams; what with Nixon and spiraling theater costs, he witnessed the disintegration of the avant-garde. "A kind of gloom fell over the audience," André says. "It was like a power failure, a dimming of the lights. A sense that everything had stopped." And so he left.... He would disappear on these strange jaunts, leaving [his family] to fend for themselves on Central Park West ... André went on hops to the Sahara and Mt. Everest and Findhorn; he communed with English eccentrics who spent time growing giant cabbages.... He thought this way he would be able to divine what was real for him. It was this internal dialectic that eventually became the core of *My Dinner with André*.[13]

According to Gregory, he then shared some of his wild and fantastic experiences with Shawn, after he returned from a trip to Poland in the late seventies.[14] He recalls:

> [Wally and I] were trying to do a theatrical version of *The Little Prince*, and we were also playing around with another script.... And one day Wally called me ... with the thought that my stories could somehow be made into ... I think his first impulse was ... some kind of talking heads comedic project for television. And the minute ... he mentioned a conversation between the two of us, I got excited, because I thought it would be funny, given the radical difference in the tone of our two voices.[15]

Gregory originally wanted to go with Shawn to a hotel room in Atlantic City (!) and co-author a musical,[16] but Shawn would not have it: "André ... kept asking me to write a play for him to direct, but I saw nothing in that project that was likely to help me with my problem. Then suddenly it occurred to me—My God, what if, instead of a play, we just did a very simple film, with lots of closeups, in which I would be talking with André? He would say absurd things, I would say absurd things, and we would just talk, as people really do."[17] Though Shawn and Gregory retained this basic form, the piece eventually became far more complex than Shawn's initial vision suggests: the playwrights reinvented themselves onscreen, as characters, and devised a fictitious scenario where they haven't seen each other for several years. In the story, "Wally," a beleaguered everyman, disgusted and exhausted with life's tribulations and scrounging for money on a daily basis, is invited (somewhat against his will) to have dinner with "André." Over a meal, Gregory details his adventures circumnavigating the globe in search of spiritual and holistic enlightenment. Aside from a brief prologue and epilogue set in the streets of Manhattan, the entire dramatic structure is built from the dinner conversation between the *artistes*.

For background research on the project, the men tape recorded countless hours of conversation where Gregory detailed his stories to Shawn; the emergent material amounted to around a thousand typed pages. They next isolated "dozens of themes" from the raw, unedited transcripts and drifted away from the aforementioned concept of a "talking heads project" to that of a movie script. Over the successive months, Shawn fashioned the dialogues into a screenplay.[18] When asked why they opted to do a film script in lieu of a stage play (given their theatrical roots and the long monologues in the piece), Gregory observes:

> For some reason, from the very beginning ... It just had always seemed a film to us. [long pause] I think somehow we'd always seen it in close-up. As a director ... I haven't had an audience larger than thirty or forty people in over thirty years. And part of the reason for that is that I think that film and television have so changed the eye of the viewer that the viewer is now used to being able to see in close-up. So if you go say to a Broadway theater, and you sit in the fifth row, which is very close, it feels now because of film and television as if you're very, very far away ... When I go to the theater, I like to be on top of the actors. I think it comes from a deep need for intimacy.[19]

Then came Louis's involvement. As Billard recounts the details of the story, they glisten with irony — the stuff of which legends are made. Malle and Guare (already a close friend of Shawn's) happened to visit a photocopy shop on lower Sixth Avenue in September 1979, to duplicate a draft of *Atlantic City*, and hit the store at the very same moment when Shawn happened to be photocopying[20] one of the drafts of his *Dinner* script. Malle met Shawn for the first time; the chance meeting sparked mutual acknowledgement and a brief conversation. (Malle possibly recognized Shawn from his debut as Jeremiah in Woody Allen's *Manhattan*, released the previous spring[21]; Shawn knew and admired Malle's films.) Afterward, Malle suggested to Guare that Shawn play a bit role in *Atlantic City*[22]; the men cast him as the waiter in the posh restaurant where Lou takes Sally for lunch.

Upon finishing the *Dinner* screenplay, Shawn and Gregory engaged in an "absurd" conversation, tossing around the names of the foremost international filmmakers as directorial candidates — *Would Woody Allen be profound enough?*, *Would Ingmar Bergman be funny enough?* and so on.[23] Accounts of what happened next differ slightly from person to person; Shawn muses, "We talked about absolutely everybody and decided that of any director we could think of, the person who was both a great storyteller and also had a great sense of humor was really Louis."[24] But Gregory disagrees. He specifically remembers that Malle's name did *not* come up in their discussion of directorial candidates, so that when Malle expressed interest by calling Shawn and later Gregory, and asked very kindly for permission to direct the script, the request came as a huge shock to the system: "[Louis] said he would *love* to do it. And he was so humble about it—he said that if we didn't think that he was the right director, he was delighted to produce the movie. He said, 'The only thing you must never do is never have flashbacks.'"[25] But how did Malle get his hands on the script to begin with?

In the Philip French interviews, Malle neglects to mention a "third party" that put him in touch with the writers, claiming Shawn approached him directly as a prospective candidate on the set of *Atlantic City*, and later had his agent the script sent to Malle.[26] Yet according to Gregory, the photographer Diana Michener,[27] a mutual friend of all three men, read the script and gave it to the director without the writers' knowledge.[28] Shawn responds to this recollection with, "I agree, except we *told* Diana to give it to him."[29]

Though quite skeptical about the piece when he first learned of it, Malle fell in love with *Dinner* at first glance. Candice Bergen remembers:

> [Louis and I] really were just starting to see each other then. And I remember that one night he came to pick me up and we were on our way to the opera, and he was very excited because he had just been sent the script, which he was completely intrigued by. One of the things that intrigued [Louis], aside from its obvious intelligence, was that it was impossible to shoot, and I think he realized that very few directors of any calibre would be foolish enough to take it on because the obstacle of two hours of even the highest level of talking heads was so daunting to people. Without resorting to flashbacks, and without compromising on the [integrity of the dialogue] ... [Louis's idea of how it would be filmed] came with time. His first idea was to shoot it live. And they did a practice run in a restaurant on the west side, I think it might've been The Ginger Man, in fact. I think it was. And he and Wally and André and maybe a script supervisor ... sat and in real time, ordering a dinner, eating dinner and talking.[30]

At this point, the script was about three hours long.[31] Gregory woke up at 5am every morning to memorize his lines note for note[32]; and Malle videotaped every rehearsal and encouraged the two actors to watch their own performances.[33] Gregory remembers, "We shot a take where I was doing it with a lot of emotion, and afterward, [Louis] said, 'What do you think?' And I said, 'Oh, it's *great!*' And he said, 'Yes, it would win a Tony, but it would never win an Oscar!' Because it didn't have the simplicity that film acting has ... [in cinema] you need to do much less."[34] The actors' biggest challenge involved learning to play themselves as characters—an excruciatingly difficult task. Gregory admits, "It was unspeakably confusing. When ... we had dinner and agreed to do the film together, Louis said to me, 'This is going to be the most difficult thing you'll ever do in your whole life.' And he was absolutely right. Because I just kept losing myself. I didn't know who I was, I didn't know who I should be..."[35] Gregory solved his problem by eventually developing four voices, each an extension of himself:

> Because we all have so many selves ... when I finally created a character, I used
> four voices. One is a kind of Peter Brook guru voice. One is the voice of a used
> car salesman. One is the voice of an upper middle class, spoiled rich kid. And
> the fourth is the voice when I'm actually being truthful. And when I was able
> to find this character based on the four voices, I could stop just being myself,
> and I could be a character based on myself ... [the voices] are isolated, depend-
> ing on which one is appropriate for different parts of the script.[36]

The aforementioned rehearsal at The Ginger Man also proved challenging for a
rather silly reason: whenever one of the actors took a bite of food, it threatened to
render the dialogue trivial and unimportant. Malle solved the problem by virtually
eliminating the moments in which André partakes of his meal, and asked Wally to
reserve his eating and drinking for occasional moments of comic relief.

As mentioned, the difficulty of soliciting funding attenuated production several
times; few financiers believed that a dinner conversation between two men could
make compelling movie material. Sue Weil, then head of PBS,[37] and British producer
Michael White[38] provided Louis, Wally, and André (who established a makeshift
production banner called "The André Company") much of the $400,000 for the film;
White came on board after Malle's first source of funding collapsed, and the director asked his two leads to bide time by performing their roles on stage, at the Royal
English Court Theater in London. To avoid unions and union fees, the crew shot the
New York restaurant scene in a non-union state—Richmond, Virginia—and re-
created a fancy New York restaurant in the ballroom of the evacuated Jefferson Hotel.
Malle and cinematographer Jeri Sopanen used specially-designed 10-minute spools
and set takes of 10 minutes each to shoot the picture. The shoot lasted three weeks;
Malle used the first week to experiment with his cameras, identified (in viewing
rushes for 10 hours, with script girl France La Chappelle) the shot angles that best
suited him, returned to the set, and reshot everything in two weeks, wrapping up
production just before Christmas, 1980. Malle co-edited *André* with Suzanne Baron
during the spring of 1981; it reached American screens in October of that year.

SYNOPSIS

Wally (Wallace Shawn), a diminutive, chubby, and balding playwright cum character actor, trudges cautiously and defensively through the sludge-covered streets of
New York, bundled up in his trenchcoat, doing his best to avoid being hit by a car.
In voice-over, he bemoans the challenges of daily life, reminding us that dramatists
must often find alternate ways to support themselves (acting in his case), and that
his days are spent "doing the errands of [his] trade"[39]—visiting the Xerox shop, buying envelopes, checking with his answering service. Dusk arrives. As Wally enters
the subway, he says he would love nothing more than to go home and have his girlfriend Debby cook him dinner; but on this particular evening, Debby is working at
her waitress job and he has been induced—to his irritation—into dining with an
old acquaintance, André (André Gregory), from whom he's been estranged for years.
A mutual friend, George Grassfield, insisted that Wally see him. Wally is unsure what

happened to André over the past several years but — given the stories he's heard about André talking with trees and an account of André leaning against a crumbling old building and sobbing uncontrollably — Wally believes André probably had some sort of nervous breakdown and despairs at the thought that he will probably be expected to help André. ("Was I supposed to be a doctor, or what?!"[40])

At a posh restaurant, Wally encounters the tall and gaunt André. To Wally's quiet dismay, André throws his arms around him in a warm hug. After the old friends sit down to dinner and order appetizers and a main course of quail, Wally (strategizing in voice-over) plans to "get through" the meal by asking André an ongoing series of questions. This he does; André responds by recounting a series of fantastic adventures to his dinner guest. He opens by detailing his decision to drop out of the theater and join theatrical guru Jerzy Grotowski in a paratheatrical improvisation in a Polish forest, with "forty women who [spoke] neither English nor French"[41] and each played a musical instrument; this led to an formation known as a "beehive," where André had only himself as an improvisatory reference. He remembers a couple who fell in love and abandoned the group following a rather banal improvisation on an imaginary airplane; he details his baptism and christening in a flower-filled castle (where the group renamed him "Yendrush") and the great, towering feast that followed. He informs Wally of his subsequent zest for life, the days when he began to relish going out to the highway and watching the lights turn from red to green. He subsequently tells the story of being called by a voice in a field to read and do a theatrical production of de Saint Exupéry's *The Little Prince*, and a wild omen involving an issue of *Minotaur* that convinced him he was on the right track. He describes his accompaniment of the Buddhist monk Kozan to the Sahara, where the two men worked on *The Little Prince* in the desert, ate sand out of sheer desperation, and threw up. He cites his decision to bring Kozan back to New York to live with the family for six months, and the little monk's comical transformation into a Gucci-wearing beefeater. And he paints the vivid picture of a hallucination in a Long Island church on Christmas Eve, where a Minotaur appeared to him with poppies growing out of its toenails and violets sprouting from its eyelids, and evoked a strange feeling of reassurance.

André speaks of his decision to buy and use for protection a giant flag, fashioned by a flagmaker in Greenwich village — a flag that spewed forth a torrent of Bosch-like demons, its cloth later burned and buried in the ground. He recalls his visit to the colony of Findhorn, a clan of English and Scottish eccentrics who dialogue with insects and grow massive cabbages — a place that blew André's mind open and engulfed him in hallucinations. And, with a passionate and terrified voice, beads of sweat appearing on his face, André flashes back on a ceremony on Montauk in which he was literally buried alive and resurrected. André concludes by repudiating all of his surrealistic experiences and — to Wally's confoundment — condemns himself as an Albert Speer–like architect of his own life.

The two men bemoan the fact that the world is growing more diseased and more horrible, and share observations that people seem to be walking around in a kind of fog, only seeing what they want to see and only expressing themselves "weirdly ... and indirectly."[42] Wally provides an example from his own experience, when he played the role of the cat in the stage production of Bulgakov's *The Master and Margarita* and his fellow performers made sneaky attempts to destroy his ego. André declares that people in general need desperately to be able "to express [themselves] with great clarity."[43] André tells Wally of Roc, the founder of Findhorn, who made great efforts to separate his dream life from his conscious life, confining himself to a state of self-perception, until he somehow fell into exchanges with fauns and the god Pan.

Wally defends the banality of his life, praising his electric blanket yet agreeing that it alters his perception in odd ways. André attempts to dissuade his friend from using the blanket, deriding it as a tool of lobotomization and warning Wally off of it; he underscores the dangers of comfort-induced mental trance. The men reflect on the loss of humanity, of kindness, of self-extension, that have grown so absent in the world — the extent to which a kind of murder is committed on a daily basis via dehumanization. The talk segues to an examination of the theater — both dinner guests agree that the stage should be used to bring one back in touch with reality, but André ultimately concludes, to Wally's utter shock, that the only remaining way to reawaken via theater is (figuratively speaking) "to take participants to Mt. Everest." In Gregory's eyes, this will involve centers like Findhorn, established around the world, used to "spiritually recharge" seekers. He argues that the zombielike states they both perceive in others could be generated by a "world totalitarian government based on money,"[44] and hypothesizes that New York has become a new incarnation of the World War II concentration camps, where prisoners exist in a state of schizophrenia, acting as both prisoners and guards.

Wally delivers a homily on the pleasures of everyday life, as something of a rebuttal to André's wild stories — the pleasures of rising each morning to his cold cup of coffee and discovering that no roach or fly has died in it; of enjoying a piece of coffee cake and of reading Charlton Heston's autobiography. He acknowledges his gross discomfort and displeasure with the highly spiritual nature of André's stories, and makes a solid defense for science, logical thinking and rational thought. André reminds him that the *worship* of science is dangerous; Wally agrees but highly questions the idea that one should simply experience *being* without purposefulness (which he perceives as the "message" of André's stories). André reminds his friend that the truly important thing in life *is* to be, to avoid at all costs the risk of going through the motions and engaging in a daily series of rituals, without any real purpose behind them. Roles, he says — a husband, a father, a wife, a mother — are meaningless, and the truly important goal is to learn to be aware of — and to listen to — the shifting feelings of one's heart. To relish each moment and live as an awakened human, not as a robotic performer. He sums up all of his experiences as a series of processes that were truly necessary for him to learn how to be a human being again. He discusses the need to make every relationship a new adventure, the sad fact that people in general are transient and tend to grow old and die instantly, before our eyes.

By this point, the restaurant has emptied; Wally is genuinely moved when André insists on picking up the check. On the way home, Wally treats himself to a cab ride and watches through the window as he passes a series of buildings, each associated with a unique childhood memory. He informs us (in voice-over) that he went home and told Debby all about his dinner with André.

ANALYSIS

Like *Atlantic City* before it, and *May Fools* a decade later, *My Dinner with André* rests on a slightly obscure, idiosyncratic contextual foundation little understood by many viewers, who thus often miss one of the critical aspects of the film. According to Pauline Kael, *Dinner* seizes upon the small group of eccentric New York theatrical directors who, in the 1970s, after growing dissatisfied with proscenium boundaries, tried to retain a sixties zeitgeist by literally dropping out (of the theater and out of society altogether) and delving into "paratheatrical cults."[45] Gregory stood at the forefront of this group; his experiences form the dramatic basis of the picture.

Through *André*, Louis Malle, Wallace Shawn and André Gregory confront a century-old weakness of cinema that had (prior to 1981) long appeared to be inherently, inextricably built into the medium, and manage to resolve this weakness with a series of groundbreaking stylistic and structural choices. The picture rests on the idea that over the decades, literature and theater have consistently remained preferable to film; unlike playwrights or belletrists, mainstream filmmakers have seldom, if ever, found a consistent way to empower the *mind's eye* and thereby avoid the risk of harnessing the audience's imaginative capacities—the risk that accompanies the existence of cinema's visual field *per se* and commercial cinema's potential for excessive visualization. On the latter note, the timing of *Dinner* was hardly accidental: if one posits *André* in the context of film history, taking into careful consideration the year in which Malle, Gregory and Shawn made the picture, one can observe how a kind of "Spielbergian visual overindulgence" had become a growing threat circa 1980—a threat that made the medium's risk of limiting the viewers' imaginations even more glaringly obvious. While filmmakers who fully harness and bind the viewer's imagination often regard the average cinemagoer as stupid and thick-headed simply by virtue of expecting their audiences to give little or nothing back to the motion picture experience, *André* rests on the opposite expectation and thus, stylistically and contextually, travels to the other extreme. The picture's approach and unusual nature—a filmed two-hour dinner conversation minus flashbacks, flash-forwards, cutaways, or other devices that would compromise the integrity of the dialogue—recall Marlon Brando's old axiom that "An audience will not take something from a film or a book or of poetry if they do not give to it."[46]

In other words, *Dinner* makes successful attempts to extend cinematic boundaries, posing the inevitable question: *Is it possible to reinvent the cinematic medium by finding a way to liberate the mind's eye from the visual prison that so often confines it in "big budget" films?* Co-screenwriters Gregory and Shawn foresaw the solution in two sources: the radio dramas of their childhood, and the work and teachings of the surrealists. As for the first, Gregory recalls:

> There's a central trick to [*Dinner*], which is the trick of radio dramas. Which is what Wally and I when we were kids used to listen to because there was no television. And the trick of the radio drama is it gives you images that activate your own imagination so that the film is actually much more visual than *Lawrence of Arabia*, because it activates each member of the audience to cre-

ating for themselves the Polish forest, the Tunisian Sahara, the journey to India.[47]

Ergo, the screenwriters' nostalgic memories of the radio programs' effects on their psyches encouraged them to heighten the use of imagistic dialogue in the picture, a process that entails moving the imagery to an offscreen fourth dimension *as the cinematic experience unfolds*.[48] Shawn and Gregory's instincts were accurate: to the viewer who surrenders himself or herself, *Dinner* is one of the most visual films ever made. One immediately thinks of the minotaur's appearance in the film.[49] Gregory recalls, "all of a sudden, a huge creature appeared, looking at the congregation, and it was about, I'd say, six foot eight, something like that, and it was half bull and half man, and its skin was blue, and it had violets growing out of its eyelids and poppies growing out of its toenails. And it stood there for the whole mass."[50] Those who dwell and meditate on this image, allowing it to gestate in their minds (in lieu of dismissing it as absurdity or refusing to summon the creature to their thoughts), will find it infinitely more overpowering than even Harryhausen's mythological Dynamatrons in, say, *The 7th Voyage of Sinbad* or *Jason and the Argonauts* because, unlike the Harryhausen creatures, Gregory and Shawn's minotaur is alive — growing and pulsating, with the ability to go through infinite changes instead of following a set, preprogrammed course. Along these lines, note the *insistence* of the verbiage at the end of this quote — violets and poppies don't *grow* out of its eyelids and toenails, they are grow*ing*. The creature is animate instead of static.

Attempts to trace the influences of the surrealism as it plays out in *André* are a bit more complicated. Though all of the stories recounted in the film are accurate,[51] Shawn reworked Gregory's aural story patterns on the page, liberally yet subtly, to take advantage of numerous facets of surrealist theory:

> What Wally did, which made it unbelievably difficult for me, was he took my verbatim stories, and he changed the language ... he didn't change my language, but he changed the order of the way that I told these stories ... it's a very subtle change. In other words, a striking example I can give you would be if I were normally telling a story about being in the Polish forest, I'd say we lived in this little castle, and every morning we'd get up, and we'd do whatever, and then for lunch, we'd eat around this great stone slab and served ... as a table.... [Wally] puts [the great stone slab] next to the tiny little castle.[52] So what you see in your mind's eye is a tiny castle and a huge table, so in fact, he's taking you into dream imagery, and he's taking you into surrealism, even though it sounds like a completely real story because of the changing of the juxtaposition of images. But that wasn't the ... that wasn't the only kind of change. Towards the end of the script when I'm talking about reality, and I say, "You know, I really think, uh, something ... when you, when you think about it, Wally, when you really think about it, I mean, really, when you think about it," the word "real" is used over and over and over and over again, so that it loses all sense of reality. So that what seems to be a real conversation between two men is in fact a hallucinogenic, surreal, dreamlike journey.[53]

The principles that Gregory describes all share the same intent: to form a *direct line* of communication with each viewer's mind, operating quite literally on a subconscious plane, so that the audience has no full or partial awareness of the process. This explains Shawn's comment, "André Gregory and I feel complimented when we realize that people don't think [*Dinner*] was written or acted"[54]: because (in cases where that comment is accompanied by viewer praise) it is proof positive that the devices, which Shawn arranged and planted so carefully throughout the text, are going unseen and thus, on a fundamental level, functioning properly. This occurs throughout the picture.

To initiate the process, Shawn and Gregory impart the discussion with a kind of surrealist prelude, or overture; if they are to carry the audience into the surrealist realm without viewer awareness, they must first preprepare the audience's minds. Thus, they give us insistent repetitions of the word "nothing" and the negation of "anything." "I told him that I didn't want to come [to Poland], because, really, I had nothing left to teach. I had nothing left to say. I didn't know anything. I couldn't teach anything. Exercises meant nothing to me anymore." It is as if the writer-turned-actors are creating a strange kind of *tabula rasa*, a blank slate, clearing their audience's minds to prepare them for the images to follow. It is completely deliberate and unaccidental that Shawn should move the Polish story from the end of André's adventures (in real life) to the outset of the film, a point immediately following the "tabula rasa": the passage in the Polish forest, with the "tiny little castle..." next to the "great stone slab," is one of the most overpowering examples of surrealistic size contrast; in the very same sentence, Shawn also condenses the audience's sense of time dramatically by juxtaposing references to night and references to day, whose proximity to each other suggest that one phase is fading into another with great rapidity. Gregory tells him, "Our schedule was that we would usually start work around sunset, and then we'd generally work until six or seven in the morning, and then, becasue the Poles loved to sing and dance, we'd generally sing and dance till about ten or eleven in the morning ..." So what we have is a kind of spatial and temporal malleabilty that implies, by its very nature, a series of adventures in the surrealistic dream plane and a departure from the realm of everyday phenomena.

Consider another example:

ANDRÉ: Yes, we went off into the desert, and we rode through the desert on camels, and we rode and rode, and then at night we would walk out under that enormous sky and look at the stars, and I just kept thinking about the same things I was thinking about at home — particularly about Chiquita — in fact I thought about just about nothing but my marriage. And I remember one incredibly dark night being at an oasis where there were palm trees moving in the wind, and hearing Kozan singing somewhere far away in a beautiful bass voice, and following his voice along the sand ... And then sometimes I would go off and meditate by myself, and I would see images of Chiquita. Once I actually saw her growing old and her hair turning gray in front of my eyes. And you know, I would just wail and yell my lungs out, out there on those dunes.[55]

Note, first, the deliberate repetition of the word "rode"— Gregory did not simply ride through the desert, he "rode and rode and rode"— the desert gains a kind of endless vastness in the viewers' minds. It is also unaccidental that the images in Gregory's descriptions should be isolated, one (or so) per sentence — Shawn relies on the metonymical use of images to create a "mental sketch," painting details in only the broadest strokes—the stars, the palm trees, the sand—and creating gaps in-between his images that allow the audience to "plug in" additional details with their own fantasies. It would not and could not achieve the same effect if the images were bundled together in one or two sentences—the imagery would be too well-defined and too overpowering, and the language would lack the conception of vastness that exists in the spaces between the individual platonic concepts of the stars, palm trees and sand. Similarly, the script encompasses a series of repetitious verbal rhythms, as when André speaks of the song of St. Francis, "In which you thank God for your eyes, you thank God for your heart, you thank God for your friends, you thank God for your life."[56] He repeats the phrase "Thank God" over and over and over again to the extent that André is not simply speaking, but half-chanting, actually evoking the repetitious and rhythmic nature of the song in his dialogue. A similar principle crops up shortly thereafter, when André recalls the American Indian dance, "with a kind of thumping persistent rhythm." But note how he reads it: "With a kind of thump-ing per-sis-tent rhy-thm." The dialogue incorporates metaphoric image repetition as well—more weighted toward the beginning of the script than the end. For instance, in describing his "beehive" theatrical formation, André uses the word seven times, until the image of a literal beehive appears before us and somehow "breaks up" into a formation of individuals.

Very occasionally, Shawn incorporates indirect references to the audience, telling them, with pure forthrightness, exactly what to picture—as when Gregory brings up the random example of a Chekhovian theatrical improvisation. "For example, you would say to them, 'All right, let's say that it's a rainy Sunday afternoon on Sorin's estate, and you're all trapped in the drawing room.'" Impossible to read this passage without actually picturing *oneself* in Sorin's estate on a rainy Sunday—the inner context of the director talking to his troupe drops away as soon as the line is spoken, and the "you're all" addressed to the imaginary theatrical troupe becomes a "you're all" addressed to the cinema audience.

Though it would be ill-advised to regard all of Gregory's words as a "gimmick," Gregory's long-windedness does, in fact, function as a defensive mechanism for his character—his attempt to avoid connecting with his friend on a deep (and thus, vulnerable) level, just as Wally cowers behind silence, muttering only occasional "Hmm"s and "I see"s for the first thirty minutes. Gregory's long monologues, to which Shawn vehemently objects on some fundamental level, as his refutation of the spiritual elements near the end of the film proves—are used to draw Wally out, and Wally's hesitations and eventual refutations encourage André to become more pensive. As Gregory notes in a 1999 *New York Times* article, "I think it's a men's movie on one level because one man [Wally] has trouble articulating. The other guy [André] just talks at him; he doesn't really talk with him. So I see one line of the movie as two men who are hidden: one through introversion, the other through extroversion."[57] The twin arcs of the picture involve a "coming together" of the two men, their growing ability to break through their barriers and form an emotional bond.

This explains, on the broadest level, Malle's shifting shot selections in the film. Many critics and commentators have assessed the film as a simple series of back-and-forth close-ups; Roger Ebert, for example, wrote of it in his 1982 review, "At first, director Louis Malle's sedate series of images (close-ups, two-shots, reaction shots) calls attention to itself, but as Gregory talks, the very simplicity of the visual style renders it invisible."[58] Ebert's observations about the subtlety and invisibility are accurate — indeed, the style becomes so natural after a few minutes that it is difficult to retain an analytical and clinical mindset without being pulled into the flow of the discussion, hypnotically. But Malle's shot choices are quite a bit more complex than Ebert's words suggest. The picture begins by using, as its most common set-up for the first 25 minutes or so, an over-the-shoulder shot of André, with Wally in the foreground, where André relies most heavily on his "Peter Brook guru voice" and, occasionally, his "used car salesman voice." When coupled with the voices representing two distinct ego states, the implication of this shot — Wally's back to us, André facing Wally and the audience — is that André is teaching everyone, or occasionally "selling" to everyone, what he experienced and learned from dropping out. Beyond these first stages in the film, the basic transition involves two trends in the shot selection as the picture unfolds: first, Malle gradually closes in, relying more and more heavily on close-ups of André and Wally, particularly at moments when André describes something deeply personal and emotionally affecting, as during his story of being buried alive. Second, Malle's shots begin to lose their angularity, facing the actor's faces more and more directly. Thus, it is only around of the end of the film (uncoincidentally, when André starts using his regular voice), both when the men's façades drop and they are able to speak directly with each other, and when the nature of the talk becomes correspondingly more "direct," that we get eye-level close-ups of André Gregory's face, not at an angle to the camera, but facing it dead-on even though his eyes are averted to Wally.

A few shots are chosen simply for utilitarian reasons, as when André tells his story about seizing the teddy bear out of pure impulse and whipping it into the air; Malle cuts to an unusual (within the shot sequence of the film) reverse two-shot of André facing Wally, with a sizeable amount of head room above them, so that as André flings his arm out and up maniacally, Malle has enough space above their heads to catch the full range of Gregory's arm movement. And similarly, in one of the film's funniest moments — when André loudly mimics the idea of bringing crazy American laughter into a Tibetan home ("If four Tibetans came together, and tragedy had just struck one of the ones, and they all spent the whole evening going *Aha ha ha ehee hee hee oho ho! Wo — ho ho ho!*") inadvertently drawing the negative attention and disapproval of the waiter ("Is everything all right, gentlemen?") Malle cuts to a kind of low-angle two shot of the two men, with the waiter between them, enabling him to catch André's intense stare of angry violation as the black-suited figure looms above them nosily.

And still other shots are so precise, angularly, that they are nearly impossible to identify onscreen; Ebert re-reviewed the film 18 years later, for its rerelease, and — perhaps catching his own oversimplicity in the first review — had apparently learned that the director's shots are judged down to the *millimeter*.[59] In *Malle on Malle*, the director tells Philip French, "Watching these takes, I somehow figured out how to deal with [Wally and André]. It became clearer to me that in shooting André, when

I wanted him to be funny or slightly pompous, a certain angle was the best, and when I wanted him to be moving, it worked better for him if the camera was a little higher."[60]

Aesthetically, the director places a series of mirrors with a single plant behind his two actors, mirrors he moves slightly from take to take,[61] rendering the background slightly animate. But the picture's most impressive aesthetic accomplishments, by all means, are spatial. *André* accomplishes something outrageously difficult: it preserves and sustains Malle's need to create and preserve an abrechtian (or Artaudian) space; we actually believe we are in a real restaurant with background action ongoing. In many of the shots of Gregory, we see the bartender walking around behind him, and Malle is able to establish a *continuity*, perhaps because so many of his shots involve cutting from one side of the room (André) to the other (Wally) that he does not have to worry about "matching" background action from shot to shot. Along similar lines (and a far more impressive feat) Malle and cinematographer Jeri Sopanen somehow manage to capture, in the mirrors behind and above Wally and André, the patrons slowly beginning to get up and leave the restaurant, the dining room emptying out at a nearly imperceptible pace as the dialogue rolls on. The very fact that the mirrored background images of the restaurant emptying are as consistent as they are from take to take, patrons gradually leaving, so that in the final scenes, we see one or two other patrons left (through the mirrors) and then, eventually, no one else in the restaurant, is astonishing — though no documentation exists of how this was accomplished, the departure of the extras must have been pre-planned and choreographed as a reverse progression, from shot to shot.

The "visual style" of *Dinner* borrows most heavily from some of the impressionist painters; one thinks in particular — *given* the mirrors behind André and Wally — of Manet's masterpiece "Bar at the Folies-Bergères," for — as in Manet — the artist uses mirrors to spread light, and a number of the colors in *Dinner* are the same as the colors in Manet's "Bar."

Narratively, though each character "arcs," *Dinner* is nonetheless far more weighted toward Shawn, simply by virtue of its dramatic architecture. Shawn is the main character, whose "desire" is twofold: on the most immediate level, to gain the courage to come out from behind his shield and express his thoughts; on a broader level, to gain a greater degree of life-appreciation. Malle and the screenwriters completely root the audience in Shawn's perspective, first with a prologue, later with an epilogue. By virtue of Shawn's full-blown transition from a *lack*-of-appreciation toward life to a spiritual awakening that enables him to see and value the beauty around him, his is the only full character transition that Malle or the writers enable the audience to witness. The prologue and the epilogue mirror the shift in Wally's internal state, the prologue cold and visually grungy, the epilogue warm, cozy and serene.

Keeping this in mind, one should observe carefully the first few minutes of the picture (in particular) to discern the visual clues that Malle and his co-writers hand the viewer. "Wally" begins the story — dwarfed by the inhumanity of the Manhattan cityscape, exhausted from doing the "errands of [his] trade," obsessed with money (or the lack thereof) and his inability to pay the bills. His outlook is generally negative, and the feeling we get is one of Wally's alienation, of his own insignificance to anyone else — during the first 20 seconds he is nearly run over by a car as he trudges through the streets and crosses an alley. Malle and his writers enable the audience to deeply feel (to share) the same alienation, beginning with the opening long shot that makes Wally appear inconsequential, and also includes a tiny, subtle, understated camera movement. Though Malle has specifically stated — many times— that he wanted to avoid tracking shots in *André* to eliminate reminders of the camera's presence, he makes one almost indiscernible exception in the first five seconds: a tiny, slow track forward that recalls an identical shot in Antonioni's *L'Avventura* (taken from a corridor in an abandoned villa, where the vanished Massari may be watching her friends from a discreet location). In *Dinner*, one cannot help but read this shot — an establishing shot — as an understated indication that we are actually *in* the frame and have "become" an unseen character; likewise, Shawn seems to be incredibly self-conscious when he is on camera, as if he is aware that we are following him.

Yet — though Shawn speaks to the audience in a voice-over — he never once turns and addresses us directly. His communication with us is oblique, indirect, so that we feel — on a deep-seated, gut level — the alienation he is experiencing.[62] On a comic note, the first impression that the screenplay (and film) hand us is that "Wally" the character is completely wrapped up in himself, although he would love to feign otherwise. Though his first line represents a half-hearted, comical attempt to demonstrate interest in making a general, slightly pretentious statement about the "life of a playwright" ("The life of *a playwright* is tough...") a kind of self-obsessed narcissism comes bursting through, completely beyond Wally's control: "*I'd* had to be up by ten in the morning ... *I'd* gone to the stationery store ... *I'd* made it to the post office," and so on. One might argue that the narcissism even extends itself into the structure of the picture — the fact that Wally as playwright only allows us to witness *his* full transition, that the picture is not balanced between Wally's arc and André's arc.

The overall implication of Wally's voice-over in *Dinner* is that — like Jeanne Tournier (Moreau) in *Les Amants*, "Wally" the character is watching his own story at some point in the distant future, and narrating the flashbacks, yet — somehow — managing to project, through his narration, the same frame of mind at every point in the story that he — as a character — had at that very stage. (He doesn't say, "This morning, the mailbox was stuffed with bills— how *am* I supposed to pay them?," but "This morning, the mailbox *had just been* stuffed with bills. What *was* I supposed to do? How *was* I supposed to pay them?") Note how this could also explain Shawn's declaration of himself as a playwright: he is subtly and indirectly mentioning the fact that he — as a playwright — is telling the story in hindsight and thus reworking it slightly, just as one must rework one's experiences through a dramatic framework, as one gives structure to a dream or a memory.

The intentional bias in Shawn's script also explains the tonal shift in the motion picture from a kind of gentle satire of the Manhattan intellectual subculture that lightly kisses off the hyper-esotericism of New York pseudo-intellectuals, before moving, during its second half, into a deeper, more sincere and dramatic Epicurean diatribe — it reflects the transition in our shifting perspective of "André" (as a character) which unquestionably rests on *Wally's* shifting perception of him. André as a character is thus hugely narcissistic, irritating, and pompous at first; he becomes sort of an amalgam of every eccentric and arcane pseudo-intellectual the viewer may have experienced, who makes crack references right and left to countless esoteric subjects.[63] And Malle uses Shawn as a tonal arbiter, interjecting carefully the shots of "Wally" (throughout the first half of the film) that align the viewer with him in spirit — wordless shots detailing his bafflement and confoundment, his slight interest but enormous disapproval. We side with Shawn automatically, simply by virtue of being "let in" on his thoughts through voice-over — it makes us close to Shawn and, via the omission of a similar voice-over from Gregory, aloof from André. Perhaps Danny Peary best summarizes Shawn's irritation and confusion when faced with Gregory's cryptic stories: "Anyone who has ever been to a party of *artistes* can identify with Shawn, who is funny."[64] A perfect example of Gregory's hyper-intellectualism arrives at the beginning of the picture, evidenced by an exchange where Wally is confounded by his inability ("What is *bramborova polevka*?") to read the Franco-Czech menu: he makes an awkward turn to André, and, with one finger on the menu, whispers, "How about this?" André roars with laughter, privy to some abstruse joke that only he understands: "*Seven swank shrimp*?!" Wally laughs along weakly, though it is perfectly clear from his baffled expression that he sits on the outside looking in, and the humor comes not from the "swank shrimp" joke, but from the lack of comprehension we share with Wally in reference to the crypticism of the joke.[65] This occurs at several points — another hilarious moment arrives when Wally, who has just been completely thrown by several of André's stories, back-to-back, hears of the minotaur and randomly interjects, "By the way, did you ever see that play *The Violets Are Blue*? When you mentioned the violets, it reminded me of that. It was about ... [long pause] ... people being strangled on a submarine. [close-up of Wally sweating]" Wally's is the confusion, the desperation (as Peary implies) of anyone who has ever struggled for an eternity to listen and pay attention to an eccentric *artiste*, and longs to be able to engage in the conversation, making desperate and consistently unsuccessful attempts to speak with that person on his or her "wavelength."

In a wonderful and moving piece of irony, the purpose of the film as a whole, in hindsight, recolors the initial implications of Wally's selfishness. The gestalt of André's dialogues involves a kind of spiritual rebirth, and a subsequent ability to appreciate *being*, to become conscious of one's feelings and stay in touch with them, to cherish the banal. This is where the lines between onscreen and offscreen reality begin to blur, for — as Gregory reveals in articles that followed the film — the real-life result of his spiritual sojourns *did* entail learning to appreciate the little things, "like Wally." What the film gives us, then, is a multi-leveled approach to the generativity that Dr. Dan McAdams describes in *The Stories we Live by: Personal Myths and the Making of the Self*. On the exterior (extratextual) level the real-life André and Wally have re-sculpted Gregory's experiences as a *formal* act of self-mythmaking, and their attempts to pass on the truths that André learned through the process, through the creation of the film — to pass on the spiritual rebirth and a heightened life appreciation, and to reawaken the viewers from the "zombielike states" that they bemoan in the conversation — lies at the core of generativity. The trick is that the film is not done in second person, as a sort of lecture, for if it were, it would be automatically dismissed by viewers everywhere as a piece of mordant and cocky pedanticism; rather, Gregory and Shawn work out the philosophical truths through the dramatic apparatus. One should recall Wally's quote from the film, "Somehow in our social existence we're *only* allowed to express our feelings weirdly and indirectly." The very fact that Gregory and Shawn resculpt themselves as characters enables them to rework something that could easily become "message material" into a legitimate drama (with satirical elements) where "Wally" the character makes a broad transition from moroseness and gloominess and a *lack* of life-appreciation to a spiritual rebirth, and then enables the audience to make the same astonishing transition via a recounting of his dinner with André. The generativity, in other words, was passed from the real-life André Gregory, to the real-life Wallace Shawn (who worked the dialogues into a screenplay and, in doing so, passed it on to the lips of Gregory's character). Then, in turn—in the framework of the story—Gregory's character passes it onto Shawn's character during the dinner conversation, who, in turn, passes it along to us, as an undeclared flashback that frames the entire film.

The prospect of tracing *André*'s influences on subsequent cinema is an interesting one indeed. While Gregory characterizes *Dinner* as so original that it failed to impact successive motion pictures, this is simply untenable. The picture would be kissed off (or, as some would argue given Fred Blassie's onscreen sincerity, *paid homage*) in the 1983 Andy Kaufman spoof *My Breakfast with Blassie*. One could make a solid case for the idea that *Dinner* had an enormous effect on the post–1980 cinema of Henry Jaglom, whose films—from the early eighties on—were intermittently successful conversation pieces.[66] *Dinner* clearly made possible the cinematic monologues of the late (and ill-fated) Spalding Gray, whose hugely entertaining cult sensations *Swimming to Cambodia, Terrors of Pleasure, Monster in a Box*, and *Gray's Anatomy* simply consist of Gray delivering surrealistic monologues to an audience from a stationary table. *Dinner* appears, as well, to have influenced an unusual and little-known 1983 made-for-cable film entitled *Mister Halpern and Mister Johnson*, directed by Alvin Rakoff; Jackie Gleason and Lord Laurence Olivier play the title characters, two elderly gentlemen who spend nearly the entire film sitting at a table in a bar after learning that they both had romantic relations with a woman who has died, and take 57 minutes to rhapsodize on the meaning of life. As we have seen, Shawn's follow-up to *André*, the much bolder exercise in style *The Designated Mourner*, would certainly never have been possible without the runaway success of *Dinner*. And Bernt Capra's 1991 indie film *Mindwalk*, dubbed "*My Dinner with André* for the Ecological Set," simply consists of Liv Ullmann, Sam Waterston and a bearded John Heard tooling around Mont Saint Michel and discussing the environmental and political teachings of the director's brother, Fritjof Capra.

Granted, one can only argue that these films pulled from *Dinner* in the loosest sense—the directors of Gray's films, for instance, tend to rely heavily on background visuals; Jonathan Demme (director of *Cambodia*) even resorts to including cutaways to scenes from a feature co-starring Gray, *The Killing Fields*. *Halpern* is filmed, more or less, with a stationary camera; though deliriously choppy, Jaglom's films from the eighties are shot more or less traditionally; Capra's film has the background of the island environment to retain visual interest. *Dinner* is one of the only pictures to film a conversation with a series of back-and-forth cuts, combined with a unity of space and time and strategically chosen shots, that moves all of the action, surrealistically, to an unseen fourth dimension.

But there is one unusual exception. *Dinner* made perhaps its most significant impact on the late Derek Jarman's experimental feature *Blue* (1994), a piece of cinematic performance art that, stylistically, is even bolder than *André*. In *Blue,* Jarman divests the screen of its visual element not partially, but fully; the film consists of only an unshifting blue matte screen, overlaid with a multilayered soundtrack of Byzantine complexity. *Blue* thus operates on the same basic principles of "radio drama" and surrealism that *André* celebrates.

CRITICAL RESPONSE

According to Gregory's recollections, *My Dinner with André* received mostly negative reviews upon release, becoming a "cult favorite" and a "runaway success" only in time, though Gene Siskel and Roger Ebert cite the film as one of the two best pictures of 1982.[67] Yet a study of the film's initial reviews suggests that Siskel and Ebert were not exceptions to the rule — it was quite well-received by most American critics. Pauline Kael, of *The New Yorker*, praises the picture as "A mad, modern Platonic dialogue about the meaning of life ... it flows smoothly and easily ... it has a beautiful structure, and the two men have turned themselves into perfect foils ... this is a bizarre and surprisingly entertaining satirical comedy."[68] Though Gregory insists that the Vincent Canby review from *The New York Times* was terrible — he remembers Canby calling it "a sweet, Winnie the Pooh kind of fable, if you like that sort of thing"[69] — a glance at Canby's review suggests quite the opposite; he evidently loved the film, and his Winnie the Pooh analogy, however ill-advised, is not used as a slur. In fact, Canby cites the picture as a "*New York Times* Critic's Pick." His review refers to the picture as, "Louis Malle's very funny, extremely special new film..." and Canby muses incisively, "the talk is not exactly Shavian but it's sometimes so provocative or nutty or freewheeling that one would like to butt it ... as the dinner progresses, André becomes a most winning character ... this film is often invigorating ... these two men respond to each other so well."[70] And Bruce Williamson, writing for *Playboy*, acknowledges his initial skepticism about a filmed two-hour conversation but heaps unbridled praise onto the film:

> Sounds dull, right? That's what I thought beforehand. But director Louis Malle, in a minor stroke of genius, fortunately saw — and has brilliantly brought out — all the potential excitement ... generated when a movie camera strips away masks to reveal character.... What results is one of the craziest, saddest, most surprising and original movies of this or any other year ... a total treat.[71]

Less enthusiastic are David Denby, writing for *New York*, who espouses mixed feelings—"[*Dinner*] is one of the most fascinating and irritating movies to come along in quite a while ... much of what [Gregory] says is foolish beyond belief, but a journey like his is not easily dismissed"[72] — and L.L. Cohn, who writes in *Variety,* "The picture fails ... in its lack of balance between the two protagonists."[73]

But these two reviews were exceptions to the rule in the States. The preponderance of negative reviews came from France and other non-English speaking countries, where — as Malle acknowledges to Philip French — the heavy emphasis on dialogue pretty much ruined the picture for European audiences, forcing them to read four or five or six subtitle lines at a time and completely miss the significance of the images.[74] Typical of these pans is Michael Chion, writing for the preeminent *Cahiers du cinéma,* who read the film as an attempt to incite the same sort of provocation, structurally and formically, that Malle had incited topically with *Murmur of the Heart* and *Pretty Baby.* Chion refers to the style as a "television style" of filmmaking and complains that the picture's formic radicalism is "unproductive."[75]

Of course, the great irony is that — as Gregory notes — *Dinner* went on to become "a classic," regarded as one of Malle's undisputed masterpieces — "very few film programs now don't teach it."[76]

17

Crackers— 1984

More Than He Needed or Wanted

> "I must be one of the last optimists, where the history and the future of the film industry in Hollywood is concerned.... Money's tight: it's 1982, and the purchasing power of the dollar is not what it once was. In 1974, when I was making *Jaws* ... the film's budget rose to $8 million. Today, because of the dollar, the franc, the yen, whatever — there's world-wide inflation besetting the film industry—*Jaws* would probably cost $27 million. And a film like *E.T.*—at $10.3 million it's the cheapest movie I've made in the last two years—would cost about $18 million in five years' time ... If we compromise, and end up having to make a film for $3 million or $4 million, when its budget ought to be more like $15 million ... we just have to do it. We are the captives of our times."
> — Steven Spielberg, asked to answer the question, "Is American cinema dying?" in Wim Wenders's documentary *Chambre 666* (1982).

> "I got some letters that [Louis] wrote from America before we went to Mexico [for the production of *Viva Maria*], and he was always putting, 'United Artists,' and following 'Artists' by an exclamation mark."
> — Jean-Claude Carrière, interview with the author

BACKGROUND

Winter, 1981-82: deeply in love with new wife Candice Bergen and riding high on the twin *succès d'estimes* of *Atlantic City* and *My Dinner with André*, Malle felt invigorated. A decade later, he would recall the period fondly, musing that he foresaw no conflicts working in the United States. He told Jamie Bruce, "'I thought, after *My Dinner with André*, that I could do *anything*."[1] His self-perceptions were astute. The triumphs of *Atlantic* and *André* opened a number of doors—several new projects for him to consider concurrently. The first involved a feature with the working title *Port Alamo*, inspired by a 1980 Ross Milloy article that Malle read in the *Sunday New York Times Magazine* about the Vietnam war reescalating on Texas soil between Vietnamese immigrants and redneck fishermen. Malle had visited Milloy in Texas, in April of 1981, to talk about a screen adaptation of the piece.[2] Though presumably

In the Mission District of San Francisco, a motley, unkempt band of social misfits, including (from left to right) Ramon (Trinidad Silva), Weslake (Donald Sutherland), Turtle (Wally Shawn), Boardwalk (Larry Riley) and Dillard (Sean Penn), devise an off-the-wall plan to rob a local pawn shop in *Crackers.*

still fresh in the filmmaker's mind late in the year (after the releases of *Atlantic* and *André*), he clearly felt, on some level, that the time wasn't yet ripe for *Alamo*, and set that project aside indefinitely. It would be produced three years later — in the summer of 1984 — under the title *Alamo Bay*, and is discussed in Chapter 18, "The Weight of the Unfamiliar."

But it was still only late 1981, and at that time, Malle's primary instinct led him back to John Guare as a collaborative partner — not only because the writer-director team culled such a positive response to *Atlantic City* (multiple Academy Award nominations, universal critical acclaim, sizeable box office draws), but because they discovered with *Atlantic* that they were on an almost identical creative wavelength, and found it a tremendous pleasure to work together. (More detail about the screenplay that came out of their second effort, *Moon Over Miami*— a strange and wonderful Guare script, originally slated to be directed by Malle in mid–1982 —can be read in Appendix A.) The ill-fated production began to collapse in March of 1982 — by no small coincidence, the same time when *Crackers* first took root.

Meanwhile, Ed Lewis (*Spartacus, Missing, The Thorn Birds*), a producer affiliated with Universal Pictures,[3,4] made other plans for Malle. He had his heart set on doing

Crackers, a contemporary American remake of the 1958 Italian caper comedy *I Soliti ignoti* (a.k.a. *Big Deal on Madonna Street*, a.k.a. *Pigeon*, a.k.a. *Persons Unknown*), a Mario Monicelli picture starring Vittorio Gassman, Marcello Mastroianni, Rosanna Rory, Toto, and Claudia Cardinale. For some unknown reason, Lewis could only foresee Malle directing the piece,[5] and repeatedly egged the director to helm this project, calling him doggedly for two years[6] and refusing to take no for an answer.[7] With *Alamo* on the shelf and the *Miami*'s future uncertain, Malle chose a path he never would have considered a year or two prior: he signed a contract with Lewis for the Monicelli remake — a contract dated March 30, 1982,[8] giving him full license to abandon the project whenever he wished. *Crackers* would begin production in December of 1982; the director spent the interim months attempting to revive *Miami*, protracting his efforts through the autumn of that year, but the project continued to slip out of his grasp, growing ever more remote and distant.

Any attempts to reestablish and reconstruct a definitive linear history of *Crackers*—which, alongside *Alamo Bay*, remains one of Malle's only unmitigated critical and commercial failures—are a bit of a challenge. Malle, screenwriter Jeff Fiskin (*Cutter's Way*, *Revenge*), film historian René Prédal, biographer Pierre Billard and assistant editor James Bruce each recount the picture's genesis uniquely — so that any discussions of the project's history (and discussions of what exactly went awry) may confuse and disorient the film historian. Moreover, after reading Fiskin and Bruce's assessment of the picture (as we shall see), one even has grounds to question *if* anything went askew in the production itself. The best this author can do is to apologize in advance, providing a series of slightly contradictory insights from several sources and encouraging the reader to draw his or her own conclusions, without being able to resolve those contradictions once and for all.

By all accounts, it is clear that *Crackers* did begin as one of Ed Lewis's pet projects. Malle implies in dialogues with Philip French that before he signed on to do *Crackers*, Fiskin became tied to the project under Lewis's aegis. He does so not only by never mentioning his attempts to seek out a screenwriter for the project, but by citing his admiration for Fiskin as one of his primary reasons for agreeing to take the assignment — as if working with Fiskin were a prerequisite.[9] Prédal affirms Fiskin's prior involvement explicitly, characterizing *Crackers* as, "[The film] that the producer ... Lewis ... had proposed to Malle several times and that the screenwriter Fiskin was in the process of writing."[10] Fiskin remembers it entirely differently: Malle, he says, became extremely interested in the project before Universal put a screenwriter under contract. According to Fiskin, Malle began to search actively for a scenarist, informally inviting Nicholas Meyer (*Star Trek 2: The Wrath of Khan*, *Invasion of the Bee Girls*, *The Human Stain*) to join him. Tied up with other endeavors, Meyer felt *Crackers* would be an assignment well suited for Jeff Fiskin and introduced the two men. Fiskin remembers:

> Louis was involved first. He had wanted to do a film, a remake of ... *Big Deal on Madonna Street* ... and Louis talked to Nick Meyer ... and Nick was busy doing something. And he said, "You know, you oughtta meet my friend Fiskin." ... When [Louis] called, I said [laughing], "Of *course* I would be interested in doing ... whatever you're interested in!" And he said, "Why don't you

take a look at the movie? ... I'm flying to New York next week ... we'll talk about
it on the plane and see if there's something we want to do." ... We discussed
it as we were flying to New York, and by the time we got off the plane, I think
he saw something in his head already.... The kind of vision that he had, it
wasn't that he said, "Go write this." It wasn't like that at all.... The first scene
... I wrote it in a particular way. I had quick cuts introducing all the characters. And what he saw immediately as he was reading it was that there could
be one tracking shot, going through this one area in the Mission District of
San Francisco.... He was a cameraman! ... And he had this vision of *exactly* how
this scene should work.[11]

One point on which everyone agrees is that Fiskin led Malle to the Mission District,
prior to the above discussion on the plane, and that the area fascinated Louis.

The director's involvement in the project *per se* raises a question that is key,
absolutely central, to this chapter: why would Louis Malle, a filmmaker so used to
creative autonomy on a movie set, so built for shooting quickly, with a smaller creative team and as much flexibility as possible, with a complete disdain for the idea
of ever working under any producer other than his brother Vincent, ever, *ever* opt
to do a $12 million motion picture for a goliathan Hollywood studio? Given an under-
standing of how the director preferred to work, this move would seem to spell the
recipe for colossal disaster — even without knowing what happened (or, circa late
1982, what would happen) when he agreed to helm *Crackers*.

The answer involves a contradiction in Malle's life and interests, identified on
the most local and immediate level by Candice Bergen. She asserts that "[Louis] was
seduced into taking [*Crackers*] for practical reasons. It obviously was not a work of
his that came from the heart. It was not a work he was passionate about."[12] But Malle
himself would perhaps have objected to Bergen's inference about his "seduction by
Hollywood" — he goes out of his way to tell Philip French that he had *no* excuse, that
Hollywood did not con him or take advantage of him, that he made the decision on
his own and had to bear the responsibility as a result.[13] He actually compliments
Fiskin's screenplay in hindsight, and believes that leviathian studio filmmaking simply ran contrary to his temperament.[14] David Hare concurs with this: "[Louis] found
it very difficult when he couldn't get his own rhythm ... [when] the rhythm was being
dictated by "Oh, we've got to go to another set-up, this'll take two-and-a-half
hours."[15]

Fiskin and (to a lesser degree) James Bruce and Pierre Billard all argue that the
problem lay elsewhere. Fiskin, for one, feels it had very little (if anything) to do with
the "studio system," and believes conflict *per se* was inherent in Malle's method. He
argues that on any project, "Louis ... considered the film an adversary ... like a bull
in a bullfight, only those old Cretan fights where they would wrestle the bull to the
ground by its horns. I don't think it had anything to do with America, or that period
of his life, that is how he approached doing things."[16] He muses, "I don't think there
was any [conflict with the studios] ... I think he pretty much had as much money as
he needed, I think that he had the script that he wanted, he had the actors that he
wanted. I didn't witness it with the studios ... No ... I don't think that's where [the
problem] happened. If it did happen."[17]

Bergen disagrees wholeheartedly with this statement. "I don't think it was an accident," she says, "that *Crackers* came out of a period where we were staying in California, which was a place [Louis] profoundly distrusted.... I think he felt that there was something in the water, and that the values were *so* screwy, and *so* skewed, that ... he felt it was ... a dangerous place for someone like him."[18]

James Bruce points to a far more interesting conclusion—and actually (given the film's initial failure) a hopeful one. He reflects, "I can tell you where the problem happened with *Crackers*. The first cut of that picture was *so* much funnier, and *so* much more interesting and better all around. They kept forcing us to cut it down. And the shorter it got, the longer it felt."[19] Likely an accurate assessment, but only a telling symptom of a much broader, insurmountable difficulty: according to Pierre Billard, Ed Lewis—godfather and overseer of the project, who devoted himself to "guiding Malle through" the studio environment, and encouraged open, creative discussions with the director about choices in the film—relinquished control of the project three weeks in. Prédal writes, "Malle had accepted the project via friendship with a producer who worked on the film for months to ensure that it would get produced, but the head of production at the studio left in the middle of the filming to pursue his career elsewhere ... and his successor found the idea execrable."[20]

This successor was Lewis's son-in-law, Robert Cortes,[21] who not only felt indifferent (as Malle suggests),[22] but began a meaningless power trip, wresting control unnecessarily from Malle and Suzanne Baron in the editing room, and thus violating Lewis's promise to give Malle full control of the final cut.[23,24] The result is a film that—as we shall see—*feels* severely truncated, a casualty of aggressive studio politics and the misguided creative instincts of a producer completely ignorant of the project he was handling.

Despite his insistence that Malle had few (if any) on set problems from the studio environment, Fiskin does recount one minor source of trouble: language. Malle demonstrated a pronounced inability to latch on to some cultural gags in the script. Fiskin reflects:

> There is a moment in *Crackers* where Jack [Warden] says at the very end ... his mother has died, he's standing there, he's seen these people who have broken into his pawn shop, and he doesn't even realize that that's what they've done. He's kind of had a few drinks to take the edge off, and he's just in this melancholy mood, and as far as he's concerned, these are his friends. And ... he is holding a huge long box that looks like long-stemmed roses ... but there is in fact smoked salmon in it. But in fact, it was not supposed to be a smoked salmon! The screenplay calls for lox, and he says, 'And she looked up at me, and her last words were 'Lox!'" This is a joke in English. A 'lox' at that time, perhaps not anymore, was a phrase quite commonly used for a worthless person ... 'He sits there like lox on a plate.' ... It would have worked in the film if it had come out exactly right. And ... Louis didn't know what to do with it ... He said, "Well, can't her last words be 'smoked sallman'?" [*sic*] ... Jack was saying [laughing], "No, no, no, Louis! I've gotta say 'lox,' it's my funny line!"[25]

Of course (as Fiskin notes) it wasn't a question of intelligence ..."Malle was a brilliant guy."[26] Instead, it was simply an undefinable "mental block" in the director's mind. As the screenwriter concludes, "I think there were subtleties that came naturally to him in his French films, that he could never master, no matter how hard he struggled, in English."[27]

The production of *Crackers* began in December of 1982 and lasted five months, through April of 1983 (an unusually long period for a Malle project, whose shoots averaged around two or three months, maximum). It appeared in U.S. cinemas in February 1984 and disappeared soon after, but did not surface in France until it aired on television, under the title *Effraction avec préméditation*, some eight years later, on July 12, 1992.[28]

SYNOPSIS

In the heavily interracial blue-collar Mission District of San Francisco, during the early years of the Reagan-era recession, security guard Weslake (Donald Sutherland); the infant-toting pimp Boardwalk (Larry Riley); thief cum electrician cum rock 'n' roll musician Dillard (Sean Penn); Dillard's diminutive, laconic partner in crime, Ramon (Trinidad Silva); and the eccentric and always-hungry Turtle (Wallace Shawn) are all neighborhood hangers-on and frequent customers of the elderly Melvin Garvey's (Jack Warden) pawn shop. Other locals include Slam Dunk (Anna Maria Horsford), one of Boardwalk's prostitutes— and meter maid Maxine (Christine Baranski), entangled in an ongoing raunchy and fetishistic love affair with Weslake.

As the story opens, Maxine cruises the streets in her vehicle, eyeing the area for illegally parked cars to ticket, while Slam Dunk saunters past, on the prowl for johns.

Weslake fritters away the afternoon playing checkers with Garvey in the shop; Boardwalk stops in and attempt to sell Garvey a baby carriage with his son Tyrone hidden inside, and almost manages to slip one past the old man when Tyrone caterwauls, giving himself away and refusing to let his father escape. Dillard and Ramon stop into the store to try to reclaim Dillard's electric guitar from Garvey—the instrument recently repossessed by the shop—but the boy is disgusted and horrified to learn that Garvey has knocked up the price for the sake of profit. As a compromise, Garvey offers to return the guitar for slightly less if Dillard follows through on his promises to wire the pawn shop's burglary system, but consistently refuses to sell the guitar for the initial buying price. Growing enraged, Dillard screams at Garvey and issues a graphically violent threat. Upon leaving the store, Dillard quietly swears revenge on the old man, planning a cunning robbery—together, he and Ramon will rig the burglary system, break into the store and crack open and rob Garvey's safe. Words about the plan pass between them in the middle of the street but fail to go unheard. An obvious mistake: Boardwalk sits in his car, only a few feet away, cradling Tyrone. Within earshot, the radio on when the words slipped out. Boardwalk insists he missed it, but later informs Weslake of the thieves' plans, the two planning (with Turtle) on joining the heist.

Meanwhile, Weslake and Turtle slip off to a bar for their weekly round of guacamole, while Dillard visits Ramon's rickety house and falls instantly in love with his luminous Hispanic sister Maria (Tasia Valenza). The girl indicates that she returns his affections, but the little thief threatens to emasculate Dillard ("I'll cut off your pesquesos") if he lays a finger on her. Ramon plans to set Maria up with a more respectable Latino gentleman, Don Fernando (Edouard de Soto). At Maxine's apartment, Weslake sits on her bed and watches ping-pong on TV while she undresses in the bathroom and warms up for sex. Weslake disappoints her with the news that this year, when Garvey makes his annual pilgrimage to visit his mother, he won't be leaving Weslake to guard the store again; Garvey plans to use the burglar alarm as an alternative, which means Weslake and Maxine won't be able to use the pawn shop for their S&M games. Maxine's let-down is a little bit deeper than usual, for this year she has furnished a huge leather riding saddle as a prop in their erotic games, inspired by a letter to Penthouse that she reads aloud to Weslake. He consoles her by revealing that if his "plan" (i.e., the heist) runs smoothly, the two of them may be vacationing in Hawaii during the coming weeks.

That night, Dillard slips up to the side of Ramon's house and, with Ramon in another room, ogles Maria through the window, his only acknowledgement from her a sidelong glance and a smile. The next morning, he huddles in a blanket on the ground outside her window and awakens her with a romantic harmonica serenade. Weslake later advises Boardwalk to try to wheedle information out of the black maid, Jasmine (Charlaine Woodard) in the apartment above the pawnshop, inhabited by a gay couple—in an attempt to learn when the couple will be out for the evening. Following suit, Boardwalk strikes up a rapport with Jasmine but actually begins to fall in love with her.

Weslake, Turtle, and Boardwalk ambush Dillard and Ramon, forcing themselves in on the burglary plan, which makes both thieves livid. Weslake informs the group—after appointing himself team leader—that they will break into the pawnshop on the evening when Garvey's trip to see his mother coincides with the "evening out" taken by the gay couple who live above the store. During the meeting, he outlines the burglary plan.

On the night Garvey leaves, the safecrackers attempt "Plan A"—to go into the pawn shop through the coal cellar—but must pursue "Plan B" (climbing up the side of the shop and over the skylight) when this fails. They find themselves trapped on the skylight, while Maxine—in the apartment beneath—flips on the light and teases Weslake by having a kinky affair with a random gentleman she has picked up.

Through a series of mishaps, the burglars eventually make their way down into the pawnshop and wire the safe for explosion, but do so seconds before a drunken Garvey stumbles into the shop, bottle of wine in one hand, a box of smoked salmon tucked under his arm. Without understanding that the men in the shop are robbing him, he reveals to his nervous friends that his mother has suddenly died. At that moment, a pussy cat runs down the stairs and paws the wire that leads to the "juice" on the safe; the safe explodes and Dillard's alarm sounds, triggering a piano, whistles, bells, sirens, the works. The cops bust in and confront the would-be robbers; Garvey insists that these are his friends, that the men would never rob him, and that they in fact protected his store from the burglars. The policemen ask for a description of the robbers but get contradictory reports from the befuddled safecrackers. After the cops leave, Garvey reveals to his embarrassed friends that his safe has actually been empty for years, and offers some smoked salmon to everyone. The men all sit down to enjoy the fish together.

ANALYSIS

Crackers represents an anomaly in Louis Malle's career. Looking beyond its status as the director's only film produced with an elephantine budget under the golden thumb of a major Hollywood studio, it also marks the first and last time Malle chose to follow a course that is intrinsically "Hollywood" and so often a sign of creative bankruptcy: shooting a contemporary remake of a long-championed classic film. In this case, Malle's picture is ostensibly an update of the 1958 Mario Monicelli caper comedy *Big Deal on Madonna Street* (I soliti ignolti).

Shot 26 years prior to the Malle/Fiskin film, *Big Deal* itself embodies the perfectly-harmonized offspring of two distinctly European genres: the caper film — epitomized by Jules Dassin's 1954 *Rififi*—and the Italian neorealist drama, exemplified by *Umberto D.*, *The Bicycle Thieves* (Ladri di bicyclette) and *Rome, Open City*. *Madonna*'s primary strength is that it works as a legitimate heist film — to whatever degree Monicelli's picture elicits hysterical laughter from audiences (and it does have a marvelous sense of the absurd, the sight gag, and comic timing *per se*), Monicelli builds the foundation of the picture from suspense, not comedy. *Big Deal* never attempts to "deconstruct," "spoof," or "kiss off" the heist pictures from which it borrows— it treats the genre reverentially, paying grand homage to it. Monicelli and his co-screenwriters Agenore Incrocci, Suso Cecchi d'Amico, and Furio Scarpelli take time and care to set up the major characters and — despite the writers' decision to never establish a clear idea of the safe's contents— the audience finds itself firmly vying for the criminals, hoping they make off with whatever loot exists inside the box. Monicelli also undertakes an extremely interesting approach to typecasting: he deliberately casts glamorous, deliriously attractive actors and actresses— Marcello Mastroianni, Vittorio Gassman, Rosanna Rory, Claudia Cardinale[29]— who exist at striking odds with their neorealist environs. The viewer, largely from reading into the characters' screen images, instinctively expects the actors to retain dignity, class, grace, and a kind of superhuman poise, as a result of their mythic celebrity status. Each gag, in turn, makes the audience more acutely aware of the characters' oafishness, clumsiness, and foolishness, and the filmmakers are able to create a chasm (much as Guare and Malle did with Burt Lancaster-Lou Pascal in *Atlantic City*) between audience expectations of the major players (combined with the characters' expectations of themselves) and reality.

Ergo, just when the viewer (without full conscious awareness of this belief) sincerely expects the criminals to break into the house gracefully and cut through the wall and crack open the safe with Rififi-like skill and cunning, the robbers perpetuate an outrageous series of gaffes: one burglar drills into a water pipe; the entire outfit breaks down the wrong wall, only to find one of their own standing on the opposite side and waving at them stupidly as he fetches a glass of water from the kitchen.

Crackers omits this chasm altogether. Malle could have gone the Monicelli route, casting a glamorous array of top American box-office draws in the early eighties (e.g., Robert Redford, Jane Fonda, Robert De Niro, Meryl Streep, Paul Newman, Jessica Lange). Instead, he assembles a ragtag bunch of deadbeat eccentrics: overwrought character actors who, as presented in this film, exist not at odds with the environs, but in perfect harmony with the environs—thus giving the picture a tremendously deadening weight of social seriousness, in lieu of comic buoyancy. The strategy may have been to encourage the audience to "root" for the characters, as underdogs. One might even be able to do so were it not for several glaring problems with the finished film.[30]

Notably, the final cut suffers from horrendously underdeveloped characterizations: like an exercise from screenwriting class, each character has been assigned one quality. Period. Turtle eats. And eats, and eats, and eats, and eats. It becomes such a lazy bit after the 13th or 14th attempt to wring humor out of it that one finds oneself wishing Wallace Shawn would disappear altogether. Maxine simply wants to get laid. She constantly hits on men — on passersby, on Weslake, on the young man she follows home to his apartment. Aside from handing out tickets, this is Christine Baranski's only function in the script. Most cryptic is Weslake (Sutherland) whose occupation and purpose — shy of becoming the ringleader for the heist — are never made abundantly clear during the course of the film; the filmmakers provide only the vaguest suggestions that he works as a security guard. Little wonder that, according to Fiskin, Donald Sutherland commented, almost six weeks into the shoot, "'You know what? I never got this character. Never have gotten this character, don't get it! Sorry! Next!'"[31]

Another of *Big Deal on Madonna Street*'s brilliant strategies involves its delicate use of tone. The screenwriters utilize Cosimo (Memmo Carotenuto) as a reference point—from one of his first scenes, in prison, where he shoves another prisoner out of the way and screams his lungs out, demanding that another prisoner stop screaming, Cosimo becomes the onscreen embodiment of negative tone — the audience delights in his being a louse (his obnoxious character is truly hilarious). But on a more sober level, Cosimo's loathsomeness magnetizes the audience, pulling viewers away from him and toward sympathy with the criminals who betray him by weasling out of him the plan to rob the safe on the della Madonna. And Monicelli's evocation of the robbers is so subtle, gentle, and delicately handled that one doesn't realize how much one cares about these characters and how much one feels the warmth, the genuine bond between them, until the caper fails and the viewer suddenly realizes—without it being said forthright in the picture — that the loyalty and friendship between the players are far more significant than anything the the safe contains. Along these lines, Monicelli includes one of the coziest and most atmospheric scenes in the history of cinema: after their robbery has failed, the criminals sit in a dimly-lit apartment kitchen, huddle around a table, and share a meal of beans and pasta in the hour of the wolf.

Such are all tonal masterstrokes. Yet *Crackers* evinces a level of complete and utter disregard for tone. It begins with an *Ishtar* casualty, by making most of the characters so stupid and blindly ignorant that the audience feels permanently alienated from them, but Fiskin lacks Elaine May's humor, good grace, and lightness of touch. More problematically, as *Crackers* unfolds, the characters begin to indulge in words and actions that obliterate the possibility of any audience sympathy. The two best examples are when Dillard screams at Garvey, "I'm gonna rip off your head and shit down your neck"; and when, at the film's lowest point, Boardwalk attempts to abandon his infant son in the middle of Melvin Garvey's pawn shop. Malle and Fiskin evidently expect the viewer to regard Boardwalk as an empathetic protagonist following this horrendous act. How the screenwriter and director could possibly treat lightly an issue that has attained such gravity over the past 30 years—in an era where stories constantly pepper the news of parents abandoning their infant children in fast food restrooms and shopping malls—is baffling.

Along these same lines, one would think—given the purpose of Cosimo in the original film—that tonally speaking, it might behoove Malle and Fiskin to include such a character. Actually, the *Crackers* video box (of all sources) has the right idea: "[Melvin Garvey] is the meanest, money-hungriest man in town." In principle: a glowing strategy. Yet the film never follows suit: as played by Jack Warden, Melvin Garvey appears neither particularly mean nor money-hungry. He simply comes across as a scrupulous businessperson. Why did Fiskin avoid writing him as a truly selfish, obnoxious, condescending, lowlife son-of-a-bitch, thus encouraging the audience to vie for the burglars? Equally questionable is the fact that Garvey turns to the robbers as *friends* in the final scene, underscoring his own victimization and worse. For at this point, the main characters come across like cruel, insensitive jackasses intent on backstabbing a close friend, and one feels deeply sorry for Garvey and instantly detests the robbers. Again: more character-audience alienation.

Similarly, one wonders why Malle and Fiskin fail to provide a clearer idea of the contents of the safe. Granted, Monicelli and his co-writers avoided this route, but Malle and Fiskin might at least have used set design to impart the impression of a heist worth undertaking. As production designer John J. Lloyd and Malle approach the *mise en scène*, Garvey's pawn shop appears to be nothing more than a hole-in-the-wall rat's nest, filled to the rafters with piles of worthless garbage. Thus, viewers are not simply alienated from the characters, but instantly alienated from the heist, from the outset of the picture.

On a positive note: as many critics overlooked (too myopic to see beyond the picture's flaws) much of the humor in *Crackers* works beautifully. The film incorporates a vivid combination of two drastically different styles of comedy. Fiskin, who came of age in Arizona ("growing up on American comedy"), is at his best with a signature style of throwaway lines; broad, coarse slapstick; and scattershot gags: Weslake mimicking numerous voices and external sound effects that will give the impression of a "wild party" as he records everything into a tape deck (a sequence that feels like it may have been cut, for although one can infer that he wants to prepare an alibi for the robbery, Malle and Fiskin never explain this sufficiently); the appearance of Maxine's massive "riding saddle" for use in her sexual games with Weslake; the parodic *Penthouse* letter Maxine reads; the shot of the men frozen, helpless, atop the skylight and the sizzling button line from Maxine's sexual partner when he looks up and sees the unwitting voyeurs hovering above their tryst: "Jesus, you're kinkier than I thought!" One can even trace the specific origins of some of the Fiskin gags to

American sources, such as the final gag — when the cops ask the robbers if they can describe the burglars, and three of the men offer up contradictory reports: "They were black!" "They were Mexicans!" "They were wearing ski masks!" (The incredulous cops: "Black Mexicans wearing ski masks...?!") This gag, or variations on this gag — when confronted by an accuser, perpetrators of a crime or a minor act of vice speak in perfect unison, offering different explanations — is everpresent on American sitcoms. It may be ancient, but it works. And it provides a crystal clear demonstration of the etiology of Fiskin's material.

The anthropological nature of Malle's comic voice — his astute behaviorist observational qualities, and his resultant ability to see and draw out the comedy in the way his characters conduct themselves (so heavily influenced by the Indian experience) are wondrous, but unfortunately add up to a comic style most sensitive to severe editing. His is the style of the small, subtle, and carefully nuanced gesture. The humor recalls Molinaro's *La Cage aux folles,* generally drawn not from what the characters do or say but how they carry themselves — the tone of their voices, the nature of their physical (nonverbal) communication: the way Dillard placates the vowels in the word "soup" (the term for the solution used to blow up the safe) with an air of complete idiocy; the undersized Ramon responding to Weslake's "tough case, Paco," by piping up with a wormy and weasly-voiced "My name is Ramon"; Ramon tasting Jasmine's ham hocks and red beans and observing woefully, "It needs chiles," to which the (deeply-in-love with Jasmine) Boardwalk growls, "It don't need *nothing.* It's fine, just the way it is."

But on a broader level, Malle's unique acuity of vision and insight also triggered the picture's downfall, leading to the same tragedy that would befall *Alamo Bay* a year later. Fiskin observes that Malle never would have felt comfortable making a "Carl Reiner comedy" or a "Garry Marshall comedy" out of the *Crackers* script. "He wanted to make a better film than that, because of that very observational quality."[32] Because of his advanced intelligence, Malle found it immeasurably challenging to work within the confines of a genre — most of his European films are so unusual and so unclassifiable that they could never be categorized *per se.* The director had a conscious need to make each project completely new, original, and different, a work that literally had never been done before. Consider *The Fire Within, My Dinner with André, Vanya on 42nd Street.* If he began with a framework, such as that of the heist comedy, in his hands the material would start to grow beyond the confines of the frame, and the genre framework itself would cripple the evolving picture. With *Crackers,* Malle felt fascinated by the interplay (interworkings) of social and racial phenomena and opted to set the picture in San Francisco where these phenomena came to a head, but the onscreen vision of economic angst and the collective struggle against impoverishment deaden the weight of the picture, giving it an unintended level of sobriety that doubles back on many of the gags and makes them feel ill-placed, even slightly offensive.

Even given Malle's studio-related disappointments, Ed Lewis's abandonment of the project, battles in the editing room with Cortes, and the director's own classification of the film as a "nightmare," *Crackers*'s critical and commercial failure — by all accounts — came as something of a shock to the system for Malle. The director did initially offer up a surprisingly favorable response to the final cut of the picture. Fiskin reflects, "He liked the movie [though] he may have changed that later."[33] According to Bergen, the critics changed Malle's mind. "He then made a film, made it interesting and original and quirky, and — within the compromise — made a film that he was happy with. But then when the reviews came out, I think he felt that he had originally been right."[34]

The treatment of *Crackers* by the folks at Universal — who purportedly hated the film — was incredibly insensitive. The one-sheet for the picture reads:

> His films have touched the hearts and minds of audiences everywhere, and the critics agree. "One of the most important filmmakers of his generation," says *The New York Times*. "Malle's films champion the discreet charm of unconventionality," cheers *The Saturday Review*. He is the popularly acclaimed director of *Pretty Baby* and *My Dinner with André*, and received an Academy Award nomination for his directorial efforts in *Atlantic City*. Now, Malle serves up a slice of American life, and the laughs are on us.[35]

This might sound quite flattering at first, until one recalls Bergen's assertion that *Crackers* "was not a work of [Louis's] that came from the heart."[36] That this is abundantly clear from the finished film raises a serious question about the integrity of Universal's marketing approach to the picture. Vincent Malle agrees with this assertion. "Universal completely dumped *Crackers*," he recalls. "And they did decide to release it as a big *auteur* film, yes."[37] In retrospect — though Vincent believes such an approach was an act of desperation and bore no ill will against his brother[38] — the marketing strategy does evince astonishing ignorance. By playing up the connection between a mediocre, subpar film and Malle's reputation as a director of brilliant cinema, Universal suggested (deliberately or undeliberately) that Malle had lost his directorial instincts, and thus directly hurt his image. Why did the studio avoid burying Malle's name in the credits? Why would it be necessary or even helpful for the studio to go out of its way to suggest that *Crackers* was one of Malle's personal films, when the film is one the director wanted to bury and forget?

CRITICAL RESPONSE

After debuting in America, *Crackers* grossed only $40,000 from a budget of some $12 million, and thus became a disaster — the biggest financial loss of Malle's career. The response was worse than a series of pans; most critics simply ignored the film.[39] Those who did write and publish reviews generally characterized the work as a mediocre effort. *Variety* summarizes it as "a letdown from director Louis Malle, with a flimsy plot that is perhaps rightly treated in a throwaway manner, film basically consists of a wide assortment of character rifs which are offbeat enough to provide moderate ... amusement but don't create a great deal of comic impact."[40] Writing for *The Monthly Film Bulletin*, Tom Milne chides the picture as:

> Yet another remake to add to the growing heap that seems to indicate either an imaginative bankruptcy in Hollywood or an unwillingness to subscribe to the Reaganite regressions that are the order of the day. A sad disappointment, at least to anyone who admired *Pretty Baby* or *Atlantic City* as daringly private explorations of inner worlds, *Crackers* is all on the surface. Much of the film is simply cribbed from Mario Monicelli's Italian original.[41]

Likewise, in *Playboy,* Bruce Williamson characterizes the film as "More a rehash than a remake ... adapted almost too loosely from Mario Monicelli's [film] ... nothing quite clicks in this comedy ... Malle's amiable secondhand spoof simply registers as a mis–*Deal.*"[42]

But most scathing and vicious is Philip French, Malle's eventual interviewer for the Faber and Faber interview volume, who writes in *The Observer,*

> *Crackers* is an ugly, unfunny, unexciting affair, a weed among the *fleurs de Malle.* Its idea of a witty line is ... Penn's threat to the elderly pawn-shop owner: I'm going to cut off your head and shit down your neck.' At the end we feel as if we've been watching Ken Russell carve up Mamet's *American Buffalo.*"[43]

On a tragic sidenote: two of the principal cast members of *Crackers* died at unusually young ages. Trinidad Silva (*Colors, The Milagro Beanfield War*), who became a cult favorite as Jesus on *Hill Street Blues,* died in 1988, in a road accident in Whittier, California; he was only 38. Four years later, the gifted and promising African American actor Larry Riley (*A Soldier's Story*) died of complications resulting from AIDS, just a few weeks shy of his fortieth birthday.

18
Alamo Bay— 1985
The Weight of the Unfamiliar

"Hyperactives dashed among the carts and coats and swollen ankles, and I was a Nazi again. I had thought I was over that stupid business, but here it was rolling back again, all the old anger like a filthy tide coming in."

— Edward Allen, *Straight through the Night*

"Of course, why not? Drive through the southwest and you're impressed with how little of the country is used. We probably have the least people per square mile in the United States than almost any place in the world."

— Marlon Brando, when asked by Larry
Grobel if he thought it realistic for the
U.S. government to begin parceling
off land to American Indians

BACKGROUND

As the first installment in an anthropological trilogy of Malle films[1] on the sociology of the United States (followed by twin documentaries, 1985's *God's Country* and 1986's *And the Pursuit of Happiness*),[2] *Alamo Bay* explores the dynamics and nuances of U.S. ethnic subcultures. Whereas *God's Country* zeroes in on the well-rooted German and Swedish denizens of a Minnesota town, *Alamo* and *Pursuit* assess the casualties and the assets of migrancy. Malle builds the films around the acculturation of immigrants who reached U.S. shores in the seventies and eighties, the majority from Asia, the Third World, and Eastern Europe. Unlike its successors, *Alamo Bay* is a fictional narrative, based loosely on fact.

As denoted briefly in Chapter 17, the seeds of *Alamo* were sown in the spring of 1980. Malle's stateside attorney, Robert Montgomery, fished out of the *New York Times Sunday Magazine* an April 6, 1980 article crafted by Texas freelance journalist Ross Milloy, entitled, "Vietnam Fallout in a Texas Town." Perhaps in acknowledgement of Malle's infatuation with social phenomena *per se*, Montgomery passed the article along to his filmmaker client, who indeed became hooked on the piece, his intrigue aggrandizing over the following year.[3]

Milloy's essay pulls readers into the world of Billy Joe Aplin, an ill-fated fisherman who spent much of his adult life suffused with wanderlust — migrating from town to town in the American South — but took several years in the late seventies to settle down with his wife in the quiet coastal village of Port Alamo, Texas. Though generally a pleasant man, "'protective and loving of his family,'"[4] Aplin slipped ever so gradually into violence, hostility and bigotry, provoked by the arrival of Vietnamese immigrant crabbers and shrimpers efficient enough at their trade — and who agreed to work for such low pay — that they nearly drove Aplin and his fellow workers out of business, draining the Gulf of its blue crab supply. Following an argument between Aplin and Vietnamese immigrant Sau Van Nguyen on the tidal flats in August, 1979, Nguyen drew a gun on the 35-year-old Aplin and murdered him, but copped a plea of self-defense and received a full judicial pardon. Nguyen's acquittal triggered racial violence in Port Alamo, culminating with the arrival of Ku Klux Klan Grand Dragon Louis Beam and his posse, who began to stir up hostilities against the Vietnamese immigrants for what they perceived as subversive attempts to incite Communist insurgence.[5] Milloy's article frames the sequence of events as a re-escalation of the Vietnam war on Texas soil.

Exactly one year following his discovery of the article, in April 1981, Malle — hot off the success of *Atlantic City*, with another triumph (*My Dinner with André*) in postproduction — flew to Texas to meet Milloy and tour the gulf coastline. He initially planned to hit the area at the tail-end of the conflict and shoot a 16mm documentary covering the deescalation, but it was, in his words, "too late."[6] Milloy longed to see the strife dramatized as a fiction film. He recalls:

Glory Scheer (Amy Madigan) and her former lover, married fisherman Shang Pierce (Ed Harris), relight old fires as they slow dance in a Texas bar in *Alamo Bay*.

Shooting *Alamo Bay* on location in South Texas circa 1984, Louis Malle instructs his cinematographer (Curtis Clark) on the placement of a shot.

> [Louis] flew into Austin, and we spent a day [there], and then drove down to
> Port Alamo, and we kind of toured that part of the Texas coast, and then drove
> back up to Austin ... and we just kept talking about the project. I think he had
> originally ... thought of it as ... a subject for a documentary, but I was ... anx-
> ious to see it made into a feature film.... [Louis's interest] was a combination
> of things.... Louis was very much ... an immigrant himself, and ... he saw that
> within the ... basic elements and events that occurred ... there was an oppor-
> tunity to tell a sort of "immigrant story." And ... then when he saw the area
> ... he just got sort of fascinated by the... "south Texas coastal culture," and ...
> also ... by the elements of the [scenery] down here, I think it was a little unlike
> anything he'd seen before ... he was particularly interested in the quality of the
> light, the cloud structure, and the ... coastal water.[7]

The question of why Malle abandoned *Port Alamo* (as he originally dubbed the
project) for almost three years (1981–4) is inextricably linked to his shifting outlook
on America. Though John Culhane asserts—in his 1985 *New York Times Magazine*
article "Louis Malle: An Outsider's Odyssey"—that Milloy's original article conveys
"[the Vietnamese immigrants'] difficult but eventual acceptance in America,"[8] and
cites Malle's self-identification with them as the reason for his interest in the project, these are both specious conclusions. Despite the brilliance and credibility of Milloy's article, its outlook on the possibility of Asian acculturation feels inescapably
angry, bitter, pessimistic. The only passage in the text that implies a smooth Viet-

namese integration into Texan society is the piece's closing line: "'Some folks are watching the Vietnamese real close; some folks are kinda hoping they'll make out O.K.'"[9] Ironically, Milloy never planned to include this line:

> That little coda there at the end [of the article] was put in at the request of the *New York Times*. They were disturbed at the time that it seemed so negative, and the editor ... said, "You know, it's just so *bleak*. Have you got any material that expresses more hope?" And what they did was they took something that was, I think, in one of the earlier drafts, and we decided to put it at the end there.[10]

That the overall trajectory of Milloy's article is clear even without learning of the *Times* imposition casts the light of incredulity on Culhane's assessment. One has trouble believing Malle originally wanted to do the adaptation as an "acceptance story." How could he have pulled the theme of "immigrant acceptance" from the Milloy article when the theme is virtually nonexistent in the piece? How can it be true that "*between inspiration and execution*, Malle came to decide ... this was no longer a film about being accepted,"[11] when the director gleaned the pessimism of Milloy's article from his initial reading of it in 1980?

Granted, Malle did originally want to do a story of an immigrant's acceptance and acculturation into the States, but not as an adaptation of Milloy — the idea germinated long prior to 1980. In 1975, Malle worked on an unproduced project entitled *The Boy*, planned as a collaboration with screenwriter and experimental filmmaker Jean-Pierre Gorin — its history is detailed briefly in Appendix A. Tonally, *The Boy* and *Alamo* sit at opposite ends of the dramatic spectrum. According to Gorin, *The Boy* told the story of a teenaged Mexican "wetback" who manages to integrate into Californian society successfully. Life-affirming and optimistic,[12] and conceived prior to Malle's move to the U.S., *The Boy* can be read as indicative of the director's hopes about the ease of his immigration into the States.

One can understand how the basic moral ambiguity of "Vietnam Fallout in a Texas Town" and the article's interesting blend of socio-cultural phenomena would appeal hugely to Malle at *any* point. But even so, one has trouble envisioning the director making an inveterately angry, damning indictment of U.S. southern narrow-mindedness and redneck culture when he first flew down to see Milloy — that is, in spring 1981, when he had three back-to-back box office successes in the can (*Pretty Baby*, *Atlantic*, and *Dinner*). Indeed, the director would soon proclaim, "I thought I was hot!"[13] and later told *Alamo* editor Jamie Bruce, "After *My Dinner with André*, I thought I could do *anything*."[14] It perhaps would have been difficult for Malle to make an anti–American film when he clearly felt so enthusiastic about himself and his new homeland. It took the disastrous *Crackers* (see Chapter 17) to change his mind and heart; he felt bitter and angry and needed to vent his frustrations.[15]

Malle next decided to find and hire a co-writer. Circa November 1982, he had attended a private screening of close friend Mike Nichols's 1983 film *Silkwood*, co-written by Alice Arlen and Nora Ephron. Impressed by Arlen's quick, sharp dialogue and ear for southern speech that are manifest in the script, Malle invited her to join the *Alamo* project as co-scenarist; they toured the Texas coast together in May 1983.[16]

In approaching *Alamo Bay*, Malle and Arlen originally followed the "blueprint" of numerous earlier Malle pictures by centering the story around an adolescent — in this case, a Vietnamese immigrant named "Dinh" in his late teens or early twenties. Fleeing Saigon, Dinh travels to the apocryphal Texas coastal community of Port Alamo to find work as a shrimper, and experiences — in his attempts to become accepted by American society — almost insurmountable obstacles, notably severe condescension from the local Texas fishermen, who pepper their sentences with the "gook" epithet and treat the immigrants like refuse. Though Arlen purportedly wrote two scenes that show Dinh becoming acculturated and accepted — Dinh with his family at Disneyworld, and Dinh and his fellow countrymen playing on the same softball team as the local Texans — these scenes were only to be used as an epilogue; the body of the picture, like Milloy's article, would remain angry and pessimistic in showing exactly how difficult it is for individuals in Dinh's position to integrate (if it is even possible *per se*). This version of the story, despite its negative overtones, held promise as interesting and multi-dimensional material.

Two of the casting choices worked beautifully: Malle recruited Ed Harris (*The Right Stuff*) and Amy Madigan (*Streets of Fire*) to portray Shang and Glory, two interlocked, adulterous lovers who take opposing stances in a racial conflict. According to Harris, he and Madigan — newlyweds at the time — met Malle when the director visited them on the set of Robert Benton's *Places in the Heart* (1984), in Texas. Harris believes that because he and Madigan had fallen deeply in love, and were slated to play lovers in *Alamo*, Malle wanted to transfer their romantic spirit to the onscreen relationship between Shang and Glory, and build on it, exploring the depths of the chemistry between two individuals passionately drawn to one another offscreen.[17]

Yet Harris and Madigan only held supporting roles in the original script, and Malle's casting decision for the young Vietnamese lead to play Dinh — on whom the entire film would hinge — proved disastrous. Culhane declares, "A change in story line also signifies how filmmaking is often a voyage of self-discovery for a director."[18] But this "self-discovery" of Malle's (if it indeed existed) only became a secondary reason, at most, for the shift-in-narrative of *Alamo Bay*. According to Malle's collaborators Ross Milloy (executive producer of the film) and Jamie Bruce, the "change in story line" on *Alamo* had everything to do with the inability of Malle and his casting associates, Juliet Taylor and Ellen Chenowith, to find a lead who could act. Jamie Bruce remembers:

> Louis was troubled by [his inability to find a lead] the way through. I mean, he was using an amateur actor [Ho Nguyen,[19] a 26-year-old research scientist from Saigon]. They looked and looked ... for somebody, and ... [Louis tried] to reloop Ho, or "Dinh" as he was called ... but that ... didn't work ... I edited [*Alamo Bay*] ... the [structural emphasis] totally changed, because the lead actor [Nguyen] was so horrible ... he was not a good actor! [Casting him] was a huge risk.... I was [casting director] Ellen Chenowith's assistant ... they went through the whole [Vietnamese community] ... [and] never found the guy. Never! And ... there was a choice between Nguyen and this other Chinese actor ... who was more of an established actor.... Louis took a huge risk [in casting Nguyen] ... thinking he could pull it off ... and ... this other guy would have been better. The bottom line: Louis went with the real deal ... he wanted to

go with a real Vietnamese instead of the Chinese-American playing the Vietnamese.[20]

Unfortunately, while the problems with Nguyen did little to complicate Harris's performance in the film by virtue of the two men sharing only a handful of confrontation scenes, Harris recalls that it was infinitely more difficult for Madigan, for she, as a professional actress, was expected to play half of the film opposite a young Vietnamese performer almost completely ignorant of the craft of acting.[21]

When Malle realized just how impossible it would be to pull the film off with Ho as the lead, he and Alice Arlen began furious on-set rewrites. Bruce remembers, "In the middle of the shooting ... [Louis] and Alice ... were rewriting constantly. I mean, *constantly* ... to adapt to the fact that ... [Nguyen] was not good!"[22] Over the weeks, Malle and Arlen attempted to bring the "second-string" subplot—a torrid affair between the politically progressive Glory (Dinh's employer) and her high school sweetheart, the racist and hateful redneck fisherman Shang Pierce (Dinh's nemesis)—to the forefront of the action; in the storyline, Glory becomes re-infatuated with Shang, but "falls rapidly and brutally out of love"[23] when she comes face-to-face with his bigotry. As a product of this shift, the narrative in the final cut feels awkward and oddly unfocused: the picture opens with Ho hitchhiking into Port Alamo, leading one to assume (naturally) that he will be the main character, but Harris and Madigan receive first billing in the opening titles—an indicator of the muddled story to follow. Indeed, Ho's story sort of "trails off," the character falling into the background and reemerging only occasionally as the Harris-Madigan story takes a front seat. But the vestiges of the original vision are present in the final cut.

Malle and Milloy set up shop in Rockport, Texas, in January and February of 1984, and used Corpus Christi for all supplies and communication needs.[24] According to Donald Moffat, who plays Wally Scheer (Glory's father) in *Alamo Bay*, Milloy and Malle flew the central actors down to Rockport during the following months, and introduced them to the man who originally started the Vietnamese shrimping business in Port Alamo.[25] He was congenial—but something of an exception within the Vietnamese community, as many of the other immigrants refused to participate. Milloy recalls:

> I remember that we had a problem ... although there were hundreds of Vietnamese there in the area where we were shooting, we couldn't get any of them to show up for casting calls, or to try and be actors in the movie, and it turned out that most of them were sort-of disciples of this priest up in Port Lavatnia ... a Catholic priest who had brought these people over from Vietnam, they came almost *en masse* as a village ... my family was from Corpus Christi, and we had a relationship with the bishop in Corpus ... and so the bishop set up a dinner where he came to Rockport, and they invited Louis and myself over there ... the bishop also invited this [Vietnamese] priest. And so we had this long Vietnamese dinner, where quite actually all the men were down around the table and all the women were bringing food, and stuff ... and the priest in a very casual and kind of gracious manner—the bishop ... [casually] let the Vietnamese priest understand that he would appreciate it if the Vietnamese would be cooperative in the making of this movie. And the bishop—I forget

his name, I think his name was Bishop Gracida, and he had been an admirer of Louis's films, anyway—he was quite an intelligent, articulate guy ... and anyway, as you can imagine the nuances of sort of delicately handling a situation like that, where the bishop wasn't *telling* the priest to do it, but sort of ... encouraging him to do it, and Louis just threaded his way through all that minefield, elegantly ... it was quite something to watch.[26]

Alongside the struggles with Ho Nguyen and the conflicts with the Vietnamese community, an ugly fight erupted between Suzanne Baron and Jamie Bruce; for an unknown reason,[27] Baron (a high strung woman, well known for "eating up and spitting out" assistant editors) grew furious with Bruce and began screaming at him without prior antagonization; this may have partially been the product of an environment poorly suited for her—she reputedly felt ill-at-ease outside of France, in the Texas heat. It is also possible, according to Bruce, that she simply felt threatened by his rising status on each new Malle project and decided his time had finally come. Baron and Malle started to quarrel endlessly; she dropped out of the production, and Malle approached Bruce the next day to edit the film; he would edit one additional film (*God's Country*) and produce another (*Pursuit*) before retiring from his professional association with Malle in 1986.[28] Working side-by-side, Malle, Bruce, and Bruce's assistant, Matthew Gaddis, edited *Alamo* in a barn behind Louis's house on the Causse during the late summer of 1984.[29] To score the film, Malle brought on-board Ry Cooder, who had just received enthusiastic notice for his compositions in Wim Wenders's *Paris, Texas.*

The first screening of *Alamo Bay*—perhaps in emulation of the *Silkwood* screening—was a private one, hosted by Malle in New York City on November 29, 1984, for several of those close to him—Candice Bergen, John and Adèle Guare, William and Rose Styron, Diane Keaton, Mike Nichols, André Gregory, Sidney Lumet, Richard Avedon, others.[30] The film received mainstream U.S. release on April 3, 1985; it debuted in France on September 18 of the same year.[31]

Synopsis

The fields of south Texas, in the late seventies: an intertitle states that over a million refugees fled Vietnam following the fall of Saigon in 1975; many traveled to the United States, seeking a better way of life. One such immigrant, Dinh (Ho Nguyen)—a boy in his early twenties—hitchhikes to the coastal town of Port Alamo, Texas, to join his fellow countrymen in a newly-settled fishing and shrimping enclave. Dinh waves a tiny American flag to showcase his allegiance to the States, but fights an uphill battle to catch a ride—a number of the xenophobic locals honk their horns angrily as they roar past; a middle-aged woman pulls over but speeds off, frightened and prejudicial, when she catches a glimpse of Dinh's Asian face. Eventually, Skinner (Rudy Young), a Vietnam vet who works for Port Alamo shrimper Wally Scheer (Donald Moffat), spots Dinh beside the road and drives him into town, offering him a Lone Star beer, rhapsodizing on the women and drugs he found in Vietnam during the war, and reassuring Dinh, "You're luckier than a pig I picked you up."

An elderly man with a heart condition, Wally runs a seafood packing plant and has—unlike most of his fellow citizens—warmed up to the Vietnamese immigrants, hiring them out as shrimpers and crabbers at a lower rate than he could ever pay the locals; he thus gleans resentment and hostility from the caucasians in the area. Wally's daughter Glory (Amy Madigan), a feisty, determined, and politically progressive young woman in her late twenties, has recently moved back into town from the city to look after her ailing father and to run the business; Luis (Martino La Salle) works alongside the father-daughter team.

As Rudy pulls into the drive of Wally's plant, he offers to try to obtain work for Dinh through the Scheers, but—shortly before introducing the boy to his employers—turns around to find Dinh gone. Meanwhile, Dinh wanders down one of the main drags of Port Alamo, and—unwittingly—across the lawn of Vietnam vet Shang Pierce (Ed Harris), a cocky, flagrantly angry and bigoted fisherman with several screaming and whining children who thrash around in a plastic wading pool and a wife, Honey (Cynthia Carle) he was forced to marry after knocking her up. Glimpsing Dinh treading on his grass, Shang leans over and screams in the boy's face, threatening to shoot him on the spot; oblivious, Dinh asks the Pierces to direct him to the Vietnamese people, smiles, and thanks the couple, wishing them a nice day. Dinh settles in with his fellow countrymen that night for a celebratory Asian banquet; Shang subsequently drives over to the Scheers' and rekindles his torrid high school affair with Glory, who has fallen in love with him, and who encourages his advances despite her father's objections.

Shang's extramarital affair with Glory unfolds, the two sneaking off to a motel together. Pierce's resentment—and the community resentment against the Vietnamese—builds to a fever pitch; as the Vietnamese are willing to work longer hours, for lower pay, they are cleaning the bay entirely of its shrimp supply. A furious Shang blames the "gooks" for his inability to make payments on his new boat, The American Dream Girl, and bemoans this to Glory; he visits the bank to try to obtain an extension on his loan, but fails in his effort, careening toward full repossession. Glory offers to try to obtain the money for Shang, by recollecting the money she loaned her father, but Wally, who is in dire financial straits himself and who loathes Shang, pointedly refuses. Meanwhile, anti–Vietnamese hostilities escalate across the town, surfacing even in the supermarket where Honey works as a checker.

As a last-ditch attempt to save himself and his treasured boat, Shang opts to return to crabbing, "like my daddy," but grows enraged upon discovering, soon after he hits the water, that Vietnamese rowboats are in full pursuit, dropping their own crab traps into the sea; Dinh leads the effort, on a tiny vessel he christened "Glory." Outraged, Shang draws a scoped hunting rifle and fires shots at the terrified migrants, cutting their nets when they flee.

Dinh strides into the town's redneck watering hole and attempts to buy a beer and an outboard motor, but drops the second request to the Grand Dragon of the KKK. A barfight ensues; Glory rushes to Dinh's defense; the two walk through the rain together until Shang pulls up, offering Glory a ride and chastizing her for spending time with a "gook." Enraged, she leaps out of the truck and sprints away. The bank collects on American Dream Girl; Shang screams at Glory once again, from across the dock, and accuses her of being "in with" the Vietnamese; she cuts him off altogether. Now jobless, Shang refuses to work for another outfit and—after Wally has a heart attack and is taken to the hospital in Corpus Christi, accompanied by Glory and Dinh, Shang leads the locals in a KKK rally against the Vietnamese, burning crosses on "Slop City," the racist nickname for the Vietnamese compound. Wally dies in the hospital; Glory and Dinh return to Port Alamo to discover the rally, which frightens all of the immigrants into hitting the road—all except for Dinh, who—to Glory's amazement, vows to stay and fight, piloting Luis's boat out onto the water despite the KKK patrols; Shang draws a scope rifle on Dinh once again, but hesitates when he catches Glory in the sight, flanking Dinh. The U.S. Coast Guard moves in and breaks up the conflict.

Leaving Dinh to guard the packing plant one night while she drives to Corpus to deliver seafood, Glory also leaves the young man open to attack from Shang, who opts to helm a raid on Wally's plant with molotov cocktails; he engages Dinh in a deadly game of cat-and-mouse, ultimately cornering the young man in an alley with a shotgun; he raises the rifle to murder Dinh in cold blood when Glory pulls up at the last minute, shooting and killing her former lover. The EMS arrive, laying Dinh on a stretcher and place him in the back of an ambulance. The film closes on a long, tortured close-up of Glory as the police lead her away from the crime scene.

ANALYSIS

Originally published in April 1980, Ross Milloy's *New York Times Sunday Magazine* feature story "Vietnam Fallout in a Texas Town" remains one of the most deliberately morally ambiguous and unbiased pieces of American journalism from the past two decades. Despite Milloy's recollection 20 years later that the Vietnamese qualified as the aggressors in their conflicts with Texas fishermen and shrimpers, and his insistence that he wanted to impart this unusual bias to the film *Alamo Bay* late into the production process ("I thought that was closer to the true situation," he muses),[32] Milloy structures the original piece of journalism so meticulously that it maintains, throughout, a perfect balance between two ends of a racial conflict, shedding an objective light on each group. Milloy thus caps and summarizes his account rather neatly with a telling passage: "As with the agonies of the conflicts in Indochina that continue even now, one sees reflected in the widening ripples of the blue-crab war of Port Alamo, Texas neither heroes nor villains, only victims."[33] He illustrates the co-mingled survival instincts, prejudicial fears, and miscommunication that spread equally to the Vietnamese and the Texans, and thus exposes the deepest proveniences of racism and bigotry. The strategy is politically incisive and gutsy—Milloy commences by encouraging his readers to fully side, on an emotional level, with the late Billy Joe Aplin, long before he reveals the man's rising tide of racism and thus colors him as prejudicial. It is a tonal masterstroke: the journalist "leaps over" the factors that would distance an audience emotionally from a bigot, and thus pulls his readers in, leading them to share the same frustrations and uncontrollable rage with Aplin as he is driven out of business, before revealing Aplin's horrific anti–Vietnamese acts. And Milloy employs the very same tonal process by building an equal level of sympathy for Aplin's murderer, Sau Van Nguyen, and his Vietnamese compatriots: "Homesick and penniless, baffled by American language and customs, [Sau] had tried several times en route to get himself returned to Vietnam, but without success.... In Port Alamo's budding refugee community, he found people who shared his memories, language and needs...."[34]

Milloy's article is morally murky, and one can foresee how this would work to Malle's advantage, given the quadruple successes of the director's films *Les Amants*, *Le Souffle au cœur*, *Lacombe, Lucien*, and *Pretty Baby*, works all rich in ethical ambiguity. One could envision him emerging from post-production of *Alamo Bay* with a modern revisionist probe of the Warner Bros. social consciousness dramas (one of the film's key influences)[35] under his arm — a Malle film that turns bigotry inside out and thus exposes the inner workings of racial hostility, illustrating clearly and succinctly how small and understandable confusions, frustrations, and miscommunications on a human level can tally up to a sweeping social tragedy.

The film falls far short of this goal; in adapting Milloy's article and bringing it to the screen, Malle and Arlen made the critical mistake of modeling *Alamo Bay*, structurally, on Fred Zinnemann's *High Noon* (1952), and on the concepts and approach of the searing old Zanuckian social consciousness dramas,[36] such as Mervyn Le Roy's *I Am a Fugitive from a Chain Gang* (1932), John Ford's *The Grapes of Wrath* (1940), Edward Dmytryk's *Crossfire* (1947), and John Sturges's *Bad Day at Black Rock* (1954). Malle was temperamentally unsuited for building one of his films around a model with such a strict narrative structure, for it prevented him from accommodating the shifts in the content of *Alamo Bay* when its characters required added dimension that would lift the film above two-dimensional, black-and-white ethos. Fred Berner echoes these insights:

> *Alamo Bay* was a story about the Anglo fishermen and the Vietnamese shrimpers/fishermen and the battles that they had. And I think going into that story ... one could easily fall into the ... "poor immigrant kid who is trying to make a living" mindset, about things, and [the Vietnamese] could have been perceived in the storytelling as the wronged party. But the more [Louis] became involved in learning about both worlds— that of the Vietnamese and that of the Texas fishermen — and the more Louis immersed himself in both worlds, there emerged two real sides to the story which Louis followed with all his heart. One of the reasons I don't think *Alamo Bay* did nearly as well as it could have is that Louis had, as a template, kind of a John Ford western, clear-cut good guys versus bad guys ... and ultimately this was a movie with a story that didn't have clear-cut good guys and bad guys. And the more deeply [Louis] immersed himself in the movie, and the more he adjusted his vision to his experiences of making the film, it became a more complex story of these two groups of people who Louis— and thus we, the audience — began to care for equally.[37]

As a result, *Alamo Bay* suffers from a complete omission of moral irony and from a full tonal evisceration. Critics have chastized the film, quite rightly, for its broad strokes; the rednecks— particularly Harris's character, Shang Pierce —come across as hate-filled, inhumane monsters—cartoons of bigotry. Compare the characterization of Shang to that of the racist Billy Joe Aplin in Milloy's original piece: the journalist quotes Aplin's wife as saying, "'[Billy] was a well-educated man. He had a 100-ton ship operator's license and they don't give those things away. He went to night school and marine college ... they even asked him to teach celestial navigation ... He was very protective and loving of his family.'"[38] It is far scarier, and far more interesting dramatically, when the descriptions of Billy Joe Aplin in Milloy's original article suggest a generally kind and sympathetic and intelligent person who somehow found himself being sucked into a racist whirlpool, than when Malle and Arlen present an ignorant demon with no traces of humanity. Peter Travers is certainly not far off when he describes Shang Pierce as a "slug"[39]: he beats his wife, cheats on her, talks down to her and consistently evinces overwhelming ignorance in his treatment of Glory and in his reasoning *per se*. One never feels that this slimebag merits an iota of sympathy.

Granted, Malle and Arlen made a wise decision to include the subplot involving the repossession of Shang's boat, "The American Dream Girl," the personal problem that heightens his racism (an intelligent strategy that could—in theory—begin to sway viewer sympathies toward Shang). But the repossession makes no *perceptible* contributions to the film's tone in light of the countless detractions from Shang's character, and Arlen structures the screenplay so ineptly that by the time the audience learns of Shang's frustrations, he has already alienated every viewer (during his first appearance) by treating Ho like a cocker spaniel, screaming his lungs out at the boy through clenched teeth, commanding Dinh off of his lawn and threatening to put a bullet through his head. For the film to work, Malle and Arlen must downplay Shang's racism (or, better yet, hold it offscreen altogether) until they have given the audience an opportunity to explore his daily life, enabling the viewer to empathize with the difficulties Shang encounters and the reasons for his hatred of the Vietnamese.

The Vietnamese (aside from their their ill-advised sexually graphic "comebacks," which they hurl at the insulting Texan fishermen) fare no better, portrayed as innocent, guileless simpletons. For some unknown reason, the screenwriter and director avoided the use of subtitles that would help the audience identify with the immigrants; without these indicators of communication; the average viewer thus feels alienated from the Vietnamese, who appear as simply a babbling mob. This is somewhat attributable the casualties of terrible casting—a product of the director and producer's inability to find a suitable Vietnamese actor to play Dinh, and Malle's unsuccessful attempts to try to "direct the narrative" away from the central figure, thus pulling it away from the dramatic crux that may have made the original script work. In the final cut, Glory Scheer emerges as the main character, and her transition from being torn between an adulterous love affair with Shang and her principles, to believing so firmly in those principles of egalitarianism that she kills Shang to defend them, constitutes the picture's central character arc. This is why the line "Glory, I don't believe you belong in this town anymore" (spoken by the ditzy barmaid, Diane) so resonated with Malle—it is perhaps the clearest indication that Glory has evolved, politically, beyond the confines of Port Alamo.

As a casualty of the central narrative shift in the picture, Dinh never once emerges as a three-dimensional character in the film. David Denby describes the character and his fellow countrymen as "morally spotless"; this only happens because Malle and Arlen never establish any of the Vietnamese characters adequately — neither Dinh nor his Vietnamese friends and family. Nguyen's wretched performance ruins the film ; Milloy and Bruce share an observation that the 25-year-old Nguyen felt confused throughout the production — a complication more than apparent onscreen. Nguyen's performance suffers most drastically from its juxtaposition alongside the comparatively skilled portrayals by Ed Harris, Amy Madigan, and Donald Moffat — not simply because one tends to compare the performances and notices repeatedly how terrible Nguyen is alongside Harris and co., but because when one watches the performances of Harris, Madigan and Moffat, and develops a tendency to read them, astutely, as performances of some depth, and the film subsequently cuts to scenes with Nguyen, one finds oneself attempting to read his portrayal on the same level — and the overall effect is not that Nguyen comes across as a bad actor per se, but that Dinh comes across as, alternately, a half-wit (he smiles unabashedly, for instance, when Harris screams at him and commands him off of the lawn) and as an individual with wretched self-esteem. Even when one takes the linguistic barrier into consideration, Nguyen's inability to pick up on universalistic overtones in the others' performances that would transcend race (such as those of hatred, in the first confrontation scene with Shang) remains a complete mystery. And it obliterates the tone of the film.

The mood of *Alamo Bay* suffers as well. While an atmosphere of suspense generally saves the old Zanuckian social consciousness dramas, Malle and Arlen build *Alamo Bay* on a foundation of pure dread. It is a terribly inadequate substitute; the audience can see the violence, hostility, and ugliness brewing from the first few minutes and feels not curious about the uncertain outcome, but repelled — forced to look away. Ergo, the mood of *Alamo Bay* — hugely dire, pessimistic, and angry — never wavers; its scenes and characters seethe with violence and hatred.

Yet one glorious exception emerges in the film, a presumably unintentional one. In the picture's finest moment, Shang returns, out of sheer desperation, to crabbing on the Texas Gulf, after being driven completely out of shrimping by the Vietnamese. The Vietnamese men not only slip in behind him in tiny rowboats, innocently sabotaging his "last resort" by dropping their own crab traps, but (in a masterstroke) Dinh floats up toward Shang, in a boat christened with the name of Shang's mistress: "Glory." We see the rage building in Shang, and for a fleeting moment, the film sings with an overtone of jet black comedy. And the kicker joke is simply that the Vietnamese are unaware of the degree to which they are pouring salt into Shang's festering wound. It brings us tremendous pleasure to see these immigrants unintentionally making Pierce seethe with rage by cutting into his Achilles heel, after all of the cruelty he has made them suffer. Unfortunately, the moment loses its comic edge in the sickening moment when Shang draws his scope rifle.

Despite innumerable flaws, *Alamo Bay* retains a few virtues. Aesthetically, Malle employs a triumphant, consistently inspired series of spatial devices. The picture opens amid the vast and unpopulated Texas fields, drawing attention to the amount of geographic space available for immigrants; every successive scene that unfolds in Port Alamo emphasizes tiny, narrow, cramped, shanty-like buildings, and the narrowness becomes not only a visual metaphor for the narrow-mindedness and the backwardness of the townspeople, but—given the seemingly endless space in the fields at the outset of the piece—a reminder of the Texans' hypocrisy about their professed inability to incorporate overseas immigrants into their community.

Ry Cooder created a brilliant score; though it initially feels almost indistinguishable from his score for *Paris, Texas*, the mental images suggested by the music gently evoke the mid–American landscape, recalling Pat Metheny's creation of an "aural metaphor" for the American Midwest: long held, twangy guitar notes conveying wide open spaces— vast, flat expanses of land, empty rail yards, suburban developments, shopping malls, etc. Yet Cooder only uses the Metheney-esque musical idiom as a launching pad, segueing smoothly and almost imperceptibly into similar guitar chords that suggest an Asian metaphor and low-whistling slide notes that paint overtones of the horrific—of inescapable doom. The message: doom and horror (a distinguishable voice in Cooder's guitar) are emerging from a union of the American midwest (given its own musical idiom by Cooder within the score, most prominent in the first few minutes of the picture) and the arrival of the Asians (given *their* own musical idiom within Cooder's score)—his use of the same acoustic instrumentation for all three overtones suggests, appropriately that the elements have become intertwined in the onscreen landscape.

Finally, the dramatic architecture in *Alamo* becomes briefly and momentarily interesting in the picture's final act. When Wally, Dinh, and Glory travel to Corpus, Malle and editor James Bruce employ quasi–Altmanesque cross-cutting between the calm and quiet of the hospital room and the raucous chaos of the Ku Klux Klan rally, and one realizes, through the use of aural and visual contrast, (given Glory's comment to Dinh that he will be accepted without racist complication in Corpus Christi) that the comparatively quiet and laid-back, hushed overtones of the hospital symbolize the peace and freedom from strife that Dinh's ethnic community needs, so desperately, to find in America.

CRITICAL RESPONSE

Thanks to its countless structural and dramatic problems, *Alamo Bay* received almost unanimously devastating reviews in the United States and opened and closed overnight. Writing for *New York* magazine, David Denby castigates the film as "a rigged morality play—a sluggish and depressed work, without surprises or clarifying insight ... Stupidity is a powerful force in the world, but I'm not sure it's dramatically interesting. *Alamo Bay* makes us feel bad without teaching us anything new about our country."[40] Denby tags Ed Harris's performance as "only half effective,"[41] and notes, as the picture's one sole virtue, "Amy Madigan's edgy, all-out performance."[42] Writing for *Variety*, Todd McCarthy similarly lambasts the effort as "a failed piece of social consciousness ... Malle and ... Arlen have only presented the surface of the dilemma and have proved singularly unsuccessful in humanizing it or providing it with any galvanizing dramatic urgency."[43] And writing for *People*, Peter Travers chides, "[Malle] didn't get either [great characters or a great story] ... Arlen's screenplay is primarily a study in stereotypes ... [Madigan and Harris's] characters remain cardboard figures ... search for human drama at your peril. You'll come away empty."[44]

The picture fared substantially better in France, perhaps because European critics were less able to judge the validity of the American context. Typical of these reviews is Ginette Delmas's critique in *Jeune Cinema*; she praises *Alamo* for handling immigration issues brilliantly and focuses more on the aesthetic and visual detail in the film than American critics, praising "the sea, the wind, the sails ... the scenes of fishing. All appears alive, soft, luminous in this kingdom of shrimp."[45] Delmas also implies (rather dubiously) that *Alamo* failed in the States because Americans, who know the context well, are too ashamed of contemporary racism to be able to acknowledge and face the picture's truths.[46] Writing for *La Revue du cinéma*, Alain Garel commends Ed Harris's "extraordinary" interpretation of Shang Pierce and characterizes Madigan's performance as cut from the same cloth as Barbara Stanwyck and Joan Crawford. He also exalts the film as a testament to Louis's own immigration experience, and — astonishingly — praises Malle for adopting the immigrant's point-of-view.[47]

19

God's Country
(Pays de dieu)— 1985 /
And the Pursuit of Happiness
(La Poursuite du bonheur)— 1986

The Well-Rooted and the Transient

"This is America
This vast, confused beauty
This staring, restless speed of loveliness
Mighty, overwhelming, crude, of all forms
Making grandeur out of profusion
Afraid of no incongruities
Sublime in its audacity
Bizarre breaker of moulds."
　　　— Amy Lowell, "The Congressional Liberty," *What's O'Clock*

"A nation, like a tree, does not thrive well till it is engraffed with a foreign stock."
　　　— Ralph Waldo Emerson, *Journals*

BACKGROUND

The production of *God's Country* (Pays de dieu), Louis Malle's premier English-language documentary, spanned six years. Circa late spring 1979, in between the release of *Pretty Baby* and the production of *Atlantic City*, the then-head of PBS Susan Weil (later one of the sources of funding for *My Dinner with André*— see Chapter 16)[1] catalyzed *Pays* by approaching Malle and asking him to shoot a documentary on any aspect of the United States that intrigued him,[2] for which he would receive funding from the Corporation for Public Broadcasting. Writing for *Cahiers du cinéma*, Charles Tesson suggests that Weil pitched the project to Malle as a kind of western follow-up to *L'Inde fantôme*: "Familiar with his documentaries on India

(*Phantom India* and *Calcutta*) ... PBS proposed that Malle do a film within a framework entitled *Phantom America*, the title referring to the silent majority in the United States."[3]

Country matured through a number of stages with the director systematically considering and rejecting prospective subthemes on American life and culture. James Bruce, at the time a production assistant under Malle's aegis, details the evolution of the project:

> [In 1979, Louis] was supposed to do another project ... a documentary about Disneyland.... He wanted to go underground [with his cameras, to film the] ... whole [technological] system [behind the theme park] ... the inner-workings of Disneyland. [But] at the last minute ... Disney said, "We need final cut," so ... Louis pulled out.... Two weeks later, Louis called me back, and said, "Hey, listen, we [have] another [project]! We're going to go do a documentary about the shopping mall, in Minnesota." The largest shopping mall, the first gigantic shopping mall ever built is in Minneapolis. So we started making the movie *God's Country* ... about shopping malls. And we went [to Minneapolis], and ... three, four days into it, Louis said, "This is not good ... and so the whole documentary changed, on the spot." ...[He] thought [the subject] was just not that interesting. There was no story ... nothing really happening. And then he [changed his mind].... The kind of documentaries he made ... weren't written [in preproduction] ... the shooting [encompassed] the research and the writing.... He was *exploring*, in the same way that he'd done *Phantom India* ... or all his documentaries, for that matter.... [So when he] changed direction, [Louis, Jean-Claude Laureux, Étienne Becker, and I] decided to get into a car and travel all over the state.... We went to Indian reservations ... to Bob Dylan's home town ... [to county fairs] ... we were touring the state of Minnesota. And ... Louis [wanted to meet] different people. [Louis would ask me to] call ahead, he would [for instance] find out we were going to be driving through this town, and I would call the chamber of commerce to find out what was happening ... find out where the big fairs were ... and we would just go to those towns. Because one thing about that time of the year — it was June ... [and in] the summer ... every town [in Minnesota] has ... something going on.... We'd [also] go to the cemeteries, to find out what the heritage of the town was, because in one town, everybody's Czech, in one town, next town, everybody is Swedish, so [Louis] found that kind of fascinating....[4]

Malle remembers that after three totally fruitless weeks of driving around Minnesota and searching for thematic fodder, he funnelled all his energies into finding a small agrarian town where he could spend quality time becoming acquainted with the inhabitants; the film crew stumbled onto Glencoe, Minnesota (pop. 5,000), while its residents were celebrating the yearly town fair; filming commenced during that event (the second sequence in the chronology of the final cut). Helplessly intrigued about the residents and their lifestyles, Malle began to cultivate trusting relationships with the indigenes.[5] He later concluded in retrospect, "I fell in love with these people."[6] Bruce recalls:

> After ... two and a half weeks of traveling to things that I might have thought more interesting and exotic, like Indian reservations ... [we were] in this town [of Glencoe, Minnesota]. At first, I thought ... "There's nothing really going

on here." But [Louis] found it fascinating, because ... it was so different than what he came from.... He was so charming that people wanted to talk to him. And they trusted him immediately.[7]

As Tesson notes, Malle ran out of money to complete the editing in the late seventies[8]; the director needed an additional $50,000 for this purpose.[9] Malle thus shelved *Country* for the five- or six-year interim that PBS needed to raise the additional funds. In August 1985, with the $50,000 in-pocket, Malle, Bruce, Becker, and sound engineer Keith Rouse (sitting in for the unavailable Jean-Claude Laureux) returned to Glencoe to do a 20-minute epilogue on how their subjects' lives had evolved or regressed over the preceding six years. Because the Reagan-era recession of the early eighties had battered the economic condition of several town residents, a tide of previously unseen racism rose in the 1985 footage, wherein the townspeople search for scapegoats who can bear the brunt of their crisis, heavily slamming the Jewish Americans in the community. *God's Country* premiered nationwide on PBS affiliates in early December 1985.

Home Box Office launched Malle's follow-up American documentary, 1986's *And the Pursuit of Happiness* (*La Poursuite du bonheur*). In January 1986, the network approached Malle to do a cinematic probe into the phenomenon of contemporary immigration, a documentary commemorating the July '86 centennial of the Statue of Liberty. HBO channeled all of the funding into Pretty Mouse Films, Inc., the independent, temporary production house that Louis and Vincent Malle set up in 1979 to handle their ill-fated Disneyland documentary. James Bruce, who graduated from editor of Malle's films (on *Alamo Bay* and *God's Country*) to producer of the HBO project, records a key detail about the origin of *Pursuit* that has generally gone undocumented in nearly every Malle filmography and uncredited in the film itself: Malle and Bruce planned and slated the film as a semi-adaptation of the July 8, 1985, issue of *Time* magazine, an issue solely dedicated to the "New Wave" of immigrants flowing into the states in the seventies and eighties, émigrés primarily from Africa, Asia, and the Third World. Malle asked Bruce to scour the issue in hand, catalog the major ethnicities it covered, and trace them to their respective metropolitan nerve centers in the states. He then sent Bruce out on a nationwide trek to locate compelling immigrant subjects at the urban hotspots on the list and talk them into appearing on camera, so that Malle's claim to René Prédal in *Jeune Cinéma*—that the featured immigrants were random, unplanned inclusions—does not stand up to scrutiny. Bruce remembers:

> [Louis and I] took [the July 8, 1985 issue of] *Time* magazine, and ... I broke it down [by ethnicity].... I said, "Okay, I'll go to all the hot spots of immigrants, and ... we'll do it by nationality." Like, Vietnamese, obviously I went to Houston, ... in Miami, I went to the Latino community ... but my emphasis [there] was, "Let's find the, you know, children of ex-dictators." ... Because ... Miami's full of the ... families of the deposed regimes that we supported. I worked my way into [the home of the Somosas] and convinced them to have Louis come and do a portrait of them, and they agreed. So that was my job. My job was to go and meet people. ... I would write files of them, and tell Louis, "These are the people I met," and I would give him a report, and he'd say, "Well,

let's go check these people out." And so we shot — we went around the country — and just filmed ... different people that I had met previously, and in the
process ... which happens all the time in documentaries ... you meet other people. But ... this [film] was ... more organized ... and structured [than] ... *God's
Country*, which was *totally* [improvisational].[10]

Pierre Billard details how Fabienne Vonier of MK2 — the force behind *Au revoir
les enfants* and *Milou en mai*— opted to blow up both 16mm documentaries, releas-
ing them theatrically across France with French subtitles over the synched English
dialogue and with Malle doing French voice-over narration in lieu of his English
commentary. In the hands of French critics, the pictures became instant sensations.[11]

SYNOPSES

God's Country

In June 1979, Louis Malle, along with his film crew of Jean-Claude Laureux, Étienne Becker, and James Bruce (none of whom appear onscreen) visit the Midwestern burg of Glencoe, Minnesota, a farming community situated approximately 60
miles due west of Minneapolis. Over the course of several days, the men tour the
community with their cameras, and — in the process— become intimately familiar
with a number of the locals. The picture opens on a chance encounter with an octogenarian named Mrs. Litzau, who whiles away her free time with summer garden-
ing and winter crocheting. A trip to the annual town fair ensues, the event laden with
heavy doses of German and Polish culture, notably jubilant polka music and ethnic
dancing. At the fair, a group of veterans gather and explain their rationale for supporting Vietnam vets, and Malle meets Rod Petticore, the assistant chief of police in
Glencoe, who expresses some hesitation about announcing his job title before the
cameras. Reverend Chapman, of the First Congregational Church of Glencoe, appears
on camera and expostulates on the ongoing conflict in Glencoe between conservatism
and progressivism, placing heavy emphasis on the climbing divorce rate. Malle depicts
the "great passion" of the Glencoeites— lawnmowing — and attends a softball game
played by the local girls' team, The Valkyries, against that of a nearby community.
The filmmakers visit the town Dairy Queen and the combination apothecary-gift
shop, run by the Barnum family, who declare that they have no familial connection
to the circus godfather Phineas T. Barnum. Rod Petticore returns and describes the
boundaries and the day-to-day of law enforcement in Glencoe and the rising tide of
drug abuse that bled over from the late sixties and early seventies. Malle and his collaborators then encounter Brian Thalman, a 10-year old who drives a massive trac-
tor onscreen and tells Malle of his efforts to help his father run a 2000-acre farm on
the outskirts of town, Thalman's Seeds. A farmer subsequently describes, in voice-
over, how the economic trends of the day involve the swallowing up of smaller farms
by larger agrarian ones.

   Malle and Co. pay a visit the Glencoe State Bank, run by Clayton Hoese and his sons, who double as farmers during off hours. Another farmer, the 28-year-old Jim McIntyre, welcomes Louis into his house and introduces, on camera, his young wife, Beverly, and his small children; the McIntyres open their home and extend their hospitality and warmth to the filmmakers. Another town resident, Mr. Beneke, speaks of his leftwing son Brad's violent act of civil disobedience that earned the boy a substantial prison sentence; Brad's mother, Mrs. Beneke, discusses her passion for writing plays, and Malle intercuts footage of one of her recent stage productions, *Much Ado about Corn*. The filmmakers visit another town resident, Steve, a bachelor who spends his days inseminating female cows with bull sperm; he illustrates the process with a Holstein while Malle films him. Later, Malle questions Steve about his bachelorhood and inquires about his marriage plans.

Jean, an attractive young woman employed as a Social Security worker at the county seat, appears on camera for an extended interview, wherein Malle questions her about her two jobs (she moonlights by running a liquor store), her bold decision to renounce Catholicism, her extramarital pregnancy as a young girl and decision to give the baby up for adoption in lieu of aborting it. She discusses sexual politics in Glencoe, including the impossibility of a homosexual lifestyle in the community, and the relevance of sexual activity in her own life.

Malle and his crew later visit the local retirement home of Glenhaven. The 1979 sequence ends with their attendance at the wedding of Robert Mark Schwanlas and Tammy Jane Judy at the Emmanuel Lutheran Church of New Auburn, Minnesota.

Six years later, in August 1985, Malle drives back into Glencoe. He reencounters Miss Litzau, now in her early nineties and still tending her garden; the Benekes—Millie Beneke has written six new plays; Rod Petticore, who has moved to a law enforcement position in a neighboring county; Steve the cow inseminator, still hard at work and still a bachelor; Tammy and Mark, now married and living in a trailer with their children; and—most significantly—Bev and Jim McIntyre, hit hard by the Reagan recession and struggling with great effort to hang onto their farm. Another farmer in the same predicament, Terry Wagner, appears in the film for the first time and complains of dire economic circumstances; Mr. Thalman, who suffers from a similar plight, discloses his dark streak of racism by blaming his misfortune on the Jews, and spends several minutes blasting the Reagan administration for increasing the national deficit. The final sequence of the film covers Malle's dinner at the home of Arnold and Minnie Beneke, whose "politically radical" son has cooled off in temperament and now sells computer software. The film concludes with a long speech from Arnold Beneke, in which he describes the emotional depression plaguing Glencoe that is a product of dire economic circumstances, and blasts the Reagan-era philosophy of greed that is sweeping the land, but insists on maintaining an optimistic outlook for the future of middle Americans.

And the Pursuit of Happiness

In early 1986, Louis Malle totes his cameras on an endless trek around the United States, and seeks out immigrants representative of the "New Wave" of émigrés from

Africa, Asia, and the southern continent, to learn of their stories and their feelings about the promise that is America. Malle journeys from ethnic borough to ethnic borough in countless major cities, flitting from case study to case study and engaging in quick, capsule-sized interviews with each subject. The picture opens with a middle-aged Romanian immigrant doing a marathon walk around the state of Texas to project the love and devotion he feels toward his new country. Malle subsequently incorporates footage of Cambodians— who have fled the Khmer Rouge ("the worst genocide since World War Two")— arriving at Kennedy Airport and undergoing a stringent inspection by the U.S. Department of Customs, and an ESL language class for a group of Cambodian refugees whose professor educates them on how to order fast food at Wendy's and Burger King. Additional subjects include (among others): a celebrated Russian stage actor who now schools American adults in what he perceives as the "complete" method of Constantin Stanislavsky; a computer specialist-in-training who has fled Cuba for Miami, leaving her beloved daughter behind but taking great pains to ensure that her St. Bernard accompanies her to Florida, and who so loathes her homeland that she vows never to return; an Asian high school student who spends much of his free time helping his parents run a grocery store, and who so excels in his courses that he "has his choice of several Ivy League universities"; a group of middle eastern taxicab drivers who— presumably sick and tired of unfair working conditions and discrimination — have banded together to become their own employers, running the Liberty Taxi Company in Dallas; and — in a much longer sequence — a Vietnamese physician, Dr. Diem, who completed his internship in Nebraska and felt so indebted to the area that he chose to stay, becoming the only Vietnamese doctor in the vicinity, and being instantly and completely accepted by the WASPish locals. The West Indian poet Derek Walcott makes an appearance, as do the Somosas, the family of the late Nicaraguan dictator, when Malle and his crew visit their home in Miami. The documentary ends with a protracted sequence on illegal immigration from Mexico and Central America, and details the countless young men and women who spend each night making rarely successful attempts to slip through the border, and are shuttled back to their homeland by U.S. Customs each morning.

ANALYSIS

God's Country takes a broad leap forward in the Malleian humanist tradition propagated and celebrated by the director's little-seen 1972 French documentary, *Place de la République* (see Chapter 11). If *Place* heightens the audience's curiosity about the random Parisian subjects who appear fleetingly before Malle's camera in "man on the street interviews"— the director probing with open-ended questions to encourage the subjects to open up and reveal their innermost feelings (i.e., the invisible inner qualities of the interviewees suddenly and unexpectedly becoming visible via their behavioral externalization)—*Country* carries this philosophy to the next level of cinematic development, with a series of highly detailed, protracted character studies. Acceptance and appreciation of the film thus become contingent on each viewer's ability to invest himself or herself, emotionally, in each subject, and the film's success should be judged by the extent to which Malle enables his audience to care.

The process of tonal empathy in *Country* begins with Malle's choice of a much smaller number of subjects than *Place*. He limits his film to between 13 and 15 individuals *in toto*, and spends an extensive amount of screen time on each. By setting his characterizations against a homogeneous midwestern backdrop, Malle is able to "blot out" the external environmental deviations, drawing the viewer's attention solely to variants in personality, outlook, and worldview among the subjects. *Country* also preserves—with its cinematographic approach—the detailed behavioral observation of *Place* and (to a lesser degree) *And the Pursuit of Happiness*. Malle's camera, largely by virtue of long-held close-ups, catches dozens of nuances that one might miss in a real-life, real-time context. For example, "dear old Mrs. Litzau," (Grace A. Litzau) the charming elderly gardener who appears at the outset of the picture and at the beginning of the 1985 epilogue, pants and breathes nervously and repeats her statements more than once. One senses from her a tremendous degree of vulnerability and self-consciousness when she stands before Malle's camera, and it is terribly affecting. Similar degrees of vulnerability and humility are displayed by Jean, the 27-year-old "free spirit" of the town, who rolls her eyes nervously and bites her lip when Malle questions her about her past decision to give up her baby for adoption, the importance of sex in her own life and the prudishness of Glencoe residents. In sum, one cannot help but feel drawn to these humans by virtue of their vulnerability.

In other words, Malle is using cinematic humanism as the core of his drama to "stack the cards," building viewer interest in his onscreen subjects with all of the aforementioned techniques. But this only embodies the first component in the process of tonal construction and balance: Malle's use of the first-person perspective (which is an inextricable component of cinema direct) enables him, in turn, to create, suspend, and sustain the illusion that the onscreen subjects share a reciprocal emotional investment in the viewer, for within the ontology of the cinematographic perspective (the subjects relating, more or less, directly to the camera), we intrinsically step into Louis's place and read the mannerisms, the gestures, and instinctively read the openness—as directed toward us. This certainly would be impossible without Malle's rare and inexplicable ability to almost instantly develop intimate confidences and bonds of trust with his subjects. Jamie Bruce observes, "Louis was so charming that people wanted to talk to him. And they trusted him immediately."[12] Malle's recollection of the interview with Jean illustrates this perfectly. He remembers sitting across from her and filming reel after reel, with only a camera between them; she felt her discretion and her emotional guard drop off and vulnerability, sensitivity and fear emerged, as she began confiding in Louis, talking directly into the camera lens and speaking candidly of her early pregnancy, the importance of sex in her life, her decision to give up her baby for adoption at a young age; she felt so comfortable opening up to Malle, in fact, that after he finished shooting, she expressed great fear about her on-camera revelations, and he reassured her about the integrity he would exercise in editing and using the footage.[13]

To a lesser degree, part of *Country*'s significance involves the film's inveterate glorification of Midwestern banality, and Malle's feelings that he need not have something *classically* interesting unfolding at any particular moment for a sequence to be incorporated into the film. More than 25 years after the initial stages of production, the film has become a period piece sketching a portrait of the mundanity of middle American life in the late seventies. The sequence that most cuts to the heart of this theme unfolds in the combination apothecary-gift shop, run by the Barnums. Malle understands that simply the flat indoor lighting, the slightly gauche décor, the hodgepodge of disparate sale items, and the "Medicine Wagon" label above the pharmacy counter earn viewer fascination. This philosophy of "beauty in the mundane" inevitably recalls observations by Richard Leacock, who complained explicitly to James Blue of commercial television's demands for "something exciting" in lieu of "something interesting," and the networks' consequent decisions to omit entire sequences from films.[14] Such sequences—as Leacock doubtless understood—may contain detail of cultural, sociological, period, or aesthetic interest and should not go overlooked or underappreciated.

To the extent that Malle's subjects automatically define—and are defined *by*—their agrarian environment, the film becomes a running social commentary on the flaws inherent in Reagan-era economics. In the 1979 footage, many (though not all) of the characters have built their lives around hope, around boundless optimism about the future. To a significant degree, the 1985 epilogue begins to answer the questions raised by the earlier segment, and the answers are largely pessimistic yet painfully realistic indictments of Reagan-era philosophy—an unveiling of Reaganite optimism as deceptive nonsense.

God's Country can also be read—to some degree—as a deliberate rectification of the problems posed by Malle's calamitous 1985 feature *Alamo Bay*. *Alamo*'s most significant casualty involves scriptwriter Alice Arlen's colossal failure to capture the challenging moral ambiguity of Ross Milloy's 1980 New York Times article on which the film was based. Milloy's strategy in that article is to help viewers enter the southern mindset and experience the frustrations of Texas fishermen, long prior to his revelations of the repellent racism that those universal frustrations may eventually produce. Though Malle never admitted so directly, it is possible—even probable—that he took the critical complaints about *Alamo Bay* to heart, and thus used *God's Country* to find its way inside racism, in a way that *Alamo* neglected to do. For this is one of *Country*'s most impressive—and bravest—accomplishments. From the 1979 footage, which constitutes the body of the documentary, one immediately sympathizes with all of the Glencoe residents who appear onscreen. No words or sentiments appear that could be characterized—to even the slightest degree—as racist or prejudicial. Only in the 1985 epilogue, and only after Malle and his subjects have revealed the devastating effects of the Reagan-era recession, does Mr. Thalman begin merciless verbal attacks against the Jews and the government for ruining his business. And significantly: we may not share his racism, but neither do we hold it against him to the degree that we would if we were first encountering him at this point, for we understand and empathize with his economic devastation and suddenly grasp, clearly and succinctly, how such devastation could bleed into the need for a scapegoat—any scapegoat at hand.

If one reads *God's Country* as an humanist excursion into several character sketches, identical claims cannot be made about *And the Pursuit of Happiness*. Though chronologically a follow-up to *God's Country* and a film that covers vaguely similar thematic ground, *Pursuit* should not be judged by the same standards as the prior film, for it operates with a unique intent. In lieu of spending a protracted amount of time on a handful of Americans set against a unified geographic backdrop, Malle paints on a vast canvas—so vast and so broad that, with only a few exceptions—it is impossible to feel a deep abiding connection to any of the onscreen individuals. Moreover, aside from Dr. Diem, the Vietnamese Nebraska physician (arguably the film's most affecting sequence), none of the subjects claim enough screen time to make a lasting impression or cultivate an ongoing tonal relationship with the viewer. The motion picture lacks the unity-of-place (the geographic cohesion) that marks *God's Country*, and as Malle and his film crew make seemingly random journeys from urban milieu to urban milieu, the film becomes a slightly coarse, scattergun carnival of immigrant life, a menagerie that only garners appeal via its ethnic diversity and whirlwind of colorful life-detail. Although Bruce and Malle preselected most of the subjects before bringing in their cameras, the film appears to lack a structure altogether. Yet, on a broader level still, if one finds the randomness and diversity of *Pursuit* somewhat frustrating, one should note the degree to which it is possible to read this diversity as Malle's very point; were the structure more cohesive, it could never convey the heterogeneity created by immigrants of numerous cultural backgrounds.

Pursuit's primary virtues are ideological. If Malle informed Philip French that his 1972 *Humain, trop humain* was not an ideologically-oriented work,[15] *Pursuit* travels to the opposite extreme; although Malle only presents—on the surface—quick, capsule-sized accounts and two or three-sentence histories that reflect on immigrant experiences, he is able to touch on deeper issues of a philosophical nature that resonate from the individualistic anecdotes. These themes include (among many others): the extent to which immigrants may be draining the country of any cohesion with their disparate languages and belief systems; the paradox that many immigrants rejoice at leaving their homelands but insist on turning major American cities into miniature ethnic versions of their indigenous countries; feelings of ethnic pride and superiority among certain immigrant groups; and the extent to which some immigrants may be draining the country of opportunities for employment in blue and white-collar spheres.

CRITICAL RESPONSE

And the Pursuit of Happiness and *God's Country* have fallen through the cracks of history; to this author's knowledge, only two collections hold copies of *Country* (the Glencoe, Minnesota Public Library and the Library of Congress) and one institution holds a copy of *Pursuit* (the University of Georgia Media Archives). As of this writing, *Pursuit* is even absent from Library of Congress holdings. It is thus perhaps unsurprising that U.S. reviews are scant. A small exception appeared in the *New York*

Times. John Corry exults the first hour of *Country* as "entirely engrossing ... [a film that] records small satisfactions." Yet he warns of the 1985 epilogue, "'God's Country' concludes with buzz words. The feeling is too smug and too neat. We're meant to be enlightened, but we're only left confused. Mr. Malle ought to have stayed with his earlier memory of Glencoe."[16] Leonard Maltin hails *Country* as, "poignant, insightful [and] occasionally hilarious."[17] *And the Pursuit of Happiness* received no English-language reviews.

European critics responded enthusiastically to the documentaries. Although Raphaël Bessan complains, in *La Révue du cinéma*, that the subjects of *God's Country* articulate the origins of their unhappiness poorly, he assesses *Country* as a "dispassionate and ..." (referring to the racist elements) "terrifying film."[18] Charles Tesson praises *Country* as "the happy flipside of *Alamo Bay*, a breathtaking plunge into the bosom of white America."[19] In *Cinéma*, Alain Carbonnier summarizes *Pursuit* as nothing more than an excellent piece of reporting on U.S. immigration, but asserts that this is not a bad thing — the film is woven around the perspective of one who is both close enough with the subject to be familiar, and distant enough to cultivate relationships with his subjects.[20] Marc Chevrie praises the film as well, in *Cahiers du cinéma:*

> What Malle demonstrates here is more than simply a perspective — it's the ability to listen ... each subject tells his or her own story and the film becomes an immense narrative comprised of many voices ... more than a theatrical film.... *Pursuit* is a marvelous document that television stations ... would be well-advised to program.[21]

20

Au revoir les enfants (Goodbye, Children) — 1987

Revisiting Old Haunts

"There was something mysterious about certain things—vague thoughts, sometimes veiled so much you felt that maybe they didn't exist, though something told you they did. What bothered you most was that you had no way of knowing if these things bothered your friends, too...."
— Sterling Hayden, *Wanderer*

"Childhood is the kingdom where nobody dies."
— Edna St. Vincent Millay

BACKGROUND

The events of 1985 and '86 recharged Louis Malle on multiple levels; in the personal sphere, his daughter Chloë's entrance into the world — on November 8, 1985[1] — renewed and reaffirmed his worldview and sense of spiritual purpose; in the professional arena, his twin documentary projects *Poursuite* and *Pays* (see Chapter 19)—which debuted on American television in July and November of 1986, respectively—entailed a return to the "hands-on" form of 16mm filmmaking Malle cherished, and the films' enthusiastic critical receptions only bolstered his confidence.

According to biographer Pierre Billard, two projects vied for Malle's attention in late spring and summer 1986: *Eye Contact* and *Au revoir les enfants*.[2] *Contact* began (and ended) with a John Guare script dramatizing the interpersonal affairs of a family on an archaeological dig in Sicily,[3] while Malle envisioned *Au revoir* as a highly personal account, something of a memory piece, recreating and dramatizing the events of January 1944 from his boarding school experiences as an early adolescent. He ultimately pushed aside the former and forged ahead with the latter—certainly crippled by an inability to devote his attention to two projects at once and by indefinite studio backing on *Contact*, but (even more so) determined to take advantage of the circumstances surrounding him at the time, that lent themselves to get-

As the show gently falls, Jean Kippelstein (Raphaël Fejtö, second from left) is led away by the Gestapo. He turns for one long, saddened final glance at his best friend, Julien Quentin (unpictured), who has just accidentally betrayed him to the Nazi militiamen. This is the haunting final scene of *Au revoir les enfants*, Louis Malle's most personal film. (From left to right: Peter Fitz, Fejtö, Damien Salot, Arnaud Henriet, Philippe Morier-Genoud.)

ting *Au revoir* produced. The conditions were optimal specifically because Chloë's birth and the successful return to documentary — when coupled — provided an enormous amount of emotional stability for the director, enabling him to reach deeply into his past, unearthing and confronting a deep-seated childhood trauma long buried, that lay at the nerve center of the *Au revoir* story. Candice Bergen observes:

> I think [Chloë's birth] gave [Louis] a comfort ... he had a sense of safety and a sense of comfort to explore, and also he had gotten to a certain age ... Louis had a very nontraditional way of family, and he was very in love with Chloë, and I think that gave him for a time a sense of comfort, and belonging, and I think that it gave him a kind of platform to dive off of ... It especially sort of replenished him to do *God's Country* and *Pursuit of Happiness* and that was very much a healing process for him, and very much an anchor, to priorities and realities.... I think it really sort-of reequilibrated him ... it brought him back to who he was.[4]

Thus, around spring 1986, the director flew to his familial estate on the Causse de Limogne in southwest France, and began taking copious notes and documenting memories in as much detail as he could summon from the past, referring constantly to friends and contemporaries to cross-check the validity of the details, and preparing to write his first draft. And though Malle initially stayed in the house alone, this isolation would be all too short-lived: Candice, Alexandra Stewart, Gila von Weitershausen, Manuel, Justine, Chloë, Chloë's nurse Ingrid Karbanneck and several friends descended on the estate when summer dawned, challenging Louis's focus and concentration.[5] As an alternative, Bergen forced Malle to return to Paris in mid–August and write his first draft *tout seul*, cut loose from all distraction.[6] Two weeks later, he emerged with the screenplay that became a blueprint for his most personal and—arguably—his most accomplished film.

But what, exactly, was the trauma that precipitated this catharsis? For the answer, one must backtrack to an event that unfolded 42 years prior. The span of 1940–8, as Billard documents it, turned young Louis's world upside down; the Germans invaded and occupied France, Pétain signed an armistice, and the Malles and Beghins hit the road for safety and self-preservation as Nazi aviators occupied their house. But most significantly, Louis began to discover himself and to come to grips with the corruption of the world. Billard writes:

> Between October 1943 and summer 1948, this child would undergo shocks, discover new territories, begin to have experiences, start to rebel, and forge a new identity. In passing from 11 to 16 years of age, the adolescent Malle would begin to turn his gaze outward to the world, using a sharp critical eye.[7]

This process of "forged identity" owed a great deal to Malle's parents' decision to put Louis on a pension, and thus begin fostering the boy's independence; the poor living conditions at St. Thérèse de l'Enfant Jésus, the boarding school where Pierre and Françoise Malle shipped their second youngest, contributed to a loss of innocence that accelerated Louis's maturation. Billard and Malle himself (in a *Cahiers* interview) each document the barely tolerable lifestyle—the indigestible food, the subthermal dormitories and classrooms (students forced to write assignments with their gloves on)—and the casualties of chilblains and pneumonia.[8]

But an unusual event that transpired in January 1944 delivered the greatest psychological impact. One of several Carmelite monks who ran St. Thérèse, Père Jacques (a.k.a. Louis Bunel, b. 1900; renamed Père Jean in Malle's onscreen fictionalization[9])—cloistered several Jews, draft evaders, and members of the *maquis* as students at the academy under assumed surnames. On Saturday, January 15, 1944, the notoriously sadistic Gestapo officer Willy Tuchel invaded the institution with his militia, and arrested three innocent Jewish students,[10] dragging them off to the gas chambers where they would later be executed with 181 other children.[11]

Opinions vary slightly on the degree to which Louis Malle interacted with a Jewish boy in his class named Hans-Helmut Michel, whom Père Jacques rechristened "Jean Bonnet" for the sake of camouflage and protection. Biographer Pierre Billard suggests that the Malle-Bonnet relationship was slightly grating, perhaps even acrimonious, that the two boys competed on an academic front but that Malle found himself oddly drawn to this older fellow student, perhaps because they shared a status as social outcasts, the 11-year-old Malle saddled with a urinary defect that made him wet the bed uncontrollably.[12] In an interview, Justine Malle (Louis's daughter) affirms her belief that Malle and Bonnet became friends, but were never as close as

Malle suggested in his finished film,[13] while according to Malle researcher and expert Stéphanie Gregoire, "Bonnet existed [and] Malle knew him but he never became his friend."[14] Malle himself sides most closely with Billard, recalling in his 1978 autobiography "A boy stood up [Michel], he was a bit older than us, always bright, always first, which irritated me. We didn't like him, he lived a bit apart from us."[15] Regardless of the degree to which these two did (or did not) grow close, it is clear that they certainly never became the best friends portrayed in the finished film, nor did Malle ever claim that it happened this way in real life.[16]

What counts is that this event—Malle rubbing shoulders with a boy close to his own age, and later watching in silence as the helpless child was arrested, deported from the school, and shipped to the death camps—changed young Louis's life forever, robbing him permanently of any lingering innocence and cutting the shackles that bound him to childhood. The director observes:

> For years I just didn't want to deal with it, but it had an enormous infuence on the rest of my life. What happened in January 1944 was instrumental in my decision to become a filmmaker. It's hard to explain, but it was such a shock that it took me several years to get over it, to try to understand it—and, of course, there was no way I could understand it. What happened was so appalling and so fundamentally opposed to all the values that we were being taught that I concluded that there was something wrong with the world and I started becoming very rebellious ... I think it sort of focused me or made me extremely curious about things happening outside the very privileged environment in which I was raised.[17]

According to Malle, the event so traumatized him that he confined himself to working it through internally, in his mind and heart, and failed to speak of it to anyone for years aside from his brother.[18] Such, at least, is the claim the director made to Philip French. Yet according to Billard, the story appeared in print in a 1963 interview with Serge July in *Clarté*,[19] and Malle told the whole story to Sarah Kant in the 1978 autobiography *Louis Malle par Louis Malle*.[20] Six years later, the story again cropped up in a discussion between Malle and Alice Arlen on the set of *Alamo Bay*, and Arlen encouraged Malle to do the project.[21] So the filmmaker was perhaps more open about it than he later cared to admit. Within the context of the story itself, Malle dramatizes the gradual collapse of barriers between his Doinel-ish onscreen alter-ego, "Julien Quentin," and the character of Jean Bonnet, as the two meet at the St. Croix boarding school and become best friends; the story hinges on its heartbreaking conclusion, Quentin's "loss of innocence" when he watches Bonnet dragged away by the Nazis.

Despite the director's recollection, in *Malle on Malle*, that Candice and Justine were crying after he finished reading the first draft to them,[22] Justine denies this vehemently ("I seriously doubt if I was in tears") and cites it as an example of her father's tendency to dramatize and imbue his life with colorful, theatrical details when recounting episodes.[23] If this is accurate, Malle likely told the story to Philip French simply as an illustration of his need to avoid excessive sentimentality in recreating the events onscreen.

Eager to rush production and begin shooting by January 1987 to obtain a wintry absence of sunlight, Malle solicited backing. He submitted his screenplay to Nicolas Seydoux at Gaumont and Claude (*Le Sex Shop*) Berri at Renn, without success, ultimately locking into Marin Karmitz at MK2. Karmitz demanded full distribution rights in exchange for seven million; pressured for time, an irked Malle conceded.[24] Supported by casting assistants Jeanne Biras and Iris Carrière,[25] the director scoured France for two young men to play his leads, posting flyers in public areas and schools, and conducting hundreds of "video screen tests." Malle ultimately cast unknowns Gaspard Manesse as Quentin and—much later—Raphaël Fëjto as Bonnet, waiting to confirm both casting assignments until he saw them together and observed their interaction, realizing that the success or failure of the film would hinge on the "chemistry"[26] between the boys. Though Malle hoped to bring Sven Nykvist on board the film as cinematographer—perhaps because the director foresaw *Au Revoir* as aesthetically identical to *Black Moon*, which Nykvist shot—the famed cinematographer was unable to do the project, recently hospitalized for exhaustion following his work on Kaufman's *Unbearable Lightness of Being*.[27] Instead, Malle hired Renato Berta. The two forged a successful partnership and would collaborate on one additional film before Louis died, *Milou en mai* (1990); they agreed to eliminate all color from the screen and to restrict shooting to the hours prior to 4 or 4:30 P.M. Malle brought Willy Holt on board to transform a modern educational facility, on the outskirts of Paris, into a period school, and discovered that, upon putting the contemporary child actors into 1944 clothes, they were instantly transported 40 years into the past and understood, inveterately, what it was like to come of age during World War II.[28]

The production of *Au revoir les enfants* spanned January and February 1987. The picture debuted in France in October 1987 and made its stateside premiere in March 1988.

Synopsis

Paris, January 1944. Immediately following the Christmas holiday, 11-year-old Julien Quentin (Gaspard Manesse) stands in the Gare de Lyon and prepares to board the train from Paris to the Ile de France, where he will return to a long semester at an exclusive Carmelite boarding school, St. Croix, administered by a group of monks.

Surrounded by a bustling crowd, he faces his mother (Francine Racette) indignantly, defensively, fighting the urge to show affection, even declaring his hatred; yet ultimately gives in and throws his arms around her; she whispers that she must also struggle to say goodbye and wishes she could disguise herself as a boy to join him. She kisses Julien on the brow, reminding him that, given the Occupation, it would never be safe for him to stay in Paris.

Julien boards the train with a lipstick-smudged forehead, and watches sadly through the window as the world whips past. Days after Quentin's arrival at school, one of the brethren, Père Jean (Philippe Morier-Genoud) inducts three new boys into the school, one of whom (Raphaël Fejtö) is introduced to his bunkmates—and to Julien—as "Jean Bonnet." Bonnet accepts the bed that flanks Julien's; and though the boys in the room immediately mock him and hurl pillows at his head, christening him "Easter Bonnet," Julien stands aside passively. When Quentin demonstrates some interest in Bonnet's novels and Bonnet attempts to introduce himself, however, Quentin responds hatefully, "I'm Julien Quentin and don't mess with me."

Over the weeks, Julien reveals some vulnerability when he accidentally wets the bed. Moreover, the hostility initially present between the two boys breaks down piece by piece; with fixated curiosity, Julien begins nonchalantly, unexpectedly catching glimpses of Jean Bonnet that indicate the boy's superior intelligence — his performance of Schubert on the piano for the music teacher (Irène Jacob), for instance, and his outstanding work on an algebraic equation before one of the classes. One evening, Père Jean — perhaps sensing a burgeoning friendship between the boys — invites Julien into his quarters and cautions him to show kindness to Jean; baffled, Julien asks if Bonnet is sick, to which the monk remains silent.

Despite Père Jean's request, the boys continue to stay slightly removed from one another until a late afternoon game of survivalist training in the woods, in which they somehow become separated from the remainder of the group and — lost and bewildered — stumble onto an open road and are picked up by two Nazi officers in a jeep, who cloak them with a protective blanket and drive the pair back to the main facility.

Curious about why Bonnet's stories of his parents never add up, Julien slips into the dormitory and rifles through Jean's locker, uncovering evidence — in a textbook — that Jean Bonnet is actually a Jewish boy named Jean Kippelstein, hiding under an assumed name. He confronts Bonnet with this discovery when the two are alone; Bonnet grows enraged. Nonetheless, Bonnet accompanies Julien, his mother, and older brother for a posh dinner in a local restaurant when Mme. Quentin arrives from Paris for a quick visit. During the meal, a French militiaman barges into the dining room and picks on an elderly Jew who dines alone at a table; irritated that the soldier would interrupt their meal, several German officers at a nearby table silence the intruder and force him to leave without arresting the gentleman.

Over the following days, any lingering hostility between Julien and Jean dissolves altogether; the boys share a number of experiences, hiding out together without attending a group air raid in a shelter, and playing a boogie-woogie piece on the piano together; Julien confides in Jean about having wet dreams and the two read passages after dark from the Arabian Nights. Yet trouble rears its ugly head when Joseph (François Négret), a slightly crippled orphan who works in the school kitchen, is kicked out of the academy for black market profiteering with the students; he grows enraged.

In the middle of a math class, a Gestapo officer bursts in and informs the students that Jews hide among them; though he is not aware of Bonnet's Semitism per se, he turns his back to the students and Julien turns his head quickly, fleetingly, eyeing Bonnet. The Gestapo catches this glance and arrests Bonnet, leading him out of the classroom. Later that morning, Julien realizes that Joseph — whom he befriended in the prior weeks — has betrayed Jean and the other cloistered Jews to the Nazis; he confronts Joseph with sheer incredulity; Joseph reprimands him for his silly piety and self-righteousness. Julien backs away in silent horror.

The Nazis line the students up in the courtyard as they lead the Jewish students — and Père Jean — away; the students all shout goodbye, in unison, to the father; he returns the greeting. Jean is the last of the arrested to leave the courtyard; as he turns to make eye contact one last time with Julien, seconds before being snatched away by a Gestapo officer, Julien lifts his hand to bid farewell to his friend. Louis Malle's voice-over, on the soundtrack, informs us that Père Jean died in Mathausen, Jean and the other Jewish boys in Auschwitz. Malle states that he will remember every second of that January morning until the day he dies.

ANALYSIS

Au revoir les enfants represents Louis Malle's cinematic apotheosis, Malle weaving into a fictional framework a handful of themes recurrent in many of his key films up through 1986, thus encapsulating and summarizing several of his lifelong preoccupations: the adult world filtered through the unblemished eyes of a child (*Pretty Baby*), the rocky passage from adolescence into adulthood (*Murmur of the Heart, Lacombe, Lucien*); the banality of evil (*Lacombe*); the desperate need for interpersonal connection with others and the defense mechanisms that some of the more emotionally broken and disenfranchised use to cope (*The Fire Within*); and even — given the Joseph character's "revenge" after being fired for black-market trading — the roots of racism and bigotry (*Alamo Bay*). In fact, the only recurrent elements in Malle's filmography that *Au revoir* omits altogether are ideological (or, more precisely, *a*-ideological): Malle's anticlericalism, anticapitalism, and relativistic moral ambiguity.[29] Ergo, while *Au revoir* explores a number of the director's fascinations, Malle never intended it as a summation of his entire worldview.

Pierre Billard terms *Au revoir* as more of a "1980s Malle film" than a "1940s Malle film."[30] This is certainly an accurate assessment: in approaching the project, Malle reflected on 1944 with 40 years of hindsight, and perceived — in a singular moment at boarding school — *the* key event that robbed him of innocence, giving birth to his lifelong need to question and severely critique and explore his surroundings. Yet the filmmaker's onscreen dramatic reconstruction reverses the chronology of events somewhat. Within the narrative, Malle does not begin with the "loss of innocence" (i.e., Jean Bonnet's arrest) and work ahead to his consequent investigation of the world. Instead, he uses the three weeks *prior* to Bonnet's arrest as the dramatic foundation, lacing the film's first few acts with the series of elements that — in real life — only became areas of curiosity in subsequent decades.[31] This transposition works because the film's shattering conclusion (i.e., Jean Bonnet's arrest) functions — in the dramatic framework — as the catalytic moment that brings everything before it into focus for Julien Quentin, and will imbue him with a retrospective curiosity, enabling him to use the events of the prior weeks as fodder in his quest for understanding in the years after the story ends.[32] It thus makes perfect sense for Malle to approach the first few acts as a sort of "loose tapestry" of early adolescence.

Yet architecturally, *Au revoir* is a bit more complex than it might appear at first glance. It marks a broad leap forward in Malle's use of "structural liberation," so evident in his films of the seventies — in fact, *Au revoir* encompasses the ultimate conciliation between the eastern-influenced narrative liberation of *Black Moon* and *Pretty Baby,* and the prototypical "Western dramatic arc" those films so sorely lack, undoubtedly gleaned from Malle's years in Hollywood. The director manages this narrative harmonization by building the structure of *Au revoir* on two levels: on the surface, he strings together a casual, laid-back dramatic web from the commonplace events of adolescence, a matter-of-fact and uneventful progression that appears to operate independently of narrative architecture *per se.* Yet the casualness is sophistic, for beneath this epidermal layer, the screenwriter-director builds an arc for the character of Julien Quentin (Malle's alter ego), that — despite its overwhelming subtlety, nonchalance, and *sublime* understatement (almost imperceptible until one has screened the film repeatedly) — is remarkably well defined and rigid. Julien's arc begins with Quentin's initial hostility and callousness and will, over the course of the narrative, involve lowering emotional barriers in his friendship with Jean Bonnet, as he allows himself to trust and to become emotionally vulnerable and open to discovery; this openness, in turn, leads him straight into the disclosure of evil and the loss of innocence.

It may help to examine the purpose and psychological function of Julien's initial defensiveness, evidenced in the opening scene with his mother at the Gare de Lyon, when Julien declares, "I don't give a damn about Dad, and I hate you!" His is a coping mechanism, an emotional shield — one might compare the harsh words of the small boy to a cat testing its claws — Julien demonstrating the aptitude of his defensive tool but immediately revealing his willingness to drop emotional armor (he hugs his mother a second time) expressly because he is able to make himself vulnerable to her without the risk of injury or insult. Such cannot happen around a majority of the other students; most telling is when Julien wets the bed, cursing under his breath ("Merde! Merde, merde, merde!"), and has the misfortune to catch the eye of a fellow student who razzes him mercilessly ("Il pisse au lit! Il pisse au lit!" he screams). It is a sign of vulnerability, much like the affection Julien expresses to his mother at the Gare, but in the case of the bedwetting, Malle places an uncontrollable weakness under the all-seeing gaze of an insensitive fellow student, in order to unveil the role of Julien's emotional callousness — its function as self-armature. Julien's hostility is also most likely the product of a miserable parochial school existence — an inner resource to shield himself against the cold, illness, and wretched food.

Julien might be comparable to Brooke Shields at a young age — tough as nails, impenetrable much of the time because he constantly raises his guard to avoid emotional abrasions; ergo, the boy virtually defies everyone to warm up to him. A telling moment has Quentin seizing a nudie magazine from a fellow student and affirming coldly as he eyes it and thrusts it back to the boy, "She has no tits." Julien's taking sudden interest in a pin-up would, of course, mean acknowledging that he exists on the same plane as the other students — equally vulnerable to the throes of pubescent lust and wet behind the ears. To whatever extent Mme. Quentin's admonition to "Be a big boy" (the film's opening line) assists Julien by reinforcing his coping mechanism, the ramifications are at least partially tragic: the words not only encourage him to avoid a public display of sadness when leaving his mother, but to carry this strategy into boarding school, which, however useful, is at least somewhat ill-advised because it stunts the growth of the initial stages of friendship between Julien and Jean. ("I'm Julien Quentin and don't mess with me," he declares.)

Malle himself may have suffered from this defensiveness to an even greater degree in early adolescence — evidenced by the fact that he seldom, if ever, extended himself to Jean Bonnet, and evidently (based on his "admission of guilt" near the end of the film — more on this later) came to harbor deep-seated regrets about his contribution to Bonnet's death through his own passivity. "Be a big boy, Julien." Mme. Quentin's words not only raise some key questions about the role and expectations of the European male during the first half of the twentieth century (Why would it be inappropriate for Julien to display emotion and sensitivity in regard to the departure from his mother? Why is vulnerability such a negative trait for *males*, and only associated with childlike behavior?) but establish Julien's defensiveness as a potent metaphor for the limitations of the male ego *per se* as defined, socially, during this period. Yet one never senses in the picture that Julien has entirely sealed himself off from emotion — he constantly reveals two layers, a surface "toughness" and a deeper vulnerability.

Julien's inner arc, as Malle sketches it, almost single-handedly determines the Quentin-Bonnet dynamic; the narrative thus unfolds, in its initial states, with indications of accessibility from Bonnet ("What's your name?") versus insurmountable defensiveness from Julien (Again: "I'm Julien Quentin and don't mess with me!") As it emerges, the friendship sits at the opposite end of the spectrum from dramatic contrivance; it happens almost fatalistically, against Quentin's and Bonnet's wills, at a deliberate pace, beginning with minor instances of Julien's curiosity about his fellow student, with a series of intriguing and unusual details he spots (Bonnet masterfully pouring out Schubert on the piano keys, for instance). Julien's vulnerabilities are accompanied by his internal need to share them, a need common to many adolescents (see the epigraphic quote from Hayden at the beginning of this chapter), revealed by his discussion of nocturnal emissions with Bonnet; Bonnet's failure to laugh or mock Julien or write him off reinforces the steps Quentin has taken toward unbridled trust in the friendship. Though one might dismiss the scene in the woods— where the two are thrown together after dark — as a piece of directorial manipulation, it retains plausibility because the children, to varying degrees, share a level of intelligence and intuition that has led each boy to separate himself from the pack, to live on the outermost edge — the fringe — of the social circle; it is a deep-seated commonality, and will draw Jean and Julien together *de facto*, with or without their becoming lost in the forest. And Quentin's indication to Bonnet that he is aware of Bonnet's Judaism — though initially perhaps mistaken by Jean as a threat (notice how Bonnet reacts with hostility and resentment upon hearing this news)— evolves into an indicator of trust over the passing days when Quentin does *not* go out of his way to rat out Jean as a refugee and thus shows himself worthy of this knowledge. Of course, the boys' piano playing together, their candid discussions about their fathers, their nocturnes reading *The Arabian Nights* to one another by flashlight, and Jean's telling acknowledgement of his own fear are all the classic elements of friendship between two boys.

With *Au revoir*, Malle works from a distinctly American cinematic genre — the memory piece — beginning with foundational subject matter that long ago become worn thin and trite in a Hollywood context, but cutting against the grain of traditional presentation in form, thus reinventing the material altogether and creating an unfamiliar voice. Ergo, while the genre content, examined independently, appears quite familiar — the motion picture taking as its raw material the process of adolescent self-discovery — Malle breaks new ground in alternate ways, reworking the presentation by draining the scenes and dialogue almost entirely of humor, as he methodically establishes the multi-faceted components of intellectual, spiritual, and physical discovery and development for the two boys, of which sexuality is a vital element. The wet dreams, like the bedwetting, evoke not amusement from the audience (as would certainly occur in a Hollywood production on the same themes) but shared empathy about the fear and confusion Julien and Jean share about the process of growing up. Consider, for instance, the misunderstanding inherent in Julien's description of a nocturnal emission as the process of waking up and finding "warm piss" on his stomach.

Within this contextual framework, Malle resists the tendency for nostalgic reminiscence. In his book *The Ethics of Memory*, Avishai Margalit provides a wonderful summary of the dangers of nostalgia of which Malle is fully conscious in his genre revisionism, a summary that perfectly befits his directorial intuition:

> An essential element of nostalgia is sentimentality. And the trouble with sentimentality in certain situations is that it distorts reality in a particular way that has moral consequences. Nostalgia distorts the past by idealizing it. People, events, and objects from the past are presented as endowed with pure innocence.[33]

To escape from this potential foxtrap, Malle begins by stripping *Au revoir*'s first few acts of a "softening" voice-over — that everpresent staple of the memory piece — and refrains from using it until the last few seconds of the final scene in the motion picture. He instead relies solely on careful framing in the opening shot to immediately paint the story visually as the recollection of one individual: Julien Quentin stands at the center of the station platform, motionless, head bowed, the crowd swirling around him[34] — as in one's own dreams and memories, wherein one posits oneself, egocentrically, at the center of the mnemonic frame.

Cinematographically, the filmmaker steers clear of any indications or evocations of nostalgia, stripping the picture entirely of romanticism from the picture's opening frames. Though the preponderance of memory pieces, particularly *coming-of-age* memory pieces, are photographed with soft focus (take Robert Mulligan's cloying and manipulative *Summer of '42*, for example) or, less commonly, with cheesecloth or dyed wedding veils over the lenses, to evoke "lost summers,"[35] Malle asked cinematographer Renato Berta to eliminate all onscreen color in *Au revoir* aside from the mother's crimson lipstick and — more importantly — to drain the film of visible sunlight, a deliberately revisionist aesthetic device with an overwhelming emotional side effect: It drains the picture of any contrived warmth, leaving a cold, haunting, and hard-edged onscreen environ that — through its brutality — forces the audience to infer and extrapolate emotional and psychological cues, *on its own*, from the friendship between the two boys. No one can ever accuse Malle of manipulation; it isn't simply that he refuses to hand the viewer emotional cues, but that he pulls his surrounding aesthetic to the alienating end of the spectrum — so that the universal aspects of adolescence in the film gain more vivid backlighting and outlines via the process of evocation. He is not forcing, but enabling.

The luminescent choices also lend the picture metaphoric significance on two levels. To grasp the first metaphor, one can begin with an essay by Cynthia Ozick, "The Shock of Teapots." Ozick uses clear and "lambent" rays of sunlight during travel as a metaphor for the clarity of memory. She writes:

> This glorious strangeness— a kind of crystalline wash — was the sunlight of a Swedish autumn. The sun looked *new*: it had a lucidity, a texture, a tincture, a position across the sky that my New York gape had never before taken in. The horizontal ladder of light hung high up, higher than any sunlight I had ever seen, and the quality of its glow seemed thinner, wanner, more tentatively morning-brushed; or else like gold leaf beaten gossamer as tissue — a lambent skin laid over the spired marrow of the sun ... I, under the electrified rays of my whitening hair, stand drawn upward to the startling sky, restored to the clarity of childhood. ... Travel returns us in just this way to sharpness of notice; and to be saturated in the sight of what is entirely new ... is to revisit the enigmatically lit puppet-stage outlines of childhood: those mental photographs and dreaming woodcuts or engravings that we retain from our earliest years. What we remember from childhood we remember forever — permanent ghosts, stamped, imprinted, eternally seen. Travelers regain this ghost-seizing brightness, eeriness, firstness.[36]

Though Louis Malle would likely agree with Ozick about the "permanence" of ghosts from childhood — evidenced by the degree to which the lingering memories of boarding school haunted him for 40 years ("I will remember every second of that January morning until the day I die," he states in his narration) he and Ozick would most certainly dispute the stasis of childhood memories. While Ozick perceives childhood ghosts as "stamped [and] imprinted," a clause that implies an unchanging nature, Malle shares his belief with Philip French that "Memory is not frozen, it's very much alive, it moves, it changes." Using *cinematic* voyages as a substitute for the geographic "travel" referenced in the above Ozick quotation, her establishment of an idiom that ties together luminescence and the clarity of memory establishes a "metaphoric spectrum" that can be applied with equal validity to the use of light in *Au revoir*. When one recognizes that Malle's own memory of boarding school was faint, somewhat uncertain circa 1986 (he was actually forced to check with friends and loved ones about the validity of his recollections and discovered that certain details had changed in his mind) and takes into consideration the use of light in the film — how cloaked and indirect and hidden the sunlight is— the overcast, wintry skies of *Au revoir* become a kind of substitution not for the *vividness* of memory, but for its dimness. A grave reminder, and a warning, of how memories can so easily become dynamic and fluid, and how personal invention and guilt, like blankets of cloud, can block out the clarity of one's hindsight with the passing years.

Ozick establishes a second metaphor, as well, that provides an equal level of insight when applied to *Au revoir*. She goes on to discuss the way in which, when travelers have "cut themselves loose from their own society, from every society..." the banal, set against an unfamiliar landscape, "arrests [them] with its absolute particularity." Note how Malle and Berta's deliberate decision to carry the onscreen realm through a dramatic aesthetic and luminescent shift renders the onscreen landscape not only strange and unfamiliar but—in Ozick's words—"Martian." When held up against this backdrop, the universality of events and experiences and relational overtones emerges with greater clarity. Ozick refers to it as "the flooding in of the real."

As the apex of this realism, however, *Au revoir*'s heartbreaking conclusion challenges the innocence of the denouements in more traditional memory pieces. If *Au revoir* borrows its basic narrative structure from films such as *Summer of '42* or *Stand by Me*, for instance—the loosely knit coming-of-age tapestry of early adolescence, that builds up to one defining moment that changes the protagonist's life forever (in the Mulligan film, Hermie's affair with Dorothy and his loss of virginity; in the Reiner film, the boys' discovery of the corpse)—Malle only retains half of the equation—self-discovery as a launching pad—and builds up to a conclusion with infinitely graver and darker overtones that actively redefines and reworks everything preceding it. And by weaving together the coming-of-age of early adolescence with one boy's arrest and deportation by the Nazis, Malle somehow accomplishes the impossible: he bridges the collective with the highly individualistic, carrying the universalist memory piece into wildly idiosyncratic territory—a destination foreshadowed, from the outset of the picture, by the film's revisionist aesthetic presentation.

A final note on Malle's genre revisionism. One might respond to the above Margalit quote ("Nostalgia distorts the past by idealizing it. People, events, and objects from the past are presented as endowed with pure innocence") by defending the idea that Malle does, actually, endow one of his characters with immaculate behavior, as when Pauline Kael bemoans Malle's desire to paint Jean Bonnet as virtually spotless:

> By the end ... you may feel pretty worn down ... by all the aching, tender shots of Jean. He's photographed as if he were a piece of religious art: Christ in his early adolescence. There's something unseemly about the movie's obsession with his exotic beauty—as if the French-German Jews had come from the far side of the moon. And does he have to be so brilliant, and a gifted pianist, and courageous? Would the audience not mourn him if he were just an average schmucky kid with pimples?

This summation glosses over at least two buried implications. First: *Au revoir les enfants*—like *My Dinner with André* a half-decade prior—is so heavily weighted toward the protagonist's recollection of his *own* development and progression as a product of the onscreen events that it cannot even begin to purport to offer the audience a full view of Jean Bonnet's character or transition (the film only encompasses one arc); and naturally, as a *guilt*-infused retrospection through Julien/Louis's hindsight, the protagonist gains a far greater ethical burden (and additional weakness) and the Jewish victim loses much of the weight of iniquity. Perhaps Quentin-Malle, like nearly every other adolescent in the world, was simply so insular in 1944, so swept up in his own inner rhythms and shifting currents, that he failed (and could not possibly be expected) to burn an accurate perception of Jean Bonnet into his psyche.

Yet even given this weightedness (the film's excessive yet intentional bias), Jean is far from perfect. The most obvious exception that emerges involves his immediate distrust and burning anger when Julien declares his knowledge of Jean's real surname, Kippelstein, and thus his Jewish identity—why would he be so gauche as to immediately assume (or infer) ill motives, such as blackmail, without definite cause from Jean? It feels like a cruel and unjust reaction.

One can also take serious issue with Kael's mention of Bonnet's "courage"; Kael is presumably sizing up Bonnet as a character whom Malle paints as a Christlike martyr simply *because* he is a Jew; for example, when Bonnet enters the classroom (days after his fellow students) he draws instant systematic attack; the boarders heave pillows at his head and hurl potshots, whooing and whooping and whistling, "Easter Bonnet! Easter Bonnet!" But a more daring implication lies buried here: certainly these children—unaware of Bonnet's Judaism—could not possibly be responding with anti–Semitic motives. Even if they have inherited anti–Semitic hostility from their parents, how could they, within two seconds, size up Jean as Jewish? Instead, note Jean's posturing as the monk guides him into the bunkhouse. His presence *exudes* self-consciousness—his snaillike gait, his tentative steps—and he becomes an easy, instant target—a credible attitude presumably because of his overfamiliarity with anti–Semitism but certainly never courageous. And though it would be insipid and rather disgusting to suggest that Jean is in any way asking for persecution, it *is* accurate to suggest that, because he has become so familiar with and used to discrimination as a Jew, he has begun to project this expectation in his body language and mannerisms, and thus draws discriminatory behavior and persecution *de facto*—in much the same way, for instance, that children who become repeat victims of molestation or rape from unrelated adults do so because they start instinctively throwing out indicators of vulnerability and thus draw predators subconsciously.

In his discussion of the history surrounding *Au revoir les enfants,* Pierre Billard spends many pages accusing Malle of toying with the real-life facts in the creation of the film. Billard's accusations inevitably recall the questions about "lying" posed by Australian novelist Peter Carey in such works as *Oscar and Lucinda,* when he deliberately attempts to spin as outrageous a tall tale as he can muster, and (for example) Robert James Waller's "deceptive" prologue to *The Bridges of Madison County,* wherein the author leads his audience into believing—erroneously—that the backstory of the characters is based on a series of real life events. Though one might take issue with the Waller example because of its presentation as fact, the concerns about a fiction author's moral character as far as *honesty* are generally ludicrous and irrelevant for one simple reason.

In her essay "Metaphor and Memory," Cynthia Ozick defines novels as "those vessels of irony and connection ... nothing if not metaphors."[37] If one accepts as valid Ozick's definition of the archetypal *roman,* the same standard should obviously apply to fictional films, including *Au revoir les enfants,* for it—like a great novel—never purports to present a context that is anything other than pure fictional re-creation. And as a metaphor, the ethic of its creator (Malle) must certainly, in turn, be judged not on the level of the "valid" or "false" facts he presents, but on the level of meaning—on the truth or falsehood of the ideas conveyed because the film is metaphoric.

And in this regard, few would dispute the validity of the deeper meanings—the "innocence lost" that Malle attempts to evoke, or the horror of Julien Quentin's discovery of evil, given his twofold realization—first, that Joseph betrayed Julien, and second, that Julien is arrested and deported despite no wrongdoing.

In case one doubts *Au revoir*'s status as a metaphor, Ozick lists several qualifying factors for "metaphor" (as contrasted with "inspiration") that would cement the motion picture even more firmly in this category, notably the idea that while "inspiration is ad hoc and has no history ... Metaphor relies on what has been experienced before; it transforms the strange into the familiar."[38] A metaphor involves a working through of the past by "interpret[ing] memory"—reaching into the past and reevaluating it, in order to work forward and learn for the future. If one concurs with all of these precepts, it is only a short deductive leap to characterize *Au revoir les enfants* as a work that lies closer to metaphor than to inspiration, given the picture's history. For Malle spent many years attempting to work through the material in his own mind, and it became, in its final form, his adidactic attempt to pass along the most personal experiences from his past to audiences and his children (note the personal dedication at the outset of the film—"Pour Cuotemoc, Justine, et Chloë") by translating raw experience, metaphorically, into fictional material with a voice of universalistic identification, as one gives structure to a formless dream in one's mind. Though the picture is not by any means a "message film" or a "fable," it retains significance as a meditation on the loss of innocence, and—significantly—on collective and individual responsibility.

On the latter note, Malle has pondered the significance of one of the picture's final moments, where Julien Quentin accidentally betrays Jean Bonnet to the Gestapo officer; Pauline Kael refers to it as "a Judas kiss, but an unintentional one."[39] Although he insists that he never included the "Judas kiss" scene as a projection of his own guilt,[40] to dispute this as Malle's central motivation would be specious; like the depiction of the passionate mother-son relationship in *Murmur of the Heart*, the director is working on a level, in *Au revoir*, where he remains completely unaware of the Freudian implications of reworking a biographical event. Malle even had difficulty shooting the sequence without bursting into tears.[41] Indeed, the scene harbors an intriguing visual clue that paints it as a trip into Malle's subconscious. As a startling and unforseeable exception to documentary-like cinematographic approach that pervades much of the picture (I speak of the *Lacombe*-like way in which the images are filmed, not of Berta's aesthetic *per se*), the classroom "betrayal" sequence is perhaps the only scene in the entire film shot like a dream. For when Herr Müller, the Gestapo officer, turns his back, and Julien does an about face and eyes Jean Bonnet, Müller's head is *not* turned to such a degree that he should be able to catch what occurred and who precipitated it. Instead, it appears—as Malle blocks the scene—that Müller somehow has eyes in the back of his head—as if the Gestapo officer has somehow superhumanly defied logic purely as a product of Quentin's (and Malle's) subconscious fear. The event unfolds completely outside the framework of the rational. It might even be comparable to a stock nightmare in which one is hiding from an individual who poses some element of danger (a murderer, a stalker), the protagonist cloistered in a completely inconspicuous and undetectable location, and yet the antagonist manages, somehow, to invariably find the hiding place of the self and zero in on his target — the stalker's knowledge and detection ability not springing from everyday logic, but directly from the sleeper's subconscious fear. Again: In this sequence, it is as if we have taken an undeclared journey straight to the core of Malle's psyche.

On a final note: *Au revoir* also investigates personal versus collective experience and — in turn — personal versus collective responsibility. Ontologically, the film adjoins the subjective and the macrocosmic; to borrow one of Avishai Margalit's terms, it functions as something of a "flashbulb memory" for Malle. Margalit writes:

> With regard to dramatic events, we are aware of the channels through which we were plugged into the shared memory. The significance of the event for us depends on our being personally connected with what happened, and hence we share not only the memory of what happened but also our participation in it, as it were.

The above concept is not difficult to apply to *Au revoir*— Malle came into close proximity ("rubbed shoulders") with — and even had the opportunity to become close friends with[42] — a victim of the gas chambers at Auschwitz. The concluding event — when Jean Bonnet-Kippelstein is ultimately dragged away — thus symbolizes the connection between personal horror (the individual adolescent's discovery of evil) and the collective horror of *shoah*.

That the Holocaust was accompanied, in time, by a collective passivity and — ultimately — growing kernels of complete ignorance, fueled Malle's moral need to craft the film and ponder this individual-collective connection. He later asserted his conviction that the French were aware of the Holocaust during the war, and have since lived in grave denial over the Nazi genocide for decades.[43] Thus, Malle bore the weight of personal responsibility — to create a monument to help the world understand, collectively. It is on this level that he most intended the film to function — as a reminder, to keep the proverbial candles burning. And just as Margalit, in turn, affirms an internal relation between memory and caring,[44] the humanistic caring in the film (which, in Margalit's terminology, is the core of *morality*— the laws governing our behavior with "thin relations," in lieu of *ethics*, which applies to "thick relations"[45]) justifies the need for a cinematic monument ensuring remembrance of Jean Bonnet and the thousands of others who were arrested and extinguished.

CRITICAL RESPONSE

It would be difficult to overestimate the critical kudos lavished on *Au revoir les enfants*; Pauline Kael's review, quoted earlier in the text, remains one of the few in print to attack the motion picture. Critics and viewers around the globe proclaimed it as an instant masterpiece, the crowning triumph of Malle's career. Among these reviews: Maurice Pons, writing for *Avant-Scène Cinéma*, praises the director as one of the most gifted and brilliant filmmakers then alive, and speaks particularly highly of Malle's ability to avoid the trap of evoking contrived emotion onscreen; he sizes up the film as genuine specifically because the memories are Malle's own.[46] Critiquing the picture for *Révue*, Marcel Martin writes eloquently, "Autobiography certainly isn't one of Malle's preoccupations, but all we can ascertain of Malle himself in *Au Revoir* ... is important ... and captivating enough to demonstate the humanist inspiration that gives Malle's œuvre its richness."[47] In the States, David Denby writes in *New York*, "From its first shot, *Au Revoir* ... feels right. The movie is concentrated and precise — a little dry — but only in the bracing and clarifying way that some of the best Truffaut movies are dry. Events and emotions are merely stated, never overstated. Malle's grasp of the material is so intuitive, so light and easy...."[48] And writing for *Variety*, Lenny Borger proclaims, "Malle ... has not betrayed his subject matter. He directs with clarity and understatement ... [his] homecoming is ... one of the best things to have happened to the French this year."[49] In Britain, Philip French rhapsodizes, "*Au Revoir les enfants* is not only the best movie on the subject of the Occupation since ... *Lacombe, Lucien*; it is also one of the best pictures ever made about childhood, and the finest French film for several years."[50]

Au revoir went on to win the Golden Lion (Malle's second, following *Atlantic City*) at the 1987 Venice Film Festival, and received a standing ovation at Telluride. And yet ironically, despite all of the acclamations, the production, release and reception of the film would lead to one of Louis Malle's few heartbreaks. He not only expected to win the Best Foreign Film Oscar for 1987, but literally had no doubt in his mind; so overwhelming was his certainty that Justine and Manuel flew to Los Angeles from Europe to attend the ceremony. When the envelope arrived, and the statue went to Gabriel Axel's Isak Dinesen adaptation *Babette's Feast*, Malle literally found it difficult to cope and almost collapsed. Candice Bergen remembers and details the shock of that evening:

> When *Au Revoir les enfants* didn't win the Oscar, it was a huge and horrible moment because Justine and Manuel came ... I mean, it was ... just ... it was really like we had all been kicked in the stomach. And then of course you're ashamed that you have such a powerful reaction to something that is ... But, I mean, [Louis] was almost out of his seat.... Our response and his response were like we had been kicked in the stomach. You know, the Academy votes the way it votes, it was just that ... we thought that there was no question. Otherwise, he never would have had the kids come with us to the awards.... So we felt even more — you feel so foolish, and it was really [Louis's] last chance to be recognized by the Academy.[51]

It all tied in, of course, to Louis's dream of paradoxically blending a tremendous artistic achievement with commercial success, and he saw the Oscar as the quintessential representation of the latter.

Yet, despite his devastation, Malle would return to America once more before his passing, and — in doing so — create yet another masterpiece of comparable weight to *Au revoir les enfants*: *Vanya on 42nd Street*. In the mean time, he needed as much emotional distance as possible from the States and remained in France for the production of his next film.

21

Milou en mai (May Fools) — 1990

Collective Mythmaking

"But all the story of the night told over,
And all their minds transfigured so together,
More witnesseth than fancy's images
And grows to something of great constancy;
But, howsoever, strange and admirable."
— Hippolyta, Shakespeare's *A Midsummer Night's Dream*, Act V, sc. 1

"The radio ... is rapidly crowning its way in among the necessities in the family standard of living. Not the least remarkable feature of this invention is its accessibility ... With but little equipment one can call the life of the rest of the world from the air."
— Robert S. Lynd and Helen Merrell Lynd, *Middletown*

BACKGROUND

If Louis Malle anticipated the runaway success of *Au revoir les enfants*, the degree of acclaim caught him off guard.[1] Disturbed — slightly bitter — about *Au revoir*'s failure to garner the 1987 Best Foreign Film Oscar, yet concomitantly swept away by the worldwide enthusiasm for the film, the director's subsequent actions paint a vivid picture of the complexity of his emotions. As Candice Bergen reveals, the "battle wounds" from the Oscars were still fresh and raw in early 1988, so Malle decided to stay as far from Hollywood as possible, remaining in France for a follow-up project.[2] Yet he happily took full advantage of the opportunity handed him by *Au revoir*'s enthusiastic public reception, hosting screenings of the film at educational institutions (universities and elementary and middle schools) at home and around the globe, and fielding questions from young viewers.[3] This lasted several months. Though it is only a loose hypothesis, the process of introducing and discussing the film before audiences perhaps functioned as yet another catharsis, enabling Malle to

The rites of spring: love, sex, *haute cuisine*, and fine wine, as Milou de Vieuzac (Michel Piccoli, right), his sister-in-law Lily (Harriet Walter) and their extended family picnic on the grounds of the deceased matriarch's estate, circa May 1968, in *May Fools* (Milou en mai). Housemaid Adèle (Martine Gautier, far left) dozes beside them.

"work through" the calamity of the Academy Awards. On still another level, Malle's decision to keep his feet planted on French soil meant reembracing his "*carte blanche* status to make any film he want[ed] in his native country"[4]—a privilege he abandoned voluntarily back in 1976, that the universal acclaim of *Au revoir* now reestablished, perpetuated and strengthened. The period was thus bittersweet.

In early 1988, Malle returned to the Causse du Lot in southwest France to recharge his batteries and chased two project leads at once: the production of John Guare's script *Eye Contact* and a single project successively titled (in its initial drafts) '68, *Les Temps de cerises* (*The Time of Cherries*),[5] and *Milou en mai* (*May Fools* or *Milou in May*). John Guare implies that Louis planned to shoot *Milou* and *Contact* about one year apart, *Milou* in the spring of 1989 and *Eye Contact* in spring 1990.[6,7]

But *Eye Contact* never took off, thanks to an absence of funding and a weak, half-hearted commitment from Hollywood studios. According to Pierre Billard, though Michel Ferry went scouting for locations in Sicily, the *haute célébré* of the American box office read the script and espoused interest, but ultimately declined. This occurred on the production end, with heavyweights such as David Puttnam and Sam Goldwyn, Jr., passing, and on the performance end, with top box office draws including Michael Douglas, Kevin Kline, Richard Dreyfuss, Meryl Streep, even Steve Martin mildly intrigued by the script, but ultimately letting the material slip from their fingers; no A-list actors or actresses, aside from Candice Bergen (who made an agreement with her husband, years prior, to avoid on-set collaboration for the sake of preserving their relationship),[8] felt compelled enough to pursue one of the lead roles.[9] Billard argues that Bergen's reason for turning down *Contact* had much to do with her acceptance of the lead role on the smash American television series *Murphy Brown*,[10] which premiered on November 14, 1988 (episodes would continue to tape over the following several years) making it impossible for her to fly to Sicily for an extended film shoot.[11] John Guare speculates that the impossibility of securing funding for the project may, in fact, have been linked to the *Crackers* debacle back in 1984:

> *Eye Contact* had a checkered past—[Louis and I] had gone to Sicily in '85, I believe, to find a story which we [wrote]. Louis loved the idea of children—step-brother and step-sister—acting out the romance of their recently married parents. We wanted Meryl [Streep] and Kevin [Kline], or perhaps Steve Martin, but we never got that far because we could not get a studio interested. Was it because of the failure of *Crackers*? Michael Eisner was interested in the script, but would not do it with Louis. I know this because I called Eisner and spoke to him about his rejection of Louis as director. Michael said the script needed Mike Nichols, that Louis was too European, which was a euphemism for "independent." I said, "Without Louis, there [is] no movie." Louis did not give up on getting it [produced] and, yes, hoped in his typical fashion that he would finish *Milou* and go right into *Eye Contact* which had to be filmed in the springtime. But we still couldn't set it up anywhere; *Milou* took over and *Eye Contact* just withered. A real sadness [overtook us].[12]

Eye Contact (a.k.a. *I Hate My Life!*) ultimately evolved into Guare's acclaimed 1992 theatrical production *Four Baboons Adoring the Sun*; see also Appendix A.

With *Contact* defunct, only *Milou* remained. Whereas many of Malle's key projects—*Lacombe, Lucien* is the quintessential example—came to fruition over years or even decades, *Milou en mai* gestated fully in only 12 months.[13] Another contradiction emerges here: although Malle never cited a specific date for *Milou*'s origin in interviews, he implies that he set to work on the treatment in mid-summer 1988, around June or July at the earliest, and invited Jean-Claude Carrière to collaborate around November.[14] Yet Pierre Billard states, forthright, that Malle began drafting *Milou* in February of that year and pulled in Carrière around mid–July.[15]

Regardless of the month *per se* when Louis began to draft the piece, the single source of inspiration for *Milou* is easy to pinpoint. In the early winter of 1988, Malle attended the Majestic Theater in Brooklyn, New York, for a performance of the Peter Brook-directed, Elisaveta Lavrova-translated stage adaptation of Anton Chekhov's *The Cherry Orchard* (a.k.a. *La Cerisaie*), starring Brian Dennehy as Lopakhin, Linda Hunt as Charlotta, and Erland Josephson as Gaev. (The production took its initial bows on January 25, 1988.)[16] Slightly dissatisfied with this ensemble of actors,[17] but enamored with Chekhov's play, Malle reflected on an experience from seven years prior, when he witnessed Brook's 1981 Parisian staging of *La Cerisaie* with an all-French cast—an adaptation scripted by Jean-Claude Carrière, with magnificent performances. And the memory, over the following weeks, sparked a new idea: a modernized cinematic adaptation of *Orchard*, a tragicomedy exploring the inner dynamics of a family of struggling sharecroppers from the Bordeaux region of France and dramatizing the family's gradual dissimilation that accompanies the sale of their palatial estate.

In mid–late 1988, after working on the treatment for a period of time, Malle hit an impasse. Enter Jean-Claude Carrière — Malle's closest friend. A world renowned "expert on script structure,"[18] the mind behind the 1981 Brook-Chekhov adaptation (i.e., the aspect of the Parisian production of *La Cerisaie* that most seduced Malle), and — most significantly — a former member of the *haute bourgeois terrienne,* born and raised (in the mid–late 1930s) in Colombières-sur-Orb, Hérault, Languedoc-Roussillon, France. This was viticulture country, the land of parceled-off vineyards whose caretakers had little to do outside of producing and selling their wines, and it lay at the heart of Malle's scenario. Carrière's intimate familiarity with the subculture or *classe* of the *vignobles* (and the like familiarity of his wife, Nicole, who hailed from the same region) thus enabled the couple to provide countless details that would enrich the story,[19] particularly the Vieuzac family's *démarche* of partitioning off the crockery to relatives (Nicole),[20] Milou's method of fishing for crawdads that entails putting his hands under the river bank and letting the crayfish bite his fingers (Jean-Claude),[21] and the backstory-laced details of the crazy and eccentric Uncle Arthur: his feat of training a feral zebra to pull his carriage and his proclivity for hunting with trained chambermaids in lieu of dogs (Nicole).[22] Though Malle and Carrière had not officially worked together since *Le Voleur* in 1966, they did uncredited collaborations on the director's *Le Souffle au cœur*; *Lacombe, Lucien*; and *Au revoir les enfants*, where — in each case — the screenwriter provided colorful details from his own experiences as a youth; the collaborative dynamic was thus familiar territory for both men.

Another series of contradictions. Although three sources concur that Malle made an initial trip to visit Carrière with an early incarnation of *Milou* under his arm, these sources divaricate on the content of the scenario that the director brought to Paris, and on the *amount* of unfashioned material: the director remembers that he had around 80 pages,[23] but according to Carrière:

> [Louis] ... came to me one day and he said ... "Listen, I have an idea, I have written twenty pages, I don't know how to go any further." I'd like to read it to you. He *loved* to read aloud. So he came to my house in Paris and he started reading *Milou en mai,* he had written the first *twenty pages*, which were, of course, to change later ... and then he stopped and ... said, "Now, I don't know how to go ... how to develop this." And then I had probably two or three possibilities, new directions to take ... and then we decided to go together[24] ... at the very beginning was the situation, the house, and different members of the same family ... gathering in the same country house. That was Louis's idea ... Of course, as usual, it's absolutely impossible to remember ... What was exactly his beginning [of the story].... I think that the very first idea of Louis was the death of the grandmother.[25]

Yet in Pierre Billard's account:

> For three months, Louis covered a *hundred pages* with notes devoted solely to
> *Milou* (though the first attempt at a scenario bore the title '68). The opening
> scene of the film never changed: Mme. Vieuzac crying while she cuts onions
> and the radio delivers a report on *les événements*; she collapses on the stair-
> case and dies. Her son Milou converses with the bees. The main storyline
> hardly changed at all: everyone is going to bury Mme. Vieuzac. Milou gath-
> ers the family together. The guests succeed one another. Emotion and conflicts.
> Problems with inheritances. A decision to compromise by drawing from a lot-
> tery. The real problem: whether or not to sell the house ... The director's notes
> multiplied the incidents, anecdotes, hypotheses among the ... twelve charac-
> ters who gather in the house. [Malle] wrote out biographical notecards on the
> most important characters.... Most extraordinary, in the attentiveness and
> meticulousness of [Malle's] work, is that he only interested himself in the char-
> acters, asking himself where they come from, what they like, who they are
> going to seduce, what are their sexual preferences. Not a word about the
> story...[26,27]

Indubitable is that Malle (not Carrière) brought to the table the unusual idea
of weaving into the story a subtextual layer that draws on the 1968 Parisian student-
worker riots—a moment in French history with a soft spot in the memories and
hearts of both men. Carrière waxes nostalgic on this era:

> In 1968, during May, we were together in Paris, Louis and me. Louis was com-
> ing back from India and he had a long beard, you know? He was in Cannes,
> at the Cannes Film Festival, when the festival was interrupted.... Louis ... had
> spent a whole year in India and made a different series of films which I love
> ... and he was getting back in Paris in the middle of May and in Cannes ... and
> he was totally involved in a movement that he didn't really understand. As a
> matter of fact, nobody really understood what [Louis] was doing [with the
> Indian documentaries]. Neither did I.[28]

Malle similarly remembers returning to Paris from India in May 1968, totally
unaware of the goings-on in the French capital, and becoming completely engulfed
and stunned by *les événements*—being jumped on and beaten by 10 policemen on the
Place St. Michel, later visiting Cannes and almost single-handedly shutting down the
1968 Festival in deference to the riots, and returning to Paris once more engulfed by
an overwhelming sense of enchantment and enthusiasm about the degree to which
everyone stopped and began to communicate with each other and question the
goings-on of the surrounding world.[29] He similarly recalls the moment when de
Gaulle disappeared, having gone to Germany to enlist the support of the French generals, and many in Paris anticipated a student-worker revolution that never
unfolded.[30] Michel Piccoli, for whom Malle and Carrière would write the lead in
Milou, helps frame this period from Malle's perspective, with over 35 years of hindsight: "We had ... a ... tender and yet extremely inquisitive [regard]—about this fear
that transpired in a certain part of France ... [in May '68], springing from this incredibly tragic revolution that had ... announced itself ... a complete change in people's
thinking, existence and religion called into question."[31]

All of these events came flooding back 20 years hence, when the French began
to celebrate the 20-year anniversary of the riots. Carrière reflects:

> So a long time after [1968], [Louis and I] ... like many people in France, of
> course ... were talking about the events of May, and one day [Louis] decided
> to make a film about it, and his great idea was to locate the film in a country
> house, you know, far from Paris, just to get the resonances, you know, of [*les
> événements*]. That was the good idea that I liked so much....[32]

As it evolved, the script thus blended a distinctly Chekhovian context — an ensemble piece on familial collapse — with a 1968-esque, lightly and briskly adidactic leftist political subtext and something of a mild, gentle satire on the *haute bourgeois
terrienne*. Piccoli observes, "This is what I would call the 'double game' of Louis
Malle. He didn't just want to do a film on May '68. He wanted to do a film on May
'68 set in the deepest and most bucolic regions of France and of the French soul —
the country of farmers and landowners, *not* of the *petit bourgeois*."[33]

   Malle fulfilled his promise, made on the set of *Atlantic City* almost a decade prior,
to eventually cast Piccoli (*La Grande Bouffe*, *La Belle Niçoise*) in a critical role, by
building the picture around him.[34] When asked what drew him to the role of Emile
"Milou" Vieuzac, the actor states candidly, "Something that overwhelmed me and
moved me was that Louis — along with Jean-Claude Carrière — had written the film
for me, and thinking of me. And that ... was very moving, very moving indeed."[35]
Malle and Carrière likewise wrote many of the other parts, in advance, for specific
French actors and actresses[36] — they had the unusual and hilarious idea to "counter-
cast" the famed alternative actress Miou-Miou (*Going Places*, *La Lectrice*) as the
uptight, reactionary bourgeois housewife Camille,[37] and opted, from the beginning,
to enlist the celebrated 78-year-old Paulette Dubost as Mme. de Vieuzac, Milou's
mother and the familial matriarch, thus making an implicit nod to Renoir's masterpiece, *La Règle du jeu*, in which Dubost plays the *soubrette*.[38] Malle brought famed
jazz violinist Stephane Grappelli on board to score the picture (who improvised in
much the same way that Miles Davis did on *Ascenseur*, over 30 years prior)[39] and
Renato Berta — held over from *Au revoir les enfants* — to photograph it.[40] TFI films
of Paris and Ellepi Film of Rome aided NEF in producing the picture and thus co-
funded *Milou*'s $35 million budget. Malle located an estate for filming, known as Le
Calaoué,[41] that sported a cherry tree in the front yard — taking this as a positive omen
(and enamored with the rest of the house), Malle asked his crew to put faux cherries on the tree, as cherry season had already ended by June.[42]

   TFI Films and Nouvelles Editions de Films of Paris and Ellipi Film of Rome co-
funded *Milou*'s $35 million budget; a French film industry executive named Fabi-
enne Volnier handled the picture's distribution after she left MK2 Films around the
beginning of 1989 and, with her husband Francis Boespflug, formed her own distribution house, Pyramide Films. The Malles gave Pyramide 20 percent of the residu-
als from *Milou* for handling distribution.[43] The production itself spanned early June
through mid–August 1989 and was — by all accounts — a joyous experience, to the
mild concern of Carrière, who warned Malle, when the director phoned him in Paris,
that screen comedy is a challenge and that one should take it as a "bad sign" when
things seem to be going swimmingly.[44] This was a case of Carrière's overcautious-
ness: the picture would go on to become a minor classic and a favorite of Malle's

admirers. Edited during the latter half of 1989, the picture reached French cinemas on January 24, 1990, and American cinemas on June 22, 1990.[45]

Synopsis

In the southwest region of France, near Le Gers, in May 1968, the 60-year-old widowed caretaker Emile "Milou" Vieuzac (Michel Piccoli) spends his days doing such light agricultural work as beekeeping and roof repair alongside an aged handyman, Léonce (Marcel Bories), and living under the protective wing of his octogenarian mother, Mme. Elisabeth Vieuzac (Paulette Dubost), as he tends his family's crumbling estate and deteriorating vineyards. In the background, rumblings are heard over the radio of the student-worker riots in Paris, which unfurl with violence and bloodshed and constantly threaten to erupt into a full-blown revolution.

As the story opens, Milou reads Virgil aloud to "calm" the bees (in the tradition of his eccentric Uncle Albert), in the fields a half-mile or so outside of the estate, while Mme. Vieuzac, who has spent the late morning in her kitchen preparing lunch, stumbles over to the staircase, collapses, and dies; the family housekeeper, Adèle (Martine Gautier) races outside and summons Milou. Milou races his bicycle up to the estate and learns (offscreen) of his mother's death.

Milou and Adèle lay out Mme. Vieuzac's corpse, and Milou contacts as many members of his immediate family as he can; prior to the arrival of the family, he offers Mme. Vieuzac's fur coat to Adèle, and attempts (unsuccessfully) to neck with her; she dissuades him. Over the next days, the family members gradually assemble at the house to participate in the wake and funeral. The guests include: Camille (Miou-Miou), Milou's daughter, a prim, conservative, and slightly snotty bourgeois housewife in the suburbs; Camille's 10-year-old daughter Françoise (Jeanne Herry-Leclerc) and twin sons (Benjamin and Nicolas Prieur); Daniel (François Berleand), the equally reactionary, slightly money-grubbing family solicitor; Georges (Michel Duchaussoy), the emotionally-backward, sexually passive and highly intellectual London correspondent for *Le Monde* (cum-freelance author); his wife Lily (Harriet Walter) an aging British flower child and unemployed actress; the diminutive Claire (Dominique Blanc) Milou's 20-something niece, raised by Mme. Vieuzac after being orphaned and slightly crippled as a child in an automobile accident with her parents, and who has now entered a lightly sadomasochistic lesbian relationship with a female lover, Marie-Laure Mounier (Rozenn Le Tallec). Late in arriving but no less important are Pierre-Alain (Renaud Danner), Georges's son from a previous marriage, who has become a fervent leftwing demonstrator and outspoken advocate of the strikes; and Grimaldi (Bruno Carette), the slightly slimy, chauvinistic, and oversexed, yet consistently affable driver of a produce rig who has no familial connection but drives Pierre-Alain to the estate.

Overtaken by grief at his mother's death, Milou climbs into bed and sobs, when a white owl visits him on the windowsill; he interprets the creature as a kind of talisman—his mother visiting him in an alternate form. The strikes outside reach the neighboring fields; Milou orders a casket for his mother as he begins to discover that basic goods and services have been severed — the petrol supply cut off, the gravediggers on strike, the neighboring shops in the process of closing. Daniel attempts to stir up a love affair with the married Camille and to collect the money Milou owes him, while Camille slips up to Mme. Vieuzac's bedroom, pocketing the family emerald.

Camille asks Françoise to awaken Claire in the "buttercup room" that once belonged to Aunt Zette; Françoise tiptoes into the *chambre* and finds Claire and Marie-Laure in separate twin beds, Marie-Laure bare-breasted, one of her wrists bound to the bedpost with rope. Meanwhile, Georges (after arriving) shies away from a head-on glimpse of his mother's corpse and must turn and bury his head in Milou's arms to pour his feelings out.

Over lunch, Camille insists, to an irritated and incredulous Claire, that Mme. Vieuzac gave her the emerald ring years ago. Meanwhile, Milou turns to his sister-in-law Lily and displays affection toward her. A number of the houseguests, led by Camille, attempt to persuade a despondent Milou to sell the estate; Milou flatly refuses and jumps up and storms away from the table, cursing. Outside, on the river bank, he removes his shirt, rolls up his pantlegs, and wades into the water, with Françoise and Lily only a few steps behind him; he demonstrates a method of catching crawfish by sticking his hands beneath the muddy river bank and letting the crawdaddies latch onto his fingers.

Following lunch, Camille, Claire, and Adèle argue about how the property in the estate (dishes, furniture, etc.) will be divvied up. Outside, after collecting a sizeable mass of crawfish in a burlap sack for dinner, Milou, his sister-in-law, and his granddaughter stroll through the woods; Lily subtly returns Milou's affections, draping a towel over his bare back and drying him vigorously. She speculates that if she had met Milou first (prior to Georges) a romance might have developed between them.

Milou charges into the house like a man renewed and reinvigorated, Lily's Srinagarian towel draped over his shoulders, and commands the women never to sell his personal books. He then parades up the stairs, chanting "L'Internationale," while Françoise informs Lily that her grandpa ("Papi") is in love.

Daniel sits the family down to discuss the portioning out of the estate, and ultimately unveils a letter Mme. Vieuzac entrusted to him a year prior, bequeathing a quarter of her estate to Adèle; the woman is so startled upon discovering her status as heiress that she falls from a ladder in the garden and loses consciousness; Milou brings her back around with a bottle of mustard that functions as smelling salt.

On a distant highway, far from the estate, Pierre-Alain has hitched a ride from Grimaldi. The rig driver brags about his experiences picking up women who are turned on by lorry-drivers, women whom (he claims) have often unzipped his fly and gone down on his lap. Back at the house, around dusk, Camille and Adèle continue to partition up the valuables, while Milou, impervious, cozies up with Lily on the couch and leafs through an old family photo album, telling his sister-in-law bizarre and hilarious stories about old Uncle Albert. Camille prepares the crawfish dinner while Marie-Laure and Claire bitch amongst themselves; suddenly a blackout hits, and Grimaldi's rig roars up outside of the house, its neon yellow lights blazing through the window. Pierre-Alain and Grimaldi join the group inside of the house, eventually partaking in a huge dinner; the men bring to the table wild stories of the riots and lovemaking in Paris. The electricity zaps back on.

The next morning, Milou discovers that the gravediggers are on strike, so the funeral must be postponed. Claire grows infuriated when she spots Marie-Laure and Pierre-Alain becoming cozy under the cherry tree; Grimaldi sets up his tomato truck outside and starts handing out produce; Milou and Lily head down to the wine cellar, and Adèle, terribly progressive of Milou, makes an unsuccessful attempt to bait him by telling Georges that his wife and brother-in-law are alone together. Camille and Daniel head off into the barn and romanticize about his former marriage proposal to her. Later on, the group picnics beneath the cherry tree and the family members pass a joint around. High on pot and slightly drunk, the Vieuzacs parade through the field arm-in-arm, and fantasize about turning the estate into a commune with a solar oven and windmills.

That night, Léonce is digging the grave when Mme. Vieuzac appears, standing at the grave above him in a white dress; he glances up at her, shrugs, and continues working. Meanwhile, in the drawing room, Claire plays the piano and everyone sings when Georges bursts into the room clad in an African mask and skirt, belting out "La Fille du Bedouin," and the family parades around the floor in a conga line. Later that evening, Monsieur (Étienne Draber) and Madame Boutelleau (Valerie Lemercier), the Vieuzacs' neighbors, appear and inform the family that De Gaulle has disappeared and that the revolution is underway, and insist that soon, hundreds of bloodthirsty Communists will show up and seek revenge on the bourgeois; just then the power goes out and the family is unable to hear the news on the radio. Terrified, they flee into the woods and eventually take refuge in a cave where a number of fights erupt among them; the next morning, Adèle appears and reveals that de Gaulle is back in Paris, and the possibility of a revolution has died. The family returns to the house, has an unexpected surprise in meeting Adèle's fiancee, and finally buries Mme. Vieuzac.

Subsequently, the relatives all leave Milou alone in the near-empty house. When they have gone, he strolls into the living room and finds his deceased mother sitting at the piano and playing joyously. She stands up; the music continues; the two embrace and begin a slow dance together.

ANALYSIS

Perpetuating the strategy inherent in much of Louis Malle's œuvre — his common disposition for cutting against the grain of his previous work for each new addition to his catalog — *May Fools* (or *Milou en mai*) represents a defiant reflex against *Au revoir les enfants*. On its broadest and most fundamental plane, *Milou* is an ensemble comedy of late spring and early summer (a reaction to the late winter of *Au revoir*). Whereas cinematographer Renato Berta drained *Au revoir* of all onscreen color aside from the crimson in Francine Racette's lipstick, *Milou* is a picture rife to bursting with aesthetic resonance (green the predominant hue throughout), and a bouncy, often prankish Stephane Grappelli score to pepper the onscreen *vie d'agri-*

cole. If *Au revoir* meditates on the gradual disclosure of evil and revels in pessimism, *Milou* exudes joy and warmth and hope and humanistic optimism, even as it paradoxically dramatizes the impending collapse of a familial structure.

Although Malle originally conceived *Milou* as a loose, modernized adaptation of Anton Chekhov's 1904 tragicomedy *The Cherry Orchard* (*La Cerisaie*),[46] he almost instantly changed his game plan, opting instead to do the project as an original work. This decision can hardly be written off as capricious. Notable in Chekhov is his universalist atemporality: the immunity of his work to the prospect of becoming "dated," and its consequent emotional and spiritual connection with generations of audience members. But this only represents half of the basic Chekhovian constitution. Near the end of his life, Malle commented on the rather arresting paradox (equally applicable to any of Chekhov's theatrical works) that Chekhovian plays demonstrate universality yet retain the specificity of their being rooted in a definite place and era, against a distinct cultural backdrop.[47] This intuition (equally applicable to any of Chekhov's masterworks) identifies a rather arresting paradox. If Shakespeare has traditionally been transferred to the screen and mounted on the stage with an unprecedented degree of temporal and geographic flexibility (consider Richard Loncraine's 1995 feature *Richard III*, for example, set in fascist Europe of the forties, or Trevor Nunn's equally brilliant 1996 film *Twelfth Night*, set in the late nineteenth century), Chekhov is perhaps, as Malle's comment indicates, quite a bit more difficult to transplant out of late nineteenth and early twentieth century Russia, because he ties his universalistic resonances to a highly particular, highly immutable time and place. Malle's decision to reslate *Milou en mai* as an original work with Chekhovian overtones, in lieu of a modern adaptation of *The Cherry Orchard per se*, thus liberated the universalistic core of the material from ties to a set era and milieu, blending Chekhov's themes, tropes, and tragicomic overtones with the zeitgeist of mid–late sixties France.

This temporality takes two forms—indeed, finds two specific historical reference points from the same era and assigns to each a highly unique function in the script. Malle and Carrière use the most obvious—*les événements* (i.e., the Parisian student-worker riots)—as a subtext, whose importance, as will become apparent later in this chapter, shifts over the course of the narrative. Its most pronounced role involves eliciting resonances contingent upon distance. For *Milou*, Malle and Carrière draw a fairly quiet and subtle correlation between temporal distance (that of 20 years between 1968 and 1988) and the geographic distance between Paris (the home of the riots) and Le Gers (the home of the Vieuzacs). In his introduction to the published script of *Milou*, Carrière writes:

> Obviously, neither in a film nor in a book, nor in any way, can one re-create such a special feeling. We recognized that it was impossible to deal with 1968 head-on, squarely and directly. But it occurred to Louis to inject a trace of what were called "les événements" ("the events") into the confines of a family story ... and suddenly, to our surprise, this "trace" of May '68 took on in the script a presence, a truth, a strength, and a comic force—the effects of which were instantly visible on the face of our characters. This simple geographic distancing, which is not dissimilar to what Lévi-Strauss calls in anthro-

pology "the detached look," can give that small breathing space which allows us to hear better and even see better what isn't shown (because it cannot be shown).[48,49]

One should observe the contrast between the overtones of key historical texts on Paris in May 1968—particularly Kristin Ross's *May 1968 and Its Afterlives*—and the overtones of *Milou*. If the Ross book feels overwrought with lurid details of violence and bloodshed and militancy, *Milou*—by virtue of its rural setting *and* its 1989 production date—stands far enough back from the volcanic event to simply bask in the relaxing warm currents that the eruption sends rippling out into the ocean, scores of miles distant. The product is a gentle and magical lyricism, impossible to catch if the setting were Paris.

To identify and grasp the role of the second historical reference point (outside of *les événements*), consider a metaphor from Lévi-Strauss's essay "The Scope of Anthropology," where the philosopher suggests a process for the formulation of myth:

> Is it not the nature of myths, which play such an important part in our research, to evoke a suppressed past and to apply it, like a grid, upon the dimensions of the present, and to do this in the hope of finding some meaning whereby two confronting faces—historical and structural—of man's own reality will for once coincide?[50]

With a key variation, one can apply the above anthropological metaphor to Malle's film. For *Milou*, Malle and Carrière utilize a process of mythmaking strikingly similar (though not identical) to the one that Lévi-Strauss describes. In the Malle film, the past functions as a historical grid, imposed not upon the "present," but upon the highly universalistic Chekhovian brand of tragicomedy with its resonances in the present (because the events are happening within the context of narrative fiction in lieu of being applied, psychoanalytically, to modern lives and events). But here, the variable plugged into *Milou* that acts as Lévi-Strauss's "historical framework" is quite a bit more obscure than *les événements*.

In his seminal work *Prelude to Revolution: France in May 1968*, Daniel Singer addresses a French agricultural crisis during the mid–late sixties that "brought about a faster increase in productivity in farming than in industry. While the agricultural population was more than halved, output per man during the same period more than tripled, thus raising the question of outlets."[51] In a subsequent chapter, he again alludes to large numbers of French farmers fleeing agrarian work and notes that, at the time of the writing (late 1969–early 1970, or only about a year-and-a-half after May 1968) more than half of the remaining farmers and rural landowners were men over 57 years old.[52] Singer likewise cites the process by which smaller farms were being devoured by larger farms. Two points are worth making here. First, coming back to the aforementioned Lévi-Strauss metaphor: although one might argue that the May 1968 Paris student-worker riots function as a grid in the Straussian sense, a grid that Malle and Carrière have superimposed atop Chekhov, this does not really work; instead, the agricultural crisis can be plugged, far more easily, into the "historical component" of the equation. It is as if, by laying this rather esoteric (to American viewers) socio-historical context — with its heightened specificity and connection to a definite time and place and series of nationally-oriented French agrarian crises— atop the universality of Chekhov's theme about the financial decline of the aristocracy and the forced sale of the family's estate in *La Cerisaie*— Malle takes two universalistic events (the familial collapse, the estate sale) and imbues them with temporally specific contour and dimension and depth. And in the process of the superimposition, Malle and Carrière create a new brand of myth and a new myth *per se*. To examine this idea from a slightly different angle: taking the above historical details from Daniel Singer into consideration, one can characterize Milou's decision to stay put on the Vieuzac property — when all of his family members have either died or left the place in previous years— as a rather neatly conceived and succinct microcosmic picture of a much broader and more sweeping social crisis that befell France in the mid-late sixties and early seventies. The family's inclination to sell the estate, presumably to a larger landowner, likewise suggests the phenomenon of smaller farms and estates and parcels of land being devoured by larger farms.

Looking beyond the question of "the temporally specific *versus* the universal," *Milou* pulls a number of unrelated elements from Chekhov. On the most rudimentary *étage*— that of theme —*Milou*, like *The Cherry Orchard*, foretells the collapse and dissolution of a family as a casualty of the forced sale of their estate, although the use of the matriarch's death as a precipitating factor for the estate sale is unique to Malle and Carrière. With regard to overtone and mood, *Milou* creates tragicomedy in the "*Cherry Orchard* mold" by building a foundation of grim drama and gently overlaying offbeat farce atop it; the end result is a highly distinct, refreshing blend of pathos and absurdity. Take, for example, the action from Mme. Vieuzac's death scene, in the opening moments of *Milou*:

> [Elisabeth] climbs a dozen or so steps, singing softly. A death-rattle sound; she collapses onto a sofa on the landing, lying amid several dolls dressed in ballgowns. Her mouth gapes open.
> The cat comes up and nuzzles her face.[53]

This excerpt appears in the published screenplay of *Milou* as quoted above, but Malle evokes the sequence uniquely onscreen. In the final cut, the cat runs up and doesn't simply nuzzle Mme. Vieuzac's face, but *licks* her face — a far more absurd accessory to the death. This coupling of the tragic and the comic inevitably brings to mind scenes in *The Cherry Orchard* such as the one where — immediately following a melancholic discussion of Lubya's social regression in Paris and an exchange between Varya and Anya regarding the sale of the estate — Lopakhin pokes his head around the corner and catches Varya's attention by mooing like a cow.[54] In both instances, the absurd event has the same function, qualifying (giving a slightly skewed perspective to) the larger and more sweeping tragic foundation that involves the death of Mme. Vieuzac (in *Milou*) and the combination of Lubya's regression with the inevitable sale of the estate (in *Orchard*). The key distinction between the tragicomic overtones in *Milou* and the almost identical tragicomic overtones in *The Cherry Orchard* is one of degree. In Malle, though his themes are indeed grave and sobering (not simply the loss of family but the loss of *identity*— as when Milou states, "But this house is the only thing that keeps us all together! We'd be nothing without the house!"), wild comedy does not simply color the play on occasion, intermittently (as in Chekhov), but acts as a sort of narrative epidermis, fully masking the graver themes that lie at the core of the drama. Thus, the picture, as mentioned previously, feels inescapably joyous and exuberant, despite its slightly graver thematic undercurrents—its surface mood captured perfectly and succinctly by Stephane Grappeli's bouncy score; in some ways, this idea of a positive exterior masking darker tropes could even be compared to Demy's *Umbrellas of Cherbourg* (though *Milou*'s themes are not as grave, its mild pessimism much easier to muster). One should note that with *Milou*, Malle and Carrière engage in selective presentation for the sake of preserving mood. The finest example involves the exclusion, from the script and from the finished film, of Milou's discovery of his mother's death. Though he presumably screams out, or breaks down and weeps, upon hearing this news, the co-screenwriters recognize that dramatizing such an event (especially placed, as it would be, at the tail end of the credit sequence, Grappelli's peppy intro number) would decimate the mood — the overtone — of the entire picture.

Narratively, *Milou en mai*, even moreso than *Atlantic City* (see the quote from John Guare in Chapter 15 on the cinematic influences behind that screenplay) feels hugely influenced by *Nashville*, not simply because of *Milou*'s Altmanesque fracturing of dramatic architecture, but because of how this fracturing — in the hands of skilled director (and co-screenwriter) Malle and co-screenwriter Carrière — alters the scope of characterization and heightens the film's demands on the audience. Malle later acknowledged that he and Carrière developed 12 major characters, each of whom arcs as the story unfolds.[55] He fails to mention that creating an ensemble cast of this size — and developing all of the characters adequately and *effectively*—facilitates the director and co-screenwriter's attempts to take a leap away from broad character transitions, particularly when the material is abetted by a short narrative timespan of two or three days. Depth exists, but on a level so subtle and so gently and quietly evocative that one must watch the film multiple times to catch the minutiae of character shifts. The narrative fracturing enables this to occur, because it reduces the amount of screen time each character has and thus cuts back on (or eliminates) the scenarists' ability to paint broad arcs. It narrows the audience's focus and suggests an advance away from histrionics and toward realism. And the characters become figures comparable to those in — say — a Cheever story or a Renoir film. Steeped in gentle and lyrical realism, but never caught in stasis. And particularly when coupled with a short narrative span (of, say, a 24-hour period), the most effective and evocative dramas will narrow their focus to steer away from contrivances and toward realism, toward more subtle arcs. More broadly, a glance at *Milou* suggests that in the case of many films, it is even possible to formulate an axiomatic relationship between the size of an acting ensemble and the scope of its individual character arcs—that, excluding melodramas[56] (at one end of the spectrum) and extreme two and three-character minimalism (at the other end — see, for example, the Pinter-Irvin production of *Turtle Diary*) the size of the ensemble is inversely proportional to the narrative span and the breadth of each character's transition.

The process behind Malle and Carrière's creation of character in *Milou* suggests

yet another parallel to *Nashville*: just as, for the latter film, scriptwriter Joan Tewkes-
bury sketched out the basic arcs in the script and Altman encouraged his cast members to flesh out their characters with quirks and nuances, each performer offering
up suggestions about how those characters would behave and developing those characters on a plane so finely-tuned that it transcends script-level indicators, Malle and
Carrière met at the Carrières' home in Paris for many a lunch, months prior to the
production, and repeatedly assisted the actors and actresses in developing their characters to an extreme degree; performers from the cast would offer up suggestions
about behavioral quirks, idiosyncracies, speech patterns, and the like, on an incredibly acute level. For instance, Malle mentions that Miou-Miou (Camille in the film)
brought into the script — influenced by one of Dominique Blanc's lines — a mild
obsession with handwashing, a hang-up she pulled from her grandmother, that
emerges in her dramatic interpretation of Camille.[57]

The best example of a subtle arc in *May Fools* involves Emile "Milou" Vieuzac
himself; at the outset of the picture, Vieuzac lives his life according to the rules of
subservience; kneeling by the beehive, in the distant fields, when he hears Adèle
yelling after him from the front steps (to notify him of his mother's death — something he does not realize until he reaches the house), his automatic response is, "I'm
late for lunch, I'll catch hell from mother."[58] His readings of the Georgics of Virgil
to the bees arguably provide a comparable illustration of his inclination to servility.
Robert Graves implies — in a comparison between Catullus and Virgil — that the latter "seems to be calling upon [poets], as posterity, to applaud a demonstration of
immortal genius"[59] and thus to become subservient to him in a way; beyond the
obvious correlations between Virgil and an agricultural worker, it thus makes perfect sense for Milou, with his passive and submissive character, to be referencing and
celebrating a poet of Virgil's ilk.[60] In fact, Milou is so passive as the story opens that
he even allows himself to be slightly intimidated by the telephone operator whom
he phones in an attempt to reach his relatives and notify them of Mme. Vieuzac's
death ("Don't shout at me, I'm just trying to call my family.") and — in the printed
screenplay (though not in the finished film) — he is reactionary enough that he even
lacks the fortitude to make the decision about which casket to order for his mother;
and never gives Monsieur Delmas a straight answer. Milou's arc will involve "rising,"
in a sense — coming into his own, to become more outspoken and assertive and thus
find a way to cling more tightly to his identity as a Vieuzac in his mother's absence.
The characters such as the uptight and slightly obnoxious Camille, the lesbian Claire,
and Georges, Milou's brother (the London correspondent for *Le Monde*), instantly
antagonize Milou with their aggressive attempts to sell the house. This has two
aftereffects. Most immediately: Milou leaps up from the table, cursing; hurries outside; and plunges himself into the cold creek, to go fishing for crawfish, which — symbolically — suggests an immersion into the presence, the inner nature, of the house,
and his childhood to which it is connected, in defiance to the idea of sacrificing his
Vieuzac identity. The submersion in the water, in turn, functions as a kind of spiritual rebirth, the water lying closer (metaphorically) to the fountain of youth than
to a baptismal pool. Following his "plunge," Milou gains virility that fuels an implied
love affair with his undersexed British sister-in-law Lily,[61] and he reemerges in the

living room more vociferous than ever, booming at the top of his lungs to Claire, "Oh, no! You're not sharing out the books! They're *mine*! I'm the only one who can read in this family!!"[62]

Tonally, a running thread unites all of these subtle characterizations and arcs; the film sports a brand of humanist acceptance that most vividly recalls (among other examples in the Malle *œuvre*) the characterization of Laurent Chevalier (Benoit Ferreux) in the director's masterpiece *Murmur of the Heart*. As discussed extensively in Chapter 10, the tone generated by Laurent is absolutely oblique because of his complexity—because, as a bourgeois archetype he has imbibed both upper-crust snottiness and a kind of likeable, "energetic amorality" and earthiness. Our feelings about Laurent thus cannot be resolved easily—we feel drawn to him, even as he grates on our nerves. *Milou* operates according to the same principles of obliqueness, throughout the picture. Ergo, if one feels some level of hostility toward the impudent and obnoxious Claire, for example, it is balanced by limited sympathy, evoked by our glimpse of her inner pain and abandonment as a child (implied in her discussion, with Marie-Laure Mounier, of the wreck that crippled her, and her experience of being orphaned by both parents, the sole survivor of the automobile crash). One can infer her subsequent need for dominance and control, which explains her implied S&M games—her inclination to tie Marie-Laure to the bedpost. The same tonal ambiguity can be applied to all of the major characters—even Milou, despite his everpresent charm, may stir up a gust of negative feelings from his lustful glimpse of 10-year-old Françoise's buttocks and bare legs, and his willingness to take advantage of Georges's sexual passivity by basically seducing his compliant sister-in-law Lily. The oblique tone, in turn, ties neatly into the picture's unique brand of humor, hugely expanding the writer-director and co-screenwriter's options.

A note on this: the humor in *Milou* operates on two levels—the individual and the collective (or macrocosmic). The former is the most immediate and accessible level—and mostly springs from the quirky behavior of specific characters. To cite only a few examples: the scene in which the "hippie" Aunt Lily picks up a palm frond before the corpse, sniffs it, and tosses it aside; the scene where 10-year-old Françoise leans over her grandmother's corpse and, attempting to shut the woman's jaw, whispers, "Close your mouth, Grandma, or you'll get dirt in it"; nearly all of Grimaldi's chauvinistic sexual advances and dirty double-entendres, which cannot help but recall Yasha's passes in *La Cerisaie*.

But on a broader plane, the film builds a running social and political commentary that weaves together the whole ensemble of actors, collectively. On this level, it would be nearsighted to color the picture as a pure satire, and a distortion to characterize it as a pure farce; more incisively, *Milou* incorporates a double-edged sword of farce and satire. The overall arc of the character ensemble thus begins with most of the characters cloaked in complete passivity and political ignorance. In the opening sequence with Mme. Elisabeth Vieuzac standing in the kitchen—the only sequence that features Paulette Dubost prior to the character's death—Malle begins in tight close-up, with "huge tears" running down Mme. Vieuzac's face. The camera pull-back to reveal Mme. Vieuzac cutting onions is an ancient bit (reminiscent of Carrière's scattershot gags in *Viva Maria*), but it gains political resonance (and depth) in light of the reports on the radio unfolding as a backdrop, behind Mme. Vieuzac. It underscores the breadth of the chasm between our assumption that Mme. Vieuzac cares for and sympathizes with the protesters, and her political ignorance and passivity, and intensifies (in our minds) not simply *her* reactionary nature, but that of the entire class of the *haute bourgeois de terrienne* that she represents.[63] Aside from the obvious necessity of its importance at the commencement of the film in light of story, the sequence is key because of what it communicates about the political and social isolation of the entire *classe*, when placed, symbolically at the outset of the narrative structure. It becomes annunciatory — philosophically indicative of the family's beliefs and values and reactionary absence of politic. This scene can be held up, next to another of great similarity — the infamous and brilliant "picnic sequence," where the members of the Vieuzac family suddenly and unexpectedly become drunk and high on marijuana and start fantasizing about turning their estate and vineyards into a hippie commune, with solar ovens and "wind for the windmills ... [where] women will belong to everyone." I juxtapose references to the "onion scene" and the "picnic scene" here because the scenes reflect about half of the film's core of humor — the farcical half. Piccoli comments in an interview with the author that Malle's running joke involved taking a leftist (Communist) revolution and putting it into the most unlikely place one could possibly imagine.[64] The central gag in the picnic sequence (never stated forthright, of course, but ever present and easily inferred) is that even if the house *per se* is decaying, these wealthy bourgeois *vignobles* are surrounded by an unfathomable amount of luxury — fine wine, a *pot au feu* of select meats and vegetables — so that, naturally, these pampered and prissied members of the bourgeois can fantasize about "dropping out." They have the financial cushion necessary to do so without ever making the necessary sacrifices.[65,66]

The constant "free will *versus* fate" in Malle's work, first observed so keenly in *Ascenseur* with the roll of thunder that jostles Louis (Georges Poujouly) awake in the room at the motor lodge, resurfaces at this point. When the Vieuzac family gathers in the house and the power cuts out (for the second time), thus preventing Milou, Camille, Georges and the others from learning of the events unfolding in Paris; when a wave of paranoia spreads among them and they fear bellicose and bloodthirsty Communists will soon appear at the door, sending "heads rolling" *à la* Robespierre and firing off guns; and when the Vieuzacs subsequently flee to the hills, one cannot help but feel that Malle and Carrière are mischievously playing the role of the prankish Satreian gods, chiding to their ensemble of spoiled and snooty characters, "Okay, if you feel like dropping out, let us see how you function when *forced* to do so — when we *make* you abandon your luxury and live off of the Earth, as you so mightily proposed when you were drunk and high on pot." In developing this element of the script — sending the Vieuzacs out into the driving rain and forcing them to shelter in a grotto, where they wind up wet and freezing and defenseless — the second "edge" of the comic sword utilized in the first half of the picture finally comes into clear view — we see clearly and sharply that the collective farcical elements functioned, doubly, as the first half of a classic, two-half, apedantic satirical structure, and that this bitter realism in the cave, after the collectively mythologized fantasy of the picnic sequence, functions as the second half of the picture's satire. Significantly, only at this point do the characters' guards begin to drop and their real feelings emerge, which could, in itself (in theory) become a positive development—a character builder, and a legitimate mechanism whereby the bourgeois members would drop the pretentious masks that they wear day in and day out. But via this "enacted" proposal of bringing the Vieuzacs down from their ivory tower, Malle and Carrière are also revealing the impossibility *of* the Vieuzacs' functioning in such a state permanently—just how incapable individuals from this bourgeois *classe* would be of sacrificing any luxury, because wealth, jewelry, fine cuisine, and fur coats function collectively as a kind of buffer against an unfathomable amount of buried insecurity and cowardice. On a broader level, the family's emotionally devastating experience in the grotto can be read as a microcosmic view of the sweeping social conflict that Malle uses as a subtext for the motion picture. It is at this point that *les événements*—used as a reference point, a subtextual layer, for much of the picture—rises to the forefront, to the surface, and gains its greatest degree of significance. Malle and Carrière are implying that such a revolution would have been quite literally impossible for French society at that time—and they do so via the emotionally-stripping circumstances in the cave, (again) using Camille, Claire, and others to reveal just how incapable an individual reactionary member of the bourgeois would be of functioning without the "luxuries" that mask his or her incredible lack of inner fortitude; from this, we can make an inductive leap and assume that collective revolution would be impossible. Thus, when her defenses are stripped, in the cave, Camille finally, once and for all, discloses her pathetic nature: "[Claire] hates me! Everyone hates me! ... I look after everyone, take care of everything, work from morning till nigh, do all the cooking, and everyone just takes advantage of me!"[67] And in retrospect, all of Camille's hateful and insulting words for the first two-thirds of the film acquire new depth and dimension given this scene; we understand that the bourgeois accoutrements function as a massive emotional shield, a defense against an astounding degree of inner vulnerability.

A final thought on the free will (Arminianism) versus fatalism (Calvinism) paradox, as evoked in *Milou*. Malle, who spent much of his life rebelling against organized western religion and who completely dissociated himself from the Christianity of his mother, continues to undercut the concept of fatalism as in *Ascenseur*, but has traveled far enough away from a pedantic, call-and-response structure—and has matured to such a degree by this point—that he is able to simultaneously reveal, via a singular action, the dual layers of a self-perpetuated mythology. Of the two most potent examples, the first involves the owl landing on Milou's window. A minute or so before this occurs, Milou walks over to his bedroom window and raises it. Standing there, he instinctively gazes up into the nighttime sky, as if he expects a visitor. Shortly afterward, while he sits in his bed and sobs, the owl arrives on the ledge. One immediately wonders, in turn, if Milou would be so inclined to read the owl's visit as a "spiritual visitor"—his mother in the form of a talisman—if his mother had not died. Likewise, when the power cuts out for the second time, the Vieuzacs convince themselves that ultraviolent Communists will instantly appear at the door, brandishing knives and guns. In both cases, Malle uses a single action to disclose the self-delusion (and the nature of collective delusions) that he perceives as the nature of mythology, which, he presumably felt, also lies at the basis of organized religion.

CRITICAL RESPONSE

Milou en mai drew a wildly mixed response in France and abroad, upon its release during the first half of 1990. Indicative of the divisive critical feelings are two *Washington Post* reviews from the oft-incongruous Hal Hinson and Desson Howe; Hinson adores the film as a piece of gently understated minimalism, rhapsodizing, "Throughout, Malle's touch remains musical, delicate and precise. All the elements— including Renato Berta's luxuriant images and Stephane Grappelli's kicky jazz score — are kept in perfect balance. The acting too."[68] Yet Howe chastizes *May Fools* as a bore: "Never trust a movie that starts out with bees ... [*Milou*] is an unending sprawl of vignettes. In a film-making career that has experienced a subtly slow decline, from good ... to moderate ... to worse ... Malle seems to have finally skeetered over the edge, into self-eulogizing sentimentality."[69] Likewise, Stanley Kauffmann, of *The New Republic*, finds the picture rather loathsome: "So desperate is the screenplay for some kind of jolt or novelty that the authors even bring the matriarch back to life — or "life"—in dream-fantasy sequences, which ... merely embarrass."[70] But Bruce Williamson, of *Playboy*, adores the film: "Malle steers ... Piccoli, Miou-Miou, and a cool French cast through an altogether sophisticated spoof of upper-crust idiocy ... While retaining his ingrained tolerance for the privileged few ... the sharp ironies of [Malle's] have-got class facing the specter of a new French revolution are tipped with vitriol."[71]

Reviewing for *The Observer*, Philip French lavishes onto *Milou* the broadest exultations it received, classing it with Buñuel's *Discreet Charm of the Bourgeoisie* and Renoir's *Rules of the Game*: "The film can stand these grand comparisons, and they in no way detract from its originality ... it offers as memorable a display of ensemble acting as we've seen in recent years ... *Milou in May* is a film of Chekhovian generosity that never strays into sentimentality or cynicism."[72]

Reactions in France were equally mixed. Writing for the leftwing paper *Libération*, Gérard Lefort accuses Malle of selling out:

> *Milou* ... is a reactionary film, literally, in the sense that Malle draws from the past all of the justifications for contenting himself with the exclusion of any social change from the future ... when one has ambitions such as the eradication in this film, he or she must have a temperament of generous ferocity ... certainly, Malle's temperament is occasionally hateful ... but a soft and stingy hatefulness ... that is afraid of its own cynicism ... The film offers a gallery of characters who are simply a series of reversals ... *Milou* is strictly and literally the modest diversion it pretends to be: a film normal, soft, gentle, titillating ... a film that would be perfect shown on television on Christmas Eve.[73]

But Marie-Françoise Leclère, of *Le Point,* characterizes the film as a small masterpiece: "How can one convey ... its sensuality, its acuity, its multiple changes in tone, and the warmth it emanates? ... The incredible intelligence of the affair lies in its refusal to show ... May '68, and to thus escape from the heavy burden of reconstructions and analysis."[74]

22

Damage (Fatale) — 1992

Double Standards

"And as the smart ship grew, in stature, grace and hue,
In shadowy silent distance grew the Iceberg too.
Alien they seemed to be: no mortal eye could see
The intimate welding of their later history.
Or sign that they were bent, by paths coincident
On being anon twin halves of one august event,
Till the spinner of the years said "Now!" and each one hears,
And consummation comes, and jars two hemispheres."
　　　　　　— Thomas Hardy, "The Convergence of the Twain"

"My stories made me tense and ill, and I wept for the fate of those poor,
bloody losers."
　　　　　　— Australian novelist Peter Carey

BACKGROUND

During the early years of Louis Malle's final decade — i.e., from January 1990
(the French debut of *Milou en mai*)[1] through December 1992 (the French and American releases of *Damage*)[2] — the director again found life alternately pleasant and vex-
ing. The year 1990 proved encouraging: NEF released *Milou* in the winter to
considerable acclaim; Malle and Bergen celebrated their tenth wedding anniversary
in September; and two months later, the director participated in a series of interviews with *Observer* columnist Philip French during French's four-day visit to his
house on the Causse. This was a defining moment in Malle's career: the edited tran-
scriptions of the French dialogues, published in mid–1992 by Faber & Faber as *Malle
on Malle*, and reissued posthumously with an appendage in February 1996[3] (the book's
authorship credited solely to the director), became the first and only volume to offer
a first-person autobiographical account of Malle's entire career, from *Monde du silence*
through *Vanya*.

But the happy moments in the early nineties were offset by calamity, notably
the death of the director's long-estranged father, Pierre Malle, in November 1990,[4]

The emotionally repressed member of Parliament Stephen Fleming (Jeremy Irons) falls into a sticky web of erotic obsession with his son's fiancée, Anna Barton (Juliette Binoche) in *Damage.*

and a series of terrifying and jolting physical afflictions with which Louis grappled. The first crisis arrived one evening around Christmas of 1990, when Bergen discovered her husband submerged in his bathtub — the water opaque with blood, his body "hemmhoraging violently,"[5] the casualty of a recent proctological operation. Horrified, Candice shuttled him to the ICU. Just shy of a year later, in December of '91 (with the preproduction of *Damage* under way), paralyzing pains racked Malle's chest. The physicians insisted on massive open-heart surgery, repairing the director's heart murmur by substituting a porcine duct for a standard plastic valve, which would have proven too narrow for Malle's heart.[6]

Both physiological complications tolled early death knells of Malle's failing health. But if these events caused brooding concern among Malle's family, friends, and collaborators, given his relatively young age (not even 60 at the time of his hospitalizations), his reactions sounded an even greater alarm. Malle's postponement of one of his operations for almost six months,[7] and the director's admission that he blatantly ignored surgeons' requests to cut back drastically on the stress of moviemaking in January '91[8] paint a picture of the filmmaker sinking into a mire of denial and apathy by refusing to come to terms with his maladies. Perhaps as an attempt to push these warning signals out of his mind, Malle plunged headlong into two projects that commanded his attention: *What Maisie Knew* and *Damage*.

Only one of these efforts, *Damage*, made it to the screen (thanks to the director's inability to find studio backing for *Maisie*) but the latter is nonetheless quite important in Malle's career. Though the fundamental idea behind *What Maisie Knew* involved doing an adaptation of Henry James's brilliant 1897 novella of the same title (where a five-year-old girl is used as a pawn in her parents' divorce and shuttled between homes), the prospect of bringing *Maisie* to the screen, in the hands of Malle and screenwriter John Guare, never once entailed an attempt to create a faithful period adaptation of the James novella, using the "equivalence" rule to rework cinematically all of James's literary tropes note-for-note. Actually, *Maisie* refers more precisely to a "project heading" than to a single project — a heading encompassing a whole series of several proposed screenplays by Guare, each with a unique take on the James novel; the basic themes remained static, while the characters, decade, milieu and mood varied from script to script. These incarnations include: *The Manchimeel Tree*, where the wife of a drug dealer flees the States with her young daughter in tow and the two jet off to the Caribbean together, setting themselves up in a hotel (the mother subsequently immerses herself in drug trafficking, and the young daughter gradually uncovers the deceit in the world that envelops her)[9]; *The Loner*, a project "suggested by Henry James' *What Maisie Knew*" and set in contemporary Hollywood, where six-year-old "Sophie," the daughter of a producer and screenwriter, becomes a casualty of her parents' custody battle; and, ultimately, *Dietrich and Marlene*, the now-legendary unproduced Guare script dramatizing Maria Riva's biography of her mother, Marlene Dietrich, and filtering the view of Dietrich through Riva's eyes as a child (in line with the original book). Greenlighted and slated to go into production during the winter of 1995-6 starring Uma Thurman as the eponymous actress, NEF abandoned *Dietrich* when Malle died. All of the aforementioned projects were, to varying degrees, loose adaptations of *Maisie*, and appear in Appendix A of this book ("Lost Horizons: Selected Unproduced Malle Projects.") and all were attempts to rework (and develop the quintessential *cinematic paragon* of) one of Malle's favorite themes: the adult world filtered through a child's eyes. On this point, Billard writes, "[*Maisie*] testifies to the permanence and the strength with which Malle focused on [the theme of] that defining instant when the adolescent learns to distinguish between good and evil."[10]

Damage began life as a short tragic novel published by Knopf and authored by first-time *bellettrist* Josephine Hart, the wealthy Irish-born wife of the British parliamentary lord and ex–advertising godfather Maurice Saatchi. Hart gained notoriety in the seventies and eighties as a director of the London-based Haymarket Publishing and (later) as a successful West End theatrical producer, before debuting as a fiction writer in early 1991. She emerged with *Damage*; the work is a sustained interior monologue, the protracted confession of an unnamed Conservative MP and former medical doctor. Hart's antihero finds himself swept up into a torrid extramarital affair with his young son's fiancée that culminates in the son's accidental violent death, the destruction of their immediate family, and his own exile to a foreign land.

While Hart made a proactive, aggressive attempt to solicit movie options on her novel by sending out copies of the proofs to film directors and studios at the outset of 1991, it is a bit difficult to determine where Malle stood on her list. Billard claims

Hart put Malle at the top of her pecking order[11]; this is perhaps a rather flippant assessment, given Malle's revelation that he had to vie for the rights with numerous interested parties, predominantly American studios.[12] No published sources document how the competition for an option played itself out. But regardless of how it materialized bureaucratically, Nouvelles Editions won the option and ultimately co-funded the picture with Skreba Films of London, Vincent Malle sharing an executive producer credit with Simon Relph.

Even more ambiguous is the degree to which Jean-Claude Carrière became involved in adapting Hart's *roman à clef* prior to David Hare (*Strapless, The Hours, Plenty*), the scriptwriter who ultimately took up the project. It is indisputably clear that Malle approached his best friend Carrière to work on the piece before he sought out Hare (Carrière corroborates this),[13] and definitive that Carrière rejected Hart's book, but something of a challenge to ascertain his rationale. Malle and Hare each maintain that Carrière found the book impossible to adapt because of its stream-of-consciousness approach; in an interview with the author, Carrière states that, to the contrary, he found the novel rather dull and uncompelling, far too *easy* to adapt—child's play, even—and passed it up for this reason:

> [Louis and I] just spent a few days together. I did not understand what Louis was looking for in *Damage*. We had long talks about it, but to me it seemed that the novel was ending where the film should start. You know what I mean? Well, it ends with the death of the son ... that's the abrupt ending of the novel. And I thought that was a very good beginning for a story.... [Louis] liked the book, he gave me the book to read, and I said to him, "There is nothing to do! It's written like a script. You have to shorten the dialogue a little bit and it's done. There is nothing a screenwriter can do about the book.... Except to consider that the book is just a sort of introduction to another story.[14]

Even less apparent is how much time the two men spent working together before reaching an impasse. Malle asserts that Carrière completed an initial draft (he even tells Philip French that their draft abandoned what made Hart's *roman* compelling)[15]; likewise, Hare agrees that Carrière completed a draft, and specifically remembers receiving Carrière's adaptation of the book from Malle and states that he holds a copy (though he never read it for fear it would throw him).[16] Yet astonishingly, Carrière denies ever even attempting to tackle the book, let alone writing an entire script from it. "No, no, no, no," he insists, "[I didn't write an adaptation of *Damage*]. [Louis and I] talked for maybe a week together ... no more."[17,18]

Malle sought out David Hare some 20 years after attending a performance of one of Hare's stage plays, *Flag*, with friend Constantin Costa-Gavras (i.e., circa 1971),[19] and left the theatre fully awed by the young man's talent. In an interview with the author, Hare reflects on the origins of his collaboration with Malle:

> I admired [Louis] like hell [from his work on *My Dinner with André*], and therefore when he rang me out of the blue, basically because he'd bought [Josephine Hart's novel], which I hadn't read ... *Damage* ... and he'd asked his regular collaborator, you know, Jean-Claude Carrière, to write a script.... Jean-Claude had written a script, and said, "This book is completely impossible, there's no way of making a film of it," and since Louis was about to give up

on it, and he said, "Look: will you take a look at it? Because ... Jean-Claude, whom I absolutely trust, says it will never work, and uh, I was slightly bewildered by what the problem was." Louis asked me to read [the Carrière script], but I said, "Look, if I'm going to write the screenplay, I really don't want to read it...." I thought it would throw me. When I read the book, I had an idea of how I would do it ... and I had a very strong reaction to it, and so ... I said, "It'll just throw me, if I read Carrière." So ... I mean, [Louis] *gave* me the Carrière, but I can't say I've ever read it. And not by the way, remotely, out of disrespect for Carrière, who is a brilliant writer.... What actually happened, is that I was due to go on holiday, in fact, and I said to Louis—I was going on holiday by myself, in France, and ... Louis said ... "Oh, well, I must leave you alone, I can see you're going off on your holiday." I said, "Yes, I'm totally exhausted," and I turned up at the hotel in France, and when I turned up, [laughing hard] they said, "Oh, there's a friend of yours staying in the hotel ... called Louis Malle." And so, that was the end of my holiday, basically. And he turned up, unannounced, and we started work.... [This] ... was in the summer of '91. And then we would sit on the beach in St. Tropez, and we just ... conceived the film together. And what [Louis] used to do was every single morning, sit you down and say, you'd have a coffee, and croissant, and you'd sit there, and he'd say, "Now, tell me the story of the film." And he would ask me the story of the film every single morning, and I would begin to tell the story of the film, and then he would say, "No, that doesn't make sense to me," and then we'd go back and then we'd say it again, until the point where I thought I was going mad! But at the end of however many days, six or seven days. ... I could tell him the story of the film. And then at the end of it, [Louis] said, "Now, go away and write it!"[20]

Malle and Hare crafted a treatment of just over 30 pages, fleshed out the characters from Hart's novel and built the basic narrative architecture of the piece.[21] Hare penned the draft in a matter of months; Louis read it in the fall of 1991 and felt enthusiastic.[22] The enlistment of Jeremy Irons (*Moonlighting, Reversal of Fortune*) and Juliette Binoche (*The Unbearable Lightness of Being, Blue*) came early on in the process, the parts of Stephen Fleming (the novel's unnamed protagonist, christened for the film) and Anna Barton (his illicit lover) more or less written exclusively for them. Irons and Malle had spoken of working together for years and considered this the pefect opportunity[23]; numerous actresses competed for the role of Anna; the two most outspoken were Jodie Foster[24] and Isabelle Adjani.[25] But Malle and Hare met with Binoche early on, over lunch, and though the director expressed a few reservations, Hare became immediately convinced of her suitability, and was responsible for persuading Malle to cast her.[26]

Hare later discusses what he perceives as Carrière's problem adapting the text, and how he himself opted to rectify it:

[Hart's novel of *Damage*] is a sustained interior monologue, and so ... I thought there were ways of making the events dramatic in a way which ... would not *need* interior monologue.... [It was my decision], entirely, [to eliminate the voice-over].... I thought the reason that[Louis] had been having so much trouble with Carrière was that those films in which people drone on about what is going on inside their heads, are a particular genre of film. Which, to be fair, the French did absolutely brilliantly, you know, there's a whole lot of ... French New Wave films, where the voice-over is used wonderfully.... Voice-over, for some reason, is much ... harder in the English language. I don't know why. French in some way seems a poetic language, that responds well to voice-over, but the English ... there are very few good voice-overs in English cinema, and very few in American cinema. And I was also very *aware* that Jeremy Irons was going to play the part ... and that he'd already done a television series, *Brideshead Revisited*, which largely consisted of him reading out bits of Evelyn Waugh's prose. The solution that the adapter had come to with *Brideshead Revisited* was simply to copy out large bits of the book! Because it was one of those books that unless you could mimic Waugh's beautiful sentences and style, through actually reading the book out... [pause] But by then I'd just heard enough films of Jeremy Irons telling us what's going on inside his head, and I didn't want this to be one of them.[27]

But the casting of Irons and Binoche brought with it an astounding degree of conflict and volatility. Plagued with emotional violence, the shoot became one of the most heated and anguished debacles of Malle's 40-year career. Hare remembers how the seeds of trouble took root and flourished: Irons adored the script and referred to it as a masterpiece ("It's fantastic!")—that is, until five days before production commenced, when he suddenly and inexplicably lambasted the screenplay and demanded a reinstatement of all the voice-overs. Hare reflects, "We had an *incredibly* attritional and painful five days ... [where] Jeremy, Louis, and I argued it out.... But basically, the damage was done in the first few days.... Jeremy had been persuaded that the route Louis and I wanted to take was right. He'd been made to accept it, but ... it didn't sit well with him."[28] Such was only the prelude; Irons and Binoche—an actor and an actress assigned to play emotionally interlocked lovers and to engage in explicit love scenes—felt mutual hatred for one another and barked at each other throughout the shoot. According to one source, during the scene where Stephen corners Barton against a cold stone wall in February Paris on the rue Férou and forces himself inside of her—a scene that required many, *many* takes—Binoche reputedly screamed out at Irons for hurting her and called him a "con" (French for idiot)[29]; another source claims that when Irons caused Binoche discomfort by becoming overly aggressive during a sex scene, Binoche stormed off the set altogether.[30]

The conflicts extended to the on-set relationship between the director and star, as well. In an interview reprinted in a periodical, Jeremy Irons offers a rather nasty and insulting reflection on the degree to which he and Malle failed to see eye to eye:

> The director, Louis Malle, is more of an *auteur* than the directors I have worked with so far. That was one of the points of friction we felt at the start. He always talked about "his" film. I told him, Louis, if it's *your* film, I wonder what I'm doing here. I'm leaving...." [Louis's] concentration is such that he does not share very much. He knows what he wants. If you know what he wants to get for you, you can help him. That's the great advantage in telling people what you expect of them.[31]

Nor was the Malle-Binoche working relationship easy and uncomplicated; according to Hare, "Juliette ... was [among] a generation of French actress who didn't really know who Louis *was*..."[32] so she perhaps failed to take the director as seriously as older actresses might have. But beyond this, Hare speculates that Malle and his leading actress failed to establish a smooth rapport simply because Malle — as a kind of documentarian — sought to photograph a pre-created, pre-planned performance, and relied hugely on his actors to create their characterizations for him, whereas Binoche expected and required specific instruction. In other words, it simply amounted to a difference in creative approach.[33]

The director fared a thousand times better with his supporting players; critics and the public quite rightly proclaimed the enlistment of Miranda Richardson as a masterstroke, although on a purely logistical level, it was — as Hare observes — one of the most bizarre and illogical casting choices in film history. Regarded by nearly everyone, including *Damage* casting director Patsy Pollock, as a genius, Richardson (*Dance with a Stranger, The Crying Game*) was only 31 at the time; Pollock, the Malles, and Simon Relph nonetheless recruited her to portray the tormented middle aged housewife Ingrid Fleming, a character some 20 years her senior, because they acknowledged the success of the picture as so contingent on the heartbreaking scene in the end of the film where Ingrid collapses onto the floor and nearly has a nervous breakdown following the death of her only son and the discovery of her husband's gross sexual and emotional betrayal, and knew for certain that only Richardson could pull this off. Pollock told Malle: "You've gotta have an actress who can play that scene, and you've got to have the greatest tragic actress in England, and it doesn't matter what age she is! ... You can [fake age] with hair and makeup, but you can't fake the few actors in England who can play Greek tragedy, and Miranda's *it*."[34] The gamble paid off; Richardson gleaned a Best Supporting Actress Oscar nomination, and unanimous raves from critics around the globe; even those who panned the film mercilessly found Richardson's portrayal mesmerizing. Malle cast Leslie Caron — an age-old friend with whom he had discussed collaborating for years and years[35] — as Anna Barton's mother, Elizabeth Prideaux.

Conflicts of a different sort erupted in post-production. Malle fought a heated, tortuous battle with the picture's American distributor, New Line Cinema, when Motion Picture Association of America president Jack Valenti threatened *Damage* with an "NC-17" rating, single-handedly guaranteeing that it would be withheld from hundreds of middle American theaters and shopping malls during the holiday movie season of 1992-3. In a prominent December 22, 1992, *New York Times* article, "Louis Malle Cuts a Film and Grows Indignant," an irate Malle castigates the MPAA's effort to "cloak *Damage* in an aura of pornography,"[36] and what he perceives as a grossly unfair American double standard for films dealing with sex versus films that feature gratuitous, explicit acts of violence. The director finally resolved the issue by capitulating — snipping about seven seconds out of one of the picture's more explicit love scenes, in which Irons and Binoche writhe naked on the floor. To compensate for the lost footage, he substituted close-ups of the two actors for the two full-body shots.[37] Though the picture avoided being slapped with the dreaded "NC-17," New Line eventually released the two alternate versions of *Damage* on home video — an R-rated cut and an "unrated" cut.[38]

Damage reached Europe before it made its stateside appearance, premiering in

France on December 2, 1992, and making its limited release debut in the United States on December 23, 1992; it received nationwide theatrical release in the states on January 22, 1993, and debuted in various European countries through summer 1993.

SYNOPSIS

In the early nineties, Dr. Stephen Fleming (Jeremy Irons), a middle-aged former medical doctor and newly appointed Conservative MP and MS in the Department of Environment, lives a quiet, contented life with his wife of over 20 years, Ingrid (Miranda Richardson) and his children, 13-year-old Sally (Gemma Clarke) and 25-year-old Martyn (Rupert Graves), in a posh house in the upscale London suburb of Hampstead. As the story opens, the British Prime Minister calls Stephen into his office and commends Dr. Fleming for his recent work. Stephen returns home to Ingrid that evening and discovers, after she finishes talking to Martyn on the telephone, that their son has taken a new girlfriend, Anna; Stephen dismisses the news and confesses rather cynically, to his embarrassed wife, that he believes his son is only interested in casual sex. Ingrid tells him that her wealthy father, Edward Lloyd (Ian Bannen), a former Member of Parliament himself, has just predicted a major promotion for Stephen, and thus implies that her father has had tremendous pull in obtaining a post for her husband. A few minutes later, Stephen walks into his costly decorated living room and pauses by the fireplace, glancing around himself uncomfortably.

At a Christmas party Stephen attends some time later, a young woman (Juliette Binoche) with chiseled masculine hair, dressed in a black trenchcoat, boldly approaches Stephen and extends her hand, introducing herself as Anna Barton—Martyn's new girlfriend. An awkward moment passes between the two as they stare fixedly into each others' eyes. Days later, when Anna and Martyn visit the Flemings' house, Anna and Stephen say nothing of the previous encounter and greet each other in front of the rest of the family as if complete strangers. Several days later, Anna rings Stephen at his office; he asks where she is and tells her he will be there in an hour. The two meet at Anna's flat; Stephen grabs her, yanks down her dress, unzips his pants, and enters her.

The affair continues, and as Stephen's obsession with Anna builds, so does Martyn's emotional commitment to her. Martyn informs his father of his promotion to deputy political editor at the national newspaper where he works; an astonished and impressed Stephen insists that the family celebrate. But the dinner turns awkward and edgy when Martyn brings Anna, and a series of uncomfortable, furtive glances pass between Stephen and his lover; Ingrid, Martyn, Sally, and Edward remain oblivious. After the dinner, Stephen lies by telling his wife he has unfinished business to attend to; minutes later, he pulls up outside of Anna's flat and glimpses Martyn bidding farewell for the evening. When Martyn has left, Stephen once again enters the flat and grabs Anna; the two indulge in passionate, animalistic lovemaking. Afterward, Anna sits naked on the bed before Stephen, and reflects on a crisis from her childhood, where her brother, Aston, developed an incestuous obsession with her and offed himself when she could not (and would not) return his affections; she tells Stephen that she is terrified of possessiveness and warns him, "Damaged people are dangerous. They know they can survive." Confused, but with ongoing interest in their love affair, Stephen suggests that she accompany him to a conference in Brussels that weekend. Anna declines, for she and Martyn are planning a romantic weekend in Paris.

When his European Commission meeting in Brussels is temporarily suspended just before dawn, Stephen slips off to Paris and phones Anna at the hotel where she and Martyn have taken a room. Anna leaves Martyn at the hotel for a few minutes and Stephen intercepts her in the street; the two duck into an alcove and make love against a cold stone wall. Anna cautions him not to follow her back to the hotel. Stephen checks into a nearby hotel and orders breakfast, taking a room with a view of the unit where Martyn and Anna are staying. After he starts to eat, and glimpses his son and his new lover in each other's arms from the window, Stephen collapses onto the bed and curls up into a ball, sobbing uncontrollably.

Back at his office in London, Stephen phones Anna and asks to meet her for lunch. She agrees; the two stroll together through a rainy park. Stephen informs Anna that he has decided to leave Ingrid for her and wants to settle down with her. She objects and tells the confused man that he would be gaining something he already has, and would certainly lose his son forever.

Days later, the family travels out to Edward's rambling country estate, Hartley, for a weekend together; Martyn brings Anna and informs the entire family that they have become engaged. Stephen is shocked and virtually speechless at the news, but manages to make a celebratory toast before the family and congratulates his son. Late that night, a restless Stephen leaves Ingrid sleeping in bed and slips out into the hallway, where he finds Anna waiting for him. The two enter one of the spare rooms and Anna fellates him, but on the way out, they cross the path of Sally, who has woken in the middle of the night. Back in Hampstead, Stephen confronts Sally in their home as she is watching television, and tells her that he and Anna met that night to discuss the engagement. Sally accepts his story on the surface but makes it clear that she doesn't buy the explanation. Still, she says nothing to anyone.

Stephen attempts to visit Anna once more at her flat, but discovers that she has another gentleman caller: Peter Wetzlar (Peter Stormare); passing the visit off as a routine, friendly call, Anna pretends to loan Stephen a book, *What Maisie Knew*, and dismisses Dr. Fleming; Stephen waits for hours in a discreet location outside of the house until Peter leaves, and storms back into the flat, furiously demanding to know who Peter is and the nature of Anna's relationship with him. Anna begins to sob and tears streak her face as she admits that she was with Peter on the night Aston died, and that she asked Peter to take her sexually immediately following Aston's suicide. Ever since, the two have forged a friendship. Stephen grabs Anna and makes passionate love to her.

Anna's mother, Elizabeth Prideaux (Leslie Caron), who has been divorced multiple times, attends a dinner with the Flemings and, having immediately sensed the trouble afoot, first attempts to warn the family of her daughter's history by commenting on Martyn's resemblance to Aston and embarrassing her daughter. She later warns Stephen — while she is riding alone with him in his car, his chauffeur driving her back to her hotel — not to stand in-between Anna and Martyn. Tormented by her words, Stephen phones Anna from his office and insists that they call off the affair, but several days later, a small package arrives at Stephen's office; it contains a silver key and the address of a nearby flat. Stephen visits the location alone and discovers that Anna has indicated the date and time when they will meet for a tryst in a journal on a glasstop table. Subsequently, while Ingrid, Martyn, and Anna sit around the kitchen table in the Fleming home and discuss wedding plans, Stephen enters. He waits until the others' backs are turned and only Anna is looking, and raises the key to his lips nonchalantly. She smiles in recognition. When the others leave the room for a minute, leaving Stephen and Anna alone together, Anna strokes her lover's hair and asks if he thinks she would be marrying Martyn if it didn't allow the two of them to be alone together.

Stephen and Anna meet in the new flat at the appointed day and time, undress, eat together, and begin an extended session of erotic lovemaking. But as they come together, Martyn, who has just accidentally learned of the flat's existence from the building landlord, steps into the apartment building and climbs the stairs. He hears the panting and moaning through the door and — as Stephen has irresponsibly left the key hanging in the keyhole — Martyn opens the door and glimpses his father and fiancée writhing naked on the bed. Torn apart, betrayal and sadness on his face, he backs away from the horror before him, but accidentally tumbles over the stairway railing and falls two stories, landing, dead, in the entry of the apartment building. Stephen flies down the stairs, naked, and lets out a cry of pain as he raises his son's body into his arms; Anna dresses and slips away from the wreckage, tears rolling down her face, as policemen and reporters crowd into the flat.

That night, when Stephen returns to Ingrid, paparazzi have engulfed the home, lights glaring, bulbs flashing. Ingrid turns to face her husband with bloody welts covering her face, and informs him that she has been beating herself. As sobs wrack her body and she collapses onto the floor, screaming out for the son that is lost to her, Stephen takes her in his arms and asks her to give him the pain and the responsibility of Martyn's death; she asks him why he never bothered to commit suicide. The next morning, she awakens to face Stephen, and tells him how much she regrets having met him; she undoes her bra and faces him, bare breasted, wondering aloud how it is possible that she could never be enough.

Stephen meets the members of Parliament in his downstairs den and resigns from his job; he then begins to search for Anna, visiting her mother in an apartment. Elizabeth denies the fact that Anna is nearby and tells Stephen she has gone to see Peter; as Stephen turns to leave, he suddenly realizes that Anna is in an adjacent room and runs over to open a door. She sits on the bed, and turns to face him, sadly, wordlessly.

An indefinite period of time passes; Stephen has grown old, his gray hair falling in wavy locks to his shoulders, his face wrinkled and weathered. He now wears sandals and loose-fitting pants, and carries a bag of fruits and cheeses as he walks down a cobblestone street, having taken a self-imposed, lonely exile in an unnamed land.[39] In voice-over, he reflects on how easy it is to withdraw from the world, and contemplates how love brings one in touch with the unknowable. After Stephen enters his spare, empty apartment, he cuts a piece of cheese on the table, and turns to open the windows, staring at the mountains against the horizon. He turns and sits down in a wooden chair before a giant photograph of himself, Anna, and Martyn, that he has enlarged and mounted on a wall. As he stares at Anna's face, he remembers that he spotted her only once more, by accident, in an airport; she did not see him, but she was with Peter Wetzlar and their small child. He muses that she looked like anyone else.

ANALYSIS

Louis Malle's 18th feature, *Damage*, received an official credit as an adaptation of Josephine Hart's erotically charged 1991 debut novel; it has identical characters and the same linear progression of events as its source material. Yet David Hare's spare script and Malle's polished film steer around a faithful note-for-note adaptation of Hart's *roman à clef*. Malle and Hare take tremendous liberties with their source novel by eliminating Hart's central literary conceit and many of her subthemes, in lieu of preserving her tropes and reinventing them for the cinematic medium within a visual context. The director and scenarist thus rely on a largely unique set of intertextual reference points and substitute an alternate set of themes for Hart's ideas. The central irony is that Malle and Hare emerge triumphant, and the motion picture poses the overwhelming (and potentially unanswerable) question of whether a screen adaptation that alters its source novel in drastic and objectionable ways but succeeds on its own terms can still be regarded as a masterwork.[40]

Josephine Hart's *Damage* remains seamy, arresting and (though seldomly acknowledged as such) one of the most intentionally deceptive and seductive pieces of literary craftsmanship in memory. The opening paragraphs of the work establish its trajectory and intent and illustrate beautifully the novel's fundamental conceit:

> There is an internal landscape, a geography of the soul; we search for its outlines all our lives.
>
> Those who are lucky enough to find it ease like water over a stone, onto its fluid contours, and are home.
>
> Some find it in the place of their birth; others may leave a seaside town, parched, and find themselves refreshed in the desert. There are those born in rolling countryside who are really only at ease in the intense and busy loneliness of the city.
>
> For some, the search is for the imprint of another, a child or a mother, a grandfather or a brother, a lover, a husband, a wife, or a foe.
>
> We may go through our lives happy or unhappy, successful or unfulfilled, loved or unloved, without ever standing cold with the shock of recognition, without ever feeling the agony as the twisted iron in our soul unlocks itself and we slip at last into place.
>
> I have been at the bedsides of the dying, who looked puzzled at their family's grief as they left a world in which they had never felt at home.
>
> I have seen men weep more at the death of their brother, whose being had

once locked into theirs, than at the death of their child. I have watched brides become mothers, who only once, long ago, were radiant on their uncle's knee.[41]

In the above excerpt and throughout the narrative, Hart confines herself (and the audience) to the prison of one male's subjective consciousness. It is a brilliant move, enabling her to take events in the story that — stripped of the interior monologue approach — could be interpreted rather easily as a damnable and highly chauvinistic series of actions. Taken objectively or given a slightly different spin, the events might gain a clearer outline as something similar to, say, Henry Miller's unabashed masculine carnality — i.e., "an undersexed middle aged father's seduction of his first-born's fiancée." Instead, Hart suspends her protagonist's "misdeeds" in an aura of moral ambiguity by filtering his affair through his own carefully constructed (though unmistakably flawed) apologetic. And the rather amusing irony — the grand paradox of the work — is that the narrator rationalizes his torrid affair with Anna, justifies it apologetically, via a feminine argument that will most dramatically persuade his female listeners: the soulmate philosophy. The subject matter of the adulterous affair and the soulmate apologetic are not necessarily mutual disqualifiers, but the subjective voice and the very convenience of the narrator's argument enable Hart to raise the question of the narrator's veracity *per se*, within a modernist framework, thus cutting herself off entirely from the ability to answer it. *Damage* is thus as delightfully ambiguous as Henry James's *In the Cage*, and Hart's novel (like *Cage*) functions as self-mythos.

The unnamed male narrator of *Damage* remains consistently and fully aware of his listening audience throughout the novel, and fleetingly drops clues of this awareness. Consider the narrator's statement, "We went to the hospital. I made the identification [of Martyn's body]. There is nothing to say. I will not speak of this."[42] Why would he refuse to "speak of this" if he were only writing or telling the story self-reflexively, as in a journal? Instead, the narrator writes — or speaks — as if fully, cognizantly addressing an audience, and thus implies that the moment is too personal, too private, to share with others. Particularly given this statement, one must interpret everything he tells (from the first sentence of the novel to the last) with a grain of skepticism. His sweeping, seductive, and overpowering voice, with its euphonic texture and metric sway, renders it challenging to stand a few steps removed and analyze the man's observations and recountances coldly and objectively; one finds oneself magnetized, helplessly swept up in the rapture of his prose. But if one detaches oneself, small lapses in the doctor's logical fabric become apparent. In these first paragraphs, he indirectly establishes a thesis about how one of the most important qualifications for a romantic relationship is that of finding a soulmate — the fleeting sense of mutual recognition that brings one into a state of inner knowledge about oneself and a feeling of "being home" in an oft cold, hostile and abrasive world — the state that provides a kind of spiritual resurrection, that can only rarely be attained from a loved one. But only sentences later, the narrator interjects a phrase that lies entirely outside of his argument, irrelevant to it: "I have watched brides become mothers, who only once, long ago, were radiant on their uncle's knee."[43] A piece of deliberately (deliriously) empty-headed rhetoric, cut free from the "soulmate" argument that surrounds it, seemingly devoid of any relevance aside from the narrator's attempt to persuade the audience of his own veracity. And why, one wonders, would he need to indulge in this persuasiveness *per se* if he did not question his own credulity on some level? Along these same lines, Hart plants in her narrative additional clues that evince the narrator casting doubt on himself: "My wife is beautiful. For that, I have the evidence of my own eyes, and the reaction of those who meet her."[44] His own word is not persuasive enough — he must call in others to back him.

The narrator's argument also reveals its heavy bias and questionability when numerous characters in the speaker's story conveniently support his own words and theories by speaking in his voice and using his metaphors. Despite Ingrid's emotional collapse in the denouement, she paradoxically affirms the narrator's basic soulmate thesis and thus contradicts herself by justifying his affair with Anna on some level: "You know, Martyn was the one for me. There is always just one person really. Anna, I suppose, for you?"[45] And later, when Ingrid observes, "My God, you never really seemed alive anyway," the narrator responds with the logical completion of his own axiom: "I never was really alive to anything until Anna."[46] The reader is expected to fill in the "logical gap" for himself or herself: how much easier to excuse an adulterous affair when, for one of the participants, it is a life or death issue. And who could deny the narrator's fundamental need for Anna when everyone in the story concurs with it?

David Denby writes, "As readers of the novel know, Stephen's passion is supposed to some sort of "higher" obsession, in which sensuality and mere pleasure are not the point."[47] More specifically, the central idea behind the narrator's decision to recount the events that led up to and followed his affair with Anna (the "higher obsession" that Denby references) involves a kind of advanced sensory perception, a coming into visual and palpable contact with the world around him, gaining life for the first time in over 50 years. Hart evokes this heightened consciousness with two scenes set in Paris, where after making love to Anna in a side street, the narrator dines in a café and later checks into the hotel room Anna and Martyn have vacated. He finds that everything before him — shapes, colors, textures, tastes— has sprung to life, a series of gifts for his rarefied senses. In the café: "I ate with a kind of rapture. The wine looked and tasted like liquid gold. The pastry seemed to explode gently in my mouth, as the salmon slipped from its crevices."[48] And later, at the room in L'Hotel: "I moved on all fours like some heavy animal from my velvet world, and fell onto the bed. In a dreamfall of colors— the green of Anna's dress, the flash of black as she slipped on her knickers, the liquid gold of the wine, and the sunlit pales of the millefeuille and salmon, the violent blood red of the chaise lounge."[49]

If such images persuade the reader sensationally, the dramatic architecture serves a like purpose. The above scene unfolds around page 57, and represents a turning point; it actually points to the novel's wickedly clever narrative structure. The narrator's apologetic spans around the first 60 pages or so (i.e., the first act) and the last 40 (i.e., the third act, pp. 161–98); the more heinous details involving the doctor's betrayal of his family span the second act (pp. 61–160). Given this structure, the reader takes the narrator's logic during the first and third acts, and "reads it into" the "unforgivable" details in the second act, particularly in retrospect.

One can imagine the team of Louis Malle and Jean-Claude Carrière being ideally suited to adapt this material, for an odd reason: the flashback structure utilized in their adaptation of Darien's *Le Voleur* (1967), so ill-suited and ill-advised for that misfire (see Chapter 8, "Deflected Emotion and the Art of Memory") would perfectly serve a faithful, tight adaptation of Hart's novel. On the level of narrative architecture, Jean-Claude Carrière naturally saw the familial collapse in Hart's novel of *Damage* as the ideal beginning of a story: as Hart builds her narrative, the family tragedy *is* the beginning — the catalytic event that precipitates the narrator's decision to relay his tale. Only at this point does the drama of the story shift from an exterior logic (melodrama) to an interior logic (psychological drama and suspense) and thus become a working through, a process of narrative catharsis, for the speaker. It almost feels as if Hart wrote the novel in reverse progression, beginning with Martyn's death, the divorce, and the narrator's exile, and working retroactively to color events and perceptions through the narrator's eyes as he, at some later point in time, reflects on the calamity chronologically. Ergo, the external tragedy informs nearly every subsequent conclusion the narrator draws, every observation he makes. For instance: when the doctor admits that "Children are the great gamble.... Instead of being ours to mold and shape after our best knowledge and endeavor, they are themselves," the speaker is reassuring himself that Martyn's decision to back away from the horror and topple over the railing, however unintentional, was Martyn's choice, not his (the speaker's); the doctor is thus making a feeble attempt to absolve himself altogether of guilt in feeling responsible for his son's death. But he does so under an objective guise, which is why the observation about children sounds so absolute, so irrevocable and universal and unbiased, when coming from his lips.

The flashback structure would thus suit *Damage* perfectly, enabling the screenwriter and director to capture the narrative reflection that lies inherent in the book. Moreover, whereas the flashback device ruins *Le Voleur* because it eliminates all suspense and excitement, instilling in the audience the foreknowledge that Georges Randal will survive throughout the story, Hare writes *Damage* as a modern tragedy, and tragedy relies to a significant degree on the audience's foreknowledge of a calamity that is fated to happen; it builds tension, in turn, from that sense of the inevitable.[50]

This is only one tipoff to the many respects in which *Damage*, the motion picture, represents a missed opportunity as an adaptation — ways it could have demonstrated far greater faithfulness to Hart's novel. Another involves the use of voice-over, and although Hare bemoaned the thought of weighing down the picture with pages and pages of "Jeremy Irons telling us what's going on inside his head," this merely represents an extreme (an *ad absurdum* argument) that could be avoided rather easily, with or without a voice-over. The voice-over could instead be reduced to a few paragraphs introducing and acting as a coda to an extended flashback confession that Stephen Fleming tells to another individual; because much of the film's narrative, in turn, would be operating within the flashback trajectory, everything onscreen would be, by its very presence, a subjectification of Stephen's recountances, and thus retain the questionability — the suspended clarity and certainty — that Hart plants, so subtly, throughout Fleming's "confession" in the novel, particularly if Malle and Carrière scattered small contradictions throughout his flashback reflection. In applying this strategy, one can even envision the filmmakers creating a cinematic equivalent for Stephen's conviction that Anna gives him heightened sensory perception; they could paint his shift in consciousness, aesthetically, during the scenes in Paris—via look shots that employ a uniquely evocative cinematographic resonance—in much the same way that Kjell Grede and Sten Holmberg do in *Hip Hip Hurrah!* (1987).

No matter. The Malle-Hare film version opts for an entirely different route by rebuilding Hart's material thematically, almost from scratch. Hare establishes alternate goals for the material and accomplishes most of them flawlessly; he also works from a set of contexts that distinguish the film from the novel, specifically classic Greek tragedy, the British cultural mythos of emotional, individual, and sexual repression; and feminine psychosexual development and trauma.

In an interview, David Hare acknowledges of his *Damage* adaptation, "I said [to Louis], 'If the book is to work as a film, it has to be a tragedy. And ... the more Greek we can make it, the better.'"[51] This claim withstands deep scrutiny when juxtaposed alongside the finished film: if Hart wrote her novel as the tragedy of one man working through his inner conflicts and struggling to come to terms with his guilt, Hare's script restructures Hart's narrative uniquely, by externalizing the sense of fatality.[52] Indeed, Hare later describes *Damage* as a contemporary Greek tragedy about "men and women struggling with their fates."[53] The tightness of the narrative architecture[54] and the inexorability of the narrative drive—i.e., its irreversibility, a product of its linear trajectory—create the overtones of tense inevitability that exist in the finished film—an impressive accomplishment (and a surprising one) given the motion picture's careful avoidance of flashback. Whereas, in the novel, the narrator makes an implicit case for his conviction that he and Anna Barton were fated to meet because they are soulmates (*born* to be together, however temporarily), in the film Malle and Hare use the pull of erotic obsession, both as a substitute for Stephen's inner knowledge of the ways in which Anna complements him psychically and spiritually, and as a dramatic counterpoint to Stephen's visible feelings of oppression (not, as David Denby ludicrously surmises, Stephen's inability to feel *per se*[55]).

In his brilliant essay "Myth into *mythos*: the shaping of tragic plot," Peter Burian lists countless additional aspects of traditional Greek tragedy, several as applicable to *Damage* as the aforementioned fatalistic narrative pull. Burian opens with the most fundamental, as illustrated by a Geoffrey Chaucer quote: "Tragedie is to seyn a certyn storie, as olde bookes maken us memorie, of hym that stood in greet prosperitee, and is yfallen out of heigh degree into miserie, and endeth urecedly."[56] As Burian acknowledges, Chaucer's definition suffers from crudeness and narrowness ("far too restrictive"[57]), for it eliminates countless exceptions to the rule within the Grecotragic canon. Yet Chaucer's narrative generalization, of course, bears haunting similarities to the story that Malle and Hare tell: Stephen Fleming begins the story amid an atmosphere of prosperity, and experiences a calamitous downfall into misery and loneliness. But even more astonishingly, as Burian describes increasingly complex Grego-tragic narrative patterns in his essay, the screen adaptation of *Damage* corresponds with like smoothness, challenging any detractors who attack the film's dramatic arc as overly simplistic or shallow (as some critics and viewers have). When evaluated according to the patterns Burian identifies, *Damage* represents a comingling of the "sacrifice" and "retribution" narrative architectures.[58] It qualifies as sacrificial in the sense that Malle pits the needs of the individual (Stephen Fleming) against the needs of the community (represented by the Fleming family). Although, as previously implied, Malle and Hare expurgate Hart's soulmate concept, they make it resoundingly clear, from the moment in the kitchen when Ingrid informs her husband that Edward (i.e., her father) has predicted a promotion for him, that Stephen suffers from an infuriating lack of control over his life; Edward (a British "Custodian" as will become apparent later) has obviously spent years pulling Stephen's proverbial marionette strings. A minute or so later, the heavily-suited Stephen strolls into his living room and, as he pauses by the fireplace, Malle intercuts a critically important close-up where Stephen turns and stares around himself awkwardly. He appears hot and uncomfortable, as if he yearns to escape from this oppressive and awkward environment, as an individual cut loose from his surroundings. The sex, in turn, becomes a kind of liberation device; initially it functions by enabling Stephen to release the pain of oppression, but over the course of the dramatic trajectory (as Stephen and Anna gradually lose their clothes from one lovemaking session to another), and particularly in the epilogue, where Stephen appears unmistakably loose and free (via his hair, his attire, even his sparse and empty room), housed in an uncluttered life, it becomes perfectly evident that the he has sacrificed the communal for the sake of the egocentric. As for the "retribution" narrative story pattern, Burian writes that it "is organized around punishment for past offenses. It may involve conflict between gods and mortals, with the mortals' challenge to divine supremacy leading to their destruction."[59] *Damage*, of course, corresponds in the sense that Stephen realizes his liberation at the cost of Martyn's death, and the destruction of his old life—his marriage, career, family[60]—and suffers for it.

Central to the Malle-Hare adaptation is the idea that—cutting against the grain of those early Malle features which dissect fate as collective free will (particularly *Ascenseur*)—the script of *Damage* gives equal weight to free will and destiny, without dissecting either. In Burian's words, "The Aristotelian tradition ... emphasizes *hamartia*, generally understood as the "tragic flaw" of overweening pride, and its punishment. The tragic hero, although caught in circumstances beyond his ken and control, is ... destroyed by the gods (or fate) because of his own failings."[61] Though one can correctly and justifiably blame Stephen for the decision to engulf himself in an illicit affair with Anna, Anna's initial chance meeting with Martyn—alluded to only in passing—(which indirectly sets into motion the wheels of Stephen's affair with Anna), as well as the landlord's decision to phone Anna about the clandestine flat at the moment when Martyn is available to answer the telephone, and Anna's decision to leave the office about four seconds before Martyn phones to question her about the flat (which indirectly set into motion the wheels of Martyn's death) are painted, unmistakably, as acts of fate because of their apparent disconnectedness from the sphere of character awareness *per se*. One could even make the same case for Stephen's decision to leave the silver lion key in the keyhole of the door at the flat, for it appears (as Malle films it) to be an unconscious (and thus uncontrollable) act—chosen and used by fatalistic forces. In the "One on One" interview at the end of the *Damage* videocassette, Malle underscores this idea: "What happens to the Jeremy Irons character and Anna is that he meets his fate in a way. Something that very well might never have happened to him. But letting fate take over, he becomes a destroyer of his own family."[62]

On the broadest level, Burian defines *story pattern* as "the shape of a narrative, constructed according to the rules of its own inner logic as storytelling rather than the probabilities of everyday life."[63] Consider how neatly this observation applies to the Malle-Hare adaptation of *Damage*. The most telling example: Martyn's death makes little sense logically; in real life, it is significantly improbable that Stephen's son would back over the railing and fall to his death. This points to the basis on which one must evaluate the events in the narrative: the dramatic developments cannot (and should not) be evaluated according to "everyday logic," (in which case they appear ludicrous, as melodramatic contrivances) but according to the inner logic of the Greco-tragic narrative patterns. For Martyn's death represents an integral, inextricable component of both the sacrificial and the retributive patterns. Without it, the sacrifice would remain incomplete and Stephen could never suffer from the same degree of palpable retribution that fate directs at his heart.

One additional point regarding the film's Greco-tragic subtext. Burian writes of "the fundamental struggle ... to wrest meaning from suffering, and the perennial question of tragic pleasure — the exaltation that accompanies the witnessing of tragic events."[64] Hare interpolates such an exaltation into the film — that is, a moral, spiritual, and psychological ascension of his primary characters — via an "explosive" narrative architecture. An integral component of the original plan for the narrative involved the idea that Malle and Hare would "plant" an emotional explosion at the end of the piece, which explains and justifies the presence of the Miranda Richardson breakdown scene. Denby complains of the picture, "Yes, but *why* does Stephen latch onto *this* woman [Anna]? And how much of Stephen's grand passion is derived from cuckolding his very handsome and accomplished son? The script is mute on all the obvious points of interest." Incorrect: the *characters* are "mute," and intentionally so. It can hardly be termed accidental that the only emotionally "explosive" scenes in the narrative arrive at the end, or that Malle and Irons withhold Stephen's voice-over until the epilogue: Hare uses the cataclysm of the adultery and Martyn's subsequent death for a set purpose. He begins with emotionally repressed and dysfunctional characters—characters that exist and function as emotional mutes on two distinct levels—and, in turn, establishes two indications of a "breaking out" for the characters that the tragedy elicits, one to represent (and, in a sense, evince a reversal of) each level. On the most fundamental, the characters exist out of touch with their emotions *per se*; thus, Malle withholds the use of voice-over until the end of the piece — it is not the first moment when the script provides a completely translucent, direct indication of Stephen Fleming's ability to feel (one can infer his feelings visually for much of the picture) but the first moment — because Stephen is narrating and discussing his own feelings in voice-over — when the film demonstrates that Stephen is in *touch with* his feelings. And note his line of dialogue, declarative of his inner arc: "Love brings one in touch with the unknowable." Prior to his involvement with Anna, Stephen's feelings are, to him, unknowable. He functions out of touch with his emotional element on a day-to-day basis; she imparts to him, *via intercourse,* a sudden détente of his icy emotional barricades. As an accessory to this (albeit an achronological one) the Miranda Richardson "breakdown" scene in the Flemings' kitchen demonstrates that the characters have not only gained access to their innermost feelings, but have, per the tragedy, suddenly gained the courage to exude them. On both counts, it is as if Hare has taken the narrator's (Stephen's) line, from Hart's book, "You are absolutely right on both counts ... I never was really alive to anything until Anna,"[65] and has given it a dramatic and stunning reinterpretation.

The process of demonstrative emancipation for the character arcs gains sociological resonance, as well—*Damage* offers an understated, scathing, and understandably controversial critique of the British cultural mythos, suggesting, in fact, that the aforementioned emotional dysfunction is not merely traceable to a single character or even several characters, but to an entire psychosocial ill that has spread like a virus across the British empire. The underrated Harold Pinter–John Irvin minimalist comedy *Turtle Diary* (1985) actually weaves itself around like trajectories for its two main character arcs, to make an identical point about the British. Yet *Damage* (unlike the Irvin film) moves beyond the question of emotional and psychological repression into examining the repression of individualism *per se,* as a product of a collectively oriented British culture that encourages class identities at the expense of individual identity and expression.[66] In his 1974 pop sociological study of England, *True Brit,* Clive Irving alludes to these collective identities when he writes of British "clubsmanship":

> Britain is run through an extensive network of private transactions. It is the most secretive ruling system in the western world. The British invented the gentlemen's club, and variations of the club principle are indispensable to the clandestine power networks.... The principle of the club is the key to understanding how British society preserves its continuity. While the more flagrant superstructure of the class system apparently disappeared, it had merely gone underground.... Today Britain is riddled with clubs. They range from the powerful to the powerless. At their most opaque they contain enormous influence.[67]

The "clubsmanship" in the film of *Damage* applies specifically to the Custodians—one of the top-ranked "clubs" for which Irving provides a concise and telling definition:

> In this supposedly model democracy, the country is not run by the people elected to run it. The power of Parliament has been systematically eroded. Real power lies elsewhere in the hands of the Custodians. This elusive entity is more extensive than the old concept of the "Establishment." It outlives governments and fashions in politics. It is not only unelected by it is self-recruited and self-sustaining.[68]

Edward Lloyd represents, on an inveterate level, the prototypical Custodian—a member of the British club who has pulled a few strings for the sake of ensuring that his son-in-law physician is elected into parliament. Lloyd is thus a critical character in the script, for, affable though he may be, he stands at direct odds to Stephen's progression as an individual and only supports Stephen's attainment of collective identity. Taking this a step further: as Malle and Hare define Lloyd, he represents the force behind the collective identity that Stephen must shuck if he is to move forward into greater individualism. This recalls the kitchen scene at the outset of the picture, where Ingrid turns to Stephen and a critically important dialogue occurs between them:

INGRID   Oh, by the way ... Edward phoned.

STEPHEN   (slightly irritated) You know, I don't *believe* your father.

INGRID   He said the prime minister had summoned you into his office.

            (long pause)

            So...?

STEPHEN   He just wanted a chat. He asked me whether power meant anything to me.

INGRID   And what did you say?

STEPHEN   The usual ... I said my family was far more important.[69]

"He said the prime minister had summoned you into his office." "You know, I don't *believe* your father." From this subtle exchange, one senses not only the inestimable amount of pull that Edward has in Stephen's (i.e., a minister of parliament's) position, but Stephen's resultant irritation becomes palpable — his accomplishments, it appears, are not entirely his own. And note the following lines of dialogue: "He asked me whether power meant anything to me.... I said my family was far more important." The "in joke" here involves the fact that for these characters, family and power are inextricably linked. Stephen's family is the source of his political power[70] and, to a large degree, his identity.

As for "hidden" British sexuality (or immorality) that the film unmasks, consider Irving's statement in *True Brit*, under his heading "Suddenly the British Are Sexy": "Not suddenly; they've just been enjoying it more — or more of them have been caught enjoying it, particularly the upper classes. The upper classes always did enjoy it, but they used not to be caught."[71] An accurate assessment that *Damage* captures, although the notion of illicit behavior revealed beneath the layers of the British upper crust is ancient news, so ancient that it even predates Profumo by a couple of centuries. In fact, it probably represents the most unrevelatory and tired aspect of *Damage*. Nonetheless, Malle's onscreen evocation of hidden British sexuality is unusual (his attempt to rescue this theme from the realm of the trite and hackneyed) and merits attention as it materializes in two distinct spheres: the ontological and the contextual.

Ontologically, Malle establishes a fascinating visual metaphor for sexual disclosure. Dr. T. Jefferson Kline, of Boston University, has written cartographic analyses of *Damage*, referencing highly lateral geographic clues throughout the novel and motion picture (beginning with Hart's opening maxim, "There is a geography of the soul — we search for its outlines all our lives"[72]); taking a second to extend Kline's ideas here: the film operates on an ontological plane as well, and, in this sphere, qualifies as purely ingressive. In keeping with the abrechtianism of so many of Malle's works, depth is a critical factor on an interpretive level in *Damage*: the picture's opening shot includes a mammoth oaken staircase of cold, laquered wood in the parliamentary building, representative of the hard, cold, proper, and immutable surface of the social structures Malle and Hare are about to explore; *behind* it (again—information communicated on an ontological plane) lies an illuminated pane of stained glass (a defiantly sexual symbol), communicating to the audience that ontological tropes will be used for much of the motion picture, and that one will be forced to look beyond deceptive surfaces. Several of the subsequent scenes employ transitional scenes that take place at greater and greater depths within an interior space, juxtaposed alongside the gradually deeper and deeper revelation of truth from characters; the most telling example, cited previously, involves the first post-credit sequence in the Fleming household, when Malle evinces surface-level shadings of discomfort and unease between Stephen and Ingrid, and subsequently follows Stephen deeper into the house, landing on the close-up of Dr. Fleming, disconcerted, rife with ennui. Likewise, in a few instances of greater potency, Malle and cinematographer Peter Biziou opt to track to greater and greater depths within a set scene, *via* a tracking shot, while characters dig into their pasts. When Stephen and Anna have made love for the second time, for instance, Anna sits nude on the tossled bed—her legs extended at an angle beneath her, her bare back and shoulders to the camera—and faces Stephen, who reclines in the bed. As the camera approaches her from a distant point, a dozen or so yards off in the house (and extends deeper into the interior space), Anna reveals her adolescent trauma with Martyn. In other words, Malle is carefully establishing a highly sexual metaphor, which suggests ever so subtly that, within the onscreen spatial relationships of his film, the deeper one ventures, the closer to truth one gets. This extends itself to Stephen's lovemaking with Anna as well—as already alluded to in passing (earlier in this chapter), the lovemaking follows a predefined arc. Malle comments in his New Line Cinema interview at the end of the video release of *Damage*, "We also knew that we had to follow a certain progression [with the sex scenes], and they had to, each time, represent the emotional moment of [Stephen and Anna's] relationship."[73] Just as the ontology of the film probes greater and greater depths onscreen to metaphorically represent levels of greater truth, the love scenes make the gradual transition from clothed to nude, and there is a sense in which, as the lovemaking becoming more explicit and less inhibited, the characters reveal more about their pasts and thus become more emotionally and intellectually vulnerable to one another. Sex becomes a tool for opening up, for inner revelation.

Contextually, the sexual activity in the film acquires a distinct meaning for each of the lovers. Stephen's motivation is far more simplistic than Anna's: for Dr. Fleming, the early sexual scenes in the film are intrinsically connected to anguish—the anguish of the "mass emotional and sexual repression" described in detail earlier in this chapter. Malle comments in his New Line interview, "[The sex scenes] shouldn't be about pleasure but should be about the revelation of something incredibly powerful and sometimes almost painful." This is predominantly true for Stephen, and the pain Malle references exists predominantly at the outset of the affair; following the "progression" to which Malle alludes, one notices that by the final love scene (just *prior to* the moment when Martyn walks in on the couple not fully aware of what—or *who*—he will find on the other side of the door), Stephen has been released of (cut free from) his sociosexual repression and thus liberated to the degree that he can express eroticism freely. To reiterate: sexual activity with Anna functions as a kind liberation for Stephen, and not temporary, but permanent. Again, because the love-making with her brings Stephen in touch with his own identity, he is able to cut him-self loose from all of the collective identity that had been imposed on him. The lifestyle of the epilogue is thus liberated, as conveyed through a unique visual approach: with its emphasis on the simplistic, the beautiful, and the spare (Stephen slicing a piece of cheese, Stephen opening his window to gaze at the mountains), the aesthetic of the epilogue suggests a cross between a cinematic still life and the writings of Carlo Levi. And lonely though this lifestyle may be, is thus far superior to his previous life; the final close-up of Stephen is one of the few moments in the picture where he appears truly content and at peace, and he comments in voice-over, "I had arrived at a life of *my own*." Anna's sexual arc, on the other hand — and the context for Anna's sexual behavior — are infinitely more complex, demanding careful scrutiny.

Malle and Hare's decision to alter the "voice" of Hart's story from Stephen's highly subjective take on Anna's psychosexual history to a more objective take on it poses a grave danger to the filmmakers. In the book, Stephen reads Anna as something of a monster — a destructive force because of her calamity with Aston and her capacity for "survival." This remains yet another area where minor characters begin to support Stephen's reasoning and logic simply by virtue of the story being filtered through his subjective stream-of-consciousness: Ingrid responds, "Aston ... and now, Martyn. Oh, God, that evil girl...." In the novel, one can dismiss the narrator's explanation of Anna's psychosis as a crack-psychiatric, slightly misogynistic, and hugely biased distortion of her as a destructive creature; one can imagine that the objectification of the film might run a high risk of entering misogynistic territory, as it leaves much of the novel's "explanation" of Anna's psychosis fully intact, despite the danger that such an explanation might severely strain credibility when carried into the objective.

Nonetheless, Malle and Hare remain fully aware of this danger, and thus alter Anna's tonal quality slightly onscreen, making her more sympathetic and less of an annihilator, and building the credibility of her psychosexual arc by giving it a developmental subtext. As Malle directs and films Anna, she first appears to be a sexually stunted adolescent — one witnesses an indisputable playfulness on her face, a young girl trapped in a woman's body. Like an adolescent girl, she enjoys toying with Stephen, treating him as a plaything. She is one "terrified of possessiveness." Thus, it is somewhat ironic that, for the duration of the motion picture until Martyn's death (her key turning point), she herself remains a prisoner to the clitoral phase of sexual development. Despite her ridiculous insistence, to Stephen, "You are my lord," (a statement that ostensibly puts him in control), *she* is the one who puts the affair in motion by phoning Stephen, and the one with complete power over Stephen's body until Martyn's death, and the one who reinitiates by renting the flat and mailing Stephen the key, days after Stephen phones her and makes a sincere attempt to sever the relationship. Anna has been stunted by the guilt associated with Aston's suicide, guilt she internalized. Simone De Beauvoir writes, "The erotic experiences of the young girl are not simply an extension of her former sexual activities; very often they are unexpected and disagreeable; and they are *always* in the nature of a new event that makes a break with the past."[74] The fact that Anna's first sexual experiences (as we are told in the novel and the film) are self-imposed, a deliberate and conscious attempt to bury the guilt of Aston's suicide by approaching Peter and demanding, "Fuck me," does not necessarily mean that this attempt has proven successful. And indeed, it has not, as Anna's mother (Elizabeth Prideaux) demonstrates, when she comments on the haunting resemblance between Aston and Martyn. Instead, the trauma created a vicious cycle of guilt — guilt she sadomasochistically is forcing herself to reexperience (over and over again). De Beauvoir describes such behavior as "true" sadomasochism:

> Now, "masochism, like sadism, is the assumption of guilt. I am guilty, in fact, simply because I am object." This idea of Sartre's is in line with the Freudian conception of self-punishment. The young girl considers herself to blame for submitting her ego to others, and she punishes herself for it by voluntarily redoubling her humiliation and slavishness.[75]

To put it another way: Anna is trying desperately to work through her guilt in the *ménage a trois* with Martyn and Stephen. Anna's is one of the sexual crises to which De Beauvoir alludes when she writes, "In certain cases the crisis in is easily passed, but there are tragic instances in which the situation is resolved only by death or dementia."[76] In Anna's case, either Stephen or Martyn will become the sacrificial victim whose death enables Anna to move forward with her sexual development.

The novel, like the film, posits the dual affairs with Stephen and Martyn as integral components of the healing process for Anna — Peter Calderon[77] tells Stephen, "It's only now that [Anna] has finally said goodbye to Aston. Anna has spoken to me of your relationship with her. You were part of the healing process. You were a vital part.... But ... it is over.... At this moment in time it is over for Anna."[78] The film supports this idea visually and, unlike the book, builds tonal sympathy for Anna around it. One can compare the film's initial aesthetic and behavioral presentation of Anna (as a kind of delayed, somewhat androgynous adolescent) with its final shot of her: as she sits on the bed in her mother's apartment, and Stephen storms in to confront her, he is visibly taken aback (as are we) for she appears unrecognizable, practically a different person — radiant with femininity, devoid of malevolence, drained of ulterior motives. Gazing at Stephen quietly and sadly. Her face is soft, gentle, supple — sculpted by diffuse light. Touched by inner peace and contentment despite fleeting indications of melancholy. She appears not to recognize Stephen, and significantly, she has fully flowered into a woman. How fitting that when Stephen last glimpses Anna — when he spots her, unaware of his presence, in an airport — she is with Peter and carrying a child. She has entered the vaginal phase and has become metaphorically capable of fecundation, in the final stages of sexual maturity. Martyn's death has become, spiritually, her sacrificial *deus ex machina* for burying the trauma of Aston's suicide, that enables her to move beyond her idiosyncratic early sexual crisis into a phase of development that is more universal among women. Thus, Stephen tells us, blatantly (in voice-over): "She was no different from anyone else."[79]

CRITICAL RESPONSE

For such an accomplished film — one of the finest of Malle's English-language works—*Damage* received surprisingly terrible reviews. Philip French notes that the critics hurt Malle's feelings with their disparagement.[80] The picture drew similar castigation in the United States, where almost no one seemed to take it seriously: David Denby mocks the film's frank sexuality, writing in *New York*, "The movie has an air of ruthless and luxurious knowledge of the world, and one wants to believe that it has special erotic wisdom, yet ... none of these chiropractic extensions looks particularly ... comfortable.... Irons gives an almost comically anguished performance ... [and] the script is mute on all the obvious points of interest."[81] Even more insulting is Joanne Kaufman, reviewing for *Time*, who states, "This adaptation of the best-selling novel by Josephine Hart would play better in French with English subtitles; then and only then might the audience be lulled into believing that something is happening onscreen ... as it is, *Damage* is an anemic, muted muddle."[82] *Damage* fared slightly better in France; writing for *le Figaro*, Daniel Toscan du Plantier observes:

> A merciless portrait of a man and a woman consumed by one another, *Damage* impresses us with the mastery of its dramatic interpretation and its direction. Shot predominantly in the twilight, the film is done in the colors of a requiem, and accompanied by the magnificent music of the Polish composer Zbigniew Preisner ... all of which contributes to this story of a savage passion, to make it the most civilized work of the year.[83]

Similarly, reviewing for *Le Monde*, Danièle Heymann commends the picture: "*Damage*, which so courageously resists giving us a happy ending, shows ... the dissolution of a bourgeois family, yet again. But it has never been shown better than it is here ... in this film so lucid and so personal, despite the British 'exoticism,' this film burns like ice and is as beautiful as desire itself."[84]

In retrospect, the critical pans in Britain and the States are terribly upsetting even a decade later, for *Damage* remains one of the few intelligent commercial motion pictures to, in Hare's words, "use sex to explore character and need,"[85] (and to examine sexual politics) in lieu of relying on erotic content solely for titillation. In this respect, it joins an elitist camp that includes such masterpieces as Machaty's *Ecstasy*, Bertolucci's *Last Tango in Paris*, Kaufman's *The Unbearable Lightness of Being*, Patrice Chereau's *Intimacy*, and Catherine Breillat's *Romance*.

23
Vanya on 42nd Street — 1994
The Process of Becoming

"Be cheerful, sir. Our revels now are ended. These our actors, as I fore-told you, were all spirits and are melted into air, into thin air; and, like the baseless fabric of this vision, the cloud-capped towers, the gorgeous palaces, the solemn temples, the great globe itself, yea, all which it inherit, shall dissolve, and, like this insubstantial pageant faded, leave not a rack behind. We are such stuff as dreams are made upon, and our little life is rounded with a sleep. Sir, I am vexed. Bear with my weakness. My old brain is troubled. Be not disturbed with my infirmity. If you be pleased, retire into my cell and there repose. A turn or two I'll walk to still my beating mind."

— Prospero, Shakespeare's *Tempest*, IV.i.146–62.

BACKGROUND

Assuming a work pattern quite typical of his later years, Louis Malle juggled dual projects in 1993–4, following the U.S. and European releases of *Damage*. The ill-fated *Dietrich and Marlene*—an aborted feature, ultimately red flagged when Malle died in November 1995, weeks before it was slated to go into production —first germinated in early 1993. The *Dietrich* project began with the death of screen siren Marlene Dietrich on May 6, 1992 (at 88 years old), an event that lifted a legal ban on the publication of Dietrich's daughter Maria Riva's epic-sized, eponymously-titled biography of her mother, and thus paved the way for Malle and John Guare to plan a big-screen adaptation of Riva's book.[1] Guare recounts how Malle happened to stop by his Manhattan apartment in 1993 and find *Marlene Dietrich* open on the nightstand — the very same book he himself was reading at that moment. Taking this as an amusing omen, the two men set to work on *Dietrich and Marlene*.[2] They planned the project not only as a cinematization of Riva, but also (and somewhat unusually) as the latest stage in their progressive attempts to rework James's *What Maisie Knew* for the screen, because the classic Mallean theme of "the corrupt adult world as perceived by an innocent" runs through both books.[3] *Dietrich* encountered few (if any) major setbacks until Louis's health failed him in mid–late 1995, but it demanded an extraor-

A look of disgust passes between Larry Pine (Dr. Mikhail Astrov) and Wally Shawn (Vanya Voynitsky) in André Gregory's makeshift stage production of Uncle Vanya, mounted in a crumbling New York theater. Louis Malle shot the production; it became his final film, *Vanya on 42nd St.*

dinarily long preproduction period and an overwhelming amount of advance planning; in the meantime, another opportunity arose, one whose first rumblings were heard several years prior, in 1989.

Though André Gregory became a legend incarnate in the seventies for his revelatory theatrical work with the Manhattan Project (a legend cemented in the minds of non–New Yorkers with the release of *My Dinner with André* in late 1981 and early 1982 — see Chapter 16), and delivered a few supporting performances in features throughout the eighties (a cameo as J.J. in the Horowitz-Hiller production of *Author, Author*; the unnamed "party philosopher" in Jaglom's *Always*; John the Baptist in Scorsese's *Last Temptation of Christ*),[4] he took a 15-year sabbatical from stage direction from 1974 to 1989. Gregory reflects on this period and the reasons for his abandonment of stage direction, that came to an end with a production of *Uncle Vanya*:

> Around 1977, I felt that theater and culture as we had known it might be ended. There were strong global forces that simply were not conducive any more to an active culture, and to works of art that had depth, complexity and ambiguity. So on a certain level, I felt there was no place for me.... I work very unconsciously. And had I not given up the theater, I would never have gone on the adventures that created the basis for *My Dinner with André*. And there would never have been a *My Dinner with André*. [Also], on a personal level, when my mother died, I wasn't sure whether I had been creating because I myself wanted to, or for her.... And ... I simply needed an active rest in order to be able to go into another period of deeper maturity. I think most artists

would be well advised to do that, otherwise there's the danger you keep repeating yourself. And when I gave it up for that long amount of time, when I finally
returned to it, I returned to it with the same passion and enthusiasm I had
had as a young man.[5]

This self-imposed theatrical exile came to an end in 1989. At an excruciatingly
difficult point, when Gregory's wife Chiquita was battling breast cancer, he dealt
with the crisis by reimmersing himself in stage work. While Gregory was performing as an actor in a Shakespeare Company production of *The Tempest*, his daughter,
Marina, approached him and asked him to informally direct scenes from Chekhov's
Uncle Vanya that she and a friend wanted to rehearse. Gregory reread David Mamet's
modern adaptation of Vlada Chernomordik's *Vanya* translation and, entranced,
immediately foresaw directing an entirely new stage production of the Chekhov play;
he hoped to cast longtime friends and associates Wallace Shawn and George Gaynes
as Ivan Petrovich "Vanya" Voynitzky and Alexandr Vladimirovich Serebryakov,
respectively.[6] Gregory also approached theatrical colleagues Larry Pine to play Dr.
Mikhail Astrov and Jerry Mayer to portray Ilya Telegin.[7] Gaynes (traumatized by the
recent loss of his son) and Shawn refused to perform in a live stage production, but
conceded to do the play privately, on the grounds that no audience members attend;
Julianne Moore—who had no prior affiliation with Gregory but came to *Vanya*
through her representation—felt completely put off by the plays that had been
proffered to her recently and by the stage directors she had met, and offered the same
condition as Gaynes and Shawn for agreeing to perform as Yelena.[8]

Actress Brooke Smith (*The Silence of the Lambs, The Moderns, Mr. Wonderful*)—
Sonya in André's *Uncle Vanya* and merely 22 at the time—recalls how she and a few
others in the cast were recruited through an agent, and how everyone managed to
coordinate incongruous (and fluctuating) schedules:

> My [theatrical] agent at the time, Jeff Hunter, was ... André's agent [as well]....
> And he ... set up all these meetings where we would get together with André
> and just talk. It was great, because you didn't have to audition, you just went
> in and talked to [André] and had tea with him, and he sort of set up this lit-
> tle group, and we just started rehearsing, just to rehearse, just because we
> wanted to work on the play.... It was bizarre logistically and hard to under-
> stand even now ... but we would basically just rehearse whenever everybody
> was available.... We we were all over the map, you know? ... Julianne [Moore]
> was going off and doing movies, and George [Gaynes] had moved to Santa
> Barbara at the time ... but every time we got together we really enjoyed it. It
> was kind of like musicians, or something, getting together and rehearsing, or
> jamming ... and for the first couple of years nobody came to see it, either.... It
> was always in André's apartment, or he rented a couple of apartments.... Larry
> [Pine], and George [Gaynes], and Wally [Shawn], certainly, and Jerry Mayer,
> they all had histories, previous histories, with André, but ... Julianne and myself
> and Lynn Cohen ... we all came in ... through Jeff Hunter.[9]

Rehearsals continued intermittently for around four years, and eventually Gregory and his cast moved from André's apartment to the abandoned Victory Theater
(on 42nd Street) and conceded to let a private audience observe, comprised entirely

of famous friends and associates. A November 1994 *Vogue* article details this stage of the project:

> [*Uncle Vanya*] was staged in a long-empty, decrepit Forty-second Street theater — which didn't stop Richard Avedon, Mikhail Baryshnikov, Robert Altman, Mike Nichols, Susan Sontag, and John Guare from braving the rickety risers and even coming back for a second, and sometimes third, viewing. They came because that *Vanya* was avant-garde director turned actor André Gregory's first directorial effort in fifteen years, and ... because it starred Wallace Shawn, George Gaynes, and then-unknown Julianne Moore, and they came because it was a continual work in progress and because no tickets were sold, no ads were placed, and the audience never numbered over 25.[10]

Malle was among these guests, and felt enchanted by the production. Gregory's company eventually moved a few blocks north, resettling in the equally decrepit New Amsterdam Theater. In late 1993, the idea arose of doing a film to document the Gregory production of *Vanya*. According to Gregory:

> We [first] approached Louis [about filming the piece] when we were performing for those small invited audiences ... and he loved the [production], but he was buried in other projects.... [That was] in '89 or '90.... When we went back to him some years later, he didn't have another project ... and because he'd had open-heart surgery, he was a little fragile, so ... I think a smaller project was very tempting to him.... We approached him probably about five or six months before we actually shot ... [and he was] immediately enthusiastic.[11]

Vanya producer Fred Berner of Sony Pictures Classics (*Miss Firecracker, The Ballad of Little Jo*), who had worked with Malle as a production assistant on *Alamo Bay*, recalls the director's next step:

> [Louis] called me and said, "I have this idea for this film, and I want to discuss it with you, and show it to you," and I said, "Okay! Sure, man." If it were Louis calling, I'd do anything, I really would. He said, "Come with me, come on, we're going to the New Amsterdam Theater, I have to show you this great *place*." So he took me to a place, which was this *hellhole* of a structure, which was half demolished — ice covering the floor and crap falling out of the ceiling. And Louis said, "Isn't it *great*? Isn't it *great??!!*" He was like a child — so enthusiastic about it! I'm like, "Yeah ... yeah. But what do you want to do here? What are you thinking?" [Louis] had the vision of the film *completely* in his head. He subsequently took me to a table reading of André's *Uncle Vanya*, and then it came together for me, as well. Louis's intention was to take this very special piece of theater and place it in this vibrant and dilapidated environment thematically perfect for the text.[12]

To determine how to best visually document the piece, Malle brought a small video camera to the New Amsterdam and shot rehearsals from various angles on a daily basis. He and Berner set a cap for the budget and eventually raised $850,000; they pulled in Declan Quinn, an Irish cinematographer; working together, Quinn and Malle invented a mechanism dubbed the "Bungee Cam," a 16mm camera on a bungee cord, suspended from a crane, that gave the two men an unlimited, unprecedented degree of cinematographic mobility — the ability to break the proscenium by filming from inside of it without (miraculously) ever once interrupting the actors, a technique Berner describes as the "fishbowl effect."[13] As discussed in greater detail later in this chapter, Malle imbued his filmization of Mamet's Chekhov adaptation with a number of explicitly cinematic devices, including a voice-over monologue, "cheated" eyelines,[14] and an allegorical, symbolic use of onscreen depth. Malle reveals in an interview that he and Quinn shot the entire picture in two weeks,[15] and according to Brooke Smith, Malle and Quinn filmed the scenes of Chekhov's play sequentially.[16]

According to George Gaynes, Malle handled the prospect of splitting directorial chores with Gregory by relying on Gregory's direction of the actors and simply supervising the technical end himself. "When we got to Louis Malle, coming in and setting up his cameras," Gaynes recalls, "He didn't direct per se. He set up his shots according to André's directions."[17] Malle dissents slightly; he tells Oren Moverman in an interview that it was necessary for him to make slight directorial adjustments to a few of the performers.[18] Brooke Smith concurs with this, revealing how — for instance — Malle took her aside and asked her, quietly, to try to avoid shedding tears in her final monologue — thus keeping it more subtle and gentle.[19] Berner resolves the slight contradiction between the Gaynes observation and the Malle-Smith observation by simply asserting the fact that Gaynes's role and performance were, by their very nature, more theatrical, and thus required little if any adjustment for the cameras,[20] unlike the performances of the other actors.

Billard records that production began on May 5, 1994, and wrapped on May 20, 1994.[21] *Vanya on 42nd Street*, as the finished film was titled, reached American screens on October 19, 1994, and debuted in France on January 25, 1995.[22] *Vanya* made its first bows exactly one year prior to Malle's death from lymphoma, and would thus become his final cinematic effort.

SYNOPSIS

Around dusk one summer evening amid the porno theaters, hot dog stands, convenience stores, and lingerie shops of New York City's Forty-Second Street, a number of seasoned stage and screen actors — George Gaynes, Julianne Moore, Wally Shawn, Brooke Smith, Larry Pine, and Lynn Cohen — approach the doors of the ruined and dilapidated old New Amsterdam Playhouse, along with stage director André Gregory. Gaynes appears, dignified and stoic, clad in a fedora and trenchcoat with his hands tucked into his pockets; Pine saunters up to the theater, sizing up the body of a svelte young woman who passes him on the street; Moore and Smith chitchat as they cross the pavement side by side, and Moore pulls Smith out of the path of a fire engine that nearly runs her down; André stares straight ahead and dangles a string of good luck beads from one hand as he walks down the street, Pine and Cohen hurry up from behind André and grasp his shoulders warmly. Shawn leans lazily against the side of the theater, munching on a knish and staring vapidly into the distance, when Gregory walks up, greets him, and takes a piece off of the delicacy without asking, sampling it for himself and marveling at the taste. Mrs. Chao (Madhur Jaffrey) appears and greets André and Wally with her friend Flip Innunu (Oren Moverman), and Wally explains to André that she is a visitor (Gregory applauds her interest and tells her he loves to have people come to watch); Wally informs André that Chao's grandfather translated Chekhov into Bengali "quite a long time ago."

The cast enters the New Amsterdam foyer and bumps into Phoebe Brand, another actress from the play, who introduces André to a third visitor, her cousin's niece Tucker from Toledo. While Gaynes and others sample food from the craft table, André throws his arm around Larry, who complains about his fear of "losing it"; as the two men stroll into the auditorium Gregory laughs and admits, "Larry, you've been losing it for twenty-five years." Jerry Mayer, the eighth *Vanya* actor to appear, sits on the stage cradling a guitar and smoking a stogie, and greets André as he enters. Wally tours the theater with Mrs. Chao and Flip, and rhapsodizes about the building's history — specifically its having been a home to the Ziegfeld Follies; he points out the old wooden facial carvings once used for Shakespearean productions. Shawn bemoans his exhaustion and makes his way up to the stage; Brooke Smith speaks to André of her concern about her performance in the first act — that it feels "very uncomfortable." André assures her, "It's supposed to feel uncomfortable. That's the point."

The performance of *Vanya* begins unannounced, with the actors in modern clothes—*sans* scenery, performed in the orchestra section as the stage itself is in ruins and the ropes have been eaten by rats. While Gregory, Tucker, Mrs. Chao, and Flip gather in the audience, Wally Shawn slips quietly into the role of the lethargic, resentful Uncle Vanya, who lies on a bench and feigns sleep while Phoebe Brand — playing Marina — and Larry Pine — playing Dr. Mikhail Astrov — sit and chitchat at a table. Within the production, Brooke Smith becomes Sonya, Julianne Moore portrays Yelena, George Gaynes is Serebryakov, Jerry Mayer plays Ilya Ilyich Telegin, and Lynn Cohen is Mariya Vasilyevna, Vanya's mother.

The basic story of the production-within-the-production follows Chekhov's original narrative. On a rural estate in turn-of-the-century Russia, Dr. Mikhail Astrov, a practicing physician and consummate environmentalist, has come to treat the 80-year-old, retired, widowed professor Alexandr Vladimirovich Serebryakov, who now keeps odd hours, working exhaustively into the night, while constantly prating about his rheumatism and gout and bemoaning his age. Serebryakov's middle aged former brother-in-law, Vanya Voynitzky, laments the degree to which he has wasted his life in academic devotion to Alexandr, his attitude much to the consternation of his mother, Mariya Vasilevna Voynitzky, who cares only for reading the scientific theories in the pamphlets she receives. There are indications that Vanya's resentment can be traced to his having fallen in love with the professor's second wife, the gorgeous 27-year-old Yelena Andreyevna, for he sees her as the incarnation of the life, luster, and youth he has squandered. Flattered on the surface but also too disgusted to return his affections (and far too faithful to her husband to ponder an infidelity) Yelena rebuffs all of Vanya's advances. Meanwhile, Sonya Alexandrovna,

Serebryakov's daughter, pines for the love of Dr. Astrov. The resentment and hostility that have cropped up between Sonya and Yelena dissolve when the two women make a truce and instantly become close friends; Yelena learns of Sonya's feelings for Astrov and agrees to chitchat with the medic privately to determine if he returns the girl's affections. In a voice-over connoting internal monologue, Yelena acknowledges her certainty that the man will not reciprocate, but she keeps her promise to confer with him, despite her private knowledge that he makes daily visits to the house only because of his romantic and sexual attraction to herself; indeed, when Yelena approaches Astrov about Sonya, he confesses his belief that Yelena is only making a cunning attempt to determine the nature of his feelings for her; Astrov makes a pass at her, grabbing her body and smothering her with kisses as Vanya saunters in. Horrified, but not entirely disinterested, Yelena frees herself from Astrov's grasp and demands that he leave the estate. Just as Sonya learns from Yelena of Astrov's irreciprocation, Serebryakov calls a meeting and informs everyone of his decision to sell the estate and buy a cottage in Finland; this infuriates Vanya, who excoriates the shocked professor in front of everyone (blasting him as a "philistine, a fraud, a swine"), and ultimately returns with a gun; he fires at the professor and misses, and the two men eventually reconcile offstage. In the fourth act, Yelena and Serebryakov prepare to abandon the estate and build a new life in Kharkov; Vanya filches a vial of morphia from Dr. Astrov in an unsuccessful suicide bid (as Ilya has hidden his revolver in the root cellar). Astrov informs Sonya of her uncle's theft and demands the vial back; Vanya ultimately complies. Astrov and Yelena exchange kisses and goodbyes. After the professor and his wife leave in a carriage, the inhabitants of the house and grounds assemble on one side of a long table. Astrov promises to return in the spring and leaves the estate. As Marina knits, and Sonya and Vanya begin to work out the accounts of the estate, Sonya delivers a monologue in which she predicts the grace, rest, and radiant beauty God will lavish on herself and her uncle when their toil on Earth comes to an end.

The four acts of the play are broken by a single, quick intermission between the second and third act, where the cast members mingle in the foyer and help themselves to food from the craft table; for the second act, set in the dining room of Serebryakov's estate at night, André and his fellow spectators sit at the table opposite the players. At each act break, Gregory sets the scene for Mrs. Chao and the others by informing them of the time and room of the estate where the forthcoming scenes will unfold.

ANALYSIS

As Louis Malle's swan song, *Vanya on 42nd Street* defies categorization. The film can be read as the cinematic equivalent of *Finnegans Wake*: a motion picture that seamlessly blends stage and narrative film in the spirit of Joyce's attempt to cross-pollinate poetry and fictional prose, thus creating an acategorical *métisse*. This interpretation is accurate in the broadest sense, with two significant qualifications. First, Malle builds his film on a theatrical foundation established by André Gregory, who, in his stage work, reduced the physical distance between the performers and the audience and thereby heightened dramatic intimacy and elicited performances more nuanced (and less histrionic) than those traditionally found on the stage. George Gaynes recalls of Gregory's *Vanya*:

> We invited [a maximum of thirty people who knew about it], and they would sit actually on the stage with us ... in chairs around the central part of the stage where the action took place. And in fact, I was next to somebody who was in the audience, most of the time! ... It had the effect on the acting to make it cinematic from the start. In other words, there was no what you might call *projection*—a word I dislike and most actors do. But no intention to have the action reach beyond the few feet around us! In other words, in the same way one might do it in a living room, or in film.[23]

In sum, the foundational chasm between theater and cinema that Malle bridges with the motion picture is not quite as broad as one might initially infer. Gregory asserts that "there was almost no gap" between the subtlety of traditional cinematic performances and the subtlety of performance in his unique brand of stage work.[24]

Second, *Vanya*'s accomplishments elevate it above the level of a sophomoric cinematic-theatrical hybrid. The motion picture constitutes a postmodern fusion of: reconstituted Jacobean theater (and an exhumation of the philosophical mannerism behind it); late Chekhovian modernism; and—most significantly—faux cinema direct (of the *Dinner with André* mold) with which Malle and cinematographer Declan Quinn give shape and voice to the aforementioned modes of thought. *Vanya* also investigates the ontology of performance and the illusion that is the theater.

In staging *Uncle Vanya*, André Gregory undertook a sustained process of theatrical reconstruction, attempting to reestablish the conditions of seventeenth century (British) Jacobean private theater[25] in late twentieth century Manhattan. He thus set up the clandestine trappings in which the original Jacobean private plays were staged (i.e., mounting *Uncle Vanya* in New York's Victory Theater an unannounced, unpublicized, "hidden" endeavor) and restricted attendance to an invitation-only audience. This bears striking similarities to the conditions in seventeenth century Jacobean productions. Historian Keith Sturgess writes:

> The [Jacobean] private playhouses hived off the more aristocratic patrons and created a coterie theatre for those able and inclined to pay more, leaving the public houses, like the Fortune and Red Bull, to provide popular theatre for a "down-market" clientele ... the boys ... attracted not only a commercially viable audience but most of the ambitious, young playwrights of the turn of the century: Jonson, Marston, Chapman, Beaumont, and Middleton.[26]

One could just as easily substitute "late twentieth century" for "turn of the century" and "Altman, Nichols, Guare, Malle and Sontag" for "Jonson, Marston, Chapman, Beaumont and Middleton"—the performance conditions are nearly identical.[27] The actual staging of Gregory's *Vanya* can be characterized as highly Jacobean as well, for Gregory eschewed all costumes, sets, and background action, and used as his source material not the Hingley Oxford translation of Anton Pavlovich Chekhov's *Uncle*

Vanya, but David Mamet's modernized 1988 adaptation of Vlada Chernomordik's literal translation; Mamet strips the Chekhov play to its barest essences, and Robert Brustein describes the Mametian adaptation as "An act of deconstruction designed to exhume the living energies of Chekhov's writing from under the heavy weight of 'masterpiece topsoil.'"[28] The overall effect was a stage production that focused entirely on performance, characterization, character motivations, character arcs, and dramatic conflict, to the exclusion of all extraneous elements—scenery and costumes had no place in this environment. Note the extent to which this mirrors descriptions of the seventeenth century stagings of Jacobean private theater, which, in Sturgess's words, "was an actor's and playwright's theatre, not a scene-painter's ... the plays and actors of the pre–Restoration ... were ... superior ... because "they could support themselves merely from their own merit—the weight ... matter and goodness of the action—without scenes and machines."[29]

Although Gregory's *Vanya* can ostensibly be regarded as a finished work, there is a sense in which Malle's production elevates it to the next level. Gregory's careful reestablishment of the conditions of seventeenth century private theater in a contemporary setting helps define Malle's role, for the director does not merely observe and film as a documentarian, but brings to the surface twin philosophies that lay at the foundations of the Gregory production, by defining and implementing the cinematic voice that best evokes those philosophical subtexts. The first philosophy in question is seventeenth century mannerism, the forerunner of twentieth century modernism and the ideological foundation of the Jacobean trappings of Gregory's production. Sturgess writes, "'Mannerist' ... is an epitome of the matrix of ideas, intuitions and aesthetic judgments prevailing in educated circles in Jacobean London which provided the intellectual climate in which the private theatre flourished."[30] Sturgess goes on to define mannerism stylistically as follows: "[it emphasizes] the artist's personal, often agonized, perception of reality and ... ignores or deconstructs conventional images of external nature."[31] The second ideological touchstone of Gregory's production involves the twentieth century modernism exuded by the *Uncle Vanya* play itself. According to scholar Ronald Hingley, Chekhov wrote *Uncle Vanya* just prior to *The Seagull*, at a point when he sought to move away from conventional drama, multiplying his number of characterizations and arcs per play—proof positive that *Vanya*, on its own (with no stylistic interpretation) constitutes a quintessential piece of early modernist theater,[32,33] for the multiple characterizations and arcs suggest a reality that is fractured into numerous perspectives. Because both modes of thought, then, share an emphasis on broken objective reality—on the distortion of reality through multiple subjective perceptions—Malle found in preplanned cinema direct a mode of expression that exhumes and gives a nearly perfect stylistic voice to the mannerism and modernism.

Gregory's theater may well have been unconventional, but the one element it did not attempt to eliminate was the kind of rudimentary theatrical multiplicativeness that enables a spectator to focus wherever (and on whatever) he or she wishes within the proscenium—to any actor's face and to any particular isolated gesture. Within the cinematic framework, Malle takes as his raw material this multiplicity of options afforded the theatrical viewer, and imposes on it a kind of rigid subjectivity, thereby severely confining each viewer's focus to a set course. More specifically, the director traps the viewer in his own perspective by his pervasive use of selectively chosen shots that filter the objective reality of the theatrical experience through his personal series of choces, and consistently refuses to cut to one objective master shot for any substantial length of time. Thus, George Gaynes remembers:

> It was left entirely to Louis to set up the shots and ... when we — the actors — first saw the completed film, we were taken aback sometimes because certain shots, certain editings we were not familiar with [would be cut in].... In other words, from constantly seeing the play as a whole, and picking our own shots for our own choice of where we would concentrate our looks and ears ... we got someone else's choice.[34]

Again: cinema direct helps Malle sustain the illusion that we are experiencing selective fragments of unfolding action alone, internalizing it, and having a highly private, highly subjective experience, and thus visualizes the concept of mannerist and modernist "broken reality." Similarly, by breaking the fourth wall with the "BungeeCam" and creating a kind of internal fishbowl effect by shooting inside of the proscenium — and via the occasional and highly deliberate shakiness of the camera on the bungee cord affixed to the crane — the director is also able to sustain the onscreen illusion (the same illusion suspended in *My Dinner with André* but via a unique set of cinematographic techniques in each film) that we are in the frame with the actors, an invisible participant in the drama.

Yet, despite these impositions, Malle inadvertently creates an unresolvable yet marvelous paradox in *Vanya*: though, as noted, the viewer essentially becomes a prisoner subject to the director's whims in editing and shot choices, Malle and Gregory, after conferring,[35] opted to strip the cinematic adaptation of any accoutrements, and to continue working from the Mamet adaptation — so that the finished picture would emphasize characterization, character arcs, and intra-character conflict to the exclusion of everything else. This emphasis is supported both by Malle's use of incredibly detailed, emotive close-ups and the Gregory-directed performances of subtle and layered nuance, and both elements are so overwhelmingly powerful that the viewer will instinctively make psychological "leaps" out of his or her own perspective and share the successive perspectives and feel the interrelationships of the many characters in the ensemble cast of the production who take the frame, so that a highly modernistic objective reality is defined as encompassing a collective array of subjectives.

Because Malle planned *Vanya on 42nd Street* as a faux (preplanned and pre-strategized) documentary of the real-life actors rehearsing the production, the tonal process of spectator-character substitution (or the "process of becoming") applies, as well, to the relationships between the viewer and each of the real-life actors as they appear onscreen. Thus, a number of important tonal events occur in *Vanya*'s prologue: first, Malle immediately paints the warmth between the characters— Julianne Moore and Brooke Smith walk shoulder-to-shoulder, buddy-buddy, as two girlfriends, and cross the street together; Larry Pine and Lynn Cohen slip up behind André Gregory and grip his back and shoulders, as all three share a chuckle; and (though it employs an overtone highly distinct from the other beats) André strolls up to Wally, so intrinsically comfortable around his old protégé that he snatches a bite of Wally's knish without so much as asking. The overarching comfort, joviality, and familiarity among all of the collaborators paints the impression of age-old friends; by including "Mrs. Chao," "Flip Innunu," and "Tucker from Toledo" (fictional characters largely unknown by members of the cast), and having Gregory reassure them, "Oh, no problem, I *love* to have people come and visit. Actually, you're coming on a great day, because we're going to run through the entire play," Malle—in an ingenious stunt—establishes a series of tonal substitutes for the otherwise-alienated viewer, enabling us to "plug ourselves" into the shoes of these new spectators and to feel ourselves personally welcomed by Gregory.

The audience's initial feelings of affability toward the actors are completely preserved toward the Chekhovian characters when the actors slip into their alter egos, as Malle implies ever so subtly that the performers and the characters are interchangeable. Brooke Smith reveals in an interview, "I remember getting this ... these three typed pages that Wally had typed up, of... [pause] you know, just explaining how we arrive at the theater."[36] None of the arrivals were unplanned—all suggest, strategically and nonchalantly, that each actor is an extension of his or her character. Ergo, within the play, Julianne Moore and Brooke Smith become the "instant best friends" Yelena and Sonya; Larry Pine becomes Dr. Mikhail Astrov, who makes *outré* advances to Yelena, grabbing her body and smothering her with (not entirely irreciprocal) kisses; and George Gaynes, who appears completely alone in the prologue, walking down the street slightly coldly and properly, back straight, fedora on his head and hands in his trenchcoat, becomes the ever-stoic and refined Professor Serebryakov in the play. This has several significant aftereffects. The seamlessness of actor-character transitions (or, more broadly, real life-stage transitions) not only makes a metaphoric comment on the extent to which a character can (should) become an extension of a gifted actor's inner self and inner life (another aspect of the process of becoming), but enables Malle to build correlative overtones between the unbrokenness and warmth that have developed between the actors offstage, and the broken (and ever-challenged) interrelationships of Chekhov's characters—the mistrust, duplicity and resentment that are sustained by the actors' relationships. One can draw a correlation, for example, between the incredible vulnerability of the (staged) conversation that transpires between André and Brooke Smith just prior to the production: (Brooke: "I'm concerned about what I'm doing in the first act." André: "How does it feel?" Brooke: "Just ... very ... uncomfortable." André [laughing]: "That's the whole point!" [Brooke rests her forehead on his affectionately]) and the tumult and heartbreak undergone by Sonya. In this and other similar instances, our impression is that, as Danny Peary writes about another film—"Only [actors] who ... really ... love ... and trust one another would dare play such emotionally devastating sequences."[37] And not only actors who love and trust *one another*, but who love and trust their direct*ors*. Indeed, as referenced in the introduction to this text, countless interviewees for this book have characterized Malle's directing environment as "safe," and the comments made by a number of the actors who reflect on their experiences acting for André in *Vanya* suggest a similar kind of emotional safety

net that Gregory builds—a safety net that allows one to take risks and explore character, allotting an "ultimate freedom,"[38] without fear of castigation.

The careful tonal control that Malle exercises in *Vanya* provides a key insight
into why—although Malle chose cinema direct—he relies on faux, preplanned
cinema direct, to merely create an illusion of a fluid play from carefully-assembled
takes, as in *My Dinner with André*: the spontaneity of the cinema direct used on, say,
Phantom India and *God's Country* would hamper and obstruct Malle and Declan
Quinn's ability to define the intra-character relationships cinematographically.
Instead, by using prearranged shots and subtly manipulative devices, the director is
able to heighten the contours of the intra-character relationships cinematically, alternately suggesting alienation and warmth between the characters depending on the
situation at hand. For example, the most understated device involves Malle's employment of spatial contrast to detail the alienation between Vanya and Yelena in Act II,
a scene that bleeds into the rejected Vanya's devastating monologue. As the under-
tones that lie just beneath the surface of the scene involve unrequited love between
Vanya and Yelena, Malle and editor Nancy Baker employ wickedly subtle and clever
editing to cut together two uniquely blocked takes: in the take filmed from over
Vanya's shoulder, facing Yelena, Yelena sits several feet away from her suitor. She
appears spatially unattainable *relative to* Vanya's position in the frame when Malle
films him from over her shoulder, for, in the latter take, Vanya sits so close to Yelena
that his intrusiveness is suffocating to Yelena and to the audience. The contrast
thus functions as a cinematographically allegorical commentary on irreciprocal
affection.

The picture's most explicitly cinematic technique involves the director's decision to reslate Yelena's soliloquy (near the outset of Act III) as an internal monologue, communicated with Julianne Moore's voice-over narration on the soundtrack,
in *lieu* of merely having Moore speak her lines aloud. Fred Berner reflects on the director's motivation behind this element:

> André's approach to things was just to continue to plumb for the truths of
> how those people were feeling at every moment; Louis was there to adjust
> those truths so that they would manifest in a way that he could capture them
> on film. He would adjust them, tweak them, so that they could be articulated
> in a way that he could capture them visually. One example—and it's a beau-
> tiful example—is the monologue that Julianne Moore gives in the third act.
> Louis's idea there, in order to be cinematic, was to make it an internal mono-
> logue. Because he felt that her still alabaster face could tell a better story at
> that particular moment of the script than it would to have her speak the words
> on camera. Louis employed such subtle cinematic techniques which elevated
> *Vanya* to the cinematic level, while maintaining a total respect both for the
> performers and for the written word.[39]

Advancing this idea by a step, another result of allowing Moore's face to tell the story
is simply that it imparts Malle with the ability to show cinematic viewers how to read
an actor's face absent dialogue, an attained insight one carries into the film's successive scenes. The film thus dissects (provides a lens into) the constituent elements of
theatrical performance *per se*.

According to Fred Berner, Malle relies on another technique that is nearly invisible onscreen, which he terms "cheated eyelines":

> [Louis] also [cheated the] "eye line," which connected the actors in a profound way.... In complementary or opposing close-ups, when one actor was acting opposite another actor, Louis would sometimes, to de-emphasize the theatrical nature of it, ask the actors to cheat their eyelines in a direction that was closer to the camera and to one another, which would allow him in the cutting to create a more intimate interaction between the two characters. In other words, instead of just playing the scene straight out to the house, if it were a scene with two people sitting next to one another, he would ask that they relate to each other in a slightly more naturalistic construct, so that when they were isolated in their singles, in their close-ups, the intimacy of the scene could be maintained by connecting their eyelines more directly.... Cheating their looks, by [turning] the camera and asking them to somehow look over in a slightly different direction, in effect what Louis achieved was a more intimate interchange which maintained the integrity of the relationships of the people and kept it from being too theatrical.[40]

In general, Malle's cinematographic strategies in *Vanya*—and his directorial function *per se*—can be thought of not merely as the shot selection referenced by Gaynes, but as a kind of identification of the emotional geography and topography of the Chekhovian subtext as interpreted by Gregory and his ensemble, and the process of tracing the dramatic contours and emotional fluctuations of the scenes—giving them shape and definition—with his camera. In other words, Malle uses the camera as a kind of emotional seismograph. Ergo, the director's utilitarian reliance on close-ups and full shots in *Vanya* mirrors the respective functions of the same shot types in *My Dinner with André*: when Malle seeks to emphasize a particularly emotional or intimate moment, for instance, he typically cuts to a close-up; at the other extreme, he occasionally dwarfs the characters in full-shot to underscore their insignificance; the preponderance of shots in the film lie in-between these two extremes yet exist on the same functional spectrum. One of the most vivid and potent illustrations falls in Act Four, in a solemn exchange between Marina (a.k.a. Nanny) and Ilya Ilych (a.k.a. Waffles), who sit in Vanya's room knitting; the two figures appear in longshot, completely inconsequential and purposeless; a few seconds later, Marina smiles broadly and asserts, "We'll live again. As we used to. I know we will!" and Malle cuts to a close-up and her face overtakes the screen. It is a moment of humanistic triumph—Nanny's stubborn refutation of a world that has thrust unimportance and triviality onto her shoulders. The shot and the line—when coupled—suggest that she will reign supreme in her humanity; with her indomitable spirit, not a force in the world can stop her.

In general, *Vanya* establishes running commentary on the illusion of the theater (and of cinema) *per se*. As in *My Dinner with André*, the brilliance of the Chekhovian dialogue and the performances render it nearly impossible to escape from being pulled into the psychic reality of the characters, a pull so overwhelming that one may find it impossible to extricate oneself from the dramatic situations on stage. It is unaccidental that Malle has Gregory appear infrequently throughout the film; his appearances are strategically placed, to quite literally provide Brechtian interruptions of the dramatic fabric that remind us of how illusory the onscreen world is that we have hypnotically been sucked into, slicing through the reality of the atmosphere visually. In the most vivid example, seconds after Sonya's haunting final monologue and just as the credits begin to roll, Gregory slips out of the darkness and into the well-lit foreground with the rest of the cast behind him, and we are reminded that a number of hands have been pulling the strings behind the darkened backdrop that has been laid out before us for two hours.

CRITICAL RESPONSE

Vanya on 42nd Street received almost unanimously enthusiastic reviews. Outside of a pan in *Variety* by Todd McCarthy — who brushes the picture aside with, "What may well have been mesmerizing in live performance becomes increasingly claustrophobic and ... exasperating on the stage,"[41] every major critic in the United States, Britain, and France hailed the film as a small masterpiece. Writing for *New York*, James Kaplan comments, "This is old-fashioned acting in the best sense ... Malle's intense, inquisitive camera puts *Vanya on 42nd Street* in a sublime no man's land between theater and film."[42] In *Sight and Sound*, Philip Strick writes, "Malle is consistent to what he has been able to bring to the play as a filmmaker ... it is a drama in which the characters learn to *look* at each other. Closely watched in turn by an unfidgeting camera, they gaze among themselves ... with a remarkable hunger ... [and] an intensity that would surely be lost in conventional theater."[43] And the reception was no less celebratory in France, where Claude Baignères proclaims the film for an intensity and a vividness unseen outside of the troupes of theatrical guru Peter Brook; he found the actors' interpretations miraculous.[44] Likewise, in *Le Point*, Michel Pascal lauds the picture as strange and beautiful, made by a humanist director who never ceases to charm, captivate, and move his audiences.[45]

24

Vive le tour (Twist encore)— 1962 / *Bons Baisers de Bangkok* (Love and Kisses from Bangkok)— 1964 / "William Wilson" (from *Histoires extraordinaires*)—1969

Brief Encounters: Three Malle Shorts[1]

"[Mirrors] are there when we are and yet they never give anything
back to us but our own image. Never, never shall we know what they are
when they are alone, or what is behind them."
— Erich Maria Remarque, *The Black Obelisk*

Vive le tour (1962)[2]

BACKGROUND

Fittingly, *Vive le tour* (a.k.a. *Twist encore*) postdates Malle's dreadful *Vie privée*
experience by only a few months. In early summer 1962, the filmmaker needed badly
to venture as far as possible from the big studio commercialism of *privée*, which left
a nasty taste in his mouth. He foresaw no better alternative than to plan and produce a nonfiction short, shooting most of the footage himself, feet-on-the-ground,
hands-on-the-camera.[3] Topically, it seemed a natural course for Malle to zero in on
the annual Tour de France, as it upholds and immortalizes cycling, his second great
lifelong passion.[4,5] Exhausted with the grave tone of *privée*, Malle naturally and
instinctively planned and shot *Vive le tour* as a quick, joyous, feel-good romp, filmed
in bright rotogravure colors with a bouncy Georges Delerue klezmer score.[6]

Synopsis

For several days in July of 1962, Louis Malle, Ghislain Cloquet, and Jacques Ertaud visit and film the annual Tour de France bicycle race, where they focus on a number of details including the cyclists' theft of food from local shops, mild and severe injuries, exhaustion, and receipt of awards.

Analysis

By virtue of its intentions, *Vive le tour* stands nearly alone among sports documentaries. Malle eschews a glimpse of the Tour de France as a competitive sport; he also carefully neglects to mention any of the major competitors' names and shies away from a visual study of the cyclists' strategies (unlike Bud Greenspan's 1986 epic *Sixteen Days of Glory*), and avoids treating the Tour as an aesthetic phenomenon (unlike Riefenstahl's 1936 *Olympia*). Intertextually, *Tour* comes slightly closer to Kon Ichikawa's *Tokyo Olympiad* (1966) or Steve James's *Hoop Dreams* (1994) from the standpoint of sociological observation, but the broad and grave concerns addressed by those films would be out-of-place and ill-advised in a film of *Tour*'s small scale and would risk violating the lyrical mood and tone Malle achieves. His concerns are lighter, simpler: he focuses almost exclusively on weaving together an impressionistic tapestry of sensationalistic images and details—material that shocks, astonishes, and inspires.[7]

Working within these boundaries, Malle and editor Suzanne Baron interweave a series of slight tonal variations to maintain audience interest: the offbeat (riders lifting food and drink from local cafés), the horrifying (severe injuries, collapses, falls), the awe-inspiring (an energy-drenched cyclist who fights exhaustion to "help his leader," so determined that he returns to the race after blacking out, and ultimately collapses by the side of the road), the lightly comic (riders cycling side by side and sharing a Fudgesicle) and the darkly comic (the ill cyclist forced to stop because he "ate fish that was not fresh the night before.") Malle frames all of this material within the reasonable assumption that many American and British viewers suffer from complete or partial ignorance of the Tour de France, and guides his viewers through this all-inclusive French subculture as if addressing an audience of strangers. The body of the film thus continually reminds each viewer ever so subtly of his or her own "foreign eye": Malle laces the opening scenes with rudimentary detail (time of year, length of race, geographical coverage of the Tour), and points a telling finger at the audience's unfamiliarity by throwing images onto the screen so inexplicable that they recall the more surrealistic work of Lindsay Anderson: the Harryhausen-like (yet static) figurehead of Apollo, perched atop a van; a bizarre, foam-core giraffe with a mobile head; an eccentric hot dog wagon. He is forcing the audience to accept their own need for explanation, to such a degree that each viewer becomes completely, consciously reliant on the director-narrator for understanding. Utilizing the opposite approach of *Bons Baisers*, Malle's voice-over carefully explains the significance of every shot following the initial surrealistic ambiguity, but the details and images are so sensationalistic that the emphasis repeatedly falls on the chasm between viewer ignorance and viewer cognizance, and the cinematographic perspective *per se* becomes a symbol of the "tourist experience." For example, we encounter an unexpectedly bloody sequence when a rider falls to the ground and fractures his skull, and begins moaning (as his head is wrapped in bandages), "Put something on my head, my head is cold." Few viewers unfamiliar with the Tour could anticipate such a heart-wrenching turn of events, could guess that the race often reaches this traumatic level, or could avoid the feelings of shock and horror Malle deliberately achieves with the sequence — so intense that each viewer becomes aware of his or her own transition from ignorance to cognizance.

The injury scene demonstrates that Malle interpolates significant emotional variations into the film, periodically diverging dramatically from the film's lighthearted and fun overtones. The director consistently tailors his gentle modulation of the film's emotional current to the contours of the onscreen events by incorporating small shifts in the mood and tone of his narration, and in Georges Delerue's klezmer score, appropriate to each scene. Initially joyous and exuberant (underscoring Malle's assertion that the Tour "travels from town to town *like a circus*"), Malle and editor Suzanne Baron pair musical variations with their onscreen visual equivalents so effectively that such shifts may pass by unnoticed on hyperinstinctive levels. The sequence of the exhausted cyclist (which provides the most harrowing moments in the film) constitutes an excellent example: Malle and Delerue protract the notes of the klezmer music, and it slows to a crawl with the man's waning energy.

Vive le tour also perpetuates Malle's exercises and experiments in multidimensional minimalist reduction, used so effectively in *Le Feu follet*. From the first frame, Malle erects and maintains two basic "reality frameworks," each represented by a unique visual perspective: the inner perspective of the cyclists (or subjective camera) and the outer, external perspective of an omnipresent bystander (or objective camera). The film opens with the lengthy establishment of the inner perspective, via one of Malle's signature abrechtian tracking shots: a fantastic image of a continually unfolding European street, presumably shot from the head of a bicycle.[8] This subjective framework emerges, periodically, throughout the first few minutes — intercut with returns to the external, "third person perspective" — yet Malle relies less and less heavily on subjective shots from the perspective of the cyclists, until the inner perspective vanishes entirely. Kinesthesia connects the two frames-of-reference associatively (as both perspectives rest on a constantly roving camera) and as in *Le Feu follet*, the director induces viewers to read the intimate kinesthetic knowledge of the "subjective" into the third-person images of the riders, thus creating a transdimensional *über*-perspective and bridging the two frameworks in the viewer's mind. Key to this multi-dimensionality is Malle's complete (or nearly complete) omission of himself and his two cinematographers (Ghislain Cloquet, Jacques Ertaud) from every frame; after the first few transitions into and out of the subjective, Malle, Cloquet, and Ertaud begin utilizing third-person shots taken from an astonishing number of perspectives — thus achieving an incredible fluidity and suspending the illusion of cinematographic omnipresence in the viewer's mind. The fact that the audience never once knows (and can easily be lulled into failing to consider) how the three cinematographers realized such shots is exactly the point — Malle, once again, is expanding the dimensionality of his film, and realizes that any appearance or indication of the cinematographers' presence could completely destroy whatever illusions of reality and cinematographic omnipresence he is heightening.[9]

Bons Baisers de Bangkok (1964)[10]
(Love and Kisses from Bangkok)

BACKGROUND

Bons Baisers de Bangkok (Love and Kisses from Bangkok) began to evolve two years after *Tour*, when Malle — having just finished *The Fire Within* and still preparing the script for *Viva Maria* with Jean-Claude Carrière — took a quick sojourn from feature filmmaking and returned to documentary work. Disturbed by the early stages of U.S. involvement in Vietnam, the writer-director approached the infamous French journalist Pierre Lazareff— then the executive producer of the French newsmagazine *Cinq Colonnes à la une*— and offered to do a piece on American military escalation in southeast Asia. Lazareff agreed to the project, yet Malle withdrew from Vietnam after a frustrating week of being swamped by competing reporters. The restless filmmaker decided instead to explore the placid, neighboring country of Thailand with his cameras.[11]

SYNOPSIS

In 1964, Louis Malle and a small film crew visit Bangkok, Thailand and offer a glimpse into various elements of Thai culture, including a floating market, dockworkers, Chinese pharmacies, astrological practices, and transsexual prostitution.

ANALYSIS

Vive le tour and *Bons Baisers de Bangkok* are sister films that both investigate the process by which a foreign traveler or spectator attains cultural understanding. Yet the documentaries rest on wholly different (though complimentary) theses, and thus, visually and aurally, approach their subjects in unique ways. If *Tour* reminds the audience of their intellectual dependence on the director-narrator for understanding in the face of an unfamiliar French subculture, yet promotes and heightens cultural discovery (Malle believing that it is possible for a *western* viewer to grasp the logistics of a *western* European subculture such as the Tour de France, with only slight narrative clarification) *Baisers* is an essay on cultural alienation, where Malle comments gravely on the "east-west schism": the futility of the American or European-born viewer's attempts to understand an eastern culture fully, and — vice-versa—the intellectual, moral, spiritual, and cultural alienation of the indigenous Thai people from American and European filmmakers, visitors, and tourists. If *Tour* makes a metonymical visual transition from scene-to-scene—a gradual segue into closer and closer detail of the cyclists that reveals their contorted bodies, furrowed brows, and the beads of sweat clinging to their faces, until empathy suffuses the frame and the audience aches with exhaustion—*Baisers* holds the viewer at a lengthy, awkward distance, Malle evoking the idea of cultural alienation with an overwhelmingly grainy, patchy, black-and-white aesthetic; oversimplified narration that fails to explain or clarify; visual ambiguity; and inexplicable, extraneous, hauntingly dissonant sounds.

Bons Baisers works on two metaphoric levels. On a primary level, the concept of the surface-level "ambiguous image" *per se* (unaccompanied by explanatory narration) becomes a sociological metaphor for the deeper, more philosophical, and abstract level of interpretive ambiguity, suggesting that an individual cannot fully grasp a culture without being an indigenous part of that culture from birth—just as Malle reasoned during the production of *Phantom India* that he, as a westerner, could never fully become Indian (and thus, gain an intimate understanding of Indian society). As Malle repeatedly reminds us, this is the central, intrinsic handicap of cinema direct method, and of documentary filmmaking *per se*. Indeed, the entire film itself is a commentary on the limitations of this form of expression. On a secondary level, Malle quite deliberately uses the presence of the cameraperson as a metaphor for the presence of an acinematic western tourist, reinforced by the subjects' pointed, awkward stares into the camera lens. This brings us back to the dubious ethos of taking a camera into a foreign culture, which will inevitably remind the subjects that they are strange, unusual, or curious enough to *be* filmed, and provides yet another intentional reflection on the difficulty of being plunged into a foreign culture for the cameramen and the audience.

The inclusion of Malle's offbeat comic voice in *Bons Baisers* represents the film's most successful and accessible element. From the first sequence—with the tiny boy attempting to mount a giant bicycle—to a shot of an entire group of men pouring blood, sweat and tears into an attempt to push a jeep over a muddy ditch, a task eventually facilitated by a small boy (!), Malle never loses his sense of the absurd. Yet unlike Buñuel's *Land without Bread* (a.k.a. *Las Hurdes,* 1932) the humor in *Bons Baisers* always empathizes with the subjects, never mocks the onscreen figures, by simple recognition of the cultural complexity that lies in front of the camera. Yet by reverse turns, Malle does occasionally flesh out and texture the film by pointing a lightly mocking finger at the viewer's ignorance, as in the darkly comic sequence when the director tempts male viewers into reading images of prostitutes and exotic dancers seductively—before revealing (a huge surprise) that the whores are all female impersonators.

To investigate cultural alienation on both sides of the east-west equation, Malle utilizes an A-B-A structure, the film divided by shifts in tone. For most of its running time, the film attempts to investigate the difficulty of the western viewer's attempts to grasp the components of Thai culture fully (A), by setting up a tension between the audience's universalistic understanding and confusion. Yet for about 15

minutes in the middle of the film, Malle incorporates a slight tonal shift, segueing —
temporarily — into the idea of Thai alienation from upper-crust American and European society (B). He subsequently returns to the initial theme of the western
audience's cultural alienation (A).

During the first third of the film, Malle plunges his European and American
viewers into the aforementioned gulf of visual and intellectual detachment that not
only reflects on the documentary's overarching theme of cultural disorientation *per
se*, but enables each viewer to experience, acknowledge, and examine his or her own
cultural disorientation self-reflexively in the face of Thai civilization. Malle maintains a constant dialectical tension between imagistic "universality" of western images
and the multiplicative imagistic ambiguity of eastern meaning, by repeatedly pulling
the same punch: he deceptively leads the viewer into the assumption that he or she
has a full understanding of onscreen events, yet subsequently slices through these
assumptions and reveals unseen cultural complexities (multiple layers) beneath, calling the western viewer's attention to his or her inability to grasp the fundamental
components of Thai culture. Ergo, seconds after Malle opens the film with a subject
familiar and relatable to anyone who has grown up in the west — a young boy attempting to mount a gigantic bicycle — he cuts to a similarly universalistic images of schoolchildren lining up single file, yet this time, accompanied by haunting, dissonant
chants overlaid on the soundtrack, noise that will strike most American and French
viewers as bizarre, quasi-disturbing, and inexplicable, given Malle's pronounced
absence of linguistic translation or narrative exposition. The tension between the
disturbing chants on the soundtrack and the universality of the schoolchildren
embodies the active tension between clarity and ambiguity, understanding and ignorance. The effect is a haunting commentary on the impossibility and futility of interpretation, and a razor-sharp dissection of Euro-American xenophobia. Watching
these scenes is like entering a dream — and attempting, by any means available — to
tie the experiences that lie within the immediate reach of the senses to a western level
of understanding, yet suddenly, frighteningly realizing that some visual or aural elements are "off," that no "familiar explanation" will suffice. It means finding oneself
at a loss, balanced precariously on the line between the universally understood and
the inexplicably foreign.

This dichotomous paradox recurs when Malle cuts to a series of signature
abrechtian shots, notably a first-person perspective filmed from the hood of a car as
it rolls down a Thai street, and an *Amants*-style cut from a close-up of a trashed automobile to a larger shot, of which the close-up is a fraction. Of these images, Malle's
driving shot is by far the most significant. The establishment of spatial depth here
might feel gratuitous (and could risk working directly against the visual, aural, and
intellectual disorientation conveyed by the film's aesthetic), were it not for the odd,
dirge-like chant on the soundtrack. Again: as in the schoolchildren sequence, the
power of the film rests on the cognizance-ambiguity tension evoked by a visual-aural
conflict, but the tone here is sharply ironic, the visual trip "into" Thailand accompanied by an unidentifiable chant that — paradoxically — distances us intellectually
and emotionally as we yet experience kinesthetic immersion.

A few seconds after the abrechtian driving shot, Malle uses a shaky hand-held camera to film a crowd of schoolchildren, heightening visually the sense of chaos and the idea that the Thai people are literally insuppressible, cannot be suppressed or governed. His narration: "Thailand is the only country the west could never colonize." This narrative comment pulls the audience back to the uneasiness of seeing and feeling western cultural elements (such as shots of American automobiles) overlaid awkwardly atop an alien culture and environment, and the feeling that such elements have been directly, cruelly, and ineffectively imposed on Thai society.

Malle interpolates an astonishing tonal reversal about 15 minutes into the film. By temporarily distancing the audience from the Americans and Europeans who appear onscreen, and facilitating a sudden emotional bond between the (western) viewers and the film's Thai subjects, Malle forces each viewer to take a step back and perceive his or her own confusion and alienation as only one half of a two-part equation: as alienated as the western audience may feel from the Thai citizens, the view is just as confusing from the other side of the looking glass. This reversal begins to emerge when two Americans appear onscreen — husband-and-wife tourists and, fascinatingly, among the strangest subjects in the motion picture. Given the director's removal of their dialogue from the soundtrack and his refusal to translate in voice-over, and given the Americans' bizarre appearances— particularly the eccentric-looking, grotesquely ugly country wife, dressed in a scarf with horn-rimmed granny glasses, smirking as she peers into Malle's camera — the audience cannot help but feel distanced from these creatures. Similarly, Malle next transitions to a shot of several wealthy, upper-crust European tourists aboard a barred boat. Because the shot is filmed from outside the bars, it not only underscores alienation from the westerners onscreen, but — significantly — limited audience identification with the Thai citizens, for the camera's position (physically separated from the westerners via the bars) conveys the very same impressions of alienation and emotional overtones of isolation that a lower-class Thai citizen would glean. The audience begins to experience a bond with the Thai subjects and understands their inability to identify fully with westerners. This process continues a few seconds later, when Malle includes shots of a Thai farmer screaming at the boat with English-language, dubbed translation (he screams at the boat: "Hello sir! How are you?") — the translation eliminates all linguistic ambiguity between the audience and the subject and fosters intellectual identification. Later in the film, Malle offers visual glimpses of Thai dockworkers, laboring in dank, sweaty, claustrophobic conditions. Given his extreme close-ups, highly textured with body sweat and facial anguish, the viewer (recalling *Tour*) cannot help but empathize with these men, on a visceral level.

In the final third of the film, highlighted by glimpses of Thai diviners and sages and a trip to a Chinese pharmacy, Malle returns to a more pronounced sense of the onscreen ambiguity that opened the film, but a palpable, almost Makavejevian physicality permeates the screen, with highly textured shots of the astrologers' wrinkled, sweaty faces that we can recognize and appreciate as symptomatic of a universal human plight (excessive, strained labor), even if the figures' words are never explained. Similarly, Malle closes on a woman crying while she digs her feet into the sand and surf (universal) yet never explains the reasons for her tears (ambiguous). This paradoxical tension between ambiguity and clarification that runs throughout the film — as the director concludes in his narrative summation — is the essence of culture itself. "One does not explain a country," he observes. "One does not relate a journey with pictures stolen on the way. I can only say it is a complicated yet simple land, incomprehensible yet familiar, irritating but beautiful."

"William Wilson" (1969)
(Second episode from *Spirits of the Dead,* a.k.a. *Histoires extraordinaires*)

BACKGROUND

According to Malle, "William Wilson" arrived at a moment of extreme emotional crisis. The genesis of "Wilson" began with the director's gut-level reaction to *Le Voleur*, his personal disillusionment and fear that an attempt to escape from the bourgeois by pursuing a career as a self-made artist had proven a futile effort, that wealth and success were forcing his backslide into the French upper crust, and that he might fall into the standard pattern of writing and directing a new feature every two years or so. He thus felt a need to try a project that was completely out-of-character. It arrived in the form of a phone call from French megastar and heart-throb Alain Delon, who invited Malle to helm the second episode of a film-as-sketch entitled *Spirits of the Dead* (produced 1967, released '69): three 40-minute adaptations of Poe stories, to be directed by an international triad of filmmakers and screened as a portmanteau feature, along the lines of *L'Amour à vingt ans* (1962), or the thematically similar *Dead of Night* (1945). Though the original three shorts of *Histoires extraordinaires* were to be directed by Vadim, Buñuel, and Orson Welles, consecutively, Malle replaced Buñuel (selecting and adapting Poe's "William Wilson"), and Fellini replaced Welles (selecting and adapting Poe's story "Never Bet the Devil Your Head," which he retitled "Toby Dammit" for the screen).[12,13]

SYNOPSIS

In nineteenth century Bergamo, northern Italy, a French soldier in the Italian army named William Wilson (Alain Delon) races through the cobbled streets and anticipates (in flashforwards) his own death, a fall from a great stone tower. Wilson bolts into a Catholic church and, though a Protestant, demands a confession on the spot. He begins recounting events from his life to a priest in the confessional.

According to Wilson, vicious, Satanic acts of cruelty and bloodshed marred his character from a young age. While enrolled as a student at the Eton boarding school, Wilson threw food in the face of a new pupil named Hans (Umberto d'Orsi). After Hans tattled on Wilson, Wilson restrained Hans with ropes, tied him to a pulley, and commanded fellow students to lower him into a pit filled with hungry rats, but a mysterious young boy with a countenance similar to Wilson's own — a *Döppel-*

6912-48

The psychotic William Wilson (Alain Delon) has strapped a naked prostitute (Katia Christina) to an operating table and prepares to place a scalpel into her live body while a group of his fellow med students watch in "William Wilson," the Louis Malle–directed second episode of the film-as-sketch *Spirits of the Dead* (Histoires extraordinaires).

ganger — appeared and ended the cruelty. The two became competitors and rivals in every arena, but one of the Eton prefects expelled Wilson after he attempted to suffocate his double.

As a young man, Wilson enrolled in medical school. One evening, he seized a young prostitute (Katia Christina),[14] stripped her, and bound her to an operating table in front of other male students. Mocking the anatomy lesson of a professor, Wilson withdrew a knife and prepared to slice into the live nude body of the whore, but his double appeared yet again, untied the ropes, and draped a cloak over the prostitute's body. Faced with two Wilsons, the prostitute ran to her tormentor's arms; the evil Wilson plunged the surgical knife into her stomach and was subsequently expelled from medical school.

A few years later, Wilson enlisted in the Italian army. At a masquerade ball, he entered a poker game with the cigar-smoking society matron Giuseppina (Brigitte Bardot). Hand after hand, she trumped him, until he began to cheat by using cards concealed in his sleeve. To collect his spoils after winning the final bet, Wilson withdrew a whip and forced Giuseppina to submit to a brutal beating, but his double appeared a third time and revealed Wilson's chicanery to the spectators, who forcibly exiled him from the town. Infuriated, Wilson withdrew a sword and raced after his double. During a duel, the evil Wilson triumphed, plunging a sword into his doppelganger's heart.

The priest treats Wilson's confessions as the hallucinations of a drunken madman. A livid Wilson races up to the top of the church bell tower and throws himself off. After his body hits the ground, the locals roll him over and find a blade plunged through his chest, the mirror image of the good Wilson's corpse.

ANALYSIS

Co-adapted with two novelists—American Clement Biddle Wood and French Daniel Boulanger—Malle's film "William Wilson" takes tremendous liberties with its source material, altering the trajectory of Edgar Allan Poe's story dramatically. Poe crafted a protracted mental dialectic between two figures who physically embody (personify) two halves of the same person—conscience and vice. The famed horror writer largely confined the personification of the two individuals to the boundaries of metaphor, and the body of the story extrapolates these conflicts and becomes a moral allegory about the inner struggle of one man between good and evil inclinations. The primary terror in the story emerges when the embodiment of evil destroys his moral counterpart, and realizes, with horror, that he is permanently, hopelessly damned. When the reader (who recognizes and relates to the universal qualities in the conscience-struggle) reads the final words of the conscience and stares into the void of damnation along with "evil Wilson": "You have conquered, and I yield. Yet, henceforward art thou also dead—dead to the World, to Heaven, and to Hope!,"[15] he or she shares this sense of damnation.

The horror of Malle's adaptation is not spiritual and eternal, but immediate and visual, and thus, infinitely more limited. It is the horror of a man living without conscience, but this horror revealed from a third person perspective, not the horror of a man looking first-person into his own future and glimpsing a complete absence of spiritual hope. The school scene (the first in Wilson's flashback) seems to have occurred long after his conscience had fallen off, and the "good half" represents a distinct individual who only bears Wilson's countenance and interferes externally, not internally. This nearly destroys the tone of the film, by permanently alienating the audience from "evil Wilson," from the first frame. (He is such a vile and disgusting sociopath that the average viewer cannot possibly relate to him.) One wonders if Malle, who reinvented the "conversation piece" so ingeniously in *My Dinner with André*, might have demonstrated more loyalty to the source material and more bravery in cinematizing Poe's "battle of conscience," had he directed "Wilson" years later.

Poe also pulls terror from ambiguity. I would not, if I could," he writes, "here or to-day, embody a record of my later years of unspeakable misery, and unpardonable crimes."[16] The author realizes, intuitively, that slight, subtle suggestions of human misdeed and vice allow the reader's imagination to run amok, into areas far darker than explicit descriptions of turpitude. But how to cinematize such ambiguity and harness the imagination in a visual medium? Malle, Biddle, and Boulanger obviously felt confined by the cinematic medium, for they abandon all traces of ambiguity, opting for a series of hyper-literal scenes—similar scenes that, back-to-back, establish the film's structural parallelism, in which "bad Wilson" commits a vice and "good Wilson" turns him in. The film never grows more complex or more ambiguous than this. A far less metaphoric and less philosophical work than Poe, the Malle-Biddle-Boulanger adaptation bears no traces of spiritual horror, shock, or terror per se; instead, the co-writers weave the story around repulsion—audience astonishment at the heartless acts of brutality that unfold before them. The film's horror is synonymous with depravity: the planned dismemberment of a live prostitute, the sociopathic abuse of a young schoolboy, whom Wilson ties up, hangs on a pulley, and systematically lowers knees-first into a tub of ravenous rats; the horror of an innocent society woman beaten with a whip until bloody welts cover her back.

And yet, despite the many weaknesses of Malle's "concrete approach," he realizes, on some level, that in addition to the power of ambiguity, Poe does use some concrete, surrealistic descriptions to involve the reader, as when he writes:

> My earliest recollections of a school-life are connected with a large, rambling, Elizabethan house, in a misty-looking village of England, where were a vast number of gigantic and gnarled trees ... at this moment ... I feel the refreshing chilliness of its deeply-shadowed avenues, inhale the fragrance of its thousand shrubberies....

Perhaps this became one justification for the "hyper-literal" visualizations within the film.[17]

Given Malle's standard penchant for anti-clericalism, it is odd, perhaps inexplicable, that he never borrows the thin layer of blasphemous mockery that laces Poe's story. Poe chides, with a tongue-in-cheek cant:

> Of this church the principal of our school was pastor. With how deep a spirit of wonder and perplexity was I wont to regard him from our remote pew in the gallery, as, with step solemn and slow, he ascended the pulpit! This reverend man, with countenance so demurely benign, with robes so glossy and so clerically flowing, with wig so minutely powdered, so rigid and so vast ... could this be he who, of late, with sour visage ... administered, ferule in hand, the Draconian laws of the academy? Oh, gigantic paradox, too utterly monstrous for solution![18]

Oddly, though Malle frames the Wilson tale as a confessional, he never examines the priest or the church itself through a darkly comic or satirical lens, leading one to question if the omission of mild sacrilege and anti-clericalism cannot be attributed to the mitigating influence of Biddle and Boulanger.

Appendix A

Lost Horizons— Selected Unfinished Malle Projects, 1949–94

Research and Initial Information
by Stéphanie Grégoire

(*Translated and Edited by Jacques Weissgerber*
and Nathan Southern)

Note: For adaptations of novels, I quoted the original title whenever I could find it — J.W.

1949 —*Petit Meurtre à l'abbaye* (Little Murder at the Abbey). At the end of the nineteenth century, three young bourgeois girls (two sisters and their cousin) are spending the summer at their family's country house on the outskirts of Paris. The sudden arrival of a first cousin upsets their lives. He seduces one of the girls, and, in doing so, calls their feelings into question and destabilizes the existing bonds between them. To reestablish their rapport, the girls murder the young man by drowning him.

1952 — Untitled 16mm documentary short on Lourdes and its pilgrims. Malle terminated the project after shooting began.

1952 —*L'Amour de vivre* (Lust for Life). A short film dramatizing one night in the life of Alfred Jarry, the eccentric Left Bank French playwright who authored the *Ubu* cycle. The film opens at a party where everything unfolds conventionally and predictably until Jarry arrives, dressed as a bicyclist. He introduces elements of absurdity and upsets the narrative. After numerous surreal episodes throughout the night in the streets of Paris, Jarry gathers all the protagonists in a clearing, convinces them to dance a minuet, and murders them.

1956–7 —*Les Lauriers sont coupés* (Laurels are cut). Julien, a graduate student majoring in literature at the Sorbonne, falls in love with Anne. The young woman introduces him to her uncle, an elderly writer. Julien becomes his secretary, then gradually his ghostwriter. When the deceit is discovered, a scandal erupts; Julien, separated from Anne, begins writing under his own name and becomes famous. But, tired of his success, he tries, and eventually succeeds in re-

341

conquering Anne. This project appears to be a variation of another, called *Emmanuel*, where a young student at the Sorbonne feels torn between his love of a woman and his political commitment to protesting France's involvement in Algeria.

1956–7 — *Monsieur Varys*, co-written with Napoléon Murat. M. Varys is a social misfit who finds it difficult to function on a daily basis. An inspector with the housing department, he leads a mediocre life in Paris. Secluded in his own world, he spends all his free time building a giant object, two meters high, using straws he steals from coffee shops. His peculiar hobby causes him to lose the only woman he has ever managed to seduce.

1956–7 — Adaptation, co-written with Hubert Heilbronn, of Arthur Koestler's novel *La Tour d'Ezra (The Tower of Ezra)*. Malle abandoned the project after scouting locations in Israel.

1958 — *Nuestra Señora de la Concepción* (Our Lady of Conception). Four youngsters sail out to sea, in search of the wreck of an old Spanish galleon, the *Nuestra Señora de la Concepción*, lost in 1641 on the reef of the Silver Bank, 60 miles off the North Coast of the Dominican Republic. During a location scouting trip in the West Indies in November 1958, Malle gradually abandoned the project and developed a completely different story, *L'Aventure (The Adventure)*.

1958–61 — *L'Aventure*, a.k.a. *Le Voyage*, a.k.a. *Liberté*, a.k.a. *The Singlehander*. Kenneth Goose, a 30 something husband and father from an American bourgeois family, decides to leave his wife, child and job and sail across the Atlantic. As he arrives at the Azores, he takes a young and pretty stowaway aboard his boat as a passenger. Their short-lived love story, which concludes with their arrival in Casablanca, provides an opportunity for Goose to assess the meaning of his existence and begin his life from scratch. François Billetdoux wrote a first draft of this story for Malle, Clement Biddle Wood a second.

1958 — *Liberté*. The second of Malle's projects during this period with the same title,

this attempted to merge several of Conrad's stories, including *Victory*, *Au bout du rouleau*, *Freya of the Seven Isles*, and *Almayer's Folly*, into one narrative. Malle and Daniel Anselme transposed the setting to Greece.

1958–9, 1979 — *Victoire* (Victory). Adaptation of Joseph Conrad's novel, that tells the story of Axel Heyst, a drifter who attempts to avoid all sorrow and disappointment by cutting himself off from the human race. Heyst is gradually drawn back into social interaction when he agrees to help run a coal company on a south seas island, but when the company collapses, he blames himself and retreats into isolation once again. Heyst subsequently encounters a British girl named Lena and saves her from a series of captors; the two begin an impassioned affair and Lena joins Heyst on his island, where she tries to help him become emotionally open and face the prospect of intimacy with her. *Victory* was one of Malle's lifelong dream projects, an idea that never died for him. It had two major incarnations, the first in 1959 and the second around 1979, when Malle co-adapted it with Susan Sarandon and Patrick Modiano (*Lacombe, Lucien*). A number of Hollywood stars including Robert Redford expressed interest in the script, and French newspapers prematurely announced a start date for production, but no parties optioned the screenplay.

1959 — *L'Epouvantail* (The Scarecrow). Adaptation, written by Ennio Flaiano, of Phyllis Hastings' novel *Rapture in my Rags*. On the outskirts of a small Atlantic coastal town, Agnes, a simple-minded woman of indeterminate age, builds a scarecrow to alleviate her loneliness. When Joseph, a fugitive from the police, dons the clothes of the scarecrow, Agnes mistakenly believes her creation has become human. Thanks to the young man's love, Agnes gains the ability to reach out to others for the first time in her life. Yet the security of the relationship is threatened by her abusive and ignorant father, and the sweet-natured romance between Agnes and Joseph eventually leads to violence when Agnes murders her dad in self-defense to save herself and Joseph. At the conclusion,

Joseph makes an astonishing sacrifice by turning himself in to the authorities in Agnes's stead. (Several years after Malle abandoned this project, Stanley Mann adapted the novel for director John Guillermin. Released in the U.S. in 1965 as *Rapture*, it stars Dean Stockwell as Joseph, Patricia Gozzi as Agnes, and Melvyn Douglas as Agnes's father, Frederick. Christian Ferry, one of Malle's best friends, produced it).

1962 — *La Grotte* (The Cave), Adaptation of a novel by Georges Buis about the Algerian war. Malle took two location scouting trips in 1962, the first preceding the Evian agreements, the second following the Algerian proclamation of independence; during the second trip, Malle shot in 16mm but never used the rushes. He subsequently abandoned the project.

1962 — *Assez de champagne* (Enough Champagne). A night in the life of a young reveler named Frantz, a former participant in O. A. S. (Organisation de l'Armée Secrète) terrorist bombings. Following an argument with his girlfriend Catherine in the early evening, the two young people spend the entire night estranged from one another, each wandering throughout Paris nightspots, until they reconnect at dawn. Malle based one of Frantz's party-going friends, loosely, on Alfred Jarry. In a subsequent version entitled *Trente ans ce soir (Thirty years old tonight)*, written in collaboration with Pierre Pelegri, the young hero commits suicide in the early morning hours. This project evolved into an adaptation of Drieu La Rochelle's novel *Le Feu follet*.

1965 — *Le Partage des eaux* (Los Pasos Perdidos, The Lost Steps). Adaptation of Alejo Carpentier's 1959 novel about a composer who flees from New York City with his lover and travels to a South American tributary that is uncorrupted by modern civilization.

1965 — *Au-dessous du volcan* (Under the Volcano). Adaptation of Malcom Lowry's 1947 novel, set in Cuernavaca, Mexico. On the Day of the Dead, Geoffrey Firmin, the U.S. Ambassador to Mexico, wrestles with alcoholism and with the infidelity of his wife, Yvonne. Note: following Malle's abandonment of this project, countless directors grappled with Lowry's novel and failed, damning this book as cinematically intractable. John Huston brought it to the screen successfully in 1984, with Guy Gallo helming the adaptation; the Huston version stars Albert Finney as Geoffrey and Jacqueline Bisset as Yvonne.

1966 — *Chasse à l'homme* (El acoso, Manhunt). Adaptation of Alejo Carpentier's 1956 novel.

1966–7 — *Le Frenchie*. Written by Claude Sautet (*Cesar and Rosalie*) and Jean-Loup Dabadie (*Pardon mon affaire*). Malle planned and commissioned this comedy as a Jean-Paul Belmondo vehicle, in which a young French boxer named François is propelled onto the American media stage (via fixed fights and various corrupt schemes) by a billionaire whose daughter he has assisted. Deeply in love with the young woman, he eventually quits boxing and she accompanies him on his return to France. Note: Malle abandoned the project, deciding instead to hire Belmondo for *Le Voleur*.

1967 — Malle contemplated assembling several uncompleted projects into one film: his idea was to combine a bulk of 22 "short film stories" of variable length (30 seconds to 20 minutes) into a feature-length compilation.

1967 — *Jelly Roll*. Co-written with Jack Gelber, the American playwright who scripted Shirley Clarke's controversial 1961 film *The Connection*. *Jelly* was a biopic of Jelly Roll Morton, one of the first jazz pianists, adapted from Alan Lomax's biography of Morton. Malle relinquished this project when he strongly disliked the script that emerged from the collaboration. Nonetheless, the central conceit — a cinematic investigation into the birth of New Orleans jazz — found its way into *Pretty Baby*.

1968–9 — *La Machine* (The Machine), a.k.a. *Mort de l'utopie* (Death of Utopia), a.k.a. *Horizon perdu* (Lost Horizon). An original drama co-written with Pierre Kast.

Three members of an expedition searching for uranium ore wind up in a remote valley of the Andes and discover a community that dates back to the arrival of an Inca tribe fleeing Pizarro and a group of British Catholics fleeing persecution in Europe. The ideal society mixes modernism and archaism, and is ignorant of war, money, and trade, by virtue of its isolation from the contemporary world. But an act of treason committed by one of the explorers, followed by a nuclear explosion, brings the utopia to a sad end. This project resembles a variation on Frank Capra's 1937 *Lost Horizon*. As an extension of the quest for spiritual meaning that led Malle to India and a reaction to Paris in May 1968, Malle speculated that a perfect, "liberated" society might be plausible, and planned to dramatize it onscreen. Yet he gave up when he deduced that a "utopia" would never work as the subject of a feature, given its obvious lack of conflict and dramatic tension. Columbia Pictures did its own remake of *Lost Horizon* four years after Malle dropped *Mort de l'utopie*; it became one of the biggest critical and commercial abominations in the history of American cinema. Barbet Schroeder (*Barfly*) also took utopian themes and used them for his 1971 psychedelic drama *La Vallée* (*The Valley Obscured by Clouds*), a critically acclaimed but rarely screened effort.

1969–70, 1985 —*Le Baron perché* (The Baron in the Trees). Adaptation of Italo Calvino's 1957 fantasy novel that tells story of a young nobleman who decides to spend his entire existence *en les arbres*, and builds his own experimental world among the branches. Malle visited the project in the early seventies, but set it aside temporarily; he returned to the idea while living and working in the U.S. (around 1985). The details are murky, but Candice Bergen believes that Richard Gere may have held the rights and expressed interest in playing one of the leads. According to John Guare, Malle abandoned the project because it was next to impossible to shoot given the subject matter.

1970 —*Ma Mère* (My Mother). An adaptation of Georges Bataille's novel that explores the troubled relationship between mother and son and ends with the boy's suicide. This became the launching pad for *Le souffle au cœur*.

1970 —*La Sauvage* (The Savage). A script dramatizing the wanderings in Italy of a young French actress and a 16-year-old British boy intent on murdering the pope.

1971, 1995 —*Robinson Crusoe*. An adaptation of Defoe's classic 1719 novel, *Crusoe* was another of Malle's dream projects, like *Victory*, that he returned to intermittently throughout his career but could never launch. One of his key plans just prior to his death involved realizing the film with an enthusiastic David Hare doing the adaptation. According to Hare, Malle felt most intrigued by those themes of the work that are unrelated to Crusoe's adventures on the desert island *per se*— presumably fate versus free will and British imperialism.

1971 —*Los Halcones*, a.k.a. *Le Faucon* (The Hawk). Malle started developing a treatment that dramatized a series of tragic events unfolding in Mexico: young men from the poor suburbs, called "porristas," who were arrested by the police for petty crimes, were being enlisted by the police to infiltrate student demonstrations and kill the young leaders. Malle's story centered around 19-year-old Chucho, who becomes a porrista in the shadow of the police and begins subtly infiltrating demonstrations on Mexican university campuses. But when a journalist photographs him killing a student during a demonstration, Chucho becomes an embarrassment to the police and is murdered by them.

1972 —*Amazon*. Malle planned a documentary series about the Amazon region in the format of *Phantom India*, to be realized through the BBC. But he failed to receive the necessary authorizations from the Brazilian government.

1974–9 —*The Boy*, a.k.a. *Chicano*, Malle wanted to tell the story of a Mexican teenager from Yucatán who becomes a "wetback" by slipping into the United States and starting a new life. *The Boy* had three incarnations. The first (c. 1974–5), Malle's planned screenplay collaboration with San Diego State professor and filmmaker Jean-Pierre Gorin, was to be a "Capraesque, feel-good film," inspired by the works of Jerzy Kosinski (*Being There*), wherein the teenager becomes the servant of a rich and eccentric, Howard Hughes–like millionaire, and inherits a fortune when his employer dies. Malle devised a variation on this *récit* after David Picker paired him up with screenwriter Polly Platt, and Malle told Platt that he wanted to do a film about the problem of illegal Mexican immigration; by this point, it had (in Malle's mind) evolved into a sober muckraking drama criticizing an element of American society. (Platt dissuaded Malle from the subject and they did *Pretty Baby* instead). The third involved Malle's quick reassessment of the project in 1979, in-between *Pretty Baby* and *Atlantic City*, without the involvement of Gorin or Platt.

1975 — *Electric Sun*, a.k.a. *Le Soleil*. A secret agent lands in a small Mexican port town, in search of an old German electrician nicknamed "Padre." This Padre is loved by everyone, yet a few suspect him of being a former Nazi war criminal; eventually, complications arise in the relationship between the two men. Malle returned to this project briefly in 1978.

1975 — *La Pornographie* (Pornography). Adaptation of Witold Gombrovicz's 1967 novel.

1977 — *The Godfather, Part III*. Charlie Bluhdorn of Paramount approached Malle (who supervised the French overdubs of *The Godfather, Part I* in 1972), and suggested that he direct *Part III*, because Francis Ford Coppola (immersed in *Apocalypse Now* at that time) refused to do a third installment. But Paramount executives rejected this as an option. Coppola directed *The Godfather III* in 1990.

1977–8 — Untitled documentary on Stevie Wonder.

1978 — *Une Comédie américaine (An American Comedy)*. A seriocomic adaptation of Theodore Dreiser's novel *An American Tragedy*.

1978 — *Le Fils de Sam (Son of Sam)*. Drama inspired by the psychopathic killer who terrorized New York City during the summer of 1977. Spike Lee made a film on the same subject in 1999: *S.O.S. (Summer of Sam)*.

1978 — *Le Consul honoraire* (The Honorary Consul) — Adaptation of Graham Greene's novel.

1979 — Untitled documentary on Disneyworld. Malle visited the theme park with his son Manuel and daughter Justine. Horrified at the commercialization and manipulation before him, he wanted to take his 16mm cameras behind the façade of the park to film its inner workings. The Walt Disney Corporation (presumably ignorant of his disgust for the park) agreed to the project but demanded final cut of the film; Malle refused to capitulate and dropped the idea.

1979 — Untitled documentary on American shopping malls. Malle read a couple of articles on the origins and sociology of the middle-American mall. Intrigued by the phenomenon, he carried his 16mm cameras and microphones to a massive indoor shopping center in Minneapolis, with James Bruce, Etienne Becker, Jean-Claude Laureux and Vincent Malle as crewmembers. Malle found the mall footage boring, however, and suggested that they look around for another interesting subject. The crew spent weeks tooling around Minnesota; during the trip, Malle alternately considered filming tourist attractions, Indian reservations, Bob Dylan's hometown, state fairs and other discoveries, until the team happened upon the farming community of Glencoe; this became the subject of Malle's documentary *God's Country*.

1981–3 — *Moon Over Miami*. Malle learned of Abscam — a Reagan-era political scandal involving an offshore tax evasion swindler — and thought it would make wonderful satirical fodder for a feature film. He suggested to John Guare that they cinematize the scandal as a contemporary political farce. Guare wrote the first draft as *Moon over Miami*, an off-the-wall comedy with musical numbers, surrealist elements and characters who frequently swap identities, and renamed the swindler "Shelley Slutski." Malle solicited the interest of John Belushi (whom he idolized) to play Slutski, and Dan Aykroyd to play a crooked FBI agent who poses as a fake Arab sheik, hired to trap Slutski. Belushi and Akyroyd signed on, Columbia greenlit the project, and Malle and Guare set up production in Florida. But when Belushi died of an overdose at the Château Marmont in March of '82, the studio lost all interest. Malle spent around a year attempting to find a Belushi substitute, and alternately considered Bill Murray, Dustin Hoffman and Bob Hoskins (among others), but without Belushi, the project remained dead in the water and could never find studio backing.

1982 — Untitled project. Marty, a wunderkind Hollywood producer hot off of a blockbuster, plans to adapt *Walden*, first with the help of an older screenwriter, later by himself.

1982–3 — Malle devised yet another variation on **Robinson Crusoe**. In this modern version, "Robinson" is a travel agent *en route* to a convention in Manila. When his plane crashes somewhere in the Philippines, he does not want to be rescued, but instead hides out in the wild and begins living like Crusoe.

1985–90 — *Necking*, a.k.a. **Ladykiller**, a.k.a. **Chloé**. Variations on the story of a man — a killer in *Necking* and *Ladykiller* — who is exasperated by the life he leads and wants to drop out and change his identity. He ends up kidnapping a little girl who witnessed one of his murders, and with whom he runs away and builds a relationship.

1987 — *Fouquet* or *Le Cœur au-dessus des périls* (**The Heart above Dangers**). A historical dramatization of the life of Nicolas Fouquet: superintendent under King Louis XIV, *bon vivant* and *cause célèbre*, Fouquet becomes caught between two merciless men intent on destroying him: Louis XIV and Colbert. At the end of the story, he develops a grave illness and is abandoned by everyone.

1987 — *Eye Contact*, a.k.a. *I Hate My Life*, by John Guare. Philip and Penny, two scholars of ancient Greece and former lovers, decide to leave their respective spouses and begin a new life together. They marry and, children in tow, leave for an archeological dig in Sicily. As they settle in the castle of a Princess, the plot gradually thickens with the murder of Dr. Cataldo (who initiated the excavation), the arrival of Phillip's ex-wife and her new lover and, finally, the arrival of Peggy's ex-husband (and his new wife) who has come to promote the building of a missile base which the local mafia is very interested in. Guare remembers that Malle was particularly fascinated by the idea of children acting out their parents' divorce (which became an element of the story); the two men wanted Meryl Streep and either Kevin Kline or Steve Martin to play the leads. Michael Eisner (of Disney) expressed interest in optioning it but refused to hire Malle as director; Guare refused to move forward without Louis. Elements of this script found their way into Guare's 1992 Broadway play, *Four Baboons Adoring the Sun*.

Late eighties/early nineties — Notes on the adaptation of Edmund White's novel **Caracole**.

1990 — *The Manchiméel Tree*, a.k.a. *The Loner*, a.k.a. *Poor Monkey*. Successive adaptations, co-written with John Guare, of Henry James' novel *What Maisie Knew*. Guare later used *Maisie*'s narrative structure — a little girl's scrutiny of her surroundings — when writing *Dietrich and Marlene*.

1990–3 — Malle planned a film with and about Commandant Cousteau, in the form of a last testament.

1992 — Untitled project. Malle made tentative plans for a documentary about truffle pickers in southwest France.

1993 — *14 juillet* (*July 14*), a.k.a. *1944*. Malle jotted down the idea for a sequel to *Au revoir les enfants*.

1993 — *My Little Madeleine*, a.k.a. *Mémoires* a.k.a. *Thumeries*. Malle devised plans for an autobiographical saga of the history of his own family, the Béghins.

1994 — *Coming Up Down Home*. An adaptation of Cecil Brown's novel about coming of age as an African American in the southern United States.

1994 — *Dietrich and Marlene*. Simultaneously a John Guare-penned adaptation of *Marlene Dietrich* (Maria Riva's 1992 biography of her mother), and the last of Guare and Malle's attempts to adapt Henry James's *What Maisie Knew*. With *Dietrich and Marlene*, Guare and Malle planned to combine both adaptations into one film. The screenplay dramatizes one day in Marlene Dietrich's life (October 30, 1934) as reminisced by Maria Riva 40 years later, in flashback. Nouvelles Éditions set up the film by pre-selling shares of it to production companies in numerous countries (patterned after the financing strategy for *Damage*) and cast Uma Thurman as Dietrich and Stephen Rea as Josef von Sternberg. NEF also began building, as the film's primary set, a 1930s-style art deco replica of Paramount Studios on the lots at Cinecitta in Rome (in lieu of Los Angeles, to reduce expenses). Louis Malle's health started deteriorating after he returned to Los Angeles in early 1995 to find a young girl to portray Riva as a child; this postponed the shoot, originally scheduled for that summer. After Malle died from lymphoma on November 22, 1995, Uma Thurman was given the option of continuing the project under the aegis of another director. She refused.

Appendix B
Filmography

Le Monde du silence (Société Filmad et Requins Associés, France, 1956); U.S./G.B.: ***The Silent World***

Co-Directors: Jacques-Yves Cousteau, Louis Malle; *Cinematographer:* Edmond Séchan (Technicolor); *Underwater Photography:* Jacques-Yves Cousteau, Louis Malle, Frédéric Dumas, Albert Falco; *Special Effects:* Noël Robert; *Music:* Yves Baudrier; *Editor:* Georges Alépée; *Narration (English version):* James Dugan; *Runtime:* 86 minutes (G.B. cut: 82 min.)

— AWARDS AND NOMINATIONS —
1956 Cannes Film Festival — Palme d'Or (win)
1956 Academy Awards — Best Documentary Feature (win)
1956 British Academy Awards — Best Documentary Film (nom)
1956 National Board of Review Awards — Best Foreign Film (win)
1957 French Syndicate of Cinema Critics — Critics Award (win)

Ascenseur pour l'échafaud (Nouvelles Éditions de Films, France, 1957); U.S.: ***Elevator to the Gallows***, a.k.a. ***Frantic***; G.B.: ***Lift to the Scaffold***

Director: Louis Malle; *Producer:* Jean Thuillier; *Screenwriters:* Louis Malle, Roger Nimier (From Noël Calef's novel *L'Ascenseur pour l'échafaud*); *Cinematographer:* Henri Decaë (black and white); *Art Directors:* Rino Mondellini, Jean Mandaroux; *Assistant Directors:* Alain Cavalier, Alain Fraisse, François Leterrier; *Music:* Miles Davis; *Sound:* Raymond Gauguier; *Editor:* Léonide Azar; *Runtime:* 90 minutes

Cast: Maurice Ronet (Julien Tavernier), Jeanne Moreau (Florence Carala), Georges Poujouly (Louis), Yori Bertin (Véronique), Lino Ventura (Inspector Chérier), Ivan Petrovich (Horst Bencker), Elga Andersen (Frau Bencker), Jean Wall (Simon Carala), Félix Marten (Subervie), Charles Denner (Inspector Chérier's assistant), Jean-Claude Brialy (chess player at motel).

— AWARDS AND NOMINATIONS —
1957 Prix Louis-Delluc (win)

Les Amants (Nouvelles Éditions de Films, France, 1958); U.S./G.B.: ***The Lovers***

Director: Louis Malle; *Producer:* Louis Malle; *Screenwriters:* Louis Malle, Louise de Vilmorin (From Dominique Vivant Denon's *Point de Lendemain*); *Cinematographer:* Henri Decaë (DyaliScope, black and white); *Art Directors:* Bernard Evein, Jacques Saulnier; *Assistant Directors:* Alain Cavalier, François Leterrier; *Music:* First and Second Movements, Brahms String Sextet No. 1, in B Flat Major; *Sound:* Pierre-André Bertrand, Poste Parisien; *Editor:* Léonide Azar; *Runtime:* 88 minutes (G.B. cut: 87 min.)

Cast: Jeanne Moreau (Jeanne Tournier), Alain Cuny (Henri Tournier), Jean-Marc Bory (Bernard Dubois-Lambert), Judith Magre (Maggy Thiébaut-Leroy), José-Luis Villalonga (Raoul Florès), Gaston Modot (Coudray), Claude Mansart (Marcelot), Georgette Lobbe (Marthe), Patricia Garcin (Catherine)

— AWARDS AND NOMINATIONS —
1958 Venice Film Festival — Special Jury Prize (win); Golden Lion (nom)

Zazie dans le métro (Nouvelles Éditions de Films, France, 1959); G.B.: *Zazie*

Director: Louis Malle; *Producer:* Louis Malle; *Screenwriters:* Louis Malle, Jean-Paul Rappeneau (from Raymond Queneau's novel *Zazie dans le Métro*); *Cinematographer:* Henri Raichi (Eastmancolor); *Art Director:* Bernard Evein; *Assistant Directors:* Philippe Collin, Olivier Gérard; *Music:* Florenzo Carpi; *Sound:* André Hervée; *Editor:* Kenout Peltier; *Runtime:* 92 minutes (G.B. cut: 88 min).

Cast: Catherine Demongeot (Zazie), Philippe Noiret (Uncle Gabriel), Carla Marlier (Aunt Albertine), Vittorio Caprioli (Pedro Trouscaillon), Hubert Deschamps (Turandot), Jacques Dufilho (Gridoux), Annie Fratellini (Mado), Antoine Roblot (Charles), Yvonne Clech (Madame Mouaque), Odette Piquet (Madame Lalochère), Nicolas Bataille (Fédor), Marc Doelnitz (Monsieur Coquetti), Louis Malle (Man with sign — uncredited)

Vie privée (Progefi, Cipra [Paris]/CCM [Rome]; France/Italy, 1961); U.S./G.B.: *A Very Private Affair*

Director: Louis Malle; *Producer:* Christine Gouze-Rénal; *Screenwriters:* Louis Malle, Jean-Paul Rappeneau, Jean Ferry; *Cinematographer:* Henri Decaë (Eastmancolor); *Assistant Directors:* Philippe Collin, Alain Gouze, Volker Schlöndorff; *Art Director:* Bernard Evein; *Music:* Fiorenzi Carpi, J. Max Rivière, Jean Spanos; *Editor:* Kenout Peltier; *Runtime:* 103 minutes (U.S./G.B. dubbed cut: 94 min).

Cast: Brigitte Bardot (Jill), Marcello Mastroianni (Fabio), Nicolas Bataille (Edmond), Jacqueline Doyen (Juliette), Eléonore Hirt (Cécile), Ursula Kubler (Carla), Gregor von Rezzori (Gricha), Dirk Sanders (Dick), Paul Sorèze (Maxime), Gloria France (Anna), Antoine Roblot (Alain), Jeanne Allard (housekeeper), Claude Day (publisher), Christian de Tillière (Albert)

Vive le tour (Nouvelles Editions de Films, France, 1962); U.S.: *Twist encore*

Director: Louis Malle; *Cinematographers:* Ghislain Cloquet, Jacques Ertaud, Louis Malle (16mm Ektachrome); *Music:* Georges Delerue; *Editors:* Suzanne Baron, Kenout Peltier; *Runtime:* 18 min.

Le Feu follet (Nouvelles Éditions de Films/Arco Film S.r.L., France, 1963); U.S.: *The Fire Within*; G.B.: *The Maddening Flame*, a.k.a. *Will o' the Wisp*, a.k.a. *A Time to Live and a Time to Die*

Director: Louis Malle; *Producer:* Louis Malle; Screenwriter: Louis Malle (From Pierre Drieu La Rochelle's novel *Le Feu follet*); *Cinematographer:* Ghislain Cloquet; Art *Director:* Bernard Evein; *Assistant Director:* Volker Schlöndorff; *Music:* Selections from Erik Satie's Gymnopedies and Gnossiennes played by pianist Claude Helffer; *Sound:* Jean Nény, Guy Villette; *Editor:* Suzanne Baron; *Runtime:* 110 minutes (G.B. cut: 107 min.)

Cast: Maurice Ronet (Alain Leroy), Léna Skerla (Lydia), Yvonne Clech (Mademoiselle Farnoux), Hubert Deschamps (d'Averseau), Jean-Paul Moulinot (Dr. La Barbinais), Mona Dol (Madame La Barbinais), Pierre Moncorbier (Moraine), René Dupuy (Charlie), Bernard Tiphaine (Milou), Bernard Noël (Dubourg), Ursula Kubler (Fanny) Also: Jeanne Moreau (Eva)

— AWARDS AND NOMINATIONS —
1963 Venice Film Festival — Special Jury Prize (win), Italian Film Critics Award (win); Golden Lion (nom)

Bons Baisers de Bangkok (ORTF, France, 1964)

Director: Louis Malle; *Cinematographer:* Yves Bonsergent; *Editor:* Nicole Lévy; *Runtime:* 15 minutes

Viva Maria (Nouvelles Éditions de Films/ United Artists [Paris], Vides [Rome]; France/Italy, 1965)

Director: Louis Malle; *Producers:* Oscar Dancigers, Louis Malle; *Screenwriters:* Louis Malle, Jean-Claude Carrière; *Cinematographer:* Henri Decaë (Panavision, Eastmancolor); *Art Director/Production Designer:* Bernard Evein; *Music:* Georges Delerue; *Sound:* José B. Carles; *Editor:* Kenout Peltier, Suzanne Baron; *Runtime:* 115 minutes (G.B. cut: 120 min.)

Cast: Jeanne Moreau (Maria I); Brigitte Bardot (Maria Fitzgerald O'Malley, a.k.a. Maria II); George Hamilton (Florès); Paulette Dubost (Madame Diogène); Gregor von Rezzori (Diogène); Poldo Bendandi (Werther); Claudio Brook (Rodolfo); Carlos Lopez Moctezuma (Don Rodriguez); Jonathan Eden (Juanito); Francisco Reiguera (Father Superior); Adriana Roel (Janine); Jose Baviera (Don Alvaro); Jose Angel Ferresquilla (El Presidente); Fernando Wagner (Maria O'Malley's father); José Luis Campa, Roberto Campa, Eduardo Murillo, José Esqueda (The Turcos); Luis Rizo (strongman)

— AWARDS AND NOMINATIONS —
1966 British Academy Awards— Best Foreign Actress, Brigitte Bardot (nom)

Le Voleur (Nouvelles Éditions de Films/ United Artists [Paris], Compania Cinematografica Montoro [Rome]; France/ Italy, 1967); U.S.: *The Thief of Paris;* G.B.: *The Thief*

Director: Louis Malle; *Producers:* Louis Malle, Norbert Auerbach; *Screenwriters:* Louis Malle, Jean-Claude Carrière, with dialogue by Daniel Boulanger (from Georges Darien's novel *Le Voleur*); *Cinematographer:* Henri Decaë (Widescreen, Eastmancolor); *Production Designer:* Jacques Saulnier; *Sound:* André Hervée; *Editor:* Henri Lanoe; *Runtime:* 120 minutes

Cast: Jean-Paul Belmondo (Georges Randal), Geneviève Bujold (Charlotte), Marie Dubois (Geneviève Delpiels), Julien Guiomar (L'Abbé la Margelle), Paul le Person (Roger-la-honte), Christian Lude (Uncle Urbain), Françoise Fabian (Ida), Marlène Jobert

(Broussailles), Bernadette Lafont (Marguerite, the maid), Martine Sarcey (Renée), Roger Crouzet (Mouratet), Jacques Debary (Courbassol), Fernand Guiot (Mr. Van der Busch), Marc Dudicourt (Antoine), Paul Vally (Le Notaire), Monique Mélinand (Mme. Maranteuil), Jacqueline Staup (Mrs. Van der Busch), Nane Germon (Mrs. Voisin), Jacques Gheusi (Prof. Boileau), Christian de Tilière (Armand), Charles Denner (Cannonier).

"William Wilson" segment, from *Histoires extraordinaires* (Les Films Marceau-Cocinor [Paris], Produzioni Europee Associati Cinematografica [Rome]; France/ Italy, 1968); U.S.: *Spirits of the Dead,* a.k.a. *Tales of Mystery;* G.B.: *Tales of Terror,* a.k.a. *Tales of Mystery and Imagination;* Italy: *Tre passi nel delirio*

Director: Louis Malle; *Screenwriters:* Louis Malle, Daniel Boulanger, Clement Biddle Wood; *Cinematographer:* Tonino delli Colli (Scope, Eastmancolor); *Art Director/Costume Designer:* Carlo Leva; *Production Designer:* Ghislain Uhry; *Music:* Diego Masson; *Editors:* Franco Arcalli, Suzanne Baron; *Runtime of Segment:* 40 minutes. (*Entire film:* 117 min.)

Cast: Alain Delon (William Wilson), Brigitte Bardot (Giuseppina), Danièle Vargas (Professor), Renzo Palmer (Priest), Marco Stefanelli (Wilson as a child); Katia Christina (Prostitute), Umberto d'Orsi (Hans)

Calcutta (Nouvelles Éditions de Films, France, 1968)

Director: Louis Malle; *Producer:* Elliott Kastner; *Cinematographer:* Étienne Becker, Louis Malle (16mm Ektachrome); *Sound:* Jean-Claude Laureux; *Editor:* Suzanne Baron *Narrator:* Louis Malle; *Runtime:* 105 min.

— AWARDS AND NOMINATIONS —
1969 Cannes Film Festival — Palme d'Or (nom)

L'Inde fantôme (Nouvelles Éditions de Films, France, 1969)

Director: Louis Malle; *Producer:* Elliott Kastner; *Cinematographer:* Étienne Becker; *Sound:* Jean-Claude Laureux; *Editor:* Suzanne Baron; *Narrator:* Louis Malle; *Run-*

time: Each episode, 54 minutes. Entire series, 378 minutes.

Segments: (1) *La Caméra Impossible,* (2) *Choses vues à Madras,* (3) *La Religion,* (4) *La Tentation du rêve,* (5) *Regards sur les castes,* (6) *Les Étrangers en Inde,* (7) *Bombay*

Le Souffle au cœur (Nouvelles Éditions de Films/Marianne [Paris], Vides Cinematografica [Rome], Franz Seitz Filmproduktion [Munich]; France/Italy/Germany, 1971); U.S.: *Murmur of the Heart;* G.B.: **Dearest Love,** a.k.a. **Dearest Heart;** Germany: **Herzflimmern;** Italy: **Soffio al cuore**

Director: Louis Malle; *Producers:* Vincent Malle, Claude Nedjar; *Screenwriter:* Louis Malle; *Cinematographer:* Ricardo Aronovich (Eastmancolor); *Assistant Directors:* Rida Draïs, Fernand Moszkowicz; *Art Directors:* Jean-Jacques Caziot, Michel Vionnet; *Music:* Charlie Parker, Sidney Bechet, Gaston Frèche, and Henri Renaud; *Editor:* Suzanne Baron; *Runtime:* 118 minutes

Cast: Léa Massari (Clara Chevalier), Benoît Ferreux (Laurent Chevalier), Daniel Gélin (Dr. Charles Chevalier), Michel Lonsdale (Father Henri), Ave Ninchi (Augusta), Gila von Weitershausen (Freda, the prostitute), Fabien Ferreux (Thomas), Marc Winocourt (Marc), Micheline Bona (Aunt Claudine), Henri Poirier (Uncle Léonce), Liliane Sorval (Fernande), Corrinne Kersten (Daphné), François Werner (Hubert), René Bouloc (Man at Bastille Day party), Jacqueline Chauvaud (Hélène), Jacques Gheusi (Hotel Receptionist), Yvon Loc (Father Superior)

— AWARDS AND NOMINATIONS —
1971 New York Film Critics Circle Awards— Best Director, Louis Malle (nom); Best Screenplay, Louis Malle (nom)
1972 Academy Awards— Best Original Screenplay, Louis Malle (nom)
1971 Cannes Film Festival— Palme d'Or (nom)

Lacombe, Lucien (Nouvelles Éditions de Films/UPF [Paris], Vides Film [Rome], Hallelujah Films [Munich]; France/Italy/Germany, 1974)

Director: Louis Malle; *Producer:* Louis Malle, Claude Nedjar; *Screenwriters:* Louis Malle, Patrick Modiano; *Cinematographer:* Tonino delli Colli (Eastmancolor); *Art Director/Production Designer:* Ghislain Uhry *Music:* Django Reinhardt and the Quintet of the Hot Club de France (performing "Manoir de mes rêves," "Minor Swing," "Nuages," "Fleur d'Ennui," "Douce ambience," and "Lentement Mademoiselle"); Irène de Trébert (performing "Mademoiselle Swing"); André Claveau (performing "Ah! c'qu'on s'aimait" and "Mon cœur est un violon"); *Sound:* Jean-Claude Laureux; *Editor:* Suzanne Baron; *Runtime:* 137 minutes

Cast: Pierre Blaise (Lucien Lacombe), Aurore Clément (France Horn), Holger Löwenadler (Albert Horn), Thérèse Giehse (Bella Horn), Stéphane Bouy (Jean-Bernard), Loumi Iacobesco (Betty Beaulieu), René Bouloc (Faure), Pierre Decazes (Aubert, the bartender), Jean Rougerie (Tonin, the police chief), Cécile Ricard (Marie, the hotel maid), Jacqueline Staup (Lucienne), Ave Ninchi (Mme. Georges), Pierre Saintons (Hippolyte, the black collaborator), Gilberte Rivet (Mme. Lacombe, Lucien's mother), Jacques Rispal (M. Laborit, the Lacombe family's landlord), Jean Bousquet (Peyssac, the schoolteacher)

— AWARDS AND NOMINATIONS —
1975 British Academy Awards— Best Film (win); United Nations Award (win); Best Director, Louis Malle (nom); Best Screenplay, Louis Malle and Patrick Modiano (nom)
1974 Academy Awards— Best Foreign Language Film (nom)
1974 New York Film Critics Circle Awards— Best Supporting Actor, Holger Löwenadler (nom)
1975 Golden Globes— Best Foreign Film (nom)
1974 National Society of Film Critics Awards— Best Supporting Actor, Holger Löwenadler (win)
1974 National Board of Review Awards— Best Supporting Actor, Holger Löwenadler (win); Best Foreign Film (nom)

Humain, trop humain (Nouvelles Éditions de Films, France, produced 1972, released 1974)

Director: Louis Malle; *Cinematographer:* Étienne Becker (Ektachrome, 16mm); *Sound:* Jean-Claude Laureux; *Editor:* Suzanne Baron *Runtime:* 75 minutes

Place de la République (Nouvelles Éditions de Films, France, produced 1972, released 1974)

Director: Louis Malle; *Cinematographer:* Étienne Becker (Ektachrome, 16mm); *Associate Director:* Fernand Moszkowicz; *Sound:* Jean-Claude Laureux; *Editor:* Suzanne Baron; *Runtime:* 94 minutes

Black Moon (Nouvelles Éditions de Films/ UFP [Paris], Vides Film [Rome]; France/ Italy, 1975); Italy: *Luna negra*

Director: Louis Malle; *Producer:* Claude Nedjar; *Screenwriters:* Louis Malle, Ghislain Uhry with dialogue by Joyce Buñuel; *Cinematographer:* Sven Nykvist (Eastmancolor); *Art Director/Production Designer:* Ghislain Uhry; *Assistant Director:* Fernand Moszkowicz; *Music:* Richard Wagner, arranged by Diego Masson; *Sound:* Nara Kollery, Luc Perini; *Editor:* Suzanne Baron; *Runtime:* 100 minutes

Cast: Thérèse Giehse (The Old Woman; Voice of the Unicorn — uncredited), Cathryn Harrison (Lily, The Girl), Joe Dallesandro (Lily, the brother), Alexandra Stewart (The sister), Louis Malle (Voice on Radio— uncredited), Justine Malle (Infant in jewel box— uncredited).

— AWARDS AND NOMINATIONS —

1976 César Awards— Best Cinematography, Sven Nykvist (win); Best Sound, Nara Kollery and Luc Perini (win)

Close Up (Sigma-Antenne 2, France, 1976)

Director: Louis Malle; Producer (N/A — Unreleased); *Cinematographer:* Michel Parbot *Music:* Erik Satie; *Editor:* Suzanne Baron; *Runtime:* 26 minutes

Pretty Baby (Paramount, U.S.A, 1978); France: *La Petite*

Director: Louis Malle; *Producer:* Louis Malle; *Screenwriter:* Polly Platt, from a story by Louis Malle and Polly Platt; *Cinematographer:* Sven Nykvist (Metrocolor); *Production Designer:* Trevor Williams; *Musical Director:* Jerry Wexler (adapted/arranged from selections by Jelly Roll Morton, Scott Joplin, Louis Chauvin, the original Dixieland Jazz Band, Mamie Desmond and others, and performed by the New Orleans Ragtime Orchestra, the Jazz Combo, The Trio, and Bob Green); *Editors:* Suzanne Baron, Suzanne Fenn; *Runtime:* 110 min. (G.B. cut: 109 min.)

Cast: Brooke Shields (Violet), Keith Carradine (E.J. Bellocq), Susan Sarandon (Hattie), Frances Faye (Madame Nell Livingston), Antonio Fargas (Claude, the "Professor"), Matthew Anton (Red Top), Diana Scarwid (Frieda), Barbara Steele (Josephine), Seret Scott (Flora), Cheryl Markowitz (Gussie), Susan Manskey (Fanny), Laura Zimmerman (Agnes), Miz Mary (Odette), Gerrit Graham (Highpockets), Mae Mercer (Mama Mosebery), Don Hood (Alfred Fuller), Eric Von Thomas (Nonny), Sasha Holliday (Justine), Lisa Shames (Antonia), Henry Braden (Harry), Philip H. Sizeler (Senator), Don Lutenbacher (Violet's first client).

— AWARDS AND NOMINATIONS —

1978 Academy Awards— Best Musical Scoring, Jerry Wexler (nom)
1978 Cannes Film Festival— Palme d'Or (nom); Technical Grand Prize (win)
1978 National Board of Review— Best Picture (nom)

Atlantic City (Cine-Neighbour/CFDC [Montreal], Famous Players Ltd./Selta Films-Elie Kfouri [Paris]; France/Canada, 1980)

Director: Louis Malle; *Producers:* John Kemeny, Joseph Beaubien, Denis Heroux; *Screenplay:* John Guare; *Cinematographer:* Richard Ciupka (color); *Production Designer:* Anne Pritchard; *Assistant Director:* John Board; *Music:* Michel Legrand, Paul Anka ("Atlantic City, My Old Friend"), Vincenzo Bellini (selections from his opera *Norma*); *Sound:* Jean-Claude Laureux; *Editor:* Suzanne Baron; *Apprentice Editor:* James Bruce

Cast: Burt Lancaster (Lou Pascal), Susan Sarandon (Sally Matthews), Kate Reid (Grace Pinza), Michel Piccoli (Joseph), Hollis Mc-

Laren (Chrissie), Robert Joy (Dave), Al Wax-man (Alfie), Robert Goulet (Singer in Hospital), Moses Znamier (Felix), Angus MacInnes (Vinnie), Sean Sullivan (Buddy O'Brien), Wally Shawn (Waiter), Harvey Atkin (Bus driver), Norma dell'Agnese (Jeanne), Louis Del Grande (Mr. Shapiro), Cec Linder (Hospital President), Sean McCaan (Detective), Vincent Glorioso (Young Doctor), Adèle Chatfield-Taylor (Florist), Tony Angelo (Poker player), Sis Clark (Toll Booth Operator), Gennaro Consalvo (Pit Boss), Connie Collins (Connie Bishop), John Allmond (Police commissioner), John Burns (Anchorman); Ann, Marie, and Jean Burns (Casino singers)

— AWARDS AND NOMINATIONS —

1980 Venice Film Festival — Golden Lion (win)

1981 Academy Awards — Best Picture (nom); Best Actor, Burt Lancaster (nom); Best Actress, Susan Sarandon (nom); Best Director, Louis Malle (nom); Best Original Screenplay, John Guare (nom)

1981 British Academy Awards — Best Picture (nom); Best Actor, Burt Lancaster (win); Best Director, Louis Malle (win); Best Screenplay, John Guare (nom)

1981 New York Film Critics Circle Awards — Best Actor, Burt Lancaster (win); Best Director, Louis Malle (nom); Best Film (nom); Best Screenplay, John Guare (win)

1980 César Awards — Best Original Score (nom); Best Original Screenplay, John Guare (nom)

1981 Genie Awards — Best Foreign Actress, Susan Sarandon (win); Best Art Direction, Anne Pritchard (win); Best Supporting Actress, Kate Reid (win); Best Cinematography, Richard Ciupka (nom); Best Costume Design, François Barbeau (nom); Best Performance by Foreign Actor, Burt Lancaster (nom); Best Performance by Supporting Actor, Robert Joy (nom)

1982 Golden Globes — Best Director, Louis Malle (nom); Best Foreign Film (nom); Best Actor in a Drama, Burt Lancaster (nom)

My Dinner with André (The André Company, for George W. George in association with Michael White; U.S.A, 1981)

Director: Louis Malle; *Producers:* George W. George, Beverly Karp; *Screenplay:* Wallace Shawn, André Gregory; *Cinematographer:* Jeri Sopanen (Color-Movielab); *Art Directors:* David Mitchell, Stephen McCabe; *Music:* Allen Shawn (Piano solo from Satie's "Gymnopedie #1," performed by Joseph Villa); *Editor:* Suzanne Baron; *Assistant Editor:* James Bruce; *Runtime:* 111 min.

Cast: Wallace Shawn (Wally Shawn), André Gregory (André Gregory), Jean Lenauer (Waiter), Roy Butler (Bartender)

— AWARDS AND NOMINATIONS —

1981 Boston Society of Film Critics Awards — Best American Film (win); Best Screenplay, Wally Shawn and André Gregory (win)

Crackers (Universal Pictures, U.S.A, 1983)

Director: Louis Malle; *Producers:* Edward Lewis, Robert Cortes; *Screenplay:* Jeffrey Alan Fiskin, from the 1958 Italian film *I soliti ignoti*, a.k.a. Big Deal on Madonna Street, a.k.a. *Persons Unknown*. Original film written by Mario Monicelli, Furio Scarpelli, Suso Cecchi d'Amico, and Agenore Incrocci; *Cinematographer:* László Kovács; *Production Designer:* John J. Lloyd; *Music:* Pal Chihara; Theme song, "More Than We Need," performed by Michael McDonald; *Assistant Directors:* Carol Green, James Quinn; *Editor:* Suzanne Baron; *Runtime:* 91 minutes.

Cast: Donald Sutherland (Weslake), Jack Warden (Melvin Garvey), Sean Penn (Dillard), Wallace Shawn (Turtle), Larry Riley (Boardwalk), Trinidad Silva (Ramon), Christine Baranski (Maxine), Charlaine Woodard (Jasmine), Tasia Valenza (Maria), Irwin Corey (Lazzarelli), Edouard de Soto (Don Fernando), Anna-Maria Horsford (Slam Dunk)

— AWARDS AND NOMINATIONS —

1984 Berlin Film Festival — Golden Bear (nom)

Alamo Bay (Tri-Star Pictures/Delphi III Productions, U.S.A, 1985)

Director: Louis Malle; Executive *Producer:* Ross E. Milloy; *Producers:* Louis Malle, Vincent Malle; *Screenwriter:* Alice Arlen, from *New York Times* articles by Ross E. Milloy;

Cinematographer: Curtis Clark (Metrocolor); *Production Designer:* Trevor Williams; *Assistant Directors:* Fred Berner, Mark McGann; *Music:* Ry Cooder; *Sound:* Danny Michael; *Editor:* James Bruce; *Runtime:* 98 minutes

Cast: Amy Madigan (Glory), Ed Harris (Shang Pierce), Ho Nguyen (Dinh), Donald Moffat (Wally Scheer), Truyen V. Tran (Ben), Rudy Young (Skinner), Cynthia Carle (Honey), Martino Lasalle (Luis), William Frankfather (Mac), Bill Thurman (Sheriff), Michael Ballard (Wendell), Gary Basaraba (Leon), Jerry Biggs (Buddy), Mark Hanks (Brandon), Khoa Van Le (Father Ky), Doris Hargrave (Mrs. Ranney), Harvey Lewis (Tex), Ed Opstad (Cal), Jeannette Hudson Gray (Rita Venable), Buddy Killen (Rev. Disney), Donna Callaway Nugent (Mrs. Disney)

God's Country (PBS/National Endowment for the Arts, U.S.A, 1985); France: *Le Pays de dieu*

Director: Louis Malle; *Producer:* Vincent Malle; *Cinematographer:* Louis Malle (color); *Sound:* Jean-Claude Laureux (1979), Keith Rouse (1985); *Editor:* James Bruce; *Runtime:* 95 minutes

And the Pursuit of Happiness (Pretty Mouse Films, U.S.A, 1986); France: *La Poursuite du bonheur*

Director: Louis Malle; *Cinematographer:* Louis Malle (color); *Sound:* Danny Michael; *Editor:* Nancy Baker; *Associate Producer:* James Bruce; *Runtime:* 80 minutes

Au revoir les enfants (Nouvelles Éditions de Films/MK2 Productions/Marin Karmitz [Paris], Stella Film/NEF [Munich]; France/Germany; 1987); U.S.: *Goodbye, Children*; Germany: *Auf Wiedersehen, Kinder*

Director: Louis Malle; Screenwriter: Louis Malle; *Cinematographer:* Renato Berta; Art Director/*Production Designer:* Willy Holt *Sound:* Jean-Claude Laureux; *Editor:* Emmanuelle Castro; *Runtime:* 104 minutes

Cast: Gaspard Manesse (Julien Quentin), Raphaël Fejtö (Jean Bonnet), Francine Racette (Mme. Quentin), Stanislas Carré

de Malberg (François Quentin), Philippe Morier-Genoud (Père Jean), François Berléand (Père Michel), François Négret (Joseph), Peter Fitz (Muller), Pascal Rivet (Boulanger), Benoît Henriet (Ciron), Richard Leboeuf (Sagard), Xavier Legrand (Babinot), Arnaud Henriet (Negus), Jean-Sébastien Chauvin (Laviron), Luc Étienne (Moreau), Irène Jacob (Mlle. Davenne), Jacqueline Paris (Mme. Perrin), Jacqueline Staup (Nurse)

— AWARDS AND NOMINATIONS —

1987 Academy Awards — Best Foreign Language Film (nom); Best Original Screenplay, Louis Malle (nom)

1988 César Awards — Best Cinematography, Renato Berta (win); Best Director, Louis Malle (win); Best Editing, Emmanuelle Castro (win); Best Film (win); Best Original Screenplay, Louis Malle (win); Best Production Design, Willy Holt (win); Best Sound, Jean-Claude Laureux, ClaudeVilland and Bernard Leroux (win); Best Costume Design, Corinne Jory (nom); Most Promising Actor, François Négret (nom)

1987 LA Film Critics Assn. Awards — Best Foreign Film (win)

1988 British Academy Awards — Best Director, Louis Malle (win); Best Film (nom); Best Foreign Film (nom); Best Original Screenplay, Louis Malle (nom)

1988 New York Critics Film Circle Awards — Best Foreign Film (nom)

1988 Golden Globes — Best Foreign Film (nom)

1987 Prix Louis-Delluc (win)

1987 Venice Film Festival — Golden Lion (win); OCIC Award (win)

Milou en mai (Nouvelles Éditions de Films/TFI Films [Paris], Ellipi Film [Rome]; France/Italy, 1990); U.S.: *May Fools*; G.B.: *Milou in May.*

Director: Louis Malle; *Producers:* Louis Malle, Vincent Malle; *Screenplay:* Louis Malle, Jean-Claude Carrière; *Cinematographer:* Renato Berta (color); *Art Director:* Willy Holt; *Music:* Stephane Grappelli, Also Cherubino's Aria from *The Marriage of Figaro* by Wolfgang Amadeus Mozart, Debussy's "General Levine," and (sung by the cast) "La Fille du Bedouin," from *Le Comte obligado*; *Editor:* Emmanuelle Castro; *Runtime:* 105 minutes

Cast: Michel Piccoli (Emile Vieuzac, a.k.a. Milou), Miou-Miou (Camille), Michel Duchaussoy (Georges), Dominique Blanc (Claire), Harriet Walter (Lily), Bruno Carette (Grimaldi), François Berléand (Daniel), Martine Gautier (Adèle), Paulette Dubost (Mme. Vieuzac, Milou's mother), Rozenn Le Tallec (Marie-Laure), Renaud Danner (Pierre-Alain), Jeanne Herry-Leclerc (Françoise), Benjamin and Nicolas Prieur (Camille's Twins), Marcel Bories (Léonce), Étienne Draber (M. Boutelleau), Valerie Lemercier (Mme. Boutelleau), Hubert Saint-Macary (Paul), Bernard Brocas (Priest), Denise Juskiewenski (Mme. Abel), Jacqueline Staup/Anne-Marie Bonange (Neighbors), Stephane Broquedis (Young Man), Serge Angeloff (Adèle's fiancé)

— AWARDS AND NOMINATIONS —

1991 César Awards—Best Supporting Actress, Dominique Blanc (win); Best Actor, Michel Piccoli (nom); Best Actress, Miou-Miou (nom); Best Supporting Actor, Michel Duchaussoy (nom)

1990 New York Film Critics Circle Awards—Best Foreign Film (nom)

1990 British Academy Awards—Best Foreign Film (nom)

Damage (Nouvelles Éditions de Films [Paris], Skreba [UK]; France/Great Britain, 1992); France: *Fatale*

Director: Louis Malle; *Producers:* Vincent Malle, Simon Relph; *Screenwriter:* David Hare (from Josephine Hart's novel *Damage*); *Cinematographer:* Peter Biziou (color); *Production Designer:* Brian Morris; *Music:* Zbigniew Preisner; *Editor:* John Bloom; *Runtime:* 112 minutes (Edited to 111 min. for U.S. theatrical release)

Cast: Jeremy Irons (Dr. Stephen Fleming), Miranda Richardson (Ingrid Fleming), Rupert Graves (Martyn Fleming), Juliette Binoche (Anna Barton), Ian Bannen (Edward Lloyd), Leslie Caron (Elizabeth Prideaux), Julian Fellowes (Donald Lindsay, MP), Peter Stormare (Peter Wetzlar), Gemma Clarke (Sally Fleming), Tony Doyle (British Prime Minister), Raymond Gravell (Raymond, Stephen's chauffeur), Benjamin Whitrow (elderly civil servant), Jeff Nuttall (Trevor Leigh Davies, MP), Susan Engel (Miss Snow), Henry Power (Henry, Sally's boyfriend), David Thewlis (Detective), Linda Delapena (Beth)

— AWARDS AND NOMINATIONS —

1992 Academy Awards—Best Supporting Actress, Miranda Richardson (nom)

1992 British Academy Awards—Best Supporting Actress, Miranda Richardson (win)

1992 Golden Globe Awards—Best Supporting Actress, Miranda Richardson (nom); 1993 César Awards—Best Actress, Juliette Binoche (nom)

1992 Los Angeles Film Critics Assn. Awards—Best Music, Zbigniew Preisner

1992 New York Film Critics Circle Awards—Best Supporting Actress, Miranda Richardson (win)

Vanya on 42nd Street (Laura Pels Productions/Mayfair Entertainment/Channel 4/Sony Pictures Classics, U.S.A, 1994)

Producer: Fred Berner; *Screenplay:* David Mamet, from Vlada Chernomordik's translation of Anton Chekhov's *Uncle Vanya*; *Cinematographer:* Declan Quinn (color); *Production Designer:* Eugene Lee; *Sound:* Ron Bochar; *Music:* Joshua Redman (Performed by the Joshua Redman Quartet); *Editor:* Nancy Baker; *Runtime:* 119 minutes

Cast: Wallace Shawn (Himself/Vanya), Julianne Moore (Herself/Yelena), Brooke Smith (Herself/Sonya), Larry Pine (Himself/Dr. Astrov), George Gaynes (Himself/Serybryakov), Lynn Cohen (Herself/Maman), Phoebe Brand (Herself/Marina, the Nanny), Jerry Meyer (Himself/Waffles), Madhur Jaffrey (Mrs. Chao), André Gregory (Himself)

— AWARDS AND NOMINATIONS —

1994 Boston Society of Film Critics Awards—Best Actress, Julianne Moore (win).

Notes

Preface

1. Several critical monographs on Malle have been published in Germany, during the director's life and in the decade since his death.

2. Billard's book is something of a disappointment because of the number of obvious factual errors it contains; several dates are substantially off, well-known actors' names are spelled incorrectly, and the material feels rather gossipy at times (as when the author suggests, erroneously, that Malle and Jean-Pierre Gorin had an acrimonious professional split). The problem is that although the book contains misinformation, it is certainly not — as the only biography published, to date, on the director's life — worthless. The Malle family and the staff of Nouvelles Éditions de Films feel positive and confident about the work and it does contain a great deal of valid information that cannot be found elsewhere without an unholy amount of archival research and interviewing. That said, though this book contains many references to Billard, I have tried to corroborate as much of the information as possible with other sources, and, in the case of information that is flatly contradicted from one source to another, I note those contradictions explicitly.

3. Manuel Malle, "Re: Louis Malle." E-mail to author, 6 June 2001.

4. Louis Malle, *Malle on Malle*, ed. Philip French, rev. ed. (London: Faber & Faber, 1996), 142–3.

5. Louis Malle and Sarah Kant, *Louis Malle par Louis Malle*, Editions de l'Athenor (Paris: Jacques Mallecot, 1978), 75 (author translation).

6. L. Malle, *Malle on Malle*, 155–6.

7. *Ibid.*, 200.

8. Philip French, introduction to *Malle on Malle*, by Louis Malle (London, Faber & Faber, 1996), xvi.

Introduction

1. Louis Malle, *Malle on Malle*, ed. Philip French, rev. ed. (London: Faber & Faber, 1996), 1.

2. Manuel Malle, interview by author, New York, NY, 20 October 2001.

3. L. Malle, *Malle on Malle*, 200.

4. A surprisingly large number of well-known, accomplished adults have, in fact, followed the same pattern. For instance, Teddy Roosevelt's transition from a physically restrained, hypersomatic childhood to intense global exploration during adulthood (see the epigraph at the beginning of Chapter 1, on *The Silent World*) epitomizes this idea.

5. L. Malle, *Malle on Malle*, 1–3.

6. Pauline Kael, "Louis Malle's Portrait of the Artist as a Young Dog," review of *Murmur of the Heart* (dir. Louis Malle). *Deeper into Movies* (Boston: Little, Brown, and Company, 1971), 307.

7. Andrew Sarris, review of *Lacombe, Lucien* (dir. Louis Malle), *Village Voice*, 17 October 1974, 78.

8. Jean Douchet and Céderic Anger, *French New Wave* (New York: DAP in Association with Editions Hazan/Cinémathèque Française, 1999), 236.

9. *Ibid.*

10. Susan Sontag, "Approaching Artaud," in *Under the Sign of Saturn* (New York: Farrar, Straus and Giroux, 1980), 15.

11. Vincent Malle, telephone interview by author, 15 December 2004.

12. Susan Sarandon, telephone interview by author, 18 November 2004

13. L. Malle, *Malle on Malle*, 28.

14. Leonard Maltin, review of *May Fools* (dir. Louis Malle), in *Leonard Maltin's Movie and Video Guide*, 20th ed. (New York: Signet Books, 1999), 889.

15. Jay Robert Nash, Stanley Ralph Ross, eds., review of *May Fools* (dir. Louis Malle), in *The Motion Picture Guide*, vol. 18 (Chicago: CineBooks, 1991), 112–13.

16. Roger Ebert, review of *Star 80* (dir. Bob Fosse). *Roger Ebert's Movie Home Companion 1993* (Kansas City, MO: Andrews-McMeel, 1992), 615.

17. Leonard Maltin, review of *Pretty Baby* (dir. Louis Malle). *Movie and Video Guide*, 1099.

18. Douchet and Anger, *French NewWave*, 261.

19. Philip French, "Malle's marvelous milieu,"

review of *May Fools* (dir. Louis Malle). *Observer*, 2 September 1990, 60.

20. Danny Peary, review of *Pretty Baby* (dir. Louis Malle). *Film Fanatic*, 338.

21. M. Malle, interview.

22. L. Malle, *Malle on Malle*, 86.

23. André Bazin, "The Myth of Total Cinema," in *What Is Cinema?*, trans. and ed. Hugh Gray (Berkeley: University of California Press, 1967), 17.

24. It is also hardly accidental that a director like Truffaut — whose discovery of cinema preceded his discovery of storytelling — would first use biographical material for cinematic fodder, as opposed to material from extrabiographical literature (as demonstrated in *Les Mistons* and *Les Quatre Cents Coups*). The opposite is the case with Malle's first four films: all are adaptations, not quasibiographical features about Malle's childhood.

25. François Truffaut, *Le Cinéma selon François Truffaut*, ed. Anne Gillain (Paris: Flammarion, 1988), 15–24.

26. L. Malle, *Malle on Malle*, 1.

27. Lest one feel tempted to argue that form-before-story is always a superior method (given the scores of celebrated filmmakers who have followed this track), one should remember that is can just as often become problematic. Even if one uses the career of Hitchcock to defend story before form — one of the most celebrated directors in history, and a man who typically devised a story as the very last step in his creative process — one can look to his last three or four films to grasp the potentially disastrous effects of relying on style at the expense of content. The same can be argued of many other *auteurs* who followed suit.

28. Manuel Malle recalls that in late 1960 François Truffaut wrote Louis a personal letter praising *Zazie*. The letter reads, "*Zazie* bowled me over; it's a madly ambitious and hugely courageous film…. I was often moved by the manipulation of the image … the close-ups against a background in motion, etc." Coming from Truffaut, these laudations are hugely significant, for it reveals the extent to which the Nouvelle Vague auteurs put form ahead of content. Like Malle's other pictures, *Zazie* places a heavier emphasis on story than on style, yet it can be misconstrued, if only because Malle's aesthetic and his stylistic devices in the film are so obtuse. Truffaut's comment reveals his misinterpretation of *Zazie*, and his erroneous belief that story takes a backseat to style in the film. From his words, we may infer that the Truffaut sensed how contrary Malle's nontheoretical *démarche* was to his own, and believed *Zazie* signaled a shift in *démarche*. It did not.

29. M. Malle, interview.

30. *Ibid.*

31. *Ibid.*

32. Kael, "Portrait of the Artist," 307.

33. Louis Malle and Sarah Kant, *Louis Malle par Louis Malle*, Editions de l'Athenor (Paris: Jacques Mallecot, 1978), 7–8 (author translation).

34. Ross Milloy, telephone interview by author, 28 March 2004.

35. L. Malle, *Malle on Malle*, 116.

36. Candice Bergen, telephone interview by author, 9 March 2004.

37. V. Malle, interview.

38. *Ibid.*

39. Bergen, interview.

40. V. Malle, interview.

41. L. Malle, *Malle on Malle*, 66.

42. Vincent Malle notes that the Indian exile and May 1968 both served the same purpose: They led Malle to the belief that a utopian society would be possible.

43. In *Murmur*, *Lacombe*, and *Black Moon*, this works; *Pretty Baby* suffers under the weight of its languor, a flaw that encouraged Malle to gravitate back to tight dramatic architecture for his follow-up American project, *Atlantic City*.

44. Although many of the Eastern-influenced qualities would continue to hallmark Malle's work, the "narrative structural liberation" came to an end with *Baby*. In his work on *Atlantic City*, John Guare reintroduced tight dramatic structure to the Malle catalog.

45. David Hare, telephone interview by author, 17 October 2003.

46. Sarandon, interview.

47. *Ibid.*

48. L. Malle, *Malle on Malle*, 94.

49. John Guare, telephone interview by author, 7 April 2004.

50. André Gregory, telephone interview by author, 15 July 2003.

51. Brooke Smith, telephone interview by author, 2 April 2004.

52. Hare, interview.

53. René Prédal, *Louis Malle* (Paris: Edilig, 1989), 141–2 (author translation).

54. Bergen, interview.

Chapter 1

1. Louis Malle, *Malle on Malle*, ed. Philip French, rev. ed. (London: Faber & Faber, 1996), 4–6.

2. Pierre Billard, *Louis Malle: le rebelle solitaire* (Paris: Plon, 2003), 555.

3. *Ibid.*, 5.

4. René Prédal, *Louis Malle* (Paris: Edilig, 1989), 8.

5. L. Malle, *Malle on Malle*, 6.

6. Richard Munson, *Cousteau: The Captain and His World* (New York: William Morrow, 1989), 39–40, 74–75.

7. Axel Madsen, *Cousteau: An Unauthorized Biography* (New York: Beaufort Books, 1986), 53.

8. In a 1992 issue of the *Calypso Log*, Malle remembers, "I'd seen Jacques' short black-and-white films and thought they were terribly interesting. Also, I was interested in underwater filming, which I'd never done. I'd never even been diving before, but I was a good swimmer, so I suppose that's how I got the job!"

9. Prédal, *Louis Malle*, 10.

10. Madsen, *Cousteau*, 84.

11. Jacques-Yves Cousteau, "'Studio' Under the Sea," *New York Times*, 16 Sep. 1956, sec. 2, p.1.

12. "The Silent Film Uses New Underwater Techniques." *Popular Photography* 40, January 1957, 116.

13. *Ibid*.

14. *Ibid*.

15. *Ibid*.

16. This running time applies only to the original French cut; the British version (with dubbed narration by James Dugan) runs 82 minutes.

17. *Le Monde du silence*, dirs. Jacques-Yves Cousteau and Louis Malle, 86 min., Filmad/J. Arthur Rank Productions/Victory, 1956, videocassette.

18. André Bazin, "Le Monde du silence," in *Qu'est-ce que le cinéma*, vol. 1, *Ontologie et langage* (Paris: Éditions du Cerf, 1958–62), 59 (author translation).

19. *Ibid.*, 60.

20. Madsen, *Cousteau*, 95.

21. Bosley Crowther, "The Real Things: Underwater Exploration in *The Silent World*." *New York Times* (30 September 1956), sec. 2, p.1.

22. Cousteau and Malle, *Monde du silence* (author translation).

23. Rachel Carson, *The Sea Around Us* (New York: New American Library, 1961), 46–47.

24. Jacques-Yves Cousteau, *The Silent World* (New York: Harper, 1953), 244.

25. Crowther, "Real Things."

26. Cousteau, "Studio."

27. Carson, *Sea Around Us*, 47.

28. Note, for example, the scene in which the men sit around the dinner table and "ad lib" conversation.

29. Interestingly, the dubbed English-language version of *The Silent World* actually heightens the imagery and the "poetic language" of the narration. For instance, the famous opening line (and metaphor), "A motion picture studio, 165 feet below the surface of the ocean" is not an accurate reflection of the original French narration. In the original film, the narrator says, "Fifty meters below the surface of the ocean, the men shoot their film."

30. It is hardly accidental that while renowned American critic Danny Peary cites *Le Monde du silence* as a "personal recommendation" in his indispensable 1986 reference book *Guide for the Film Fanatic*, he omits the picture from his list of historically significant films. Yet one may add a historically significant footnote to the film: *Monde* was the first motion picture in history to incorporate footage shot at a depth of 247 feet below sea level.

31. This sense of "unbroken reality" can be directly traced to one of Malle's most significant influences — Jean Renoir — and also to Malle's interpretation of André Bazin's teachings.

32. A final note: given the inevitability of cinematic subjectivity, absolute truth is nonexistent onscreen, which is why Malle objects so vehemently to the term *cinéma vérité* and states that he prefers cinema direct. The latter refers not only to a set of techniques, but (as we have seen) to a series of kinesthetic principles, yet avoids the moral imperative suggested by "*vérité*" (the truth) that carries pretentious and hypocritical connotations. In his reference volume *Documentary: A History of the Nonfiction Film*, Eric Barnouw lists another crucial distinction between cinema direct and *cinéma vérité*. "The direct cinema documentarist," he writes, "took his camera to a situation of tension and waited hopefully for a crisis; the Rouch version of *cinéma vérité* tried to precipitate one. The cinema direct artist aspired to invisibility' the Rouch *cinéma vérité* artist was often an avowed participant." Ergo, in this sense as well (i.e., the fact that Louis attempts — as much as possible — to avoid influencing the events before him) the Malle segments of *The Silent World* are cinema direct but cannot by any means be classified as *cinéma vérité*.

33. Erik Barnouw, *Documentary: A History of the Nonfiction Film* (New York: Oxford, 1993), 235.

34. *Ibid.*, 231.

35. Once again, this recalls Bazin's ubiquitous "Myth of Total Cinema" essay (see Introduction), which suggests that ideas for the development (or destination) of a medium arrive many years prior to the technical means for realizing it.

36. Erik Barnouw, *Documentary: A History of the Nonfiction Film* (New York: Oxford, 1993), 234–5.

37. *Ibid.*, 235–6.

38. L. Malle, *Malle on Malle*, 8.

39. Jacques-Yves Cousteau, interview by Mose Richards, *Calypso Log* 12, no. 2 (June 1985): 6.

40. Bazin, "Monde," 59 (author translation).

41. Bosley Crowther, "Screen: Beautiful Sea," *New York Times*, 25 Sep. 1956, late ed.: p. 30.

42. "Le Monde du silence." *Monthly Film Bulletin* 23 (1956): 12.

43. Gene Moskowitz, review of *Le Monde du Silence* (dirs. Jacques-Yves Cousteau and Louis Malle), *Variety* 203, 6 June 1956, 6.

44. Louis Malle and Sarah Kant, *Louis Malle par Louis Malle*, Editions de l'Athenor (Paris: Jacques Mallecot, 1978), 16 (author translation).

45. Philip French, Introduction to *Malle on Malle*, 8.

46. Madsen, *Cousteau*, 103, 113–116.

Chapter 2

1. Released in 1961, *Vie privée* (A Very Private Affair) falls in-between *Zazie* and *Le Feu follet*. *Privée* breaks Malle's succession of "acclaimed literary adaptations" on two counts: first, though the film began as a cinematization of Coward's *Private Lives*, it immediately became an original script, not an adaptation; second, a disastrous critical and commercial reception turned the film into Malle's first unmitigated bomb. See Chapter 6 for a full discussion of this motion picture.

2. The accreditation of the "cinematic equivalence" rule to François Truffaut is erroneous. Truffaut did discuss the idea extensively in his "Une Certaine

Tendance" essay, but published the work in a 1954 issue of *Cahiers,* three years after Bazin's essay on *Diary of a Country Priest* appeared in the same publication. One can thus infer that Truffaut lifted the idea from the teachings of Bazin, his mentor. Unlike Bazin, Truffaut deliberately sought to incite a revolution in French film culture, and thus saw no problem in "borrowing" Bazin's ideas. It is hugely ironic that Malle often lists Bresson as one of his biggest influences, given the fact that Malle's approach to Zazie seems to celebrate Truffaut/Bazin cinematic equivalence, and thus works directly *against* Bresson's "word for word faithfulness" in the adaptation process. (This could offer yet another explanation for the letter Truffaut wrote Malle, congratulating him on *Zazie:* perhaps Truffaut sensed a more faithful allegiance to Bazin than Malle typically demonstrated.)

3. André Bazin, "*Le Journal d'un curé de campagne* and the Stylistics of Robert Bresson," in *What Is Cinema?,* trans. and ed. Hugh Gray (Berkeley, CA: University of California Press, 1967), 126–8.

4. Stephen Geller, lecture to Graduate Level Screen Adaptation class, Boston University, Boston, MA, 8 October 1999.

5. Louis Malle, *Malle on Malle,* ed. Philip French, rev. ed. (London: Faber & Faber, 1996), 11.

6. *Ibid.*

7. Louis Malle and Sarah Kant, *Louis Malle par Louis Malle,* Editions de l'Athenor (Paris: Jacques Mallecot, 1978), 16–17.

8. L. Malle, *Malle on Malle,* 10.

9. René Prédal, *Louis Malle* (Paris: Edilig, 1989), 12 (author translation).

10. Malle and Kant, *Malle on Malle,* 17.

11. *Ibid.*

12. L. Malle, *Malle on Malle,* 10–11.

13. Eric Rohmer, review of *Ascenseur pour l'échafaud* (dir. Louis Malle), *Cahiers du cinéma* 80, February 1958, 59.

14. Jean Herman, review of *Ascenseur pour l'échafaud* (dir. Louis Malle), *Cinéma* 20, February 1958, 115 (author translation).

15. L. Malle, *Malle on Malle,* 11.

16. *Elevator to the Gallows,* dir. Louis Malle, 90 min., New Yorker Films, 1958, videocassette.

17. As Paul Schrader argues in his groundbreaking 1972 essay "Notes on Film Noir," *film noir* and *postnoir* should not be mistaken for genres. They represent specific periods in American and European cinema, characterized by tone and mood (whereas genres are characterized by theme and conflict).

18. This table generally speaks for itself, with a few exceptions. Naturally, some noir films are unclassifiable [for instance, *Vortex* (1982)]. A few films are dynamic, beginning as observational and detached, yet suddenly, unexpectedly becoming empathetic. The transition from empathetic to observational, on the other hand, rarely occurs in successful noirs. Granted, we may feel the need to associate "Observational" with *crime noir,* and "Empathetic" strictly with *suspense noir.* This generally holds, but one discovers significant exceptions, and *Ascenseur* represents the quintessential example. Most would

label the film a "thriller" (as does Pauline Kael) but Malle approaches it as an observational crime noir.

19. Daniel Lopez, *Films by Genre* (Jefferson, NC: McFarland & Company, 1993), 118–19 (noir/postnoir classification of individual films *only*—table is an original work).

20. Philip French, Introduction to *Malle on Malle,* by Louis Malle (London, Faber & Faber, 1996), xiii.

21. This explains why *Cahiers* (with its overwhelming emphasis on style) regarded the sudden inclusion of Florence's voice-over monologue as a flaw—a lapse in style.

22. Rohmer, *Ascenseur* review, 60.

23. Carl Jung, "On Synchronicity," in *The Portable Jung* (New York: Penguin Books, 1971), 505–9.

24. Interestingly, it is unnecessary for Malle, even once, to cloak the audience in the distortion of Julien's subjective outlook; the god's-eye-view offers far more interesting possibilities. Through it, we can not only make the inference about Julien's interpretation of the crime, but gain the superior oversight necessary to critique the distortion of his limited perspective.

25. Walter Weideli, *The Art of Bertolt Brecht* (New York: New York University Press, 1963), 61.

26. *Ibid.,* 16.

27. Eric Rohmer, "A New Generation," in *French New Wave,* ed. and trans. Jean Douchet and Céderic Anger (New York: DAP in Association with Editions Hazan/Cinematheque Francaise, 1999), 110. Originally published in *Arts,* 12 November 1958.

28. Pauline Kael, review of *Umberto D.* (dir. Vittorio De Sica). *5001 Nights at the Movies* (New York: Owl Books, 1991), 803.

29. L. Malle, *Malle on Malle,* 31–32.

30. Herman, 115 (author translation).

31. Kael, review of *Ascenseur.*

32. Jacques Doniol-Valcroize, "La Pouvoir de la nuit," review of *Les Amants* (dir. Louis Malle), *Cahiers du cinéma* 89, November 1958, 43.

33. French, Introduction to *Malle on Malle,* xiii.

Chapter 3

1. Louis Malle, *Malle on Malle,* ed. Philip French, rev. ed. (London: Faber & Faber, 1996), 20.

2. Philip French, explanatory notes to *Malle on Malle,* by Louis Malle (London, Faber & Faber, 1996), 16.

3. L. Malle, *Malle on Malle,* 20.

4. *Ibid.,* 20–21

5. Chris Wiegand, "Jeanne Moreau: Profile." *BBC Four* [online]. (cited 2002-12-8). Available from internet:<http://www.bbc.co.uk/bbcfour/cinema/features/jeanne_moreau_profile.shtml>

6. L. Malle, *Malle on Malle,* 20.

7. René Prédal, *Louis Malle* (Paris: Edilig, 1989), 18.

8. Jacques Doniol-Valcroize, "La Pouvoir de la nuit," review of *Les Amants* (dir. Louis Malle), *Cahiers du cinéma* 89, November 1958, 43.

9. Eric Rohmer, "A New Generation," in *French New Wave*, ed. and trans. Jean Douchet and Céderic Anger (New York: DAP in Association with Editions Hazan/Cinematheque Francaise, 1999), 110. Originally published in *Arts*, 12 November 1958.

10. *Ibid.*

11. One ambiguous element is Bernard's decision to leave the turntable running. It directly precipitates Jeanne's visit downstairs and thus leads one to question if Bernard's decision was premeditated. Did he consciously or subconsciously attempt to lure Jeanne to the lower level of the house with the music? Or, was it simply an accident that happened to lead to a romantic encounter? If the latter is true, the choice can certainly be described as "fate-driven." But Malle leaves it open to interpretation.

12. L. Malle, *Malle on Malle*, 22.

13. *Ibid.*, 20.

14. Louis Malle and Sarah Kant, *Louis Malle par Louis Malle*, Editions de l'Athenor (Paris: Jacques Mallecot, 1978), 19.

15. *Les Amants*, dir. Louis Malle, 88 min., New Yorker Films, 1959, videocassette.

16. Doniol-Valcroize, "Pouvoir," 44 (author translation).

17. Vincent Lavoie, "Amities et autres catastrophes: la carte du tendre (exposition)." *Parachute: Contemporary Art Magazine* (1 January 1998). In HighBeam Research [database online]. Available from internet: <http://www.highbeam.com/library/doc3.asp?docid=1G1:30479993&ctrlInfo=Round9c%3AProd2%3ATYF%3AContinue> (author translation).

18. Valerian Tornius, *Salons: Pictures of Society through Five Centuries* (New York: Cosmopolitan Book Corporation, 1929).

19. Danny Peary, review of *The Discreet Charm of the Bourgeoisie* (dir. Luis Buñuel). *Guide for the Film Fanatic* (New York: Fireside Books, 1986), 124.

20. Karen Mankovich Geller, lecture to Introduction to Screenwriting class, Boston University, Boston, MA, 20 February 1998.

21. L. Malle, *Malle on Malle*, 22.

22. Danny Peary, review of *The Lovers* (dir. Louis Malle). *Guide for the Film Fanatic* (New York: Fireside Books, 1986), 253.

23. L. Malle, *Malle on Malle*, 22–24.

24. Claretta Micheletta Tonetti, *Bernardo Bertolucci: The Cinema of Ambiguity* (New York: Twayne, 1995), 140–141.

25. Gene Moskowitz, review of *Les Amants* (dir. Louis Malle), *Variety* 212, 17 September 1958, 7.

26. Martin Quigley, Jr., and Richard Gertner, *Films in America 1929–1969: A Panoramic View of Four Decades of Sound* (New York: Golden Press, 1970), 262.

27. *Ibid.*, 353.

28. Moskowitz, 7.

29. Eric Rhode, review of *Les Amants* (dir. Louis Malle), *Monthly Film Bulletin* 26 (1959): 154.

30. L. Malle, *Malle on Malle*, 22.

31. Rohmer, "New Generation," 110.

32. Richard Roud, review of *Les Amants* (dir. Louis Malle), *Sight and Sound* 28 (1959): 22.

33. L. Malle, *Malle on Malle*, 21.

34. Malle and Kant, *Louis Malle par Louis Malle*, 18 (author translation).

Chapter 4

1. Because of my own limitations with French semantics and period slang, I have used Barbara Wright's author-supervised English translation when incorporating quotations from Queneau's novel. Because Wright made a series of meticulous and extraordinary attempts to preserve Queneau's wordplay, and received author supervision, this substitution seems reasonable and appropriate.

2. Gilbert Adair, introduction to *Zazie dans le métro*, Raymond Queneau, trans. Barbara Wright (New York: Penguin, 2001), xiii.

3. Pierre Billard, *Louis Malle: Le Rebelle solitaire* (Paris: Plon, 2003), 191.

4. Louis Malle, *Malle on Malle*, ed. Philip French, rev. ed. (London: Faber & Faber, 1996), 26.

5. This time frame is approximate; the specific month of *Zazie*'s initial publication, the date when Nouvelles Éditions purchased the rights from Iéna, and the date when Malle and Rappeneau began their adaptation are not documented in any published source.

6. Unsigned interview with Louis Malle, on *Zazie dans le métro. L'Express* (27 October 1969): 38.

7. *Ibid.*

8. Billard, *Rebelle,* 196.

9. Despite Démongeot's indisputable triumph in the role [she would go on to make three additional screen appearances, including an uncredited cameo as Zazie in Godard's 1961 *Une Femme est une femme*], Malle later commented, in *L'Express,* that she defiantly remained herself, never fully identifying with Zazie, never referring to Zazie in the first-person, and developing unshakable, highly individualistic opinions on the character of Zazie.

10. Philippe Noiret, telephone interview by author, 30 June 2004 (author translation).

11. *Ibid.*

12. *Ibid.*

13. *Ibid.*

14. Unfortunately, this jaw-dropper did not end up in the finished film.

15. Noiret, telephone interview.

16. "Release dates for *Zazie dans le métro*." *Internet Movie Database* [online]. (cited 2004-12–06). Available from internet: <http://www.imdb.com/title/tt0054494/releaseinfo>

17. L. Malle, *Malle on Malle*, 29.

18. *Ibid.*, 26.

19. See Chapter 7, "Only a Paper Moon," for a detailed discussion of *Maria*.

20. Stéphanie Grégoire, "Les Débuts de Louis Malle 1956–1963: un cinéaste humain, trop humain pour la Nouvelle Vague" (master's thesis, Université Michel de Montagne, 1998), 35–6.

21. *Ibid.*

22. Raymond Queneau, *Zazie dans le Métro*, trans. Barbara Wright (New York: Penguin, 2001), 3.

23. *Ibid.*, 42.

24. *Ibid.*, 124.

25. *Ibid.*, 112.

26. *Ibid.*, 74.

27. L. Malle, *Malle on Malle*, 26.

28. Adair, introduction to *Zazie*, xi.

29. A certifiably odd exception to this rule exists in Queneau's book: at the outset of Chapter 3 (pages 22–3 in the Penguin-published English translation) Zazie explores the physical space of her uncle's house while Gabriel sleeps. Though this scene remains as far as possible from rich neorealist description of, say, Carlo Levi or Jan Wolkers, it is so spatially credible and lucid relative to the rest of the work that one cannot help but wonder if Queneau is indulging in pure ontological stylistic experimentation.

30. L. Malle, *Malle on Malle*, 26–7.

31. Grégoire, "Débuts de Malle," 35–6.

32. Norman F. Cantor, *The American Century: Varieties of Culture in Modern Times* (New York: Harper Collins, 1997), 44.

33. *Ibid.*, 46.

34. Grégoire, "Débuts de Malle," 34.

35. Billard argues that *Zazie dans le métro* is directly related to Malle's student short, *Crazeologie*, which was influenced by the theater of the left bank, such as Samuel Beckett. Note the extent to which Beckett's *Godot*, for example, retains a surface-level linearity but lacks progression.

36. Adair, introduction to *Zazie*, xiii.

37. *Ibid.*

38. *Zazie dans le métro*, dir. Louis Malle, 92 min., New Yorker Films, 1960, videocassette.

39. K.L. Billingsley, *The Seductive Image* (Westchester, IL: Crossway Books, 1989), 26.

40. Pauline Kael, review of *Zazie dans le métro* (dir. Louis Malle). *5,001 Nights at the Movies* (New York: Owl Books, 1991), 864.

41. Gene Moskowitz, review of *Zazie dans le métro* (dir. Louis Malle), *Variety* 220 (23 November 1960).

42. Geoffrey Nowell-Smith, review of *Zazie dans le métro* (dir. Louis Malle), *Sight and Sound* 32 (1963): 37.

43. Marcel Martin, review of *Zazie dans le métro* (dir. Louis Malle), *Cinéma* 52 (December 1961): 117 (author translation).

44. *Ibid.*, 117–18.

45. André S. Labarthe, "Au pied de la lettre," review of *Zazie dans le métro* (dir. Louis Malle). *Cahiers du cinéma* 114 (December 1960): 58–60.

Chapter 5

1. MGM has only released the expurgated, 95-minute English-language cut of *Vie privée* on videocassette, *sans* approximately 20 minutes of footage, excised from the third act. An analysis of the original was thus impossible, and the discussion in this chapter pertains to the dubbed, truncated version.

2. For a discussion of the second "accident," please see Chapter 17, "More Than He Needs," on *Crackers* (1983).

3. Louis Malle, *Malle on Malle*, ed. Philip French, rev. ed. (London: Faber & Faber, 1996), 29.

4. *Ibid.*, 36.

5. Ibid, 33.

6. Brigitte Bardot, fax to author, 26 July 2004 (author translation).

7. L. Malle, *Malle on Malle*, 33.

8. Pauline Kael, review of *Vie privée* (dir. Louis Malle). *5,001 Nights at the Movies* (New York: Owl Books, 1991), 813.

9. In the case of *Feu follet*, the broader arguments about a critical locus as the subtext of the film do not apply, for Malle withholds judgment from his characters.

10. Lest it seem unnecessary for the screenwriters to craft Jill as a deep character (what if she were simply shallow from the outset?) one should note that shallowness, as a weakness, blankets the entire film: *none* of the characters, particularly Fabio Rinaldi, demonstrate depth. This is how we can make the critical distinction between two layers: the shallowness of Jill and the shallowness of the film itself. It would be quite a different issue if Malle and his co-writers crafted Jill as a naïve, superficial bubblehead and surrounded her with multi-layered characters.

11. Donald Gutierrez, "The Mass-Media Celebrity: Big Star, Little Fan," in *Breaking Through to the Other Side: Essays on Realization in Modern Literature* (Troy, NY: Whitson Publishing Co., 1994), 154.

12. The need for a contrapuntal relationship between context and subtext applies to nearly every fictional narrative where the director and screenwriter(s) build the film around criticism of a particular issue.

13. For three fascinating, intelligently written, and frequently resourced books on this subject, see: *Illusions of Immortality: The Psychology of Fame and Celebrity* by David Giles; *The Frenzy of Renown: Fame and Its History* by Leo Braudy; and Joshua Gamson's *Claims to Fame: The History of Celebrity in Contemporary America*.

14. De Beauvoir published the essay and a revealing photographic spread of Bardot for a 1959 issue of *Esquire* (not *Playboy*, as Malle told Philip French); the article and photos later appeared in the 1960 book referenced above.

15. In his 1978 film *Pretty Baby*, Malle revokes the dimple-legged Parisian "nymphette" first immortalized by Bardot, by resurrecting the "green fruit"–*femme fatale* confluence in the personage of 12-year-old whore Violet (Brooke Shields). See Chapter 14, "A Tainted World Through Innocent Eyes."

16. Simone De Beauvoir, *Brigitte Bardot and the Lolita Myth* (New York: Reynal & Co., 1960), 12.

17. *Ibid.*, 8.

18. Walter Weideli, *The Art of Bertolt Brecht* (New York: New York University Press, 1963), 61.

19. L. Malle, *Malle on Malle*, 34.

20. Bardot, fax.

21. Richard J. Calhoun and Robert W. Hill, *James Dickey* (Boston: Twayne Publishers, 1983), 49.

22. Bardot, fax.

23. Kael, review of *Vie privée*, 813.

24. Tom Milne, review of *A Very Private Affair* (dir. Louis Malle). *Monthly Film Bulletin* 29 (1962): 152.

25. Marcel Martin, review of *Vie privée* (dir. Louis Malle). *Cinéma* 64 (March 1962): 105–7.

Chapter 6

1. Louis Malle, *Malle on Malle*, ed. Philip French, rev. ed. (London: Faber & Faber, 1996), 36.

2. *Ibid.*

3. Despite critical acclaim, *Zazie* failed financially after achieving great success during its opening weekend at the box office. (See Chapter 4.)

4. In an interview, Justine Malle acknowledges the fact that, although Louis rebelled ideologically from his grand bourgeois upbringing, he never renounced the wealth of the Beghins.

5. L. Malle, *Malle on Malle*, 43.

6. *Ibid.*

7. *Ibid.*, 39.

8. See also Appendix A, "Lost Horizons," for a brief discussion of the aborted projects that led to *Feu Follet*.

9. L. Malle, *Malle on Malle*, 39.

10. Louis Malle and Sarah Kant, *Louis Malle par Louis Malle*, Editions de l'Athenor (Paris: Jacques Mallecot, 1978), 25.

11. *Ibid.*

12. *Ibid.*, 25–26.

13. *The Fire Within*, dir. Louis Malle, 110 min., New Yorker Films, 1963, videocassette.

14. L. Malle, *Malle on Malle*, 38.

15. For a more detailed discussion of similarities between the work of Malle and Guare, see Chapter 15, on *Atlantic City* (their one produced collaboration), and Appendix A for a brief discussion of *Moon Over Miami*, a scripted but unfilmed Malle/Guare project, which Guare eventually rewrote as a stage play, *Moon Over Miami*.

16. Though the 1971 Braucourt interview pertains to *Murmur of the Heart*, Malle uses part of the discussion to sketch an analogous relationship between the musical/contextual union in *Murmur* and the musical/tonal union in *Feu Follet* (which — as Malle discloses explicitly, and as I will explore in my analysis of *Souffle*— are similar but not identical devices). See Chapter 10, "East Meets West," on *Le Souffle au cœur*.

17. Lest the reader doubt the connection between Malle and Beckett, it may help to recall the fact that Malle's first short, at IDHEC, pulled heavy influence directly from the Left Bank playwright.

18. In some ways, this anticipates Derek Jarman's final film, *Blue* (1993): a piece of cinematic performance art where a multi-layered stereo soundtrack atop an unshifting blue field harnesses the mind's eye by inducing the viewer to "read" images into the empty space. See Chapter 16, on *My Dinner with André*, for a discussion of a film with similar intent.

19. Recall Schrader's observation that in the noir and postnoir periods, a majority of the scenes are "shot for night," to convey a highly stylized, romantic, *arealist* milieu. It thus seems perfectly appropriate that at the other end of the spectrum, the psychorealist subgenre should utilize scenes shot for *day* as an integral part of its aesthetic strategy.

20. French, *Malle on Malle*, 36.

21. Pauline Kael, "Louis Malle's Portrait of the Artist as a Young Dog," review of *Murmur of the Heart* (dir. Louis Malle). *Deeper into Movies* (Boston: Little, Brown, and Company, 1971), 308.

22. *Ibid.*

23. Gene Moskowitz, review of *Le Feu follet* (dir. Louis Malle), *Variety* 232 (11 September 1963): 22.

24. *Ibid.*, 26.

25. *Ibid.*

26. Peter John Dyer, review of *Le Feu follet* (dir. Louis Malle), *Monthly Film Bulletin* 30 (1963): 114.

27. Pierre Loubière, review of *Le Feu follet* (dir. Louis Malle), *Télé Ciné* 113–14 (Dec.–Jan. 1964): 136 (author translation).

Chapter 7

1. Louis Malle, *Malle on Malle*, ed. Philip French, rev. ed. (London: Faber & Faber, 1996), 49.

2. Justine A. Malle, telephone interview by author, 19 March 2004

3. L. Malle, *Malle on Malle*, 44–45.

4. "Louis Malle: Biography." *Internet Movie Database* [online]. (cited 2004-04-18). Available from internet: <http://www.imdb.com/name/nm0086443/>

5. Carrière served as uncredited consultant on *Souffle au cœur*; *Lacombe, Lucien*; and *Au revoir les enfants*.

6. L. Malle, *Malle on Malle*, 49.

7. Jean-Claude Carrière, telephone interview with author, 14 February 2004.

8. *Ibid.*, 20.

9. In one of those "movie connections" that seems closer to a theft than an homage, William Friedkin's 1968 comedy *The Night They Raided Minsky's*— also produced for United Artists— uses this very same plot point, verbatim, where wet-behind-the-ears Amish girl Britt Ekland comes to Manhattan and "accidentally" invents the striptease.

10. Daniel Lopez, *Films by Genre* (Jefferson, NC: McFarland & Company, 1993), 35.

11. *Ibid.*

12. A great conundrum emerges when one compares the "classical femininity" of *Les Amants* to the sexual equality of *Viva Maria*. Even if Malle were the most stylistically and thematically diverse director on earth, one wonders how in the world the same person could craft both of these films.

13. Intertextually, one can argue (given the substi-

tution elements) not that *Maria* influenced all female buddy films in the ensuing decades, but rather a small handful of cross-cultural films (again, see Table 8-A) within its subgenre: Alain Tanner's *Messidor*, Arthur Hiller's *Outrageous Fortune*, Ridley Scott's *Thelma & Louise*, and a few others. All adhere, more or less, to the same idea.

14. Before examining the multiple meanings of this division, one must acknowledge and accept by default the massive, insurmountable ideological differences between the "two-world" structure of *Les Amants* (see Chapter 3) and the architecture of *Maria*. Although they may appear similar at first glance, the two dramatic structures are as different as night and day.

15. L. Malle, *Malle on Malle*, 52.

16. It is hardly accidental that Carrière earned his first credit co-scripting *The Diary of a Chambermaid* with Buñuel, the Mexican surrealist and Dali-collaborator.

17. K.L. Billingsley, *The Seductive Image* (Westchester, IL: Crossway Books, 1989), 26.

18. Carrière reveals that part of what Malle expected of him — via his experiences with Étaix and Tati — was the ability to provide gags.

19. Although, for *Atlantic City*, the reverse was true: the American public and press welcomed it with open arms; Europeans failed to appreciate it because they lacked contextual understanding. See Chapter 15.

20. L. Malle, *Malle on Malle*, 54.

21. Ralph Blum, "He Let the Film Get Away." Review of *Viva Maria*. *Vogue* 147 (1 February 1966): 101.

22. Tom Milne, review of *Viva Maria*. *Monthly Film Bulletin* 33 (1966): 40.

23. Marcel Martin, "Zazie au Mexique." *Cinéma* 102 (January 1966): 112 (author translation).

24. *Ibid.*, 113 (author translation).

25. François Chevassu, review of *Viva Maria*. *Image et Son* 192 (March 1966): 114.

Chapter 8

1. Louis Malle, *Malle on Malle*, ed. Philip French, rev. ed. (London: Faber & Faber, 1996), 55–6.

2. *Ibid.*, 54.

3. Louis Malle and Sarah Kant, *Louis Malle par Louis Malle*, Editions de l'Athenor (Paris: Jacques Mallecot, 1978), 26–7 (author translation).

4. It is hardly an accident that almost immediately after co-writing and directing this film, Malle took his concerns a step farther by abandoning feature filmmaking and the wealth and comfort of Western civilization altogether to "drop out" of society and head for poverty-stricken India.

5. Randal's forgery of his uncle's will constitutes far more satisfying revenge, but does not arrive until almost 90 minutes into the picture, and thus fails to elicit a big emotional payoff from the audience.

6. Georges's theft of Armand's jewels (Charlotte's

dowry) could also represent some form of revenge against Urbain (note Urbain's virulent chagrin when he discovers the theft), but Randal's more immediate need to preserve Charlotte's romantic availability overtakes and obscures whatever vengeful, anti–Urbain motivations may also belie this theft.

7. L. Malle, *Malle on Malle*, 58.

8. One wonders why a screenwriter (and structuralist) as brilliant as Carrière would not attempt to move the source of the flashbacks to a point earlier in the narrative, and move the audience forward in time from this point, along the narrative continuum, *sans* awareness of future events, to generate a hefty dose of suspense and excitement.

9. For further discussion of the use of tonal splits, see also Chapter 11, "East Meets West," on *Le Souffle au cœur*.

10. Pauline Kael, review of *The Thief of Paris* (dir. Louis Malle). *5,001 Nights at the Movies* (New York: Owl Books, 1991), 756–7.

11. L. Malle, *Malle on Malle*, 56.

12. For another, more effective exploration of this idea, see Chapter 22, "Double Standards," on *Damage*.

13. Sigmund Freud, "The Neuro-Psychoses of Defence," in *The Standard Edition of the Complete Psychological Works of Sigmund Freud*, ed. James Strachey (New York: W.W. Norton, 1976), 3:45–61.

14. Recall Malle's perception of Randal as an autobiographical character — so autobiographical that he compares the personal significance of *Le Voleur* to that of *Le Feu follet*. When coupled with his descriptions of the period during and immediately following *Le Voleur*— rife with recollections of wanting to abandon feature filmmaking and question everything about his own life — (not to mention his indication that he was suicidal during the filming of his next project, "William Wilson") we may infer that Malle, like Randal, was stricken by a staggering amount of self-disgust at this time and desperately needed the reassurance and encouragement India brought.

15. It is important not to confuse the *cinematic interruptus* technique of Malle-the-director with the emotional needs of Randal the character. Though Malle and Carrière consistently terminate suspense and allow Randal to emerge undetected by police and unscathed (and might benefit by including more emotional payoffs from the robberies — thus including the audience more), Randal *the character* would never opt for more extreme emotional follow-throughs, as they would mean increasing the probability of his detection and capture!

16. Kael, review of *Thief of Paris*, 757.

17. Gene Moskowitz, review of *Le Voleur* (dir. Louis Malle). *Variety* 246 (15 March 1967): 26

18. Samuel Lachize, review of *Le Voleur* (dir. Louis Malle). Excerpt in *Télé-Cine* 133 (February–March 1967): 59 (author translation).

19. Jean-Louis Bory, review of *Le Voleur* (dir. Louis Malle). Excerpt in *Télé-Cine* 133 (February-March 1967): 59 (author translation).

20. Albert Cervoni, review of *Le Voleur* (dir. Louis

Malle). Excerpt in *Télé-Cine* 133 (February–March 1967): 59 (author translation).

21. Janick Arbois, review of *Le Voleur* (dir. Louis Malle). Excerpt in *Télé-Cine* 133 (February–March 1967): 59 (author translation).

Chapter 9

1. Louis Malle, *Malle on Malle*, ed. Philip French, rev. ed. (London: Faber & Faber, 1996), 64.

2. For a more detailed discussion of this period, see the introduction to Chapter 10, "Deflected Emotion and the Art of Memory."

3. L. Malle, *Malle on Malle*, 66.

4. For a detailed discussion of William Wilson, see Chapter 25, "Brief Encounters."

5. L. Malle, *Malle on Malle*, 64.

6. *Ibid.*, 68.

7. *Ibid.*, 69.

8. Candice Bergen, telephone interview by the author, 9 March 2004.

9. Louis Malle and Sarah Kant, *Louis Malle par Louis Malle*, Editions de l'Athenor (Paris: Jacques Mallecot, 1978), 29.

10. "Quand Louis Malle se remet en question," *Jeune Cinéma* 39 (May 1969): 21 (author translation).

11. René Prédal, *Louis Malle* (Paris: Edilig, 1989), 74.

12. Malle and Kant, *Louis Malle par Louis Malle*, 30 (author translation).

13. *Ibid.*

14. "Quand Malle remet," 18 (author translation).

15. Malle and Kant, *Louis Malle par Louis Malle*, 81.

16. "Quand Malle remet," 18 (author translation).

17. *Ibid.*

18. "Le Point de vue de Suzanne Baron, monteuse," *Jeune Cinéma* 39 (May 1969): 18 (author translation).

19. "Quand Malle remet," 18 (author translation).

20. *Ibid.*

21. Jean-Pierre Oudart, "Les Trajets et les lieux," review of *Calcutta*, *Cahiers du cinéma* 213 (June 1969).

22. Prédal, *Louis Malle*, 181.

23. *Ibid.*

24. *Ibid.*

25. For some indeterminate reason, *Phantom India* did not open in French cinemas until 1975.

26. "Television,'" *New York Times*, 7 December 1971, p. 95.

27. "Arts and Leisure," *New York Times*, 20 May 1972, p. 7.

28. A common misconception (as listed on a popular film reference website) is that *Phantom* made its American premiere on October 7, 1972. Not accurate. The New Yorker Theater did screen all of the episodes back-to-back on 10/7/72, but only following the success that came from showcasing the episodes individually over the preceding months.

29. "Arts and Leisure," *New York Times*, 17 Sep. 1972, p. D10.

30. Malle and Kant, *Louis Malle par Louis Malle*, 82.

31. *Calcutta*, dir. Louis Malle, 100 min., NYFA Films, 1969, videocassette (author translation).

32. The inspiration for the "Grand Maja Sequence" in *Pretty Baby*, perhaps?

33. *L'Inde fantôme*—Episode 1: "La Caméra impossible," dir. Louis Malle, 54 min., Fil à film, 1969, videocassette (author translation).

34. *Ibid.*

35. *Ibid.*

36. *Ibid.*

37. *L'Inde fantôme*—Episode 2: "Choses vues à Madras," dir. Louis Malle, 54 min., Fil à film, 1969, videocassette (author translation).

38. *Ibid.*

39. Malle never mentions the name of the film in his narration; it was obtained here through research.

40. *L'Inde fantôme*—Episode 2.

41. *Ibid.*

42. *L'Inde fantôme*—Episode 3: "La Réligion," dir. Louis Malle, 54 min., Fil à film, 1969, videocassette (author translation).

43. *Ibid.*

44. *Ibid.*

45. *Ibid.*

46. *Ibid.*

47. *L'Inde fantôme*—Episode 4: "La Tentation du rêve," dir. Louis Malle, 54 min., Fil à film, 1969, videocassette (author translation).

48. *Ibid.*

49. *Ibid.*

50. *L'Inde fantôme*—Episode 5: "Regards sur les castes," dir. Louis Malle, 54 min., Fil à film, 1969, videocassette (author translation).

51. *L'Inde fantôme*—Episode 6: "Les Étrangers en Inde," dir. Louis Malle, 54 min., Fil à film, 1969, videocassette (author translation).

52. *Ibid.*

53. *L'Inde fantôme*—Episode 7: "Bombay," dir. Louis Malle, 54 min., Fil à film, 1969, videocassette (author translation).

54. *Ibid.*

55. *Ibid.*

56. An anticipation of Malle's 1974 documentary *Humain, trop humain*, perhaps?

57. Malle, *Malle on Malle*, 225.

58. Because Malle shot *Phantom* and *Calcutta* with an almost identical style, the motion pictures will fist be discussed interchangeably here, prior to a brief commentary on the distinction—and interconnectedness—of the two projects.

59. When asked, in an interview, if her father would ever have attempted to use one of his films to "teach" or "educate," Justine Malle responds with an emphatic "no" and affirms the fact that he never put himself above a viewer, always placed himself in the same "process of discovery" as his audience.

60. Though only accurate as a general rule, the overall gestalt of *Phantom* also encompasses Malle's decreasing reliance on "aural dating" in voice-over

(e.g., "Tuesday, January 18, Delhi. First day of shoot-ing...") instances of which grow more and more in-frequent as the series progresses. This occurs within episodes and from episode to episode, so that by the time episode five arrives: such reminders no longer exist (though episode seven has one), the sequences have grown longer and longer, and the viewers have lost "time awareness" *per se*. Malle thus imposes on the audience a gradual "loss of time" in the western sense. This also metaphorizes the mental and spiri-tual easternization that the filmmakers undergo dur-ing their Indian immersion. The only clue that the di-rector provides of this process lies in his opening narration to Episode Four, "La Tentation du rêve."

61. L. Malle, *Malle on Malle*, 213.

62. In this regard, the film even incorporates match cuts similar to those typically found in a fea-ture, and identifiable in the opening shots of *Les Amants* (see Chapter 3).

63. Andrew Sarris, "Nasty Nazis: history or myth-ology," review of *Lacombe, Lucien* (dir. Louis Malle), *Village Voice* 19 (17 October 1974): 77.

64. Oudart, "Trajets et lieux."

65. *Ibid.* (author translation).

66. Jonathan M. Richards, interview by author, 23 May 2004.

67. Oudart also views it as a kind of active decon-structionist regression — so that society can ulti-mately arrive, by virtue of meanings lost, at a unified "opaqueness."

68. To clarify: though the Naipaul block quote ap-plies specifically to Indian Islam, he intimates in a subsequent passage that Hinduism suffers from the same disconnectedness within Indian society, as signified by the ease with which conquerors imposed Islam (a new set of rituals) on Hinduism (an old sys-tem of rituals), and by the continued existence in largely Muslim areas of Hindu names dissociated from their histories and interpretations.

69. V.S. Naipaul, *An Area of Darkness* (New York: Macmillan, 1964), 135–7.

70. Oudart, "Les Trajets et les lieux."

71. *L'Inde fantôme* 1—"La Caméra impossible."

72. It would be a mistake to infer that Malle de-liberately chose to use an alternate style while filming the city of Calcutta; the consistency of approach uti-lized throughout the shooting of the Indian docu-mentaries completely negates any readings on that level. But Malle and Baron's editing decisions are an-other story; only at this stage did he choose to delay narration and to open the film with a series of im-pressionistic images. It may also be viable to suggest that because Malle and Becker shot most of the Cal-cutta footage around the beginning of the journey, the freshness of their eyes and perspectives as new-comers to India — are automatically conveyed through that footage.

73. Pauline Kael, review of *Calcutta* (dir. Louis Malle). *5,001 Nights at the Movies* (New York: Owl Books, 1991), 115.

74. Gene Moskowitz, review of *Calcutta* (dir. Louis Malle), *Variety* 254, May 1969, 35.

75. Max Tessier, review of *Phantom India* (dir. Louis Malle), Écran 39, 15 September 1975, 68 (au-thor translation).

76. Gauston Haustrate, "La Vie, une illusion," re-view of *Calcutta* (dir. Louis Malle), *Cinéma* 137, June 1969, 133–34

Chapter 10

1. Louis Malle, *Malle on Malle*, ed. Philip French, rev. ed. (London: Faber & Faber, 1996), 82.

2. Louis Malle and Sarah Kant, *Louis Malle par Louis Malle*, Editions de l'Athenor (Paris: Jacques Mallecot, 1978), 37.

3. *Ibid.*, 75.

4. *Ibid.*, 36.

5. L. Malle, *Malle on Malle*, 81.

6. Ibid, 82.

7. Pauline Kael, "Louis Malle's Portrait of the Artist as a Young Dog," review of *Murmur of the Heart* (dir. Louis Malle). *Deeper into Movies* (Boston: Little, Brown, and Company, 1971), 306.

8. L. Malle, *Malle on Malle*, 82.

9. Paul Chutkow, "Louis Malle Diagnoses His 'Murmur of the Heart,'" *New York Times*, 19 Mar. 1989, sec. 2, p.20.

10. L. Malle, *Malle on Malle*, 82.

11. Louis Malle, interview by Guy Braucourt, *Cinéma* 157 (June 1971): 106–7.

12. *Ibid.*, 106 (author translation).

13. L. Malle, *Malle on Malle*, 69–70.

14. This idea also applies hugely to Malle's tri-umph *Lacombe, Lucien* (See Chapter 12, "The Politics of Detachment," for a discussion of *Lucien*).

15. As we have seen, at least two of Malle's pre–1967 films fall into the category of anti-bourgeois satire (*Les Amants, Le Voleur*) though none are nearly as vitriolic as, say, some of Buñuel's efforts (e.g., *The Discreet Charm of the Bourgeoisie, That Obscure Ob-ject of Desire*), or evince Buñuel's surrealism. One should remember that even in the instance of Buñuel, who flaunted atheism and mocked Christianity with-out abandon, the filmmaker relied on a knowledge of western morality to establish his framework of criticism, and — in satirizing the dualistic hypocrisy of the bourgeois— revealed some allegiance to west-ern morality himself. Malle is aware of the same framework — and references it in (for instance) the embodiment of Père Henri, and in the characters' re-version to western ethos at the end (when Clara tells Laurent, "[The incest] will never be repeated.") We see quite clearly the half-hearted surface layer of western ethos. But for the most part, *Souffle* is an ex-ercise of working against this moral framework, rel-ativistically, by revealing the characters' partial evis-ceration of it — and siding with them, not criticizing them.

16. Alexandre Astruc, "Un Film osé qui se termine par un grand et sain éclat de rire." *Paris Match* (24 April 1971).

17. Kael, "Portrait of the Artist," 306.

18. The film's incredible empathy for the characters *per se* does not disqualify it as a satire — a number of satirical comedies (see Michael Ritchie's *Smile*, Alex Payne's *About Schmidt*) employ a careful enough tonal balance that enables character empathy and light criticism to coexist.

19. Daniel Lopez, *Films by Genre* (Jefferson, NC: McFarland & Company, 1993), 265.

20. Danny Peary, review of *Discreet Charm of the Bourgeoisie* (dir. Luis Buñuel), in *Guide for the Film Fanatic* (New York: Fireside Books, 1986), 124.

21. L. Malle, interview by Braucourt, 108.

22. Though she adored *Souffle* and praises it at length, Pauline Kael criticizes Malle's portrayal of Father Henri (Michel Lonsdale), the priest with an implicit fondness for young boys, as a failure — a caricature. As one of the only blatant instances of anti-bourgeois satire in the film, this scene does violate the film's tone, and thus feels slightly out-of-place (even given Malle's penchant for anti-clericalism).

23. Kael, "Portrait of the Artist," 306.

24. *Ibid.*, 310.

25. Philip Strick, review of *Murmur of the Heart* (dir. Louis Malle), *Monthly Film Bulletin* 38 (1971): 204.

26. This same tie between the individual and the social (communal) applies to *Lacombe, Lucien*, as well (see Chapter 12, "The Politics of Detachment").

27. L. Malle, *Malle on Malle*, 70.

28. Sigmund Freud, "A Special Type of Choice of Object Made by Men (Contributions to the Psychology of Love I)," in *The Complete Psychological Works of Sigmund Freud, Vol. XI* (London: Hogarth Press, 1957), 166.

29. *Ibid.*, 167.

30. *Ibid.*

31. Danny Peary, review of *Deep End* (dir. Jerzy Skolimowski), *Film Fanatic*, 117.

32. Freud, "Special Type," 168.

33. *Ibid.*, 168–9.

34. Robert Hatch, review of *Le Souffle au cœur* (dir. Louis Malle), *The Nation* 213 (1 November 1971): 446.

35. Jeffrey Alan Fiskin, telephone interview by author, 24 October 2003.

36. Stanley Kauffmann, review of *Le Souffle au cœur* (dir. Louis Malle), *The New Republic* 165 (13 November 1971): 32.

37. Richard Schickel, "Deft handling of an old taboo," review of *Murmur of the Heart* (dir. Louis Malle), *Life* 71 (12 November 1971): 16.

38. Kael, "Portrait of the Artist," 305.

39. Alexandre Astruc, "Éclat de rire." (Author translation).

40. Guy Braucourt, "Tout cela, mon pere, n'est qua moitie votre faute," review of *Le Souffle au cœur* (dir. Louis Malle), *Cinéma* 157 (June 1971): 109 (author translation).

41. Paul Chutkow, "Malle Diagnoses 'Murmur'" *New York Times,* 19 Mar. 1989, sec. 2, pp. 19–20.

Chapter 11

1. Pierre Billard, *Louis Malle: Le Rebelle solitaire* (Paris: Plon, 2003), 326–9.

2. *Ibid.*, 329–30.

3. Tristan Renaud, review of *Humain, trop humain* and *Place de la République* (dir. Louis Malle), *Cinéma* 187 (May 1974): 122.

4. Richard Leacock, "One Man's Truth," interview with James Blue. In *The Documentary Tradition: From Nanook to Woodstock*. ed. Lewis Jacobs (New York: Hopkinson & Blake, 1971), 406–7.

5. Louis Malle, *Malle on Malle*, ed. Philip French, rev. ed. (London: Faber & Faber, 1996), 162.

6. Vincent Malle, telephone interview by author, 15 December 2004.

7. *Ibid*

8. Thérèse Giraud, "*Attica/Humain, trop humain*: deux conceptions du cinéma direct." Review of *Humain, trop humain* (dir. Louis Malle) and *Attica* (dir. Cinda Firestone). *Cahiers du cinéma* 250 (May 1974): 51.

9. Albert Maysles, interview by G. Roy Levin. In *Documentary Explorations* (Garden City, NY: Doubleday, 1971), 275–6.

10. Pauline Kael, review of *Humain, trop Humain* (dir. Louis Malle). In *5,001 Nights at the Movies* (New York: Owl Books, 1991), 344.

11. Tristan Renaud, review of *Humain, trop Humain* and *Place de la République*. *Cinéma* 187, 122–3.

12. *Ibid.*, 123 (author translation).

13. Jean Delmas, review of *Humain, trop Humain*. *Jeune Cinéma* 78, May 1974, 4 (author translation).

14. *Ibid.* (author translation).

15. *Ibid.*, 5 (author translation).

Chapter 12

1. *Louis Malle par Louis Malle* offers the most detailed and thorough discussion of *Lacombe*'s genesis; the discussion in *Malle on Malle* is a bit more vague and cursory.

2. The occasional references to scene numbers in this chapter (e.g., "Scene Twenty-four") are those used in the published script from Éditions Gallmard (c. 1974).

3. Louis Malle and Sarah Kant, *Louis Malle par Louis Malle*, Editions de l'Athenor (Paris: Jacques Mallecot, 1978), 41.

4. *Ibid.*

5. Louis Malle, *Malle on Malle*, ed. Philip French, rev. ed. (London: Faber & Faber, 1996), 36.

6. Malle and Kant, *Louis Malle par Louis Malle*, 43 (author translation).

7. L. Malle, *Malle on Malle*, 90.

8. See Chapter 26, "Lost Horizons," for a more detailed discussion of *Les Halcones*.

9. Malle and Kant, *Louis Malle par Louis Malle*, 46.

10. *Ibid.* (author translation).

11. Michel Sineux, "Le Hasard, le chagrin, la nécessité, la pitié," review of *Lacombe, Lucien* (dir. Louis Malle), *Positif* 157 (March 1974): 25 (author translation).

12. Pauline Kael, review of *Lacombe, Lucien* (dir. Louis Malle), in *Reeling* (Boston: Little, Brown, & Co., 1976), 335.

13. Manuel Malle, interview by author, New York, NY, 20 October 2001.

14. Lest one place an overabundance of faith in Kael's comment, believing that Lucien lacks a conscience and empathy *altogether*—note the striking moment when the boy encounters a wounded horse, strapped to a pushcart and minutes away from death. Lucien gently, softly strokes its mane and evinces remorse for its suffering. His desire to care for France Horn postcoitally (running his hand gently over her nude back) draws the same insight.

15. Pierre Blaise, as quoted by Margaret Ronan in review of *Lacombe, Lucien* (dir. Louis Malle), *Senior Scholastic* 105 (15 December 1974): 18.

16. In this regard, *Lacombe, Lucien* critiques Occupation-era Frenchmen as Fred Schepisi's *A Cry in the Dark* attacked Australians, and as *Damage* critiques the British (see Chapter 22)—it encapsulates an entire cultural mythos within its narrative.

17. John Simon, review of *Lacombe, Lucien* (dir. Louis Malle), *Esquire* 82 (December 1974): 26.

18. Louis Malle and Patrick Modiano, *Lacombe, Lucien: The Complete Scenario of the Film by Louis Malle* (New York: The Viking Press, 1975), 11.

19. Claretta Micheletta Tonetti, "Re: Thanks." E-mail to author, 17 September 2002.

20. Interesting to note how eerily (for 1974) this dynamic foreshadows the psychological factors inherent in the current behavioral patterns of wayward inner city youths—most from broken families—who enlist in violent street gangs.

21. Jan Dawson, review of *Lacombe Lucien* (dir. Louis Malle), *Monthly Film Bulletin* 41 (1974): 149.

22. Danny Peary, review of *Slaughterhouse-Five* (dir. George Roy Hill), in *Guide for the Film Fanatic* (New York: Fireside Books, 1986), 390.

23. *Ibid.*

24. From one end of Malle's œuvre to another, one senses a constant vacillation between two trends—in certain films (*Ascenseur, Milou*) the tendency to establish the force of fate (or "desking") and radically dissect it as collective mythmaking in the others, an inclination to give equal weight to fatality and determinism without dissecting either. *Lacombe* belongs in this camp, as does *Damage.*

25. Jean Delmas, review of *Lacombe, Lucien* (dir. Louis Malle), *Jeune Cinéma* 77, March 1974, 33.

26. Kael, review of *Lacombe*, 336.

27. L. Malle, *Malle on Malle*, 92–3.

28. Friedrich Nietzsche, *The Will to Power*, ed. Walter Kauffmann (London: Lowe & Brydone, 168), 13.

29. Kael, review of *Lacombe*, 341.

30. *Ibid.*

31. Andrew Sarris, "Nasty Nazis: history or mythology," review of *Lacombe, Lucien* (dir. Louis Malle), *Village Voice* 19 (17 October 1974): 77.

32. Bruce Williamson, review of *Lacombe, Lucien* (dir. Louis Malle), *Playboy* 21 (November 1974): 34.

33. René Andrieu, "*Lacombe, Lucien* et l'Occupation: Louis Malle's explique, René Andrieu conteste." *Humanité Dimanche*, 3 April 1974, 19 (author translation).

34. *Ibid.*

35. Marcel Martin, review of *Lacombe, Lucien* (dir. Louis Malle), *Écran* 23 (March 1974): 50 (author translation).

36. "Pierre Blaise." *Internet Movie Database* [online]. (cited 2004-03-07). Available from internet: <http://www.imdb.com/name/nm0086443/>

Chapter 13

1. For a more detailed discussion on this transition, please see the Introduction to this text.

2. Pauline Kael, review of *Lacombe, Lucien* (dir. Louis Malle), in *Reeling* (Boston: Little, Brown, & Co., 1976), 339–41.

3. Jean-Claude Carrière, telephone interview by author, 14 February 2004.

4. Louis Malle, *Malle on Malle*, ed. Philip French, rev. ed. (London: Faber & Faber, 1996), 106.

5. Louis Malle and Sarah Kant, *Louis Malle par Louis Malle*, Editions de l'Athenor (Paris: Jacques Mallecot, 1978), 54.

6. "Release dates for *Lacombe, Lucien* (1974)." *Internet Movie Database* [online], (cited 2004-03-23). Available from internet: <http://www.imdb.com/title/tt0071733/releaseinfo>

7. Either way, *Black Moon*'s preproduction coincided with the timing of Malle's second child. In autumn 1973, he conceived a baby with French-Canadian actress Alexandra Stewart, who gave birth to their daughter, Justine, on June 11, 1974.

8. L. Malle, *Malle on Malle*, 106.

9. Malle and Kant, *Louis Malle par Louis Malle*, 55 (author translation).

10. L. Malle, *Malle on Malle*, 106.

11. Malle and Kant, *Louis Malle par Louis Malle*, 54 (author translation).

12. L. Malle, *Malle on Malle*, 107.

13. *Ibid.*, 106.

14. "Release dates for *Black Moon* (1975)." *Internet Movie Database* [online], (cited 2004-03-24). Available from internet: <http://www.imdb.com/title/tt0072709/releaseinfo>

15. "What? Art film curios from around the globe." *The Pimpadelic Wonderland* — *Weird World of 70s Cinema* (Cited 2004-03-24). Available from internet: <http://www.pimpadelicwonderland.com/art.html>

16. Jean de Baroncelli, "Un Film rêve," review of *Black Moon* (dir. Louis Malle), *Le Monde* (27 September 1975): 1, 23 (author translation).

17. Louis Malle, interview by Susan Sontag, in *Louis Malle par Louis Malle*, Editions de l'Athenor

(Paris: Jacques Mallecot, 1978), 104 (author translation).

18. David Mamet, *On Directing Film* (New York:
Penguin, 1992), 6.

19. René Prédal, *Louis Malle* (Paris: Edilig, 1989),
124 (author translation).

20. Malle and Kant, *Louis Malle par Louis Malle*, 56.

21. L. Malle, *Malle on Malle*, 110.

22. André Breton, "Limits not Frontiers of Surrealism," in *Surrealism* (London: Faber and Faber,
1971), 103.

23. *Ibid.*, 104.

25. *Black Moon*, dir. Louis Malle, 100 min., Fil à
film, 1975, videocassette.

26. Gilles Colpart, review of *Black Moon* (dir.
Louis Malle), *La Revue du cinéma* 300 (November
1975): 86.

27. Note the transition between *Black Moon*
(1975), which has as its heroine a "Lily" (symbol of
purity) and Malle's 1978 follow-up *Pretty Baby* (see
Chapter 15), which has as its central character the 12-
year-old prostitute "Violet," a flower emblematic of
seduction. Bear in mind, of course, that Al Rose, the
author of *Storyville, New Orleans* (on which *Pretty
Baby* is based) is the one who gave the real-life "trick
baby" the pseudonym "Violet," to protect her identity, so this irony did not originate with Malle.

28. L. Malle, *Malle on Malle*, 110.

29. Jean Chevalier and Alain Gheerbrant, *The Dictionary of Symbols* (London: Penguin, 1996), 673–4.

30. Bruce Williamson, "Pretty Baby." *Playboy* 25
(March 1978): 104.

31. The pig chased by the naked children can be
read both as an intertextual allusion to William
Golding's *Lord of the Flies* and — possibly — as an
homage to Thierry Zeno's aforementioned *Vase de
Noces* (a.k.a. *Wedding Trough*), an arthouse shocker
in which a demented man strips, chases a giant sow
through the mud, and ultimately penetrates the animal from behind.

32. Louis Malle, interview with Susan Sontag, in
Louis Malle par Louis Malle, Editions de l'Athenor
(Paris: Jacques Mallecot, 1978), 107 (author transla-
tion).

33. It was this theory that — in an interesting cinematic parallel to *Black Moon* — Stanley Kubrick
fleshed-out cinematically. He did so by subtly suggesting that Alex de Large in *A Clockwork Orange* and
the Starchild in *2001: A Space Odyssey* are incarnations of the same entity at varying evolutionary
stages.

34. L. Malle, *Malle on Malle*, 113

35. *Ibid.*

36. André Breton, "Manifesto of Surrealism," in
Manifestoes of Surrealism (Ann Arbor: University of
Michigan Press, 1969), 46.

37. Chevalier and Gheerbrant, *Penguin Dictionary
of Symbols*, 673–4.

38. *Ibid.*, 1054–6.

39. Peter Bogdanovich, *The Killing of the Unicorn*
(New York: Bantam, 1985), 224–5.

40. C.A.S. Williams, *Chinese Symbolism and Art
Motifs* (Edison, NJ: Castle Books, 1974), 413–15.

41. Chevalier and Gheerbrant, *Penguin Dictionary
of Symbols*, 608–9.

42. *Ibid.*, 65.

43. Chevalier and Gheerbrant, *Penguin Dictionary
of Symbols*, 339.

44. *Ibid.*, 788–9.

45. C.A.S. Williams, *Chinese Symbolism*, 175.

46. Chevalier and Gheerbrant, *Penguin Dictionary
of Symbols*, 323–8.

47. *Ibid.*, 164.

48. *Ibid.*, 753.

49. *Ibid.*, 526–7.

50. C.A.S. Williams, *Chinese Symbolism*, 362–3.

51. Chevalier and Gheerbrant, *Penguin Dictionary
of Symbols*, 1047–9.

52. *Ibid.*, 529–30.

53. *Ibid.*, 530–1.

54. Pauline Kael, review of *Black Moon* (dir. Louis
Malle), in *When the Lights Go Down* (New York: Holt,
Rinehart, & Winston, 1980), 83–4.

55. Jean Roy, review of *Black Moon* (dir. Louis
Malle), *Cinéma* 202 (September–October 1975): 203.

56. L. Malle, *Malle on Malle*, 112.

57. Gilles Colpart, review of *Black Moon* (dir.
Louis Malle), *La Revue du cinéma* 300 (September
1975): 86.

58. Gene Moskowitz, review of *Black Moon* (dir.
Louis Malle), *Variety* 280 (24 September 1975): 22.

59. *Ibid.*

60. "User comments for *Black Moon* (1975)." *Internet Movie Database* [online], (cited 2004-03-29).
Available from internet: <http://www.imdb.com/
title/tt0072709/usercomments>

61. L. Malle, *Malle on Malle*, 112–13.

Chapter 14

1. Maureen Orth, "The Americanization of Louis
Malle," *New West* 3, 24 April 1978, 59.

2. Louis Malle, *Malle on Malle*, ed. Philip French,
rev. ed. (London: Faber & Faber, 1996), 118–19.

3. Karen Pedersen, telephone conversation with
author, 12 April 2004.

4. Playing a similar role as studio president
Picker but in a far more immediate capacity, Polly
Platt's Associate Producer role on the *Pretty Baby* set
meant guiding Malle through the schematics of
launching his first American picture. She recalls,
"Even though I was only the Associate Producer, it
was Louis's first film in America, and I really functioned as a producer ... [Louis] certainly wasn't in a
position to really produce. For instance he wanted
Sven Nykvist to be the cinematographer, and Sven
had no green card, and no work permit to work here
in America, and I engineered that, I got him into the
union, and I got him his card, and ... things that Louis
wouldn't have the faintest idea how to do. Bureaucratically and politically."

5. L. Malle, *Malle on Malle*, 118.

6. *Ibid.*, 118–19.

7. Louis Malle's request that Picker "partner him up" with another screenwriter seems a bit unusual, not only given Malle's impeccable English, but given his co-authorship of an unproduced English-language screenplay (*Jelly Roll*) almost a decade prior. Whatever the reason for it, it set a definite pattern: the "American phase" of Malle's career is marked by the decision to work with one major creative force on every American feature — forces whose input generally equaled his own. For *Pretty Baby*, he had Polly Platt; for *Atlantic City*, John Guare; for *My Dinner with André*, the team of Shawn and Gregory; for *Crackers*, Jeffrey Fiskin, and for *Alamo Bay*, Ross Milloy. From 1970 until his arrival in America, and certainly for *Au revoir, les enfants* (for which he returned to France in 1986), he would assume his "triple threat" status of solo writer-director-producer.

8. Polly Platt, telephone interview by author, 2 July 2003.

9. "Polly Platt." *Internet Movie Database* [online], (cited 2004-04-12). Available from internet: < http://www.imdb.com/name/nm0686895/>

10. Peter Biskind, *Easy Riders, Raging Bulls* (New York: Simon & Schuster, 1998): 215–16.

11. "Polly Platt." *Internet Movie Database* [online].

12. Platt, interview.

13. This is the same ill-fated project that began as a collaboration with Jean-Pierre Gorin back in 1976. Alternately called *The Boy* and *Chicano*, Malle would briefly resume work on this film in-between *Pretty Baby* and *Atlantic City*, without Gorin. See Appendix A for more information.

14. Platt, interview.

15. Louis Malle, as quoted in author's telephone interview with Polly Platt, 2 July 2003.

16. Though only notable for its loose thematic connection to *Pretty Baby*, Malle and American playwright Jack Gelber (*The Connection*) drafted a screenplay on the life of Ferdinand "Jelly Roll" Morton — entitled *Jelly Roll* — back in the late sixties, but it went unproduced. Platt states that she neither read the Gelber script nor discussed it with Malle. See Chapter 26, "Lost Horizons," for a more detailed discussion of *Jelly Roll*.

17. Platt, interview.

18. *Ibid.*

19. *Ibid.*

20. *Ibid.*

21. "Antonia Bogdanovich." *Internet Movie Database* [online], (cited 2005-01-02). Available from internet: < http://www.imdb.com/name/nm0091668/>

22. Platt, interview.

23. *Ibid.*

24. Danny Peary, review of *Pretty Baby* (dir. Louis Malle), in *Guide for the Film Fanatic* (New York: Fireside Books, 1986), 338–9.

25. Vincent Malle, telephone interview by author, 15 December 2004.

26. Susan Sarandon, telephone interview by author, 18 November 2004.

27. There is a lack of consensus about which photos of Shields inspired Malle to cast her. The controversial Garry Gross photographed Shields at 10, fully nude, in a bathtub; this yielded a series of seductive, disturbing images that — given Brooke's heavy makeup and "woman-child" appearance — echo the film's themes and bathtub scene only vaguely. Many others have suggested that the refined and asexual Scavullo images of bare-chested Brooke (in lieu of the Gross photographs) led to her involvement in *Pretty Baby*. This seems far more likely given the film's tastefulness. Moreover, Platt has no recollection of ever seeing the Gross images, but did review the Scavullo photographs with Louis and Maureen Lambray in casting.

28. Sarandon, telephone interview.

29. Platt, interview.

30. Johnny Wiggs, as quoted in Al Rose, *E.J. Bellocq: Storyville Portraits* (London: Scolar Press, 1970), 8.

31. Platt, interview.

32. *Ibid.*

33. Keith Carradine, telephone interview by author, 31 March 2003.

34. *Ibid.*

35. Platt, interview.

36. *Ibid.*

37. *Ibid.*

38. *Storyville, New Orleans* (Tuscaloosa: University of Alabama Press, 1970), 149.

39. *Ibid.*

40. Referenced once in Malle's film, Emma Johnson — a Storyville madam and brothel owner — can be safely assessed as the walking embodiment of evil. She was notorious in her day for masterminding the sex slavery of children and hosting hardcore stage shows, where she forced the participants (mostly minors) to indulge in whatever perversions or barbarities her audience could dream up. Al Rose writes, "She caviled neither at kidnapping nor at functioning as accessory to rape. She forced brandy down the throats of 10-year-old girls to make them amenable to sexual overtures."

41. *Ibid.*

42. *Ibid.*, 150.

43. Michael Costello, review of *Pretty Baby* (dir. Louis Malle). *Internet Movie Database* [online], (cited 2004-04-18). Available from internet: <http://www.allmovie.com/cg/avg.dll?p=avg&sql=1:39087>

44. *Ibid.*

45. Danny Peary, review of *Pretty Baby* (dir. Louis Malle), in *Guide for the Film Fanatic* (New York: Fireside Books, 1986), 338.

46. "Film Directors' Erotic Fantasies." *Playboy* 25 (January 1978): 108.

47. Bruce Williamson, "Pretty Baby." *Playboy* 25 (March 1978): 101–5, 218–19.

48. Officially, Malle and Maureen Lambray share credit for the photographs, but according to Sarandon, Lambray alone took the pictures.

49. V. Malle, interview.

50. Loïc Malle, "Detachment," in *Lee Friedlander* (New York: Random House, 1988).

51. Uncoincidentally, Platt reveals that she drew most heavily from the impressionist works of Au-

guste Renoir — hence the picnic on the banks of the river.

52. *Pretty Baby*'s structural liberation had a high cost indeed: most of the critics who responded unfavorably to the picture chided its lack of narrative momentum as the picture's central flaw, and John Guare (Malle's collaborator on *Atlantic City*) approached Malle after the screening with, "Too bad you didn't work with a writer."

53. The film qualifies as a piece of deconstructionism in another respect: concurrent with Bellocq's attempts to see prostitutes as prostitutes, they are, in the deconstructionist sense, self-referential figures.

54. Polly Platt, telephone interview by author, 2 July 2003.

55. To accomplish this visual element, it should be noted that *Pretty Baby* was the first Malle film to employ the use of a Steadicam (invented around 1976 by Garrett Brown).

56. L. Malle, *Malle on Malle*, 122.

57. Peary, review of *Pretty Baby*.

58. *Pretty Baby*, dir. Louis Malle, 110 min., Paramount Pictures, 1978, videocassette.

59. Carradine, interview.

60. Molly Haskell, "When a House Is a Home," review of *Pretty Baby* (dir. Louis Malle). *New York* 11 (17 April 1978): 97.

61. Kenneth Turan, "No Help from the Stars," review of *Pretty Baby* (dir. Louis Malle). *Progressive* 42 (July 1978): 38.

62. Richard Corliss, "The Stranger Equations of Love and Art," review of *Pretty Baby* (dir. Louis Malle), *New Times* 10 (1 May 1978): 70–1.

63. Gilles Cebe, review of *La Petite* (dir. Louis Malle). *Écran* 71 (15 July 1978): 61.

64. Henri Behar, review of *La Petite* (dir. Louis Malle). *La Révue du cinéma* 329 (June 1978): 321.

65. Peary, review of *Pretty Baby*.

66. Sarandon, interview.

Chapter 15

1. Pierre Billard, *Louis Malle: Le Rebelle solitaire* (Paris: Plon, 2003), 389–92.

2. Maureen Orth, "The Americanization of Louis Malle." *New West* 3 (24 April 1978): 62.

3. Billard, *Rebelle*, 389–92.

4. *The Neighbor* would eventually be adapted by Leila Basen and co-screenwriter-director Max Fischer as *Killing 'Em Softly* (1982).

5. Despite the fact that neither Malle or Guare have ever acknowledged a connection between *The Neighbor* and *Atlantic City*, the stories do have a couple of fleeting similarities: both feature — as their central characters — elderly men whose lives are touched by the drug trade and who become involved, unexpectedly, with murder.

6. Billard, *Rebelle*, 387.

7. Louis Malle, *Malle on Malle*, ed. Philip French, rev. ed. (London: Faber & Faber, 1996), 125.

8. John Guare, telephone interview by author, 7 April 2004.

9. *Ibid.*

10. Pauline Kael, "Chance/Fate," review of *Atlantic City* (dir. Louis Malle). *Taking It All In* (Boston: Little, Brown, and Company, 1984), 176.

11. Author's note: there exists a small contradiction between this recollection of Guare's and Malle's recollection (the director claims that a *dentist* from Winnipeg — not a rabbi — backed the picture).

12. Malle remembers spending a straight 24 hours in Atlantic City, not 8 to 10 hours.

13. For a discussion of a Malle film that bears even more pronounced similarities to Altman's *Nashville,* see Chapter 21, "Collective Mythmaking," on *Milou en mai* (1990).

14. Kael, *Taking It All In*, 176.

15. *Ibid.*

16. Paul "Skinny" d'Amato (1908–84): the Atlantic City nightclub owner whose story is well told in Jonathan Van Meter's 2003 biography, *The Last Good Time*. d'Amato founded The 500 Club and eventually became host to scores of mobsters, and the unofficial godfather and founder of the Rat Pack, as well as close friends with Frank Sinatra; Den Martin; Sammy Davis, Jr." Eddie Fisher; Jerry Lewis; and countless other entertainers. Though Guare refers to d'Amato as a "mob boss," all of Van Meter's evidence suggests that d'Amato was never actually in the Mafia. When Guare alludes to d'Amato's "humiliating situation," he is referring to the fact that the nightclub impresario became a recluse for the last several years of his life, living out of his bedroom in his silk pajamas. It was in this state — in his bedroom — that d'Amato received Louis Malle and John Guare in the summer of 1979. Perhaps an inspiration for Grace's lifestyle in *Atlantic City*?

17. Guare, interview.

18. Kael, "Chance/Fate," 176.

19. Susan Sarandon, telephone interview by author, 18 November 2004.

20. This contradicts what Malle told Philip French in *Malle on Malle*, p. 129: "I have to be honest with you — my first choice was Robert Mitchum."

21. Guare, interview.

22. *Ibid.*

23. *Ibid.*

24. Guare, interview.

25. *Ibid.*

26. Billard, *Rebelle*, 396.

27. L. Malle, *Malle on Malle*, 129.

28. Guare, interview.

29. Sarandon, interview.

30. L. Malle, *Malle on Malle*, 129.

31. Sarandon, interview.

32. Guare, interview.

33. Gene A. Plunka, *The Black Comedy of John Guare* (Newark, NJ: University of Delaware Press, 2002), 140.

34. Guare, interview.

35. John Guare, introduction to *The House of Blue Leaves* (London, Faber & Faber, 1996), xiii.

36. Plunka, *Black Comedy*, 231.

37. Of the many contextual resources used to analyze and understand the films in this volume, one of the best — by far — was Dr. Dan McAdams's brilliant *Stories We Live By: Personal Myths and the Making of the Self,* which serves beautifully not only an analysis of *Atlantic City,* but an analysis of *My Dinner with André.* I reference and footnote McAdams's book several times in this and the next chapter, and use its terminology throughout. While published over a decade after Paramount released *Atlantic* and *André,* the volume is an absolutely essential resource if one desires a full understanding of the psychoanalytic context of Malle's second and third English-language films.

38. L. Malle, *Malle on Malle,* 132.

39. Jonathan Van Meter, *The Last Good Time: Skinny d'Amato, the Notorious 500 Club & the Rise and Fall of Atlantic City* (New York: Crown, 2003), 15.

40. Charles Funnell, as quoted in Van Meter, *Good Time,* 23.

41. The "contemporary" Atlantic City — i.e., post–1978 — lacks the same mythos. It became clear, when Steve Wynn, Donald Trump and Hugh Hefner first began to build golden towers on the Jersey Shore (circa 1978–79), that these renovations did not spring from a void — that most of the founders were already self-made, with the enormous and overpowering evidence of wealth used to start the renovations. Not so with Lou or with the "old Atlantic City" that Pascal personifies in the early stages of the picture.

42. Dan P. McAdams, PhD, *Stories We Live By: Personal Myths and the Making of the Self* (New York: William Morrow & Company, 1993), 128.

43. *Atlantic City,* dir. Louis Malle, 105 min., Paramount Pictures, 1980, videocassette.

44. Pauline Kael, "Anybody home?" Review of *Zelig* (dir. Woody Allen). *State of the Art* (London: Arrow Books, Ltd., 1987), 25.

45. McAdams, *Personal Myths,* 12.

46. *Ibid.,* 124.

47. L. Malle, *Malle on Malle,* 131.

48. Pauline Kael, "Chance/Fate," review of *Atlantic City* (dir. Louis Malle). *Taking It All In* (Boston: Little, Brown, and Company, 1984), 176–7.

49. David Denby, "Avenging Angel," review of *Atlantic City* (dir. Louis Malle). *New York* 14 (6 April 1981): 56, 58.

50. Bruce Williamson, review of *Atlantic City* (dir. Louis Malle). *Playboy* 28 (June 1981): 32.

51. Philip French, "Desperate Losers," review of *Atlantic City* (dir. Louis Malle). *Observer* (25 January 1981): 32.

52. Claude-Michel Cluny, "Voilà donc l'Amérique?," review of *Atlantic City* (dir. Louis Malle). *Cinéma* 262 (October 1980): 82 (author translation).

53. Max Tessier, review of *Atlantic City* (dir. Louis Malle). *La Révue du cinéma* 353 (September 1980): 20 (author translation).

54. Plunka, *Black Comedy,* 140.

Chapter 16

1. Pierre Billard, *Louis Malle: Le Rebelle solitaire* (Paris: Plon, 2003), 559.

2. The U.S. release date of *Atlantic City* was April 3, 1981, and the date for *My Dinner with André* was October 11, 1981.

3. John Guare, telephone interview by author, 7 April 2004.

4. L. Malle, *Malle on Malle,* 137.

5. Billard, *Rebelle,* 406–9.

6. Philip French, introduction to *Malle on Malle,* by Louis Malle (London: Faber & Faber, 1996), xv.

7. Billard, *Rebelle,* 406.

8. Billard even titles his chapter on this period, "New York. My lunch with Candice. My dinner with André." Though *Le Rebelle solitaire* purports to provide an in-depth analysis of the Malle-Bergen relationship, one might find it preferable — for a more accurate and balanced account of Bergen's early relationship with Malle — to consult Bergen's 1984 biography, *Knock Wood,* published by Simon & Schuster.

9. Billard, *Rebelle,* 406.

10. L. Malle, *Malle on Malle,* 136.

11. *Ibid.,* 414.

12. Marie Brenner, "My Conversation with André." *New York* 14 (19 October 1981): 37.

13. *Ibid.,* 40.

14. Note that as André recalls his real-life experiences, his trip to Poland seems to have come at the end of his search, whereas, in the carefully restructured script, the Poland trip precedes everything else.

15. André Gregory, telephone interview by author, 15 July 2003.

16. Brenner, "Conversation," 40.

17. Wallace Shawn, Introduction, *My Dinner with André* by Wallace Shawn and André Gregory (New York: Grove Press, 1981), 13.

18. *Ibid.*

19. *Ibid.*

20. On an amusing note, one wonders if the line at the outset of *Dinner* about the Xerox shop mightn't be an inside nod to this event.

21. Shawn had only appeared in one film at this point; *Starting Over* and *All That Jazz* would not be released until later in 1979.

22. Billard, *Rebelle,* 401.

23. Gregory, interview.

24. William Grimes, "Our Dinner with Louis." Interview with Wally Shawn and André Gregory. *New York Times Magazine* (31 December 1995), 42.

25. Gregory, interview.

26. L. Malle, *Malle on Malle,* 136.

27. Michener's frequent presence in the credits of the Grove-published *Dinner* screenplay — she is co-credited with still photographs of the production and credited in the acknowledgments alongside her husband — would seem to corroborate the Shawn-Gregory account.

28. Gregory, interview.

29. Grimes, "Our Dinner," 42.

30. Candice Bergen, telephone interview by author, 9 March 2004.

31. Wally Shawn, "Some notes on Louis Malle and *My Dinner with André*," *Sight & Sound* 51 (1982): 119.

32. Bergen, interview.

33. Gregory, interview.

34. A slight contradiction: Gregory places this Malle comment in early rehearsals; Prédal (p. 138) places it around the time of the Royal Court Theater performance of *André*.

35. Gregory, interview.

36. *Ibid.*

37. *Ibid.*

38. Brenner, "Conversation," 40.

39. *My Dinner with André*, dir. Louis Malle, 111 min., Pacific Arts Video, 1981, videocassette.

40. *Ibid.*

41. *Ibid.*

42. *Ibid.*

43. *Ibid.*

44. *Ibid.*

45. Pauline Kael, review of *My Dinner with André* (dir. Louis Malle). *New Yorker* 57 (4 January 1982): 82.

46. Larry Grobel, *Conversations with Brando* (New York: Hyperion, 1991), 72.

47. Gregory, interview.

48. Looking strictly at Malle's achievements: he directed a production of *Lydie Breeze*, one of John Guare's most captivating and underappreciated stage plays, in New York circa 1982 — i.e., shortly after *André*'s stateside release. *Breeze* pulls directly from *André*, by moving a preponderance of the action to an unseen visual field and thus continuing the "fourth dimension" idea on stage. Much of this action unfolds in long monologues, through characters' revocations of the past. The play's approach was so groundbreaking that it failed to be noticed or appreciated.

49. Gregory's story of the Saharan desert — see the block quote later in this chapter — is another fantastic example.

50. Wallace Shawn and André Gregory, *My Dinner with André* (New York: Grove, 1981), 45.

51. *Ibid.*

52. Another such example that uses *contrasting size* to paint a mental tableaux of surrealistic landscapes and characters (strikingly similar to the illustration of the castle-slab juxtaposition) is André's comical description of Kozan: "This tiny little Buddhist, who when I first met him, you know, was eating a little bowl of milk, hot milk with rice, was now eating huge *beefs*!"

53. Shawn and Gregory, *My Dinner with André*, 145.

54. Wally Shawn, "Some Notes," 118.

55. Shawn and Gregory, *My Dinner with André*, 42.

56. *Ibid.*

57. Mel Gussow, "My Lunch with André (and Wally): A Dialogue Resumes," interview with Wally Shawn and André Gregory. *New York Times* (16 May 1999): 5.

58. Roger Ebert, review of *My Dinner with André*.

Cinemania '96 [software]. (cited 2004-07-22). Microsoft Publishing, 1997.

59. Roger Ebert, review of *My Dinner with André*. *Chicago Sun-Times* [online]. (cited 2004-07-22). Available from internet: <http://www.suntimes.com/ebert/ebert_reviews/1999/01/andre1118.html >

60. Louis Malle, *Malle on Malle*, ed. Philip French, rev. ed. (London: Faber & Faber, 1996), 139.

61. *Ibid.*, 138.

62. To progress beyond the obliqueness (the indirectness) of Shawn's attempts to address the audience, one must leave the sphere of the film and examine Shawn's small oeuvre as screenwriter: he scripted (and David Hare filmed) *The Designated Mourner* largely (though not entirely) as a series of second-person monologues by Mike Nichols, Miranda Richardson, and David de Keyser, done straight into the camera and thus implying full acknowledgment of the audience.

63. The irony, of course, is that the more one familiarizes oneself with Gregory's first few monologues through repeated viewing and script readings, the more clarity his words and passages gain, until one can discern the major themes perfectly (even if the individual situations in which André finds himself remain completely unrelatable) and grasp just how the bizarre details fit in — for example, it quickly becomes clear that Gregory's trips out to the highway to "watch the lights turn from red to green" are meant to signify the degree to which he has learned to extract and value tiny magical details from everyday occurrences — to regard even the most banal incidents as sources of wonder.

64. Danny Peary, review of *My Dinner with André* (dir. Louis Malle), in *Guide for the Film Fanatic* (New York: Fireside Books, 1986), 288.

65. This arcanum is completely unaccidental, a deliberately empty postmodern reference: this author did an extensive internet search for the meaning of "seven swank shrimp" and turned up nothing, aside from ads for a shrimp appetizer at the Swank Bar.

66. André Gregory even appears in a wonderful Jaglom film, *Always*, four years after shooting *Dinner*. He plays the "life is a stone" party philosopher, in a marvelously comic bit that appears to be influenced by the Malle film.

67. Gregory, interview.

68. Pauline Kael, review of *My Dinner with André* (dir. Louis Malle). *New Yorker* 57 (4 January 1982): 81–3.

69. Gregory, interview.

70. Vincent Canby, review of *My Dinner with André* (dir. Louis Malle). *New York Times* (8 October 1981). [online]. (cited 2004-07-22). Available from internet: <http://movies2.nytimes.com/gst/movies/movie.html?v_id=34015>

71. Bruce Williamson, review of *My Dinner with André* (dir. Louis Malle). *Playboy* 29 (June 1982): 34.

72. David Denby, "Boeuf à la Mode," review of *My Dinner with André* (dir. Louis Malle). *New York* 14 (26 October 1981): 96.

73. L.L. Cohn, review of *My Dinner with André*. *Variety* 304 (16 September 1981): 16.

74. L. Malle, *Malle on Malle*, 141.

75. Michael Chion, "Bouvard et Pécuchet dînent à New York," review of *My Dinner with André* (dir. Louis Malle). *Cahiers du cinéma* 346 (April 1983): 50–1.

76. Gregory, interview.

Chapter 17

1. Louis Malle, *Malle on Malle*, ed. Philip French, rev. ed. (London: Faber & Faber, 1996), 134.

2. Pierre Billard, *Louis Malle: Le Rebelle solitaire* (Paris: Plon, 2003), 428.

3. *Ibid.*, 430.

4. Pierre Billard writes on p. 430 of *Louis Malle: Le Rebelle solitaire* that Lewis only had *ties* to Universal. Malle himself, who describes the "musical chairs" played when Lewis left Universal to be replaced by Robert Cortes, implies that Lewis was actually one of the heads of production. It is thus unclear from any published source what Lewis's business relationship was, exactly, with Universal.

5. Why did Lewis seek out Malle, of all directors? Though such a comparison risks insulting John Guare, perhaps Lewis viewed an early cut of *Atlantic City* and saw qualities in it that he wanted to carry over into *Crackers*—a fascinating *Nashville*-like narrative structure, with crosscutting between several subplots that unfold concurrently; a ripe sense of humor; and the story of "small-timers" trying to "make it" with a "big score." These are, of course, only surface-level similarities. The elements of *Atlantic City* that give the picture its kick are Guare's sizzling dialogue and characterizations, and the delightful eccentricity of his story twists—none of which are shared by *Crackers*.

6. The approximate date of when Lewis began to contact Malle is uncertain, but given Malle's wording, we can infer that it was probably sometime in mid–1980.

7. René Prédal, *Louis Malle* (Paris: Edilig, 1989), 142.

8. Billard, *Rebelle*, 430.

9. L. Malle, *Malle on Malle*, 143.

10. Prédal, *Louis Malle*, 142 (author translation).

11. Jeffrey Alan Fiskin, telephone interview by author, 24 October 2003.

12. *Ibid.*

13. L. Malle, *Malle on Malle*, 144.

14. *Ibid.*, 146.

15. David Hare, telephone interview by author, 17 October 2003

16. Fiskin, interview.

17. *Ibid.*

18. Bergen, interview.

19. James Bruce, telephone interview by author, 16 April 2004.

20. Prédal, *Louis Malle*, 145 (author translation).

21. Author's note: Cortes produced only one additional film, *The River* (1984), that same year, and

(according to the IMDB) has done no production or directorial work since.

22. L. Malle, *Malle on Malle*, 146.

23. Billard, *Rebelle*, 433.

24. Is it possible that a longer cut of *Crackers* may still exist in a vault — either a print or a videocassette (telecined by Malle or Ed Lewis)? Or that Universal may still hold the trim from which a longer cut could *be* reconstructed, using Malle and Baron's notes? Jamie Bruce's recollections of the initial cut certainly make this option sound appealing. The author speculated on the first possibility in an interview with Bruce, who seemed pleased by the suggestion, yet dubious. As for the second: although Universal probably still holds the trim in their vaults, the odds of their believing in a box-office bomb enough to pull it out and allow it to be reedited are second to none. (As of this writing, *Crackers* is one of Malle's few recent releases to have long since fallen out of print on videocassette in the States.) It is, however, possible that given the films' resounding success in France in the early nineties, someone in Europe may try to buy back the rights and release a director's cut. Here's hoping.

25. Fiskin, interview.

26. *Ibid.*

27. *Ibid.*

28. Billard, *Rebelle*, 434.

29. Making her cinematic debut as Carmela in Monicelli's film, Cardinale is limited to a bit part but manages to deliver one of the strongest first impressions in movie history with only a few minutes of screen time. She is *astonishingly* sexy.

30. As it stands, it is impossible to tell if the flaws mentioned are the fault of a poorly developed screenplay from Fiskin, or of Robert Cortes becoming splicer-happy and having Malle, Baron, and their platoon of co-editors chop sequences out of the picture.

31. Fiskin, interview.

32. Fiskin, interview.

33. *Ibid.*

34. Bergen, interview.

35. "*Crackers* movie posters and memorabilia at MovieGoods." *MovieGoods* [online]. (cited 2004-06-10). Available from internet: <http://www.moviegoods.com/movie_product.asp?master%5Fmovie%5Fid=7577&movie%5Fnss=19830110>

36. Bergen, interview.

37. Vincent Malle, telephone interview by author, 15 December 2004.

38. *Ibid.*

39. L. Malle, *Malle on Malle*, 151.

40. Todd McCarthy, review of *Crackers* (dir. Louis Malle). *Variety* 313, 25 January 1984.

41. Tom Milne, review of *Crackers* (dir. Louis Malle). *Monthly Film Bulletin* 52 (1985), 19.

42. Bruce Williamson, review of *Crackers* (dir. Louis Malle). *Playboy* 26 (March 1984), 26.

43. Philip French, review of *Crackers* (dir. Louis Malle). *The Observer* (27 January 1985).

Chapter 18

1. Ross Milloy, telephone interview by author, 28 March 2004.

2. See Chapter 19, "The Well-Rooted and the Transient," for an extended discussion of these films.

3. Milloy, telephone interview.

4. Ross Milloy, "Vietnam Fallout in a Texas Town," *New York Times Sunday Magazine* (6 April 1980): 39.

5. *Ibid.*, 58.

6. Louis Malle, *Malle on Malle*, ed. Philip French, rev. ed. (London: Faber & Faber, 1996), 148.

7. Milloy, interview.

8. John Culhane, "Louis Malle: An Outsider's Odyssey," *New York Times Sunday Magazine* (7 April 1985): 28.

9. Milloy, "Vietnam Fallout," 58.

10. *Ibid.*

11. Culhane, "Outsider's Odyssey," 28.

12. Jean-Pierre Gorin, telephone interview by author, 2 July 2004.

13. L. Malle, *Malle on Malle*, 134.

14. James Bruce, telephone interview by author, 14 April 2004.

15. L. Malle, *Malle on Malle*, 148.

16. Pierre Billard, *Louis Malle: Le Rebelle solitaire* (Paris: Plon, 2003), 437.

17. Ed Harris, telephone interview by author, 17 November 2004.

18. Culhane, "Outsider's Odyssey," 28.

19. No relation to the Sau Van Nguyen who shot B.J. Aplin.

20. Bruce, interview.

21. Harris, interview.

22. *Ibid.*

23. David Denby, "Gulf Coast Blues," review of *Alamo Bay* (dir. Louis Malle). *New York* 18 (15 April 1985): 97.

24. Billard, *Rebelle*, 438.

25. Donald Moffat, telephone interview by author, 6 April 2004.

26. Milloy, interview.

27. As Baron died in 1996, her motivations cannot be clarified.

28. Bruce, interview.

29. *Ibid.*

30. Billard, *Rebelle*, 443.

31. "Release dates for *Alamo Bay* (1985)." *Internet Movie Database* [online], (cited 2004-08-08). Available from internet: <http://www.imdb.com/title/tt0088689/releaseinfo>

32. Milloy, interview.

33. Ross Milloy, "Vietnam Fallout," 58.

34. *Ibid.*, 48.

35. L. Malle, *Malle on Malle*, 146–7.

36. L. Malle, *Malle on Malle*, 146, 148–9.

37. Fred Berner, interview by author, New York City, 7 March 2003.

38. Milloy, "Vietnam Fallout," 38.

39. Peter Travers, review of *Alamo Bay* (dir. Louis Malle). *People Weekly* 23 (15 April 1985): 16.

40. Denby, "Gulf Coast Blues," 97, 99.

41. *Ibid.*, 97.

42. *Ibid.*

43. Todd McCarthy, review of *Alamo Bay* (dir. Louis Malle). *Variety* (3 April 1985): 15.

44. Peter Travers, review of *Alamo Bay* (dir. Louis Malle). *People Weekly* 23 (15 April 1985): 16.

45. Ginette Delmas, review of *Alamo Bay* (dir. Louis Malle). *Jeune cinéma* 170 (November 1985): 42.

46. *Ibid.*

47. Alain Garel, "Un Autre Guerre du Viêt-nam," review of *Alamo Bay* (dir. Louis Malle), *La Revue du cinéma* 409 (October 1985): 35–7.

Chapter 19

1. André Gregory, telephone interview by author, 15 July 2003.

2. Louis Malle, *Malle on Malle*, ed. Philip French, rev. ed. (London: Faber & Faber, 1996), 155.

3. Charles Tesson, review of *God's* Country (dir. Louis Malle). *Cahiers du cinéma* 386 (July 1986): 64 (author translation).

4. James Bruce, telephone interview by author, 14 April 2004.

5. L. Malle, *Malle on Malle*, 157.

6. *Ibid.*, 156–7.

7. Bruce, interview.

8. Tesson, review of *God's Country* (dir. Louis Malle). *Cahiers du cinéma* 386 (July 1986): 64 (author translation).

9. L. Malle, *Malle on Malle*, 158.

10. Bruce, interview.

11. Billard, *Rebelle*, 448.

12. Bruce, interview.

13. L. Malle, *Malle on Malle*, 158.

14. Richard Leacock, "One Man's Truth," interview by James Blue. In *The Documentary Tradition: From Nanook to Woodstock*. ed. Lewis Jacobs (New York: Hopkinson & Blake, 1971), 414–15.

15. L. Malle, *Malle on Malle*, 162.

16. John Corry, "Malle's 'God's Country' in Minnesota," review of *God's Country* (dir. Louis Malle). *New York Times* (11 December 1985): C29.

17. Leonard Maltin, review of *God's Country* (dir. Louis Malle), in *Leonard Maltin's Movie and Video Guide*, 25th ed. (New York: Signet Books, 2004), 541.

18. Raphaël Bassan, review of *God's Country* (dir. Louis Malle). *Révue du cinéma* 419 (September 1986): 49 (author translation).

19. *Ibid.*, (Author translation).

20. Alain Carbonnier, review of *La Poursuite du bonheur*. *Cinéma* 400 (22 May 1987): 13.

21. Marc Chevrie, review of *La Poursuite du bonheur*. *Cahiers du cinéma* 397 (June 1987): 40.

Chapter 20

1. "Today in History Basic Datebook — November 8th." *Dave's Date Book* [online]. (cited 2004-08-

22). Available from internet: <http://www.daves-datebook.com/630/630d1108.htm>

2. Pierre Billard, *Louis Malle: Le Rebelle solitaire*. (Paris: Plon, 2003), 459–60.

3. The title page of the second draft of *Eye Contact* suggests that Billard's version of the story is at least partially inaccurate: the script does not bear a date of 1986, but a date of March 1987 — at least one month after production wrapped on *Au revoir*. For a slightly more detailed discussion of *Eye Contact* — the project's history, a summary of the screenplay, and how it evolved, by turns, into a Tony-nominated Guare stage triumph in the early nineties — see Appendix A, "Lost Horizons."

4. Candice Bergen, telephone interview by author, 9 March 2004.

5. Billard, *Rebelle*, 466–7.

6. L. Malle, *Malle on Malle*, 168.

7. Billard, *Rebelle*, 48 (author translation).

8. Serge Toubiana, "Souvenirs d'en France," interview with Louis Malle, *Cahiers du cinéma* 400 (October 1987): 34.

9. L. Malle, *Malle on Malle*, 181.

10. Pierre Billard, *Rebelle*, 54.

11. *Ibid.*, 60–1.

12. *Ibid.*, 50.

13. Justine A. Malle, telephone interview by author, 18 May 2004.

14. Stéphanie Grégoire, "Some points...," email to author, 21 August 2004.

15. Louis Malle and Sarah Kant, *Louis Malle par Louis Malle*, Editions de l'Athenor (Paris: Jacques Mallecot, 1978), 11.

16. S. Grégoire, "Some points..."

17. L. Malle, *Malle on Malle*, 167–8.

18. *Ibid.*, 168.

19. Billard, *Rebelle*, 463.

20. Malle and Kant, *Louis Malle par Louis Malle*, 11–12 (author translation).

21. L. Malle, *Malle on Malle*, 168.

22. *Ibid.*, 169.

23. J. Malle, interview by author.

24. Billard, *Rebelle*, 475–6.

25. "Full cast and crew for *Au revoir les enfants*." *Internet Movie Database* [online]. (cited 2004-08-22). Available from internet: <http://www.imdb.com/title/tt0092593/fullcredits>

26. L. Malle, *Malle on Malle*, 176.

27. Billard, *Rebelle*, 478.

28. *Ibid.*, 174–8.

29. Some might object to my idea that the film excludes anticlericalism, arguing that *Au revoir* does incorporate one mildly anticlerical element: the priests' refusal to give Jean Bonnet (Kippelstein) wine and a communion wafer. This may appear cold or hostile to a viewer unfamiliar with the Christian church or with biblical teaching; I disagree completely. The priests are only remaining loyal to their beliefs and thus cannot be accused of hypocrisy — how could the one small act of excluding a non-Christian from communion outweigh the selfless and compassionate act of hiding the refugees in the school *per se*? If one doubts the director's sympathy toward

the clerical leaders in *Au revoir*, one should compare the politically astute, warm and sincere monks in that film to the lecherous homosexual priest (Michel Lonsdale) in Malle's earlier *Souffle au cœur*.

30. Pierre Billard, *Louis Malle: Le Rebelle solitaire* (Paris: Plon, 2003), 459–60.

31. Consider, for example, the character of Joseph — practically indistinguishable from Lucien Lacombe — whose genesis came not from the St. Thérèse boarding school in 1944, but from several experiences Malle had in the sixties and seventies — e.g., the encampment in Algeria, the discovery of the "Halcones" in Mexico, etc.

32. It is hardly accidental that Malle planned, tentatively, to do a sequel to *Au revoir*.

33. Avishai Margalit, *The Ethics of Memory* (Cambridge, MA: Harvard University Press, 2002): 62.

34. One should note, as well, how the director draws contrast between the stillness of Julien's movement and the bustle of the crowd to "pull" the audience's attention to Julien.

35. Danny Peary, review of *Picnic at Hanging Rock*, in *Guide for the Film Fanatic* (New York: Fireside, 1986): 330.

36. Cynthia Ozick, "The Shock of Teapots," in *Metaphor & Memory* (New York: Knopf, 1989): 143.

37. C. Ozick, "Metaphor and Memory," in *Metaphor & Memory*, 282.

38. *Ibid.*, 280.

39. Pauline Kael, review of *Au revoir les enfants* (dir. Louis Malle). *New Yorker* 64 (22 February 1988): 86.

40. L. Malle, *Malle on Malle*, 180–1.

41. Billard, *Rebelle*, 479.

42. On this note, consider another of Margalit's statements: "Even if it turns out that flashbulb memories are not on the whole reliable, that fact would not undermine the point that we find it important to report (even falsely) the channels by which we become related to a shared event when that event is of immense importance to us."

43. L. Malle, *Malle on Malle*, 181.

44. Margalit, *Ethics of Memory*, 30.

45. *Ibid.*, 44–5.

46. Maurice Pons, "Un Premier Film signé Louis Malle," review of *Au revoir les enfants* (dir. Louis Malle). *Avant-Scène Cinéma* 373 (July 1988): 5.

47. Marcel Martin, "Louis Malle, humaniste inclassable," review of *Au revoir les enfants* (dir. Louis Malle). *La Révue du cinéma* 431 (October 1987): 48.

48. David Denby, "Past Perfect," review of *Au revoir les enfants* (dir. Louis Malle). *New York* 21 (22 February 1988): 70.

49. Lenny Borger, review of *Au revoir les enfants* (dir. Louis Malle). *Variety* 328 (2 September 1987): 18.

50. Philip French, "A Guilty Occupation," review of *Au revoir les enfants* (dir. Louis Malle). *Observer* (9 October 1988): 43.

51. Bergen, interview.

Chapter 21

1. Louis Malle, *Malle on Malle*, ed. Philip French, rev. ed. (London: Faber & Faber, 1996), 185.

2. Candice Bergen, telephone interview by author, 9 March 2004.

3. *Ibid.*

4. Maureen Orth, "The Americanization of Louis Malle," *New West* 3, 24 April 1978, 59.

5. Pierre Billard, *Louis Malle: Le Rebelle solitaire* (Paris: Plon, 2003), 494, 496.

6. Billard incorporates a significant piece of misinformation here; he seems to imply (p. 491) that Malle planned to shoot *Milou* from May to June of '88 and *Contact* from September to October of '88. Absolutely impossible. Because Malle worked on co-writing *Milou* for most of 1988 (and began a treatment — at the *absolute* earliest — in February of that year), he never could have expected to get two drafts of *Milou* written and completed, secure financing, and finish location scouting and casting within three months, particularly if he had *Eye Contact* in the works as well. The projected schedule detailed by Billard would only begin to make sense if reposited in 1989. Indeed, when talking to Philip French, Malle remembers, "I started to *think* about Milou in the spring of 1988" and "I was anxious to shoot in the spring or summer of the following year, 1989." But if a production start date for *Milou* in May of '89 is accurate, one cannot assume that Malle planned to shoot *Eye Contact* from September to October of that year, because Guare reveals (see extract) that although Malle did plan to do *Milou* and *Contact* back-to-back, *Contact* could have only been filmed in the spring. One can thus infer that Malle slated the production of *Eye Contact* for spring 1990.

7. Billard, *Louis Malle*, 491.

8. *Ibid.*

9. *Ibid.*, 492.

10. *Ibid.*, 492–3.

11. "Release dates for 'Murphy Brown.'" *Internet Movie Database* [online]. (cited 2004-09-13). Available from internet: <http://www.imdb.com/title/tt0094514/releaseinfo>

12. John Guare, "Re: Verifying info from Billard," email to author, 19 September 2004.

13. Billard, *Rebelle*, 493.

14. L. Malle, *Malle on Malle*, 187.

15. Billard, *Rebelle*, 493.

16. Frank Rich, review of *The Cherry Orchard* (dir. Peter Brook). *The Broadview Press Adjunct Website.* [online]. (cited 2002-12-30). Available from internet: <http://www.broadviewpress.com/drama/cherryorchard.htm>

17. L. Malle, *Malle on Malle*, 215.

18. *Ibid.*

19. Though Carrière finds it impossible to remember all of the contributions that came specifically from him (He told this author, "It's always impossible to say in a script, when you share the writing ... 'Who? How? What?'") one catches throughout the *Milou* many of these eccentric and marvelously vivid details of rural life that, by their very nature, must

have sprung directly from the Carrières' experiences or from Malle's experiences rather than from loose invention — details such as the anecdote about Uncle Albert reading Virgil to the bees to calm them, Milou use of mustard as a kind of "primitive smelling salt," to awaken Adèle after her fall, and Milou screaming his lungs out in a kind of wild Tarzan cry to savor the silence it leaves in its wake.

20. Billard, *Rebelle*, 495.

21. L. Malle, *Malle on Malle*, 187.

22. Billard, *Rebelle*, 495.

23. L. Malle, *Malle on Malle*, 187.

24. Carrière is speaking of "going together" to Louis's house, on the Causse du Lot, to co-write the script.

25. Jean-Claude Carrière, telephone interview by author, 14 February 2004.

26. Billard, *Rebelle*, 495 (author translation).

27. This would accord with another interviewee's recollection about Malle's *processus* for creating a screenplay. In an interview with the author, *Alamo Bay* producer Ross Milloy — like Billard — suggests that Malle (in the mode of the great screenwriters) was almost exclusively preoccupied with minute character detail and believed the story should proceed from the characters instead of being imposed on the characters.

28. Carrière, interview.

29. Richard Bernstein, "Louis Malle Uncorks the '68 Crop," interview with Louis Malle. *New York Times* (17 June 1990): 20.

30. L. Malle, *Malle on Malle*, 182–4.

31. Michel Piccoli, telephone interview by author, 7 July 2004 (author translation).

32. Carrière, interview.

33. Piccoli, interview (author translation).

34. L. Malle, *Malle on Malle*, 133.

35. Piccoli, interview (author translation).

36. L. Malle, *Malle on Malle*, 193.

37. *Ibid.*

38. *Ibid.*, 194.

39. *Ibid.*, 196–7.

40. Louis Malle and Jean-Claude Carrière, Introduction, *Milou in May* (London, Faber & Faber, 1990), ix.

41. Billard, *Rebelle*, 497.

42. L. Malle, *Malle on Malle*, 188.

43. Fabienne Volnier, "Re: Louis Malle/Milou en Mai," email to Jacques Weissgerber, 16 September 2004 (author translation).

44. L. Malle, *Malle on Malle*, 194–5.

45. "Release dates for *Milou en Mai*." *Internet Movie Database* [online]. (cited 2004-09-14). Available from internet: <http://www.imdb.com/title/tt0097884/releaseinfo>

46. Marie-Françoise Leclère, "Louis Malle: La Recherche du bonheur," review of *Milou en Mai*. *Le Point* 905 (22 January 1990): 14.

47. L. Malle, *Malle on Malle,* 216.

48. Malle and Carrière, Introduction to *Milou*, viii.

49. The idea to use some essays by Claude Lévi-Strauss as one (of several) contextual reference points in this chapter thus comes directly from Carrière,

who references the great French anthropologist's concept of the "detached look" in his eloquent foreword to the *Milou* script.

50. Claude Lévi-Strauss, "The Scope of Anthropology," in *Structural Anthropology Volume II* (New York: Basic Books, 1976), 3–4.

51. Daniel Singer, *Prelude to Revolution: France in May 1968* (Cambridge, MA: South End Press, 2002), 75.

52. *Ibid.*, 225.

53. Louis Malle and Jean-Claude Carrière, *Milou in May* (London: Faber & Faber, 1990), 2–3.

54. Anton Chekhov, *The Cherry Orchard*, in *Five Plays*. Trans. Ronald Hingley. (New York: Oxford University Press, 1998), 245.

55. L. Malle, *Malle on Malle*, 191.

56. Certainly, in the hands of an American director (other than Altman) the material might risk veering into the melodramatic. A *Newsweek* review compares *May Fools*— simply by virtue of its ensemble cast and the idea of a mass of characters gathering in a house — to Larry Kasdan's insipid Sayles rehash *The Big Chill* (1983); such a comparison is a shallow and grievous offense to Malle and Carrière, but yields an interesting insight, because it discloses how much closer the Kasdan-Benedek scripted American film lies to contrived melodrama. Like the Kasdan picture, P.T. Anderson's wildly overrated *Magnolia* (1999) also works with a collective scope but lacks any understatement and veers absurdly into the melodramatic. But these directors are less adroit and less sensitive than someone working on the level of Altman or Malle, perhaps too insensitive to take advantage of the aforementioned "equation." And in the case of *Milou* and *Nashville*, the arcs are infinitely more minimalist then the pictures by Kasdan and Anderson, minimalist and subtle almost to the point of invisibility.

57. L. Malle, *Malle on Malle*, 194.

58. *May Fools*, dir. Louis Malle, 109 min., MGM/UA Home Entertainment, 1990, videocassette

59. Robert Graves, *The White Goddess* (New York: Farrar, Straus, and Giroux, 2000), 392.

60. The Virgil references may also be something of an "in joke" within French culture, as a correlation exists between residents in the south of France — with their frequently mocked accents (rolling "R's") and the Roman poet, whose "musical and rhetorical skill ... fine-sounding periphrases, and ... rolling periods are ... designed to dazzle and overpower," according to Robert Graves. This could explain the humor in Léonce's line, "Yes, but dialect works as well, with bees from 'round here, anyway."

61. Note the kitschy symbolism of Lily stroking the rhinoceros's horn with a broad smile on her face, as if the horn is an erect penis.

62. Malle and Carrière, *Milou*, 28–9.

63. How appropriate it is, then, that Mme. Vieuzac is the one major character of the 12 (whom Malle describes as a "crucial character, ever present ... a constant reference point") to exist, figuratively speaking, at the center of the circle. She thus becomes a figure used, via her placement in the narrative framework, to help define the attitudes of the rest —

representing the shared paradigm of her relatives. Note how this is foreshadowed by the visual metaphor, at the outset of the picture, of the honeybees swarming around a single queen.

64. Piccoli, interview (author translation).

65. Structurally, one cannot help but recall Albert Brooks's (similarly inspired) comic masterpiece *Lost in America,* in which he and wife Julie Hagerty drop out of society "to live off of the land" with a nest egg of several hundred thousand dollars, and are immediately forced into a blue collar life after losing all of the money at a Las Vegas casino.

66. The similar celebratory scene of the Vieuzacs parading around in a conga line as they belt out "La Fille du Bedouin" in front of the matriarch's body, colored by Philip French as Malle challenging the audience's sensibilities, also feels like a direct *homage* to a scene from an underscreened little masterpiece that Malle appeared in (one of his only appearances as an actor) circa 1969. In Nelly Kaplan's *La Fiancée du Pirate,* several village buffoons and idiots "dishonor" an emotionally beleaguered woman by making drunken merriment around her mother's dead body, even (at one point) attempting to pour wine down the corpse's throat.

67. Malle and Carrière, *Milou*, 74.

68. Hal Hinson, review of *May Fools* (dir. Louis Malle). *The Washington Post* [online]. (cited 2004-09-25). Available from internet: <http://www.washingtonpost.com/wp-srv/style/longterm/movies/videos/ mayfoolsrhinson_a0a98d.htm>

69. Desson Howe, review of *May Fools* (dir. Louis Malle). *The Washington Post* [online]. (cited 2004-09-25). Available from internet: <http://www.washingtonpost.com/wp-srv/style/longterm/movies/videos/mayfoolsrhowe_a0b28e.htm>

70. Stanley Kauffmann, review of *May Fools* (dir. Louis Malle). *The New Republic* 203 (9 July 1990): 32.

71. Bruce Williamson, review of *May Fools* (dir. Louis Malle). *Playboy* 37 (July 1990): 24.

72. Philip French, "Malle's Marvelous Milieu." Review of *Milou in May* (dir. Louis Malle). *Observer* (2 September 1990): 60.

73. Gerard Léfort, "Honni soit qui Malle y pense." Review of *Milou en Mai* (dir. Louis Malle). *Libération* (4 January 1990): 1.

74. Leclère, "Recherche du bonheur," 14–15.

Chapter 22

1. "Release dates for *Milou en Mai* (1990).'" *Internet Movie Database* [online] (cited 2004-10-14). Available from internet: <http://www.imdb.com/title/tt0097884/releaseinfo>

2. "Release dates for *Fatale* (1992)." *Internet Movie Database* [online]. (cited 2004-10-15). Available from internet: <http://www.imdb.com/title/tt0104237/releaseinfo>

3. "Amazon.com: Books—*Malle on Malle.*" *Amazon.com* [online]. (cited 2004-10-15). Available from

internet: <http://www.amazon.com/exec/obidos/tg/
detail/-/0571178804/qid=1097870921/sr=1-1/ref=
sr_1_1/104-5721201-2000704?v=glance&s=books>

4. Billard, *Rebelle*, 504.

5. *Ibid.*, 505.

6. *Ibid.*, 506.

7. *Ibid.*

8. Louis Malle, *Malle on Malle*, ed. Philip French,
rev. ed. (London: Faber & Faber, 1996), 201.

9. Billard, *Rebelle*, 502.

10. *Ibid.*, 503 (author translation).

11. *Ibid.*, 507.

12. L. Malle, *Malle on Malle*, 200.

13. Jean-Claude Carrière, telephone interview by
author, 14 February 2004.

14. *Ibid.*

15. L. Malle, *Malle on Malle*, 201.

16. David Hare, telephone interview by author, 17
October 2003.

17. Carrière, interview.

18. A dubious statement that borders on the absurd. If Carrière wrote an entire script, how is it con-
ceivable that he cannot remember doing so? And if,
in turn, he did *not*, why would Hare and Malle—on
separate occasions—each fabricate a story about the
existence of a Carrière adaptation? The greatest im-
plausibility in Carrière's recollection of the book as
"too easy" means that he, arguably the most brilliant
screenwriter in Europe, completely missed the complexity of the text—a highly unlikely occurrence. As
Stephen Geller has proven on many an occasion,
filming an interior monologue is by no means impossible—quite literally *anything* can be adapted—but
on the other hand, the adaptation of a first person,
stream-of-consciousness narrative can hardly be
written off as facile, even by someone as gifted and
experienced as Carrière.

19. Hare, interview.

20. *Ibid.*

21. L. Malle, *Malle on Malle*, 201.

22. *Ibid.*

23. Billard, *Rebelle*, 509.

24. Hare, interview.

25. Billard, *Rebelle*, 509.

26. Hare, interview.

27. *Ibid.*

28. *Ibid.*

29. Billard, *Rebelle*, 510.

30. "Trivia for *Fatale* (1992)." *Internet Movie
Database* [online]. (cited 2004-10-15). Available from
internet: <http://www.imdb.com/title/tt0104237/
trivia>

31. Danielle Heymann, "Louis Malle Tackles Desire." Interview with Jeremy Irons. *World Press Review* 39 (September 1992): 53.

32. Hare, interview.

33. *Ibid.*

34. *Ibid.*

35. Leslie Caron, telephone interview by author,
7 May 2004.

36. Bernard Weinraub, "Louis Malle Cuts a Film
and Grows Indignant." *New York Times* (22 December 1992): C15.

37. *Ibid.*

38. Although the differences between the two versions of the film are almost unnoticeable, discussions
of *Damage* in this chapter pertain to the unrated "Director's Cut" that Nouvelles Editions released in Europe.

39. Unnamed in the film and in Josephine Hart's
book, Philip French reveals, in his synopsis, that the
location of the final scene is, in fact, "the medieval
town of Villefranche de Rouergue in south-west
France." He most likely pulled this information from
a source that details the shooting locations.

40. One can make an identical case for Adrian
Lyne's hugely underrated *Lolita* (1997), also starring
Jeremy Irons—a work mercilessly panned for its lack
of tonal faithfulness to Nabokovian satire, but that
nonetheless achieves brilliance when evaluated independently of the book.

41. Josephine Hart, *Damage* (New York: Knopf,
1991), 3–4.

42. *Ibid.*, 161.

43. *Ibid.*, 4.

44. *Ibid.*, 10.

45. *Ibid.*, 167.

46. *Ibid.*, 168.

47. David Denby, "One from the Heart." Review
of *Damage* (dir. Louis Malle). *New York* 25 (14 December 1992): 90.

48. Hart, *Damage*, 53.

49. *Ibid.*, 55.

50. Hare's primary objection to the flashback involves what he perceives as the need for suspense on
the plot level in the motion picture ("[One] structural
idea was just the tension of whether this man was
going to get away with it, and the planned explosion
when he doesn't.") But as Peter Burian suggests in his
wonderful essay on Greek tragic architecture, the creation of tragic structures and the evocation of suspense at the plot level (both of which Hare sought)
traditionally sit at odds to one another. Burian writes,
"The dramatist is, in effect, relieved of the require-
ment of providing suspense at this level of the plot,
but instead he must find ways to make fate work for
him as a tool for building dramatic tension." The
irony is that in Hare's case, *despite* the absence of a
flashback, the sense of fate still emerges strongly in
the picture, and this completely eliminates the sense
of suspense, rendering Hare's above "structural idea"
completely moot. One never experiences suspense in
Damage, on the plot level—only a sense of the fated,
of pure inevitability.

51. Hare, interview.

52. Little wonder, then, that the French title for
the picture is *Fatale*.

53. Hare, interview.

54. Such narrative tightness represents one of a
number of drastic improvements that Hare makes on
Hart's novel. The final act of the book, in particular,
is nothing short of exhausting—Hart spends dozens
of pages unnecessarily and anticlimactically detailing Stephen's attempts to end his day-to-day com-
mitments, whereas Malle and Hare cut their denouement to only the most necessary and pivotal scenes.

More generally (taking into consideration the spareness of the film's entire narrative) consider the opening scenes in Stephen's home and how stripped they are of clutter: Stephen learns of Anna (necessary), is told that Edward has predicted a major promotion for him (necessary, as it reveals Stephen's lack of control over his life), walks into the living room and feels visibly uncomfortable and oppressed (necessary), and visits a Christmas party where he meets Anna and they experience an instant, hypnotic connection (necessary). The dramatic architecture quite literally incorporates nothing gratuitous. It is as tight as a narrative could possibly be.

55. Denby, "One from the Heart," 90.
56. Peter Burian, "Myth into *mythos*: the shaping of tragic plot," in *The Cambridge Companion to Greek Tragedy* (Cambridge, England: Cambridge University Press, 1997), 178.
57. *Ibid.*
58. One could also make a fairly solid case for the argument that *Damage* corresponds to Burian's "return-recognition" tragic story pattern, but this really only applies to Hart's novel, wherein the affair with Anna brings the narrator in touch with who he is (the "geography of his soul").
59. *Ibid.*, 187.
60. Though presumably not at the cost of his daughter (Sally's) love—as one can infer from the thick stack of letters Stephen has amassed in his new home at the conclusion of the story.
61. Burian, "Myth into *mythos*," 181.
62. "One on One with Louis Malle," on *Damage* video, 15 min., New Line Home Video, 1993, videocassette.
63. Burian, "Myth into *mythos*," 186.
64. *Ibid.*, 182.
65. Hart, *Damage*, 168.
66. This is not entirely unique to the film. Though the cultural and sociological resonances in Josephine Hart's novel are not nearly as pronounced, the narrator does address, at length, the extent to which his own father dictated the course of his life and how, as a result, he was too deluded to be able to grasp his need to make his own choices, independently of a desire to please his father. The narrator states, "Even as I went my own way, I felt I served some purpose of his. So it is with powerful personalities. As we swim and dive away from them, we still feel the water is theirs." And later: "All had been my own choice. It was a blessed life. It was a good life. But whose life?"
67. Clive Irving, *True Brit* (London: Jonathan Cape, 1974), 36.
68. *Ibid.*, 37.
69. *Damage*, dir. Louis Malle, 112 min., New Line Home Video, 1993, videocassette.
70. Notice, as well, an interesting little metaphor in the picture: when Sally, Jonathan (Sally's boyfriend), Ingrid, and Stephen drive to Hartley for the weekend, Ingrid drives and Stephen sits in the passenger seat.
71. Irving, *True Brit*, 17.
72. Hart, *Damage*, 3.

73. "One on One with Louis Malle."
74. Simone De Beauvoir, *The Second Sex* (New York: Vintage, 1989), 371.
75. *Ibid.*, 400.
76. *Ibid.*, 371.
77. Calderon is his surname in Hart's novel; for some unknown reason, Malle and Hare changed it to Wetzlar for the screenplay.
78. Hart, *Damage*, 190.
79. *Damage*, dir. Louis Malle.
80. Philip French, introduction to *Malle on Malle*, rev. ed. (London: Faber & Faber, 1996), xvi.
81. Denby, "One from the Heart," 89–90.
82. Joanne Kaufman, review of *Damage* (dir. Louis Malle). *Time* 39 (18 January 1993): 15.
83. Daniel Toscan du Plantier, review of *Fatale* (dir. Louis Malle). *Le Figaro* (12 December 1992).
84. Danièle Heymann, review of *Damage* (dir. Louis Malle). *Le Monde* (9 December 1992).
85. Hare, interview.

Chapter 23

1. Pierre Billard, *Louis Malle: Le Rebelle solitaire* (Paris: Plon, 2003), 519.
2. John Guare, telephone interview by author, 7 April 2004.
3. Billard, *Louis Malle*, 502–3.
4. "André Gregory." *Internet Movie Database* [online]. (cited 2004-11-02). Available from internet: <http://www.imdb.com/name/nm0339737/>
5. André Gregory, telephone interview by author, 11 November 2004.
6. Billard, *Louis Malle*, 522–3.
7. Brooke Smith, telephone interview by author, 2 April 2004.
8. Billard, *Louis Malle*, 522–3.
9. Smith, interview.
10. Vanessa Friedman, "A Hard Act to Swallow: André Gregory and Louis Malle chew the fat about their new collaboration, *Vanya on 42nd Street*." *Vogue* 184 (November 1994): 182.
11. *Ibid.*
12. Fred Berner, interview by author, New York City, 7 March 2003.
13. *Ibid.*
14. *Ibid.*
15. Louis Malle, *Malle on Malle*, ed. Philip French, rev. ed. (London: Faber & Faber, 1996), 209.
16. Smith, interview.
17. George Gaynes, telephone interview by author, 15 February 2003.
18. L. Malle, *Malle on Malle*, 208.
19. Smith, interview.
20. Berner, interview.
21. Billard, *Louis Malle*, 561.
22. "Release dates for *Vanya on 42nd Street*." *Internet Movie Database* [online]. (cited 2004-11-02). Available from internet: <http://www.imdb.com/title/tt0111590/releaseinfo>.
23. Gaynes, interview.

24. Gregory, interview.

25. Strong emphasis here on *private* theater. As David Sturgess notes in his 1987 book on the subject, *Jacobean Private Theatre* (quoted and cited liberally in this chapter), and as will become clear to anyone who has read or skimmed Alexander Leggatt's sister volume, *Jacobean Public Theatre,* a world of difference existed between the private and public modes of the Jacobean stage.

26. Keith Sturgess, *Jacobean Private Theatre* (Routledge & Kegan Paul: London, 1987), 13, 17.

27. Though Gregory, Shawn and their contemporaries heightened the privacy of their endeavor and restricted attendance to those they knew, one could make a case for the argument that financial restrictions proved every bit as insurmountable to seventeenth century patrons as Gregory's acquaintances-only restrictions did to average New Yorkers in the early nineties. The completed film, of course, incorporates a beautiful paradox: it somehow carries into a public forum the sense of privacy that one would obtain from watching a "closed" performance of Gregory's *Vanya.*

28. Anton Chekhov. *Uncle Vanya,* adapt. David Mamet (New York: Grove, 1988), back cover.

29. Sturgess, *Jacobean Private Theatre,* 37–8.

30. *Ibid.,* 5.

31. *Ibid.,* 6.

32. By placing a modernist play in a reconstructed Jacobean (and thus, mannerist) setting, Gregory essentially — independently of Malle's film — poses the question of whether the two philosophical modes are not essentially one and the same at differing historical points.

33. Anton Chekhov, *Five Plays,* ed. Ronald Hingley (London: Oxford, 1998), xiv–xv.

34. Gaynes, interview.

35. From the recollections of the interviewees, Malle and Gregory at one point — "early, early on" in the process according to Brooke Smith — did give some serious consideration to the idea of staging *Uncle Vanya* on an estate with period costume.

36. Smith, interview.

37. Danny Peary, review of *Made for Each Other* (dir. Robert B. Bean), in *Guide for the Film Fanatic* (New York: Fireside Books, 1986), 257.

38. Smith, interview.

39. Berner, interview.

40. *Ibid.*

41. Todd McCarthy, review of *Vanya on 42nd Street* (dir. Louis Malle), *Variety* 356, 12–18 September 1994.

42. James Kaplan, review of *Vanya on 42nd Street* (dir. Louis Malle), *New York* 27, 12 September 1994, 62.

43. Philip Strick, review of *Vanya on 42nd Street* (dir. Louis Malle), *Sight and Sound* 64, January 1995, 61.

44. Claude Baignères, "Tchekhov parmi nous," review of *Vanya on 42nd Street* (dir. Louis Malle), *Le Figaro* (25 January 1995).

45. Michel Pascal, review of *Vanya on 42nd Street* (dir. Louis Malle), *le Point* 1166 (21 January 1995): 1.

Chapter 24

1. Because Malle's shorts drew almost no formal critical attention (aside from brief reactions to "William Wilson" in *Spirits of the Dead* reviews), the film analyses in this chapter will largely omit the discussions of critical summaries included for Malle's features.

2. The original French version of this film appeared in 1962, as listed; Malle prepared an English-language version (handling the voiceover himself) with the narration rewritten slightly for U.S. and British audiences, in 1976. The discussion of *Tour* in this chapter pertains to the English version — the only cut publicly available on videocassette.

3. Louis Malle, *Malle on Malle,* ed. Philip French, rev. ed. (London: Faber & Faber, 1996), 36–8.

4. Malle listed "cycling" as his primary hobby in *International Who's Who.*

5. L. Malle, *Malle on Malle,* 37–8.

6. Note that this very same intra-project transition from "dour and pensive" (*Vie privée*) to "joyous and exuberant" (*Vive le tour*) recurred one year later, when Malle developed the idea for *Viva Maria* as an escape from the melancholia of writing and directing *The Fire Within.*

7. Though a comparison to Gualtiero Jacopetti's reprehensible *Mondo Cane* (1963) would do grave injustices to *Vive le tour*, the films share a foundation of sensationalism, and *Tour* does attempt non-exploitatively to do for the most eccentric facets of a domestic French subculture what Jacopetti would purport to do one year later for exotic foreign cultures. But unlike Jacopetti, Malle does so honestly, without falsification or misrepresentation of evidence, and the most amusing irony is that he finds such eccentric and fascinating subject detail in his own backyard.

8. At least three intertextual cross-references for this shot, from Malle's oeuvre alone: the scooter shot of *Monde du silence* (see Chapter 2); the abrechtian "driving shot" at the outset of *Bons Baisers* (see the discussion of *Baisers*, later in this chapter); and the closing credits shot of *My Dinner with André* (see Chapter 17). One could make the same argument about the opening credit sequence shot from *Zazie* (of a train), were it not for the continual jump cuts.

9. Malle also suspends the illusion of "cinematographic omnipresence" in *Vanya on 42nd Street,* made 42 years hence, with a technique producer Fred Berner describes as the "fishbowl effect." See Chapter 23 for a more detailed explanation of how the director accomplishes this effect.

10. Most film guides and databases list *Bons Baisers de Bangkok* as a 15-minute documentary. Yet the 15-minute version referenced by these sources constitutes only half of a 31-minute program entitled *Cinq Colonnes à la une — De Thailande: Bons Baisers de Bangkok,* directed entirely by Malle and produced for the Office de Radiodiffusion Télévision Française (ORTF) television network. The program debuted in its entirety on French television on March 1, 1964.

In preparing this chapter, the research copy of *Bons Baisers* that we received includes all of the footage. Our discussion thus pertains to the full version. Yet because Malle filmographies typically include the truncated cut, the Malle Filmography at the end of this book (see Appendix A) references that version.

11. L. Malle, *Malle on Malle*, 50.

12. The accounts of how *Histoires extraordinaires* evolved vary slightly from text to text. In discussions with Philip French in *Malle on Malle*, Malle lists the replacement order cited above (stating that "Vadim was not someone I greatly admired," and "the third was meant to be directed by Orson Welles," which suggests that Malle himself replaced Buñuel and Fellini replaced Welles). Yet Mike Always's fascinating essay "Toby Dammit: Never Bet the Devil Your Head" states that the original lineup consisted of Welles, Buñuel, and Fellini — that the first change arrived when Vadim replaced Welles, and that Malle subsequently replaced Buñuel. According to Always, Fellini was a permanent fixture from the beginning.

13. L. Malle, *Malle on Malle*, 64–8.

14. A few sources mistakenly list Bardot in a "double role, as the prostitute and the cigar-smoking poker player Giuseppina." This is not accurate: though the prostitute bears a striking resemblance to Bardot, she is portrayed by 21-year-old Katia Christina (*Don Giovanni in Sicilia*).

15. Edgar Allan Poe, "William Wilson," in *Tales* (New York: Dodd, Mead & Company, 1952), 24.

16. Poe, "William Wilson," 1.

17. *Ibid.*, 2.

18. *Ibid.*, 3.

Select Bibliography

Transcriptions from Films and Reprints of Source Material (chronological)

de Vilmorin, Louise. "*Les Amants* (extracts)." *Cahiers du cinéma* no. 90, December 1958, 41–46.

Vivant-Denon, Dominique. *Point de Lendemain.* Reprinted in *Cinéma* 35, April 1959, 85–96.

Les Amants (text), in *L'Avant-scène Cinéma* no. 2, 15 March 1961, 184.

Le Feu follet (text), in *L'Avant-scène Cinéma* no. 30, 15 October 1963, 184.

Calcutta (commentary), in *Jeune Cinéma* 43, January 1970, 41–8.

Published Correspondence to and from Malle

Malle, Louis. Letter to Henry Chapier. *Combat*, 7 February 1966, 8.

_____. Letter to Alfred Fabre-Luce. *Le Monde*, 20 May 1971.

_____. Note to Jacques-Yves Cousteau. *Calypso Log* 17, no. 3 (June 1990): 3.

Articles—Interviews with Malle (chronological)

Malle, Louis. "Entretien: *Zazie dans le métro*." *L'Express* (27 October 1960): 38–9.

_____. Interview by André Fontaine. *Le Monde* (27 October 1960). (On *Zazie dans le métro*)

_____. "Zazie ... vous connaissez?" Interview by René Gilson. *Cinéma* 51 (December 1960): 5–11. (On *Zazie dans le métro*)

_____. "Talk with the Director." *Newsweek* 58 (27 November 1961): 88. (On *Zazie dans le métro*)

_____. Interview by Michèle Manceaux. *L'Express*, 25 July 1963. (On *Le Feu follet*)

_____. "Louis Malle (30 ans) et le suicidé." Interview by Robert Benayoun. *France-Observateur* (29 August 1963). (On *Le Feu follet*)

_____. "Louis Malle nous parle de son film *Vie privée*." Interview by Yvonne Baby. *Le Monde* (1 February 1962)

_____, and Jean-Claude Carrière. Interview by Pierre Billard. *Cinéma* 102 (January 1966): 52–62. (On *Viva Maria*)

Malle, Louis. "Louis le fataliste." Interview by Anne Capelle. *Arts* 74, 22 February 1967. (On *Le Voleur*)

_____. "Malle des Indes." Interview by Guy Braucourt. *Cinéma* 135 (April 1969): 27–31. (On *Calcutta*)

_____. Interview by Jean-Louis Comolli, Jean Narboni and Jacques Rivette. *Cahiers du cinéma* 211 (April 1969): 27–30, 32–4, 60–1. (On *Calcutta*)

_____, and Suzanne Baron. "Quand Louis Malle se remet en question." *Jeune Cinéma* 39 (May 1969): 18–22. (On *Calcutta*)

Malle, Louis. "Louis Malle, *Le Souffle au cœur*: l'inceste, le délire et l'humiliation." Interview with Gérard Langlois. *Les Lettres françaises* (28 April 1971).

_____. Interview by Guy Braucourt. *Cinéma* 171 (June 1971): 106–9. (On *Le Souffle au cœur*)

_____. Interview by Gilles Jacob. *Positif* 157 (March 1974): 28–35. (On *Lacombe, Lucien*)

_____. "*Lacombe, Lucien* et l'occupation." Interview by René Andrieu. *Humanité dimanche* (3 April 1974): 19–22.

_____, et al. "En direct avec Louis Malle, Joël Santoni, Agnès Contat, Claude Champion." Interview by Guy Braucourt. *Écran* 25 (May 1974): 22–4. (On *Humain, trop humain* and *Place de la République*)

Malle, Louis. "Louis Malle on *Lacombe, Lucien*." Interview by Jan Dawson. *Film Comment* (Sep.-Oct. 1974): 36–7.

_____. Interview by Thérèse Fournier. *France-Soir*, 22 September 1975. (On *Black Moon*)

_____. "Fires Within: The Chaste Sensibility of Director Louis Malle." Interview by Jonathan Cott. *Rolling Stone* no. 262 (6 April 1978): 39–41, 43–5. (On *Pretty Baby*)

_____. "Louis Malle: Images of Decay and Change." Interview by Jonathan Cott. *Rolling Stone* no. 342 (30 April 1981): 39–41, 43–5. (Overview of filmography through 1981)

_____. "Stranger in a Strange Land: A French Take on the American Dream." Interview by Jonathan Cott. *Vogue* 175, March 1985, 128, 132. (Overview of American films through *Alamo Bay*)

_____. "Souvenirs d'en France." Interview by Serge Toubiana. *Cahiers du cinéma* 400 (October 1987): 21–2. (On *Au revoir les enfants*)

_____. "La Blessure d'une amitié'" Interview by Danièle Heymann. *Le Monde* (4 October 1987). (On *Au revoir les enfants*)

Pascaud, Fabienne. "Qu'avez-vous fait de mon enfance?" *Télérama* (09 October 1987): 24–5. (On *Au revoir les enfants*)

Malle, Louis. "A chaque fois, recommencer à zéro!" Interview by François-Régis Barbry. *Cinéma* 411 (7–13 October 1987): 2 (On *Au revoir les enfants*)

_____. "Un Cinéma du regard." Interview by Ginette Delmas, Bernard Nave and Andrée Tournès. *Jeune Cinéma* 184 (December 1987): 4–15. (On filmography through 1987)

_____. "A Tale of Two Cultures." Interview by Maia Wechsler. *U.S. News and World Report* 104 (15 Feb 1988): 69. (On *Au revoir les enfants*)

_____. "Childhood's End." Interview by Elvis Mitchell. *Rolling Stone* no. 522 (24 March 1988): 48. (On *Au revoir les enfants*)

_____. "Dialogue on Film: Louis Malle." *American Film* 14 (April 1989): 22–4, 26, 28.

_____. "Louis Malle en mai." Interview by Jacques Julliard. *Le Nouvel Observateur*, 25 January 1990, 102–3. (On *Milou en mai*)

_____. "My Déjeuner with Louis." Interview by Kathy Bishop. *American Film* 15 (July 1990): 64. (On entire filmography)

_____. "Quiet Rebel." Interview by Paul Rambali. *Vogue* 180, July 1990, 232–5, 280.

_____. Interview by John Guare. *New Yorker* 70 (21 March 1994): 137. (On *Vanya on 42nd Street* and *Dietrich and Marlene*)

_____. "Les Trucs un peu dingues, c'est toujours moi qui les fais." Interview with Pierre Murat. *Télérama* (18 January 1995): 27.

Articles, Essays, and Published Letters by Malle

"Avec *Pickpocket*, Bresson a trouvé." *Arts*, 3 January 1960.

"Le Feu follet." *Cahiers du cinéma* 146, August 1963, 33.

"*Lacombe, Lucien*: un enfant perdu dans un monde chaotique." *France-soir*, 31 January 1974, 13.

"*Black Moon*: Guetter les signes." *Le Monde*, 27 September 1975, 1, 23.

"Human Landscapes: 25 Years of Photographs by Mary Ellen Mark." *Rolling Stone* no. 614, 3 October 1991, 49–53, 140.

Articles—Criticism, Production Detail of Films (by film title)

LE MONDE DU SILENCE (THE SILENT WORLD)

Bazin, André. Analysis of *Le Monde du silence*. In *Qu'est-ce que le cinéma?* Collection "Septième art" 29, 33: vol. 3, "Ontologie et Langage" (Paris: Editions du Cerf, 1958–62), 59–64.

Caussou, Jean-Louis. Review of *Le Monde du silence*. *Télé-Ciné* 58, Fiche filmographique no. 277, June 1956, 1–4.

Cousteau, Jacques-Yves. "'Studio' Under the Sea: Sub-Marine Scientist Scans Problems of Shooting in Lower Depths." *New York Times*, 16 September 1956, sec. 2, p. X7.

Crowther, Bosley. "The Real Things: Underwater Exploration in *The Silent World*." *New York Times*, 30 September 1956, late city edition, sec. 2, p.1.

_____. "Screen: Beautiful Sea." Review of *The Silent World*. *New York Times*, 25 September 1956, late city edition, p. 30.

de Baroncelli, Jean. Review of *Le Monde du silence*. *Le Monde*, 07 February 1956.

Dubreuilh, Simone. Review of *Le Monde du silence*. *Libération*, 20 February 1956.

Genêt, Jean. Review of *The Silent World*. *New Yorker* 32, 31 March 1956, 84, 86.

Knight, Arthur. Review of *The Silent World*. *Saturday Review* 39, 20 October 1956, 59.

Malle, Louis. "Filming the Silent World." *Calypso Log* 19, no. 2 (April 1992): 11.

Mauriac, Claude. Review of *Le Monde du silence*. *Le Figaro*, 18 February 1956.

McCarten, John. "Down in the Depths." Review of *The Silent World*. *New Yorker* 32, 13 October 1956, 181.

Moskowitz, Gene. Review of *The Silent World*. *Variety* 203, 6 June 1956, 6.

Ranchal, Marcel. "Rien que l'aventure." Review of *The Silent World*. *Positif* 18, November 1956, 35–7.

Review of *The Silent World*. *Monthly Film Bulletin* 24, 1957, 12.

Review of *The Silent World*. *Newsweek* 48, 24 September 1956, 114, 116.

Review of *The Silent World*. *Time* 68, 1 October 1956, 90.

Rochereau, Jean. Review of *Le Monde du silence*. *La Croix*, 24 February 1956.

"*Silent World* Uses New Underwater Techniques." *Popular Photography* 40, January 1957, 116.

Thévenot, Jean. "Le Film de Cousteau poisson-pilote du cinéma français." *Les Lettres françaises*, 23 February 1956.

"World Under Water." *Newsweek* 47, 13 February 1956, 96–8.

Ascenseur pour l'échafaud
(Elevator to the Gallows)

Arnault, Hubert. Review of *Ascenseur pour l'échafaud*. *Image et Son* 244, fiche filmographique, hors série, 1970, 7–12.

Chauvet, Louis. Review of *Ascenseur pour l'échafaud*. *Le Figaro*, 31 January 1958.

Chevallier, Jacques. Review of *Ascenseur pour l'échafaud*. *Image et Son*, March 1958, 15.

de Baroncelli, Jean. Review of *Ascenseur pour l'échafaud*. *Le Monde*, 1 January 1958.

Doniol-Valcroze, Jacques. Review of *Ascenseur pour l'échafaud*. *France-Observateur*, 5 February 1958.

Dubreuilh, Simone. Review of *Ascenseur pour l'échafaud*. *Libération*, 3 February 1958.

Guimard, Paul. Review of *Ascenseur pour l'échafaud*. *Arts*, 15 January 1958.

Herman, Jean. Review of *Ascenseur pour l'échafaud*. *Cinéma* 25, February 1958, 114–15.

Houston, Penelope. Review of *Ascenseur pour l'échafaud*. *Monthly Film Bulletin* 27, 1960, 62.

Kael, Pauline. Review of *Elevator to the Gallows*. In *5,001 Nights at the Movies* (New York: Owl Books, 1991), 215.

Monjo, Armand. Review of *Ascenseur pour l'échafaud*. *Les Lettres françaises*, 22 December 1957.

Moskowitz, Gene. Review of *Ascenseur pour l'échafaud*. *Variety* 211, 7 May 1958, 22.

Rohmer, Éric. Review of *Ascenseur pour l'échafaud*. *Cahiers du cinéma* 80, February 1958, 59–60.

Sadoul, Georges. "Quel feuillage séché dans les cités sans soirs..." Review of *Ascenseur pour l'échafaud*. *Les Lettres françaises*, 30 January 1958.

Salachas, Gilbert, et al. Review of *Ascenseur pour l'échafaud*. *Télé Ciné*, 1958.

Sonnenberg, Ben. Review of *Elevator to the Gallows*. *Nation* 255, 13 July 1992, 67.

Vivet, Jean-Pierre. "Ascenseur pour le succès." Review of *Ascenseur pour l'échafaud*. *L'Express*, 30 January 1958.

Les Amants
(The Lovers)

Arnault, Hubert. Fiche filmographique of *Les Amants*. *Image et Son* 244, 1970, 1–6.

Clavel, Maurice. "Paradoxe sur deux scandales." *Combat*, 13 November 1958, 2.

de Baroncelli, Jean. Review of *Les Amants*. *Le Monde*, 1 January 1958.

Doniol-Valcroze, Jacques. "Le Pouvoir de la nuit." Review of *Les Amants*. *Cahiers du cinéma* 89, November 1958, 43–46.

Flacon, Michel. Review of *Les Amants*. *Cinéma* 32, December 1958, 104–108.

"Funny and unfettered." Review of *Les Amants*. *Newsweek* 58, 27 November 1961, 88.

Genêt, Jean. Review of *Les Amants*. *New Yorker* 34, 24 January 1959, 94–5.

Jeander. Review of *Les Amants*. *Libération*, 10 November 1958.

Kauffmann, Stanley. "New directors, old directions." Review of *Les Amants*. *New Republic* 141, 7 December 1959, 21.

Lefèvre, Raymond. Review of *Les Amants*. *Image et Son* 116, November 1958, 15.

Magnan, Henri. "Ces Amants que nous voudrions être." Review of *Les Amants*. *Combat*, 10 November 1958.

Moravia, Alberto. "Mais l'amour reste dehors." Review of *Les Amants*. *Espresso*, 19 April 1959.

Moskowitz, Gene. Review of *Les Amants*. *Variety* 212, 17 September 1958, 7.

Rhode, Eric H. Review of *Les Amants*. *Monthly Film Bulletin* 26, 1959, 154.

Rohmer, Éric. "*Les Amants*: Finesse et rigueur." *Arts* 696, 12 November 1958, 7.

Roud, Richard. "The Festivals: London." Review of *Les Amants*. *Sight and Sound* 28, 1959, 21–22.

Sadoul, Georges. "Enfin, un film d'amour." Review of *Les Amants*. *Les Lettres françaises*, 14 November 1958.

Siclier, Jacques. "Verroterie de clair de lune." Review of *Les Amants*. *Radio cinéma télévision*, 19 November 1958.

Truffaut, François. "Louis Malle a filmé la première nuit d'amour au cinéma." Review of *Les Amants*. *Arts* 687, 9 September 1958, 1.

Vincent, Denis. Review of *Les Amants*. *L'Express*, 06 November 1958.

ZAZIE DANS LE MÉTRO
(ZAZIE IN THE MÉTRO)

Aubriant, Michel. Review of *Zazie dans le métro*. *Paris-Presse*, 1 November 1960.

Capdenac, Michel. "Zazie ou la comédie infernale." Review of *Zazie dans le métro*. *Les Lettres françaises*, 13 November 1960.

Dor, Étienne. Review of *Zazie dans le métro*. *Télé Ciné* 93, Fiche filmographique no. 374, January 1961, 1–16.

d'Yvoire, Jean, and C.M. Trémois. Review of *Zazie dans le métro*. *Télérama*, 13 November 1960.

"L'Enfant le plus terrible." *Time* 76, 21 November 1960, 61.

"Funny and Unfettered." Review of *Zazie dans le métro*. *Newsweek* 58, 27 November 1961, 88.

Gill, Brendan. "High spirits and low." Review of *Zazie dans le métro*. *New Yorker* 37, 25 November 1961, 204–5.

Guyo, Pierre-Jean. Review of *Zazie dans le métro*. *La Croix*, 05 November 1960.

Kael, Pauline. Review of *Zazie dans le métro*. In *5,001 Nights at the Movies* (New York: Owl Books, 1991), 864.

Kauffmann, Stanley. "French novels into French Pastries." Review of *Zazie dans le métro*. *New Republic* 145, 18 December 1961, 28–9.

Labarthe, André S. "Au pied de la lettre." *Cahiers du cinéma* 114, December 1960, 58–60.

Macdonald, Dwight. Review of *Zazie dans le métro*. *Esquire* 57, February 1962, 24, 28.

Martin, Marcel. Review of *Zazie dans le métro*. *Cinéma* 52, December 1961, 117–18.

Milne, Tom. Review of *Zazie dans le métro*. *Monthly Film Bulletin* 30, 1963, 20.

Moskowitz, Gene. Review of *Zazie dans le métro*. *Variety* 220, 23 November 1960, 20.

Nowell-Smith, Geoffrey. Review of *Zazie dans le métro*. *Sight and Sound* 32, 1963, 37.

Palinure. Review of *Zazie dans le métro*. *Radio cinéma télévision*, 16 April 1960.

Pilard, Philippe. Fiche filmographique of *Zazie dans le métro*. *Image et Son* 274, 1973, 161–7.

Queneau, Raymond. "Du livre au film." Review of *Zazie dans le métro*. *L'Express*, 27 October 1960, 38.

Sadoul, Georges. "À Zazie." Review of *Zazie dans le métro*. *Les Lettres françaises*, 13 November 1960.

VIE PRIVÉE
(A VERY PRIVATE AFFAIR)

Billard, Pierre, and Marcel Martin. Review of *Vie privée*. *Cinéma* 64, March 1962, 105–09.

Bory, Jean-Louis. Review of *Vie privée*. *Arts*, 08 February 1962.

Champenier, Serge. Review of *Vie privée*. *Revue du Cinéma* 274, 1973, 147–59.

Colet, Jean. Review of *Vie privée*. *Télérama*, 18 February 1962.

de Baroncelli, Jean. Review of *Vie privée*. *Le Monde*, 03 February 1962.

Delahaye, Michel. "Interconnections." Review of *Vie privée*. *Cahiers du cinéma* 129, March 1962, 62–3.

Dort, Bernard. Review of *Vie privée*. *France-Observateur*, 08 February 1962.

Genêt, Jean. Review of *A Very Private Affair*. *New Yorker* 38, 3 March 1962, 127–8.

Gill, Brendan. "Under Fire." Review of *A Very Private Affair*. *New Yorker* 38, 13 October 1962, 191.

Guyonnet, René. Review of *Vie privée*. *L'Express*, 1st February 1962.

Jeander. Review of *Vie privée*. *Libération*, 03 February 1962.

Kael, Pauline. Review of *Vie privée*. In *5,001 Nights at the Movies* (New York: Owl Books, 1991), 813.

Martin, Marcel. Review of *Vie privée*. *Cinéma* 64, March 1962, 105–7.

Miller, Claude. Review of *Vie privée*. *Télé-Ciné* 104, Fiche filmographique no. 402, May 1962, 1–12.

Milne, Tom. Review of *Vie privée*. *Monthly Film Bulletin* 29, 1962, 152.

Rochereau, Jean. Review of *Vie privée*. *La Croix*, 21 February 1962.

"Sad Affair." Review of *Vie privée*. *Newsweek* 60, 1 October 1962, 61.

"Sex Tabby." Review of *A Very Private Affair*. *Time* 80, 26 October 1962, 99.

LE FEU FOLLET
(THE FIRE WITHIN)

Arnault, Hubert. Review of *Le feu Follet*. *Image et Son* 167/168, November 1963, 103–5.

Benayoun, Robert. "*Le Feu follet*, c'est a dire l'echappatoire." Review of *Le Feu follet*. *Positif* 56, November 1963, 5–7.

Bory, Jean-Louis. Review of *Le Feu follet*. *Arts*, 23 October 1963.

Collet, Jean. Review of *Le Feu follet*. *Télérama*, 27 October 1963.

Comolli, Jean-Louis. Review of *Le Feu follet*. *Cahiers du cinéma* 148, October 1963, 29–30.

Cournot, Michel. "Bravo Malle." Review of *Le Feu follet*. *L'Express*, 05 September 1963.

de Baroncelli, Jean. Review of *Le Feu follet*. *Le Monde*, 19 October 1963.

Dyer, Peter John. Review of *The Fire Within*. *Monthly Film Bulletin* 31, 1964, 114–15.

Genêt, Jean. Review of *The Fire Within*. *New Yorker* 39, 16 November 1963, 148–50.

Gill, Brendan. "A+." Review of *The Fire Within*. *New Yorker* 40, 22 February 1964, 112, 114.

Hatch, Robert. Review of *The Fire Within*. *Nation* 198, 9 March 1964, 252.

Kauffmann, Stanley. "Seven Days, Fulsome Praise." Review of *The Fire Within*. *New Republic* 150, 7 March 1964, 35.

"Lemorningafter." Review of *The Fire Within*. *Time* 83, 6 March 1964, 84.

Loubière, Pierre, et al. Fiche filmographique of *Le Feu follet*. *Télé-Ciné* 113/114, December 1963–January 1964.

Moskowitz, Gene. Review of *The Fire Within*. *Variety* 232, 11 September 1963, 22, 26.

"On the mirror — July 23." Review of *The Fire Within*. *Newsweek* 63, 2 March 1964, 83–4.

Sadoul, Georges. "Le Cœur d'y mourir." Review of *Le Feu follet*. *Les Lettres françaises*, 17 October 1963.

VIVA MARIA

Benayoun, Robert. "Vive la différence!" Review of *Viva Maria*. *Positif* 74, March 1966, 95–100.

Billard, Pierre. "Avé Maria y Maria" Review of *Viva Maria*. *L'Express*, 13 December 1965.

Blum, Ralph. "He Let the Film Get Away." Review of *Viva Maria*. *Vogue* 147, 1 February 1966, 100–1.

Bory, Jean-Louis, and Roger Boussinot. "Viva Maria: Le Bric à brac d'un enfant gâté." Review of *Viva Maria*. *Arts*, 08 December 1965.

Carrière, Jean-Claude. "La Véritable Histoire de Viva Maria." Review of *Viva Maria*. *L'Express*, 17 May 1965.

"Carnival in Brio." Review of *Viva Maria*. *Time* 86, 31 December 1965, 77.

Chevassu, François. Review of *Viva Maria*. *Image et Son* 192, March 1966, 114.

Collet, Jean. Review of *Viva Maria*. *Télérama*, 26 December 1965.

Comolli, Jean-Louis. "Tous dans le même cul-de-sac." Review of *Viva Maria*. *Cahiers du cinéma* 177, April 1966, 75.

Delmas, Jean. "*Viva Maria*, film liberateur." Review of *Viva Maria*. *Jeune Cinéma* 11, January 1966, 17–18.

Fovez, Jean E. Review of *Viva Maria*. *Télé-Ciné* 126, December 1965, 36.

Gill, Brendan. "Sharpshooters." Review of *Viva Maria*. *New Yorker* 41, 25 December 1965, 56, 58.

Hatch, Robert. "The 10th Victim: *Viva Maria*." Review of *Viva Maria*. *Nation* 202, 3 January 1966, 27–8.

Houston, Penelope. Review of *Viva Maria*. *Sight and Sound* 35, 1966, 90–91.

Kael, Pauline. Review of *Viva Maria*. In *5,001 Nights at the Movies* (New York: Owl Books, 1991), 818.

"Malle-adroit." Review of *Viva Maria*. *Newsweek* 67, 3 January 1966, 56.

Martin, Marcel. "Zazie au Mexique." Review of *Viva Maria*. *Cinéma* 102, January 1966, 112–15.

Milne, Tom. Review of *Viva Maria*. *Monthly Film Bulletin* 33, 1966, 39–40.

Moskowitz, Gene. Review of *Viva Maria*. *Variety* 241, 8 December 1965, 6.

Rochereau, Jean. "Viva Maria I Maria II." Review of *Viva Maria*. *La Croix*, 20 December 1965.

Sadoul, Georges. "Que viva Bardot" Review of *Viva Maria*. *Les Lettres françaises*, 09 December 1965.

Schickel, Richard. "Two Sexpots in a Fine, Old-Fashioned Fantasy." Review of *Viva Maria*. *Life* 60, 28 January 1966, 8.

Le Voleur (The Thief of Paris)

Arbois, Janick. "Il ne faut pas cracher dans la soupe." Review of *Le Voleur*. *Télérama*, 05 March 1967.

Benayoun, Robert. "La Belle France et l'en dehors." Review of *Le Voleur*. *Positif* 84, May 1967, 33–40.

Billard, Pierre. "Louis Malle enterre la bourgeoisie." Review of *Le Voleur*. *L'Express*, 20 February 1967.

Chapier, Henry. Review of *Le Voleur*. *Combat*, 02 February 1967.

Chauvet, Louis. Review of *Le Voleur*. *Le Figaro*, 24 February 1967.

Crist, Judith. "Needless Smuggery." Review of *The Thief of Paris*. *Vogue* 150, 1 September 1967, 226.

de Baroncelli, Jean. Review of *Le Voleur*. *Le Monde*, 24 February 1967.

Gardies, René. Review of *Le Voleur*. *Image et Son* 204, April 1967, 114–15.

Gilliatt, Penelope. "Moonlight." Review of *The Thief of Paris*. *New Yorker* 43, 2 September 1967, 74–6.

Jacob, Gilles. "Louis Malle: au pied du mur." Review of *Le Voleur*. *Cinéma* 115, April 1967, 52–62.

Kael, Pauline. Review of *The Thief of Paris*. In *5,001 Nights at the Movies* (New York: Owl Books, 1991), 756–7.

Le Goff, Jean Paul. Review of *Le Voleur*. *Télé-Ciné* 134, Fiche filmographique no. 471, August 1967, 1–11.

Michaud-Mailland, Jean. "En regardant Louis Malle travailler." Review of *Le Voleur*. *Les Lettres françaises*, 20 October 1966.

Moskowitz, Gene. Review of *The Thief of Paris*. *Variety* 246, 15 March 1967, 26.

Rabine, Henry. Review of *Le Voleur*. *La Croix*, 06 March 1967.

Reif, Tony. Review of *The Thief of Paris*. *Film Quarterly* 23, Fall 1969, 47–8.

"Robber Barren." Review of *The Thief of Paris*. *Time* 90, 1 September 1967, 65.

Roulet, Sébastien. Review of *Le Voleur*. *Cahiers du cinéma* 188, March 1967, 71.

Salachas, Gilbert. Review of *Le Voleur*. *Télé-Ciné* 133, February 1967, 59.

Schickel, Richard. "Belmondo on Crime and Sensibility." Review of *The Thief of Paris*. *Life* 63, 22 September 1967, 19.

Zimmerman, Paul D. "No Exit." Review of *The Thief of Paris*. *Newsweek* 70, 28 August 1967, 83.

Histoires Extraordinaires (Spirits of the Dead)

Aumont, Jacques. "Tobie et le diable." Review of *Histoires Extraordinaires*. *Cahiers du cinéma* 203, August 1968, 62–3.

Gili, Jean A. "Disparate Amalgame." Review of *Histoires Extraordinaires*. *Cinéma* 129, October 1968, 127, 130–1.

Gilliatt, Penelope. "Getting Warm." Review of *Spirits of the Dead*. *New Yorker* 45, 13 September 1969, 144–5.

Gross, Robert A. "The Telltale Heart." Review of *Spirits of the Dead*. *Newsweek* 74, 15 September 1969, 102.

Kauffmann, Stanley. Review of *Spirits of the Dead*. *New Republic* 161, 27 September 1969, 22.

Moskowitz, Gene. Review of *Histoires Extraordinaires*. *Variety* 251, 5 June 1968, 6, 18.

Rayns, Tony. Review of *Spirits of the Dead*. *Monthly Film Bulletin* 40, 1973, 76.

Schickel, Richard. "A Sandwich of Baloney and Fellini." Review of *Spirits of the Dead*. *Life* 67, 5 September 1969, 12.

Sineux, Michel. "Une Oasis de fatalité dans un Sahara d'erreurs." Review of *Histoires Extraordinaires*. *Positif* 98, October 1968, 58–60.

"Two Dead Spirits Out of Three." Review of *Spirits of the Dead*. *Time* 94, 12 September 1969, 96.

Calcutta and *L'Inde fantôme: Reflexions sur un voyage* (Phantom India)

Arbois, Janick. Review of *Calcutta*. *Télérama*, 06 August 1975.

Bory, Jean-Louis. Review of *Calcutta*. *Le Nouvel Observateur*, 21 April 1969.

Chapier, Henry. "Une Réalité hallucinante." Review of *Calcutta*. *Combat*, 15 April 1969.

Chauvet, Louis. Review of *Calcutta*. *Le Figaro*, 22 April 1969.

Dawson, Jan. Review of *Phantom India*. *Monthly Film Bulletin* 42, 1975, 13–14.

de Baroncelli, Jean. Review of *Calcutta*. *Le Monde*, 17 April 1969.

Gauthier, Guy. Review of *Calcutta*. *Image et Son* 229, June-July 1969, 97–9.

Gilliatt, Penelope. "Self-Colloquy about a Subcontinent." Review of *Phantom India*. *New Yorker* 48, 8 July 1972, 55–7.

Gitlin, Todd. Review of *Phantom India*. *Film Quarterly* 27, summer 1974, 57–61.

Haustrate, Gaston. "La Vie, une illusion." Review of *Calcutta*. *Cinéma* 137, June 1969, 132–4.

Kael, Pauline. Review of *Calcutta*. In *5,001 Nights at the Movies* (New York: Owl Books, 1991), 115.

Michener, Charles. "Louis in Wonderland." Review of *Phantom India*. *Newsweek* 79, 12 June 1972, 97–8.

Moskowitz, Gene. Review of *Calcutta*. *Variety* 254, May 1969, 35.

Oudart, Jean-Pierre. "Les Trajets et les lieux." Review of *Calcutta*. *Cahiers du cinéma* 213, June 1969.

"Le Point de vue de Suzanne Baron, monteuse." *Jeune Cinema* 39, May 1969, 21–2.

"Quand Louis Malle se remet en question." *Jeune Cinéma* 39, May 1969, 18–21.

Rolland, Béatrice. Review of *Calcutta*. *Positif* 113, February 1970, 81–5.

Tessier, Max. Review of *L'Inde fantôme*. *Écran* 39, 15 September 1975, 67–9.

LE SOUFFLE AU CŒUR (MURMUR OF THE HEART)

Astruc, Alexandre. "Un Film osé qui se termine par un grand et sain éclat de rire." *Paris Match*, 24 April 1971.

Birstein, Ann. Review of *Murmur of the Heart*. *Vogue* 158, 1 November 1971, 170.

Braucourt, Guy. "Tout cela, mon pere, n'est que moitie votre faute." *Cinéma* 157, June 1971, 106–11.

Capdenac, Michel. "L'État de grâce." Review of *Le Souffle au cœur*. *Les Lettres françaises*, 05 May 1971.

Chapier, Henry. Review of *Le Souffle au cœur*. *Combat*, 29 April 1971.

Chauvet, Louis. Review of *Le Souffle au cœur*. *Le Figaro*, 29 April 1971.

de Baroncelli, Jean. Review of *Le Souffle au cœur*. *Le Monde*, 29 April 1971.

Chutkow, Paul. "Louis Malle Diagnoses His 'Murmur of the Heart.'" *New York Times*, 19 March 1989, 15, 20.

Cocks, Jay. "I Remember Mamma." *Time*, 25 October 1971, 89–90.

Delmas, Jean. Review of *Le Souffle au cœur*. *Jeune Cinema* 55, May 1971, 40–1.

Fabre-Luce, Alfred. "Morale et cinéma." *Le Monde*, 13 May 1971, 19.

Hatch, Robert. Review of *Le Souffle aů cœur*. *Nation* 213, 1 November 1971, 446.

Kael, Pauline. "Louis Malle's Portrait of the Artist as a Young Dog." Review of *Le Souffle au cœur*. *New Yorker* 47, 23 October 1971, 139–43.

Kauffman, Stanley. Review of *Le Souffle au cœur*. *New Republic* 165, 13 November 1971, 24, 32.

Legrand, Gérard. Review of *Le Souffle au cœur*. *Positif* 131, October 1971, 71–2.

Moskowitz, Gene. Review of *Le Souffle au cœur*. *Variety* 262, 14 April 1971, 16.

Nourrissier, François. "Louis Malle: un talent d'enfer." Review of *Le Souffle au cœur*. *L'Express*, 26 April 1970.

Oudart, Jean-Pierre. Review of *Le Souffle au cœur*. *Cahiers du cinéma* 230, July 1971, 58–9.

Rochereau, Jean. Review of *Le Souffle au cœur*. *La Croix*, 05 May 1971.

Schickel, Richard. "Deft Handling of an Old Taboo." Review of *Souffle au cœur*. *Life* 71, 12 November 1971, 16.

Strick, Philip. Review of *Le Souffle au cœur*. *Monthly Film Bulletin* 38, 1971, 203–4.

Tallenay, Jean-Louis. "L'Inceste est-il le secret du bonheur?" Review of *Le Souffle au cœur*. *Télérama*, 16 May 1971.

HUMAIN, TROP HUMAIN AND *PLACE DE LA RÉPUBLIQUE*

Chazal, Robert. "Deux Témoignages de Louis Malle." Review of *Humain, trop humain* and *Place de la République*. *France-Soir*, 13 April 1974.

Delmas, Jean. Review of *Humain, trop humain*. *Jeune Cinéma* 78, May 1974, 4–5.

Gauthier, Guy. Review of *Humain, trop humain* and *Place de la République*. *La Revue du cinéma, Image et Son* 285, June/July 1974, 98–9.

Giraud, Thérèse. "*Attica / Humain, trop humain*: Deux Conceptions du cinéma direct." *Cahiers du cinéma* 250, May 1974, 47–51.

Kael, Pauline. Review of *Humain, trop humain*. In *5,001 Nights at the Movies* (New York: Owl Books, 1991), 344.

Remond, Alain. "Vivre, pour quoi faire?" Review of *Humain, trop humain* and *Place de la République*. *Télérama* 1264, 06 April 1974.

Renaud, Tristan. Review of *Humain, trop humain* and *Place de la République*. *Cinéma* 187, May 1974, 122–4.

Toubiana, Serge. "Donner la parole au peuple pour mieux lui clouer le bec." Review of *Humain, trop humain* and *Place de la République*. *Libération*, 09 April 1974.

LACOMBE, LUCIEN

Bonitzer, Pascal. "Histoire de sparadrap." Review of *Lacombe, Lucien. Cahiers du cinéma* 250, May 1974, 42–7.

Bory, Jean-Louis. "Servitudes et misères d'un salaud." Review of *Lacombe, Lucien. Le Nouvel Observateur,* 28 January 1974, 56–7.

Chapier, Henry. "L'Histoire au bistouri." Review of *Lacombe, Lucien. Combat,* 20 January 1974.

Chevassu, François. Review of *Lacombe, Lucien. Revue du Cinéma* 282, March 1974, 110–14.

Cluny, Claude-Michel. Review of *Lacombe, Lucien. Cinéma* 184, February 1974, 94–5.

Clurman, Harold. Review of *Lacombe, Lucien. Nation* 219, 19 October 1974, 379.

Cocks, Jay. "Corruption's Toys." Review of *Lacombe, Lucien. Time* 104, 14 October 1974, 4, 8.

Cooper, Arthur. "Lovers, Traitors, Con Men." Review of *Lacombe, Lucien. Newsweek* 84, 14 October 1974, 131.

Dawson, Jan. Review of *Lacombe, Lucien. Monthly Film Bulletin* 41, 1974, 149–50.

de Baroncelli, Jean. "Lacombe Lucien, un adolescent dans la Gestapo." Review of *Lacombe, Lucien. Le Monde,* 31 January 1974.

Delain, Michel. "Le Dernier Zigzag." Review of *Lacombe, Lucien. L'Express,* 14 January 1974.

Delmas, Jean. Review of *Lacombe, Lucien. Jeune Cinéma* 77, March 1974, 33–5.

Drexler, Rosalyn. Review of *Lacombe, Lucien. Vogue* 164, November 1974, 110.

Flacon, Michel. "Sans chagrin ni pitié." Review of *Lacombe, Lucien. Le Point,* 28 January 1974, 62–3.

Fournier, Thérèse. "'C'est beau,' ont dit les lecteurs de *France-soir* premiers spectateurs de *Lacombe, Lucien.*" *France-soir,* 31 January 1974, 13.

Kael, Pauline. Review of *Lacombe, Lucien. New Yorker* 50, 30 September 1974, 94–100.

Kauffmann, Stanley. Review of *Lacombe, Lucien. New Republic* 171, 5 October 1974, 18, 33.

Martin, Marcel. Review of *Lacombe, Lucien. Écran* 23, March 1974, 50–1.

Meillant, Jacques. "Un Gamin à la Gestapo" Review of *Lacombe, Lucien. Télérama,* 02 February 1974, 66.

Milne, Tom. Review of *Lacombe, Lucien. Sight and Sound* 43, 1974, 176.

Moskowitz, Gene. Review of *Lacombe, Lucien. Variety* 273, 30 January 1974, 14.

Sarris, Andrew. "The Nasty Nazis: History or Mythology?" Review of *Lacombe, Lucien. Village Voice* 19, 17 October 1974, 77–8.

Simon, John. Review of *Lacombe, Lucien. Esquire* 82, December 1974, 23, 26, 32, 35–6.

Sineux, Michel. "Le Hasard, le chagrin, la nécessité, la pitié." Review of *Lacombe, Lucien. Positif* 157, March 1974, 25–7.

BLACK MOON

Brunn, Julien; Rochu, Gilbert. Review of *Black Moon. Libération,* 29 September 1975.

Chapier, Henry. "Le Changement de cap..." Review of *Black Moon. Le Quotidien de Paris,* 26 September 1975.

Chazal, Robert. "L'Ultime Refuge." Review of *Black Moon. France-Soir,* 25 September 1975.

Colpart, Gilles. Review of *Black Moon. La Revue du cinéma* 300, November 1975, 86–7.

Crist, Judith. "Confession of Sins Past." Review of *Black Moon. Saturday Review* 3, 29 November 1975, 37–8.

de Baroncelli, Jean. "Un Film rêve." Review of *Black Moon. Le Monde,* 27 September 1975, 1, 23.

Delmas, Jean. Review of *Black Moon. Jeune Cinéma* 90, November 1975, 25–9.

Flacon, Michel. " Louis Malle prend ses distances." Review of *Black Moon. Le Point,* 22 September 1975.

Garson, Claude. Review of *Black Moon. L'Aurore,* 29 September 1975.

Ionesco, Eugène. "Le Mariage de la douleur et de la beauté." Review of *Black Moon. Le Figaro,* 30 September 1975.

Kael, Pauline. "Becoming an American." Review of *Black Moon. New Yorker* 51, 24 November 1975, 168, 171.

Mohrt, Michel. "De l'autre côté du miroir." Review of *Black Moon. Le Figaro,* 25 September 1975.

Moskowitz, Gene. Review of *Black Moon. Variety* 280, 24 September 1975, 22.

Roy, Jean. Review of *Black Moon. Cinéma* 202, September-October 1975, 293.

PRETTY BABY (LA PETITE)

Béhar, Henri. Review of *La Petite. Revue du Cinéma* 329, June 1978, 121.

Billard, Pierre. Review of *La Petite. Le Point,* 22 May 1978.

Bonitzer, Pascal. Review of *La Petite. Cahiers du cinéma* 290–291, July/August 1978, 41.

Bory, Jean-Louis. "Alice au pays des plaisirs."

Review of *La Petite*. *Le Nouvel Observateur*, 22 May 1978.

Cebe, Gilles. Review of *La Petite*. *Écran* 71, 15 July 1978, 61–2.

Corliss, Richard. "The Stranger Equations of Love and Art." Review of *Pretty Baby*. *New Times* 10, 1 May 1978, 70–1.

de Baroncelli, Jean. "Les Fleurs et le fumier." Review of *La Petite*. *Le Monde*, 24 May 1975.

Delmas, Jean. Review of *La Petite*. *Jeune Cinéma* 55, May 1971, 34–6.

Douin, Jean-Luc. "Une Partie de colin paillard." Review of *La Petite*. *Télérama*, 24 May 1978, 60.

French, Philip. Review of *Pretty Baby*. *Observer*, 28 September 1979.

Garsault, Alain. Review of *La Petite*. *Positif* 208, July/August 1978, 115–16.

Gili, Jean A. Review of *La Petite*. *Écran* 71, 15 July 1978, 61–2.

Gilliatt, Penelope. "His Finest Yet." Review of *Pretty Baby*. *New Yorker* 54, 10 April 1978, 126–7.

Haskell, Molly. "When a House Is a Home." Review of *Pretty Baby*. *New York* 11, 17 April 1978, 97–8.

Hatch, Robert. Review of *Pretty Baby*. *Nation* 226, 22 April 1978, 484–5.

Kauffmann, Stanley. "Pretty Awful." Review of *Pretty Baby*. *New Republic* 178, 15 April 1978, 18–19.

Kroll, Jack. "Alice in Brothel Land." Review of *Pretty Baby*. *Newsweek* 91, 10 April 1978, 106–7.

Magny, Joël. Review of *La Petite*. *Cinéma* 235, July 1978, 112–14.

Milne, Tom. Review of *Pretty Baby*. *Sight and Sound* 48, 1979, 261.

Murphy, A.D. Review of *Pretty Baby*. *Variety* 290, 5 April 1978, 23.

Orth, Maureen. "The Americanization of Louis Malle." *New West* 3, 24 April 1978, 59–62.

Pym, John. Review of *Pretty Baby*. *Monthly Film Bulletin* 46, 1979, 231–2.

Rich, Frank. "A Child's Garden of Sin." Review of *Pretty Baby*. *Time* 111, 10 April 1978, 70.

Rochu, Gilbert. "Un Ange dans l'alcôve." Review of *La Petite*. *Libération*, 17 May 1978.

Schlesinger, Arthur, Jr. "A Waif in Storyville: Sweet Bordello Baby." Review of *Pretty Baby*. *Saturday Review* 5, 27 May 1978, 40–1.

Simon, John. "A Stroll on the Wild Side." Review of *Pretty Baby*. *Maclean's* 91, 15 May 1978, 84, 86.

ATLANTIC CITY

Ansen, David. "Boardwalk of Dreams." Review of *Atlantic City*. *Newsweek* 97, 6 April 1981, 103.

Baudin, Brigitte. "Louis Malle: anaylse spectrale d'une capitale de hasard." Review of *Atlantic City*. *Le Figaro*, 20 June 1980.

Benayoun, Robert. "Toujours un coup de dés..." Review of *Atlantic City*. *Positif* 236, November 1980, 69–70.

Cervoni, Albert. Citizen Malle. Review of *Atlantic City*. *L'Humanité*, 03 September 1980.

Cluny, Claude-Michel. "Voilà donc l'Amerique?" Review of *Atlantic City*. *Cinéma* 262, October 1980, 82.

de Baroncelli, Jean. "Le Destin d'un perdant" Review of *Atlantic City*. *Le Monde*, 06 September 1980.

Denby, David. "Avenging Angel." Review of *Atlantic City*. *New York* 14, 6 April 1981, 56, 58, 60.

French, Philip. "Desperate Losers." Review of *Atlantic City*. *Observer*, 25 January 1981, 32.

Hatch, Robert. Review of *Atlantic City*. *Nation* 232, 25 April 1981, 508–9.

Jackson, Martin A. Review of *Atlantic City*. *USA Today* 110, 9 July 1981, 68–9.

Kael, Pauline. "Chance/Fate." Review of *Atlantic City*. *New Yorker* 57, 6 April 1981, 154, 157–8, 160.

Kauffmann, Stanley. "Images Fine and Fuzzy." Review of *Atlantic City*. *New Republic* 184, 18 April 1981, 29–30.

Lardeau, Yann. Review of *Atlantic City*. *Cahiers du cinéma* 316, October 1980, 186.

Milne, Tom. Review of *Atlantic City*. *Monthly Film Bulletin* 48, 1981, 3.

Moskowitz, Gene. Review of *Atlantic City*. *Variety* 300, 3 September 1980, 25.

Murat, Pierre. "Lou le planqué et Sally l'ambitieuse." Review of *Atlantic City*. *Télérama*, 03 September 1980.

O'Toole, Lawrence. "Murmur of the Heartless." Review of *Atlantic City*. *Maclean's* 94, 27 April 1981, 50–51.

Pulleine, Tim. "The Vanished Swashbuckler." Review of *Atlantic City*. *Sight and Sound* 50, 1981, 137.

Reed, Rex. Review of *Atlantic City*. *Vogue* 171, June 1981, 40.

Rochu, Gilbert. "Un Voyeur au pays des miracles." Review of *Atlantic City*. *Libération*, 03 September 1980.

Schickel, Richard. "Boardwalk." Review of *Atlantic City*. *Time* 117, 6 April 1981, 68.

Sragow, Michael. "Tinhorns Triumph in

Boomtown." Review of *Atlantic City*. *Rolling Stone* no. 342, 30 April 1981, 38.

Tessier, Max. Review of *Atlantic City*. *Revue du Cinéma* 353, September 1980, 20–22.

Turan, Kenneth. "Acting up." Review of *Atlantic City*. *New West* 6, May 1981, 112, 114.

Wolcott, James. "Making a Grand-Slam Movie: The Astonishing Louis Malle." *Vogue* 171, August 1981, 216.

Yvinec, Alain. "La Ville dont le prince est le flambeur." Review of *Atlantic City*. *Le Quotidien de Paris*, 09 September 1980.

MY DINNER WITH ANDRÉ

Amiel, Mireille. "Une Expérience originale et ambitieuse." Review of *My Dinner with André*. *Cinéma* 292, April 1983, 34.

Baignères, Claude. "À la recherche du bonheur." Review of *My Dinner with André*. *L'Aurore*, 2 March 1983.

Bolduc, Albert. Review of *My Dinner with André*. *Postif* 268, June 1983, 74.

Brenner, Marie. "My Conversation with André." *New York* 14, 19 October 1981, 36–40.

Carrère, Emmanuel. "L'aventure du bavardage." Review of *My Dinner with André*. *Télérama*, 2 March 1983.

Chazal, Robert. "Un Long Tête-à-tête." Review of *My Dinner with André*. *France-Soir*, 12 March 1983.

Chion, Michel. "Bouvard et Pécuchet dînent à New York." *Cahiers du cinéma* 346, April 1983, 50–1.

Cohn, L.L. Review of *My Dinner with André*. *Variety* 304, 16 September 1981, 16.

Denby, David. "Boeuf à la mode." Review of *My Dinner with André*. *New York* 14, 26 October 1981, 96–7.

Godard, Colette. "Wally écoute." Review of *My Dinner with André*. *Le Monde*, 03 March 1983.

Grimes, William. "Our Dinner with Louis." Interview with Wallace Shawn and André Gregory. *New York Times Magazine*, 31 December 1995, 42–3.

Gussow, Mel. "My Lunch with André and Wally: A Dialogue Resumes." *New York Times*, 16 May 1999, 5.

Hatch, Robert. Review of *My Dinner with André*. *Nation* 233, 7 November 1981, 483–4.

Jebb, Julian. Review of *My Dinner with André*. *Sight and Sound* 51, 1982, 208.

Kael, Pauline. Review of *My Dinner with André*. *New Yorker* 57, 4 January 1982, 81–3.

Kauffmann, Stanley. "A Dinner and a Disaster."

Review of *My Dinner with André*. *New Republic* 185, 25 November 1981, 22–3.

Kauffmann, Stanley. "The Facts of Some Matters." *New Republic* 185, 23 December 1981, 25.

Kroll, Jack. "Conversation Piece." Review of *My Dinner with André*. *Newsweek* 98, 26 October 1981, 78.

Lahr, John. "An Amazing Journey." Review of *My Dinner with André*. *Vogue* 171, November 1981, 446, 491.

O'Toole, Lawrence. "A Still Life with Conversation." Review of *My Dinner with André*. *Maclean's* 95, 29 March 1982, 60, 63.

Pym, John. Review of *My Dinner with André*. *Monthly Film Bulletin* 49, 1982, 109.

Schickel, Richard. "Small Bore." Review of *My Dinner with André*. *Time* 118, 26 October 1981, 94.

Seguret, Olivier. Review of *My Dinner with André*. *Libération*, 03 March 1983.

Serceau, Daniel. "Tu causes, tu causes..." Review of *My Dinner with André*. *Revue du cinéma* 382, April 1983, 30–1.

Shawn, Wallace. "Some notes on Louis Malle and *My Dinner with André*." *Sight and Sound* 51, 1982, 118–20.

Teisseire, Guy. Review of *My Dinner with André*. *Le Matin*, 04 March 1983.

CRACKERS

Crist, Judith. "Once More with Feeling." Review of *Crackers*. *Saturday Review* 10, Jan-Feb. 1984, 40–1.

Hey, Kenneth R. Review of *Crackers*. *USA Today* 112, May 1984, 97.

McCarthy, Todd. Review of *Crackers*. *Variety* 313, 25 January 1984.

Milne, Tom. Review of *Crackers*. *Monthly Film Bulletin* 52, 1985, 19.

Schickel, Richard. "Rushes." Review of *Crackers*. *Time* 123, 13 February 1984, 74.

ALAMO BAY

Chazal, Robert. "Violence au Texas" Review of *Alamo Bay*. *France-Soir*, 21 September 1985.

Combs, Richard. Review of *Alamo Bay*. *Monthly Film Bulletin* 53, 1986, 5.

Corliss, Richard. "An Immigrant Tragedy in Texas." Review of *Alamo* Bay. *Time* 125, 8 April 1985, 83.

Culhane, John. "Louis Malle: An Outsider's Odyssey." *New York Times Magazine*, 7 April 1985, 28–31, 68.

Daney, Serge. "Malle fait de la série Bay." Review of *Alamo Bay*. *Libération*, 26 September 1985, 37.

de Baecque, Antoine. Review of *Alamo Bay*. *Cahiers du cinéma* 376, October 1985, 64–5.

Delmas, Ginette. Review of *Alamo Bay*. *Jeune Cinéma* 170, November 1985, 43–5.

Denby, David. "Gulf Coast Blues." Review of *Alamo Bay*. *New York* 18, 15 April 1985, 97–9.

Douin, Jean-Luc. "Les Crevettes de la colère." Review of *Alamo Bay*. *Télérama*, 18 September 1985, 40.

Garel, Alain. "Une Autre Guerre du Viêt-nam." Review of *Alamo Bay*. *Revue du Cinéma* 409, October 1985, 35–7.

Gentile, Michaël. "Emigrant Malle." *World Press Review* 32, November 1985, 59.

Kroll, Jack. "Fire in the Gulf." Review of *Alamo Bay*. *Newsweek* 105, 8 April 1985, 85.

Magny, Joël. "Le Bon, la brute, et le chalut." Review of *Alamo Bay*. *Cinéma* 321, 18 September 1985, 4.

McCarthy, Todd. Review of *Alamo Bay*. *Variety* 318, 3 April 1985, 15.

O'Toole, Lawrence. "Pride and the Prejudiced." Review of *Alamo Bay*. *Maclean's* 98, 22 April 1985, 74.

Pérez, Michel. "Texas, ton univers impitoyable." Review of *Alamo Bay*. *Le Matin*, 18 September 1985.

Ramasse, François. "Cow-Dinh, the all–American boy." *Positif* 297, November 1985, 71–3.

Siclier, Jacques. "Alamo Bay: la guerre des crevettes." Review of *Alamo Bay*. *Le Monde*, 14 September 1985.

Travers, Peter. Review of *Alamo Bay*. *People Weekly* 23, 15 April 1985, 16.

GOD'S COUNTRY
(LE PAYS DE DIEU)

Bassan, Raphaël. Review of *Le Pays de dieu*. *La Révue du Cinéma* 419, September 1986, 49.

Boujut, Michel. "La Clé de l'Amérique profonde." Review of *Le Pays de dieu*. *L'Evènement du Jeudi*, 10 July 1986.

Chazal, Robert. "L'Amérique profonde." Review of *Le Pays de dieu*. *France-Soir*, 21 July 1986.

Corry, John. "Malle's 'God's Country in Minnesota.'" Review of *God's Country*. *New York Times*, 11 December 1985, C29.

Derobert, Eric. Review of *Le Pays de dieu*. *Positif* 308, October 1986, 72.

Maltin, Leonard. Review of *God's Country*. In *Leonard Maltin's 2005 Movie Guide*. (New York: Signet, 2004), 541.

Montaigne, Pierre. "Louis Malle au cœur du Middle West." Review of *Le Pays de dieu*. *Le Figaro*, 16 July 1986.

Perez, Michel. "La Fin des petits arpents du bon Dieu." Review of *Le Pays de dieu*. *Le Matin*, 16 July 1986.

Revault d'Allonnes, Fabrice. Review of *Le Pays de dieu*. *Cinéma* 362, 9 July 1986.

Roy, Jean. "Les Deux Faces du $." Review of *Le Pays de dieu*. *L'Humanité*, 16 July 1986.

Schidlow, Joshka. "Dieu est américain." Review of *Le Pays de dieu*. *Télérama*, 16 July 1986.

Tesson, Charles. Review of *Le Pays de dieu*. *Cahiers du cinéma* 386, July/August 1986, 64.

Waintrop, Edouard. "Le Petit Arpent américain dans le viseur de Louis Malle." Review of *Le Pays de dieu*. *Libération*, 22 July 1986.

AND THE PURSUIT OF HAPPINESS
(LA POURSUITE DU BONHEUR)

Carbonnier, Alain. Review of *La Poursuite du bonheur*. *Cinéma* 400, 22 May 1987.

Chevrie, Marc. "L'Amérique et les autres." Review of *La Poursuite du bonheur*. *Cahiers du cinéma* 397, June 1987, 40.

Ciment, Michel. Review of *La Poursuite du bonheur*. *Positif* 317–318, July-August 1987, 70–1.

Tessier, Max. Review of *La Poursuite du bonheur*. *La Revue du cinéma* 429, July-August 1987, 43.

Tournès, Andrée. Review of *La Poursuite du bonheur*. *Jeune Cinéma* 182, July-August 1987, 35.

AU REVOIR LES ENFANTS
(GOODBYE, CHILDREN)

Andreu, Anne. "Louis Malle signe son chef-d'oeuvre et, déjà, les politiques rappliquent..." Review of *Au revoir les enfants*. *L'Evénement du jeudi*, 1 October 1987, 96–7.

Ansen, David. "A School for Sorrow, Friendship, and Betrayal in Wartime France." Review of *Au revoir les enfants*. *Newsweek* 111, 15 February 1988, 70.

Baignères, Claude. "Au plus profond de l'être." Review of *Au revoir les enfants*. *Le Figaro*, 7 October 1987.

Barbry, François-Régis. Review of *Au revoir les enfants*. *Cinéma* 411, 7–13 October 1987, 1.

Benayoun, Robert. "Un Ailleurs infiniment proche." Review of *Au revoir les enfants*. *Positif* 320, October 1987, 29–31.

Bernard, René. "L'Enfance nue de Louis Malle"

Review of *Au revoir les enfants*. *L'Express*, 09 October 1987.

Borger, Lenny. Review of *Au revoir les enfants*. *Variety* 328, 2 September 1987, 18.

Chase, Donald. Focus: Foreign Affairs. *American Film* 13, January/February 1988, 7.

Denby, David. "Past Perfect." Review of *Au revoir les enfants*. *New York* 21, 22 February 1988, 70–1.

French, Philip. "A Guilty Occupation." Review of *Au revoir les enfants*. *Observer*, 9 October 1988, 43.

Genin, Bernard. "Bonjour la haine." Review of *Au revoir les enfants*. *Télérama*, 7 October 1987, 17–18.

Heymann, Danièle. "L'Ami perdu." Review of *Au revoir les enfants*. *Le Monde*, 2 September 1987.

Jefferson, Margo. "Childhood's End." Review of *Au revoir les enfants*. *Vogue* 178, February 1988, 82.

Kael, Pauline. Review of *Au revoir les enfants*. *New Yorker* 64, 22 February 1988, 85–6.

Kauffmann, Stanley. "Under the Gun." Review of *Au revoir les enfants*. *New Republic* 198, 22 February 1988, 24.

Kemp, Philip. "Childhood's End." Review of *Au revoir les enfants*. *Sight and Sound* 57, 1988, 283–4.

Kramer, Jane. "The French and Louis Malle." *Vogue* 178, March 1988, 496–7, 557.

Leclère, Marie-Françoise. Review of *Au revoir les enfants*. *Le Point*, 05 October 1987.

Lefort, Gérard. "Le Malaise Malle." Review of *Au revoir les enfants*. *Libération*, 08 October 1987.

O'Toole, Lawrence. "A Child's Brush with Nazi Brutality." Review of *Au revoir les enfants*. *Maclean's* 101, 11 April 1988, 60.

Pons, Maurice. "Un Premier Film signé Louis Malle." Review of *Au revoir les enfants*. *L'Avant-Scène Cinéma* 373, July 1988, 5.

Sweet, Louise. Review of *Au revoir les enfants*. *Monthly Film Bulletin* 55, 1988, 296.

Toubiana, Serge. "Regards d'enfants." Review of *Au revoir les enfants*. *Cahiers du cinéma* 400, October 1987, 18–20.

Travers, Peter. Review of *Au revoir les enfants*. *People Weekly* 29, 29 February 1988, 12.

MILOU EN MAI
(MAY FOOLS; MILOU IN MAY)

Audé, Françoise. "La Mort et l'utopie." Review of *Milou en mai*. *Positif* 348, February 1990, 62–3.

Baigères, Claude. "Le Pavé dans la mare." Review of *Milou en mai*. *Le Figaro*, 24 January 1990.

Bernstein, Richard. "Malle Uncorks the '68 Crop." Review of *May Fools*. *New York Times*, 17 June 1990, 13, 20.

Borger, Lenny. Review of *May Fools*. *Variety* 338, 14 February 1990, 34.

Bowman, James. "Wild Metropolitan Fools." Review of *May Fools*. *American Spectator* 23, November 1990, 39.

Braudeau, Michel. "L'Héritage, camarade." Review of *Milou en Mai*. *Le Monde*, 25 January 1990.

Brisset, Stéphane. Review of *Milou en Mai*. *Cinéma* 463, January 1990, 26–27.

de Gaspéri, Anne. "... 68, côté jardin." Review of *Milou en mai*. *Le Quotidien de Paris*, 24 January 1990, 26.

Denby, David. "Big Shop of Horrors." Review of *May Fools*. *New York* 23, 25 June 1990, 61, 64.

Fabre, Maurice. "Un Chaud Printemps." Review of *Milou en mai*. *France-Soir*, 23 January 1990.

Forbes, Jill. Review of *May Fools*. *Monthly Film Bulletin* 57, 2 September 1990, 67.

French, Philip. "Malle's Marvelous Milieu." Review of *May Fools*. *Observer*, 2 September 1990, 60.

Grassin, Sophie. "Malle, c'est bien." Review of *Milou en mai*. *L'Express*, 19 January 1990, 104–5.

Kauffmann, Stanley. "Figures from the Past." Review of *May Fools*. *New Republic* 203, 9–16 July 1990, 32–3.

Kroll, Jack. "French Revolution, Family Style." Review of *May Fools*. *Newsweek* 116, 9 July 1990, 66.

Le Morvan, Gilles. "Un Pavé de douce dérision." Review of *Milou en mai*. *L'Humanité*, 24 January 1990, 23.

Leclère, Marie-Françoise. "Louis Malle: La Recherche du bonheur." Review of *Milou en mai*. *Le Point*, 22 January 1990, 14–5.

Lefort, Gérard. "Honni soit qui Malle y pense." Review of *Milou en mai*. *Libération*, 24 January 1990.

Mayne, Richard. Review of *May Fools*. *Sight and Sound* 59, 1990, 201–2.

Nave, Bernard. Review of *Milou en mai*. *Jeune Cinéma*, March/April 1990, 35–36.

Novak, Ralph. Review of *May Fools*. *People Weekly* 33, 2 July 1990, 12.

Pérez, Michel. "Le fond de l'air est rose" Review of *Milou en mai*. *Le Nouvel Observateur*, 25 January 1990, 104.

Rafferty, Terrence. "Picnic on the Grass." Review of *May Fools. New Yorker* 66, 16 July 1990, 73–5.

Rainer, Peter. Review of *May Fools. American Film* 16, May 1991, 54.

Toubiana, Serge. "Fantômes sans liberté." Review of *Milou en mai. Cahiers du cinéma* 428, February 1990, 66–7.

Travers, Peter. Review of *May Fools. Rolling Stone* no. 581, 28 July 1990, 32.

DAMAGE (FATALE)

Ansen, David. "Fatal and Foolish Obsessions." *Newsweek* 121, 4 January 1993, 50.

Baignères, Claude. "Mélo physique." Review of *Fatale. Le Figaro*, 09 December 1992.

Boujut, Michel. "Le Feu sous la glace." Review of *Fatale. L'Evènement du jeudi*, 10 December 1992.

Buck, Joan Juliet. "Passion and Lust." Review of *Damage. Vogue* 182, December 1992, 101, 4.

Conlin, Jennifer. "Like Father, Like Son." *Premiere* 6, December 1992, 31, 34.

Corliss, Richard. "Stiff Upper Libido." Review of *Damage. Time* 141, 11 January 1993, 50–1.

Danel, Isabelle. Review of *Fatale. Télérama*, 09 December 1990.

de Bruyn, Olivier. "Honni soit qui mal y pense!" Review of *Fatale. Positif* 382, December 1992, 48–9.

de Gaspéri, Anne. "Les Nouveaux Amants." Review of *Fatale. Le Quotidien de Paris*, 09 December 1992.

Denby, David. "One from the Heart." Review of *Damage. New York* 25, 14 December 1992, 89–91.

French, Philip. "Loving Dangerously." Review of *Damage. Observer*, 7 February 1993, 50.

Heymann, Danièle. "Les Amants '92." Review of *Fatale. Le Monde*, 09 December 1992.

Johnson, Brian D. "Lethal Women." Review of *Damage. Maclean's* 106, 25 January 1993, 45.

Jousse, Thierry. Review of *Fatale. Cahiers du cinéma* 463, janvier 1993, 63.

Kaufman, Joanne. Review of *Damage. People Weekly* 39, 18 January 1993, 15–16.

Kauffmann, Stanley. "Basic Ingredient." Review of *Damage. New Republic* 208, 1 February 1993, 50–51.

Lefort, Gérard. "Fatale, dommages sans intérêts." Review of *Fatale. Libération*, 09 December 1992.

Macia, Jean–Luc. "Les Amants, le retour." Review of *Fatale. La Croix*, 10 December 1990.

McCarthy, Todd. Review of *Damage. Variety* 349, 7 December 1992, 70–1.

Philippe, Claude-Jean. "Loyal et rigoureux." Review of *Fatale. France-Soir*, 12 December 1992.

Rafferty, Terrence. "Baser Instincts." Review of *Damage. New Yorker* 68, 25 January 1993, 96–7.

Riou, Alain. "Fleurs de Malle." Review of *Fatale. Le Nouvel Observateur*, 03 December 1992.

Romney, Jonathan. Review of *Damage. Sight and Sound* 62, February 1993, 41.

Travers, Peter. Review of *Damage. Rolling Stone* no. 647, 7 January 1993, 51.

Weinraub, Bernard. "Louis Malle Cuts a Film and Grows Indignant." *New York Times*, 22 December 1992, C15–16.

VANYA ON 42ND STREET

Baignères, Claude. "Tchekhov parmi nous." Review of *Vanya on 42nd Street. Le Figaro*, 25 January 1995.

Friedman, Vanessa. "A Hard Act to Swallow: André Gregory and Louis Malle Chew the Fat about Their New Collaboration, *Vanya on 42nd Street.*" *Vogue* 184, November 1994, 182, 184.

Frost, Polly. Review of *Vanya on 42nd Street. Harper's Bazaar*, November 1994, 102, 110.

Grassin, Sophie. Review of *Vanya on 42nd Street. L'Express*, 26 January 1995.

Guilloux, Michel. "Quand théâtre et cinéma avancent main dans la main." Review of *Vanya 42nd Street. L'Humanité*, 25 January 1995.

Johnson, Brian D. "Lovers and Exiles." Review of *Vanya on 42nd Street. Maclean's* 108, 15 May 1995, 73–4.

Kaplan, James. "Louis Malle's 42nd Street 'Uncle Vanya.'" *New York* 27, 12 September 1994, 62–3.

Kauffmann, Stanley. "From Russia with Love." Review of *Vanya on 42nd Street. New Republic* 211, 7 November 1994, 34–6.

Kroll, Jack. "Saying Uncle in New York: A Classic Comes to Life." *Newsweek* 124, 31 October 1994, 67.

Lalanne, Jean-Marc. Review of *Vanya on 42nd Street. Cahiers du cinéma* 488, February 1995, 59.

Marcabru, Pierre. "Une Miraculeuse Rencontre." Review of *Vanya on 42nd Street. Le Figaro*, 4 February 1995.

McCarthy, Todd. Review of *Vanya on 42nd Street. Variety* 356, 12 September 1994, 40.

Mérigeau, Pascal. "Louis Malle dans les coulisses." Review of *Vanya on 42nd Street. Le Monde*, 26 January 1995.

Pascal, Michel. "Malle-Tchekhov Off Broadway

ou la rencontre inspirée." Review of *Vanya on 42nd Street*. *Le Point*, 21 January 1995.

Rafferty, Terrrence. "Plays on Film." Review of *Vanya on 42nd Street*. *New Yorker* 70, 31 October 1994, 105–6.

Sineux, Michel. "Un Mélange unique de théâtre et de cinéma." Review of *Vanya on 42nd Street*. *Positif* 408, February 1995, 46–7.

Strick, Philip. Review of *Vanya on 42nd Street*. *Sight and Sound* 64, January 1995, 61.

Travers, Peter. Review of *Vanya on 42nd Street*. *Rolling Stone* no. 694, 3 November 1994, 106.

Trémois, Claude-Marie. Review of *Vanya on 42nd Street*. *Télérama*, 18 January 1995, 24–6.

COVERAGE OF MULTIPLE FILMS

Grégoire, Stéphanie. "Les Débuts de Louis Malle 1956–1963: un cinéaste humain, trop humain pour la Nouvelle Vague." Master's thesis, Université Michel de Montagne, 1998.

Prédal, René. "L'Oeuvre de Louis Malle, ou les étapes d'une évolution personnelle." *Jeune Cinéma* 190, September/October 1988, 19–26.

Articles—General Interest on Malle

Haller, Scot. "Malle's American Connection." *Saturday Review* 9, June 1982, 19.

Kauffmann, Stanley. "New Directors, Old Directions." *New Republic* 141, 7 December 1959, 21.

Lambert, Pam. "As Winter Comes." *People Weekly* 44, 11 December 1995, 73–4, 76.

"Louis Malle." *Variety* 361, 27 November 1995, 92. (Obituary).

Martin, Marcel. "Louis Malle, humaniste inclassable." *Revue du Cinéma* 431, October 1987, 48.

Nesselson, Lisa. "20th Century Rebels." *Harper's Bazaar* 122, April 1989, 106.

Wolf, William. "Louis Malle's Love Affair with America." *New York* 14, 1 June 1981, 48–9.

Books

Billard, Pierre. *Louis Malle: Le Rebelle solitaire*. Paris: Plon, 2003.

Chapier, Henry. *Louis Malle*. Cinéma d'Aujourd'hui, no. 24. Paris: Éditions Seghers, 1964.

Frey, Hugo. *Louis Malle*. Manchester: Manchester University Press, 2004.

Malle, Louis. *Malle on Malle*. Edited by Philip French. Rev. ed. London: Faber and Faber, 1996.

_____, and Sarah Kant. *Louis Malle par Louis Malle*. Paris: Jacques Mallecot, Éditions de l'Athenor, 1978.

Prédal, René. *Louis Malle*. Paris: Edilig, 1989.

Published Screenplays

Malle, Louis. *Au revoir les enfants*. London: Faber and Faber, 1989.

_____. *Le Souffle au cœur*. Paris: éd. Gallimard, 1971.

_____, with Patrick Modiano. *Lacombe, Lucien*. New York: Viking Compass, 1975.

_____, with Jean-Claude Carrière. *Milou in May*. London: Faber and Faber, 1990.

Source Material—Malle's Films

Calef, Noël. *Ascenseur pour l'échafaud*. Paris: Librairie Arthème Fayard, 1957.

Chekhov, Anton Pavlovich. *Uncle Vanya*. Adapted by David Mamet, from a Literal Translation by Vlada Chernomordik. New York: Grove Press, 1988.

Darien, Georges. *Le Voleur*. Paris: P.-V. Stock, 1898.

Denon, Baron Dominique Vivant. *Point de lendemain*. Strasbourg: Vve Berger-Levrault, 1861.

Friedlander, Lee, and Bellocq, E.J. *Storyville Portraits*. New York: Museum of Modern Art, 1970.

Hart, Josephine. *Damage*. London: Chatto & Windus, Ltd., 1991.

La Rochelle, Pierre Drieu. *Feu follet*. Paris: Gallimard, Éditions de la Nouvelle revue française, 1931.

Milloy, Ross. "Vietnam Fallout in a Texas Town." *New York Times Sunday Magazine*, 6 April 1980, 38–9, 42, 44, 46, 50, 56, 58.

Poe, Edgar Allan. "William Wilson." In *Tales*. New York: Dodd, Mead, 1952, 1–24.

Queneau, Raymond. *Zazie dans le métro*. Paris: Olympia Press, 1959.

Rose, Al. *Storyville, New Orleans*. Tuscaloosa, AL: University of Alabama Press, 1974.

Time 126, 8 July 1985. (Entire issue on immigration, that forms the basis of *Poursuite du bonheur*).

Index

Numbers in **bold italics** indicate photographs